THE GREENWOOD ENCYCLOPEDIA OF
LOVE, COURTSHIP,
& Sexuality THROUGH HISTORY

THE GREENWOOD ENCYCLOPEDIA OF LOVE, COURTSHIP, AND SEXUALITY THROUGH HISTORY

The Ancient World, Volume 1
James W. Howell

The Medieval Era, Volume 2
William E. Burns

The Early Modern Period, Volume 3
Victoria L. Mondelli and Cherrie A. Gottsleben, with the assistance of Kristen Pederson Chew

The Colonial and Revolutionary Age, Volume 4
Merril D. Smith

The Nineteenth Century, Volume 5
Susan Mumm

The Modern World, Volume 6
James T. Sears

THE GREENWOOD ENCYCLOPEDIA OF
LOVE, COURTSHIP,
& Sexuality THROUGH HISTORY

THE MODERN WORLD

Volume 6

Edited by
JAMES T. SEARS

GREENWOOD PRESS

Westport, Connecticut • London

Dedicated to
Robert Sargent Jr. and Janie Sargent

Library of Congress Cataloging-in-Publication Data

The Greenwood encyclopedia of love, courtship, and sexuality through history /
volume editors, James W. Howell ... [et al.].
   p. cm.
  Includes bibliographical references and index.
   Contents: v. 1. The ancient world / James W. Howell, editor—v. 2. The medieval era / William
E. Burns, editor—v. 3. The early modern period / Victoria L. Mondelli and Cherrie A. Gottsleben,
editors—v. 4. The colonial and revolutionary age / Merril D. Smith, editor—v. 5. The nineteenth
century / Susan Mumm, editor—v. 6. The modern world / James T. Sears, editor.
  ISBN-13: 978–0–313–33359–0 (set : alk. paper)—ISBN-13: 978–0–313–33583–9 (vol. 1 : alk.
paper)—ISBN-13: 978–0–313–33519–8 (vol. 2 : alk. paper)—ISBN-13: 978–0–313–33653–9 (vol. 3 :
alk. paper)—ISBN-13: 978–0–313–33360–6 (vol. 4 : alk. paper)—ISBN-13: 978–0–313–33405–4
(vol. 5 : alk. paper)—ISBN-13: 978–0–313–33646–1 (vol. 6 : alk. paper)
  1. Sex—History—Encyclopedias. 2. Love—History—Encyclopedias. 3. Courtship—History—
Encyclopedias. I. Howell, James W. II. Title.
  HQ21.G67125 2008
  306.703–dc22   2007023728

British Library Cataloguing in Publication Data is available.

Library of Congress Catalog Card Number: 2007023728
ISBN-13: 978–0–313–33359–0 (set code)
       978–0–313–33583–9 (Vol. 1)
       978–0–313–33519–8 (Vol. 2)
       978–0–313–33653–9 (Vol. 3)
       978–0–313–33360–6 (Vol. 4)
       978–0–313–33405–4 (Vol. 5)
       978–0–313–33646–1 (Vol. 6)

First published in 2008

Greenwood Press, 88 Post Road West, Westport, CT 06881
An imprint of Greenwood Publishing Group, Inc.
www.greenwood.com

Printed in the United States of America

∞

The paper used in this book complies with the
Permanent Paper Standard issued by the National
Information Standards Organization (Z39.48–1984).

10 9 8 7 6 5 4 3 2 1

Contents

List of Entries

Set Preface

Sex and love are part of the very fabric of daily life—universal concepts that permeate every human society and are central to how each society views and understands itself. However, the way sex and love are expressed or perceived varies from culture to culture, and, within a particular society, attitudes toward sex and love evolve over time alongside the culture from which they arose. To capture the multicultural and chronological dimensions of these vital concepts, the six-volume *The Greenwood Encyclopedia of Love, Courtship, and Sexuality through History* explores the array of ideas, attitudes, and practices that have constituted sex and love around the world and across the centuries.

Each volume of alphabetically arranged entries was edited by an expert in the field who has drawn upon the expertise of contributors from many related disciplines to carefully analyze views toward sex and love among many cultures within a specified time period. Students and interested general readers will find in this work a host of current, informative, and engaging entries to help them compare and contrast different perceptions and practices across time and space. Entries cover such topics as customs and practices; institutions; legislation; religious beliefs; art and literature; and important ideas, innovations, and individuals. Users of this encyclopedia will, for instance, be able to learn how marriage in ancient Rome differed from marriage in Victorian England or in colonial America; how prostitution was viewed in medieval Europe and in the contemporaneous Islamic societies of Africa and the Middle East; and how or even if celibacy was practiced in eighteenth-century India, ancient Greece, or early modern Europe.

Edited by James W. Howell, Volume 1, *The Ancient World*, explores love and sexuality in the great societies of Europe, Africa, and Asia in the period before around 300 CE. Entries include Marriage, Homosexuality, Temple Prostitution, and Sex in Art. Volume 2, *The Medieval Era*, by William E. Burns examines sex and love in Europe, East Asia, India, the Middle East, Africa, and pre-Columbian Mesoamerica in the period between around 300 and 1400. Entries in this volume include Arthurian Legend, Concubinage, Eunuchs, Krishna, Seclusion of Women, *Thousand and One Nights*, and Virginity.

Volume 3, *The Early Modern Period*, edited by Victoria L. Mondelli and Cherrie Ann Gottsleben, with the assistance of Kristen Pederson Chew, focuses on sex and love in Europe, India, China, the Middle East, Africa, and the Americas in the fifteenth and sixteenth centuries. Some important entries in this volume are Bastardy, Confucianism, Dowries, Sex Toys, Suttee, and William Shakespeare. Edited by Merril D. Smith,

Volume 4, *The Colonial and Revolutionary Age*, looks at love and sexuality in western Europe, eastern Asia, India, the Middle East, Africa, and the Americas in the seventeenth and eighteenth centuries. The volume offers entries such as Bestiality, Castration, Berdache, Harems, Pueblo Indians, and Yoshiwara.

Volume 5, *The Nineteenth Century*, edited by Susan Mumm, explores sex and love in the Victorian period, primarily in Europe and the United States, but also in India, Asia, and the Middle East. Entries in this volume include Birth Control, Courtship, Fetishism, Native Americans, and Ottoman Women. Edited by James T. Sears, Volume 6, *The Modern World*, explores major topics in sex and sexuality from around the world in the twentieth and twenty-first centuries. Entries include AIDS/HIV, Domestic and Relationship Violence, Internet Pornography, Politics and Sex, Premarital Sex, Television, and the Women's Movement.

Each volume is illustrated and several cross-references to entries are provided. The entries conclude with a list of additional information resources, including the most useful books, journal articles, and Web sites currently available. Other important features of the encyclopedia include chronologies of important dates and events; guides to related topics that allow readers to trace broad themes across the entries; bibliographies of important general and standard works; and useful appendices, such as lists of Chinese dynasties and selections of important films and Web sites. Finally, detailed subject indexes help users gain easy access to the wealth of information on sex, love, and culture provided by this encyclopedia.

Preface

The Greenwood Encyclopedia of Love, Courtship, and Sexuality through History: The Modern World provides 85 entries, ranging in length from 1,000 to 3,000 words, that evidence the range of topics that have come to prominence during the last tumultuous 11 decades. Most of the entries are multicultural and cross-national in their content and the contributors bring their expertise and insight from North and South America, Europe, the Middle East, and Asia. Entries about the many aspects of sexuality and the roles that love has played in world cultures throughout this time period include bibliographies of important books and articles as well as annotated Web sites. Although no entry material is drawn exclusively from one geographical region or culture, some entries that may have their basis in American culture (e.g., Popular Music, Alfred Kinsey) may, in fact, bleed over into other cultures as found in related entries (e.g., Popular Culture, Sexual Science/Sexology). This cultural diffusion (and, in some cases, cultural hegemony) is, in fact, one important phenomena of the twentieth and twenty-first centuries. Entries also consider issues of gender, race, social class, ethnicity, or alternative sexualities. In most cases, inclusion of one or more of these issues is relevant and, thus, integrated into the entry. Even entries that on the surface might appear to focus exclusively on one gender or sexuality often impact or are influenced by other sexualities (e.g., pregnancy or single mothers are not restricted to women or to heterosexual-identified women).

The goal of this volume, therefore, is not to be exhaustive but to be representative and inclusive of various peoples and beliefs. It is intended for a general readership and for students at the secondary and college levels. As such, entries should be seen as gateways into a particular topic with specific avenues for further exploration. Every entry is indexed with additional assistance provided by boldfaced cross-references to other entries and recommendations to consult other entries in the "See also" section at the end of each contribution. Photographs and other visuals also illuminate some of the entries. A Chronology helps readers quickly identify key events of the twentieth and twenty-first centuries and a helpful general bibliography lists important information resources. A detailed Introduction puts the study of love, courtship, and sexuality during the last century into perspective for users of the entries. Finally, a Guide to Related Topics allows the reader to gain a quick synoptic understanding of the interconnections among various entries.

Introduction

A thirteen-year-old growing up in Athens, Georgia, and another in Athens, Greece, are linked—consciously and unconsciously—through a mediascape of shared experiences barely conceivable eleven decades ago when H. G. Wells penned his 1895 novella, *The Time Machine*. In fact, the futuristic world of AD 802,701 is more similar to Wells's late nineteenth-century class-ridden London than it is to the present day city on the south bank of the River Thames, boasting its new "Millennium Wheel."

George, the Time Traveler, returning from his adventures in a new world divided between the sheep-like Eloi who live leisurely above ground and the working class subterranean Morlock cannibals, explained the time-space phenomenon to his doubting colleagues as follows:

> There is no difference between time and any of the three dimensions of space except that our consciousness moves along it.... Our mental existences, which are immaterial and have no dimensions, are passing along the Time-Dimension with a uniform velocity from the cradle to the grave.

Our mental constructions about sexuality and love are not uniform, however. They change over a lifespan as a function of individual aging and social transformation. So, too, has cultural consciousness about sex and love changed through the generations. At no time in recorded history is this more apparent than between the twin centuries that first ended the Victorian Era and then birthed the digital one.

At the end of the nineteenth century and with advancing modernism and rising revolutionary movements from politics to the arts, conceptions about love and sex altered. Medical and technological advances coupled with forces for democratization shifted Western mores and morals. Global wars, mass communication, and monopoly capitalism also significantly influenced twentieth and early twenty-first century sexual beliefs and behaviors. Thus, a thirteen-year-old Londoner reading Wells's time traveling tale in W. E. Henley's magazine *The National Observer*, from the autumn of 1894 through the spring of 1895, would probably have been more stunned with the scope of changes if she had only traveled across a mere five generations.

Many of these changes are material: television, penicillin, jet planes, the Internet, cloning, air conditioning, and oral contraceptives. All these scientific and technological advances have impacted sexual beliefs and behaviors. Penicillin, for instance, discovered in 1928, was an antibiotic antidote to sexually transmitted diseases. By the 1940s, when it was mass produced, public advertisements promised a four-hour cure for gonorrhea.

Meanwhile, modern air travel reduced geographic and cultural distances while also facilitating the transmission of HIV and the transportation of sex tourists.

These material changes have also transformed our mental existence, which, in turn, has shifted our consciousness about ourselves and our relationships with others. The very concept of a "teenager" and this pseudo purgatorial separation of childhood from adulthood by an ever increasing span of years now called "adolescence" would have been surprising to this late nineteenth century young adult. So, too, would have been the steady—albeit uneven—openness about sex and love. From Margaret Sanger and Sigmund Freud to Alfred Kinsey and Betty Friedan to Dr. Ruth and Judith Butler, sex and love were researched and popularized. These individuals reflected *and* contested their cultural beliefs while significantly altering our sexual beliefs and behaviors.

Arguably, the transformation of American consciousness from the nineteenth to the twentieth centuries began with the World's Columbian Exposition held in Chicago in 1893. More than 27 million visitors had the opportunity to see exhibits in 200 buildings, including those of Westinghouse and Western Electric, which displayed the power of alternating electric current. There, too, were amusements, including the world's first "Ferris Wheel." Another popular Midway attraction was the Street in Cairo. Here audience eyes danced over the exotic dancer, Farida Mazar Spyropoulos, as she performed her famous "danse du ventre" or belly dance. Other firsts included different types of breakfast cereals. A year later, Dr. John Harvey Kellogg and his brother inadvertently invented corn flakes, which they patented under the name Granose, believing it aided in the prevention of masturbation—among other supposed ailments.

Other turn-of-the-century marvels of science and technology also promised sexual health. The Sears Roebuck Catalog, for example, offered the Giant Power Heidelberg Electric Belt for various afflictions, including male impotency. A 1900 advertisement claimed: "The constant soothing alternating electric current is ever at work, touching the weak spots, building up the system, stimulating the circulation." Later, the catalog featured the first electric vibrator for $200, which before was sold only to physicians. Advertising of any birth control merchandise, of course, was illegal under the Comstock Law of 1873, as was mailing any type of "obscene material," including condoms.

In 1901, Anthony Comstock, who founded the New York Society for the Suppression of Vice and amassed his private collection of confiscated materials, challenged the publication of the first modern marriage manual, *The Wedding Night*. Telling the court that the booklet, designed to enhance the sex experience of married couples, was "so obscene" that it should not be viewed by either judge or jury, Comstock was rewarded with the conviction and suicide of its author, Ira Craddock.

"Comstockery," a term coined by playwright and social critic George Bernard Shaw, himself a censorship victim and whose *Man and Superman* (1903) articulated women as the "life force" and initiators of marriage, continued well past the death of Comstock in 1915. Modern science, though, was unrelenting. In 1919, Frederick Killian revolutionized the condom by developing natural rubber latex (rubber cement, of dubious quality, had previously been used). By the mid-1930s, manufacturers were producing 1.5 million condoms a day. Meanwhile, publications like Edward Carpenter's *The Intermediate Sex* (1908), Edward Irenaeus Prime-Stevenson's *Intersexes* (1908), Magnus Hirschfeld's *The Transvestites* (1910), and Havelock Ellis's final volume, "Sex in Relation to Society" (1910), in his *Studies of Psychology of Sex* offered scholarly insights into alternative sexualities. Research on sex also advanced as Hirschfeld, a German physician, administered 3,000 psychobiological questionnaires to male polytechnic students in Berlin; a year later, in 1904, 5,000 metalworkers were surveyed. Results included the scientific finding that 5–6 percent were bisexual or homosexual—and the political action brought by several students against Hirschfeld for disseminating obscene material. Around this same time, Viennese endocrinologist Eugen Steinach began an effective line of research documenting the role hormones play in sexual and gender behaviors.

By the 1933 Century of Progress Exposition in Chicago, despite the depths of the Great Depression, most Americans were optimistic about the future, given the progress of the first three decades, including that of sex researchers and activists such as Sigmund Freud and Margaret Sanger. In contrast to the "White City" and its Grecian-style buildings of the 1893 World's Columbian Exhibition, the 1933 World's Fair followed the cubist, art nouveau architectural modernism of Art Deco with rainbow color buildings. Under the motto "Science Finds, Industry Applies, Man Conforms," cooperation among science, business, and government would lead to progress and a brighter economic future for all consumers. Among the exhibitions were incubators displaying babies and, in the Hall of Science, the Transparent Man, a life-size model made of "cellon" making all human organs clearly visible. Homes of Tomorrow exhibited futuristic kitchens with features designed to save women housekeeping time, like the new electric dishwasher. However, unlike the 1893 fair, there were no women's exhibits or a women's building. The only exhibit arguably featuring women was on the Midway. Here, like the 1893 exposition, the hit was female dancing, this time in the person of Sally Rand, whose striptease show made the Streets of Paris concession one of the crowd's favorites.

Across the Atlantic, two months before the fair's opening day, the "Law for Removing the Distress of the People and the Reich" passed in the German Reichstag by a vote of 441 to 84; the law effectively ended German democracy and legally granted Adolf Hitler dictatorial rule. Two weeks before the "Century of Progress" had opened, Hirschfeld's Institute of Sex Research was sacked by Nazi youth and its contents, including 20,000 books and 5,000 images, were publicly burned. By the arrival of the 776-foot German airship *Graf Zeppelin* in Chicago on October 26, 1933, the Exposition's theme of a "century of progress" appeared, at least to some, as hollow or, worse, as deeply troubling.

The new German government set forth a series of draconian decrees, including the 1933 "Law for the Prevention of Hereditary Diseased Offspring," which established "genetic health courts" to rule on the mental and familial fitness of citizens to bear children. In addition to forced sterilizations, the Nazis soon created the Reich Central Office for the Combating of Homosexuality and Abortion, and the sterilization program against Blacks, Jews, and gypsies was soon fully underway based on the genetic research of Dr. Eugen Fischer, who had been funded by the Rockefeller Foundation. Rape research on women and gypsies was also performed in concentration camps. Following the rape and murder of the female subjects, Dr. Hermann Stevie performed autopsies to study the anatomical effect. He concluded that "all women were inferior to men and had 'weak' reproductive systems that could 'easily be injured'" (http://www.bigeye.com/sexeducation/nazirape.html). Thus, as the celebration of modernism was at its zenith, the golden era of progressive sex research and reform in Germany had been shattered. A third of the new century had already passed, and with that passing, the major contributions of Margaret Sanger and Sigmund Freud had been made.

Margaret Sanger, the world's advocate for birth control, was editor of the short-lived militant periodical *The Woman Rebel: No Gods, No Masters*. Suppressed by U.S. postal authorities under the Comstock Law, its motto was "A woman's body belongs to herself alone." Its premier issue (March 1914) recruited female rebels with the following attributes:

> Who demand that those desiring to live together in love shall be provided with such knowledge and experience as Science has developed, which would prevent conception.... Who have the courage and backbone to fight with "THE WOMAN REBEL" against this outrageous suppression, whereby a woman has no control of the function of motherhood. (http://historymatters.gmu.edu/d/5084/)

In the third issue, Sanger advocated a boycott of the Baptist Church, denounced the YWCA as "brothels of the Spirit and morgues of Freedom!," and castigated the Catholic Church for "turning woman into a mere incubator." She also pronounced that " 'criminal' abortions arise from a perverted sex relationship under the stress of economic necessity, and their greatest frequency is among married women." Sanger, as a leader in the first wave of feminism, believed that "marriage laws abrogate the freedom of woman by enforcing upon her a continuous sexual slavery and a compulsory motherhood"; she separated from her husband that same year. Two years later, in 1916, Sanger opened the first birth control clinic in the United States. Her long-standing monthly, *Birth Control Review*, included articles by H. G. Wells and other reform-minded authors, scientists, and public policy advocates.

Sigmund Freud's first major work, *Studies of Hysteria*, was published the same year as *The Time Machine*. He followed up, in 1900, with *The Interpretation of Dreams* and five years later with *Three Essays on the Theory of Sexuality*. These and other books examined the inner worlds of the unconscious. Psychosexual concepts like libido, Oedipal and Electra complexes, id and superego, as well as phrases like "Freudian slips" and "penis envy" entered the popular vocabulary.

The idea that a little girl "would rather be a boy" was first broached in *On the Sexual Theories of Children* (1908), but the psychosexual concept of penis envy was developed in *Observations and Analyses Drawn from Analytical Practice* (1913) and *On Narcissism* (1914). It was the failure of the girl's mother to provide her with a penis, Freud surmised, that caused her to reject the mother and to become envious of and attracted to the father as a love-object. She then assumed diminutive status in relationship to him—and all men—while eventually identifying with her mother with whom she could vicariously share (and ultimately replace) the father. The resolution of the Electra complex could occur as father was displaced by husband—the source for the grown up girl's search for a penis (and power through control of the man).

Freud was not without his critics. Psychoanalyst Karen Horney criticized the deficit female mode as patriarchal and misogynistic and C. G. Jung shifted emphasis from sex and individual consciousness to the spiritual and the collective unconscious. Nevertheless, Freud's theories were popular among professionals and the public during the first several decades of the twentieth century.

By mid-century, the United States (and much of the Western world) had experienced an odd social juxtaposition. On the surface, post-World War II life was almost as Victorian as Norman Rockwell's romanticized "nuclear family" illustrations that appeared on covers of *The Saturday Evening Post*. Suburbs sprouted around urban centers, Perry Como and Rosemary Clooney crooned on the airways, and *The Ten Commandments* and *Pillow Talk* (starring Rock Hudson and Doris Day) attracted theater-goers. Below this idealized world was an underground inhabited by "beats," fallen women, and homosexuals. Jack Kerouac's *On the Road* (1957), Allen Ginsberg's *Howl* (1956), and William S. Burroughs's *Naked Lunch* (1959) articulated a nascent counter-culture's beliefs about sex and love. Meanwhile, women who found themselves "in trouble" had little recourse aside from a march to the marriage altar or a midnight visit to a back-alley abortion shop while heterosexual men continued to enjoy greater sexual freedom, including the newly available *Playboy* magazine. Queering the veneer of family life, gay men and lesbians went on "fake dates" and entered into false marriages as a small phalanx of activists organized through the Mattachine Society and the Daughters of Bilitis. And, despite President Harry S. Truman's racial integration of the Armed Services in 1948, *de facto* segregation, including laws against interracial marriage, remained a fact of American life.

Alfred Kinsey, a professor of zoology at a sleepy southern Indiana university, turned this post-war everyday black-and-white TV land upside down with his scientifically based but graphic descriptions in *Sexual Behavior in the Human Male* (1948) and *Sexual Behavior in the Human Female* (1953). Findings from sex histories of thousands of Americans shocked and titillated the public. The silence over sex was shattered along with assumptions about premarital sex (two-thirds of boys by the age of 18 and one-half of girls), masturbation (92 percent of males and 62 percent of females), homosexuality (one-third of adult men and one-in-ten exclusively), and extramarital sexual activity (a quarter of married women and half of married men)—to name just a few. Far from engaging in publicly prescribed and religiously mandated sexual practices, persons of all ages engaged in all types of sex behind the façade of their Rockwellesque white picket fence homes.

Nearing the end of this era and in the same year as President John F. Kennedy's assassination, Betty Friedan launched the second wave of the women's movement. *The Feminine Mystique* (1963), which eventually would sell more than 3 million copies, challenged American myths about sex and love. Most pernicious was her imagery of the fulfilled housewife dutifully tending to the needs of husband and children. Arguing that women had won the battle for suffrage but lost the war between the sexes, Friedan challenged the folk belief that a woman's fulfillment could be found in "sexual passivity, male domination and nurturing maternal love." She went on to challenge the centuries-held prejudice against women that had reappeared in "Freudian disguise." Central to it was "the concept 'penis envy,' which ... was seized in this country in the 1940s as the literal explanation of all that was wrong with American women." (Chapter 5, The Sexual Solipsism of Sigmund Freud, http://www.marxists.org/reference/subject/philosophy/works/us/friedan.htm). Three years later, in 1966, Friedan co-founded the National Organization for Women (NOW), which, in turn, engaged in its own internal battles over racism, classism, and lesbianism. In the process, Friedan opened the door for other feminist writers—Shulamith Firestone, Kate Millet, Germaine Greer—thus further challenging women's familial and social roles.

The role women played in the bedroom, however, was most forcefully challenged by practitioners through post-1970 publications, such as the highly influential *Our Bodies, Ourselves*, by abortion rights advocates who secured the landmark Supreme Court decision *Roe v. Wade* (1973), and through the everyday work of sexologists and therapists like Virginia Johnson, Shere Hite, and Ruth Westheimer.

"Sexually Speaking" was first telecast in September 1980. This fifteen-minute taped show (broadcast after midnight in New York City) soon expanded to a live one-hour call-in show airing at 10 p.m. Syndicated as "The Dr. Ruth Show," another one for adolescents, "What's Up with Dr. Ruth," was developed later. Through these shows and publications, including *Dr. Ruth's Encyclopedia of Sex* and *Sex for Dummies* as well as videos such as *Terrific Sex*, sex talk went from the lab of the sexologist, the banter in the locker room, and the therapist's office to everyday and very public worlds.

Westheimer, like other sex educators of her day along with the prior generation of 1960s' identity-based activists, understood sex, gender, and sexuality to be a fixed and essential part of the human condition. But, just as the lines of seemingly fixed and bounded musical *Billboard* genres of pop, country-and-western, and soul were blurring (e.g., "rockabilly") with cross-over artists (e.g., Hammer's *Please Hammer Don't Hurt 'Em*) and imploding genres (e.g., house music, acid house), so was our thinking about sex and gender.

From the 1980s onward, academics, most notably Jean Francois Lyotard, Michel Foucault, and later, Judith Butler, used postmodern and poststructural social theories to analyze and critique modernist understandings. Here the role that language, "discourse," played in how we understood and acted upon concepts such as gender or sexual identity was central to their thinking. Rather than viewing categories of gender (masculine/feminine), sex (male/female), or sexuality (gay/straight) as essentially biological, these were, they argued, historically and culturally constructed. Thus, just as being "a homosexual" was not possible prior to the mid-nineteenth-century invention of the term "homosexual," neither could one be "gay" prior to the usurpation of this word by homosexuals in the mid-twentieth century. In fact, just as the invention of "homosexuality" allowed for its social regulation and medicalization so, too, the re-appropriation of the everyday word "gay" (and later "queer") by oppressed homosexuals underscored both the power of language and the dispossessed to challenge their oppression, queering the very categories created by the oppressor.

Literary theorist Judith Butler, beginning with *Gender Trouble* (1990), questioned whether any identity had an essential core. She argued that its naturalness appeared so only because of these identities' repeated performance and that their binary oppositions, presented in both language and performance (masculine/feminine, gay/straight, male/female), were as arbitrary as the social texts that produced and governed them. The impact of Butler and other postmodern scholars on the academy was immense. They challenged the very foundations of identity-based social movements that had fueled the modern women's, gay, and civil rights movements.

Far from a mere academic theory, postmodernism could be seen in everyday life throughout the 1980s and 1990s. Disjunctive, contradictory, and unsettling are apt descriptors for these decades. Take, for instance, the year 1984, made infamous by Wells's social critic successor, George Orwell. On the floor of the Rift Valley of Kenya, a 5-million-year-old jawbone of *Australopithecus afarensis*, our earliest ancestor, was unearthed. While DNA analysis revealed the genetic difference between chimpanzees and humans to be barely 1 percent, the Texas Board of Education debated a decade-old ban on the teaching of evolution as scientific fact. In Paris and Atlanta, researchers announced the discovery of HIV as a half million AIDS cases were reported worldwide while *Advocate Men* premiered in gay bookstores. Meanwhile, a stunned and long closeted Rock Hudson was diagnosed with AIDS and later traveled to Paris for treatment while his agent—a former homosexual leader of the Mattachine Society—denied rumors of his illness and homosexuality. Hudson's longtime friend, President Ronald Reagan, failed to address the issue for another two years. By then, 20,849 Americans had died and AIDS had spread to 113 countries.

Never distant from popular culture, sex and love also appeared contradictory or unsettling. From the mid-1980s through the early twenty-first century, the top-rated television shows changed from steamy plot lines in *Dallas* and *Dynasty* to seemingly unscripted "reality shows" like *Big Brother* and *American Idol*, but the lure of romance and lust remained constant. Strong female-centered shows also emerged, notably *Roseanne, Murphy Brown,* and *Ellen.* These fictional characters of courage and conviction paralleled their real life stories: Roseanne Barr's working class life, Candace Bergen's real life out-of-wedlock pregnancy, and Ellen DeGeneres's "coming out" as a lesbian. Each of these shows challenged gender and sexual taboos like teenage masturbation, birth control, and lesbianism.

Perhaps most disjunctive was that of *Ellen.* On the night of April 30, 1997, 42 million viewers watched as the character, Ellen Morgan, came out along with its star, Ellen DeGeneres. The disjunctive connection between fantasy and reality was even more apparent, as detailed at the time in *Z Magazine:*

> For those who really follow pop culture, in all its intertextual meandering, the show was only half the story. In the midst of all the publicity about Ellen's coming out, another young blond Hollywood starlet, Ann Heche—whose career as a romantic lead in blockbuster movies was just taking off, after years of working in such lower-profile genres as soap opera and independent cinema—found herself "powerfully drawn" to de Generes.... This "piggy back" coming out was in many ways even more significant, because Heche was on the verge of a big-time career her new disclosure could easily demolish. She does not, after all, have the clout and bankability of an established star like de Generes.... But Heche—whose father had been a closeted Protestant minister who died of AIDS in his early 40s—was determined to live "honestly and truly" as her father had not been able to. So her decision comprised an act of courage and potentially great sacrifice. (http://www.zmag.org/zmag/articles/rappingjuly97.html)

Openness about sex during the twentieth and early twenty-first centuries has advanced and retreated much like women's hem lines. Just as in the Victorian era, behaviors and attitudes about sexuality were far from uniform. If anything, as sex and love became more public, it became more contested as "wars" among various cultural factions, such as between religious conservatives and progressive secularists, erupted. Thus, the regulation of sexuality—often under the guise of protecting public morals and health—is an equally important phenomenon during this eleven-decade period. For instance, after Comstockery and as technology advanced, the Hays Production Code mandated that the film industry portray the "correct standards of life" and "the sanctity of the institution of marriage and the home shall be upheld," baring scenes that "stimulate the lower and baser element" such as "excessive and lustful kissing," "sex perversion or any inference to it," "sex relationships between the white and black races," and "indecent or undue exposure" (http://www.artsreformation.com/a001/hays-code.html). Thus, in the 1934 film, *Men in White,* nurse Barbara Dennin's back-alley abortion is only hinted at, although the film ends with her death—mirror-opposite to the play in which she marries and enjoys the good life. From postal authorities seizing copies of *Life* magazine due to photos of childbirth and United States Customs prohibiting importation of *Tropic of Cancer* and *Lady Chatterley's Lover* to Charles Keating founding the Citizens for Decent Literature to congressional passage of "Don't Ask, Don't Tell" anti-gay military policies and the Defense of Marriage Act, the superego of the United States sought to suppress its bawdiness, licentiousness, and fetishes.

Another characteristic of this era is the increased homogenization of cultures. In reading this volume, one cannot escape the fact that, over time, cultural landscapes have become more alike. Western constructs like being "gay," social movements such as feminism, and popular culture—ranging from the bikini to the Beatles—have become nearly ubiquitous. And, at the cultural vortex is the United States—its science and technology, its ideals and images, its media and language. From President William McKinley's "little war" in Cuba that brought the United States world colonial power status at the end of the nineteenth century to President George W. Bush's "war of liberation" in Iraq that may well signal the end of American hegemony, the United States has wielded enormous economic, political, and social influence. This influence has manifested itself in the arena of sex and love during these eleven decades: the Jazz and Big Band eras, the Harlem Renaissance and Greenwich Village scenes, the women's and gay rights movements, Elvis and Madonna, penicillin and Viagra, abortion rights and abstinence-based sex education.

Despite the tectonic changes during this 110-year period, we are, in some ways, at a similar consciousness—one that joins the Londoner of 1895 with her counterpart today. At both points in time, the world was at a threshold. The end of the Victorian era marked the dissolution of old European empires, the evolution of industrialization, and the emergence of new sciences. Wars of nationalism, assembly line mass productions, and ego psychology and quantum physics transited youthful soldiers across an ocean of experience; transported young lovers to dark, dead-end, dirt roads; and transformed our understanding of innermost realities. Around the beginning of this new millennia, the Cold War's end and the bipolar world it created and then vaporized, the rise of the service and information sectors, and advances in molecular biology have transformed sexual science fiction into scientific fact through birth control patches, cloning of human embryos, date rape drug spotters, robot reproduction and evolution along with sexbots, and Viagra. It is this timeline that is encompassed by this encyclopedic volume and anticipated by the one that follows this new century.

Guide to Related Topics

ARTS
Censorship
Cinema
Politics
Popular Culture
Popular Music
Pornography
Pornography, on the Internet

BIRTH CONTROL
Abortion
Birth Control
Celibacy
Feminism
Heterosexuality
Homosexuality
Masturbation
Morality and Ethics
Pregnancy
Premarital Sex
Sanger, Margaret
Sex Education
Virginity
Women's Movement

CHILDREN AND YOUTH
Adolescence
Child Abuse
Childhood
Dating
Drugs and Alcohol
Families
Incest
Pederasty
Pregnancy
Premarital Sex
Prostitution

Puberty and Puberty Rituals
Romance
Sex Education

COMMERCE
Advertising and Sex
Colonialism/Postcolonialism
   and Sex
Cosmetics
Fashion
Popular Culture
Popular Music
Pornography
Pornography, on the Internet
Prostitution
Sports
Workplace

EDUCATION
Internet
Psychoanalysis
Psychotherapy
Puberty and Puberty Rituals
Sex Education

GENDER AND GENDER IDENTITY
Cross Dressing/Drag
Feminism
Gender Roles
Masculinity
Sexism
Transgender/Transsexual

HEALTH
Abortion
AIDS/HIV
Birth Control

Domestic and Relationship
   Violence
Drugs and Alcohol
Erectile Dysfunction (ED)
Fetishes
Incest
Masturbation
Mental Health and Sex
Orgasm
Pregnancy
Premarital Sex
Prostitution
Psychoanalysis
Psychotherapy
Sex Education
Sexually Transmitted Infections
   (STIs)

INDIVIDUALS
Freud, Sigmund
Hirschfeld, Magnus
Kinsey, Alfred Charles
Reich, Wilhelm
Sanger, Margaret

LAW
Abortion
Birth Control
Censorship
Child Abuse
Divorce
Incest
Indigenous Peoples
Interracial/Ethnic Intimate
   Relationships
Morality and Ethics
Politics

Chronology of Selected Events

1900   Roebuck catalog offers the Giant Power Heidelberg Electric Belt for impotent men.

1901   Ida Craddock authors one of the first known "marriage" manuals entitled *The Wedding Night*.

1904   The first electric vibrator, "The Chattanooga," is sold to doctors only for $200.

1905   Sigmund Freud publishes his *Three Essays on the Theory of Sexuality*.

The League for the Protection of Motherhood is formed in Germany under the leadership of Helene Stöcker.

1908   Edward Carpenter's *The Intermediate Sex* is published in England.

Xavier Mayne (pseudonym for Edward Irenaeus Prime-Stevenson) publishes *Intersexes*, which includes some of the earliest writing in English about homosexuality.

1909   Webster's dictionary first defines homosexuality as a "morbid sexual passion for one of the same sex."

1910   Magnus Hirschfeld publishes *The Transvestites*.

1911   Women's rights activist Jin Yi publishes *Women's Bell* in Shanghai advocating freedom from arranged marriages.

1912   Dr. Eugen Steinach, a pioneer in the field of endocrinology, alters sexuality with his work on hormones.

The National Education Association (NEA) endorses sex education.

1913   Sigmund Freud publishes *Totem and Taboo*.

1914   Margaret Sanger publishes *The Woman Rebel*.

Magnus Hirschfield publishes *The Homosexuality of Men and Women*.

1916   First U.S. birth control clinic is opened in Brooklyn, New York, by Margaret Sanger.

1918   Margaret Sanger's successful suit allows New York doctors to advise their married patients about birth control.

Sears, Roebuck & Co. catalog sells a portable vibrator.

1919   Germany's Scientific Humanitarian Committee becomes the Institute for Sexual Research, the first major center for sexual science.

1920   Latex condoms are commercially marketed for the first time.

Ratification of the Nineteenth Amendment to the U.S. Constitution gives women the right to vote.

Soviet Union legalizes abortion (Stalin bans it in 1936).

Sigmund Freud publishes *Beyond the Pleasure Principle*.

1923   The British Parliament passes the Matrimonial Causes Act, which makes grounds for divorce the same for women and men.

1924   Society for Human Rights, the first U.S. gay organization, is incorporated in Illinois by Henry Gerber.

1927   Actress Mae West is convicted for using obscenity for her stage show, "Sex."

1928   *The Well of Loneliness*, a lesbian novel by Radclyffe Hall, is censored in England.

Margaret Mead publishes *Coming of Age in Samoa*.

1929   Bronislaw Malinowski publishes *The Sexual Life of Savages*.

1930   The Hays Production Code, which prohibits scenes that "stimulate the lower and baser element," becomes mandatory in the film industry.

Denmark first country to decriminalize homosexual sexual activity.

1931   The Federal Council of Churches endorses the use of birth control by married couples.

Eighty-five percent of college women wore rouge, lipstick, face powder, and nail polish.

1933   The Nazis destroy Magnus Hirschfeld's Scientific-Humanitarian Committee and library.

Denmark repeals its anti-sodomy laws.

1934   United States Customs prohibits importation of Henry Miller's sexually graphic novel, *Tropic of Cancer*.

1936   Havelock Ellis revises his *Studies in the Psychology of Sex* from four to seven volumes.

1938   Copies of *Life* magazine are seized because they contain photos of childbirth.

1940   The Birth Control Federation of America becomes The Planned Parenthood Federation of America.

1944   Lillian Smith publishes *Strange Fruit*, her novel of interracial love.

Seventeen magazine premiers.

Sweden repeals its anti-homosexual laws.

1946   The "bikini" is created in Paris by designer Louis Reard.

Benjamin Spock publishes his famous and highly influential *Common Sense Book of Baby and Child Care*.

1947   Publication of *Vice Versa*, the first lesbian magazine.

1948   Alfred Kinsey et al. publish *Sexual Behavior in the Human Male*.

U.S. divorce rate falls.

1949   Theodor Reik publishes *Of Love and Lust*.

1950   Founding of the Mattachine Foundation, the first effective gay rights group.

1952   Christine Jorgensen is the first person from the United States publicly known to have a "sex change," creating international notoriety.

1953   Alfred Kinsey et al. publish *Sexual Behavior in the Human Female*.

George Jorgensen undergoes a highly publicized sex operation to become Christine Jorgensen.

Simone de Beauvoir publishes *The Second Sex*.

Hugh Hefner publishes his first issue of *Playboy* magazine.

The term "gender role" first appears.

1956   *The Ladder*, a lesbian magazine, is published in San Francisco.

Allen Ginsberg publishes his long poem "Howl," about the destructive impact of materialism and conformity on American society.

1957   The Wolfenden Report recommends the decriminalization of homosexuality in the United Kingdom.

Kinsey's Institute for Sex Research is given the right to import erotic/pornographic materials for research purposes.

The U.S. Marital Fertility rate reaches its highest level in 25 years.

Roth v. United States establishes legal standards for the publication of pornography.

1958   Charles Keating founds Citizens for Decent Literature in Cincinnati, Ohio.

1959   D. H. Lawrence's *Lady Chatterley's Lover* is confiscated by U.S. postal authorities.

1960   The Playboy Club opens in Chicago.

The first oral contraceptive, Enovid, is approved by the FDA.

1961   Illinois decriminalizes homosexuality.

Drag performer Jose Sarria runs for a seat on the San Francisco Board of Supervisors, thus becoming the first openly gay person to seek public office.

New Motion Picture code allows treatment of homosexuality.

1962   James Baldwin publishes *Another Country*.

The Catholic Church council known as Vatican II is convened by Pope John XXIII.

1963   First gay rights pickets.

Betty Friedan publishes *The Feminine Mystique*.

1964 Founding of the Sex Information and Education Council of the United States.

Title VII of the Civil Rights Act prohibits employment discrimination on the basis of race, color, religion, national origin, or sex.

1965 *Griswold v. Connecticut* establishes the "right to privacy" in the use of contraceptives.

Family life version of sex education becomes compulsory in all schools accepting federal funds.

1966 Harry Benjamin publishes *The Transsexual Phenomena*.

Transsexual clinic opens at Johns Hopkins.

William Masters and Virginia Johnson publish *Human Sexual Response*.

The National Organization for Women (NOW) is formed.

1967 The CBS Special "The Homosexual" is reported by Mike Wallace.

The Abortion Law Reform Bill legalizes abortion in Great Britain.

"Hair," a play that includes nudity, opens on Broadway.

U.S. Supreme Court rules anti-miscegenation laws unconstitutional in *Loving v. Virginia*.

Great Britain legalizes consensual adult homosexual activity.

1968 Creation of the President's Commission on Obscenity and Pornography.

1969 The Stonewall Riots, a confrontation between New York City police and groups of gay people, begin June 27, the day of Judy Garland's funeral; the rights become a watershed for the gay rights movement.

California adopts the nation's first "no fault" divorce law.

Paragraph 175, outlawing homosexual acts, is finally repealed in West Germany.

Denmark becomes first country to legalize "hardcore" pornography.

GAY, the first weekly gay magazine, is issued with two southerners as the editors.

1970 The Campaign Against Moral Persecution (CAMP), the first Australian gay rights organization, is formed.

Shulamith Firestone publishes *The Dialectic of Sex*.

The First International Erotic Film Festival is held in San Francisco.

John Money publishes *Sex Reassignment*.

Our Bodies, Ourselves, a book about women's health and sexuality, is published by the nonprofit organization Our Bodies Ourselves.

1970 The first shelter for abused women opens (England).

1972 Kathy Kozachenko of the Human Rights Party becomes the first openly gay person to be elected to public office when she wins a seat on the Ann Arbor, Michigan City Council.

Release of the erotic movie *Deep Throat*, which eventually grosses more than $100 million.

Ms. Magazine is first published.

In *Eisenstadt v. Baird*, the Supreme Court gives an unmarried person the right to use contraceptives.

Broadcast of *That Certain Summer*, the first made-for-TV movie about homosexuality.

U.S. Congress passes Title IX prohibiting the exclusion of participation in a federally funded activity based on gender.

The American Psychiatric Association votes to remove homosexuality from the *DSM*.

1973 *Roe v. Wade* makes abortion legal in the United States.

The *Rocky Horror Picture Show*, a musical with a transsexual as a leading character, debuts in theaters.

1974 Phyllis Schlafly rallies women against the Equal Rights Amendment (ERA) to the Constitution.

Larry Flynt publishes *Hustler*.

Cleveland Board of Education v. LaFleur declares it illegal to force pregnant women to take maternity leave.

1975 International Women's Year with the United Nations's first conference on women.

1976 Shere Hite publishes *The Hite Report on Female Sexuality*.

1977 Anita Bryant launches her Save Our Children campaign opposing gay rights.

First National Women's Conference is held in Houston.

Charlotte Wolff publishes *Bisexuality*.

Although as yet unnamed and undiagnosed, AIDS cases begin appearing in the United States.

1978 Defeat of California Proposition 6, which would have banned homosexual teachers from the state's public schools.

The Pregnancy Discrimination Act bans employment discrimination against pregnant women.

Gay rights activist and San Francisco supervisor Harvey Milk is assassinated by former supervisor Dan White.

The Moral Majority, an evangelical Christian political organization, is founded by a group that includes Rev. Jerry Falwell.

1979 *DSM-III* includes gender identity disorder.

1981 Gay-related immune deficiency (GRID) is identified by the CDC.

1982 Alice Walker publishes *The Color Purple*.

Wisconsin becomes the first state to pass a gay rights statute.

1983 The HIV virus is identified.

1984 Berkeley, California, becomes the first city with a domestic partner law.

1985 Death of actor Rock Hudson due to AIDS.

1986 In *Bowers v. Hardwick*, the Supreme Court votes 5–4 to affirm state sodomy statutes.

1987 The controversial film *The Last Temptation of Christ* is released.

The first condom commercial airs on U.S. television.

1989 *Webster v. Reproductive Health Services* affirms the right of states to deny public funding for abortions and to prohibit public hospitals from performing abortions.

Denmark becomes the first country to legalize same-sex marriage.

1990 Congress passes the Americans with Disabilities Act (ADA), which includes job protections for persons with HIV and AIDS.

1991 The Clarence Thomas-Anita Hill hearings before the U.S. Senate revolve around the Supreme Court nominee's alleged sexual harassment of Hill.

Madonna publishes her book *Sex*, which contains sexually explicit photos of the singer.

1993 *Philadelphia*, a movie about a gay lawyer with AIDS, appears in theaters.

President Bill Clinton issues an executive order creating the "Don't Ask, Don't Tell" policy for gays in the military.

The USDA approves a female condom.

1994 Rape in marriage is made a crime in Great Britain.

1995 *Angels in America* debuts on Broadway.

1996 The Defense of Marriage Act passes in the U.S. Congress.

1997 Divorce legalized in Ireland.

First marital rape law passed in the United States.

1998 Maine rescinds the state's gay non-discrimination statute.

Introduction of Viagra for male impotence.

1999 Margaret MacGregor becomes the first woman to box and beat a man in an officially sanctioned bout.

An estimated 340 million new cases of curable sexually transmitted infections occur worldwide.

The Sex Discrimination (Gender Reassignment) Regulations make discrimination against transgender persons illegal in Great Britain.

2003 The U.S. Supreme Court declares sodomy laws unconstitutional.

2004 Massachusetts gives state sanction for gays and lesbians to marry.

2005 HBO's *Sex and the City* airs in syndication on network television.

2006 *Brokeback Mountain*, a movie about a sexual relationship between two cowboys, wins three Academy Awards.

2007 New Hampshire becomes fourth state to sanction civil unions.

The Encyclopedia

A

ABORTION. Abortion is widely defined as the intentional termination of a **pregnancy**. Medical practitioners often refer to an induced abortion as elective, voluntary, or therapeutic; a miscarriage is a spontaneous, unplanned abortion. Though performed since antiquity and practiced at all levels of societies, attitudes about abortion vary widely across social groups and eras. These attitudes reveal a great deal about the status of women, the intersections of gender with other markers of social status, relations between the sexes, and interconnections between religion and state. As such, abortion has a significant relationship to cultural beliefs and behaviors regarding sex and love. Technological changes, feminist movements, and ongoing re-examinations of social conceptions of life, the individual, gender, and family make the twentieth century a particularly noteworthy period in the history of abortion.

Abortions are performed by a variety of means, some of which are not safe. Herbs that induce abortion, the insertion of thin implements through the cervix, eliminating or restricting food intake, vigorous physical activity such as jumping up and down, and applying external pressure are among the methods that have been used; some of these are still in use. According to a 2004 report by the World Health Organization, 19 million abortions are performed under unsanitary or medically inappropriate conditions and 68,000 of the women die; out of every 10 pregnancies, one will result in an unsafe abortion—the largest numbers of these occur in Asia, Africa, and Latin America. Precise numbers of induced abortions worldwide are frequently hard to calculate due to inaccuracy or absence of data. The UN Population Division (2002) estimates that of the 50 million abortions performed each year, perhaps 40 percent are performed illegally. Of the total number of abortions, the majority are performed on women who are in long-term relationships, many of whom have children.

Abortions are performed for a wide variety of reasons and under innumerable circumstances. The decision may be individual, shared, or imposed. A woman may wish to end an unplanned or planned pregnancy for reasons related to the circumstances under which she became pregnant and other aspects of her life such as her economic situation, personal relationships, and health.

During the twentieth century, attitudes on abortion have become more liberal. Abortion was legalized following the Russian Revolution, a decision reversed by Stalin in 1936 to increase the rate of population growth. Iceland legalized abortion in 1935. Sweden did so in 1938, and Japan broadened the circumstances under which abortion was allowed in 1948. Most of Europe had legalized abortion by the 1970s, although some countries such as Ireland have only recently done so.

Abortion rights advocate Inga Coulter, left, and anti-abortion advocate Elizabeth McGee express their opposite views during a demonstration outside the Supreme Court in Washington, 1993. © AP Photo/Joe Marquette.

Prior to the mid-twentieth century, abortion was primarily discussed and conducted in private settings. Prominent social movements beginning in the United States and Europe in the 1960s and 1970s, in particular, the women's movement and the "sexual revolution," were key factors in moving discussions of abortion to the public sphere and bringing about the legalization of abortion or liberalization of abortion laws. The landmark 1973 *Roe v. Wade* ruling by the U.S. Supreme Court allowed abortions to be legally performed during the first two trimesters. This ruling did not end the controversy, however. In 1977, the U.S. Congress passed a law that made it impossible to use Medicaid funds for abortions other than for a narrow set of circumstances and therapeutic reasons. In recent years, numerous states have passed more restrictive abortion laws as the politics of abortion have extended from elections to court appointments. In 2001, President George W. Bush imposed a "global gag" rule that requires all organizations applying for U.S. funds to sign a document stating that they will not provide abortion services or any related counseling that involves advising women to seek an abortion. In 2006, the British government's Department for International Development began donating funds to organizations offering safe abortions, helping to make up for the loss of U.S. funding.

Changes in abortion laws around the world continued between 1988 and 1998 as there was a general shift from retribution to a greater emphasis on women's physical health, social welfare, and human rights. Government policies regarding abortion are also influenced by a perceived need to increase the size of the population (e.g., USSR under Stalin and Romania under Ceausescu) or to decrease it (e.g., China). During these ten years, twenty-six additional jurisdictions extended the circumstances in which abortions are legal and four countries limited the condition under which an abortion may be obtained. In the majority of Latin America countries, abortion remains illegal. Cuba and Puerto Rico and a few Caribbean countries allow it. Countries such as Chile, El Salvador, and Nicaragua prohibit abortions under all circumstances and actively prosecute women who have them. Other countries, such as Argentina, Bolivia, and Peru, allow abortion only in instances of rape or when the pregnant woman's life is in danger.

A study (Henshaw, Singh, and Haas 1999) of all countries with populations over one million and in which abortion was legal found that most have low rates of abortion and that strict limitations on abortion do not always result in a low rate. There is growing evidence, however, that the availability of safe and reliable contraceptives reduces the number of induced abortions. For example, abortion rates dropped sharply in central and eastern Europe when family planning services were instituted. According to the United Nations Population Fund, between 1995 and 1999 abortion rates for women in Romania, ages 15–44, fell from 52 to 11 per thousand. Overall, the evidence indicates that legalizing abortion reduces infant mortality and enhances the conditions of children's lives.

As the laws governing abortion differ tremendously across cultures, so, too, do attitudes. Abortion is widely approved of by women in Japan, as choices of other forms of birth control (e.g., oral contraceptives) were very limited until recent years. Some areas of China have banned prenatal tests conducted for the purpose of ascertaining the sex of the fetus, as has India. Nevertheless, there is evidence that in China, as well as Taiwan and Korea, sex selective abortions are common. Legal restrictions aside, cultural and economic reasons undergird a strong preference for sons over daughters in parts of Asia and South Asia.

Morality and ethics also inform the debate about abortion leading to questions such as: Is aborting a fetus the equivalent of the taking of a life after birth? Does a fetus have rights? Are they the equivalent to the rights of an adolescent or adult? Is abortion ethical under some circumstances and unethical under others? If so, how and where should these lines be drawn? For example, some people and groups argue that abortion is acceptable when it is a consequence of rape or incest, but not when the pregnancy is a result of consensual sexual intercourse. Some believe that abortion for any reason during the first trimester of pregnancy is unobjectionable but that later in the pregnancy there should be restrictions on the conditions under which it may be performed. As the UNFPA points out, the tendency to define pregnancy entirely as a "woman's issue," may reduce men's participation in many of the responsibilities it entails. Who can or should be empowered to make decisions regarding abortion?

There are many factors influencing attitudes towards abortion, including gender, age, education, urban or rural location, religious beliefs, and sexual liberalism. Despite the important role of feminists in pressuring Western governments to expand the range of circumstances under which a woman may legally obtain an abortion, there is no uniform feminist position on abortion. While there are numerous and prominent organizations that aim to keep abortion legal, there are also organizations of feminists who oppose abortion. Some argue that the pro-choice and pro-life debate reduces the complexity of the subject of abortion and fails to address the needs of women from marginalized communities.

Overall, those with the most traditional religious views are most likely to favor strongly restricting access to abortion. Since 1869, the leadership of the Catholic Church has not distinguished between the fetus at various stages of development and has condemned all abortions. Similar views are held within traditional Jewish, Muslim, and Hindu religious communities. Buddhist beliefs and practices vary across cultures. For example, there is much greater tolerance for abortion in Japan than in Thailand.

Abortion is not an issue that only pertains to heterosexuals. Women who identify as lesbian or bisexual who become pregnant as a result of consensual or nonconsensual sex sometimes seek abortions. LGBT organizations, like the National Gay and Lesbian Task Force, have taken stances for abortion, and others, like the Pro-Life Alliance of Gays and Lesbians, oppose it.

Major changes in available medical technologies generally make abortion a less dangerous procedure for the pregnant woman. They have not, however, simplified the worldwide debate. Procedures such as amniocentesis and ultrasound provide ways of learning more about the status of the fetus, including sex and abnormalities, raising increasing concerns about diminishing the value of some lives on the basis of such factors. RU-486, Mifepristone, and their successors have the potential to greatly reduce the cost of medical abortions and move the decision to end a pregnancy back to the private sphere. *See also* Birth Control; Feminism; Religions, Eastern; Religions, Western.

Further Reading: Basu, Alaka Malwade, ed. *The Sociocultural and Political Aspects of Abortion: Global Perspectives.* Westport, CT: Praeger, 2003; Guttmacher Institute. "Abortion." http://www.guttmacher.org/sections/abortion.php. A nonprofit organization for sexual and reproductive health research, policy analysis, and public education, 2006; Henshaw, Stanley K., Susheela Singh, and Taylor Haas. "The Incidence of Abortion Worldwide." *International Family Planning Perspectives* 25 (Supplement) (1999): S30–38; available at http://www.guttmacher.org/pubs/journals/25s3099.html; Kulczycki, Andrzej. *The Abortion Debate in the World Arena.* New York: Routledge, 1999; Levine, Philip B. *Sex and Consequences: Abortion, Public Policy, and the Economics of Fertility.* Princeton and Oxford: Princeton University Press, 2004; Mundigo, Axel I., and Cynthia Indriso, eds. *Abortion in the Developing World.* London and New York: Zed Books, 1999; Silliman, Jael, Marlene Gerber Fried, Elena Gutierrez, and Loretta Ross. *Undivided Rights: Women of Color Organize for Reproductive Justice.* Cambridge, MA: South End Press, 2004; United Nations Population Fund. "Reproductive Health: A Matter of Equity." Chapter 4 of the UNFPA State of the World Population 2005. http://www.unfpa.org/swp/2005/english/ch4/index.htm. Focuses on reproductive health conditions worldwide including the problem of unsafe abortions, 2005; United Nations Populations Division. *Abortion Policies: A Global Review.* Vols. I–III. New York: United Nations Publications, 2002; Woliver, Laura R. *The Political Geographies of Pregnancy.* Urbana: University of Illinois Press, 2002.

Karen Lovaas

ADOLESCENCE. Adolescence is a period of social and personal development that falls between **childhood** and adulthood. Over the course of the nineteenth century, improvements in health and nutrition lowered the average age at which North American youths entered **puberty**. Yet as they matured and entered into sexual relationships earlier, these youths simultaneously chose to delay their commitment to marriage. The net result, by the early 1900s, was a lengthened period of adolescence, whose individual and cultural impact continued throughout the twentieth century. Importantly, this impact extended to research on love and sexuality. Just as romantic and sexual attachments became integral to the experience of adolescence, so, too, adolescence has proven a key site for investigations of sex and **romance**.

Although psychologist G. Stanley Hall did not coin the word *adolescence*, his groundbreaking 1904 study popularized the term to such an extent that he is often viewed as the man who invented, rather than studied, the modern adolescent. Today, most Westernized adults conceive of adolescence as a crucial stage of biological, emotional, and cognitive growth, one frequently accompanied by anxiety and tumult. It is fair to credit Hall with carving out this space between childhood and adult maturity, but it is important also to note that these boundaries are constructed. Adolescence is not a biological given, nor is it historically or geographically universal. Himself a product of late-Victorian Era and a man committed to Darwin's theory of evolution, Hall cast adolescence as a culturally specific experience. Whereas all humans passed through a stage of puberty (after which they became capable of sexual reproduction) adolescence, he believed, was limited to members of "civilized" races, who tried to impose a buffer between the possibility of sexual reproduction and its actual occurrence. Reflecting his ambivalent views on sexuality, Hall considered adolescence as a sort of safety net: a cultural and developmental stage meant to fill the dangerous space between puberty and marriage. In this sense, adolescence, as defined by Hall, was not just a stage of life in which sexuality played a part, but one originally *defined by* sexuality.

Following the mid-twentieth-century work of psychologists like Erik Erikson and Henry Stack Sullivan, much of the current research on adolescent sexuality endows it with a dual importance. First, sexual and romantic experiences during adolescence are thought to contribute to the formation of one's identity. This includes sexual identity but functions more broadly to encompass all the ways individuals are situated in relation to our peers, families, and to society. Second, adolescent experiences may predict future sexual behavior as adults and the nature of the relationships likely to be formed with others. However, these correlations are both far from exact, as evidenced in recent research with same-sex romantic relationships. Not all teenagers who experience same-sex attractions or encounters identify themselves as gay, nor will they necessarily do so as adults. Similarly, not all adults who identify as gay or lesbian experienced same-sex relations as adolescents (though they may have desired them). The connection, then, between relationships in adolescence and those in adulthood is neither obvious nor direct.

Slightly easier to investigate than the future impact of adolescent sexual and romantic relations are the biological, psychological, and social factors that structure these relations in adolescence. Literally meaning "covered in fine hair," puberty is a time of accelerated physical growth and hormonal activity, determined by a combination of genetic, nutritional, and environmental factors. It is characterized by the maturation of sexual organs, which results both in the physical capability of parenthood and an increased sex drive. Alongside and actually preceding these physical changes by about a year, increased hormone levels play a key role in the development of sexual organs and secondary sex characteristics.

While itself primarily a biological phenomenon, puberty expands in significance when physical changes bring psychological and social consequences. These can be seen quite clearly at the beginning moments of pubertal change. For males, early maturation often presents itself as an advantage: increased physical size for boys has been linked to greater self-assurance, popularity, and even academic performance. Early initiation into both heterosexual and same-sex relations is linked to androgen levels produced in males during puberty. For girls, however, social factors, rather than hormone levels, are the most reliable predictors of sexual activity. Additionally, an early onset of puberty means something very different to most girls than to their male counterparts: breast development can lead to harassment or other unwanted attention, in addition to more private emotional responses, which are often negative. Thus, a tangle of factors, of which gender and the age of puberty onset are only two, contribute to the picture of sexuality in adolescence. Peers, families, schools, and cultural context influence and are influenced by experiences of love and sex.

Familial relations influence adolescent sexual experiences in several ways. Parents enact relationships for the benefit or detriment of their children, setting examples through their marriages, divorces, and child-rearing practices. The adolescent's personal relationship with a parent—whether it be loving, disappointing, distant, or abusive—also influences what he or she seeks from peer and romantic relations. In general, teens with more secure and fulfilling parental relations are likely to delay sex and to have fewer partners. While these findings encourage parental involvement, excessive or intrusive control has been linked to increased sexual activity among adolescents.

Although parents also wield significant influence through their attitudes about adolescent sexuality, the role of one's peers is often even more powerful. Broadening of one's peer group to include members of the other sex characterizes the early stages of adolescence (assumed between 11 to 14 years of age). These cross-gender friendships are hugely important because most adolescents' **dating** experience develops from them. Group dating and eventually couples dating are largely possible through this pool of friends. Peer relationships within one's gender are also important since it is in adolescence that one's friends become a support system alongside, and often supplanting, the family. More broadly, one's peers exert influence on sexual and romantic relationships by becoming sources of information (sometimes incorrect) and attitudes about sex. In high school, teenagers continue to cite "social status" as one of the many factors that influence their dating choices. Interestingly, they also frequently overestimate the sexual experience of their peers.

School is, of course, not only the stage for the formation of friendships and romantic relationships, but a site for educating adolescents about sexuality. Formal sexuality education varies considerably across cultures. In Sweden, for instance, students begin compulsory sex education between the ages of 10 and 12, and there, as in much of western Europe, adolescent sex is viewed as a predictable and acceptable part of development. In the United States, sex education retains the faulty stigma of being a catalyst for sexual activity. A recent study, for example, found that thirty percent of middle and high schools maintain an "abstinence-only" program, which conflicts with what most parents desire for their children (Kaiser Family Foundation). Education, however, takes many forms. In Cameroon and much of sub-Saharan Africa, for instance, formal **sex education** has been described as "a conspiracy of silence" that ill equips sexually active teenagers to negotiate the risks of HIV (Brown, 83). In the region's more traditional societies, rites of passage at puberty provide youths with information about sexual hygiene and activity as well as gender expectations. Some of these rituals may instill more accurate information than the schools, while others, such as female circumcision, have proven controversial. Recently, female legislators in Cameroon began formally campaigning to outlaw the practice of genital mutilation.

Experiences of adolescent sexuality in Sweden, the United States, and Cameroon do not merely differ according to each country's means of sex education. An array of historical and current cultural factors influence youths at every step along the way. In sub-Saharan Africa, female fertility has long been seen as a necessary component of womanhood. Consequently, some girls continue to view teenage **pregnancy** as a means of avoiding the stigma of infertility. This clearly contrasts to the prevalent attitudes in the United States, where teenage motherhood is typically cast as a problem to be solved. In the Swedish context, it is even more complicated, for teenage pregnancy is arguably even more unacceptable than in the United States; where sex is tolerated, pregnancy is not, thus the stress on a more comprehensive approach to sexual education.

In addition to differences across cultures, adolescent relationships clearly change over time. The gulf between physical maturity and **marriage** grew over the course of the twentieth century, leading to increased rates of **premarital sex**, particularly among white females. In 1930, adolescents in the United States began dating at age 16; by the 1970s, the age had dropped to 13. The age of first sexual contact likewise dropped during the twentieth century. Whereas only 7 percent of girls under 16 had experienced sexual intercourse in 1950, that figure rose to almost 45 percent by the early 1980s. Recent figures for American adolescents place their first sexual encounter at about age 17; nearly one-half of adolescents between the ages of 15 and 19 have had sex at least once.

But facts like these do not fully capture the picture of adolescent sexuality. For instance, statistics on **virginity** do not reveal whether someone's "first time" was an isolated event or initiative of a pattern. Further, much of what is known about adolescent sexuality comes from psychological and sociological studies, most of which concentrate on only one adolescent's account of their relationships without seeking information from his or her partner. Moreover, the experiences of heterosexual, white, middle-class adolescents dominate, at the expense of ethnic and sexual minorities (though this is changing). Perhaps the most difficult to grasp, however, is the qualitative nature of sexual and romantic activity among adolescents. For example, the most common adolescent sexual experience (not lending itself to the statistical breakdowns) is erotic fantasy. Solitary and clearly non-coital, fantasizing is almost ubiquitous.

Studies of adolescence have excelled at investigating some topics while falling short on others. The question of adolescent love, for example, is an elusive one for most adults, be they parents or researchers. Younger adolescents very frequently label their desires as "love," perhaps idealizing their emotions but nevertheless announcing them as powerful and legitimate. And yet, many adults resist viewing these emotions in the terms that adolescents ascribe to them. "Puppy love," maybe, but not "true love." Psychologists currently working against this tendency suggest that we may have come full-circle from G. Stanley Hall on this point. If Hall and his contemporaries viewed adolescent sexuality as the largest threat to the values and order of society, adolescent love might perform a similar role for us today. *See also* Heterosexuality; Homosexuality.

Further Reading: Advocates for Youth. http://www.advocatesforyouth.org. Advocates programs and policies for helping adults and youths negotiate an array of sexually related topics; site provides recent statistical fact sheets on adolescent sexual behavior in a global context, October 2006; Brown, B. Bradford, et al. *The World's Youth: Adolescence in Eight Regions of the Globe*. Cambridge: Cambridge University Press, 2002; Guttmacher Institute. "Facts on American Teens' Sexual and Reproductive Health." Available at http://www.guttmacher.org/pubs/fb_ATSRH.html, 2006; Hall, G. Stanley. *Adolescence: Its Psychology and its Relations to Physiology, Anthropology, Sociology, Sex, Crime, Religion, and Education*. 2 vols. New York: D. Appleton and Company, 1904; Kaiser Family Foundation. "Sex Education in America." Available at http://www.kff.org/newsmedia/upload/Sex-Education-in-America-Summary.pdf, 2004; Moore, Susan, and Doreen Rosenthal. *Sexuality in Adolescence*. London: Routledge, 1993.

Wendy Korwin

ADULTERY. *See* Infidelity/Extramarital Sex

ADVERTISING AND SEX. Advertising is a technique to draw public attention to commercial and non-commercial services and products through a variety of **media**. Wall or rock painting for commercial advertising is a manifestation of an ancient media advertising form, which remains popular in many parts of Asia, Africa, and South America. Since the 1920s, advertising has grown massively, and current advertising expenditures are 80 times greater than in that decade. By the mid-twentieth century, advertising had been transformed by a modern, more scientific approach in which creativity was allowed to shine, producing unexpected messages that made advertisements more tempting to consumers' eyes—particularly with images and language relating to love or sex. Such images are drawn from society at large and reflect cultural values, but advertisers also shape the status and roles of their target audiences, thus influencing the sexual values and attitudes of the society as a whole. Advertisements enter **popular culture** through media such as billboards, printed flyers, radio, cinema and television advertisements, Web banners and pop-ups, bus stops, magazines, newspapers, sides of buses, taxicab doors, subway platforms and trains, and the backs of event tickets and supermarket receipts. Advertising techniques employed by different advertisers include emotional transfer (love, sex, and friends), **humor**, and testimonial. Others employ violence, stereotypes, and controversial topics. Stereotypical **gender role** portrayal and sexual content in advertisements are among the most popular.

As far back as in the 1930s, most print advertisements featured woman in the home, taking care of the children while her husband worked. In a *Campbell's Soup* advertisement, which appeared in a 1936 issue of *Life,* a woman was featured in a colonial log cabin setting, cooking soup over the fireplace as she prepared the meal for her husband. There was a shift in the 1940s, as men went to the war, and print advertisements portrayed the changing times. Campbell's Soup ads now featured working mothers who needed quick and easy meals to feed their children after a long day of factory work. After World War II, female factory workers were replaced by secretaries, nurses and homemakers as depicted in many print advertisements.

The rise of mass circulation magazines, radio broadcasting, and television provided new media for advertisers to reach consumers. Sexual messages were incorporated into these advertisements. Perhaps one of the most famous examples of these was launched in 1955, when Marlboro, a minor cigarette brand formerly marketed for its mildness and aimed at women smokers, was transformed. The "Marlboro Man" modeled a rugged cowboy (and later included a Marine, cab driver, and sailor) smoking "a cigarette designed for men that women like." Despite the heterosexual makeover, "The first 'Marlboro Country' featured skinny models, several of them gay, wearing Dingo boots and spurs mistakenly mounted upside down with the San Francisco Bay Bridge between their legs" (Carrier 2005, paragraph 6). Marlboro eventually became one of the world's best-selling cigarette brands and the "Marlboro Man," an advertising icon—one of whom later became an AIDS activist. In fact, the macho and muscular Marlboro clone became visible in the 1970s gay communities as Marlboro cigarettes became the most popular brand among gay men.

The roles of women multiplied and diversified in many countries during the second half of the twentieth century. Women across cultures, including Asian women brought up in traditional and conservative ways, who for centuries had accepted their roles as wives, mothers, and inferiors to men, began demanding equal footing. However, advertisers were slow in picking up on this change. From 1960 to 1979, a time when women entered the workforce in unprecedented numbers, advertisements failed to depict a significant increase in women's employment outside the home. Women continued to be portrayed in traditional female roles: cooking, cleaning, and caring for children. Men were far more likely than women to be presented as experts or authorities. Advertisements, such as those featuring stylishly dressed and independent looking women for Virginia Slims cigarettes under the 1968 moniker "You've come a long way baby," were the exception.

Advertisements are still telling us what it means to be a desirable individual—in a sexist and sexualized way. Cover girls sell magazines that picture perfect female models while those magazines catering to men show wealthy, powerful, and confident men. Topless masculine men and beautiful voluptuous women portrayed in such magazines' advertisements convey a sexual message. Sexually explicit pop-up windows, **Internet** banners, spam e-mail messages, and search results are also used by advertisers to grab attention. Although many Internet users find these advertisements offensive, they are not illegal.

Most people realize that such media images rarely reflect reality. However, that does not mean that these images are not influential, otherwise they would not be used. Advertisements often represent an ideal image of the way that life should be like, especially how an ideal woman or man should appear and behave. In addition to reinforcing sexist notions about ideal women, advertisements exploit sexuality and love. Perfume, lingerie, and designer jeans are often sold on the very purpose of attracting a sexual partner. Advertisers also appeal to the audience's need for love, affection, and belongingness. Whether buying a diamond ring, purchasing a dozen roses, or subscribing to a supplementary credit card for their loved ones on Valentine's Day, advertisers recognize the power of romance and the lure of desire: buy the beer, get the girl. Bodies are equated with commodities, and presented as the rewards of consumption.

Sexually laced advertisement topics are far more explicit in the twenty-first century than they were a decade or two ago. This, however, varies across societies. Nudity is generally regarded as offensive in the United States. Although partial nudity is acceptable, it may result in some boycotting the product. One commonly sees men and women in intimate and suggestive poses, but advertisers refrain from any display of frontal nudity, except in some fashion print ads and men's magazines. However, in European countries, such as Denmark, Germany, Italy and France, consumers generally do not have a problem with nudity in advertisements. French advertisers frequently show partially clad or nude women and use sexually suggestive language. Conversely, countries in Asia and the Middle East tend to be more conservative, frowning upon all kinds of salacious displays and indirect sexual references and prohibiting the advertising, in any form, of pantyhose, contraceptives, sanitary napkins, and toilet papers. Women cannot be seen even in advertisement for fear of arousing the sexual interest and desire of men. Advertisers in Iran, therefore, use simile (objects) to illustrate product attributes. One advertisement for hair shampoo used a cat (replacing woman's hair) to illustrate softness of hair (via the cat's fur), strong roots (minimize hair falling versus cat's hairball), and ease to groom (comb).

There is usually no simple explanation of why a particular advertisement is considered offensive, although advertising guidelines dictate what is sexy, sexist, or indecent. Different standards of taste, modesty, and even sexual imagery exist around the world based on cultural values and social norms, and these standards are constantly shifting. Religion and other value systems are certainly crucial in defining these standards.

The representation of **homosexuality, bisexuality**, and **transgender** people in advertisements have also increased since the 1990s, although specialized advertisements within gay or lesbian magazines existed two decades earlier. Globally, Swedish home furnishing retailer IKEA has a long history of including homosexual and transgender themes in its advertising, from featuring a same sex couple buying furniture together to featuring a woman in a hospital who has just undergone gender reassignment surgery with the theme "Redecorate Your Life." Philip Morris, the cigarette producer, placed the first ever cigarette advertisement in a gay men's periodical, *Genre*, in 1992. Today, many companies incorporate gay, lesbian, bisexual, and transgender themes into mainstream advertisements, especially in Western

European countries. In the Netherlands, a print advertisement showed a girl and her two daddies, one kissing the other on the cheek; another advertisement in Germany depicted two men in bed together. Other companies who have targeted gay, lesbian, bisexual, and transgender consumers include Unilever, Volkswagen, PepsiCo, General Electric, and Levi Strauss. However, advertising stereotypes, ranging from diva queens to scary leather men, remain.

Advertisements are made to sell products, not create social change. Nevertheless, advertising is generally more influential than literature in spreading ideas given its high accessibility. Many people have protested the portrayal of sexual themes in advertisements. Nevertheless, advertisements can be a useful means of dispensing information about sexuality and health, as seen in the increase of contraceptive advertisements on television. *See also* Cosmetics; Fashion; Sexism.

Further Reading: Boddewyn, Jean J. "Sex and Decency Issues in Advertising: General and International Dimensions." *Business Horizons* 34, no. 5 (1991): 13–22; Borchers, Timothy A. *Persuasion in the Media Age.* 2nd ed. New York: McGraw-Hill, 2005; Carrier, Jim. "Marlboro Man at 50—Icon or Illusion?" *San Francisco Chronicle*, January 5, 2005. Available at http://www.sfgate .com/cgi-bin/article.cgi?f=/c/a/2005/01/07/EDGOQALLP11.DTL; Engel, Jack. *Advertising: The Process and Practice.* New York: McGraw-Hill, 1980; Goffman, Erving. *Gender Advertisements.* New York: Macmillan, 1979; Greenberg, Jerrold S., Clint E. Bruess, and Debra W. Haffner. *Exploring the Dimensions of Human Sexuality.* 2nd ed. Sudbury, MA: Jones and Bartlett, 2004; *Wikipedia, The Free Encyclopedia.* "Sex in Advertising." http://en.wikipedia.org/wiki/ Sex_in_advertising (accessed February 6, 2007). Provides a variety of sexual images employed by advertisers, December 2006.

Reiko Yeap

AGING. The passage of time changes people and it is generally believed that the character of love and sex also changes with age, specifically, that passionate love and sexual **desire** fade away. The notion that "old people" are not sexual—they are not supposed to have sex, to want to have sex, or even be able to have sex—dates at least as far back as Socrates, who reported that he was glad to be rid of "that mad and furious monster," sexual love. Love is supposed to grow less physical and more spiritual with age—culminating in the "platonic" ideal where physical love (i.e., sex) has no part. The explanation has been that as one matures physically and intellectually, one gains better mastery of the physical self and becomes more reasonable and rational; therefore, one's actions are less likely to be controlled by emotion, passion, or instinct. Similarly, while passion, sex, and sexual desire are often described as "hot," old age is often viewed as a time of cooling down—when the flames of passion are extinguished. Similarly, love in later life has been said to be neither passionate nor physical but rather paternal, companionate, platonic, or even patriotic. Old people are supposed to love their country, their children, and their spouses—in a best-friends sort of way. The ubiquity and tenacity of these ideas are remarkable: As one authority put it: "Every elderly man should feel content to see his virility die a natural and easy death" (Sperry 1900: 104). If the scientific and medical models of sexuality that dominated the twentieth century, tied sexuality and gender very closely to reproductive biology, perhaps the twenty-first century, which began with the baby-boom generation entering later life, might come to see sexuality as a more complex aspect of identity that transcends the simple biological drive to reproduce.

Historically, age has been measured with a sexual yardstick: old age and sexual vitality have been treated as mutually exclusive—you can't be both old and sexual at the same time. One result of the lack of a model for "healthy" or "normal" sexuality in late life is that expressions of sexual activity or desire in the elderly have been cast as abnormal, deviant, neurotic, or even pathological. Thus, ironically, the aged have been believed to be particularly prone to sexual misbehavior and deviance, from comparatively "passive" crimes like voyeurism and exhibitionism, to the more supposedly socially threatening transgressions of **homosexuality** and **pederasty**. This is, in part, because *any* expression of sexuality is seen as abnormal and an indication that the person is either sick, demented, or perverted. Older men, for example, who were believed to be incapable of "normal" sexual relations, were said to be prone to being attracted to young people, and particularly to young men or boys. Interestingly, the "pederast" historically has been an older man attracted to a younger man, who is doubly damned for combining the violation of cultural norms about same-sex liaisons with the violation of norms about intergenerational relations. Menopausal women, too, have been said to be subject to a kind of hysterical urge to have sex with inappropriate partners, including other women; their increased sex drive was attributed to their "masculinized" state. Similarly, young people attracted to older people are thought to suffer from a condition called "gerontophilia."

Though the model of a sexless old age has dominated Western civilization since well before the twentieth century, there have been alternative visions. Sex-reformer Marie Stopes, for instance, argued in the 1930s: "There is no inherent physical reason why mutual married love should not last till death" (Stopes 1936: 264). Later in the century, feminist theorists proposed that menopause can be experienced as sexually liberating because a woman is freed from the social constraints of potential motherhood.

Aging is a complex phenomenon that varies according to a person's sex, class, ethnicity, and culture. Not only does being old have different meanings, but the physical experience can also differ. Years of manual labor can age someone differently than a desk job. Diet can affect the course of aging, as can cultural expectations. Some scholars claim that the pains of old age are fewer in cultures where the aged are supposedly revered, such as Japan. The claim that it is easy to grow old in Japan, however, has been questioned by other scholars.

There is much evidence that, despite social pressure and expectations, many people have not been at all content to embrace a sexless old age. The wildly popular "rejuvenation" therapies of the 1920s (including testicular grafts from ape to man) are testament to aging men's desire to resist an impotent old age and a persistence in seeing sexual vitality as a sign of youth. This was also the era when sex hormones were discovered, identified, synthesized, and marketed. Menopause—now considered a hormonal crisis treatable by pharmaceutical intervention—replaced the "female climacteric" which had described a more general transitional time of life. The corresponding "male climacteric" was for a time eclipsed, but resurfaced several decades later in the medicalized form of "male menopause" or "andropause." While hormone replacement therapy remains controversial, drugs like Viagra promise ever-greater sexual ability in later life.

Despite medical advances, little is actually known about aging in relation to sex and love. Those who have studied and theorized about sex (e.g., **Freud** and **Kinsey**) have rarely considered old age; authorities on aging and geriatrics have seldom addressed sexual issues. Nevertheless, the relationship of aging to sex and love is full of enduring, unproven, and often contradictory assumptions: old men are believed to be both impotent and sexually dangerous; aging women are both sex-crazed and frigid; intergenerational relationships are both rejuvenating and life-threatening. The first-ever survey of the sexual feelings and behaviors of adults over age 45 was not conducted until 1999, and the results indicated that sex and sexuality remain an important part even into extreme old age. Other studies have found two-thirds of the unmarried population over 70 remains sexually active, and that half of the people over 80 claim that sex is at least as important to them in the present as it has been in the past.

While many older, retired people have sex lives that would be envied by those in mid-life, mid-career, or mid-child-rearing, it is true that average rates of sexual activity, at least as measured by traditional penile-vaginal intercourse, tend to drop off with age. However, concluding that this reflects a loss of interest is a mistake. The most common limitation on the sexual activity of older men is their physical ability, which can be either directly or indirectly related to health. For example, many people take beta-blockers, drugs notorious for causing **erectile dysfunction**. Thus, while high blood pressure would not itself affect a man's sex life, the medication he takes for this condition might very well do so. Similarly, surgery for prostate cancer, another condition that does not in itself affect the sex drive, frequently results in impotence. Interestingly, the most significant limitation on older women's sexual activity is not their health, but the availability of an able partner. In addition to the medical problems facing many men, since women tend to live longer than men, there are many more aged women than men (in the United States, by the age of 80, the ratio is 10:7; by 85 it is greater than 2:1). Not surprisingly, ageism has been called a feminist issue. French existentialist philosopher Simone de Beauvoir, for example, noted that old women are doubly invisible: once for being old and again for being women.

Love and sex remain important parts of life to the very end, and have begun to be recognized as quality of life issues for the aging and aged. There is a need for **sex education** for older, institutionalized populations (and, importantly, for those staff members who serve them), including access to condoms and STI testing. Until very recently, for instance, **masturbation** in these institutional settings was considered unacceptable, anti-social behavior, and justified both sedation and restraint of the perpetrator. Today, progressive nursing homes recognize the importance of their residents' rights to sexual expression, privacy, and respect. *See also* Mental Health and Sex.

Further Reading: AARP Policy & Research. http://www.aarp.org/research/family/life-styles/2004_sexuality.html. This site contains the report on the 1999 AARP/Modern Maturity survey on the sexual attitudes and behavior of adults over 45 and a 2004 update on the report. Also, see related articles in its online magazine at http://www.aarpmagazine.org/lifestyle/relationships/great_sex.html, May 2005; Cohen, Lawrence. *No Aging in India.* Berkeley: University of California Press, 1998; Friedan, Betty. *The Fountain of Age.* New York: Touchstone Press, 1993; Gullette, Margaret. *Aged by Culture.* Chicago: University of Chicago Press, 2004; Sperry, Lyman. *Husband and Wife.* New York, 1900; Stearns, Peter. *Old Age in Pre-industrial Society.* New York: Holmes and Meier Publishers, 1982; Stopes, Marie. *Change of Life.* New York: G.P. Putnam's Sons, 1936; Traphagan, John. *Taming Oblivion.* Albany, NY: SUNY Press, 2000; Walker, Bonnie. *Sexuality and the Elderly: A Research Guide.* Westport, CT: Greenwood Press, 1997.

Sarah Goodfellow

AIDS/HIV. AIDS, the international pandemic of the late twentieth century, is caused by the human immunodeficiency virus (HIV), an insidious virus that slowly weakens and destroys the immune system, leaving the body vulnerable to deadly assaults from bacteria and other viruses. HIV is generally transmitted through the exchange of body fluids, such as blood and semen. The common routes of HIV transmission are needle sharing in intravenous drug use and unprotected sexual intercourse (both vaginal and anal). Although recent research suggests that HIV has been around for several decades, the medical establishment did not officially recognize it until 1981, when the first reported cases were documented in the United States. Since then, HIV has quickly spread to affect just about every region in the world; close to 40 million people worldwide are living with HIV (UNAIDS 2006). AIDS/HIV affects children and adults, women, men, and transgender people, wealthy and poor, educated and uneducated, people of different ethnicities, religions, and cultures, and individuals across the spectrum of sexual identities. Africa remains the epicenter of the epidemic where AIDS is the leading cause of death in the sub-Saharan region. However, HIV prevalence is increasing in both South and Southeast Asia, most notably China, Indonesia, Papua New Guinea and Vietnam.

This international pandemic has revealed how sexuality is intricately connected with the invisible dynamics of race, social class, gender, and culture as individuals and communities attempt to deal with, and, at times, ignore and elude, the rapid spread and harsh realities of HIV infection. Because of the powerful cultural stigma associated with certain sexual practices and drug use, many public officials from different regions of the world initially denied the existence of HIV in their communities, which resulted in further marginalization and denial of care for individuals and groups living with the virus. After more than a quarter of a century since its inception, AIDS has become the pandemic of the "Other"—African Americans, Latinos, the poor, people living in inner cities in the United States, and mostly black and poor people from developing countries in the southern hemisphere.

United Nations staff members and a child of a U.N. employee unfold a section of the AIDS Memorial Quilt at the U.N., 2001, in preparation for its display at the U.N. General Assembly Special Session on HIV/AIDS. © AP Photo/Marty Lederhandler.

AIDS/HIV has essentially become two parallel epidemics, one at the biomedical and another at the cultural level. The biomedical epidemic—the chronicle of an infectious disease and the search for a cure—has gone through three distinct periods. The first was searching for a causal agent, understanding modes of transmission, and attempting to develop a cure. In 1984, researchers Luc Montagnier in France and Robert Gallo in the United States isolated a new retrovirus, which later became known as HIV, as the causal agent for AIDS. An HIV antibody test was licensed a year later. Medical researchers identified exchange of body fluids (primarily blood and semen) as the primary modes of HIV transmission. Clinical trials for the first antiretroviral agent for AIDS, zidovudine or azidothymidine (AZT), started in 1986 and the drug was later approved by the U.S. Federal Drug Administration (FDA) for treating people living with AIDS/HIV. In the next several years, a number of antiretroviral medications were tested; however, the efficacy of these drugs was limited.

The second period was characterized by the introduction of a different class of HIV drugs—protease inhibitors—around 1995. These new medications were added to existing HIV drugs—a combination that was later known as highly active antiretroviral therapy (HAART) to treat individuals living with HIV infection. During this period, a viral load test was also developed. HAART's success and the development of a viral load test significantly decreased deaths due to AIDS in the United States and other wealthy nations. AIDS/HIV quickly evolved from a fatal and acute illness to a chronic health condition, a major shift that signaled the third period of the epidemic. However, HAART is not a cure for AIDS; many people experience from mild to severe side effects and the number of drug-resistant strains of HIV has increased in recent years. Although testing for an AIDS vaccine continues, the promise of a safe and effective one does not appear realistic in the immediate future. Further, in developing nations, most people living with AIDS/HIV cannot afford the expensive HIV drugs, and relatively straightforward HIV interventions—such as condom use—have not been implemented.

AIDS/HIV, however, is not simply a medical condition and the story of an infectious disease. It is also a cultural struggle over scientific, sexual, and social processes of signification associated with the biomedical epidemic. Indeed, the pandemic created conflicts over definitions and meanings, questions of **desire** and pleasure, and struggles over representation.

Cultural struggles over definitions and meanings started at the onset of the biomedical crisis. The definition of AIDS itself has evolved and changed over the years. In 1981, medical researchers called the newly identified medical condition GRID (gay-related immunodeficiency). The process of coupling a medical condition with a sexual identity served to create, maintain, and perpetuate discursive dichotomies and social hierarchies in the contemporary Western world (for example, homosexual/the "general population"; us/them; guilty/innocent; perpetrator/victim; anus/vagina; love/death; normal/abnormal). As disease and marginal groups in society (such as gays, injecting drug users, and commercial sex workers) became linked by the dominant biomedical discourse of AIDS, the notion of "high-risk" groups emerged. As the name suggests, "high-risk" groups focus on identity—who people are personally, socially, and culturally—rather than behavior—what people do that might put them at risk for HIV infection. This focus maintains a safe distance between the mainstream (heterosexuals) and the disenfranchised (homosexuals and drug users) in First World nations.

AIDS activist groups, such as AIDS Coalition to Unleash Power, or ACT UP, in various U.S. cities, have emerged to respond to the social, symbolic, and material inequities produced by medical, political, and social institutions. The biomedical discourse of AIDS has also perpetuated discursive dichotomies between the First and Third World. "African AIDS," for example, characterizes Africa as a dark and infectious continent where death, disease, filth, and decay are rampant and Africans as primitive people of unbridled lust and uncontrollable passion. The discourse of African AIDS draws on colonial narratives by tacitly comparing the rationality, civility, and cleanliness of the West to the irrationality, primitivism, and filthiness of the "Other."

AIDS/HIV also drew attention to cultural contestations over questions of desire and pleasure. The notion of safer sex in HIV education and prevention programs requires acknowledgement of sexual desire and pleasure, recognition of multiple forms of sexual interaction, and explicit talk about sexual activity. This has been challenging and complex in different cultural contexts. In Latin American countries, churches have been resistant to **sex education** but often played a positive role in combating AIDS-related stigma. In Thailand, the "100 percent Condom Use Programme" was successfully implemented to empower the workers in the commercial sex industry, and other Asian nations (such as Cambodia, China, and the Philippines) have adopted it for their populations.

Although often sensationalized by corporate **media**, the HIV epidemic brought discussions of same-sex sexuality and sexual practices into the mainstream. Gays and lesbians are now increasingly visible in public discourse through transnational media. The U.S. gay media has sensationalized "barebacking," the deliberate engagement in unprotected anal intercourse. Barebacking is now an important subject of discussion among gay men, **mental health** professionals, public health workers, and AIDS educators. "Bug chasers"—individuals who deliberately seek to become infected with HIV—and "gift givers"—people who infect bug chasers—have also received national attention in U.S. media.

Disputes over representation are another facet of the cultural epidemic associated with AIDS/HIV. Representations of AIDS have gone through periods of "gaying" (association of AIDS with homosexuals), "de-gaying" (uncoupling the association of AIDS with gays by emphasizing heterosexual transmission and vulnerability), and "re-gaying" (returning to the focus on AIDS and male-to-male sexual transmission). Since the onset, AIDS has been mostly associated with white homosexual men in First World nations. Such connection has been costly to women, who were generally neglected and ignored in HIV funding, outreach, and care, and prompted the need of "gendering AIDS." In the United States, African American and Latino women, men and transgender persons continue to be disproportionately affected by HIV, revealing how race, class, gender, and sexuality operate as simultaneous systems of oppression and have brought about the process of "coloring AIDS" in the United States.

Internationally, the Global Programme on AIDS (GAP) represents AIDS/HIV in terms of three patterns (Patton 2002). Pattern One, commonly known as "AIDS," refers to locations characterized by sexual intercourse between men (e.g., North American and European nations). Pattern Two, generally known as "African AIDS," suggests locations characterized by sexual intercourse between women and men (e.g., African nations). Pattern Three refers to locations where "AIDS arrived late" but is quickly spreading (e.g., Asian nations). As the pandemic continues to evolve and change, these representations are likely to shift as conceptions of sexuality, pleasure, love, and health interplay with social, cultural, economic, and political conditions. *See also* Heterosexuality; Homosexuality; Race and Racism; Sexually Transmitted Infections.

Further Reading: Frasca, Tim. *AIDS in Latin America*. New York: Palgrave Macmillan, 2005; Kalipeni, Ezekiel, Susan Craddock, Joseph R. Oppong, and Jayati Ghosh, eds. *HIV and AIDS in Africa: Beyond Epidemiology*. Malden: Blackwell, 2004; Narain, Jai P. ed. *AIDS in Asia: The Challenge Ahead*. New Delhi: Sage, 2004; Patton, Cindy. *Globalizing AIDS*. Minneapolis: University of Minnesota Press, 2002; Stockdill, Brett C. *Activism against AIDS: At the Intersections of Sexuality, Race, Gender, and Class*. Boulder: Lynne Rienner, 1999; Treichler, Paula A. *How to Have Theory in an Epidemic: Cultural Chronicles of AIDS*. Durham: Duke University Press, 1999; UNAIDS. *Report on the Global AIDS Epidemic: An Executive Summary—A UNAIDS 10th Anniversary Edition*. See http://www.unaids.org/en/HIV_data/2006GlobalReport/default.asp. UNAIDS offers a variety of subjects related to AIDS ranging from policy and research to speeches and photo journals, 2006; Yep, Gust A., Karen E. Lovaas, and Alex V. Pagonis. "The Case of 'Riding Bareback': Sexual Practices and the Paradoxes of Identity in the Era of AIDS." *Journal of Homosexuality* 42, no. 2 (2002): 1–14.

Gust A. Yep

ALCOHOL. *See* Drugs and Alcohol

ASEXUALITY. From a traditional biological view, asexuality refers to organisms that do not use sex (i.e., male and female variations) to reproduce. Asexual reproduction is usually characteristic of simpler animals, such as invertebrates. For example, many small sea creatures such as anemones or starfish reproduce by asexual reproduction, using mitosis (a parent cell splitting into two daughter cells) to produce offspring. In the social sciences (e.g., psychology or sociology), the word asexuality has been used infrequently. Asexuality has been used recently within the context of some models of human sexual orientation to describe people without any sexual attraction. In contrast to **heterosexuality** (attraction to the other sex), **homosexuality** (i.e., attraction to the same-sex), or **bisexuality** (attraction to both sexes), asexuality is attraction to neither sex (or to anything, for that matter). An asexual orientation would presume an enduring (perhaps lifelong) absence of attraction, just as the other three orientations presume an enduring pattern of sexual attraction toward others. People who conform to this definition of asexuality may still have some level of sexual **desire** and arousal. They may, for example, still masturbate but they would not connect these sexual feelings and responses to others. People who lack sexual attraction may also have some level of romantic/affectionate attraction for others. They could marry or have other loving/affectionate relationships with adults. This is not surprising because recent models of sexual orientation are consistent with the notion that one's erotic or sexual orientation may be independent of, and hence differ from, one's romantic orientation.

Asexuality may also refer to very low or no sexual desire (rather than just attraction). Thus, asexual people who are not interested in any sexual activity would likely choose to forgo all kinds of sexual activity, not just with a partner but also solitary sex (**masturbation**). However, lack of sexual desire does not necessarily mean a lack of arousal or a lack of romantic/affectionate attraction for others. Note that this definition of asexuality as a lack of sexual desire may overlap with a clinical or psychiatric diagnosis known as Hypoactive Sexual Desire Disorder (HSDD). However, what may distinguish asexual people who lack desire from an HSDD diagnosis is that some (perhaps many) of the former may not be distressed by their condition, an important consideration when applying a diagnosis of HSDD.

Three other considerations with regard to definitions of asexuality are notable. First, asexuality (as defined as lack of sexual attraction or desire) is not the same as **celibacy**. Celibates are individuals who voluntarily abstain from sexual activity for religious or other reasons. Thus, celibates may still have strong sexual attraction and/or desire. Second, some people may have periods of their life (e.g., after the loss of a partner) where they lack sexual desire or attraction. These people would not likely conform to a strict definition of asexuality (e.g., never having felt sexual attraction), but they may still identify as "asexual" for a part of their life. Third, there is significant overlap between the definitions of asexuality as a lack of sexual attraction and as a lack of sexual desire. After all, those who lack sexual desire are likely to lack sexual attraction and vice versa. But some level of distinction is important between these two definitions because each likely captures valid variation among people who lack some aspect of traditional sexual expression. It also likely captures distinctions among self-identified "asexual" people.

A lack of sexual behavior has occurred throughout history. Sometimes this is without choice, as some people would not have found mates and, of course, may not have masturbated. Also, as Elizabeth Abbott indicates in her book *The History of Celibacy*, some people had abstinence forced upon them. For example, young males were castrated to encourage loyal service to Chinese emperors during the Ming and other dynasties, as they were in a number of royal courts throughout European history. A lack of sexual behavior has also been a choice throughout history, reflecting the value (often religiously inspired) placed on celibacy. Vestigial virgins occurred in ancient Rome and monks, priests, and nuns continue a tradition of the vow of celibacy. However, celibacy and asexuality—lack of attraction or desire—can be construed as different phenomena. Has asexuality occurred throughout history?

The historical record is unclear, although it is plausible there have been many kinds of sexual variations. Some reports suggest that Isaac Newton and Emily Brontë, among others, were asexual. Newton was reported to have lived a very solitary life, never married (although he became engaged), and was wholly preoccupied with his science. Nevertheless, lack of evidence for sexual relations does not necessarily mean that they were indeed asexual. It may only mean that they had atypical sexual inclinations (e.g., same-sex attraction), that were unrecorded by historians.

Although asexuality has likely occurred throughout history, the self-identification of "asexual" ("I am asexual") is probably a Western, twenty-first-century phenomenon. In addition, the word "asexual" is a relatively common part of modern speech or parlance in the West, which reflects recent events such as a high level of **media** attention surrounding the publication of an academic article by psychologist Anthony Bogaert and a popular scientific paper by Sylvia Pagán Westfall in 2004, along with the recent promotion by members of Asexual Visibility and Education Network.

How many people lack sexual attraction or desire? It is difficult to provide an accurate estimate because the rate of asexuality may vary over time and across cultures. It also depends on how asexuality is defined. In 1990, approximately 1 percent (total sample: 195) of British adults reported never having had sexual attraction to anyone (Bogaert 2004). Ten years later, analysis of a new national sample in Britain found approximately one-half of 1 percent had "never felt sexual attraction to anyone at all." Other surveys have asked about low or absent sexual desire. In a representative sample of Danish residents, Søren Ventegodt (1998) found that 11.2 percent of women and 3.2 percent of men reported low sexual desire. In the United States, about one-third of women and one-in-seven men reported low desire in the past year (Laumann et al. 1999). However, "low" desire is not the same as the absence of desire. Further, it is unclear to what degree these individuals would report low or even absent desire over, for example, a prolonged period of years. In a recent national sample of China re-analyzed by Anthony Bogaert, 7 percent reported "no" desire for a year or more. However, again, it is not clear whether these individuals would report no desire for a very long period of time. Perhaps most importantly, no representative research study has ever included a survey item that would allow a respondent to self-identify as asexual.

The origins of asexuality are unknown and research on its causes is likely to be in its infancy for a number of years. However, there are a number of plausible correlates or associated factors. One is gender. More women than men have reported lifelong lack of sexual attraction and most general surveys show that women are more likely than men to report low or no sexual desire. Some social psychologists have suggested that women are more "plastic" than men in their sexuality (or, at least, their sex drive). As such, situational and cultural influences may play a larger role in women's sexual development, including promoting asexuality if life circumstances become unusual or sexually restrictive. In addition, some researchers have found women often less aware than men of their own sexual arousal. If so, women relative to men may be less likely to perceive or label as sexual objects males or females; hence, they may report that they have no attraction to either gender.

Ethnicity may also be associated with asexuality. For example, in one recent study (Bogaert 2004), it was found that a higher percentage (14 percent) of the asexual participants were ethnic minorities (e.g., Asian, East Indian) relative to the sexual individuals (4.5 percent). If this difference appears in other samples, an important question is why ethnicity relates to asexuality. Perhaps processes related to Western acculturation play a role. Western society is often considered more sexual than some parts of the non-western world, and some ethnic minorities may not have had the same learning experiences and exposure to the (potentially) sexualizing forces that pervade the West.

Biological factors have also been shown to be associated with asexuality and may play an important role in its development. Prenatal (before birth) mechanisms may affect some people's asexuality and there is some evidence that atypical hormone levels may underlie some people's low sexual desire. Whether such hormonal factors play a significant role in a majority of asexual people remains to be seen, however. Given the potential diversity of people who are asexual, it is likely that multiple factors, perhaps both biological and psychosocial, contribute to the origins of this phenomenon, just as multiple causes are likely to contribute to the origins of other forms of sexual variability. *See also* Birth Control; Romance.

Further Reading: Abbott, Elizabeth. *The History of Celibacy.* New York: Da Capo Press, 2001; Asexual Visibility and Education Network. http://www.asexuality.org. An online resource for people whose identity is asexual; Bogaert, Anthony F. "Asexuality: Its Prevalence and Associated Factors in a National Probability Sample." *The Journal of Sex Research* 41 (2004): 279–87; Bogaert, Anthony F. "Toward a Conceptual Understanding of Asexuality." *Review of General Psychology* 10 (2006): 241–50; Laumann, Edward O., Anthony Paik, and Ray C. Rosen. "Sexual dysfunction in the United States: Prevalence and predictors." *Journal of American Medical Association* 281 (1999): 537–44; Pagán Westfall, Sylvia. "Glad to Be A." *New Scientist* 184 (2004): 40–43; Prause, Nicole, and Cynthia A. Graham. "Asexuality: Classification and Categorization." *Archives of Sexual Behavior.* (2006); Ventegodt, Søren. Sex and Quality of Life in Denmark. *Archives of Sexual Behavior,* 28 (1998): 295–307.

Anthony F. Bogaert

B

BIRTH CONTROL. A term coined in 1914 by Margaret **Sanger**, birth control describes natural or artificial methods voluntarily employed by humans to regulate births. Because the term "birth control" includes all actions, medications, or devices aimed at preventing or reducing the likelihood of fertilization of an ovum by a spermatozoon, it has been used interchangeably with "contraception." However, unlike "contraception," which literally means opposing conception, "birth control" sometimes includes measures or substances taken to induce **abortion**, after fertilization has occurred. Some also consider that the killing of a newborn—infanticide—constitutes a form of birth control. Although, from a biological point of view, heterosexual intercourse serves a reproductive function, and many cultures also believe that sex represents the ultimate way of sharing intimacy or expressing the feeling of love. The development and spread of new birth control methods during the twentieth century have untied the links between sex and reproduction, allowing sexual pleasure to occur without a high possibility of **pregnancy**.

Although a wide range of birth control methods exist, their use varies according to several factors, such as geographical location and social class. The most effective method of birth control is abstinence—refraining from sex. Barrier methods consist of putting a block between the man's sperm and the woman's egg. These include the diaphragm; a rubber dome inserted into the vagina and placed over the cervix to prevent sperm from entering the uterus. A similar device, the cervical cap, is smaller, firmer and held in place over the cervix by suction. Barrier methods also include female and male condoms. The female condom is a lubricated polyurethane pouch worn by women during sex. It covers the inside of the vagina and prevents the sperm from reaching the ovum. While not very popular in North America, the female condom is widely used in South Africa, Zimbabwe, Brazil and Ghana, where governments—with support from the Joint United Nations Programme on HIV/AIDS (UNAIDS)—have encouraged its use and distribution. Women, in particular, have welcomed the introduction of the female condom because it gives them control over their fertility and contributes to the prevention of **sexually transmitted infections** (STIs). The male condom—the most commonly used barrier method (and often the cheapest and most readily available one)—is a thin sheath made of rubber (latex) fit to the erect penis before sexual contact. Spermicides (chemicals that destroy or immobilize sperm) are sometimes added to, or used with, condoms for additional protection. The condom collects semen from the penis and stops it from entering the vagina, thus preventing pregnancy. The only contraceptive device currently available for men, the male condom also helps to prevent STIs. For this reason, it can also be worn by men who have sex with men.

Barrier birth control methods are sometimes criticized for taking away from the experience of sex, by limiting direct skin-to-skin contact, or by preventing the sperm from entering the vagina. Some blame male and female condoms for ruining the spontaneity of sex. These reasons, among others, may explain the popularity of hormonal methods. The best-known hormonal birth control method is the oral contraceptive (also called the pill). Two types of pills are usually available. The combined pill contains two synthetically produced hormones (progestogen and oestrogen), which stop the release of eggs by the ovaries, thicken cervical mucus, and change the lining of the womb. Particularly suited to women who breastfeed or have medical conditions that prevent them from taking the regular pill, the mini-pill contains only progestogen and works by thickening cervical mucus, thus not letting the sperm reach the ovum. Injections and implants of hormones (progestogen) are also available as birth control methods. Injections last for three months; implants last up to three years. Both present a definite advantage for women who have difficulty remembering to take a pill every day.

Various other contraceptive devices or techniques exist in addition to barrier and hormonal methods. A tiny t-shaped plastic and copper device, the intrauterine device (IUD), is inserted in the uterus to prevent the implantation of the embryo. Since the IUD must be inserted by a doctor and because it does not protect against STIs, this birth control method especially suits women who are in long-term monogamous relationships. Natural family planning consists of abstinence during the presumed fertile days of a woman—a technique particularly favored by those who have objections to artificial birth control methods, for religious or ethical reasons. The withdrawal method (*coitus interruptus*) is another natural pregnancy prevention technique. It consists of withdrawing the penis from the vagina just before ejaculation. Although its efficiency has been questioned many times by scientists, the withdrawal method has been used for more than two millennia. Like the male condom, this method allows men to participate more actively in birth control. There are also two permanent birth control procedures (also known as sterilization): vasectomy for men and tubal ligation for women. A vasectomy is a minor surgery during which a doctor generally cuts the tubes that carry sperm from the testicles to the penis. Also a surgical operation, tubal ligation is the blockage of fallopian tubes, the tubes linking the ovaries to the uterus. Although male and female sterilization can sometimes be reversed, these procedures are usually permanent. When barrier, hormonal or other methods fail (or when no contraceptives were used), emergency birth control methods like the emergency contraception (EC)—also known as the morning-after pill—and the IUD can be considered. These techniques do not end pregnancies, but rather prevent them after the act of sex. Up to several years ago, most countries limited the availability of the EC by requiring a prescription. However, because the EC's efficiency increases if taken less than 72 hours after sex, countries like Israel, France, Norway, South Africa, and Portugal have permitted its over-the-counter access. The U.S. Food and Drug Administration only recently approved over-the-counter access to Plan B, a type of EC, for women 18 and older. If a woman gets pregnant, and the EC cannot be used, the only birth control option left is abortion.

Although this variety of relatively efficient birth control methods is available in many countries, scientists are still trying to develop new ones. For example, in recent years, researchers have tried to develop a hormonal contraceptive to provide men with their version of the pill. This research has contributed to the development of hormonal and non-hormonal male contraceptives. Although they have yet to be commercialized, a hormonal implant and an intra vas device (IVD) have already been tested on men.

This multiplication of birth control methods in the second part of the twentieth century, and the research associated with their development contrast with earlier decades. Before the 1960s, birth control consisted essentially of natural and barrier methods. Most countries forbade the distribution, import, or promotion of contraceptives. However, the declining birth rate in certain countries such as England suggests that the use of birth control techniques or devices was more common than governments would have liked.

In the initial decades of the twentieth century, two women significantly influenced the evolution of birth control in their respective countries, and their activities also had an impact on various parts of the world. An American nurse, Margaret Sanger (1879–1966) started distributing information on contraception in the 1910s, thus infringing the law. She opened the first American birth control clinic in 1916, but the authorities forced her to close it shortly after. Four years later, she founded the American Birth Control League (ABCL) and then established a new birth control clinic in New York in 1923. Marie Stopes (1880–1958), a Scottish doctor of science published *Married Love* in 1918 and a contraception guide, *Wise Parenthood*. She became interested in birth control after meeting Margaret Sanger, and established a birth control clinic in London in 1921.

Both Sanger and Stopes opposed abortion, but they recommended the use of contraceptives such as the diaphragm and the cervical cap (at the time called pessaries). Some of their ideas had a strong eugenic component. For example, although their literature and clinics seemed to have attracted middle-class and upper-class women, Sanger and Stopes were preoccupied especially by the fertility of the working class. Eugenics, a theory developed by Sir Francis Galton in 1865, sought improvement of the human race by encouraging the procreation of the "fit" and breeding out the "unfit"—meaning the poor, the mentally deficient, physically handicapped, and certain ethnic groups. Sanger and Stopes's desire to provide contraceptive advice—particularly to the working class—was shared by other organizations, such as the Racial Hygiene Association (RHA) of New South Wales. In 1933, the RHA opened a birth control clinic in Sydney, emphasizing that providing contraceptive advice to married women would contribute to the prevention of abortion and reduce the number of children born of poor or mentally ill parents. Many of these birth control clinics and organizations joined the International Planned Parenthood Association, created in 1952 in Bombay, and some of them, like the RHA, became family planning associations.

Often cited as one of the most important medical developments of the twentieth century, the birth control pill appeared on the American market in the mid-1960s. A rich American heiress, Katharine McCormick agreed to fund the research necessary for the creation of Sanger's most important project, a pill that would allow women to control their own fertility, and an important concern for Second Wave feminists fighting for reproductive rights. Legal from 1965 in the United States, the pill was made available in family planning clinics. The use of the pill spread quickly to the rest of the world, although in some countries its legalization took much longer such as in Japan where it was not legally available until 1999.

Birth control is not confined to the bedroom only. It also affects population management since it can be used to limit its size or control its "quality." In the first half of the twentieth century, several countries adopted compulsory sterilization programs.

As early as 1907, some American states enacted such legislation for eugenic reasons and Nazi Germany sterilized more than 400,000 individuals on the basis of mental or physical illness. Other countries like Canada (provinces of Alberta and British Columbia) and Sweden also adopted similar programs in the 1930s. China, well known for its one-child policy, adopted it as a temporary measure in 1979 to limit the population growth, and it is still in place today. In the case of a second pregnancy, a family risks fines, forced abortion, or subsequent sterilization. This policy has created a gender imbalance in China. Particularly in rural areas, where married couples value boys for their manual labour, sex-selective abortion and infanticide has been used to respect the single-child policy without abandoning the idea of a son.

China's policy has been criticized, notably by the Roman Catholic Church, which considers birth control (with the exception of total abstinence and some forms of natural family planning) as a threat to the unity of the family. Though Islam also strongly values **families**, most schools of Islamic law permit birth control (with the exception of abortion, infanticide, and sterilization), when used by married couples. Judaism prefers hormonal methods to barrier ones because these methods do not "waste" sperm. Hindu religion does not forbid birth control and is normally open to most methods. In contrast, most Buddhists who believe in reincarnation oppose abortion and, believing conception occurs when the egg is fertilized, also oppose emergency contraception. *See also* Religions, Eastern; Religions, Western; Women's Movement.

Further Reading: McLaren, Angus. A *History of Contraception: From Antiquity to the Present Day*. Oxford (UK) and Cambridge (USA): Blackwell, 1990; Medline Plus. U.S. National Library of Medicine. http://www.nlm.nih.gov/medlineplus/birthcontrol.html. Comprehensive website that includes the latest news on birth control research, general information, statistics and useful links, October 2006; Sanger, Margaret. My *Fight for Birth Control*. London: Faber, 1932; Stopes, Marie Carmichael. *Married Love*. New York: The Critic and Guide Company, 1918.

Émilie Paquin

BISEXUALITY. Bisexuality is commonly understood as having **desire** for persons of both sexes; male and female. Just as desire is manifest in various ways, bisexuality may be expressed through various means, including close friendship, romantic gesture, or sexual relationships. Bisexuality is most commonly understood as a marker of sexuality, although it does not determine lifestyle. Just as many heterosexuals and homosexuals choose polyamorous relationships, many bisexuals choose monogamous relationships while still identifying with their bisexuality. Bisexuality exists in many world cultures and throughout history, which is particularly important because often queer sexualities are represented as being specific to Western culture. In fact, it may be the mundane aspect of bisexuality that has sometimes caused it to be overlooked or dismissed as a legitimate category of identity, particularly in light of twentieth-century gay rights movements.

Anthologies like *Bisexuality: A Critical Reader* (1999), *Bisexuality in the Ancient World* (1994), and *Getting Bi: Voices of Bisexuality Around the World* (2005) have identified and studied bisexual practices in historical and contemporary cultures on every continent. Historically, bisexuality has existed in men's baths in Turkey, Roman gymnasiums and in the Japanese practice of Shudo—though these histories are primarily focused on structured, intergenerational relationships between men and or/boys, known as **pederasty**. More contemporary histories include early-twentieth-century

Paris and Berlin as an important gathering place for bisexual artists and intellectuals, as well as The Bloomsbury Group in London. Women's bisexuality can be found during the Harlem Renaissance of the 1920s and 1930s and among Mexican artist Frieda Kahlo's circle of friends and colleagues. This is not to suggest that women were not participants in bisexual practices in the previously mentioned examples. But rather, this points to established global feminist histories of the public and private spheres as well as how these have affected access to social networks and have encouraged women to create networks that challenge or operate outside of male-dominated ones. During the 1970s in the United States and Canada, in particular, feminist movements emphasized the concept of "womyn-identified womyn," which not only created stronger lesbian communities but made it more acceptable for bisexual women to engage in same sex relationships.

Labels like bisexual, homosexual, and heterosexual are relatively recent and, limited inventions to describe human expressions of sexuality, love, and desire. Thus, it is somewhat problematic to identify bisexual individuals in history (primarily, Western) as revisionist historians have shown. It is difficult to accurately say whether a person was gay and entered into heterosexual relationships due to social pressures, or if a person was bisexual and lived life monogamously. Unlike those involved in today's politically charged bisexual movement, previous to the twentieth century individuals were almost never defined solely on the basis of their sexual practices. Thus, there were many instances of people in heterosexual relationships who would not have considered—and might still not consider—any same sex relations to be relevant to their identity. For this reason, we might consider bisexuality as a historical marker to describe attempts to resist compulsory identity, and second, as a more recent political marker of identification.

As a political movement, bisexuality is not only driven by a belief in freedom of sexual expression but, perhaps more importantly, by a commitment to the idea that love is not a concept easily restrained by social boundaries. Many bisexual individuals see themselves as transgressing conventional perimeters of love in relationships and challenging perceptions that love must be identified as either platonic or romantic. Bisexuality provides an opportunity to explore the wide range of expressions that love might take. For example, in many educational institutions (both secondary and collegiate) in the United States around the early twentieth century, younger female students were encouraged to develop crushes on older female students who might act as a sort of mentor for them (and similar situations were encouraged for male students). In all-female schools, students might accompany each other to dances and carry on correspondences over summers.

In contemporary cultures, bisexuals have fought against stereotypes that would de-legitimize their sexual orientation. Generally speaking, bisexuality has been integrated into queer communities as signified by the standard LGBT abbreviation, though it has also sometimes been glossed over. Bi pride might be expressed by wearing bisexual colors (pink, purple, and blue), or a male/female symbol, which is certainly less common than the standard rainbow symbol. Established bisexual awareness groups throughout the world are also more accessible due to the **Internet**. For example, The Australian Bisexual Network's website provides links to groups associated with the Bisexual Network of the Philippines, The New Zealand Bisexual Network, The Dutch Bisexual Network, Bi India, and the Boston-based Bisexual Resource Center.

Youth are much more likely to come out as bisexual than in previous generations, and in fact, often embrace bisexuality as a more inclusive way to express themselves through both friendship and romantic relationships. Stephen Russell's research is especially useful to better understand the unique challenges facing queer youth today, considering that they are "growing up in the first period in history in which 'gay issues' have been prominent in the public consciousness" (258). He suggests that "family, faith, and education" are the three main formative institutions for youth, and that most bisexual (and other LGT) youth have overwhelmingly negative experiences in their respective institutions. Russell posits Internet culture and gay-straight alliances as two examples for the development of queer-positive culture. Such opportunities are essential for bisexual youth to strengthen their sense of self and to combat unclear or harmful images often perpetuated by peers and other institutions, such as **media**.

Bisexuality has been given more or less attention by popular media depending on the political climate, and is often framed as a passing trend, rather than a legitimate identity. At varying moments in recent Western **popular culture**, the term "bisexual chic" has been used to refer to actors (Margaret Cho, Angelina Jolie, Alan Cumming), singers (TATU, Michelle Ndegeocello, Michael Stipe), and other public figures who have openly declared non-heterosexual identity.

Bisexual women tend to receive more attention and validation than bisexual men, and many heterosexually-identified women are encouraged to engage in same-sex acts with women as part of a current popular culture trend, in a way that mirrors the playboy model of a female performance of sexual acts for the male gaze. These performances should not necessarily be confused with bisexual experimentation, such as Jen Sincero advocates in *The Straight Girl's Guide to Sleeping with Chicks*. While Sincero does suggest that inviting another woman into a heterosexual relationship might be fun for the male in the relationship, she also gives advice to women who want to engage in relationships with other women, unmediated by a male figure. Perhaps it is not surprising that no parallel guide yet exists that encourages either inviting another man into a heterosexual relationship, or even for heterosexual men to experiment with bisexuality (as opposed to coming out as gay).

Many women—and men, though again this does not receive as much attention in the media—enjoy the freedom to experiment without having to adhere to a political identification. Heterosexual people who engage in same-sex acts may not call themselves bisexual. One example of this is what is commonly known as the "Down Low" within African-American male communities in the United States. These are straight-identified men who have sexual relationships with men. Arguably, with more support from African-American cultures for gay identity, some of these men might no longer feel the need for the heterosexual pretense; others may feel equally comfortable in relationships with men and women and thus, with support, come to identify as some version of bisexual.

Bisexuality often appears more palatable to mainstream tastes, particularly in the case of women. However, the assumption that bisexuality is a transitional identity or an experimental phase makes it easier to ignore it as a sexual orientation or to simply disregard the underlying issues. Bisexuals, for instance, are sometimes labeled as opportunists and dismissed by both heterosexuals and homosexuals. Bisexual identity, too, has often been conflated with **infidelity** and promiscuity. Unlike sexual orientation, monogamy is a choice that is made regardless of sexuality. Bisexual individuals who choose monogamous relationships illustrate this as much as non-bisexual individuals who do not, and exclusion of or resistance to bisexuals within queer communities is certainly an unfortunate irony. Finally, bisexuality is a specific identification that many people are not comfortable with. Thus, although gay and straight individuals may engage in bisexual behaviors, they might not choose to politically identify as such.

Bisexuality is sometimes described as having desire for both genders. This presupposes a gender binary (male and female) in which sex is synonymous with gender and that as a result there are only two options. Here the term "bisexual" is limiting, as it does not account for multiple expressions of gender. For example, based on the understanding that there are only two genders, a **transgender** person has no place in either the gender binary or a definition of bisexuality, such as is the case with Two Spirit persons in some native North American tribes. Known historically as "berdache" (this problematic term likely originated during French colonization of native peoples), many assume a contemporary gay or lesbian identity as a means of assimilation, rather than maintaining a more fluid gender identity.

Emotional ties develop across a spectrum of genders as does sexual attraction. Acknowledging this in our language has resulted in new terms, such as "omnisexual" and "pomosexual," or even the ubiquitous "queer." The term queer, in particular, is increasingly popular in youth cultures that emphasize self-expression, creativity, and ingenuity. Younger generations are more likely to look beyond fixed categories of identity if there are greater interests at stake. Such fluid politics contribute to an overall queer aesthetic that becomes evident through DIY (Do It Yourself) events, such as indie music concerts and craft shows, and collective culture on the Internet like community blogs and sites like Myspace that allow for diverse and uncensored expression of identity. *See also* Heterosexuality; Homosexuality; Polygamy/Polyamory.

Further Reading: Cantarella, Eva, and Cormac O. Cuilleanin. *Bisexuality in the Ancient World.* New Haven, CT: Yale University Press, 1994; Garber, Marjorie. *Vice-Versa: Bisexuality and the Eroticism of Everyday Life.* New York: Simon & Schuster, 1995; Haworth Press, *Journal of Bisexuality.* https://www.haworthpress.com/store/product.asp?sku=J159. Includes academic/research articles, as well as movie reviews and other popular culture-themed essays; Hutchins, Loraine, and Lani Kaahumanu, eds. *Bi Any Other Name: Bisexual People Speak Out.* Boston, MA: Alyson, 1991; International bisexual organization links. http://www.bi.org. Providing extensive links to bisexual awareness and activist organizations around the world, this website focuses on current political events and provides links to the annual International Conference on Bisexuality. Russell, Stephen. "Queer in America: Citizenship for Sexual Minority Youth." *Applied Developmental Science* 6 (2002): 258–63; Rust, Paula C. Rodriguez. *Bisexuality in the United States.* New York: Columbia University Press, 1999; Sincero, Jen. *The Straight Girl's Guide to Sleeping with Chicks.* New York: Fireside, 2005.

Elizabeth Whitney

C

CARTOONS AND COMICS. A cartoon is a form of visual art in which drawings and dialogue are used to tell a story, either in print as a comic, or on film as an animated cartoon. In the United States, Britain, and a few other countries, most people regard comics and cartoons as primarily a children's medium. Therefore, censors watch them very carefully and sexual practices, non-heterosexual identities, and all but the most conventional forms of heterosexual romance are absent or appear only in the form of subtexts and in jokes. However, underground comics, privately printed and distributed, feature sex and **romance** as key themes. In France and Latin America, explicit heterosexual behavior and romance appears in comics and animated cartoons with some frequency. Japan, too, has a long tradition of same-sex behavior and romance.

The earliest comic strips to appear in U.S. newspapers during the latter part of the nineteenth century shied away from even conventional heterosexual romance. Instead, they featured grotesquely caricaturized husbands and wives, like Maggie and Jiggs in *Bringing Up Father*, or groups of friends with only a passing interest in romance. However, they often featured shielded references to heterosexual and same-sex practices. Winsor McKay's *Dreams of a Rarebit Fiend* (1904), for instance, depicted people who had eaten too much Welsh rarebit (grilled cheese on toast) having nightmares that involved transvestism, gender transgressions, nudity, and sexual obsessions. Early animated cartoons privileged sexual practices over romance. *Betty Boop* (Fleischer Studio, 1930) had the sexually provocative stage presence of a Mae West and was constantly defending herself from lecherous wolves, but rarely went on a romantic date. Both comic strips and cartoons featured stereotyped gay men.

The 1934 Hays Code spelled an end to this period of relative freedom. For the next fifty years, comic strips, comic books, and animated cartoons produced in the United States would be strictly censored. Heterosexual romance appeared, if at all, in "working girl" comic strips like *Tillie the Toiler*, and in the "true romance" genre of comic books. Animated cartoons all but eliminated heterosexual romance; it appeared rarely, in idealized, almost mythological form, as in Disney's feature-length *Snow White and the Seven Dwarfs* (1937).

Sexual behavior, including nudity, sexual situations, and "perversion," was strictly forbidden. Nevertheless, comics continued to provide ample fodder for erotic fantasy. Milt Caniff's *Terry and the Pirates* (1934) featured an endless number of shapely, minimally-clothed women; during World War II, there was even an R-rated version for distribution on military bases. Comic book covers often featured well-endowed women in bikinis or having their clothes torn off. Readers interested in men were not neglected: comic strip heroes like *Tarzan*, *Flash Gordon*, and *Prince Valiant* were superbly muscular and minimally clothed; the comic book market was dominated by superheroes in skintight costumes. In animated cartoons, attractive people were rare, but sexual practices, gender transgression, and same-sex desire appeared through innuendo. For instance, in the Warner Brothers cartoon "For Scent-imental Reasons" (1949), the amorous skunk Pepe LePew gleefully pursues a cat, even after finding out that it is male.

A few more explicit depictions of heterosexual romance and even sexual behavior began to appear in the 1970s and 1980s, mostly in independent feature-length animation aimed at adults, like *Fritz the Cat* (1972). On television, heterosexual romance remained rare, but heterosexual behavior began to appear in the 1990s, in such adult-oriented prime-time cartoons as *The Simpsons* (1989) and *Futurama* (1999). Even heterosexual fetishes were fair game for the new adult-oriented animation. In an episode of *Family Guy* (1999), Peter and Lois calmly discuss their children's problems while preparing for an S&M scene. Same-sex behavior was less common and same-sex romance unheard of, though stereotyped gay men and lesbians often appeared as homophobic jokes.

Comic strips in the United States were still heavily censored through the 2000s. Conventional heterosexual romance occasionally occurred, but there was little or no reference to heterosexual behavior and an almost complete erasure of gay men and lesbians. In 2001, when a character in the *For Better or for Worse* comic strip asked a gay friend to be best man at his wedding, there was a vocal outcry by conservative watchdog groups like the American Family Association. Many editors refused to run the strip. Cartoonist Lynn Johnson was forced to produce two versions, one in which the friend mentions being gay, and one in which he does not.

Beginning in the 1990s, comic books were usually sold as graphic novels, longer, with more complex plots and situations, and a greater exploration of heterosexual behavior; but they still tended to be highly stylized and to promote heterosexual romance as the only worthwhile goal in life. Daniel Clowes' *Ghost World* (2001), for instance, follows the life of a recent high school graduate as she cynically explores the futility of heterosexual behavior; but she ends up establishing a conventional heterosexual romance not much different in substance from that of Snow White in 1937. Only a few graphic novels, such as Ned Gaiman's *Sandman* (1993), contain any reference to same-sex desire or to lesbian, gay, bisexual, or transgender (LGBT) people.

Before the 1990s, readers looking for an alternative to the heavily censored comic strips, comic books, and animated cartoons could turn to underground comics, so called because they were written and produced without the authority of the mainstream comic industry. The first underground comics were the "Tijuana Bibles," eight-page books containing two or four panels per page, drawn in an extremely crude, amateurish style, like a dirty picture scribbled in the margin of a junior high schooler's notebook. There were no plots, just comic strip characters or celebrities engaging in explicit sexual acts

This is a detail from the cover of the thirtieth-anniversary issue of *Zap Comix*, released in 1998. Racy and anarchic, *Zap Comix* rebelled against the restrictive comics code of the 1950s and feasted off the sex, drugs, and rock and roll of the late 1960s. © AP Photo.

(usually heterosexual), along with racist and homophobic jokes. Hundreds of separate titles were produced and distributed from the 1930s through the 1960s.

Later in the 1960s, the alternative bookstores and collectives of counterculture began to produce the works of professional or semi-professional artists. Instead of appropriating mass culture icons, they created original characters, like R. Crumb's *Mr. Natural,* with more sophistication in style and plot, often including political and social satire rather than nonstop sexual encounters. However, images of sexual and ethnic minorities were still heavily stereotyped; for instance, one of the recurring characters in *Zap Comix* was a nude African caricature named Angelfood McSpade.

LGBT people, ignored by the mainstream and stereotyped by underground comics, began producing their own comic strips in the late 1950s, when the artist Tom of Finland published stories in European and American gay magazines. They showed a great deal of artistic precision, though they were minimally plotted and virtually dialogue-free, about cops, soldiers, construction workers, and other macho types, almost always White, having sex with each other. There were also **humor** strips, such as the James Bond parody Harry Chess in *Drum* magazine (1964). The first comic book to specialize in lesbian stories, *Come Out Comix,* appeared in 1973. Today many gay-themed comic strips appear regularly in local and national gay newspapers, and there is a huge industry of gay-themed graphic novels.

Comics in France and Belgium, called *bandes dessinée,* generally appear in anthology style magazines, and later in bound hardback volumes. They have suffered from fewer restrictions on subject matter, and heterosexual practice is common. Superhero *Jacques Flash* (1957) falls for a different woman in nearly every installment, and space wanderer *Barbarella* (1962) is often displayed in sexual situations. Same-sex **desire** and practice tends to be more subtle and coy, as in *Alix* (1949) and Enak, teenage partners from ancient Rome, or contemporary adventurers (and domestic partners) *Spirou* (1938) and Fantasio.

In Japan, *manga* are thick, hefty hundred-page volumes offering dozens of stories in every conceivable genre, and *anime* are animated cartoons, often based on manga. Same-sex romances (*shonen-ai*) among characters not otherwise identified as gay are quite common in manga and anime, especially those marketed at preteen and teenage girls. Scholars speculate that heterosexual girls find these relationships more attractive than heterosexual relationships, since they are not "competing" with other girls for the affection of the boys. *Seijin manga* ("adult manga"), usually called *hentai* in the West, involve explicit sexual behaviors, including sadomasochism, incest, bestiality, pedophilia, and uniquely Japanese fetishes (like sex with tentacled monsters). Two specialized types of hentai provide images of same-sex behavior: *yaoi* when the partners are both men, and *yuri,* when they are both women. Many gay and lesbian artists in Europe and America have adopted the distinctive hentai style for their graphic novels. *See also* Censorship; Cinema; Fetishes; Popular Culture.

Further Reading: Cohen, Carl F. *Forbidden Animation: Censored Cartoons and Blacklisted Animators in America.* Jefferson, NC: McFarland, 2004; Kinsella, Sharon. *Adult Manga: Culture and Power in Contemporary Japanese Society.* New York: Curzon Press, 2000; Markstein, Donald D. "Toonopedia." See http://www.toonopedia.com/index.htm. An encyclopedia of comic and cartoon characters and their creators, February 2006; Ramakers, Micha. *Dirty Pictures: Tom of Finland, Masculinity, and Homosexuality.* New York: St. Martin's Press, 2000; Rosenkranz, Patrick. *Rebel Visions: The Underground Comix Revolution, 1963–1975.* Seattle: Fantagraphics, 2003.

Jeffery P. Dennis

CELIBACY. Celibacy is the state of not being married and abstention from sexual intercourse or abstention by vow from **marriage**. More generally, celibacy is the act of abstaining from sex either as a lifetime commitment, as in the case of certain members of the clergy, or for a specific purpose or period of time, such as until one is in a committed relationship. Although individual instances of a celibate lifestyle differ, in many cases, the decision to practice celibacy is not based on a dissatisfaction or disinterest in sexuality or sexual activity. Rather, celibacy often is chosen with the intent to focus the energy usually devoted to sexual activities more directly on some other area of one's life. In many instances the desire is to turn the focus from the sexual act to a focus on love within one's personal relationships. This idea, seen across cultures and within varying religious modes of thought, recognizes sexual activity as secondary to intimacy and love. Although in most instances celibacy is chosen freely by a given individual, there are some of instances where it is forced or is adopted by default rather than by choice. Incarcerated populations or individuals unable to locate a desirable sexual partner are examples of this. In these cases, celibacy is not based on any beliefs or ideas about the primacy of love over sex or about the use of sexual energy, but is rather an outcome of an individual's situation.

Although there are certain similarities between celibacy and virginity or asexuality, there are marked differences. Celibacy assumes a certain denial of sexuality rather than a lack of sexual **desire**. So, for example, to be celibate does not imply that one lacks sexuality, or is asexual, but that one is in a position, chosen or not, where one's sexual desires cannot be acted upon. On the other hand, to be a virgin means that one has not had sexual intercourse, whereas a celibate individual may or may not have been previously sexually active.

In most Western societies, celibacy is associated with religion and, more specifically, with certain members of the clergy in Latin-Rite Catholicism like priests and nuns. Consecrated celibacy includes not only abstention from sex and marriage, but being chaste, which places restrictions on all types of sexual activity. In this arena, celibacy is a necessary pre-requisite to membership in the clergy as well as an act of charity on behalf of the individual who has chosen to take the vow.

Consecrated celibacy has a certain practicality. It allows one to use the energies usually devoted to sex/sexuality to service for the Lord. Also, it is understood as a charitable act in that the vow of celibacy is the gift of full devotion by way of this sacrifice of one's sexual pleasure for the greater good of God's work. Candidates for certain clerical positions have already chosen to live a life of celibacy in a life of religious devotion *prior* to the assumption of one's role as a priest or nun.

In Eastern Christianity celibacy is associated not with the clergy but with monasticism. Here celibacy is ascetic and the representation of the purest kind of love. Celibacy serves as only one aspect of a cultural tradition of asceticism wherein the practice of self-denial and discipline are essentially related to spirituality. In this sense, celibacy is necessary only insofar as it reveals the true meaning of love, of which all other types of human affection are mere reflections. Celibacy, in this view becomes the necessary counterpart to sexual love, each act of sex and love, needing the other to give itself meaning.

Following the cultural tradition of asceticism in Eastern societies, the practice of radical celibacy, *brahmacharya*, among Eastern religions centers around a similar notion of self-denial and discipline. Within Hinduism and Buddhism, celibacy is practiced as one of many forms of self-discipline meant to allow one to achieve divine happiness through the renunciation of material pleasures. Celibacy elevates the status and the experience of love, although in this case it is only one aspect of an overall quest toward spiritual enlightenment.

In secular society, individuals choosing a celibate lifestyle for reasons other than religion or spirituality often do so in order to devote their energies to other tasks such as educational, artistic, or professional aspirations. Or, in other cases, as a form of self-denial for the purpose of heightening the enjoyment of future sexual encounters. In some instances, individuals may devote a period of celibate time to the process of developing or coming to understand their own sexuality apart from any partner. The practice of celibacy in all of these instances varies widely from their religious counterparts as they are defined almost exclusively at the individual level and may allow **masturbation** or other sexually gratifying activities.

Historically, celibacy has predominately emerged within secular culture in relation to women's recognized roles and/or status in a given society. Because lack of available **birth control** was, and remains to be in some societies, a problem until the second wave of the feminist movement in the United States, women who did not want to reproduce were forced to turn to celibacy. During the early decades of the twentieth century, women were also routinely forced into a celibate lifestyle in order to conform to the cultural ideal of women as pure or chaste. In some societies this would mean that a woman unable to find a suitable mate would be forced to remain a virgin throughout her life. Or, along the same lines, a woman who had been widowed was expected to practice celibacy until her death. In some Eastern cultures, women were routinely segregated beginning at the onset of their menstrual cycles and were expected to remain celibate during that time as they were viewed as "unclean."

In the United States, voluntary celibacy among secular populations within all genders and sexualities has become more common in recent decades. Some scholars attribute this to the AIDS epidemic and the rise in public awareness of **AIDS/HIV** and other **sexually transmitted infections**. Quite often individuals who are diagnosed with HIV will choose to be celibate due to fear of infecting others or of rejection. For others, celibacy has become an alternate manner of achieving intimacy in a culture that promotes sex as a purely casual activity. In this sense, celibacy becomes a kind of affirmation of the fulfillment of love relationships. There, too, are individuals who choose celibacy not as a life-long endeavor, but as a means to ensure that future sexual activity becomes an expression of love rather than physical need. *See also* Asexuality; Prisons, Sex in; Religions, Eastern; Religions, Western; Virginity; Women's Movement.

Further Reading: Catholic Answers. "Celibacy and the Priesthood." Available at http://www.catholic.com/library/celibacy_and_the_priesthood.asp. October 18, 2004; Davies, Maximos. "Celibacy in Context." *First Things: A Monthly Journal of Religion & Public Life* (December 2002): 13–15; DMOZ: Open Directory Project. "Celibacy." http://dmoz.org/Society/Sexuality/Celibacy. Provides list of links to articles and forums on the topic of celibacy, 2006; Foston, Nikitta. "Is Celibacy the New Virginity? Living the Single Life without Sex." *Ebony* 59, no. 3 (2004): 118, 120, 122; Siegal, Karolynn, and Eric W. Schrimshaw. "Reasons for the Adoption of Celibacy Among Older Men and Women Living with HIV/AIDS." *The Journal of Sex Research* 40, no. 2 (2003): 189–200; Watson, Candace. "Celibacy and Its Implications for Autonomy." *Hypatia* 2, no. 2 (1987): 157–58.

Shannon Kelly

CENSORSHIP. Censorship is both symbolic and material, a matter of subjective interpretation and law, and something with which we are simultaneously uncomfortable and supportive. Even those who practice control over the speech, art, or behaviors of others often do not wish to be known as "censors." Censorship is a potent term because it conveys power and social control. Its exercise ranges from the formal control of behavior by state authorities to the personal control of expression. Censorship has existed almost as long as human society. Indeed, some argue that controlling sexual expression has a very high societal value by establishing social identity boundaries that define behaviors in which "people like us" do not participate. Levels of censorship also vary across time and culture. Like other social boundary mechanisms, what is censored often change to the more "liberal" and sometimes back to the "conservative." For instance, up until the 1970s works of literature now considered classic, like *Ulysses* by James Joyce and J. D. Salinger's *Catcher in the Rye*, were censored in the United Kingdom and the United States.

Although attitudes toward censorship range from the extremely liberal to extremely restrictive ideas about what can be expressed, some level of censorship exists in every society. For example, most individuals would support the suppression of materials that feature sexual behavior with non-consenting individuals, especially children; some would support the control of materials that represent extreme forms of sexual violence or intolerance.

Censorship may be practiced by governmental bodies or industrial groups, or even citizens. In Australia and Singapore, censorship decisions generally rest with a national body. Public servants termed "censors" or "classifiers" review materials covered by the authority of their board or commission and issue classification ratings that govern the audiences for whom particular materials are suitable, what sorts of shops they may be sold in, venues in which they may be viewed/performed, or even whether they may be consumed in the country/province. In these jurisdictions, ratings are based on published standards available to all citizens, as well as producers/distributors of sexually explicit materials. The restrictiveness of the ratings and what is allowable under the standards, however, varies widely across nations/provinces, as one might expect given differences in culture.

For example, in Australia the Office of Film and Literature Classification (OFLC) comprises a board made up of appointed citizens and public servants who screen, review, and rate each movie, video, and magazine to be sold in Australia. The categories of ranking are publicly available with explanations of what moves an offering from "G" (general audience) to "R" (Restricted) to "X" (sexually explicit). A vendor may appeal a rating if it is believed the rating is too restrictive. The number of products submitted for review, the decisions reached for each product, and the results of appeals are published annually at the OFLC Web site.

The "X" rating in Australia is reserved for videos and films that depict actual sexual activity, rather than simulated sexual activity. One can depict sexual intimacy without showing the penetration or sexual manipulation of the actors and receive an "R" rating. Once the sexual activity is shown graphically, the rating is placed into the "X" category. One of the interesting debates about these two ratings centers on the issue of violence. Sexualized violence can be shown in an "R" rated product without explicit sexual scenes, but any type of violence with explicit sexual activity renders a film "unclassified," or banned.

The rating received also limits the outlets available to the distributor. "R" rated products can be shown in general cinemas, with proper adult supervision. "X" rated products must be sold or rented/hired in only those locations where they are legal (generally the Northern Territory and Australian Capitol Territory). "X-rated" films are rarely shown in general **cinema** settings. Local authorities continue to prosecute "adult shop" owners who provide "X-rated" videos for sale or rental in the Australian states, though the enforcement appears to be less vigorous than it was in the late 1990s. Thus, the rating a product receives restricts the market to which it can be legally distributed and the audiences exposed to that product, but in a generally consistent manner across the nation.

By contrast, in the United States the concept of "community standards" guides censorship decisions. This results in a patchwork set of standards that vary by what a prosecutor in a particular jurisdiction wishes to pursue. "Ratings" of films are provided by independent boards heavily dominated by representatives from media industries. There is no standard or absolute meaning to the ratings of films or books provided nationally in these settings. What might be acceptable in one locale might not be acceptable in another. The notion of "prurient interests" versus "ideas having even the slightest redeeming social importance" from the *Roth v. United States* 1957 decision still allows for a non-standard approach to the availability of sexually oriented materials throughout the United States.

From the "Production Code" or "Hays Code" of the 1930s to the existing ratings of the Motion Picture Association of America (MPAA), what is acceptable is what is not prosecuted. Thus, while the top grossing film, *Deep Throat* may have been openly played at a theater in New York City during the 1970s, showing that same film in Tampa would have resulted in the arrest and prosecution of the theater owner, as well as the person running the projection booth. Even now, authorities in cities within the greater Atlanta area seek to stop the operation of "adult shops" that sell or rent sexually explicit videos and print materials through zoning laws or criminal prosecution. Other cities or unincorporated areas of the same county may allow the operation of these shops and sale/rental of their products.

While the *Roth* decision relied on the notions of "prurient interest" and "community standards" to guide local classification of sexually-themed materials, in the United Kingdom the *Obscene Publications Act of 1959* employed the "tendency to deprave and corrupt" standard for deciding whether something was in need of censorship. Some analysts believe that the Act was an attempt to navigate a path between artistic freedom and a "legally sanctionable social harm." In short, the Act was a way of protecting artists from those who do not enjoy the aesthetic experience of the educated. While "works of art" (e.g., *Lady Chatterley's Lover*) are protected from censorship, skin flicks are not.

Time and membership in the European Union have brought changes to the way in which the United Kingdom makes censorship decisions. The United Kingdom's classification scheme now occupies a middle ground between the national government agency and the industry voluntary group. The British Board of Film Classification (BBFC) is an independent body whose classifications are subject to local council approval or disapproval. For videos, the BBFC is chartered by the government to provide classification services. While local councils may choose to ignore a BBFC rating and stop the availability of a film or video in that jurisdiction, the national ratings provide a published standard against which those decisions as well as personal choices can be made.

Regardless of the authority from which censorship decisions come, enforcement is generally provided by a national customs or local law enforcement force. Customs agencies are generally charged with preventing censored materials from entering a country; local law enforcement agencies generally react to citizen complaints about materials. In extreme cases and especially in those areas where decision-making is local, religious groups or civic organizations seek enforcement.

The level of legal safeguard provided to one accused of violating the community standard or national standard varies from country to country and often within various regions of a nation. Even in the countries generally considered the most progressive in their prosecution practices, the cost and time involved in appealing a decision or fighting a criminal charge can lead to bankruptcy and others into simply "giving in." This leads to the "chilling effect" of censorship on sexual expression. From the prosecution of Larry Flynt on obscenity charges in Cincinnati, Ohio, or Gwinnett County, Georgia for publication in *Hustler* magazine, or a group of "leather pride" professors protesting the decision to ban all video depictions of mild bondage and sadism in Australia, some believe that their sexual expression is unjustifiably censored.

The impact of censorship also has a chilling effect on artists from print to video and audio media. They have expressed dismay at the limitations placed on their artistic expression by censorship schemes around the world. From D. H. Lawrence to Wendy O. Williams, individual artists have explained how censorship of materials that express their sexual desires leads them to self-doubt and a negative self-image. Some see artistic sexual expression as a way to "normalize" certain sexual practices, and censorship as a continuation of the "deviant" status applied to minority sexual practices. Whether it is Hugh Hefner, Bob Mizer, Nina Hartley, or even Andrea Dworkin, artists (and everyday people) often view such censorship as a hegemonic tool to control sexual behavior by marginalizing and discrediting those who do not follow in the normalized path.

As the sociologist Emile Durkheim pointed out more than a century ago, this struggle over the boundaries of what is socially acceptable behavior will continue in regard to sexual expression whether it involves a formal, national body or a community standard. Censorship is always with us, only the level at which it is applied changes across time and space. Despite new technological development in media, many of the same issues of censorship arise. For example, there are those who assert that **pornography** has pushed the technological boundaries from the invention of the home video player through the current state of the **Internet**. In each case there have been reactions to those developments, such as the *Communications Decency Act of 1995*. Thus, technology plays a role in boundary testing and maintenance. In some instances the boundaries around what is censored will be loosened; at other times the boundaries will tighten. There appears to be only one absolute: for each new sexual expression, someone will attempt to censor it. *See also* Cartoons and Comics; Pornography, on the Internet.

Further Reading: Australian Office of Film and Literature Classification. http://www.oflc. gov.au/special.html; MacKinnon, Catherine. *Only Words.* London: Harper-Collins, 1994; National Coalition Against Censorship. http://www.ncac.org; Hunter, Ian, Stephen Heath, Colin MacCabe, and Denise Riley, eds. *On Pornography: Literature, Sexuality, and Obscenity Law.* London: Macmillan, 1993; Index for Free Expression. http://www.indexonline.org; Potter, Hugh. *Pornography: Group Pressures and Individual Rights.* Sydney: Federation Press, 1996; Potter, Lyndy, and Roberto H. Potter. "The Internet, Cyberporn, and Sexual Exploitation of Children." *Sexuality & Culture* 5, 3 (2001): 31–48; Strossen, Nadine. *Defending Pornography: Free Speech, Sex, and the Fight for Women's Rights.* New York: Scribners, 1995; Wilson, Paul. *In Defence of Pornography.* Sydney: The University of New South Wales Press, 1995.

Lyndy A. Potter and Roberto Hugh Potter

CHILD ABUSE.   Several forms of child abuse exist: neglect, physical, emotional, sexual abuse, and exploitation. Yet, varying cultural practices, ideas about child development, moral values, and legal notions influence what specific acts are considered abuse. A child is generally defined as someone "below the age of 18 years unless the laws of a particular country set the legal age for adulthood younger" (UNICEF 2006). According to the World Health Organization:

> Child abuse or maltreatment constitutes all forms of physical and/or emotional ill-treatment, sexual abuse, neglect or negligent treatment or commercial or other exploitation, resulting in actual or potential harm to the child's health, survival, development or dignity in the context of a relationship of responsibility, trust or power.

In general, health and **mental health** professionals agree that child abuse threatens the social, spiritual, moral, psychological, and physical well-being of children and interferes with their development. Broadly speaking, media violence, **pornography**, use of firearms, war, poverty, capital punishment, and social inequities are forms of abuse of children insofar as children live in cultures that support these and to the extent their lives are influenced by them. Most research, however, is on abuse that is neglect, physical, and sexual. Child abuse in any form disrupts the development of children along typical lines that would lead to healthy relationships, the ability to love, the ability to co-exist with others, and the ability to form a healthy sexual identity as well as develop healthy desires and outlets for such.

It is difficult to know how prevalent any form of child abuse is within any country or among any group of people because any estimate of child abuse is likely to be an underestimate. For example, counting only substantiated cases of abuse by a social service agency or those coming to police attention eliminates many possible cases. Adult retrospective surveys are limited by memory and subjectivity with regard to what counts as abuse. In certain Asian cultures, for example, there is high agreement that sexual abuse does not occur, and so disclosure and identification may be even more difficult. Many forms of abuse have no physical evidence and, thus, research depends on verbal description by victims, offenders, or bystanders. And the youngest have little capacity to report abuse. In cases of parental maltreatment or sexual abuse, there are indeed other reasons that prohibit children who could disclose abuse from reporting, such as threats, fear of being sent away, or a relationship with the offender.

Neglect is a term used to describe acts of omission, that is, the failure to care. When a caregiver fails to provide for a child's safety, physical needs such as food, warmth, and shelter, give medical attention, provide for education, and even meet emotional needs, this is neglect. Neglect also includes the failure to properly supervise and protect children from harm. Many caregivers around the world cannot provide for their children the way they would like to and the circumstances under which children live in some countries might look like neglect in other societies. However, in general, a child is said to be neglected when minimal community standards for the care of the child are not met. The association between neglect and poverty is very strong; one can quite possibly blame society rather than parents for failure to care. When parents do neglect, it rarely indicates a lack of love or caring as it may be caused by a **drug or alcohol** addiction or mental illness, and exacerbated by isolation and lack of social supports. Neglected children are at risk for a number of developmental problems. Still, the outcome depends on other factors such as the severity of the neglect, the age of the child at the time of the neglect, how long the neglect lasts, and whether or not there are more positive activities and other supportive adults in the child's life.

Emotional abuse or psychological maltreatment may be at the core of all maltreatment. Historically, the notion that a child needs love for proper development arose in the late nineteenth century. Nevertheless, there is ample evidence from historical documents that the love of children by their parents is no modern phenomenon. Parents or caregivers who convey to children that they are worthless, flawed, unloved, unwanted, or are only of value if they meet the caregiver's needs, and who spurn, terrorize, isolate, denigrate, threaten, scare, exploit, or deny them emotional responsiveness, commit acts of psychological maltreatment. Growing up with emotional abuse puts children at risk for low self-esteem, poor interpersonal relationships, and, in particular, aggressive and angry behavior.

The World Health Organization defines physical abuse of a child as that which results in actual or potential physical harm to a child caused by some interaction or lack of interaction that was in the control of the parent or caregiver. There may be a single or repeated incidents and it is the form of maltreatment most likely to lead to death. Physical abuse is not caused by a lack of love or caring; parents who tend to hit their children are more likely to see their children's noncompliance as defiant and intentional and have developmentally inappropriate expectations of their children. Parents who physically abuse their children are also more likely to have low income, lack of education, and be socially isolated. A child may suffer physical injuries such as skin lesions or fractures. A child is also more likely to approve of violence and, as he or she grows up, more likely than other children to become depressed, anxious, or to act out in aggressive ways.

One controversial topic in the area of physical abuse is corporal punishment, using physical punishment to coerce or control a child. In almost all the countries around the world, save for Denmark, Finland, Germany, Italy, and a few others, corporal punishment is permitted in the home. About half of the countries around the globe permit it in schools. Some child advocates have argued, however, that this is a form of physical abuse because it has the potential to cause injury and is strongly associated with a host of negative outcomes in children.

Child sexual abuse involves a child in sexual activity that she or he is unable to give informed consent to and for which she or he is not developmentally ready. Also it is any sexual act with a child that violates the law or social taboos of society. It includes fondling as well as penetration as well as non-contact acts such as exposing oneself to a child or exposing a child to pornography. Generally, an arbitrary difference of five years of age categorizes an act as sexual abuse if children report mutual consent. No age difference is necessary if the victim reports that she or he was coerced. Girls are more likely to be sexually abused than boys; however, boys are also sexually abused. The major gender difference appears in the perpetrators, with over 90 percent of sexual abuse acts committed by men. Sexually abused children have been found to be depressed, anxious, and aggressive and to be more at risk for future drug and alcohol problems, depression, and chronic low self-esteem. One of the characteristics that best distinguish sexually abused children from physically abused children in terms of outcome is a tendency to engage in sexualized behavior like exposing themselves, inserting objects into their anus or vagina, and compulsive masturbating.

Several controversies have emerged around child sexual abuse questions: can children be seductive? Do women sexually abuse children? Is child play sexually abusive? How reliable are repressed memories (false memory syndrome)? Will long-term effects be likely? Today, few professionals believe that a child's seductive behavior leads to sexual abuse. In fact, rarely will a clinician even label a child's behavior as "seductive" because experimenting and learning about their sexuality is a natural part of development and it is the adult's responsibility to respond to that appropriately. There was a time, however, when children were labeled as seductive and adults were let "off the hook." Before the Romantic era, Christian societies like the Puritans viewed children as wild and more capable of influence by the devil, thus female children could be considered temptresses. When **Freud** gave up his "Seduction Hypothesis" (his original theory that explained sexual abuse as the cause of neurosis) to create his theory of the unconscious (children only *fantasized* about sex with their parents), Western cultures entertained the idea of the sexual child. It is true that children do present sexualized behavior, particularly after being sexually abused or exposed to inappropriately sexual material, however, professionals now consider this behavior as a symptom rather than a seduction.

Another controversy surrounds women's sexual abuse of children. While this is much rarer than male perpetrated abuse (less than one-in-ten cases), it occurs and the effects can be just as devastating on children. Some cultures' fascination with such may be a way to diffuse blame from men in societies that support male entitlement to women and by extension girls. It may also be because women who sexually abuse defy two stereotypes: women as nurturers and women as not sexually driven.

A third controversy has to do with whether children can be considered sex offenders as they are in some places by law. Sexual play between children is a natural part of development, and, depending on the exposure of the child to adult material, some of this play can appear adult-like. If one child bullies another child, that is, coerces the child into sexual play, this is a form of abuse. If one child is older than the other child and uses the power as an older child to get the younger child to consent, this is a form of abuse. Whether these acts are considered "sex offenses" is a matter of legal terminology and public opinion about childhood as well as normative sexuality.

A fourth controversy is whether people can have false memories of abuse or forget their abuse. Cognitive psychologists of the 1980s and 1990s asserted that it was impossible to forget traumatic memories believing, perhaps wrongly, that all abuse was traumatic. Since the controversy exploded, researchers have shown that sexual abuse victims (some that had witnesses to their abuse to verify it) have forgotten and then later remembered their abuse and that creating a false memory is highly unlikely even though it is possible. The most likely circumstance for the creation of a false memory is under hypnosis; this form of therapy is no longer used with sexual abuse victims.

The final controversy that has arisen from an interest in child sexual abuse is whether outcomes from **sexual abuse** are uniformly poor. One study (Rind, Tromovitch, and Bauserman 1998) showed that over 50 percent of children who had been sexually abused as children displayed no symptoms by their early twenties. It was condemned for purportedly indicating that sexual abuse was not so bad for all children.

Children are exploited through physical labor in many countries across the globe, with sub-Saharan African countries leading in the percentage of children employed in hazardous working conditions. Since the beginning of the twentieth century, laws have existed to protect children; these laws vary by country, and in many countries these are not enforced. Thus, child labor continues and can be detrimental to their health and well-being.

Child rape during war is another issue of concern with regard to exploitation. For example, in Cambodian refugee camps run by the Khmer Rouge, the Khmer, and Thai soldiers routinely used children for sex. Children are also trafficked for sex as evidenced in the "sex tourism industry" catering to men who travel to foreign countries to have sex with children. Child **prostitution** as well as trafficking exists in the West as well as in the East, with the majority of prostitutes beginning work before the age of 16. Boys as well as girls are induced to work in the sex industry. In El Salvador, one-third of child prostitutes are boys. In some poorer countries, daughters (less valued than sons) are sold into prostitution as a way for their parents to make money. Some West African and Middle Eastern countries circumvent child trafficking laws through early **marriage** (*sique*). And fear of **AIDS/HIV** infection has created a demand for younger sex partners.

A further form of child sexual exploitation is child pornography, which is illegal in most countries. A *New York Times* article (Eichenwald 2005) noted a disturbing trend in the recruitment of children into pornography: Pedophiles and "johns" enter online chat rooms for teens with web cameras linked to their computers and then seduce them into performing sex acts for money in front of the camera. These activities are to the detriment of the child's physical and mental health, education, spiritual, moral, and social-emotional development. *See also* Childhood; Colonialism/Postcolonialism and Sex; Domestic and Relationship Violence; Incest; Morality and Ethics; Scandals; Sex Crimes.

Further Reading: Eichenwald, Kurt. "Through His Webcam, a Boy Joins a Sordid Online World." *New York Times*. December 19, 2005, available at http://select.nytimes.com/gst/abstract. html?res=F30617FC3C540C7A8DDDAB0994DD404482; EPCAT International (End Child Prostitution, Child Pornography and Trafficking in Children for sexual purposes), available at http://www.ecpat.net/eng/CSEC/faq/FAQ_English.pdf; Fontes, Lisa Aronson, ed. *Sexual Abuse in Nine North American Cultures: Treatment and Prevention.* Thousand Oaks, CA: Sage, 1995; Gabarino, James, Edna Guttman, and Janis Wilson Seeley. *The Psychologically Battered Child: Strategies for Identification, Assessment, and Intervention.* San Francisco: Jossey-Bass, 1986; Global Initiative to End All Corporal Punishment of Children, available at www. endcorporalpunishment.org; Hines, Denise A., and Kathleen Malley-Morrison. *Family Violence in the United States: Defining, Understanding, and Combating Abuse.* Thousand Oaks, CA: Sage, 2005; Lamb, Sharon, ed. *New Versions of Victims: Feminists Struggle with the Concept.* New York: New York University Press, 1999; Myers, John, Lucy Berliner, John Briere, C. Terry Hendriz, Carol Jenny, and Teresa A. Reid. *The APSAC Handbook on Child Maltreatment.* 2nd ed. Thousand Oaks, CA: Sage, 2002; Rind, Bruce, Philip Tromovitch, and Robert Bauserman. "A Meta-analytic Examination of Assumed Properties of Child Sexual Abuse Using College Samples." *Psychological Bulletin* 124 (1998): 22–53; UNICEF, Convention on the Rights of the Child, available at http://www.unicef.org/crc/index_30177.html; World Health Organization. Report of the Consultation on Child Abuse Prevention, Geneva, 29–31 March 1999, Social Change and Mental Health, Violence and Injury Prevention.

Sharon Lamb

CHILDHOOD. Childhood is a chronological, biological, social, political, cultural, and sexual condition characterized by generalizable stages of development, during which children are seen as both sources and objects of love. Childhood, including the age range which it encompasses, has changed over the course of the twentieth century as culture has changed, yet there still remains a lack of research and writing on how children experience childhood, especially with respect to love and sexuality. The early years of life are commonly understood as a preparation for adulthood, including the way the child will seek loving relationships as an adult. Romantic Western philosophies hold children in a reverent light that emphasizes the love that is inborn in all children. But understandings of what constitutes an appropriate childhood change as society changes. At any given time, what is acceptable for some children is unthinkable for others. Because childhood is temporary and constructed, the time of childhood must be understood in terms of the precise form and manner particular groups of children are educated into society within a specific generational cohort.

During childhood, children love their parents and siblings without question across cultures. At about the age of three, they become interested in their peer group and are particularly attracted to children older then them. Sigmund **Freud**'s discovery of the power of the unconscious at the turn of the twentieth century made adults aware of negative experiences during childhood and their continuing effects. Reformers during the first part of the twentieth century founded a number of institutions dedicated to child welfare. Some children gained by these reforms, depending on their class, gender, and race. Children were not passive victims, however, and they figured out ways to resist the "curricularized" life enforced on them. For poor children, this often meant going from the school classrooms to an extended care program within the same classrooms. Escape with their friends from so much structure in their lives was one way children resisted, which distanced themselves from parental influence.

Although childhood usually is considered a sexless period of life, children engage in curious games that are often sexual in nature. Adults label friendships between boys and girls as "puppy love," implying play (the child not agents of love) and mild bestiality (the child not fully civilized). As *objects* of love, children across cultures receive gifts and their parents often work very hard to give to their children what they perceive was missing from their childhood. Sociologists have combined the ethnographies of anthropologists with a focus on children's experiences to reveal a much more complex field in which children, given their limited access to resources, do possess agency.

There is also a biological component to childhood. For girls and boys, the onset of **puberty** is the end of childhood biologically. At the turn of the twentieth century, menarche (a girl's first period) occurred at sixteen or seventeen. As the century progressed, the age of menarche steadily declined until today it usually occurs at eleven or twelve and is still declining. Twenty-first-century marketing aimed at even younger children who idolize teen stars and want to emulate them has created a false puberty that begins when a child goes to school.

This construction of childhood, however, is a relatively recent phenomenon. For the working-class child, education became mandatory during the course of the twentieth century. This had an effect on the length of childhood. No longer could children pick up what they needed to succeed as adults by hanging around parents or other adults. Due to extended formal schooling, adults felt they must take childhood seriously and more importantly, that children must take childhood seriously.

In the United States, before the passage of the Fair Labor Standards Act in 1938, children worked under dangerous conditions in several industries, including textile mills, factories, coal mines, and a plethora of odd jobs such as "newsies," fruit pickers, bootblacks, bowling alley boys, postal telegraph deliverers, oyster shuckers, and breakers in lumber camps. During this time, childhood ended at age seven for some children because this was the age they began to work either on the family farm or in various industries associated with the increase of urban populations. Between 1908 and 1912, Louis Hines traveled across the United States photographing children as young as three laboring under dangerous conditions. His photographs depict how quickly children as young as five adopted the working-class habits of adults. They smoked, played craps and poker for money, and saw prostitutes after they turned twelve.

Before World War II, characters such as those portrayed on film by Shirley Temple provide examples of what Valerie Walkerdine has termed the "child woman," a street-smart and irresistible orphan who takes care of everyone in her life. Adults speak to her on an adult level while she rearranges the lives of the adults so that everyone is happy. Another example of the child-woman is Orphan Annie. Her relationship to Daddy Warbucks in the famous comic strip that spanned much of the twentieth century is a love relationship. Warbucks does not want romantic love from Annie; he wants child love. Orphan Annie and most of the characters played by Shirley Temple are working-class girls who have lost their parents and hit upon hard times. It is their purity, common sense, and love that make them so irresistible.

While working-class children fared no better in Europe than North America, theirs was an older and more embedded culture of child labor. At the same time, children who lived in middle- and upper-middle-class European homes were clothed in highly stylized and traditional outfits, while adults saw childhood as a time of innocence and play. They were formally educated into the class system in which they were born, living highly idealized lives.

For the working class child, education became mandatory during the course of the twentieth century; for the middle class child, higher education became mandatory. This had an effect on the length of childhood. No longer could children quickly pick up what they need to succeed as an adult by hanging around parents or other adults. Due to extended formal schooling, adults felt they must take childhood seriously and more importantly, that children must take childhood more seriously. School has become the principal site for work by children in the last half of the century. School also provided age-graded extra-curricular activities such as dances that structured the child's initiation into romantic relationships with each other.

Childhood intersects with sexuality in more nuanced ways culturally. Corporate culture, aimed at children, creates classrooms out of public places. However, this *kinderculture* does not have any responsibility in respect to the developmental stages of children's lives. Because television has replaced parents as authorities in the child's life, children have sophisticated introductions to adult life without the benefit of years to distinguish the inappropriate from the appropriate. Simultaneously, the "empty nest" most children arrive to after school means they have a site for child-constructed social situations without parental oversight. Love relationships portrayed by television are possible in the empty nest. Children are also unprotected from predators. Parental warnings are stringent because of this and children may experience the hours before the parent's arrival as threatening.

Because of the increasing violence toward children and the unhealthy social relationships often fostered by institutionalized schooling, many parents increasingly choose alternative schools or home schooling. In 2003, the U.S. Department of Education reported 1.1 million home-schooled children in the United States. Though a majority chooses to home school for religious reasons, there are many "boutique" reasons for choosing the flexibility of home schooling. This includes slowing down the social aspects of childhood, including peer pressure to engage in relationships, which include love and sexuality, while expanding learning experiences. Home and alternative schooling also provide a buffer zone from bullying, which emerged as a crucial issue after two victims of bullying expressed their resentment towards their peers through violence in Columbine, Colorado.

Childhood became shorter and more commodified as the twentieth century progressed, even as adolescence was extended. Parental love is often symbolized by conspicuous consumption of children while children themselves live in more and more virtual worlds. Richard Louv labels the condition children suffer as "nature-deficit disorder." Children have limited access to nature, with negative implications for health and child development, including love and sexuality. In 1986, Robin Moore charted the loss of natural play spaces in urban England that had occurred in a fifteen-year period. Another study in Great Britain found that the average eight-year-old could identify more characters from the Japanese card trading game Pokémon than native animals in the community where they lived. This estrangement from nature and increasing use of indoor spaces removes the opportunities for children to engage in experiences that are planned and carried out by them, as well as health consequences. Love and sexuality, as it is portrayed on television, become more important in structured indoor programs from which the child wishes to escape. *See also* Adolescence; Cartoons and Comics; Child Abuse; Families; Romance.

Further Reading: Ariès, Phillipe. *Centuries of Childhood*. Translated by Robert Baldick. London: Pimlico, 1996; Child Trends DataBank. www.childtrendsdatabank.org. Research on "key indicators" of childhood and youth, including love and sexuality, February 2006; Fass, Paula S., and Mason, Mary Ann, eds. *Childhood in America*. New York: New York University Press, 2000; Heywood, Colin. *A History of Childhood*. Malden, MA: Polity Press, 2001; James, Allison, Chris Jenks, and Alan Prout. *Theorizing Childhood*. Cambridge: Polity Press, 1998; Lillard, Paula Polk. *Montessori Today: A Comprehensive Approach to Education from Birth to Adulthood*. New York: Schocken, 1996; Louv, Richard. *Last Child in the Woods: Saving Our Children from Nature-Deficit Disorder*. Chapel Hill, NC: Algonquin, 2005; Pollock, Linda. *Forgotten Children: Parent-Child Relations over Three Centuries*. Hanover, NH: University Press of New England, 1987; Walkerdine, Valerie. *Daddy's Girls: Young Girls and Popular Culture*. Cambridge, MA: Harvard University Press, 1998.

Pamela Autrey

CINEMA. Sex and love are highly popular themes in mainstream, independent and marginal cinema. The American movie industry, effecting most of the world cinema, has attempted to visualize and dramatize the spectator's most intimate fantasies, basic instincts and desires, to expose and celebrate human bodies and to idealize particular patterns of female and male physique, creating influential iconographies of sex symbols, stars and starlets that often communicate popular values of machismo, power, femininity and formulated sex appeal. During the twentieth century and early 2000s, diverse romantic and erotic film genres and subgenres gradually emerged. These include melodramas, bedroom farces, erotic thrillers, romantic TV sitcoms and melodramatic soap operas and telenovelas, erotic animation, musicals and westerns, the New Queer Cinema, and **pornography**.

Since its beginning, cinema has portrayed blissful **romance** and unfulfilled love, yearning and courtship, infatuated and frustrated couples, fidelity and **infidelity**. Thomas Alva Edison's blockbuster, *The May Irwin Kiss* (U.S. 1896), featured passionate kisses between May Irwin and John Rice. Georges Méliès's *A Trip to the Moon* (France 1902) presented a bevy of starlets in girdles and garters, cheering the male astronauts about to leave Earth on their way to explore new stars (and starlets) in the universe. George Loane Tucker's commercially successful *Traffic in Souls* (U.S. 1913), dramatizing an actual "white (women) slavery" scandal in New York City, attracted about 30,000 viewers in its first week. The ultimate female vamp, the femme fatale Theda Bara (Theodosia Goodman) made her debut in Frank Powel's *A Fool There Was* (1915), about a married diplomat who falls under the spell of a dangerous woman.

Tatsuya Fuji (as Kichizo Ishida), left, and Eiko Matsuda (as Sada Abe), right, star in Nagisa Oshima's 1976 film, *In the Realm of the Senses*. Courtesy of Photofest.

These "passionate" motion pictures faced legal and moral challenges. In 1913, the U.S. Supreme Court, defined movies as a form of business not a form of art, and thus not constitutionally protected. Consequently, the Pennsylvania Board of Censorship prohibited the screening of pimping, **prostitution**, white slavery, brothels, nudity, knifing, **abortion**, **birth control**, parodying the Church, fornication, and even honeymoon scenes and lingerie display. In an effort to prevent further government control, the Association of Motion Picture Producers established, in 1930, the Hays Code, promising to produce no film that would lower the moral standards of those of see it. Explicitly prohibited were adultery, excessive and lustful kissing, seduction, rape, interracial intercourse, homosexual relationships, and scenes of actual child birth.

The restrictions on representation of passionate romance and erotic practices created a challenge for the great female film stars like Joan Crawford and Mae West, who were often perceived as sexual role models. While many female idols represented the myth of the sexy but dangerous *femme fatale*, male stars such as the melodramatic Rudolph Valentino and the ultimate sex symbol James Dean, were glorified as irresistible lovers, reinforcing patriarchal codes of dominance and idolization. Ironically, these men are now considered gay or bisexual icons.

The romantic melodrama is a powerful cinematic genre that effectively mediates and communicates human experience—while conforming to censorship codes of the times. It promotes emotional response and compassionate identification with its suffering protagonists who feel trapped within society's norms. Victor Fleming's *Gone with the Wind* (U.S. 1939), for example, features the hopeless love of Scarlett O'Hara (Vivien Leigh), a spoiled young southern woman for Rhett Butler (Clark Gable), a married man, before and after the Civil War. One of the characteristics of the classic melodramas is the extraordinary sense of frustration and dissatisfaction found in their central female characters. Ahmed Dia Aladdin's *My Lost Life* (Egypt 1956), for instance, articulates the hardship of Aliya, a young woman, whose mother pairs her off with Aziz, a rich old man, who abuses her. Finally, Aziz is killed and Aliya finds her true love.

Another significant melodramatic pattern is that of the Love Triangle, as manifested in François Truffaut's *Jules et Jim* (France 1962); and Bernardo Bertolucci's *The Dreamers* (France/Italy/UK 2003). Given the different cultural mores and legal restrictions, the latter includes some nude scenes, articulating the intimate relationship between the female character, her twin brother, and their male friend. In his spectacular and sensational manner, Bertolucci also featured Marlon Brando and Maria Schneider's unforgettable and (at the time) shocking anal scene in *The Last Tango in Paris* (France/Italy 1973), but still the most controversial is Nagisa Oshima's *In the Realm of the Senses* (Japan 1976), the story of a servant and former prostitute, who becomes obsessed with her male employer. For the ultimate erotic pleasure, she finally strangles him, then cuts off his penis as a keepsake. This film exemplifies the borderline between pornography and art, and marginal versus legitimate cinema, in a realm of growing porn industries around the world, stimulated by the popularity of home movies, video, CDs, computer games, and the **Internet**. These sources provide a wide range of erotic images—from softcore nude photography to hardcore pornography and are characterized by graphic depictions of every imaginable sexual practice, targeted at diverse audiences.

Today, family objection, in particular, is a common theme in many queer adolescent melodramas. Hettie MacDonald's *Beautiful Thing* (UK 1995), for instance, articulates the love story of two working-class high-school students from East London: Jamie, a delicate boy, and Ste, the football captain who is frequently beaten by his drug-dealing older brother and his abusive father.

Mainstream romantic comedies usually avoid explicit sex scenes. Their pursuit plots, according to Mark Rubinfeld (2001), usually portray the man's quest for conquest, his refusal to accept "no" for an answer, and his eventual winning of the girl. This subgenre, as manifested in Hollywood classics like Ernst Lubitsch's *The Shop around the Corner* (U.S. 1940) with James Stewart and Margaret Sullavan, emphasizes the male's loving paternalism, and enforces the social imperative for woman to accede to men. In comedies based on a redemption plot, in contrast, the coldhearted, bitter hero is less easily redeemed by his vivacious female suitors: Vivian (Julia Roberts), for example, a prostitute who becomes a lady and finally wins the coldhearted businessman Edward (Richard Gere) in Gary Marshal's classic film *Pretty Woman* (U.S. 1990).

More sensitive, brokenhearted, and lonely male protagonists find their love in fairy tales. In this subgenre, the female protagonist is obliged to accept the man's offer (and to become a human being), or be perceived as a heartless woman as in *Splash* (U.S. 1984), in which the ultimate mermaid (Darryl Hannah) finds the lonely man Allen (Tom Hanks). Romantic comedies based on foil plots include the prick foil plot, the dweeb foil plot, the bitch foil plot, and the temptress foil plot. In the first two, the woman is the one to choose between two men, one of whom is more socio-economically successful (but sometimes nothing but a snobbish bore), while the other is more common but also more attractive and witty, as in Howard Hawks's classical comedy *His Girl Friday* (U.S. 1940), in which the former journalist Hildy (Rosalind Russell), returns to her ex-husband and editor (Cary Grant), abandoning her fiancée Bruce Baldwin (Ralph Bellamy).

In the bitch and the temptress plots, it is the man who must choose between two women who love him. The female protagonist is the typical good wife, confronting her rival, the stereotypical bad girl. Such a formulation turns a comic love story into a comic hate story, representing women as bitter and angry at other women, rather than at the patriarchal establishment. For example, in Warren Beatty's *Dick Tracy* (U.S. 1990), Madonna plays the sexually aggressive temptress, contrasted to Dick's prudent girlfriend. The comic "permission plots" portray the difficulties of a hero and a heroine in love, often dealing with parental resistance to their relationship, as in Assi Dayan's *Hill Halfon Doesn't Answer* (Israel 1975), in which a father will not allow his beautiful, younger daughter to marry a young soldier before her older and less attractive sister is married.

Ethnic comedies are an important romantic subgenre characterized by inter-cultural collisions producing comic situations, interracial eroticism, mistaken identifications and hyper-stereotypical portrayals of ethnic minorities. Ephraim Kishon's *Sallah* (Israel 1964) depicts the affair of Habooba (Geula Noni), the daughter of Sallah (Chaim Topol)—a hyper-stereotypical, low-class Jewish immigrant—and Ziggy (Arik Einstein), a privileged, handsome native-Israeli of western Jewish origins who lives on a Kibbutz, and the parallel romance between Sallah's son Shimon (Shayke Levy) and Bat-Sheba (Gila Almagor), a female kibbutz member. Sometimes these comedies deal with sexual transgression, particularly in the New Queer Cinema of the 1990s and the 2000s. This is exemplified in the **interracial relationship** between a Taiwanese gay man and his white lover in Ang Lee's *The Wedding Banquet* (Taiwan 1993), and Emile Gaudreault's flamboyant farce *Mambo Italiano* (Canada 2003), which portrays the erotic relationship between the sissified Italian-American Angelo (Luke Kirby) and the muscular, bisexual policeman Nino (Peter Miller), who are confronted by their bigoted, hysterical parents. Notably, gayness is associated by Angelo's family with decadent Western culture, contrasted with "authentic" Italian (straight) machismo.

The bedroom farce is one of most popular subgenres of the romantic comedy. Originating in popular comedies-of-errors in the French theater in the late nineteenth century, it focuses on unexpected, erotic couplings and surprising infatuations. This extravagant, carnivalesque genre includes many blockbusters. The American youth trilogy *American Pie* (the first film directed by Paul Weitz, U.S. 1999), captures the coming of age, **puberty** rites, and romantic lives of middle and upper class teenage boys encountering their first sexual experiences, finding a girlfriend, and maintaining their male bonds in high school and college. Into this category falls *Boat Trip* (Mort Nathan, U.S. 2003), a comedy about two straight mates, chubby Nick (Horatio Sanz) and handsome Jerry (Cuba Gooding, Jr.) who mistakenly join a gay cruise ship, while Edouard Molinaro's French classic *Cage Aux Folles* (France/Italy 1978) focuses on an effeminate gay couple, Renato (Ugo Tognazzi) and Albin/ZaZa (Michel Serrault), who try to camouflage their sexuality to help their child marry the daughter of a conservative heterosexual couple.

A more conservative perspective on masculinity and machismo is reflected in many westerns, focusing on the lonely rider who has to choose between wandering and settling down, or the sheriff who has to choose between fighting white bandits and/or demonized native Americans, and his duties as a family guy; his modest wife (who dresses his wounds) and the town's exotic, unruly woman (who undresses his muscular body). Westerns often underscore sexual symbols—particularly phallic weapons like pistols, rifles, guns, knifes, and arrows—to overcome the censors, such as Howard Hawks's *Red River* (U.S. 1948), in which two handsome young cowboys, played by Montgomery Clift and John Ireland, homoerotically compare their private shooting tools. The all-male intimacy in the wilderness is much more explicit, however, in Ang Lee's *Brokeback Mountain* (U.S. 2005), which portrays Ennis Del Mar (Heath Ledger) and Jack Twist (Jake Gyllenhaal), as two cowboys who fall in love.

Sex and love are also common themes in musicals, a utopian genre, typically featuring the hardship of a young couple and their attempts to overcome ethnic differences, bigotry, and narrow-mindedness. For example Jerome Robbins and Robert Wise's *West Side Story* (U.S. 1961), which presents the love affair of Maria (Natalie Wood), the sister of Bernardo, a Puerto-Rican street gang member, and Tony (Richard Beymer), who belongs to a rival (white) street gang; the popular Bollywood musical *Sangam* (Raj Kapoor, India 1964) featuring the attempts of Gopal (Rajendra Kumar) to fulfill his love for Radha (Vyjayantimala), the sister of his best friend Sunder (Raj Kapoor); and the romance between the 1950s high-school students Sandy (Olivia Newton-John) and Danny (John Travolta) in Randal Kleiser's *Grease* (U.S. 1978). *See also* Adolescence; Censorship; Families; Fetishes; Heterosexuality; Homosexuality; Masculinity; Popular Culture.

Further Reading: Abel, Richard. *The Cine Goes to Town: French Cinema 1896–1914.* Berkeley, Los Angeles and London: University of California Press, 1994; Artsreformation. See http://www.artsreformation.com/a001/hays-code.html. Information about the Motion Picture Production Code of 1930 (Hays Code), 2000; Braun, Eric. *Frightening the Horses: Gay Icons of the Cinema.* Richmond, UK: Reynolds & Hearn, 2002; Buehrer, Beverley Bare. *Japanese Films: A Filmography and Commentary, 1921–1989.* Jefferson, NC, and London: McFarland & Co., 1990; Dyer, Richard. *The Culture of Queers.* London and New York: Routledge, 2002; Filmsite. See www.filmsite.org/romancefilms.html. Review of romance films from the 1890s to the present, 2003; Levy, Emanuel. "The New Gay and Lesbian Cinema." In *Cinema of Outsiders: The Rise of American Independent Film,* edited by Emanuel Levy, 442–93. New York: New York University Press, 1999; Padva, Gilad. "Edge of Seventeen: Melodramatic Coming-Out in New Queer Adolescence Films." *Communication and Critical/Cultural Studies* 1, no. 4 (2004): 355–72; Rich, B. Ruby. "New Gay Cinema." *Sight and Sound* 2, no. 5 (1992): 31–34; Rubinfeld, Mark, D. *Bound to Bond: Gender, Genre, and the Hollywood Romantic Comedy.* Westport, CT: Praeger, 2001.

Gilad Padva

COLONIALISM/POSTCOLONIALISM AND SEX. To colonize a land means to settle the land, to populate as well as to govern. It is through the notions of settling and populating that the most basic relationship between "colonial" and "sex and love" become apparent. Populating demands procreation, so settlers of colonial holdings were expected to emigrate as **families** and to expand their influence and dominance through future generations. This process took place with an eye to maintaining boundaries between the colonized and the colonizer. Racial and ethnic differences were central concerns, as most colonizing nations were anxious to avoid miscegenation (the mixing or interbreeding of different racial or ethnic groups) and maintain a sense of racial "purity." The emphasis on heterosexual family led to a culture of patriarchal and paternalistic assumptions, a power hierarchy dependent on maintaining a sense of superiority in terms of gender, sexuality, and race.

The era of European colonialism—in which England, France, Belgium and the Netherlands played a major role—began in the Renaissance or early modern period and reached its greatest heights in the nineteenth century, stretching across Africa, Asia, Australia, and the Americas. Most, if not all, of these colonial holdings were motivated by the desire for wealth, as increased trading depended on the acquisition and exchange of natural resources. The resources were varied and included minerals (such as gold and silver) and foodstuffs (such as tea or tobacco).

Slavery is a critical institution in considering colonization. Not only were human beings "farmed" out of colonial holdings in West Africa as part of the "resources" of the land, native populations were further used in retrieving and processing local natural resources. Colonization was often rationalized on the basis of cultural or religious superiority, and most European nations approached colonization with the idea that they were bringing enlightenment and civilization to primitive and barbaric peoples. Most contemporary research notes the way such rationalizations instead allowed for cruelty, enslavement, genocide, and oppression.

The historical period of European colonization comes to a close at the beginning of the twenty-first century. Most African nations achieved independence in the mid- to late twentieth century, while some areas (such as those in the Middle East) still function under what many describe as colonization. The most basic definition of "postcolonial" concerns the many cultural and historical effects of colonization, and seeks to understand the complex interplays of power, identities, place, and history emerging out of the dynamics of colonization. While the "post" in "postcolonial" may seem to signal a straightforward historical difference (insofar as postcolonial comes after colonization), such simple distinctions ignore the complexities of the relationships between the two terms. Many critics use the term "neocolonialism" to signal the kinds of power imbalances that still exist today as part of the pressures of globalization. Sex tourism represents one form of contemporary neocolonialism. It entails wealthy travelers from first-world countries seeking sexual companionship from sex workers in developing countries (most typically in Asia or the Caribbean).

During the nineteenth century, sexuality became one of the spaces where racial difference was explored. One infamous episode involved Saartjie Baartman, who became known as the "Hottentot Venus." She was taken from her land in South Africa and displayed as an example of racial difference, her genitalia interpreted as indicating some essential and biological difference between white and black humans. While alive she was paraded through European capitals and examined by a range of medical "experts," who sought to tease out the presupposed link between her anatomy (size of her buttocks, clitoris, etc.) and her sexual nature. Upon death her organs were preserved and continued their bizarre journey to medical societies and universities.

Bartram's experience points to the complex relationship between colonial power and sexual knowledge. The concept of the "exotic other" also informs other constructions of sexuality in twentieth century colonialism. The idea of "going native" is based on the threat of a degenerative primitive culture infecting the morally superior colonizing culture and indicates a link between racism and sexuality. Edgar Rice Burrough's popular "Tarzan" series (begun in 1912) based its appeal on the concept of a white child with aristocratic background who becomes an "Ape Man" when he is left to survive in the jungles of Africa. It is worth noting that Tarzan's appeal lasted well into the twentieth century, as the popularity of the "Tarzan" film series and television show attest.

Joseph Conrad's 1899 novella *Heart of Darkness* also depends in part on this concept of "going native." Although the story is a response to the horrors of colonial domination, its meanings nevertheless depend, in large part, on colonialist perceptions. The character of Kurz, for example, may exemplify one form of European corruption, but his madness nevertheless comes out of his isolation in a native culture and makes sense within the assumptions of "going native." Kurz's madness is further linked to his association with a powerful and mysterious African woman, a figure that contrasts in the text with Kurz's European fiancée, his "Intended." Conrad's description of the African woman, "a wild and gorgeous apparition of a woman," reflects the ambivalent European fascination with black female sexuality and power (Conrad 1988, 60).

Twentieth century postcolonial texts often work against such stereotypes. Kenyan writer Ngugi Wa Thiong'o considers the role of women in a socialist postcolonial Africa. His fiction often contains strong women characters that participate actively in the revolution and are in full control of their sexuality. His 1980 novel, *Devil on the Cross*, exemplifies this trend.

Edward Said's *Orientalism* (1978) offers an analysis of how the Western imagination has constructed the idea of the Orient. Said argues that the East (and here he includes what we might term the "Middle East") is more a projected ideal than a separate reality, a place and people imbued with peculiar expressions of exoticism. Part of this imagined exoticism takes on a peculiarly sexual or gendered nuance, as the East became a place for Westerners to project their desires onto a space replete with seduction, sexuality, and loose sexual mores. As Conrad's novel and Said's theory imply, the metaphorical language of sex and love are mutually informing when it comes to considering the dynamics of the colonial and postcolonial.

Recently, crossovers between "queer theory" and the "postcolonial" have led to rich explorations of their shared thematic interests. These include such elements as questions of representation, identity, and agency. While postcolonial reading might tend to focus on representations and identities of race, ethnicity, and nationality, feminist and queer inquiries will attend most closely to those of gender and sexuality. Analyzing the power relationship between the colonizer and the colonized is perhaps the central occupation of postcolonial criticism, and one that is shared by contemporary gender and sexuality studies. South Asian critic Gayatri Gopintha, for example, explores postcolonial representations of sexuality through a range of Indian film and fiction. Her work on Bollywood films reveals the conservative sexual politics that influence such productions. While the influential African writer Franz Fanon considered non-normative sexualities such as homosexuality, to be a European colonial import, more recently critics have considered ways that gay, lesbian, bisexual, and **transgender** expressions offer useful spaces for re-imagining desire, identities and kinship. Queer experience, for example, resonates with the sense of displacement and outsider status that are in many ways central to Diaspora, a key experience in the postcolonial. *See also* Childhood; Cinema; Feminism; Heterosexuality; Homosexuality; Masculinity; Politics; Race and Racism; Religions, Western; Sexual Science/Sexology.

Further Reading: Ashcroft, Bill, Gareth Griffiths, and Helen Tiffin. *Post-Colonial Studies: The Key Concepts*. New York: Routledge, 2000; Bahri, Deepika. "Emory University Postcolonial Studies." http://www.english.emory.edu/Bahri/index.html. A resource for students of postcolonial literature, but also provides information and an introduction to general postcolonial studies, with short discussions of major theories and ideas; Conrad, Joseph. *Heart of Darkness: An Authoritative Text, Backgrounds and Sources, Criticism*. 3rd ed. New York: Norton, 1988; Fanon, Frantz, and Charles Lam Markmann. *Black Skin, White Masks*. New York: Grove Press, 1967; Gilman, Sander L. "Black Bodies, White Bodies." In *"Race," Writing, and Difference*, edited by Henry Louis Gates, 223–61. Chicago: University of Chicago Press, 1985; Patton, Cindy, and Benigno Sánchez-Eppler, eds. *Queer Diasporas*. Durham, NC: Duke University Press, 2000; Said, Edward W. *Orientalism*. Harmondsworth: Penguin, 1995; wa Thiong'o, Ngugi. *Devil on the Cross*. London: Heinemann, 1982; Young, Robert. "Postcolonialism." In *Very Short Introductions*, p. 98. Oxford: Oxford University Press, 2003.

Lorena L. Russell

COSMETICS. Cosmetics can be broadly defined as referring to techniques and materials used to enhance the appearance of persons according to the cultural norms of a social group to which they belong or identify. These techniques may be temporary or permanent ways of decorating or manipulating the body. Modern cosmetic practices include embellishing the bodily surface (e.g., face makeup, henna (*mehndi*) decoration of the feet and hands, skincare, perfume, tattoos) or the addition of objects to the body (e.g., earrings, false eyelashes, body piercings). Cosmetic surgery is also a permanent form of bodily augmentation and re-invention—from scarification to rhinoplasty. Cosmetics spin in and out of the orbits of sex, love, and culture. Above all, cosmetics establish identity, both social and sexual. There are expressions such as "I must put on my face," and "I feel naked without makeup." The act of putting on cosmetics becomes a habit or routine, almost an unconscious part of getting dressed. The body is like a canvas on which the artist paints a pattern that creates a desired self-image. Cosmetics are both a mask (to disguise oneself or create a new identity) and a mirror (to reflect a desired identity). We call this "cosmetic behavior."

The twentieth-century emphasis on skin, eyes, and mouth in cosmetic practice illustrates the paradoxical resonances of cosmetics. Makeup and seduction are inextricably linked and facial features are symbols of sexuality. Different cosmetic practices convey different aspects of bodily performance and sexual references, whether it be the blankness of a Kabuki white face, the black-eyed menace of Goths, the overtly sexualized red lips of a Hollywood siren, the stylized, color-coded masquerade of Chinese opera, or the exaggerated makeup of a female impersonator.

While Western culture usually makes blended products made from artificial ingredients, other cultures use natural ingredients. The myrrh (camphor) and frankincense (conifer) carried by the biblical three wise men are such an example. All kinds of natural ingredients can be used to make cosmetics: floral or vegetable extracts (patchouli, jasmine, henna, belladonna), animal products (lanolin, bones, egg whites, cochineal), and minerals and natural substances (ochre, antimony, charcoal, cinnabar, lead, arsenic). Some ingredients have been used in the pursuit of beauty despite serious health side-effects.

Cosmetic practices are as variable as the cultures in which they are practiced, but within a culture, such practices are regarded as natural. They are internalized and repeated as an essential component of belonging to that culture or subculture. Such historical and cross-cultural uses and meanings of cosmetics have shaped the ways in which modern cosmetics are understood and re-interpreted today.

If cosmetic practices are relative and context-specific, they are linked also to the "previous" uses that they reject and deliberately differ from as "not statements." Cosmetics are used as means of identifying with or visually rejecting particular social roles by drawing on sets of opposites: casualness versus control; exposure versus concealment; and plasticity versus fixity. Different ways of scenting the body illustrate the infinite play of cosmetic between these polarities.

Deodorants may be used to *conceal* natural body odors and *control* bodily excretions (perspiration, mucous, and other excretions), while scents may be used to *expose* the "desirable" body or *cover* unpleasant smells (such as body odor, halitosis, infected flesh). Deodorant brands often use **sports** stars to promote their products since the athletic performance of the star can be metonymically linked both to the performance of the product (in stopping perspiration) and the wearer of the product (in implying enhanced social performance).

Cosmetic manufacturers also segment the market, for example, scents come in different forms: concentrates, aerosols and *eau de toilette* indicating different strengths of scent and associated cultural connotations and priced according to their social value. Like deodorants, perfumes use advertisements to project the attributes of the perfume onto the attributes of the intended consumer. By imbuing the magical powers of perfumes to transform the wearer, consumers purchase the desire to transcend the everyday and assume another perhaps more glamorous, successful or seductive identity. An effective technique is to use a popular role model as the face of the brand or product.

The word "cosmetic" is also used to mean "false" or "superficial." Throughout history cosmetics have been perceived as a moral problem that poses a threat, incites inappropriate passions, conceals the "real" person, or creates an "undesirable" persona. Very often, this has been an attack on "unruly" women along with the implication of sexual impropriety. Cosmetics, it is argued, cause women to concentrate on the body instead of the spirit; stray from the path of virtue; deceive people by appearing unnaturally attractive; and drive the quest for conformity by making all women look the same. Terms such as vamp, harlot, painted woman, *femme fatale* and siren, all connote a sexually provocative woman who displays her sexuality through her body.

Ambivalent resonances of cosmetics can be found throughout history in religious tracts, philosophical writings, moral codes, fiction, poetry and theatrical traditions (from burlesque to Shakespeare). A catalog of makeup routines were used to portray distinct character traits of actors and roles in Chinese opera and Japanese Noh theater. This tradition of seeing cosmetics and especially face color in moral terms also invoked racial stereotypes. Conventions about desirable and undesirable traits and makeup routines coincide with established racial hierarchies. Common colors of cosmetics (red, black and white) signified specific attributes as visual shorthand of personality, sexuality, and role. These symbolic markers persisted into the twentieth century and shape contemporary understandings of cosmetics. For example, "A Book of Make-up," published in 1930 as a manual for stage and film actors, detailed cosmetic techniques to portray male and female characters by different ways of contouring the face, highlighting and shaping the lips, and embellishing the eyes to create particular character types. Instructions to create racial and ethnic types were also given.

By the late nineteenth century, the use of cosmetics was more accepted and a cottage industry developed often by women who manufactured and marketed their products. Pale skin was a sign of gentility and status so products that whitened the skin were especially popular though discreetly used. There were also successful cosmetic firms offering products for black women, such as Madam C. J. Walker and Annie Turnbo Malone. They advocated the importance of beauty management for black women but rejected skin whitening and hair straightening techniques, instead promoting shades suited to dark skin tones and products to manage complexion and hair. A recent study of makeup in the workplace found that women of color (African American, Asian, or Mexican) believed that wearing makeup was essential for enhancing their professional status by either concealing or highlighting racial or ethnic features.

This tolerance of subdued cosmetic usage was about to change due to a number of social upheavals. No longer were pioneer women mixing potions at home. Women's niche businesses quickly were transformed into major companies complemented by aggressive marketing and retailing. Successful products became brand leaders, and some companies became multi-nationals marketed globally. Examples include Harriet Hubbard Ayer, Cyclax, Helena Rubinstein, Elizabeth Arden and Estée Lauder. Sales of hundreds of thousands of dollars in the 1910s multiplied to hundreds of millions in the 1920s.

The advent of Hollywood was particularly important for advances in the manufacture and marketing of cosmetics. Max Factor, an immigrant wig maker and former cosmetics advisor to the Russian court, was an especially important figure using his knowledge of theatrical makeup to overcome the extremes of light and dark produced by early color filmstock. Not only was he a brilliant wig maker but in 1938 revolutionized filming by inventing water soluble pancake that would not cake or crack under studio lights and lip gloss to enhance a lasting moist look. Later he diversified into other products, including lipsticks, eye shadow, mascara, eye pencils, and false eyelashes as well as skincare products.

Factor was regarded as a magician who could conjure images in his laboratory-like beauty salons. He treated cosmetics as a science yet constructed a mystique around the application of these principles to disguise "defects" in shape, size, angle, and complexion. Actresses sought him out to create a unique individual look. His salon featured four color-coded celebrity consulting rooms designed to best enhance hair and skin tones—blue for blondes, mint green for redheads, dusty rose pink for brunettes, and pale peach for brownettes. As actresses became popular icons, demand to recreate their looks followed and the marketing of Max Factor's "Society Makeup" enabled ordinary women to acquire a touch of Hollywood glamour without sacrificing their morals.

This transformation of the production and consumption of cosmetics coincided with major changes in women's lives. The 1920s was particularly important. More women than ever were employed giving them disposable income to make discretionary purchases. The consumer revolution was underway and cosmetics were one of the early products to be heavily promoted in the media, film, department stores, and fashion photography. Cosmetics acquired connotations of women's new freedom, independence, individuality, and sense of sexuality.

Throughout the 1930s, the mass marketing of cosmetics reached new heights. Women could choose from three thousand different face powders and hundreds of rouges and lipsticks. Cosmetics became big business and with that, a normal part of everyday life and an essential part of femininity. While there was still moral concern about overly made-up women, by 1931, 85 percent of college women wore rouge, lipstick, face powder, and nail polish. In 1941, Helena Rubinstein alone marketed 629 cosmetic items and, despite war-time rationing, sales of cosmetics rose by 65 percent between 1940 and 1946.

The postwar period saw the consolidation of the cosmetics industry with new entrants such as Revlon and increasingly aggressive marketing. Cosmetics were a low cost, high profit industry. As little as eight cents in the dollar covered the cost of ingredients, while marketing accounted for twenty-five cents. Known brands inflated prices with profit margins up to 900 percent. For department stores, cosmetics were especially profitable with ground floor positioning attracting customers and acting as a "traffic generator."

In the search for new consumers, **advertising** and new products in the 1950s and 1960s were directed towards the emergent youth or teenage market and products promoted as a means to escape the everyday and traditional female roles and transform oneself into a thoroughly liberated participant in modernity and consumerism. Names of products reflected the ambiguous messages and attributes being conveyed by cosmetics: sexual (*Passion*); exotic (*Shalimar*); magical (*Pure Poison*); rebellious (*Shocking*); transgressive (*Tabu*); youthful (*Miss Dior*); status-laden (*Top Brass*);

scientific (*Chanel No. 5*); and romantic (*Heart*). Meanwhile, the black power movement in the United States, for example, led to a "Black is Beautiful" mantra and growth of cosmetic products specifically for non-Caucasian markets such as Fashion Fair Cosmetics, Naomi Sims Beauty Products, Sleek Cosmetics, and Cover Girl Queen Collection. Throughout the 1970s and 1980s, as popular culture came to dominate public debate, new social movements, subcultures, and ethnic groups created new subsectors of consumerism and new ideals of beauty, social mores, and sexual codes. The "natural" look was popularized and makeup developed to enhance "natural beauty."

Responding to these trends, new cosmetic market segments emerged in the late millennium. The emergence of gay pride movements and explosion of Mardi Gras celebrations internationally fanned the growth of specialist cosmetic providers and products for non-heterosexual markets. This was ironic since non-heterosexuals had always been prominent in the cosmetics arena in beauty salons (Elizabeth Arden), in the theater (Noël Coward, Jean Cocteau), as fashion photographers (Cecil Beaton, George Hoyningen Huene), and as fashion designers (Christian Dior, Cristóbal Balenciaga). In fact, fashion designer Rudi Gernreich and perfumery expert Edward Sagarin (Donald Webster Cory) were very active in the early gay rights movement. Moreover, cosmetics were a key part of the performance of non-heterosexual identities (drag shows, female impersonators, butch and femme roles, androgyny, transvestites, transsexuals, cross-dressers, and clones). Making up social identities went hand in hand with re-constructing sexual identities just as cosmetics were used to construct other identities among subcultures like hippies, punks, rappers, Goths, new romantics, and Japanese pop cultures such as black Ganguros.

The role of cosmetics as a body technique for constructing particular desired attributes and traits is more potent than ever. Alongside Hollywood glamour, **popular music** and street **fashion** increasingly set the desired role models to emulate. The use of cosmetics by popular musicians, models, and television stars as trend setters is partly reflected in the use of celebrities to promote brands accompanied by a vast media industry of cross-promotion of stars, lifestyles, celebrity glamour and consumer culture. Some celebrities (Elizabeth Taylor, David and Victoria Beckham, Britney Spears, and Paris Hilton) also own cosmetic lines and perfumes. The development of Botox, collagen, laser treatments and similar products called cosmecuticals offer skin rejuvenation without surgery and have proven extremely popular with celebrity devotees and rich clientele.

At the same time, the emphasis on enhancing the face has been shifting from surface cosmetics to skin care products (moisturizers, cleansers, and exfoliants) designed to improve the canvas upon which "the look" was created. Competition between brands and product lines has become ever fiercer with the globalization of the cosmetics industry and entry of new players into the industry, especially fashion designers diversifying into cosmetic lines. Some designers like Calvin Klein, Dolce and Gabbana, and Ralph Lauren, have added extra spice to their products due to their sexual preferences or ambiguity. Makeup artists such as Kevyn Aucoin created new cosmetic regimes and in the process became a gay icon and role model. With all this frenzied activity within the cosmetic industry and new market sub-sectors to entice, cut-throat competition between brands and their distributors has become the norm.

By the new millennium, significant cultural re-alignments were occurring from the banning of cosmetics by the Taliban in Afghanistan to prohibiting veiled women in Turkish universities. Elsewhere, there was a nominal integration of ethnic and racial diversification with accompanying moral panics and divisions. Within identity politics, the period saw a proliferation of sexual identities and subcultures with specific cosmetic practices and codes. As before, cosmetic practices are the subject of heated debate for example, concerning drag and transsexual/transvestite uses of cosmetics, the sexual connotations of elaborate makeup worn by child beauty contestants, and debates between radical and moderate Islamic groups about appropriate performances of femininity. Cosmetics are tokens of dissent and struggle. Behind the look run strong currents of debate and ambivalence surrounding the sensual, sexual and moral innuendoes behind the act of putting on one's face. *See also* Cross Dressing/Drag; Gay and Lesbian Movement; Gender Roles; Popular Culture; Race and Racism; Women's Movement.

Further Reading: Brain, Robert. *The Decorated Body*. London: Hutchinson, 1979; Craik, Jennifer. "Cosmetic Attributes: Techniques of Make-up and Perfume." In *The Face of Fashion. Cultural Studies in Fashion*, 153–75. London and New York: Routledge, 1994; Fashion Era. http://www.fashion-era.com. Provides a comprehensive overview of fashion history including the history of cosmetics and perfume; Polhemus, Ted. *Hot Bodies, Cool Styles. New Techniques in Self-Adornment*. London: Thames & Hudson, 2004; Wax, Murray. "Themes in Cosmetics and Grooming." *The American Journal of Sociology* 62, no. 6 (1957): 588–93.

Jennifer Craik

COURTSHIP. *See* Dating

CROSS DRESSING/DRAG. Cross dressing occurs when a man or woman dons the clothing of the other gender. Reasons for cross dressing include personal preference, expression of a sexual orientation, and theatrical performance. In most cultures, it is more acceptable for women to dress in the clothing of men than for men to dress in the clothing of women. Transvestites believe that their **desire** to cross dress is natural, becoming aware of this desire at a very early age. Cross dressing for pleasure usually begins in **childhood** or **adolescence** and is initiated by the child. Sometimes it starts as nonsexual activity then becomes an activity that provides sexual pleasure at **puberty**. Most male cross dressers are heterosexual.

The negative evaluation of males who adopt, in any way, characteristics of the female stems from many societies' traditional conception of the female as the inferior sex. For this reason, theatrical cross dressing, such as when male comedians and actors appear in drag, has traditionally sparked laughter in the West. These actors do not necessarily attempt to appear as the other gender, but instead seek to look ridiculous. There are few circumstances in which men can wear the clothing of women without triggering laughter or rage. In contrast, there is considerable lenience for the type of female cross dressing that involves stylish dress. The threat to cultural norms from cross dressing women is not as great.

Cross dressing became an increasing concern in the nineteenth century Western world as middle-class men in the United States and Europe began to suffer from a growing anxiety about the meaning of **masculinity**. In 1910, transvestism emerged as a term for cross dressing with sexologist Magnus **Hirschfeld's** *Transvestites*. To many people in the nineteenth and twentieth centuries, transvestism was a sexual perversion. The German sexologist Richard von Kraft-Ebing first categorized it as a pathological behavior. By 1952, the American Psychiatric Association listed male, but not female, transvestism as an illness in its *Diagnostic and Statistical Manual*. Only in the late twentieth century did this label come under heavy attack. As part of the sexual

Treechada Petcharat, right, a competitor in Miss International Queen 2004 transvestite competition held in Thailand, reacts to winning the crown as fellow competitor Arisha Rani, left, of India earns the runner-up spot. © AP Photo/David Longstreath.

revolution of the 1960s, transvestites began to organize. In 1961, Virginia Price, also known as Charles Price, founded Hose and Heels (also known as the Society for Personal Expression), the first support group for male cross dressers. The majority of its members were heterosexual men, including Price. By the 1970s, cross dressing was identified in the West as a sexual neurosis that facilitated pleasure.

Different societies define cross dressing as negative or positive. A traditional exception to the Western concept of maleness with respect to skirts, occurs in the Scottish Highlands where men don kilts without being suspect. In some parts of Scotland during the first years of the twentieth century, a newly born child was dressed in the other gender's clothes. The Scots did so to encourage the child to eventually marry a person of the other sex.

In Latin America, the transvestite community is far less visible than it is in the United States. Often **prostitution** is the only career avenue open to men who feel a need to dress publicly as women, even if they are heterosexual. Such an occupation is linked to discrimination against cross dressers, though many men express interest in other lines of work if only they were open to them. In Costa Rica, these men are known as *paqueteos*, a term for male cross dressers who render themselves so feminine in appearance that they are able to pass for women. In Brazil *travesties* are homosexual men who adopt female names, clothing styles, hairstyles, and body features such as silicone breasts and silicone expansive buttocks. They do not identify as women and are not transgendered. *Travesties* try to find love with other men by becoming an object of **desire** for those men.

Cross dressing also has a long history in the East. In India's Dhed community, men dress as women and, as such, are temporarily possessed by goddesses or female demons. Cross dressing males, called *kathoey* in Thailand, enjoy a degree of social acceptance. Although there are no legal sanctions against cross dressing, such dressers are widely scorned. At the Thailand National Games in 1996, half of the volleyball team, *Satri Lek* (Iron Ladies), consisted of cross dressing men. The team became the center of attention whenever they appeared on the volleyball court because of their pony-tail hairstyles, heavy makeup, and effeminate screams and gestures. Although *Satri Lek* beat the national team and captivated audiences, the Volleyball Association of Thailand refused to allow this team to represent Thailand in international competition because such men would "humiliate" the nation. Despite the visibility of some cross dressers in the East, especially in the entertainment industry, most choose the safety of remaining hidden rather than risk social condemnation.

Women cross dressers are typically not as visible as males, and are often part of the butch-femme lesbian community where they have historically found support. However, women who dressed in drag as a life choice faced arrest for donning attire inappropriate to their sex and were persecuted by police in the United States until the 1960s.

Women occasionally cross-dressed for reasons more political than sexual: male attire allowed them to travel, work, and live independent lives in eras and cultures in which the movement and activities of women were highly circumscribed. Babe Bean, for example (also known as Elvira Virginia Mugarrieta), was exposed by the Stockton, California police during the summer of 1897 as a woman posing as a man. After garnering some local notoriety, Bean took up residence in San Francisco in about 1900 and briefly resumed wearing women's clothing. He discovered that the attire still limited his freedom to roam at night and donned a man's suit once again. In 1903, San Francisco passed an ordinance banning the wearing of "opposite sex" apparel and Bean feared arrest. He adopted his mother's maiden name to become Jack Bee Garland and faded from view. Garland died on September 18, 1936 in San Francisco of generalized peritonitis following the perforation of a peptic ulcer. Garland had been suffering from abdominal pains for some time but, like many transgendered women, feared that a physician would expose his secret. Predictably, the autopsy surgeon undressed the body, discovered Garland's sex, and publicized the findings.

Similar cases popped up throughout the twentieth century with cross-dressing women typically exposed at death. Nicholai de Raylay, a secretary to the Russian consul, was found after his 1906 death in Chicago to be a woman. The twice-married de Raylay had been divorced from his first wife after ten years of **marriage** for indiscretions with chorus girls. His second wife was a chorus girl. De Raylay, slight in build, wore a long-waisted coat to disguise the lines of his figure. Another case was that of Murray Hall, a Scottish-born Tammany Hall politician who died in New York City in 1901. Living and working as a man for more than 30 years, her mannerisms were so masculine that no one ever questioned him.

In other cases, colleagues apparently knew about cross dressing. Hundreds of Russian women disguised as men were believed to have fought in World War I. It is possible that some of the male soldiers knew that their comrades were women but they were indifferent to the news. Most of the Russian soldiers were peasants who knew from experience that women were capable of enduring such hardships as the privations of war. Russian women had long worked as hard as men in the fields. The motives of the Russians are not as clear as those of Captain Flora Sanders, an Englishwoman who served in the Serbian Army during this war. Sanders had wanted to be a boy since she was a small child. Most of her fellow Serbian soldiers knew that she was cross dressing, but did not care since they valued the language, military, and nursing skills. Sometimes the demands of war exposed cross dressers who had successfully passed in civilian life.

Albert F., a lesbian Londoner drafted in World War I, was exposed as female during the military medical examination and was not permitted to enlist.

Drag, a relatively new style of cross dressing, does not obviously involve either sexuality or increased professional opportunities. Drag is a theatrical type of cross dressing that is often part of a drag show. Drag queens are men who dress as women, generally elaborately, and who display exaggerated feminine gestures and expressions. Drag kings are women who dress in men's attire and perform in a masculine manner that underscores the social construction of gender. It is not clear when drag king behavior began but it became a central feature in queer clubs around the world in the 1990s. Unlike male impersonators (which has a long theatrical tradition), drag kings draw attention to the theatrical nature of masculinity itself. They do not attempt to fool the audience into believing that the performers are male. Likewise, the drag king is not the same as a butch lesbian who dons male attire. A butch lesbian is not dressing for theatrical effect. However, many lesbians do dress as drag kings and seek to perfect their likeness as men. Some femme lesbians use exaggerated drag costumes to highlight the very falseness of their attempt to pass as men. *See also* Cinema; Fetishes; Gender Roles; Heterosexuality; Homosexuality; Indigenous Peoples; Transgender/Transsexual.

Further Reading: Bullough, Vern L., and Bonnie Bullough. *Cross Dressing, Sex, and Gender*. Philadelphia: University of Pennsylvania Press, 1993; Jackson, Peter A., and Gerard Sullivan, eds. *Lady Boys, Tom Boys, Rent Boys: Male and Female Homosexualities in Contemporary Thailand*. Binghamton, NY: Haworth Press, 1999; Kulick, Don. *Travesti: Sex, Gender, and Culture Among Brazilian Transgendered Prostitutes*. Chicago: University of Chicago Press, 1998; Rupp, Leila J., and Verta Taylor. *Drag Queens at the 801 Cabaret*. Chicago: University of Chicago Press, 2003; Schifter, Jacobo. *From Toads to Queens: Transvestism in a Latin American Setting*. Binghamton, NY: Haworth Press, 1999; Talamini, John T. *Boys Will Be Girls: The Hidden World of the Heterosexual Male Transvestite*. Lanham, MD: University Press of America, 1982; Tri-Ess (The Society for the Second Self). http://www.tri-ess.org. Tri-Ess is a U.S.-based social and support group for heterosexual cross dressers and their families, December 2006.

Caryn E. Neumann

CYBERDATING. *See* Dating; Sociobiology

CYBERSEX. *See* Internet; Pornography, on the Internet

D

DATING. Dating is an appointment or a series of appointments with a person one is socially, romantically, or sexually interested in. Although it is often part of the mate selection and courtship process, dating is also a popular leisure activity in its own right among many adolescents and adults. The meaning, purpose, and activities of dating, which have changed over time, are influenced by culture, religion, social norms and conventions, and family and friends.

During the Victorian Era (mid-1800s until World War I) courtship norms for middle and upper classes varied considerably from those of the working class. In the former case, strict rules of etiquette existed, which required a man interested in a young woman to "call" on her at her parents' home. The meeting took place in the presence of a parent or chaperone. Subsequent "dates" were under adult supervision until close to **marriage**, although the relatively spacious homes of the upper classes afforded some privacy. Women were in control of the interaction between the two partners. In the case of the lower classes, however, men and women met in public given the limited space in their homes. Thus, men would take women to restaurants, movies, and dances. Because men incurred the costs associated with these activities, men controlled these interactions.

By the 1920s, the middle and upper classes had begun to emulate the working class. Dating no longer took place in the living room and on the front porch but moved to the backseat of the automobile, providing couples with considerably more mobility and privacy. Not surprisingly, sexual activity began to increase, especially given that many women felt pressured to give their date a good time in return for his expenses. However, the majority of women had sexual intercourse only after they were engaged or married.

Among college students, the purpose of dating began to shift from love and mate selection to competition and consumption. Men's status and reputation depended on how many beautiful and popular women they dated and with how many of them they were sexually active. Women's popularity depended on whether their male dating partners were athletic, wealthy, and owned a car.

Since the 1920s and 1930s, dating has become much less formal, ritualized, and gender scripted. The women's movement and the improvement of methods of **birth control** account for this. Although in the 1930s and 1940s sexual activity, such as petting, often took place prior to engagement, sexual intercourse became much more common during the 1970s. Girls began dating at age fourteen and began going steady and having **premarital sex** at age sixteen.

Today, almost 90 percent of young people in the United States have dated someone by their seventeenth birthday, and about three-fourths have been in a serious, steady dating relationship by age eighteen. The age at which adolescents today begin to date, however, varies, with some religions influencing the age to begin dating. Members of the Church of Jesus Christ of Latter-Day Saints, for example, are encouraged not to date before age sixteen, and then not to enter a romantic relationship too soon. Abstinence from sexual activity until after marriage is expected within many religions and female **virginity** is valued in many cultures.

Regardless of when people begin to date, most men and women in the United States and other countries in the world (e.g., Germany, Netherlands, Russia, and Japan) desire to date someone who possesses a variety of desirable characteristics such as attractiveness, friendliness, sociability, emotional stability, kindness, wealth, social status, intelligence, and a sense of humor. The extent to which people are able to attract others depends on their own "market value." A person who possesses few desirable qualities and many repellant ones is less likely to attract a person with high market value than a person who possesses many sought after traits and few negative characteristics. People typically pair up with a partner of roughly equal market value.

Generally, men and women seek similar qualities in a potential partner, they differ, however, in regard to their emphasis on particular characteristics. Men place greater value on partners who are attractive and healthy, whereas women value status and wealth more. This is true not only in the United States but many other countries in the world. Both, men and women are equally selective with respect to their dating partners. Because men and women tend to seek partners with a high market value, they are often inclined to engage in activities that increase their market value. Women typically use a variety of deceptions that enhance their physical appearance such as **cosmetics** or clothing, whereas men tend to exaggerate their income or wealth potential.

Personal ads and **Internet** matchmaking services, which have increased dramatically in recent years, bear witness to the qualities men and women look for in a dating partner and to their tendencies toward exaggeration of their market value. Increasingly, more singles use the Internet to search for a dating partner, because it allows them to review lists of potential candidates within a short period of time without excessive expenses. Moreover, once contact with a potential dating partner is established, this technology provides a relatively safe environment in which to get to know the other person.

Whether meeting a person online or face-to-face, men and women worldwide engage in a variety of flirting behaviors to convey romantic interest in a potential dating partner and to signal that romantic overtures are welcomed. In face-to-face situations, they may move closer to the potential partner, smile, laugh, and intently gaze into the other's eyes. They also frequently make themselves physically more attractive such as smoothing their hair, tightening their abdomen, and arching their back. In online situations, verbal forms of flirting are used to convey interest, such as joking and teasing the other person.

Two people who are interested in each other may set up a "first date." According to social scripts or conventions, men are expected to initiate this event. Many men, however, would prefer women to take a more active role as well, which women have in recent years. Women also increasingly share dating expenses.

Men and women interested in a partner typically initiate a dating relationship to have fun, to learn more about the other person, and to develop a loving, caring relationship. Although men and women tend to have similar reasons for initiating a dating relationship and share similar ideas of what happens during a first date, they also differ somewhat in their expectations. Men, much more so than women, initiate dating relationships to be sexually intimate. Not surprisingly, they tend to expect more than a "good night kiss" on a first date. Sometimes men's and women's differing expectations lead to faulty decoding of the other's signals. Whereas a woman may smile to show that she likes her dating partner, he may interpret it as sexual attraction and innuendo. Misinterpretations like these sometimes lead to men's unwanted sexual advances. Several studies suggest that 12–15 percent of men, and 21–40 percent of women have been involved in some form of dating and courtship violence. Interestingly enough, levels of violence tend to be similar to same-sex couples.

Although reported rates of physical violence within lesbian relationships vary widely, most studies found that between 30 and 40 percent of lesbian participants have been involved in at least one physically violent lesbian relationship. Unlike in heterosexual relationships, however, lesbians are more likely to leave an abusive relationship, and violent behavior exhibited by one gay partner tends to be more likely reciprocated by the other male partner.

Young homosexual men and women find it generally more difficult to establish and maintain romantic relationships than their heterosexual counterparts. These difficulties can be attributed to their social environments, which are often characterized by stigmatization, victimization, isolation, and lack of support. For instance, in communities intolerant of **homosexuality**, gay and lesbian individuals frequently fear physical victimization, verbal harassment, peer rejection, and public humiliation. Communities such as these also often do not provide homosexual youth and support groups. Thus, opportunities to meet and interact with other homosexual individuals are severely constrained, and fear of repercussions great. If gay and lesbian individuals, despite these odds, successfully establish relationships, they often do so at the cost of having to hide their relationship from **families**, friends, peers, and other significant individuals.

Partners, be they heterosexual or homosexual couples, with favorable impressions of one another during their first and subsequent dates often begin to increase contact, disclose more personal information, and decide to date each other exclusively. They also often become physically intimate with each other.

It is not unusual for homosexual and heterosexual couples to experience conflict in their relationships, and the successful resolution of these conflicts plays a pivotal role in the continuation and development of their relationship. Partners who successfully negotiate their relationship, who express more affection, who become more intimate, and who reveal more about themselves, are also likely become more committed to each other. How deep their commitment to their partner and relationship is depends not only on how satisfied they are with their relationship, but also on how much their needs are met and how much time, emotional energy, and possessions they have invested. Moreover, influences from within (like sense of compatibility) and without (such as approval of the relationship from parents and friends) can result in changes in commitment over time.

Unlike heterosexual couples, however, gay and lesbian couples frequently experience unique sources of conflict, such as when and to whom to disclose their sexual identity or relationship. They also often experience additional stressful life events that can put extra strain on their romantic relationships, such as hate crimes, discrimination, concealment of sexual identity, insults, etc., and these additional factors can seriously undermine the longevity of their relationships.

Whereas dating in the early stages is often used as a form of recreation and leisure, serious dating and engagement are generally used to determine partners' compatibility and their potential as future spouses or lifelong partners. Increasingly, more couples test their compatibility by living together for a while. In 1950, approximately 50,000 unmarried people in the United States were cohabiting; today, more than half of all first marriages are preceded by cohabitation. Moreover, many same-sex couples, who tend to have dating approaches and expectations similar to those of cross-sex couples, show their commitment to each other and test their compatibility by cohabiting, which in some localities can also result in domestic partnerships, civil unions, or marriages.

Ineffective mate selection tends to be associated with later marital failure. In the United States, compatibility testing rests in the hands of the individual partners. This is not the case in many other places in the world, such as in several Asian and African countries, where the family, rather than the individual, determines a compatible mate. Dating and courtship traditionally have not existed in these countries, and marriages were arranged by the families rather than based on partners' romantic feelings for each other. In recent years, many of these countries have been influenced by Western ideas of romantic love, and consequently increasingly more marriages are now based on free choice rather than arranged. *See also* Adolescence; Celibacy; Divorce; Domestic and Relationship Violence; Gender Roles; Heterosexuality; Interracial/Ethnic Intimate Relationships; Romance; Sociobiology.

Further Reading: Bailey, Beth L. *From Front Porch to Backseat: Courtship in Twentieth Century America.* Baltimore: The Johns Hopkins University Press, 1988; Cate, Rodney M., and Sally A. Lloyd. *Courtship.* Newbury Park, CA: Sage, 1992; Hamon, Raeann R., and Bron B. Ingoldsby. *Mate Selection across Cultures.* Thousand Oaks, CA: Sage, 2003; Huston, Ted L. "The PAIR Project." http://www.utexas.edu/research/pair/ourresearch/index.html. Information on courtship, its effect on marriage and divorce, and much more, February 2002; Lloyd, Sally A., and Rodney M. Cate. "The Developmental Course of Conflict in Premarital Relationship Dissolution." *Journal of Social and Personal Relationships* 2 (1985): 179–94; Niehuis, Sylvia, Ted L. Huston, and Reva Rosenband. "From Courtship into Marriage: A New Developmental Model and Methodological Critique." *Journal of Family Communication* 6 (2006): 23–47; Regan, Pamela. *The Mating Game: A Primer on Love, Sex, and Marriage.* Thousand Oaks, CA: Sage, 2003; Rose, Suzanna M., ed. *Lesbian Love and Relationships.* Binghamton, NY: Haworth Press, 2002; Waller, Willard. "The Rating and Dating Complex" *American Sociological Review* 2 (1937): 737–39.

Sylvia Niehuis

DESIRE. The word "desire" conjures up many ways of thinking about its meaning: one can think of desire as physical (need to eat), emotional (need for "other"), political (need for freedom), religious (need for the spiritual), social (the need for communities), economic, and so on. Are these desires related, are they "innate"? Are they universal? Are the expressions of desire dependant on cultural context? Any discussion of the concept "desire" brings to mind "sexual desire" although when the term is explored further, it is evident that desire goes beyond sex.

Many more questions arise when one is confronted with the term "desire." For instance is desire a conscious recognition of a lack? Does one need a language to express desire? If desire depends on language, does that mean that different language users desire different objects? Is desire culturally determined? Is desire that moment when an indefinable ache that is an absence is articulated into a need? Is desire physiological? Is it psychological? In sexual terms, can one separate desire from lust? Can one distinguish between desires for someone from desire of something? Is desire learned? And if so, can it be taught? What is the connection between desire for something(s) and the daily onslaughts of advertising in the various media? Is desire gendered? Is it racialized? Is desire entirely selfish? Is desire only for what is not? When fulfilled, what does desire become?

These questions gesture toward desire as not quite definable, and yet many words are dedicated to trying to understand what desire is, how to control it, regulate it, universalize it, and fundamentally grasp it.

At the turn of the last century, Victorian ideologies ruled in the English-speaking world. Sexual desire was rampant yet strictly regulated. This was a time when, in the public domain, men were required, even forced, to express their sexual desires only within the circumscribed norms of heterosexual **marriage**. In private, they were allowed (and perhaps expected) to express and act on their desires, however perverse or exotic. Women, on the other hand, were perceived as passionless, devoid of sexual desires, except of course, if they were slovenly or promiscuous, in which case they were "fallen women." It was a time when sexologists like Richard von Krafft-Ebing, Havelock Ellis, Otto Weininger, Albert Moll, and Edward Carpenter categorized and classified human sexual desires. In doing so, they were regulating, redefining and controlling what could be expressed and what was to be kept secret through the nascent field of **sexual science**.

The Victorian era rang with a cacophony of discourses about desire and sexual desire, specifically, a time "of blatant and fragmented perversions" (Foucault, 47). It was also a time when various "perversions" were transformed from "sins" to "identities." For instance, desiring sex between two men or sex with animals were "sins" in the eighteenth century; in the late nineteenth century, sexologists transformed such "desires" into discreet categories from which identities could emerge: **homosexuality**, bestiality. From such categories, identities, like the "homosexual," later emerged.

As sexologists were categorizing and classifying sexual desires in Europe- some made legal, others illegal- in other parts of the world these same desires were embodied differently. For instance, North American **indigenous people** understood ambiguously gendered people as "Two Spirited" (erroneously labeled *berdarche* by European missionaries and, later, mis-labeled as gay). In Egypt, where women were not allowed to dance or perform in public, young men, disguised as women, acted these roles. They came to be known as *khawal*, a word that was taken up more recently as a pejorative term to indicate a "gay man." In India, Pakistan, and Bangladesh, *hijras* were/are **transgender** or intersexed people. Their culture stems from medieval Islam when, being neither male nor female, they guarded the private realm of women. Today, *hijras* are often not tolerated and, in some cases, persecuted.

In the early part of the twentieth century, sexual desires were recognized only when they were acted upon or articulated in some way. But it was Sigmund **Freud**, the "father" of **psychoanalysis**, who first spoke of desire and drives not defined by acts alone, but of the unconscious lacks that shape and determine concepts of self, or ego. In *Three Essays on the Theory of Sexuality* (1905), Freud both agreed with previous sexologists (e.g., Krafft-Ebing) and challenged earlier conceptions of sexual desires and perversions. In effect, argues Davidson, Freud claimed that there is no natural object of the sexual instinct, but that the sexual object and sexual instinct are intricately connected. In saying so, Davidson claims, Freud dealt a conceptually devastating blow to the entire structure of the nineteenth century theories of sexual psychopathology. These theories were invested in proving that the object of a man's desire was "instinctively" a woman, and that any desire outside of this "natural" desire was pathological.

Jacques Lacan, writing in the 1950s to 1970s and building on Freud's theories, is the theorist most noted for his treatment of the concept of desire. For Lacan, once an individual acquires language, desire is to be found in the social structures, the prohibitions, and fantasy version of reality, which are determined by and reliant on language. Where for Freud "the unconscious can be compared to a language without grammar," Lacan, using structuralist linguistics that depend on language to understand the structure of thinking, took up Freud's contention that the unconscious is like a language without grammar. But, Lacan argued that "it speaks" ("ça parle"). By that he understood the unconscious to be more accessible. So, Sharpe sums, Lacan argued that meaning is formed prior to verbal communication, a belief that goes against many philosophical accounts. Thus, for Lacan, speech is a process in which the subjects get their meanings back from another person (real or imagined), or "the Other" in an inverted form, like in a mirror image. Lacan maintained that a child's recognition of an "Other" begins when itself as distinct from anyone else, as in a mirror image. He offers his famous theory of the "Mirror Stage" in which the child first sees itself in the mirror and begins to conceive of an "other," eventually extrapolating the notion of a self as different from others.

Like Lacan, Michel Foucault wrote extensively about desire. However, in his *History of Sexuality*, one is left with a sense of ambiguity as to his meaning of this term. It was a concept he tried to discard but found he could not do without. Foucault needed this concept because it led him to recognize how, through the production of desire and its regulation in the mid-nineteenth century, notions of sexual identities were being created.

With the second wave of the **women's movement** in the mid-1960s came **feminism** and with it, a demand for women's perspectives on desire and the reclaiming of women's bodies. In effect, this is the era when history heard, perhaps for the first time, desires such as these incorporated and defined by women *for* women. Feminists, like Marilyn Frye or Anne Koedt, challenged male theorists' conceptualizations of female desires, and as such, revealed that desire, in general, is gendered. In the same decade, the **gay and lesbian movement** produced the discourses that recognized the political dimensions of same-sex desires. Same-sex or homosexual desires, historically seen as "sinful" from a religious perspective and "perversions" from a social point of view, were reclaimed as neither a sin nor sickness. From these categories, however, political and social identities emerged as men and women "came out" and demanded political recognition, and legal rights and protections, along with a legitimate place in society. Gay and lesbian desires expanded to incorporate a rainbow of diverse desires and identities—from **transgender** to queer, from **bisexual** to questioning—the whispered perversities of the Victorian era became legitimated desires in the late twentieth century.

The postcolonial era, at the end of the twentieth century, also redefined desire. Scholars are now recognizing that desire, although universal, is culturally specific and, perhaps even racialized. If, as Lacan and Foucault (from differing theoretical perspectives) claim, desire is dependant on language, then a change in language results in differing desires, and, presumably, a change in culture would also determine and define desire. For instance, in a culture that conceives of "teen" years as that space between **childhood** and adulthood, such as North America, it is a time of schooling and fun, the beginning of a consciousness of sexual desires. In other cultures, teenage years do not exist as a definable period; therefore there is no word to describe those years. After childhood, in some cultures, comes a time of progressive responsibilities, a time for **marriage** and reproduction, toil and sweat, a time when the child becomes an adult, often with a transition such as **puberty** rites.

We also can understand desire as racialized when thinking, for instance, of concepts of beauty, who is considered "desirable," who defines "desirable," whose desires are acknowledged, whose are recognized, and who is "exoticized." Black male genitals, for example, are perceived as better endowed, as measured against white.

Living at the beginning of the twenty-first century and within an electronic global village more than ever before, desire is sold to us all, taught to us, and often defined for us. Desire for things has become the universal rule as bodies are commodified and anything can be bought, sold, or advertised. Desire is bought in telephone sex, sexual exchanges occur and mates found on-line, and **Internet** pornography downloaded for a fee. Despite these developments, desire remains that inexplicable ache for what we think is lacking. *See also* Adolescence; Colonialism/Postcolonialism and Sex; Fetishes; Gender Roles; Heterosexuality; Pornography, on the Internet; Race and Racism.

Further Reading: Foucault, M. *The History of Sexuality: Volume I.* English translation copyright 1978. New York: Vintage, 1980; Raitt, S. "Sex, Love and the Homosexual Body in Early Sexology." Bland, L., and L. Doan, eds. *Sexology in Culture: Labeling Bodies and Desires.* Chicago: University of Chicago Press, 1998; Sharpe, M. "Jacques Lacan." *The Internet Encyclopedia of Philosophy,* 2005; See http://www.iep.utm.edu./l/lacweb.htm; Stoler, A. L. *Race and the Education of Desire: Foucault's History of Sexuality and the Colonial Order.* Durham, NC: Duke University Press, 1995; Suhagi, Leyla. "Muslim Hijras in India and Pakistan." See http://www.geocities.com/leylasuhagi/hijra?200617. Historical and contemporary information provided.

(*Note:* The contributor thanks Celia Haig-Brown for her untiring editing and support.)

Didi Khayatt

DIVORCE. Divorce is a social event and process, regulated by law and ideology, which leads to the legal dissolution of a marital union. This legal dissolution is associated with the breakdown of a marital relationship between two spouses. The breakdown of a marital relationship, however, is experienced privately whereas divorce is experienced publicly. Thus, marital breakdown occurs in all societies whereas the possibility to divorce differs cross-nationally.

The ability of a couple to seek divorce, and the process through which divorce is granted, differs cross-nationally because of the legality of divorce. The divorce laws of a nation reflect the cultural values and practices that a particular society or nation hold about the meaning of marriage and divorce, gender relations, and love, sex and sexuality.

Cultural values towards divorce can be restrictive, where there are many laws and social norms in place to regulate the ability of a couple to divorce, or they may be less restrictive, leaving room for a variety of possible behaviors that are acceptable. Throughout the twentieth and beginning of the twenty-first century, the constant changing cultural values and laws regulating divorce can be seen cross-nationally. At the beginning of the twenty-first century, divorce had become a taken-for-granted component of family life for most North Americans and Europeans. For instance, in 2002, 38 percent of all marriages in Canada were projected to end in divorce before their thirtieth wedding anniversary and one in every two marriages within the United States.

Nevertheless, most people who divorce remarry or re-partner, demonstrating the continued commitment to finding satisfying intimate relationships.

Prior to the beginning of the twentieth century divorce was rare and inaccessible to the majority of adults living in North American and European societies. This was due to rigid laws and social ideologies around the meaning of **marriage** and family life. In Britain and Canada, legal dissolution of a marriage was nearly impossible due to the inconsistent regulation of marriage. Until 1857 there were no provisions for divorce except through a private act of Parliament, leaving legal divorce rarely sought-after except by wealthy males.

At this time, women were particularly disadvantaged by divorce law, economic structure, and rigid ideology. To petition for divorce, women had fewer means economically and more stringent burdens legally than men. Moreover, there were few opportunities for women in the workplace, which limited their ability to financially provide for themselves and their children in the event that divorce was granted. These conditions remained well into the twentieth century.

Restrictive divorce laws, prior to and throughout much of the twentieth century, were characterized by the belief that one member of the marital union was at fault for the breakdown of the marital relationship. Countries had different fault grounds on which divorce could be sought. Between the period of 1884 and 1975, France had three bases for divorce including adultery, sentence for a crime, or the violation of marital duties, which included cruelty and abuse. Similarly, the United States fault grounds for divorce included adultery, desertion, physical or mental cruelty, long imprisonment for a felony, and/or drunkenness. Individuals wishing to receive a divorce had to prove these grounds.

The restrictive nature of laws and regulations surrounding divorce reflected dominant social ideologies about the family. Marriage was an institution entered into for the economic, political, and family ties it provided. Love was not necessarily part of marriage. Nonetheless, sex and sexuality were seen as highly connected to marriage, but for reproduction rather than love. In this sense, sexual relationships were only socially acceptable within marital unions. Extramarital sex was one of the few grounds for divorce. Yet men could divorce women on the grounds of simple adultery but women had to prove men had committed aggravated adultery, or adultery along with cruelty or desertion. By 1925, in Canada, this distinction was changed, but it did not alter the restrictive ideologies about divorce. At this time, less than 1 percent of marriages ended in divorce. It was not until the mid-twentieth century that attitudes began to change dramatically in North America and Europe.

After World War II, economic and social conditions supported an ideological shift in the meaning of marriage, family, and the state's role in regulating citizens' private lives. These conditions included changes in women's rights and employment, and the post-war economic boom. Women's access to higher education and participation in the workforce increased, effectively moving women into the public sphere and lowering their economic dependency on their husbands.

In industrial nations, the meaning of marriage shifted from a necessary economic relationship to a partnership, focusing on love and companionship. Consequently, divorce began to shift from the deficiency of one spouse to a means to rectify unhappy and unfulfilling relationships.

Governments experienced increasing pressure to make divorce more accessible to the public. An acute cross-national intensification of liberalized divorce laws occurred after 1960 when no-fault divorce was introduced. Consequently, many nations adopted this idea that marital breakdown and the desire for a divorce could occur without being either spouse's fault. Thus, divorce could now be granted due to irreconcilable differences or incompatibility in the couple. Nations that liberalized divorce laws included the United States, Canada, Britain, and Sweden in 1969 and Italy, France, China, and Ireland, in 1970, 1975, 1981, and 1997, respectively.

Liberalization of divorce law, however, did not take a uniform course. While Sweden eliminated fault grounds for divorce, other nations' divorce law reform used both fault and no-fault grounds. In 1970, Italy was one nation that chose to include fault and no-fault grounds in divorce reform, resulting in many couples still using fault grounds since these divorces were granted faster.

Although most industrial nations liberalized divorce legislation in some way or another, not all nations followed this legal or social pattern. In many countries, especially those heavily influenced by religion, divorce continues to be restricted through law and ideology. The Philippines has a pro-marriage ideology where dominant social beliefs concerning love, sex, and sexuality are highly connected to the maintenance and stability of marital unions. Severe legal restrictions leave annulment as the only option to legally dissolve a marital union. Divorce is illegal and a socially undesirable option for Filipinos.

Divorce was also illegal, through a constitutional ban, in another heavily Catholic country, Ireland. This created a much greater obstacle for divorce reform than other nations where divorce reform was introduced through legislation. Though divorce was legalized in 1997, reforms were made to the constitution. Thus, further changes to divorce law would have to be made through a referendum, making social change and further liberalization difficult.

Chile did not legalize divorce until 2004. Before this, marriages could only be ended through annulment. However to make dissolution possible, informal practices, such as reporting incorrect information at the time of the wedding, were used to provide possible future grounds for annulment.

In contrast to the Philippines, Ireland, and Chile, there are also nations and cultures that have been traditionally permissive in their divorce laws and ideologies. For example, in Ethiopia divorce is an accepted and common practice that can be traced back to as early as the sixteenth century. The social acceptance of divorce continues to be supported within a culture that supports individuals leaving unsatisfactory marriages. Similarly, Muslim nations have also been permissive, but predominantly for men.

National diversity also existed in the liberalization of divorce law. In the United States, divorce law regionally differs because divorce legislation is introduced at the state level. The liberalization of divorce law began in the state of New York, through the introduction of a number of grounds for divorce. In 1969, California was the first state to introduce "no-fault" divorce. By 1985, all states had a "no-fault" divorce option. Changes in laws surrounding marriage and divorce are continually evolving. One example, in the U.S. South, is that covenant marriages are being introduced, where couples have the option to enter legal marriages tied with pre-no fault divorce restrictions.

In North America, women are more likely than men to file for divorce. There is some evidence, too, that the increased possibility of divorce encourages couples to work harder on their marriages while increasing gender equality in marriage. Yet there is also evidence that women, more so than men, continue to experience declines in their economic standard of living following divorce. Having sufficient economic resources is important for adjusting to divorce and ensuring the fewest negative consequences for adults and dependent children.

As cultural values evolve, divorce laws and procedures will inevitably change. With the legalization of same-sex marriage, for instance, there will be the need to change divorce laws to include same-sex couples. Other formal and informal processes of uncoupling also will emerge with the widespread practice of long term common-law and cohabiting relationships. *See also* Domestic and Relationship Violence; Families; Heterosexuality; Homosexuality; Infidelity/Extramarital Sex; Politics; Religions, Eastern; Religions, Western; Sexism; Workplace.

Further Reading: Amato, Paul. "The Consequences of Divorce for Adults and Children." *Journal of Marriage and Family* 62 (2000): 1269–87; Burley, Jenny, and Francis Regan. "Divorce in Ireland: The Fear, the Floodgates and the Reality." *International Journal of Law, Policy, and the Family* 16 (2002): 202–22; Cherlin, Andrew J. "The Deinstitutionalization of American Marriage." *Journal of Marriage and Family* 66 (2004): 848–61; Feliciano, Myrna S. "Law, Gender, and the Family in the Philippines." *Law & Society Review* 28 (1994): 547–60; Hackstaff, Karla. *Marriage in a Culture of Divorce.* Philadelphia: Temple University Press, 1999; Fine, Mark, and David R. Fine. "An Examination and Evaluation of Recent Changes in Divorce Laws in Five Western Countries: The Critical Role of Values." *Journal of Marriage and the Family* 56 (1994): 249–63; Goode, William J. *World Changes in Divorce Patterns.* New Haven, CT: Yale University Press, 1993; Trent, Katherine, and Scott J. South. "Structural Determinants of the Divorce Rate: A Cross-Societal Analysis." *Journal of Marriage and the Family* 51 (1989): 391–404; United Nations Statistics Division. "Social Indicators." http://unstats.un.org/unsd/demographic/products/socind. Useful data on marital trends, August 2006.

Adena Miller and Carrie Yodanis

DOMESTIC AND RELATIONSHIP VIOLENCE. Domestic and relationship violence include acts carried out by an intimate partner with the purpose of causing physical pain, injury, fear, intimidation, or with the intent to coerce a person through control or domination. Anyone in a close relationship can be a victim of domestic violence, including spouses, same-sex and dating partners, as well as relatives. Relationship violence, typically between partners in a romantic couple, includes physical and **sexual abuse**, destruction of property and pets, neglect and deprivation, and emotional abuse. Rates of relationship violence are difficult to assess given that victims of relationship violence are reluctant to report and records are kept independently for different types of abuse, such as violence between adolescent partners, spousal violence, and elder abuse. In the United States, where extensive domestic violence research has been conducted, it is estimated that relationship violence occurs in 10 to 20 percent of marital relationships and same-sex relationships; violence is also common in adolescent and adult dating relationships although the estimates are less reliable. Although more commonly reported by families of lower socioeconomic status, domestic violence occurs among **families** at all income levels and of all racial and ethnic groups.

Relationship violence between intimate partners and domestic violence among family members has been documented in the majority of countries that have been studied. However, the ways relationship violence is committed and understood varies cross-culturally. For example, brother-to-sister abuse is common in Saudi Arabia, while adultery among women is commonly defined as relationship abuse in other countries like Nicaragua and Lebanon. In most countries, there are legal protections from relationship violence, often covered under The United Nations Commission for Human Rights or by local laws and regulations. In many countries where relationship violence is legally prohibited, however, domestic violence laws are rarely enforced or prosecuted.

Legal definitions of relationship violence are also diverse, varying by country and region. Child abuse was the first type of domestic violence acknowledged. The first documented court case of domestic violence occurred in 1874; child protective laws soon followed. Nevertheless, it wasn't until 1962 when an American doctor used x-ray evidence to disprove parents' claims that their children's injuries were caused by accidents, that the extent of domestic violence against children was exposed. Child sexual abuse laws also evolved to protect children from sexually exploitative behavior between adults and children starting in the 1970s within the United States.

Wife abuse has been legal throughout history in most countries. In the United States, the first spouse abuse laws to address wife abuse were enacted in the 1870s when it became illegal to beat one's wife, pull her hair, choke her, or spit in her face. These, though, were rarely prosecuted. In the 1960s, the **women's movement** raised public awareness of the subordinate status of women, thereby increasing attention to wife abuse. Research documenting the problem of wife abuse soon followed, with studies showing 24 percent of families experienced at least one incident of relationship violence. Although there is some evidence that rates of wife abuse have decreased in the past decade, it is estimated that about one-fourth of U.S. couples experience one act of violence in a year. Because of differences in the methods of data collection for wife abuse, it is difficult to know how this rate compares with other countries; however, it is typical for the level of wife abuse to be consistent with a countries' overall rate of violent crime. For example, the U.S. homicide rate for women is five times that of all other high-income Western countries combined; violent crime against men and women overall is epidemic in U.S. society.

The first shelter for abused women opened in England in 1971. Treatment facilities for abused women and male perpetrators of violence were subsequently established. Organizations such as the National Organization of Victim Assistance, The National Clearinghouse for the Defense of Battered Women, and The National Coalition Against Domestic Violence were formed in the United States. Most countries have governmental and non-profit organizations to address wife abuse (e.g., National Council for Women's Rights [Brazil]; Women's Rights Promotion Committee [Taiwan]; National Network on Violence Against Women [South Africa]) and most major cities provide hotline services to women seeking support.

Marital rape and elder abuse are relatively recent additions to domestic violence. Every year approximately two million older adults are maltreated by family members and care providers, and those who are maltreated tend to die earlier than non-abused elders. Laws dictating mandatory reporting of elder abuse now exist in 46 U.S. states and in many countries, while agencies such as Adult Protective Services are responsible for overseeing protection of elders. The traditional definition of rape was sexual intercourse forced by a man on a woman with whom he was not married, therefore forced sexual relations in marriage were not considered to constitute rape until 1997 when the first marital rape law was passed. Although spousal rape is considered a crime in all U.S. states and in most countries, marital rape is considered a less serious offense than most other forms of rape, which often results in less punitive charges or consequences for perpetrators of marital rape.

Relationship violence can have severe physical and emotional consequences, even resulting in death. Violence committed against partners is the number one cause of injury for women in the United States. Even so, only one of every two female victims reports injuries, and just one-in-five seek medical treatment. Following an assault a victim often experiences helplessness, anger, or anxiety, and some victims may develop post-traumatic stress disorder, which is a mental impairment marked by nightmares, intrusive thoughts, intense anxiety, and fears associated with the violent treatment. Many victims suffer neurological damage, physical illness brought about by stress, or impairment to cognitive and problem-solving skills as a result of violence. Repeated violence may lead to learned helplessness, a psychological state in which victims no longer attempt to remove themselves from a painful situation because of failed attempts.

Other research suggests, however, that victims of relationship violence respond with help-seeking efforts, either finding support from family or friends, reporting the incident, or making preparations for leaving the relationship. Although it is estimated that it takes women victims of relationship violence several times to ultimately leave a violent relationship, most victims do end the relationship. Other women find ways to maintain the relationship while ensuring the safety of themselves and their children, typically when the perpetrator receives treatment or finds other ways to resolve conflict.

Making the decision to leave an abusive relationship is immensely complex. Love relationships develop over time and once a couple has formed a close attachment, it is difficult to break—even without issues of power and control between partners. Relationship violence is often maintained through power and coercion, causing the partner who is abused to perceive herself as helpless and dependent upon the abuser. In addition, many victims of violence are economically dependent on the perpetrator. They simply have nowhere to go should they leave their abuser in the absence of supportive family members or shelters, which are found in major cities throughout the world (although still very limited in most regions). Leaving a violent relationship is no guarantee of safety either, when victims try to leave their violent partners, laws often fail to protect them, and many victims experience an increase in violence when they physically leave the relationship.

Cultural expectations of relationships may also contribute to a person remaining in an abusive relationship. Across cultures, women are rewarded for committed relationships and, in many countries, a **divorce** or separation is difficult to obtain. Many women victims of relationship violence also lose custody rights to their children if they initiate a divorce or formal separation. Traditional **gender roles** can contribute as well. Women are reinforced for nurturing and maintaining relationships, and maintaining hope that the violent partner will change plays a major role in perpetuating violent relationships.

Male victims of violence and partners in same-sex relationships have additional stress given that few resources are available to assist them. Across cultures, traditional male gender roles emphasize physical strength and independence. Therefore, male victims of violence have difficulty reporting violent acts and seeking help as "victims" of violence. Authorities often interpret violence between same-sex partners as a fair fight or perceived to be sexual in nature; few shelters, hotlines, or treatment groups exist for people abused in same-sex partnerships.

How a person becomes abusive toward his or her romantic partner or family member is a complex and unclear process. However, there are some factors that appear to contribute to the likelihood of a person becoming violent. Exposure to violence in **childhood**, parental abuse, alcoholism, and mental illness consistently have been shown to be related to later adult partner violence. Violent perpetrators are often clinically depressed, anxious, and suicidal. In addition, being anxiously attached during childhood can play a role in later violence in adulthood. Men who are violent toward partners tend to hold sexist views toward women and to favor aggression as a means to resolve conflict. Some biological factors such as head injuries and brain traumas are also important in male perpetrated violence. Perpetrators also have more difficulty with interpersonal relationships, have inadequate problem-solving skills, and often misinterpret their partners' actions or behaviors, resulting in jealousy and lack of trust. Many violent men appear to use violence to control women, have excessive needs for power and lack empathy for their partners. These are all related factors and not causes of domestic violence. There is no one cause of violence against relationship partners or family members; rather, there are numerous ways that individuals learn to become violent toward loved ones. Fortunately, there are many means to unlearning violent behavior such as individual and group therapy, practicing peaceful conflict resolution skills, and seeking out support to manage interpersonal conflict as well as anxiety and stress. *See also* Drugs and Alcohol; Mental Health and Sex; Politics; Psychotherapy; Sexism.

Further Reading: Barnett, Ola, Cindy Miller-Perrin, and Robin Perrin. *Family Violence across the Lifespan*. 2nd ed. Thousand Oaks, CA: Sage, 2005; Domestic Violence International Resources. The Zero 5.0laf: Official Website of Andrew Vachss. See http://www.vachss.com/ help_text/domestic_violence_intl.html. International contacts and resources for domestic violence throughout the world, April 2006; Greenfeld, Lawrence, Michael Rand, Diane Craven, Patsy Klaus, Craig Perkins, Cheryl Ringel, Greg Warchol, and Cathy Maston. *Violence by Intimates*. NCJ Publication No. 167237. Washington: U.S. Department of Justice, 1998; Malley-Morrison, Kathleen, ed. *International Perspectives on Family Violence and Abuse*. Mahwah, NJ: Lawrence Erlbaum, 2004; National Coalition Against Domestic Violence. See http://www.ncadv. org. A grassroots non-profit organization that works to end domestic violence, this site is a clearinghouse of resources and education on community-based, non-violent alternatives, including safe homes and shelter programs, for victims of violence, April 2006; The National Domestic Violence Hotline, Texas Council on Domestic Violence. See http://www.ndvh.org. This is a telephone service, available in more than 140 languages, for victims of domestic violence available 24/7, April 2006.

Sharon Horne

DRAG. *See* Cross Dressing/Drag

DRINK. *See* Food and Drink

DRUGS AND ALCOHOL. Drugs and alcohol are mind-altering substances that influence a user's physiology and mental state; because of the disinhibiting effect often associated with their use, it is not surprising that these substances have been historically linked to sexual behavior in various cultures. Alcohol and drug use often intersects with sex and love through the use of substances that are thought to be aphrodisiacs, or thought to enhance the sexual experience. The pursuit of alcohol, drugs, sex, or love (in any combination) may be part of an individual's general tendency toward pleasure-seeking. Attitudes towards alcohol and drugs can also be illustrative of historical eras and cultural norms, and may be interpreted as key markers

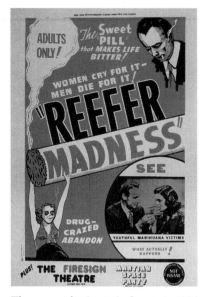

The poster for Louis J. Gasnier's 1936 film, *Reefer Madness*. Courtesy of Photofest.

of societal attitudes toward sexuality, religion, or other personal freedoms. Noted alcohol and drug historian David Musto emphasizes that a shift in attitudes regarding these substances from widespread tolerance to disapproval is often signaled by the identification of a feared mind-altering drug with a particular marginalized cultural or ethnic group. Historical trends in the United States and in other societies have followed this pattern. Because that which is exotic or unknown is often eroticized, a complex interplay between drugs and alcohol, sexuality, and cultural identity has punctuated human history.

The history of alcohol and drug use in the United States has been more documented than in other countries; other societies are often described in terms of their marked contrast to America. For example, the Netherlands is seen as a country with more experimental policies: marijuana and many hallucinogens have been available for over a quarter of a century, and **prostitution** is a legalized (and unionized) profession. Dutch society is often cited as an example of the success of such policies; for example, marijuana use has not been linked to driving accidents or to violence. In other parts of the world, culturally sanctioned use of mind-altering drugs include betel chewers in southern Asia (a stimulant plant estimated to be frequently used by one tenth of the world's population), the chewing of coca leaves in South America (a stimulant from which cocaine is derived), and San Pedro cactus extract users in Peru (a ceremoniously used form of mescaline).

In the early twentieth century, drugs and alcohol were legal and mostly unregulated in the United States Products containing morphine and opium could be marketed without legal dictates about the chemical content or the labeling of these products. Anti-liquor and anti-drug sentiments were emerging, however. Opium had emerged as a problem during the 1800s—connected with the Chinese populations who had entered the country as part of the railroad workforce. The government soon began looking at ways to decrease opium and opiate use and addiction. In 1914, the Harrison Narcotic Act prohibited the sale of narcotics (in particular opiates and cocaine) except as indicated by a doctor's prescription. With tighter controls on narcotics, the narcotic addict was reframed as a criminal, seeking thrills through drugs and sexual behavior. Consequently, addiction treatment programs that came about in the 1930s were very similar to prisons of the time.

In addition to narcotics, there were also concerns about alcohol and the "saloon lifestyle." From this movement arose the Anti-Saloon League of America. This group began as a moral movement operating through local churches aiming to combat prostitution, liquor, and the saloon lifestyle. The League ultimately sought federal prohibition of alcohol by proposing the adoption of the 18th Amendment to the U.S. Constitution. This amendment, which prohibited the sale, manufacture, and transportation of alcohol, went into effect in 1920. Other countries, such as the Netherlands, experienced a similar anti-alcohol movement, but simply used social movements to reduce alcohol intake.

Movements to repeal prohibition quickly emerged. Proponents argued for personal rights but maintained a stance against drunkenness, seeing use of alcohol in moderation as a solution. During the Great Depression, the Democratic Party advanced repeal as a method to generate revenue from alcohol taxes, which could aid in the reconstruction of the economy. The 18th Amendment was repealed in 1933.

The formation of Alcoholics Anonymous (AA), in 1935, heralded another major shift in public perception about alcohol. Despite espousing a medical model of addiction, AA was originally grounded in Christian religious principles. Its abstinence-based model reflected mid twentieth century attitudes toward substance use. At this time, a generally repressive culture in the United States was represented by a stereotyped middle-class American family, where the topics of sexual behavior and alcohol problems were inappropriate for public discussion. This soon changed.

Perhaps no other era in U.S. history is as punctuated by drug use as the 1960s and 1970s. This was an era of widespread use of marijuana and hallucinogens, as well as increased acceptance of variations in sexual behavior. Marijuana use had been illegal since 1937, following a series of government publications and films targeting the drug. The most notorious of these, *Reefer Madness*, depicted youth transitioning into rapists, homicidal maniacs, and mentally ill individuals after smoking marijuana. Such propaganda had the opposite of the intended effect, and marijuana smoking became associated in the 1960s with **free love**, peace, and creativity.

The 1980s marked a return to the employment "rat race" and competitiveness. Marijuana and hallucinogen use declined, and cocaine consumption rose markedly. Governmental policies in this conservative era reflected increasing penalties for use, possession, and distribution of illicit drugs; the "war on drugs" became part of the cultural lexicon. Treatment for individuals with alcohol or drug programs took second place to fighting this "war" through criminalizing users and fighting anti-drug campaigns in other countries.

In the past two decades, use of alcohol, marijuana, heroin, powder cocaine, and hallucinogens has remained relatively stable in the United States. Many concerns around illicit drug use have centered on refined or synthetic versions of stimulant drugs, such as crack cocaine and methamphetamine, which have equal or greater addictive potential to their counterparts (powder cocaine and amphetamines), but often cost significantly less. Both of these newer drugs have been identified with marginalized groups.

In the late 1980s and early 1990s, reports began to appear of "crack babies," whose mothers (typically urban, African American poor women) used crack cocaine while pregnant, resulting in compromised offspring. Later studies examining the effects of crack cocaine on the developing fetus indicated that poor prenatal care and use of legal drugs (alcohol and nicotine) while pregnant were more damaging than crack use *per se*. With regard to methamphetamines, "crystal meth" first emerged in reports as a club drug, often used by gay men in urban centers or at rave parties. Stimulant drugs were linked to the heightening of sexual experiences: "if a sexual experience is combined with intranasal or smoked cocaine or crystal methamphetamine, powerful and reciprocally enhancing experiences occur. Fears of rejection or overwhelming reactions to rejection are diminished" (Guss 2000, 108). The caveat to the increased pleasure of pairing sex with drugs is that the risk of acquiring **sexually transmitted infections**, such as **AIDS/HIV**, escalates when the user is disinhibited by the substance and less likely to use sexual protection or inject a drug with infected needles, or both. Changing meanings of both drug use and sexuality in current society represent both the pleasure and the danger inherent in these activities, often described as "risky" behaviors.

There is a tremendous amount of variability in social norms regarding sex, alcohol, and drugs. Use of drugs and alcohol, and some manifestations of sexuality, occur only "behind closed doors" in some communities despite being part of cultural ritual or social history. In those countries that observe Islamic law, such as Saudi Arabia, alcohol is prohibited and possession or use of alcohol can result in public flogging. Additionally, in some Middle Eastern countries same-sex sexual intercourse is punishable with the death penalty, though recent political movements are challenging these laws (in Lebanon, for example). The use of drugs and alcohol interplays with attitudes regarding sexuality as defining aspects of the societies in which we live. The relative visibility or invisibility of these universal aspects of the human experience remains an important marker of cultural context. *See also* Food and Drink; Politics.

Further Reading: Guss, Jeffrey R. "Sex Like You Can't Even Imagine: 'Crystal,' Crack and Gay Men." *Journal of Gay and Lesbian Psychotherapy*, 3 (2000): 105–22; McNeece, C. Aaron, and Diana M. DiNitto. *Chemical Dependency: A Systems Approach.* 3rd ed. Boston: Pearson Education, 2005; Musto, David, ed. *Drugs in America: A Documentary History.* New York: New York University, 2002; Perrine, Daniel M. *The Chemistry of Mind-altering Drugs: History, Pharmacology, and Cultural Context.* Washington, DC: American Chemical Society, 1996; Porter, Roy, and Mikulas Teich, eds. *Drugs and Narcotics in History.* Cambridge: Press Syndicate of the University of Cambridge, 1995; Schaffer Library of Drug Policy. http://druglibrary.org/ schaffer/history/CASEY1.htm. Provides an historical overview of drugs and alcohol in relation to U.S. society, November 1978 [last date updated]; Transform Drug Policy Foundation. http:// www.tdpf.org.uk. Works at both the research and the policy levels to minimize drug-related harm; Wilson, Robert A. *Sex, Drugs & Magick: A Journey Beyond Limits.* Tempe, AZ: New Falcon Publications, 2000.

Bryan N. Cochran and Annesa Flentje Santa

E

ED. *See* Erectile Dysfunction

EDUCATION. *See* Sex Education

ERECTILE DYSFUNCTION (ED). The fear of "impotence," the inability to obtain or maintain an erection sufficient for intercourse, has pervaded the male psyche throughout the ages as well as across cultures, age, race, and sexual orientation. The word "impotence" connotes a loss of power and worth as a man, not just a sexual dysfunction. In 1998, the introduction of Viagra led to a revolutionary shift regarding the medical and public view of this problem. A new term, "erectile dysfunction" (ED) replaced "impotence." Traditionally, when men experienced ED, they felt humiliated and like a failure as men. These feelings were commonly expressed nonverbally by avoiding sexual relations. This had a dramatic impact on couple intimacy and loving feelings. However, the belief that taking a pill would revitalize sex *and* love was a seductive promise, but misplaced.

Since the publication of the **Kinsey** reports in the 1940s, erection problems were believed to be caused by psychological factors and were commonly viewed as a sign of weakness. Other cultures attributed erectile failure to a "curse" or "black magic"; some encouraged men to increase their virility by taking purported aphrodisiacs (such as potions derived from the tusks of animals) or having sex with virgins or prostitutes. The introduction of Viagra and the reduction in stigma surrounding ED led to a dramatic shift to a physiologically based perspective and a cure through medical intervention.

Across both time and cultures, there has existed a strong association between **masculinity** and sexuality. For example, in Western cultures, images of manhood are closely linked to ideals of virility and the ability to achieve an erection. Specifically, adolescent men learn that sexual responses and erections are easy, highly predictable, controllable, and most importantly, autonomous (i.e., a man can experience **desire**, arousal, and **orgasm** without needing anything from a partner). Typically, erectile failure has been viewed as a devastating symbol of failed manhood caused by anything from "God's punishment" to "being crazy." The common mythology is that only men who have a secret homosexual orientation experience ED. This misperception dramatically increased heterosexual men's fears of ED and prejudice towards gay men.

In truth, the perfect erectile and intercourse performance is a mythical image that intimidates and worries most men. For example, it is estimated that one in four males has an unsuccessful first intercourse experience. This usually is a function of ejaculation before the penis entered the vagina or losing erection before or after intromission. Rather than discussing his concerns with a physician or sex therapist, the man might brag to friends about how great the sexual encounter was and claim the woman begged him to return.

Anxiety about the penis also is reflected in the report that as many as three in four men are afraid that his penis is smaller than average. Other than being a statistical impossibility, this concern reflects the anxiety generated by the traditional male perfect sexual performance model. Many of these anxieties and insecurities are the side effects of cultural belief systems that consider erectile capacity, specifically, the ability to generate an erection easily, quickly, with total control, and autonomously, to be the prime measure of masculinity.

Before 1998, psychologists and sex therapists attributed erectile problems to psychological issues (performance anxiety, depression, or taking a spectator role) or relationship issues (anger or alienation). The groundbreaking laboratory and clinical research of William Masters and Virginia Johnson, during the 1960s and 1970s, evaluated the vascular, neurological, and hormonal factors in the etiology of ED. They pioneered the biopsychosocial model of diagnosis and treatment of sexual dysfunction, including ED.

The introduction of Viagra in 1998 by a group of urologists/researchers working with Pfizer, a large drug company, revolutionized the medical and public approach to treating ED. The drug and the term, ED, were touted in all forms of **media** from professional journals, doctor's offices, popular magazines and newspapers, but most successfully with the use of commercials and famous spokesmen, such as former Senator and presidential candidate Bob Dole.

The marketing of Viagra is a prime example of medical oversimplification and promises of a cure. "Impotence" was no longer a stigmatized male problem; ED is now viewed as a common medical problem that can be easily and totally treated with a tiny blue pill. In a matter of months, Viagra prescriptions increased dramatically, not just in the United States, but throughout the world.

It has been estimated that there are approximately 30 million men throughout the world taking pro-erection medications. The marketing industry replaced the role of physicians and researchers with the use of a very simple and seductive message: ED was a medical problem that could be successfully treated. The woman's only role was to encourage her partner to ask his physician for the prescription. Thereafter, he would be able to perform for her like a teenager.

The medical intervention promised to restore a totally predictable erection resulting in a 100 percent successful intercourse performance. This promise encouraged heterosexual as well as homosexual men to use this "medical breakthrough" with the expectation that this stand-alone medical intervention would return them to total erectile control and predictability. There is some anecdotal evidence that gay men use erection aides and medications more frequently than straight men. In many cultures Viagra became a "lifestyle drug" that purportedly enhances sexual performance. For example, in Brazil, the modal age of a Viagra user was 22.

Despite the exciting promise of a quick cure, psychologists and sex therapists questioned the medicalization of male sexuality. In fact, the data regarding the success of Viagra challenged the lofty promises of the drug marketers. It appears that although Viagra is quite helpful for men with moderate to severe medical problems as well as for men with mild or no medical impairments, a return to total predictability and control of erections is not the reality. More commonly, when a pro-erection medication is used, successful intercourse is achieved at a rate of about 65–85 percent. Whereas this is a significant outcome, it did not conform to the traditional erection and intercourse performance model. Consequently, roughly 40–80 percent of men, often holding unrealistic expectations, have stopped using the medication. Following discontinuation, men generally have felt demoralized and avoided partner sex.

When heterosexual couples stop being sexual it is almost always the man's decision. The most common cause is that he has lost his comfort and confidence with having an erection and intercourse. The male falls into a cycle of anticipatory anxiety, tense and failed intercourse performance as well as embarrassment, inhibited sexual desire, and avoidance.

Rather than confronting the psychobiosocial problem of ED, two other drugs, Levitra and Cialis, furthered medication as a "stand alone" intervention. Levitra was very similar to Viagra, but claimed stronger, firmer erections. Cialis offered longer effects, lasting up to 36 hours. In Europe, Cialis was nicknamed the "weekender." There exists no solid scientific evidence that there is a difference in the efficacy of these three drugs although each has different side effects and preferences. Specifically, some men and couples prefer the degrees of freedom allowed by Cialis whereas other men prefer the time-limited (four-hour time frame) structure of Viagra and Levitra.

Psychologists and sex researchers now believe that the best way to assess, treat, and prevent relapse for ED is to adopt a couple psychobiosocial approach. This means recognizing that sexuality is primarily an interpersonal process, not an autonomous one. Psychologically, the man must let go of the pass-fail intercourse performance criterion and replace it with a greater understanding of his sexual body. Furthermore, he must rely more on psychosexual skills, particularly relaxation, developing a cognitive and sexual arousal continuum, be open to partner stimulation in developing an erection, and the most challenging, accept the "Good-Enough Sex" model of variable, flexible male and couple sexuality. Biologically, he assesses vascular, neurological, and hormonal function, specifically the effects of illness and side-effects of medications. He changes those health habits that might interfere with sexual functioning, particularly fatigue, alcohol and drug abuse, and smoking. Relationally, he learns to value his partner as his intimate, erotic friend with whom he shares pleasure rather than performs for.

In the traditional perfect erectile and intercourse model, the man is always one erectile experience from feeling like a "sexual loser" and falling into an avoidance trap. The key to successful treatment of ED is to set positive, realistic expectations of erections and for couple sex and to adopt the "Good-Enough Sex" model of sharing pleasure. In this model, 85 percent of sexual encounters result in successful intercourse. When that does not occur, however, the man and couple are comfortable transitioning to an erotic non-intercourse scenario or a sensual, "cuddly" scenario. Pro-erection medication needs to be integrated into the couple's sexual style of intimacy, pleasuring, and eroticism. However, it is critical for both partners to understand that it is normal for a sexual encounter not to always end with intercourse, whether this occurs once every ten times or once a year.

The more educated and psychologically minded the man, the more easily the Good-Enough Sex model is accepted and the more likely that sexual life can be extended well into his eighties. Men who hold the traditional perfect performance model typically stop being sexual in their fifties and sixties. They often try a pro-sex medication or other medical interventions but when these do not deliver totally predictable erections, they feel like a failure as a man and withdraw. These men not only stop engaging in intercourse, but sensual, playful, and erotic touch as well because "I don't want to start something I can't finish."

Although fear and stigma about ED is prevalent across cultures, social class, and sexual orientation, over 90 percent of men over age 40 have had at least one experience of not obtaining or maintaining an erection sufficient for intercourse. Thus, some type of ED is a virtually universal experience for older men. However, age per se does not cause ED. Increased illness and the side effects of prescription and non-prescription medications affect erectile functioning. And, as the man's vascular and neurological systems become less efficient, psychological, relational, and, most importantly, psychosexual skill factors, become more important for erectile function. *See also* Aging; Mental Health and Sex; Sex Therapists; Sexual Science/Sexology.

Further Reading: McCarthy, Barry, and Michael Metz. *Men's Sexual Health.* New York: Routledge, 2007; Metz, Michael, and Barry McCarthy. *Coping with Erectile Dysfunction.* Oakland: New Harbinger, 2004; WebMD. http://www.webmd.com/diseases_and_conditions/impotence. htm. WebMD provides medical advice, information, and up-to-date research about a number of different medical conditions including ED, January 2007.

Barry McCarthy and Maria Thestrup

ETHICS.   *See* Morality and Ethics

ETHNIC INTIMATE RELATIONSHIPS.   *See* Interracial/Ethnic Intimate Relationships

EXTRAMARITAL SEX.   *See* Infidelity/Extramarital Sex

F

FAMILIES. For most middle-class North Americans the ideal family is a nuclear one, composed of a husband and wife and their biological children. However, United States Census statistics indicate that less than one-half of all families fit this model. During the last thirty years the concept of who is a family has broadened to include cohabiting individuals, divorced, single and re-married parents, and gay, lesbian, and childless couples. While families historically were formed for economic reasons as well as to bear and socialize children, today families are formed to satisfy individual desires for love, sex, and intimacy. The notion of marrying for love, however, is a fairly recent and Western ideal. In the past, families arranged marriages for the purposes of economics, political positioning, or convenience. **Marriage** marked the formation of a new household, the initiation of a sexual relationship, and the birth of children. Today, in the Western world, marriage, sexuality, and childbearing have been separated. There is an increasing social acceptance of **premarital sex**, childbirth outside of marriage, and remaining single. It also is becoming typical for people to cohabit for long periods of time, forming families without a traditional legal commitment. These trends are accompanied by a rapidly decreasing fertility rate.

In non-Western parts of the world, other paths and traditions are associated with family formation. Premarital sexual activity tends to be forbidden, some variation of arranged marriages is not uncommon, and strong sanctions against out of wedlock childbirth continue to persevere. Yet, whatever family traditions are emphasized, every contemporary society is characterized by complex public debates about the nature of marriage and families. Attitudes toward love, sex, marriage, and families are not stagnant but, instead, are influenced by the larger society—by culture, law, **politics**, and economics. Furthermore, in every society "family" experiences are not uniform, differing on social class, race, ethnicity, and gender.

Throughout much of Western history, love and sex did not play a significant role in marriage and the founding of families. Until about 1900, passion was thought to be a dangerous emotion that should not be part of the marriage process. Instead, parents played an important role in helping choose a mate for their children, taking into account suitable family background, economics, and empathy. Women did not expect marital sex to be desirable and enjoyable but married for stability, social acceptance, and to bear children. Men married in order to have access to women's reproductive and domestic labor.

However, children did not enjoy the same privileged status they have today. Children were thought to have been conceived "in sin" and, thus, were brought up very strictly. It was only in the late 1800s that attitudes towards children began to shift. Children were now thought to be morally pure and closer to God than adults, which led to our contemporary more permissive parenting techniques.

Between 1890 and 1960 attitudes towards families, marriage, and sex radically changed. Sexual attraction and romantic love came to be seen as the most important criteria in choosing a mate. Individuals did not just marry in order to produce children. With the introduction of **birth control** and better health practices **childhood** mortality sank and concepts of family and marriage began to change. Further, the increasing industrialization of Western societies led to a sharper division of labor within families. Men increasingly worked outside of the home while middle and upper class women and children remained homebound. In poorer families, men and children and, at times, women, worked for wages.

During this time period, families shifted from a unit of production to one of consumption and emotional intimacy rather than economic necessity being the prime criteria for family formation. Additionally, better health practices and medical innovations resulted in "bean pole families"—families that are larger due to the longevity of their members rather than the presence of many children.

From 1960 onwards, sexual activity became an increasingly private matter not under the purview of the state. Laws dealing with contraception, abortion, miscegenation, and sexual behavior were increasingly overturned. Families with few or no children, single parent families, mixed-race, and same-sex families became more common. In particular, gay and lesbian families have become a recognized albeit contested family form in Western families. Gay and lesbian couples have similar criteria that other men and women search for in their relationships: commitment, stability, companionship, as well as satisfying sexual relationships. Gay and lesbian couples, however, tend to be more egalitarian than heterosexual couples. Current legislation preventing same-sex marriage or adoptions in many parts of the United States and other countries present unique challenges in family formation. Nevertheless, the "gayby boom" has led to a significant number of same-sex partners and gay and lesbian individuals choosing to have children through adoption, artificial insemination, and other means.

In much of the West, marriage and the formation of a family is based on concepts of individualism, **romance**, love, and passion. Elsewhere, family, ritual, and tradition dictate how couples meet, marry, and begin their families. In North Africa, the Middle East, South Asia, and Southeast Asia, some variation of arranged marriages remains common. Sexual activity outside of marriage, especially for women, is often forbidden, and young couples are closely chaperoned until their wedding day. In these societies, love is expected to come after marriage, a consequence of commitment and support.

In North Africa and the Middle East, many couples are introduced by elderly relatives who take a consummate interest in marrying off their younger family members. First cousin marriage is still perceived as ideal due to the importance placed on marrying someone of a compatible family background. In contemporary India, tradition and modernity have intertwined. Thus, it is quite common for families to advertise for a potential marriage partner through local newspapers, listing education, employment, and hobbies as well as a personality description. If the family approves, a background check is conducted on the interested candidate and the couple is allowed to date once. If they still like each other after this one meeting, the couple is engaged. Unlike the West, family involvement in the marital process is based on the rationale that marriage is not an individual matter.

While at one point researchers predicted that families around the world would adopt Western characteristics such as **dating** and sex before marriage, cross-cultural data reveal that this has not occurred. Instead, there has been a backlash in certain countries and cultures against what is seen as the moral decay and the breakdown of the family in the West. In Latin American, Middle Eastern, and some Asian countries, new social movements point to the importance of preserving traditional cultural and family values as a means of avoiding the perceived destructive trends found in Western societies. Over time, global influences fueled through improvements in communication and technology may ultimately spread Western values despite such opposition.

Even in the United States, multiple beliefs about sexuality, love, and marriage co-exist. Although the "ideal" of marriage remains significant to a majority of men and women, different racial and ethnic groups may not always have access to appropriate marital partners. Recent studies illustrate that cohabitation is the primary type of partnership for raising children among low-income minority group members. Interestingly, many of the women who live in these cohabiting unions believe in love and highly value marriage but refuse to bind themselves legally to partners who are economically unstable.

Marriage and family are also defined differently by various ethnic groups. For example, there are profound differences among Japanese Americans between how first and second generations view marriage and family. First generation Japanese Americans tend to believe that duty (*giri*) is of primary importance. Older Japanese Americans feel that duty and ethical commitment are the foundation of marriage and family, recognizing that intense emotional bonds may develop but are not essential for a strong marriage. An alternative view of marriage that intertwines romantic love with duty is held by second generation Japanese Americans.

Profound social and economic transformations have altered conceptions of what constitutes a family. Since marriages and families today are founded on love, it is much more likely that they will be dissolved in the absence of love. In contemporary times **divorce**, blended families, and single-parent families have become more common. Divorce rates are on the rise, which brings on a concomitant increase in single-parent families. Economic stress factors make single parenting a difficult challenge, a challenge often faced by women. For many children, the "new" extended family is the one formed through the remarriage of their biological parents. Also, increasingly children are growing up in mixed-race families. Although there is still some stigma in American society when individuals marry across racial lines, this is slowly disappearing. In particular, Asian/White and Hispanic/White marriages are becoming common. *See also* Child Abuse; Gender Roles; Heterosexuality; Homosexuality; Incest; Interracial/Ethnic Intimate Relationships; Religions, Western; Sociobiology.

Further Reading: Aulette, Judy. *Changing American Families*. Boston, MA: Allyn and Bacon, 2002; Bailey, Beth. *From Front Porch to Back Seat: Courtship in Twentieth-Century America*. Baltimore: Johns Hopkins Press, 1988; Cherlin, Andrew. *Public and Private Families*. 4th ed. Boston: Allyn and Bacon, 2005; Coontz, Stephanie. *The Way We Never Were: American Families and the Nostalgia Trap*. New York: Basic Books, 2000; Fine, Reuben. *The Meaning of Love in Human Experience*. New York: John Wiley & Sons, 1985; Ingoldsby, Bron, and Suzanna Smith, eds. *Families in Global and Multicultural Perspective*. Thousand Oaks, CA: Sage, 2006; Lewin, Ellen. *Lesbian Mothers*. Ithaca, NY: Cornell University Press, 1993; National Council of Family Relations. www.ncfr.org. Premier organization dealing with family issues where research reports and briefs can be accessed, 2007; National Survey of Families and

Households. www.ssc.wisc.edu/nsfh. Information on major national surveys dealing with family issues, 2007; Smock, Pamela. "Cohabitation in the United States: An Appraisal of Research Themes, Findings, and Implications." *Annual Review of Sociology* 26 (2000): 1–20; Yangisako, Sylvia. *Transforming the Past: Tradition and Kinship among Japanese Americans.* Stanford, CA: Stanford University Press, 1985.

Bahira Sherif Trask and Melina McConatha-Rosle

FASHION.   Fashion refers to a system of dress where the governing logic is that of deliberate and continual changes in style. In the twentieth century, women's fashions, in particular, have been designed to enhance the sexual allure of the wearer while men's dress has tended to de-sexualize the body. Recently however, there has been an increasing eroticization of men's fashions.

One of the most influential fashion theorists to address the role that fashion plays in sexual attraction has been James Laver. Writing in the 1960s, he put forward the proposition that while the primary purpose for men's clothes has been to enhance their status (the "Hierarchical Principle"), sexual attraction has been the main motivation behind women's fashions (the "Seduction Principle"). According to him, this is due to the fact that throughout history, men have tended to choose their wives according to their attractiveness while women have chosen their husbands for their capacities to maintain and protect a family. He thus interprets the numerous changes in women's fashions as being motivated primarily by the **desire** to eroticize different parts of the female body. In his view, female fashions over the years have drawn attention to various areas of women's bodies—sometimes emphasizing the breasts, the legs, the abdomen, the hips, or the buttocks. These constant shifts in which parts of the body are revealed or concealed have served to stimulate and enhance erotic interest in the female body.

Laver's theory, however, has been criticized for its broad generalizations and simplifications. For instance, as Valerie Steele points out, there are many reasons other than sexual attraction for the clothes that women wear. Sometimes women may dress to impress rather than to be seductive. Even when they wish to be attractive, this is not necessarily with the aim of actually seducing the viewer. Conversely, there have been many occasions in the history of Western fashion when men have adopted styles not just to enhance their status but also their sex appeal. Furthermore, although different fashions emphasize different parts of the female body, it is dubious whether these changes are due solely to men's shifting sexual interest in these various parts of the body.

Nevertheless, since the nineteenth century, female dress has become the focus of erotic interest while male dress, at least until very recently, has tended to de-emphasize the body. Whereas in the past, both male and female dress had frequently enhanced and drawn attention to the body, throughout the twentieth century, male dress has generally been much plainer and more practical than women's clothing and less subject to the vagaries of fashion. Fashion theorist J. C. Flugel refers to this significant reduction in the decorativeness of male dress that has been a hallmark of twentieth-century men's fashion as the "great masculine renunciation" (1976 [1930], p. 110).

This is particularly evident in the suit, which has been the "uniform" for the middle class male for most of the twentieth century. In contrast to the more decorative modes of male apparel of earlier centuries, the suit disguises the contours of the body, thereby de-sexualizing it, in order to convey an air of seriousness, professionalism, and authority. While the suit may indirectly enhance the wearer's attractiveness to women insofar as it symbolizes power and status, its primary purpose is to project an image of respectability. It signals a concern with the intellectual rather than the bodily. Men, in contrast to women, are not supposed to take too much interest in their appearance. Men who do generally have been criticized as being vain and self-indulgent.

At the beginning of the twentieth century, theorists of fashion such as Adolf Loos, regarded male fashion as being more "rational" and "civilized" than that of females' clothing in its avoidance of sensual display. As Loos argued in his 1902 essay on "Ladies' Fashion," the evolution of women's dress has fallen behind that of men's in its continued adherence to frivolous decoration and its lack of comfort and practicality. By contrast, male dress was superior insofar as it was more functional and less concerned with superficial ornamental effects than female dress. Loos also regarded European man's rejection of ornament as proof of the superiority of Western culture over "primitive" cultures, which indulged in elaborate forms of body decoration such as tattooing.

During the course of the twentieth century, even as women have entered the workforce and adopted elements of male dress such as trousers and tailored jackets, their clothing has continued to be invested with greater erotic significance than those worn by men. A good example of this can be seen in the different attitudes to male and female underwear. Because of its close connection to the body, it might be expected that underwear would be regarded as intrinsically erotic insofar as it draws attention to the body it conceals. However, women's underwear has generally been regarded as "sexy," men's underwear has not.

As increasing numbers of women first began to wear closed underpants during the early twentieth century, great efforts were made to feminize what had previously been a garment worn mainly by men or women of low moral repute. They were made of delicate, sensuous fabrics such as silk and were elaborately decorated with ribbons, embroidery, and lace. Advertisers promoted the new garment to women as a means of becoming more attractive to their husbands. At the same time, designers were careful to ensure that the style of these garments was not too immodest to deter the respectable middle-class woman from purchasing and wearing them. While the expense of these garments meant that they were mainly worn by well-to-do women, later on, with the development of synthetic materials such as rayon, nylon, and Lycra, fancy underwear became affordable to women of all social classes.

As the century progressed, women's underpants became increasingly skimpy and body revealing, facilitated by the newly manufactured fabrics that made possible the creation of styles which closely followed the contours of the body. Advertisements also became more and more overt in promoting the seductive qualities of female lingerie. By contrast, male underwear, until relatively recently, has been largely devoid of erotic connotations. Up until the 1940s, the most popular underpants for men were drawers (subsequently known as boxer shorts) that concealed the contours of the body. Mostly plain and utilitarian in nature, they usually were made of less sensuous materials than female underwear, such as cotton. When the more body-revealing, though still relatively modest, Y-fronts were introduced in 1939, there was resistance to them, particularly amongst upper class men who continued to prefer boxer shorts. It was not until the 1960s that men began to embrace skimpier and more figure hugging briefs. But even then, they were promoted more for their sporting associations than for their sexual allure.

Generally speaking, female fashions in the twentieth century have tended to be more body revealing than those of men. Where men's bodies have been exposed, this has usually been in non-erotic contexts such as manual labor or sport; the exposure of women's bodies has been primarily designed to titillate the viewer. A good example of this has been the exposure of women's legs. Prior to the twentieth century, women's legs had always been hidden beneath long skirts. During the course of the twentieth century, skirt lengths rose, reaching the extreme mini-skirt of the 1960s. Although this could be seen as liberating insofar as it allowed a greater freedom of movement, it extended the eroticization of the female body. This was further enhanced by the wearing of seamless, sheer panty hose, which, unlike the seamed stockings of the past, made women's legs appear naked.

Even where women's dress has sought to be modest, it has often still been interpreted as having sexual connotations. An example is the skirt suit, first made popular by Coco Chanel in the 1950s and adopted by professional women in a bid to command the same degree of respect as their male colleagues. While the tailored skirt suit borrows elements of the male suit, it is still considered to be a more sexually appealing garment than the male version firstly because the skirt reveals the legs. Furthermore, it is normally teemed with a frilly "feminine" shirt made of a more sensuous material than the male equivalent. Thus, although the skirt suit is designed to keep in check the eroticism of the female body, it still maintains feminine elements that enhance the sexual attractiveness of the wearer.

During much of the twentieth century women's clothes have been the focus of erotic interest. However, during the last couple of decades, there has been a discernable trend towards the greater eroticization of the male body through the design and advertising of men's fashion. One of the factors behind this, as Susan Bordo points out, has been the recognition by the fashion and **advertising** industries of the potentially lucrative market amongst gay men. As the stigma associated with **homosexuality** has lessened, advertisers have increasingly sought to incorporate this group of male consumers into its marketing strategies. Mindful of the fact that single gay men without family responsibilities tend to have higher disposable incomes than their heterosexual counterparts, fashion designers (some of whom are gay) recognized the greater interest of many gay men in their personal appearance. During the 1980s, for example, Calvin Klein launched a series of advertisements for men's underwear that stressed its sex appeal. Similarly, in a 1980s advertising campaign to promote Levi jeans, the male model seductively stripped off his clothes in a laundromat.

Fashion has been a predominantly Western phenomenon. Recently, it has spread across the globe as capitalist modes of production and consumption have become more and more widespread. In the process, however, the traditional dress of non-Western cultures has not disappeared but, in many cases, adapted itself in new and creative ways. An example is the Indian sari, which has been given a new lease of life as a fashionable garment, designed to appeal to the modern sensual Indian woman through a wide choice of color, design, and fabric. Another traditional Indian garment, the *churidar-kurta*—a loose, knee-length shirt worn over pajama pants—has also become a fashion item promoted to young women leading active lives outside the home. Similarly, in Nigeria, the Western suit has been combined with elements of traditional male apparel to produce a hybrid garment known as the conductor's suit.

As non-Western dress has come under the influence of the Western fashion system, fashions in the West have increasingly incorporated elements of traditional costume. Thus, Japanese fashion designers Issey Miyake, Rei Kawakubo, Yohji Yamamoto, Kenzo, Kansai, and Matsuda have infiltrated both Parisian couture and street fashion, infusing key elements of Japanese aesthetics such as irregularity, imperfection and asymmetry into Western fashions. *See also* Cosmetics; Gender Roles; Masculinity; Popular Culture.

Further Reading: Bordo, Susan. "Beauty (Re)Discovers the Male Body." In *The Male Body*, 168–225. New York: Farrar, Straus and Giroux, 1999; Craik, Jennifer. *The Face of Fashion*. London and New York: Routledge, 1994; Encyclopedia: Fashion-Infoplease.com. *The Columbia Electronic Encyclopedia*. 6th ed. Columbia University Press. www.infoplease.com.encyclopedia/1fash.html. Provides a brief definition of fashion and a link to a fashion timeline from 1858 to the 1990s, Last updated 2006; Entwhistle, Joanne. *The Fashioned Body*. Cambridge: Polity Press, 2002; Flugel, J. C. *The Psychology of Clothes*. New York: AMS Press, 1976; Laver, James. *Modesty in Dress*. London: Heinemann, 1969; Loos, Adolf. "Ladies' Fashion." In *Spoken into the Void: Collected Essays 1897–1900*, 99–103. Cambridge, MA: MIT Press, 1982; Steele, Valerie. "Clothing and Sexuality." In *Men and Women: Dressing the Part*, edited by Claudia Brush Kidwell and Valerie Steele, 42–63. Washington, DC: Smithsonian Institution Press, 1989.

Llewellyn Negrin

FEMINISM. Feminism seeks social justice for women and the end to **sexism** of all types. It is grounded in two interrelated beliefs: that society systematically denies women individual choice, political power, economic opportunity, intellectual recognition, and control of their persons; and that oppression is illegitimate and unjustified. Derived from the French *féministe*, the term came into English usage beginning in the late 1890s to indicate advocacy of rights and freedoms for women that were equal to those of men. In contemporary usage "feminism" refers both to feminist theorizing and to social movements working to end the political, economic, social, cultural, and sexual subordination of women. Both theoretically and politically, feminists advocate unqualified physical and social equality, the right to love persons of one's own choosing, and to control one's sexual agenda, including reproductive choice.

Advocates of equality for women reach into antiquity, as evidenced in Plato's argument in *Republic* that social roles should be based on merit, rather than gender. However, the first theoretical work that was unambiguously feminist was Mary Wollstonecraft's *A Vindication of the Rights of Woman* (1792). Full of democratic zeal, she extended the notion of inalienable rights of "man" to women, which would allow women to develop fully their intellectual and physical attributes. Wollstonecraft further argued that only fully developed women can serve as suitable intellectual and romantic companions for educated men; love relationships should be based first and foremost upon friendship, which can exist only between equals.

Twentieth century feminists have focused on political institutions and socio-cultural practices that perpetuate women's subordination. They have analyzed why women are oppressed in ways that men are not and have suggested strategies for attaining equal political and social freedoms that are morally desirable and politically viable. Their analyses, however, are far from uniform.

Marxist feminists argue that women must enter the **workplace** *en masse* and must advocate for socializing child care and domestic work. They contend that only economic independence will allow women to free themselves from gender oppression and hope to enter into equitable relationships with men. Psychoanalytic feminists, in contrast, believe that women's subordination results from socializing influences that make loving relations with significant others more important than individual development. Women's capacity for deep relationships leaves them vulnerable to control by the needs and wants of significant others rather than developing a sense of agency. These feminists suggest that women must re-define themselves as individuals, not just in relation to the men or women that they love. Further, they maintain that men must be re-socialized both to value relationships more highly and to see the relational benefits of gender equity. Radical feminists insist that women's subordination is a result of men's control of women as child bearers and child-rearers. Drawing a distinction between biologically determined and culturally determined behavior, radical feminists argue that justice for women must be more far-reaching than political or legal rights. It must include women's freedom to choose the men or women who will be their life and/or sexual partners, to determine their roles within love relationships, and to control their sexual and reproductive decisions. Despite these differences, feminists agree that women *as a group* suffer the same injustices, and that men *as a group* reap the same benefits from women's second-class status.

In the 1970s, lesbians, women-of-color and differently-abled women criticized the assumption that "women" could be treated as a homogeneous group. They charged that the issues that had taken center stage in feminist theorizing had been those faced by Western, white, middle-class women while claiming to represent all women. It is impossible, they argued, to separate gender oppression from other oppressions such as socio-economic class, race, and sexual orientation. Thus, in the last two decades postmodern feminists have shifted to specific and local analyses of the ways in which sex intertwines with other forms of oppression. Nevertheless other feminists charge that postmodern feminists have so splintered the feminist movement that collective social action becomes impossible on important issues like domestic violence, equal pay for equal work, reproductive freedom, all of which have been the province of feminism.

Within feminist social movement historians commonly refer to "waves" of feminism. The "First Wave" began in the United States, England, and western Europe during the mid-1800s, campaigning for women's rights to suffrage and control of their property and persons. Even though it was only in the early decades of the twentieth century that women won the right to vote in the United States, England, France, and Germany, there were earlier victories like the rights of women to inherit, own, or purchase property, to sue for **divorce**, to enter some professions, and to attend college. Much organized feminist movement waned until the "Second Wave," which emerged in North America and Europe in the 1960s, becoming known as the "women's liberation movement."

Many scholars charge that this "Wave" approach to feminist history implies that resistance to male domination is the province of only a few, primarily white middle-class women in a handful of countries, during a specific timeframe. It ignores struggles in non-Western societies and by women of color or working class women. For example, from the early nineteenth through the early twentieth century hundreds of women in the Kwantung region of China became "marriage resisters." These women either rejected **marriage**, or once ceremonially married, refused to consummate their marriages or live with their husbands. Sworn sisterhoods of marriage resisters pledged their lives to one another; lesbian practices were fairly common.

In the United States, Britain, France, and Germany, the "new woman" emerged in the late nineteenth and early twentieth centuries. Because the feminist movement had opened new jobs for women that allowed them financial independence, many of these educated and articulate women formed romantic and/or sexual relationships with other professional women, referred to as "Boston Marriages," or when between college professors, "Wellesley Marriages." Similarly, in urban centers female schoolteachers often formed communities in boarding houses and apartment buildings that promoted separatist cultural centers in which many women formed long-term companionate and/ or romantic relationships. All of these women were radical departures from the middle-class tradition in which middle-class women structured their lives around men.

World War II opened many opportunities for increased independence to women of the middle and lower socio-economic classes in the United States, Britain, and their allies. Because so many men were in the military, jobs in manufacturing and many professions were available to women for the first time. Posters like "Rosie the Riveter" showed women of strength making important contributions to the war effort. These women were rewarded with good pay, advancement, and the excitement of working out of the home with other women.

When the war ended, a combination of social and governmental factors effectively discouraged women from remaining independent or single. Women were asked to resign their jobs so that returning veterans could be re-employed and professional schools of law and medicine reversed their policies of admitting women. In addition, government assistance through the G.I. Bill offered mostly men opportunities to further their educations and purchase homes.

With the contraction of women's opportunities for paid labor, men once again became the sole "breadwinner" for families and the notion of "professional homemaker" took hold for women. Marriages skyrocketed followed by the "baby boom." The enthusiasm for living prescribed **gender roles** increased further as teams of scientific experts claimed that indulgent mothering and effeminate fathering caused **homosexuality**, **premarital sex**, and juvenile delinquency. There was strong societal pressure to conform to the ideal of the heterosexual nuclear family and many **families** retreated into affluent consumerism in the newly created suburbs.

Feminism began to gain a foothold once again in the late 1950s and early 1960s. The financial demands of living a consumer-laden middle-class lifestyle began to require women's re-entrance into the workforce. But, this time, in so-called "pink collar" jobs in traditional women's roles such as secretaries, teachers, and nurses. With the advent of landmark books, notably *The Second Sex* and *The Feminine Mystique*, agitation increased for greater equality in employment opportunities and for equal pay.

A second, far more militant, strain of feminism grew out of the leftist movements that supported the Civil Rights Movement and protested the Vietnam War. These women, schooled in consciousness-raising and organization of large collectives, began the fight for "women's liberation." Avowing that "the personal is political," they advocated not just women's civil and political rights, but also radical transformation of marriage, family, and sexuality. Books like *Sexual Politics* and *The Dialectic of Sex* challenged traditional gender roles in the workplace to be sure, but also in the kitchen and the bedroom. Feminists demanded that men in their lives assume more responsibilities for household duties and child-rearing. Gaining knowledge about their bodies and sexuality from literature published by groups like the Boston Women's Health Book Collective, they demanded equality in sexual relationships and fought for women's choice in reproductive decisions. There were grassroots campaigns in living rooms, community centers, and church basements for women to understand their bodies, expect sexual fulfillment, demand equitable treatment by life partners, and access to contraception and **abortion**. Feminists asserted that women's control over their own persons to be fundamental to liberation. In addition they fought for rape victims' rights, and worked for changes in laws and policies guarding against **domestic and relationship violence**.

Even though lesbians were prominent in the leadership of both wings of the feminist movement, there was little commitment for including lesbian issues in the agenda of feminist political associations. In 1969, Betty Friedan, president of the National Organization of Women (NOW), called lesbians the "lavender menace." She argued that association with lesbian issues would hamstring the organization's ability to effect serious political change because stereotypes of "man-hating" lesbians made it easy to dismiss the movement. Lesbians in NOW resigned and organized a group calling itself "The Lavender Menace," which took over the stage at the NOW-sponsored Second Congress in 1970, expressing their anger about homophobia in the feminist movement and the relationship between sexism and heterosexism. As a result, at the next national conference of NOW, delegates passed a resolution recognizing lesbianism and lesbian rights as a legitimate concern of feminism. Lesbian feminists established women-centered cultural centers and extended feminist theory by demonstrating the link between compulsory heterosexuality and patriarchy and emphasizing lesbianism as a choice, a deliberate and passionate orientation to other women in a misogynist, heterosexist society.

Since the 1960s feminists have been involved in intense political activity in virtually every part of the world, all of which have been influenced by other progressive movements within their respective societies. For instance, in addition to lobbying for equal opportunities in education and the workplace, North American feminists have raised public awareness about violence against women and girls, and continue efforts to ensure reproductive freedom for women. In Latin America feminists campaigned for garment workers; in Afghanistan and Iraq, education for girls; in Uganda, Nigeria, and Namibia, reserved legislative seats for women.

Feminists, too, have challenged traditional misogynist practices such as *sati* (widow burning) in India, clitoridectomies in Africa, foot binding in China, and international trafficking of women in former Iron Curtain countries and throughout Asia. In parts of the world where rapid industrialization has worsened social problems, such as in Mexico, Korea, Malaysia, and the Philippines, feminists have helped create social services, health services, and community projects designed specifically to improve women's overall and reproductive health. They have lobbied governments to intervene in the systematic rape of women in war-torn regions like Bosnia and Sudan, and worked to protest the rapes and murders of hundreds of Juarez women who worked in *maquiladoras* (sweatshops). Feminist organizations are urging these U.S.-owned businesses to institute safety measures to protect the women in their employ. These varied feminist projects around the world all share a commitment to social justice for women and the belief that control of one's body is crucial to achieving political and social equality. *See also* Colonialism/Postcolonialism and Sex; Heterosexuality; Politics; Psychoanalysis; Sanger, Margaret; Sex Crimes; Sexual Abuse and Assault; Women's Movement.

Further Reading: Collins, Patricia Hill. *Black Feminist Thought: Knowledge, Consciousness, and the Politics of Empowerment.* New York and London: Routledge, 1991; Donovan, Josephine. *Feminist Theory: The Intellectual Traditions of American Feminism.* New York: Continuum, 1994; Feminist Majority Foundation. "Global Feminism." See http://www.feminist.org/global. Articles about feminist struggles for equality worldwide, 2005; Schneir, Miriam. *Feminism in Our Time: The Essential Writings, World War II to the Present.* New York: Vintage, 1994; Smith, Barbara, ed. *Home Girls: A Black Feminist Anthology.* New Brunswick, NJ: Rutgers University Press, 2000.

Susan Birden

FETISHES. Sexual fetishes and sadomasochism, as a set of sexual practices, are collectively known as "perversions" and form the boundaries or limits of human sexuality. A fetishist attains sexual gratification from the encounter with a particular object or body part, like shoes or breasts, or from an action, like spanking or being watched. Sadomasochists express a fetish for power by inflicting or receiving pain and/ or humiliation. These acts are often accompanied by a variety of stage-setting props, such as whips or riding crops, and restraints of rope or leather. People who identify as fetishists and sadomasochists place a priority on safe, consensual relations with their sexual partners and often make their perversion, or "kink," part of their sexual relationship with a loved one. Love and fetishism are not mutually exclusive as long as reciprocity and communication are present in the relationship. "Paraphilia," on the other hand, is an extreme condition in which a person's sexuality focuses exclusively on an object or an activity, without which he or she is unable to attain sexual arousal and satisfaction. As paraphilia, fetishism can involve turning people into objects such as when the fetish object comprises members of a particular racial or ethnic group.

European traders in coastal West Africa in the sixteenth and seventeenth centuries coined the word "fetisso" in an attempt to explain objects of religious significance to Africans. Their attempts to understand cultural difference in order to maximize monetary profit were influenced by the assumption of the superiority of their Judeo-Christian religious tradition. In 1757, Willem Bosman developed the concept of fetishism as central to his theory of "primitive" religions. He defined a fetish as a random object to which Africans ascribed magical powers. To West Africans, however, these talismans, containing bone, fur, hair, or wood, were vital to their spiritual well-being.

During the late nineteenth and early twentieth centuries, the concept of fetishes developed as a way to describe Western and, more broadly, modern social and sexual behavior. Alfred Binet first used the word "fetishes" in 1887 within a psychosexual sense to mean the unhealthy sexual fixation on an inanimate object. Psychologists such as Havelock Ellis and Richard von Krafft-Ebing traced the origin of this sexual fascination with an object rather than another human being to a previous traumatic experience in the life of the fetishist. In sharp contrast, Magnus **Hirschfeld** proposed in 1920 that fetishism was a normal part of human sexual activity, asserting that cases of true paraphilia were rare compared to the number of people who enjoyed a fetish object or sadomasochistic act as a healthy sexual expression.

Krafft-Ebing also first used the words "sadism" and "masochism" to describe sexual pleasure obtained by inflicting or receiving pain. He derived the first term from the works of the Marquis de Sade, a French aristocrat whose books mixed violent pornography with political philosophy. The second term comes from Baron von Sacher-Masoch's novel *Venus in Furs,* the story of a man who wishes to be dominated by a woman wearing fur. Sigmund **Freud** later argued, in 1905, that there is an intimate connection between sadism and masochism: they are merely opposite roles taken up by people in orbit around the same perversion. Today, this is widely recognized by the sadomasochistic, or S&M, community.

In 1927, Sigmund Freud presented his theory of fetishism, which detailed the exact nature of the trauma that results in a sexual attraction towards an object instead of a person. Freud thought that only men could have a fetish. Fetishism was based on a boy's "disavowal," or refusal to acknowledge, his mother's lack of a penis. Instead, the boy's psyche seizes on an object that stands in for the missing penis and invests all of his erotic energy into the object. Objectively, the boy knows that women don't have

Fetish model and artist Ms. Veronique, left, flogs David Larson as his wife Lisa Larson, right, watches during the 10th Annual Fetish & Fantasy Halloween Ball at the Las Vegas Sports Center, 2005. © Ethan Miller/Getty Images.

penises, but through the construction of a fetish object, he is able to hold this knowledge at bay. In this way, the boy is able to assuage his own castration anxiety: the fear that his own penis is in danger of disappearing.

Freud's theory argues for a fundamental split in the fetishist's ego, which is at odds with Hirschfeld's idea that fetishism exists on a sliding scale. But Freud's most basic insight is that the creation of a fetish object occurs when an important piece of reality is disavowed by a person's ego, or conscious mind, in such a way that the person is able to continue living with reality.

During the 1980s and 1990s, Freud's general claim was taken up and expanded by the academic fields of gender studies and queer theory in order to explain female fetishism, with particular reference to the lesbian sadomasochistic community. While many feminists declared sadomasochism to be intrinsically degrading to women, proponents of lesbian S&M either took a libertarian approach, claiming it as a right of individual free expression, or said that engaging in ritualistic S&M scenes could be a process that aided women in their recovery from prior, non-consensual abuse.

Gay and straight practitioners of S&M took their lead from this lesbian discourse, and began referring to their activities as "BDSM," from the terms "bondage, discipline, sadism, and masochism," in order to differentiate their activities from the negative associations surrounding the word perversion. The words "top" or "dom" (short for dominant) describe the sadist's role in a BDSM scene, while "bottom" or "sub" (short for submissive) describe the masochist's role. In this way, S&M practitioners sought to present themselves to society at large as normal people engaged in an alternative lifestyle.

Karl Marx's theory of commodity fetishism, which he first proposed in 1867, also had a significant influence in the twentieth century. Marx asserted that in a capitalist economic system, the use value of goods is separate from their exchange value. Some commodities like luxury goods—from Prada bags to Porsche sports cars—are expensive and desired, bought and sold, because they seem to promise more than just practical use. The growth of global capitalism, accompanied by increasingly sophisticated **advertising** and marketing techniques, resulted in all human **desire** becoming increasingly fetishistic in developing and developed nations. Commodity fetishism promises to add a certain mystique or desirability to a person's identity: particularly to her or his sexual identity. Luxury goods are commodity fetishes to the extent that they seem to make people sexier. This is different from sexual fetishists, who find sexual satisfaction from the object itself, not in the way that possessing the object makes them feel about themselves or appear to others.

The late twentieth century saw the rise of fetish parties, a cultural phenomenon linking the two concepts of fetishism. Beginning in London during the mid-1980s, these spread across Europe, North America, Australia, and Japan. They combined two earlier types of events: small S&M gatherings and large "gay mix" dance or rave parties.

Following the sexual liberation movement of the 1960s, heterosexuals interested in S&M began to form groups in the early 1970s. Later in that decade, in conjunction with the homosexual rights movement, gays and lesbians followed suit. Both began gathering in increasingly public venues, some of which became known as S&M or fetish clubs, in which they could participate in BDSM role playing or scenes. In the 1980s, gay mix dance parties became popular in several urban centers around the world. Predominantly gay, but open to everybody, these events began to create a queer atmosphere in which people of any gender and sexual orientation were welcomed, as long as they were tolerant of others.

Fetish parties originated when the two scenes mixed together. S&M practitioners attended and did performances, both organized and spontaneous, in which formerly secret and forbidden practices were conducted in front of new, appreciative audiences. The various alternative lifestyles and identities represented at fetish parties include bisexuals, transgendered people, and cross-dressers as well as rubber and leather fetishists.

By encouraging or requiring participants to wear costumes that incorporate or embody their particular fetish fantasies, fetish parties emphasize fashion: high heeled shoes or boots; clothing made from latex, shiny vinyl, leather; whips, chains and collars. Perhaps the most emblematic item of fetish clothing, however, is the corset. When corsets went permanently out of fashion in the early twentieth century, they reappeared as eroticized, fetish costumes. Through tight-lacing, the corset has the ability to alter body shape while simultaneously displaying the wearer's ability to bear pain.

Uniforms, especially those of nurses, doctors, and military officers, are sometimes seen at fetish parties. The wearing of certain uniforms, especially those of Nazi Germany, has caused controversy in the fetish community. These uniforms recall an anti-Semitic and homophobic historical period in which people were enslaved, tortured, and killed by a fascist regime. The wearers of such outfits believe that making the uniforms of Nazi oppressors into a fetish is the ultimate transgression and claim doing so provides a sexual thrill that liberates them from the weight of history. Others maintain that this practice denigrates the memories of the millions murdered by the Nazis and constitutes a denial of history.

Fetishism and sadomasochism are not confined to Western cultures. The historical practice of Chinese foot binding has often served as a non-Western example of fetishism. In Japan, however, fetishism and sadomasochism have developed both independently of and in exchange with Western cultures. Rope bondage was first developed as a form of punishment during the Edo period (1603–1867). Many ukiyoe, or Japanese prints, included jail scenes with depictions of criminals tied with complicated knots. Their social class and the type of crime they had committed could be discerned by looking closely at the knots and style of bondage. Japanese rope bondage was invoked as a fetish by its first photographer, Seiu Itoh, in 1919. With his wife as a model, he did a series of photographs intended not only to show bondage, but also to test her endurance. However, his photographs were never widely known and the rise of the fascist military government in Japan soon put an end to such activities.

Although copies of the American fetish pulp magazine *Bizarre* appeared in Japan as early as 1946, probably brought by occupation troops, the Japanese S&M boom was sparked in 1952, by *Kitan Club*. This domestic magazine, switched from nude photography to bondage and S&M photos after a police crackdown on **pornography**. As Japan's postwar economy developed, commercial clubs where customers paid to engage in S&M appeared, but it wasn't until the late 1980s that the fetish scene began. The first fetish clothing shop opened in Tokyo in 1988 and the first fetish party was held two years later. Both were heavily influenced by the London fetish scene. Soon, the cross-cultural connections began to flow both ways, and Japanese rope bondage became a fixture of fetish parties around the world. It remains so today. *See also* Cross Dressing/Drag; Fashion; Feminism; Psychoanalysis; Race and Racism.

Further Reading: Akita, Masami. *Nihon Kinbaku Shasinshi* [The History of Bondage Photography in Japan]. Vol. 1. Tokyo, Japan: Jiyu-kokuminsha, 1996; Apter, Emily, and Pietz, William, eds. *Fetishism as Cultural Discourse*. Ithaca, NY: Cornell University Press, 1993; Koshi, Shimokawa. *Fuzoku Kenkyu Shiryo Sousho: Keibatsu Hentai Seiyoku Zufu* [An Illustrated Bibliographic Study of the Demimonde: Punishment, Perversion and Sexual Desire]. Vol. 1. Tokyo, Japan: Kouseisha, 1996; McCallum, E. L. "How to Do Things with Fetishism." *Differences: A Journal of Feminist Cultural Studies* 7, no. 3 (1995): 24–49; Medhurst, Andy, and Sally R. Munt, eds. *Lesbian and Gay Studies: A Critical Introduction*. London: Cassell, 1997; Sexuality.org: The Society for Human Sexuality. http://www.sexuality.org. Dedicated to improving the quality and scope of the sex education material available on the Internet, includes information on fetish and BDSM communities; Steele, Valerie. *Fetish: Fashion, Sex and Power*. Oxford: Oxford University Press, 1996; Weinberg, Thomas S., ed. *S&M: Studies in Dominance and Submission*. New York: Prometheus Books, 1995.

Joshua Paul Dale

FOOD AND DRINK.   In every culture, beliefs and behaviors pertaining to food and drink, or "foodways," constitute a system of meaning that contributes to the organization of the natural and social world. Food and drink are important symbolically and materially. Like sex and love, sharing them binds people together and assures the continuation of the social group. And similar to prohibitions pertaining to sexual practice, all cultures have rules about what particular groups of people, such as women or men and children or adults, should and should not consume. Still, human eating and drinking behaviors are highly variable over time and across cultures.

The twentieth and early twenty-first centuries experienced dramatic transformations in what and how humans eat and drink. Yet, food and drink remain central to our definitions of society, self, and other. In every part of the world, foodways represent an ordered system that reflects and reproduces other cultural systems. Food and its preparation also create a bridge between nature and culture. That is, when humans transform an item into something edible—through harvesting, cleaning, and cooking— they remake the "natural" into the "cultural." Because of its strong transformative symbolism, food is often central to rites of passage. For example, among the Mihinaku Indians of the Amazon, specific prohibitions around eating and drinking accompany the symbolic passage of girls into women and boys into men. Similarly, the tiered wedding cake and champagne toast have long been important features of **marriage** ceremonies throughout much of the West. Thus, food and drink act as a means for communicating not only social relationships and boundaries, but also thoughts and feelings, including those pertaining to love and sex.

Food and drink stir the emotions due to their sensual properties and social meanings. On the one hand, the physical characteristics of foodstuffs—their aroma, texture, and taste—are central to the affective responses they evoke. Biting, chewing, and swallowing food are sensual experiences that frequently engender emotions, either consciously or unconsciously. On the other hand, such emotional responses to food and drink are intricately linked to their symbolic significance. The smell of baking cookies or fresh bread brings about not only hunger, but also feelings of warmth and security. And while alcohol clearly has physiological effects in that it relaxes, elevates mood, and reduces inhibitions, these effects are tightly bound up with the cultural significance of drinking alcohol, including intimacy and **romance**.

Some of the strongest emotional meanings of food and drink derive from their association with the home. However, the nature of "home cooking" has changed dramatically. During the early 1900s, domestic cooking in Western countries was done on wood-burning stoves; iceboxes were a novelty; indoor running water was unusual. Most food was fresh and locally produced, and seasonable vegetables, lard, butter, fresh meats, sugar, and potatoes dominated the Western diet. As agricultural techniques advanced, a wider variety of foodstuffs became available. These included pre-prepared items such as John Harvey Kellogg's breakfast cereal (the forerunner of today's Kellogg's Cornflakes). Originally intended to do more than fill the stomach, the cereal was actually designed as a cure for what Kellogg believed were the common ills of the day— namely constipation and **masturbation**. In his mind, the two were closely linked, the common cause being a lack of fiber, both dietary and moral. Like processed foods, dining out in restaurants became increasingly widespread during the mid-1900s. Combining American favorites such as hamburgers and milkshakes, the service of often scantily clad, roller-skating carhops and the opportunity for sustained romantic activity, drive-in restaurants became popular during the 1950s.

It is not only in Western countries that food, drink, and romance are culturally and symbolically linked. For example, among the Mihinaku Indians, "to have sex" is literally defined as "to eat to the fullest extent possible." Like copulation and reproduction, sharing food and drink ensures the survival of the group. It signals intimacy and trust, particularly when the items shared are highly symbolic, as in the case of special feasts and holiday celebrations. Because intimacy and trust are so central to both food consumption and intercourse, all societies have rules concerning "appropriate" eating and sexual practices as well as partners. In many cultures, gifts of food are used to initiate sexual liaisons. More generally, food exchanges provide a crucial means for maintaining good relations with extended family and those outside the family group, especially when food is scarce.

The association of food and sex derives, in part, from the fact that both eating and intercourse are acts of "incorporation." That is, each involves the passage of some external object into the body. In the context of eating, incorporation is fraught with a range of potential dangers, not only because some substances are fatal, but also because the characteristics of foods consumed are transferred, physiologically and symbolically, to the eater. The principle of incorporation—and the threat it entails—underlies many cultural prohibitions surrounding both eating and copulation.

Like social rules pertaining to sexual practice, shared perceptions of what constitutes "food," what foods should be eaten together, when they should be eaten and the manners required in doing so, not only define communities but also differentiate "us" from "them." At the same time, such distinctions are linked to factors such as stage in the life course, gender, place, and social class. For example, while infants' consumption of their mother's milk is considered appropriate and even desirable, the consumption of another woman's breast milk and of breast milk by older children are not commonly accepted in the West; both practices are unproblematic in some non-Western tribal societies.

Food, drink, and sex are also relevant to gender and gendered social relations. Entitlements to foodstuffs differ for men and women in most parts of the world. Within egalitarian cultures, food prohibitions tend to apply equally to males and females, such that some foods and drinks are thought to be either beneficial or dangerous for men, while others are considered so for women. Among the Hua of Papua New Guinea, for instance, *koroko* foods (defined as wet, cold and soft) are believed to make the eater more feminine, while *haberi'a* foods (which are dry, warm and hard) are thought to impart masculine characteristics. The situation is very different in gender-stratified western societies like the United States, in which males tend to have greater access to larger quantities of food and, particularly, to foodstuffs that are especially scarce or valuable, such as red meat and alcohol.

At the same time, Western women have long been responsible for most aspects of food provision within **families**, and continue to be so even today. That responsibility, in combination with women's role in childbirth and their production of breast milk, ties females symbolically to both feeding and reproduction. Despite that connection, Western women have historically been expected to limit their food consumption in order to conform to ideals of femininity and female slimness, in much the same way as they have been required to restrain their sexual interest and activity. In some cases, however, women have responded to such expectations through means that either they or others deem socially, personally, or politically empowering. For example, Victorian "fasting girls" abstained from food and drink to gain public esteem for their refinement, delicacy, and morality, characteristics that were highly regarded in females of the period. In a somewhat different way—and a very different social context—modern day anorexics deny themselves food in pursuit of what they consider to be physical and moral perfection.

Like its relevance to gender relations, food is central to family life and child socialization. Feeding is one of the primary means of establishing bonds between parent and child, not only in the West but in other cultures as well. For example, in Kalauna, Goodenough Island in New Guinea, feeding is so important to the establishment of parent-child relations that the very act of *being* a parent—for both males and females—is defined in terms of food provision. Feeding is also central to personality formation. In fact, Sigmund **Freud** (1962) argued that the child's earliest eating experiences establish his or her personality for life. Furthermore, breast-feeding plays a significant part of the process of individualization. As children come to recognize that the source of food lies outside themselves, they begin to establish an autonomous, bounded subjectivity. With maturation, children may also use food and drink as a means for enacting an individual sense of self. That is, by voicing preferences for some items over others, they demonstrate their personality and unique taste.

For these reasons and others, the "family meal," in which mother, father, and children consume home-cooked foods, is often characterized as an essential foundation of Western family life. However, the late twentieth and early twenty-first centuries have witnessed the increasing availability of pre-packaged snacks and a growing popularity of fast foods, many of which are marketed in ways that cast cooking as drudgery and meals as discretionary. Yet, making and sharing food and drink remain sacred events that are even more central to human life than sex. After all, only occasional sex is required to continue the species, but humans must eat and drink regularly if we are to survive. *See also* Childhood; Drugs and Alcohol; Gender Roles; Indigenous Peoples.

Further Reading: Association for the Study of Food and Society. http://food-culture.org. Addresses a range of issues related to food habits, dietary change, nutrition, government policy/programs, food history, marketplace ethics, agriculture/production, and hunger, 2006; Brumberg, Joan Jacobs. *Fasting Girls: The Emergence of Anorexia Nervosa as a Modern Disease.* Cambridge, MA: Harvard University Press, 1988; Counihan, Carole. *The Anthropology of Food and the Body: Gender, Meaning and Power.* New York: Routledge, 1999; Freud, Sigmund. *Three Contributions to the Theory of Sex.* New York: Dutton, 1962.

Debra Gimlin

FREE LOVE. Free love describes the act and ideology of sharing sexual relations and/or personal intimacies with multiple rather than single partners. Free love is often understood as an alternative to sexual and romantic monogamy. This is slightly ambiguous, though, because each social context creates different standards and alternatives. Some free love practitioners advocate for unfettered sexual relations. Others advocate for multiple romantic relationships involving love and commitment. Still others define free love as the right to freely choose a lifelong loving partner. Social, cultural, political, and economic situations influence these differing views. Free love in Japan during the 1920s was not the same as 1970s free love in North America, and, despite its cross-cultural status, twentieth-century free love is absent in certain parts of the world. Despite these differences, free love is often anchored in a spirit of rebellion, overlapping with **feminism**, sexual revolutions, women's rights, lesbian, gay, bisexual, and **transgender** (LGBT) rights, the rejection of traditional **marriage**, and the fight for **birth control** and contraceptives.

Free love, as a movement and/or individual practice, frequently emerges during times of social change, specifically at the onset or fruition of industrialization. This explains free love's frequent association with anti-capitalism and anarchism. For instance, Emma Goldman (1869–1940), a famous early century transatlantic feminist anarchist, argued that capitalist societies tend to be patriarchal, authoritarian, and hierarchical. Such conditions, she argued, cast interpersonal relationships in terms of private ownership, designate women as the property of men, and arrange traditional two-person heterosexual **families** with children as social necessity. Emma Goldman rejected random promiscuity and called for emotional commitment. She believed that human beings have the capacity, and thus, should have the socio-legal right, to love more than one person. Goldman's free love revolted against monogamous heterosexual marriage, and sought to break the subordination and privatization of interpersonal relationships.

During the first quarter of the twentieth century, Britain, France, Germany, Holland, Russia, and the United States encountered separate but related free love movements. These movements often connected with socialism and workers' rights. The socialist writings of Karl Marx and Friedrich Engels sparked calls for alternative economics based on shared rather than private wealth and ownership. True human freedom, they argued, entails not just economic, but also, and perhaps more importantly, sexual and intimate sharing. Fighting for individual and social freedom necessitates sexual and romantic liberation, and sharing rather than hording our bodies, sex and love creates a more satisfying human existence.

Ernest Juin (1872–1962), a Frenchman known as Emile Armand, was one prominent free love advocate of this era. Armand called for plural love, libertarian sexuality, and a sexual communism that entailed a free contract of sexual association. Armand believed that human beings should have the right to freely give themselves to, and keep themselves from, whomever they chose. This involved more than physical attraction. Outward appearances, he thought, should be a secondary rather than primary credential for sexual encounters, and sexual communism involved overcoming sexual repression and conjoining negative emotions—e.g., jealousy, possessiveness, fears of rejection, and low self-esteem.

Early twentieth century Japan experienced a free love emergence, albeit, different from the above examples. Japanese free love primarily concerned legalities of chastity, fidelity, and **divorce** between married heterosexual couples. Japanese law upheld a double standard: it allowed, and accepted as natural, male extramarital sex, but outlawed female infidelity. Women were subordinate to their male spouses, while men were free to love whomever. This debate was more about legal equality than the **morality** of infidelity. Japanese free lovers argued that males and females should receive one standard legal treatment regardless of the specific law. If men can have extramarital sex, so can women, and if women cannot, then neither can men.

Japanese free love also concerned free marriage. Traditionally, Japanese marriages were arranged by parents according to familial lineage and property inheritance. Japanese free lovers countered this tradition, believing that each person should freely marry out of mutual love—not familial or economic obligation. This strand of Japanese free love connects to that of the West's, and was no doubt influenced by Japan's blossoming print **media** industry. Japanese intellectuals of that time, like Murobuse Koshin, and Niizuma Kan, were reading many of the same authors as the Western free lovers, thus producing similar perspectives.

The United States experienced a free love revival during the 1960s and 1970s. Free love of this period is often associated with the hippie movement—a youth subculture politically involved with various social upheavals, particularly, the anti–Vietnam War movement. Hippie free love involved a sense of hedonism in which all human experiences should be embraced and sought after. Hippies—borrowing theories from Wilhelm **Reich**, Herbert Marcuse, Abraham Maslow, and others—argued that a proliferation of experiences could expand human consciousness, freeing individuals from the mores of a repressive social system. Hippie free love critiqued monogamy and sexual repression, and argued that people are not truly free until they can have sex with whomever, whenever, however, and wherever. Free love, sometimes advocated as sex with numerous and unknown partners in public spaces, was understood by Abbie Hoffman, John Sinclair, and many others as a political act that undermined the social order. Similar youth subcultures and free love revivals were prominent in Britain and France.

During the mid- and late-1970s, free love was more commonly practiced by mainstream middle-class North American couples. The term "open marriage," popularized by researchers Nena and George O'Neill, began to eclipse the term "free love." Open marriage described middle-class couples' willingness to have extramarital sexual relations. Open marriage advocates rejected notions of **infidelity** and argued that multiple sex partners were normal and healthy. Open marriage couples joined clubs and social circles that fostered numerous sex partners, one-night stands, group sex, exhibitionism, and voyeurism. Many of these folks also began to experiment with same-sex partners, arguing that love—be it sexual or emotional—precedes and exceeds socially constructed **gender roles** and sexual identities. Unlike many of the previously mentioned free love movements, open marriage partners did not link their sexual practices with such political upheavals as anti-capitalism or rebellion against the state.

During roughly the same time period, North American and European LGBT citizens were coming to political consciousness, fighting for civil rights, and gaining social visibility. The socio-cultural milieu of the 1970s cultivated a sense of non-heterosexual identity as LGBT communities emerged with participants openly engaging in freer sexual and romantic relationships, and visible "gay only" establishments, opening in greater numbers, encouraging sexual openness, experimentation, and sharing. While much of this activity occurred in urban centers, LGBT free love also occurred away from the city's spotlight. Matriarchal villages, for instance, were populated by free-spirited, gypsy-like lesbians who communed in makeshift towns and neighborhoods. All participants openly shared **food**, clothes, money, housing, chores, and sexual relationships.

The 1980s and 1990s witnessed the rise of the **AIDS/HIV** pandemic and the social fear of **sexually transmitted infections**. Non-monogamy, polygamy, and polyamory became new terms for free love, and the act itself became a private and personal choice rather than an overt political tool.

Different forms of free love emerged at the start of the twenty-first century. Shanghai youth, partially influenced by economic globalization, articulate public affection, sex talk, and freedom to choose sexual partners as positive social progressivism. Also, "cuddle parties," first emerging in New York City in 2004 and spreading to Berlin and Amsterdam, involve consensual group cuddling among adults. Cuddle parties provide space for intimate contact among strangers while prohibiting nudity, French kissing, and any form of sexual intercourse. Such free love strongly differs from previous, more radical forms. But free love persists as a social theme despite, or perhaps because of, these generational and cultural differences. *See also* Gay and Lesbian Movement; Homosexuality; Pederasty; Politics; Women's Movement.

Further Reading: Falk, Candace Serena. "Chapter Four: Promiscuity and Free Love." In *Love, Anarchy, and Emma*, 67–78. New Brunswick, NJ: Rutgers University Press, 1990; Farrer, James. *Opening Up: Youth Sex Culture and Market Reform in Shanghai*. Chicago: University of Chicago Press, 2002; International Institute for Social History. *Free Love and the Labor Movement: Second Workshop in the Series on Socialism and Sexuality*. Workshop papers posted online at http://www.iisg.nl/womhist/freelove.php, 2000; Loving More: New Models for Relationships. See http://lovemore.com:8888/home. Posts conferences, definitions, discussions, and a magazine for multiple partner participants; Munson, Marcia, and Judith P. Stelboum, eds. *The Lesbian Polyamory Reader: Open Relationships, Non-Monogamy, and Casual Sex*. Binghamton, NY: Haworth Press, 1999; O'Neill, Nena, and George O'Neill. *Open Marriage: A New Lifestyle for Couples*. New York: Evans; 1984; Polyamory Society. See http://polyamorysociety.org. A nonprofit organization supporting multi-partner relationships and families; Selth, Jefferson P. *Alternative Lifestyles: A Guide to Research Collections on Intentional Communities, Nudism, and Sexual Freedom*. Westport, CT: Greenwood Press, 1985; Stoehr, Taylor. *Free Love in America: A Documentary History*. New York: AMS Press, 1979; Tipton, Elise. "Sex in the City: Chastity and

Free Love in Interwar Japan." *Intersections: Gender, History and Culture in the Asian Context* 11 (August 2005). See http://www.sshe.murdoch.edu.au/intersections/issue11/tipton.html#t48.

Jason Del Gandio

FREUD, SIGMUND (1856–1939).   An Austrian neurologist credited with founding the psychoanalytic movement, Sigmund Freud was born in 1856 to Jewish merchant banker Jacob Freud and his second wife Amalia. Freud had two older half-brothers and six younger siblings. It is apparent, however, that Sigmund was his mother's "darling," and by far the family's most intellectually precocious child. Excelling in his secondary education, he entered the medical school at Vienna University in 1873, choosing medicine, which—along with law—was the only other respectable profession available to talented Jewish men in the Austro-Hungarian Empire of which Austria was then a part. Today, it is difficult to engage in any kind of serious speculation on the nature of love and sexuality without an understanding of Freud's work.

Although his name is most often associated with the psychological theory of **psychoanalysis**, Sigmund Freud's initial training was as a medical doctor with a particular interest in neurology. During his medical studies at Vienna University (formally completed in 1881) he worked with the neurologist Ernst Bruecke at the Institute of Physiology. He befriended fellow researcher and clinician Joseph Breuer, whose patient "Anna O"—a woman whose amnesia seemed to be alleviated by hypnosis—inspired much of Freud's theorizing about the subconscious mind, and perhaps also his emphasis on the "talking cure."

In 1885, Freud received a one-year scholarship to study under the imminent Paris neurologist Jean-Martin Charcot. Here he observed the clinical practice of hypnosis to treat hysteria. This was a formative period in the development of his subsequent theoretical and clinical work, during which he converted from a purely anatomical understanding of mental disorders to an approach more closely resembling what today is called psychology.

After a brief residency as a neurologist and director of a children's ward in Berlin, Freud returned to Vienna and began his private clinical practice, specializing in the treatment of nervous disorders. This clinical experience furnished him with a wealth of evidence for the notion that psychological neuroses might arise not, as was thought, from purely biological or physiological disorders but from disturbances in the patient's mind. Although this supposition ran counter to the prevailing medical wisdom of the time, it was not entirely without precedent. Intellectual historians critical of what they call "the Freud legend" point to his correspondence with Wilhelm Fliess as an example of how ideas that would eventually be specifically outlined in Freud's theory of psychoanalysis were already circulating in the medical community during this period.

These controversies serve to highlight the importance of understanding the emergence of psychoanalysis (or "development of Freud's theories") in relation to the scientific spirit of Europe during the late nineteenth and early twentieth centuries. The intellectual climate was still coming to grips with the profound implications of Charles Darwin's theory of evolution by natural selection, which radically altered biological accounts of human evolution by suggesting that species (including humans) change or adapt from one generation to the next.

Undated portrait of Sigmund Freud. Courtesy Library of Congress.

During the next fifteen years Freud's publications testify to his mounting suspicions concerning the development of mental disorders. In 1895, he published *Studies of Hysteria*, which outlined a number of case studies of individual patients and detailed their treatment. Freud's six children—three daughters and three sons—were also born during the period from 1887 to 1895. Later, his youngest daughter, Anna, became a successful psychoanalyst, specializing in the developmental analysis of children.

This was followed five years later by *The Interpretation of Dreams*, in which Freud suggested that the images experienced in dreams have both a manifest (or readily apparent) meaning and—more importantly—a latent content. This, in turn, suggests that there are different modes of consciousness at work in the individual human mind beyond the purely conscious or rational. In 1901, Freud published *The Psychopathology of Everyday Life*, in which he elaborated two basic themes that became important in his later thinking.

First, Freud argued that **childhood** memories have a direct and lasting impact on the future development of the individual; the memory "exercises a certain amount of selection among the impressions at its disposal." From this Freud concluded that the manner in which a child's mind deals with these "impressions" is fundamentally different to that of an adult, thus laying the groundwork for his developmental theory.

The second and more comprehensively discussed theme in *Psychopathology* is that an individual's acquisition and use of language reveals important insights into how the mind works. It is through errors in speech—the famous "Freudian slips" or "slips of the tongue"—that we can come to a psychoanalytic understanding of the mind's functioning. The fact that what is actually said and what is intended by the "dynamic unconscious" are often two very different matters provides further evidence for Freud's early proposition in *The Interpretation of Dreams* that the mind can be split into a number of different categories, including the conscious and the unconscious.

In 1905, Freud joined the Faculty of Medicine at the University of Vienna, a position he held until 1920, when he was granted a full professorship. During this period, he further elaborated on the developmental aspects of psychoanalysis, most specifically and controversially in his 1905 paper, *Sexuality*. Freud asserted the primacy of two triebe (or "drives") in the human organism: the sex drive and the death drive, or *eros* and *thanatos* in Greek (*eros* can be understood as the drive to growth, vitality and creativity, whereas *thanatos* is the drive toward dissolution and death). It was Freud's frank and clinical discussion of the former of these instincts that generated the most criticism from the prudish social environment in which his work was received.

After the German occupation of Austria in 1938, Freud's family escaped to London, where he was to spend the remaining year of his life. He was aided by the French psychoanalyst Princess Marie Bonaparte (great-grand niece of Napoleon I of France) and the Welsh psychologist Ernest Jones, who later published a three-volume biography of Freud. Jones's books, although dated and subject to criticism from intellectual historians, are perhaps the most comprehensive analysis of Freud's life and work published to date. It was in London that Freud, having been diagnosed with cancer of the jaw in 1937, died in 1939.

Since Freud's death, his psychoanalytic theory and clinical practice have been subjected to a great deal of criticism, most notably by feminists, who challenged his categorization of female sexual development in terms of what he called "penis envy." According to Freud, in order to differentiate herself from her male counterpart, the female child engages in a struggle similar to the Oedipus complex, in which she must acquire *something* that stands in for the male phallus. This conception of feminine identity, critics like Julia Kristeva and Juliet Mitchell argue, implies a sexist understanding of **masculinity** as a "default" position, relegating femininity to the position of a variant on this universal male category of humanity. Similarly, Freud's descriptions of **homosexuality** as a problematic and pathological "stage" along the road to a "healthy" **heterosexuality** have been questioned by critics who find these statements at odds with Freud's writing elsewhere that people are at least potentially "bisexual."

Although Freud's psychoanalytic theories have born the brunt of what Paul Robinson calls an "anti-psychoanalytic turn" in the 1980s, his intellectual influence is felt across disciplines, ranging from psychology to literary study, linguistics, and the philosophy of mind. Even the most ardent feminist criticisms contain a profound respect for Freud's contributions. Practicing psychoanalysts of many different persuasions can be found in the United States and Europe and the persistence of phrases such as "the unconscious" and the "Freudian slip" testify to the lasting effect of Freudian thought on the popular cultural imagination. *See also* Bisexuality; Feminism; Psychotherapy; Reich, Wilhelm; Sexual Science/Sexology.

Further Reading: Ellenberger, Henry. *The Discovery of the Unconscious: The History and Evolution of Dynamic Psychiatry.* New York: Basic Books, 1970; Elliott, Anthony, ed. *Freud 2000.* Carlton, Victoria: Melbourne University Press, 1998; Freud, Anna. *Normality and Pathology in Childhood.* New York: International Universities Press, 1965; Green, Christopher. "Classics in the History of Psychology." York University, Ontario, Canada. http://psychclassics.yorku.ca/Freud/Psycho/. Several of Freud's more important writings; Mitchell, Juliet. *Feminism and Psychoanalysis.* New York: Basic Books, 2000; Neu, Jerome, ed. *The Cambridge Companion to Freud.* Cambridge and New York: Cambridge University Press, 1991; Roazen, Paul. 1976. *Freud and His Followers.* London: Allen Lane, 1976; Robinson, Paul. *Freud and His Critics.* Berkeley: University of California Press, 1993, also available at http://ark.cdlib.org/ark:/13030/ft4w10062x; Strachey, James, ed. *The Standard Edition of the Complete Psychological Works of Sigmund Freud.* London: Hogarth Press, 1953–1975.

David Nel

G

GAY AND LESBIAN MOVEMENT. The gay and lesbian movement refers to collective action by people who share identities defined by same-sex desire. People with such identities have existed in many historical periods, but social and political movements opposing hostility towards people who define themselves as "homosexual," "lesbian," and/or "gay" have only emerged since the end of the nineteenth century. Social reformers began to propose that a newly identified group of men and women described by medical experts as "homosexuals" should be defended from stigma they faced in society, and allowed to legally engage in private same-sex sexual behavior. The Stonewall riots in New York in 1969 signaled the emergence of the "gay liberation movement." Subsequently, an increasingly assertive gay and lesbian movement claiming equality, citizenship, and rights has emerged in Western societies, and, increasingly, worldwide.

The concept of a "gay and lesbian movement" is problematic for a variety of reasons. Historians and social theorists such as Mary McIntosh and Michel Foucault have argued that the idea of a "homosexual" as a type of person defined by same-sex **desire** has not always existed, and that the actual sexual behavior of people is more complex and diverse than such categories suggest. For example, many people who define themselves as "heterosexual" sometimes in practice have sex with people of the same sex. Furthermore, the concepts "gay" and "lesbian" have different meanings and histories from "homosexual." The term "homosexual" appeared in the late nineteenth century, used to label people by psychologists and psychiatrists, implying inferiority relative to **heterosexuality**. "Lesbian" also tended to be used by experts rather than ordinary people. By contrast, "gay" is a word which emerged from everyday city life in the early twentieth century; it was sometimes used as an insult but could also be used as a code word without arousing suspicion of **homosexuality**, and tended to become used by men to describe themselves. However, early homosexual movements sought to represent people who identified as "gay" and "lesbian," so they can be considered when surveying the "gay and lesbian movement."

The concept "gay and lesbian movement" also does not ostensibly include "bisexuals." Bisexuals have been welcomed in and participated in some movements with gay and lesbian people, but not others. The contribution of bisexuals should be recognized where it has existed, but we should not misrepresent movements as inclusive if they have not been. Similar questions can be considered concerning the contribution of **"transgender"** people who do not conform to dominant binary understandings of sex ("male" and "female") and/or gender ("men" and "women"). In general, these

Hundreds of thousands of gay rights activists carry a mile-long rainbow banner in New York, 1994. 1994 marked the twenty-fifth anniversary of the Stonewall Inn riots, considered the birth of the gay rights movement. © AP Photo/Eric Miller.

considerations suggest the need to reject the idea of a single homogenous "gay and lesbian movement" operating across long periods of history in favor of discussion of a shifting, evolving, and internally divided movement, or multiple movements which have been historically and socially specific, and variously "gay" (men only), "lesbian" (women only), "gay and lesbian," and "gay, lesbian, bisexual, transgender."

Finally, "gay" and "lesbian" are concepts in the English language that do not always translate directly into words in other languages and cultural categories. For example, in Brazil the traditional term *bicha* is a stigmatizing word for a man who has sex with men, which implies the person is sexually passive, feminized and subordinate to other men.

Gay and lesbian movements have generally been concerned with issues of both sex and love. However, some religious traditions such as Roman Catholicism have focused on condemning same-sex sexual acts (particularly anal intercourse), more than condemning homosexual desires or feelings. This has implied scope for gay and lesbian Christian movements to challenge Church discrimination even where they do not challenge prohibitions on sexual behavior. Gay and lesbian movement culture has tended to support an ethical questioning of traditional assumptions that sex and love should always go together, such as in **marriage**.

In the early twentieth century a new science of sex, "sexology," was explored in Europe by sexologists such as Richard von Krafft-Ebing in Germany, Havelock Ellis in Britain, and Sigmund **Freud** in Austria. Many of these sexologists researched the sex lives and experiences of homosexuals and, together with writers, artists, and intellectuals such as the Bloomsbury Group in the United Kingdom, became campaigners for "sex reform," including education and more tolerant social attitudes. Magnus **Hirschfeld**, who developed a theory of people with same-sex desires being a third "intermediate sex" between men and women, founded the Scientific Humanitarian Committee in 1897, which campaigned against harsh punishment of same-sex sexual behavior. Hirschfeld organized the first Congress for Sexual Reform in 1921, which led to the formation of the World League for Sexual Reform and further congresses.

In the United States, there, too, were fledgling efforts to organize homosexuals, the most notable being the Society for Human Rights, chartered in the state of Illinois in 1924. Its founder, Henry Gerber, leaned heavily on his experience and knowledge of the reform efforts in Germany, but it quickly disbanded. After the Second World War, organizations and publications could still be found in Europe such as the magazine *Der Kreis*, but the first "homophile" (chosen because of its reference to "love" as opposed to "sex" in the word "homosexual") organization in the United States was the Mattachine Society, formed in 1950. It was followed by the Daughters of Bilitis for lesbians. Publicly reformist and liberal organizations advancing claims for tolerance emerged such as the Homosexual Law Reform Society in the United Kingdom, formed in 1958.

The earliest gay and lesbian movement in which those involved publicly invoked the label "gay" rather than "homosexual" was the "gay liberation movement." This is widely understood as having its symbolic beginning in the Stonewall Inn riots during three nights in June 1969 in which New York gay men, lesbians, and transvestites in the Stonewall bar in Greenwich Village fought back against police aggression. The emergence of gay liberation can be seen as associated with the political climate created by the civil rights movements of the 1960s and the political uprisings of the radical left in 1968, as well as with the sexual libertarianism of the 1960s radical counterculture.

Although second wave **feminism** began in the early 1960s and influenced gay liberationists' critique of "sexism," the **women's movement** in the early 1970s became a source of divisions within the gay and lesbian movement. Many women initially involved in gay liberation came to find a more sympathetic or significant political environment in the women's movement. Lesbian feminists participated in building a women's counterculture intended to challenge patriarchy—a social system of male domination. Hence during the 1970s and early 1980s, in many countries, there was both a gay liberationist movement and a lesbian feminist movement.

Lack of diversity within the movement in relation to racially defined groups, ethnicity, class, disability, and other forms of social difference has been apparent, particularly among movement leaders. The predominance of able-bodied white middle-class gay men has been subject to increasing criticism, just as **sexism** and homophobia have been criticized in socialist and anti-racist movements. However, some radicals in different social movements have been reaching out to each other for decades. For example, in 1970 at the Revolutionary People's Constitutional Convention in Philadelphia, Black Panther leader Huey Newton issued "A Letter from Huey to the Revolutionary Brothers and Sisters about the Women's Liberation and Gay Liberation," inviting homosexuals as "maybe … the most oppressed people" to the Convention to unite with other oppressed groups (Blasius & Phelan 1997: 404–5).

After the flourishing of gay liberation, new formal organizations emerged to spearhead movement activity. These tended to focus on claims for "non-discrimination," "equality," "rights," and (more recently) "human rights." But dynamics varied greatly even among Western countries. For example, in France during the early 1980s, the gay movement was generally lacking in formal organization, partly because of a republican context in which for historical reasons the state's sex laws did not heavily discriminate against same-sex behavior. By contrast, in Protestant northern European states, such as the United Kingdom and Denmark, which had experienced stronger social purity movements in the late nineteenth century, gay movements tended to become more organized to combat repressive laws. The lack of established community organizations in French lesbian and gay politics had disastrous consequences when **AIDS/HIV** emerged in the 1980s. Responses from the French gay community to press for public health and education campaigns, research, treatments, and funding, were not as strong as in the United Kingdom.

In poorer non-Western states, the gay and lesbian movements and organizations have appeared more recently. These have been shaped by HIV/AIDS necessities and Western lesbian and gay identities and forms of culture, typically in tension with indigenous forms. Thus, although the contemporary gay and lesbian movement is global, it is also highly differentiated.

Tensions over the appropriate form and direction of the movement are apparent in comparing the two leading international lesbian and gay non-governmental organizations. The International Lesbian and Gay Association (ILGA) is the only worldwide federation of national LGBT groups. Formed in the 1970s with a liberationist ethos, it is a democratic organization run largely by unpaid volunteer representatives from a variety of nations. By contrast, the International Gay and

Lesbian Human Rights Commission (IGLHRC), formed in the 1990s with an explicit human rights focus and more paid staff, is U.S.-based. Where ILGA struggled to find funding to establish itself as an effective lobbying group, IGLHRC has found resources and engaged strategically to influence human rights agendas. Both have contributed positively to transforming the lives of lesbian, gay, bisexual, and transgender (LGBT) people worldwide, but debates continue over who should lead such organizations and how. Critics, for instance, suggest that Western-led lesbian and gay movements misrepresent the identities and concerns of groups in the "developing world."

A key event for the global gay and lesbian movement occurred in July 2006. The International Conference on LGBT Rights was held (together with the first World Outgames) in Montreal, Canada. The *Declaration of Montreal* (http://www .declarationofmontreal.org) summarizes the demands of the international LGBT movement. On December 1, 2006, 54 states supported a statement by Norway to the United Nations's new Human Rights Council that called upon the Council to pay "due attention to human rights violations based on sexual orientation and gender identity" (p. 1). Additionally, an organization representing lesbian and gay people—ILGA-Europe (the European Region of ILGA), and German and Danish national organizations, were granted consultative status at Economic and Social Council of the United Nations (which had previously been held then lost by ILGA, and was already held by International Wages Due Lesbians). Together, these developments suggest gathering momentum for change at a global level.

A central issue for the worldwide gay and lesbian movement is how to negotiate a global political context structured by profound religious and cultural differences as well as legacies of Western colonialism, including profound economic and social inequalities between the global north and global south. One concern is that formerly colonized states have sought to forge national identities by emphasizing their difference from aspects of Western culture, including Western tolerance of homosexuality. For example, leaders of Trinidad and Tobago, in the Caribbean, and Zimbabwe in Africa have used rhetoric and policy changes that present homosexuality as a white, foreign threat to the family and nation while simultaneously denying the existence of indigenous black homosexuality. Another concern is that, within the context of the United States and United Kingdom military intervention in the Middle East, Islamist radicals represent human rights and gay freedom as Western degeneration. Thus, Western lesbian and gay activists defending sexual freedoms around the world risk contributing to the perception that human rights are simply an imposition of Western culture, so need to support and empower third world activists. *See also* Bisexuality; Colonialism/Postcolonialism and Sex; Gender Roles; Men's Movements; Politics; Religions, Western; Sexual Science/Sexology; Sodomy.

Further Reading: Adam, Barry D., Jan Willem Duyvendak, and André Krouwel, eds. *The Global Emergence of Gay and Lesbian Politics: National Imprints of a Worldwide Movement.* Philadelphia: Temple University Press, 1999; Alexander, M. Jacqui. "Not Just (Any) Body Can Be a Citizen: the Politics of Law, Sexuality and Postcoloniality in Trinidad and Tobago and the Bahamas." In *Sexualities and Society: A Reader,* edited by Jeffrey Weeks, Janet Holland and Matthew Waites, 174–82. Cambridge: Polity Press, 2003; Blasius, Mark, and Shane Phelan, eds. *We Are Everywhere: Historical Sourcebook in Gay and Lesbian Politics.* London: Routledge, 1997; Carter, David. *Stonewall: The Riots That Sparked the Gay Revolution.* New York: St. Martin's Press, 2004; Chauncey, George. *Gay New York.* London: Flamingo, 1995; Drucker, Peter. "Reinventing Liberation: Strategic Questions for Lesbian/Gay Movements." In *Different Rainbows,* edited by Peter Drucker, 207–20. London: Millivres Ltd., Gay Men's Press, 2000;

The International Gay and Lesbian Human Rights Commission (IGLHRC). http://www.iglhrc. org/site/iglhrc/. Timely regional information along with publications and resources; The International Lesbian and Gay Association (ILGA). http://www.ilga.org/. Includes world legal survey of state laws and links to regional ILGA bodies; Johnston, Jill. *Lesbian Nation: The Feminist Solution.* New York: Simon and Schuster, 1973; Martel, Frédéric. *The Pink and the Black: Homosexuals in France since 1968.* Stanford, CA: Stanford University Press, 1999; Phillips, Oliver. "Zimbabwean Law and the Production of a White Man's Disease." In *Sexualities and Society: A Reader,* edited by Jeffrey Weeks, Janet Holland, and Matthew Waites, 162–73. Cambridge: Polity Press, 2003; Sears, James. *Behind the Mask of the Mattachine.* Binghamton, NY: Haworth Press, 2006.

Matthew Waites

GENDER ROLES. A gender role consists of the expectations for behavior and qualities for people in a particular gender category within a particular culture. Gender roles are socially constructed—not determined by "nature"—and are developed by groups of people through interactions in personal encounters and in social institutions such as schools, churches, and the **media**. Different cultures have different gender roles related to sex and love, which change over time. Most cultures have the gender categories "man" and "woman," and many cultures include additional gender categories. For example, traditional Thai culture includes three gender categories: women, men, and *katoey* (coming from ancient words meaning "another kind of person"). *Katoeys'* anatomy is like men but they express themselves (through dress and speech) like women. Indonesia, too, has three genders: women (*wanita*), men (*pria*), and *waria*. *Waria* combines the "*wa*" from *wanita* and the "*ria*" from *pria*. In Hindu culture in India, there are women, men, and *hijras*. *Hijras* are usually born with male genitals, but participate in a religious initiation in which these are removed. Many Native American cultures also have more than two genders. For example, Navajo culture has traditionally included male and female *nádleehé* (meaning a person who is in a constant process of change) in addition to the categories of man and woman. Children become *nádleehé* because of the type of work tasks in which they are interested. For example, a female child who was interested in tasks usually performed by boys could become a *nádleehé,* and would then perform the same work tasks as boys and men. The existence of more than two genders influences how Navajo people have thought about **homosexuality** and **heterosexuality**. Sex between a woman and a male *nádleehé* and between a man and a female *nádleehé* have been considered homosexual and have been stigmatized. However, sex between a man and a male *nádleehé* or between a woman and a female *nádleehé* has been accepted.

Gender categories can change over time. For example, the traditional gender roles for *nádleehé* have disappeared on many reservations in the United States due to colonization; although today the term "Two Spirit" is used among some Native Americans. *Katoeys, waria, hijras,* and *nádleehé* are gender categories that have existed since before 1900. More recent categories have also emerged. For example, since the 1990s, the new term *genderqueer* has appeared in the United States. Some *genderqueer* people consider their gender to be a combination of man and woman. Others consider themselves to be neither man nor woman. Many people who identify as *genderqueer* question the very idea of gender categories.

There are varying cultural expectations regarding who can have sex with whom. In some cultures, people are expected not to have sex before they are married, while this is less important in other cultures. For example, in 1998, 60 percent of people in the Philippines said that sex before marriage was wrong, while less than one-in-ten Germans believed so (Widmer et al. 1998; cited in Galliano 2003: 173). Expectations regarding sex before marriage also differ for men and women. Women are often stigmatized or punished more harshly for sex before marriage than men. In Egypt, men gain pride and prestige *both* from their **premarital sex** experiences and from the virginity of their brides. Egyptian families go to great lengths to preserve girls' **virginity** through gender segregation and female circumcision (removing part or all of the labia minora, labia majora, and clitoris). This process, it is believed, will prevent girls from engaging in sex until marriage. In 1980, approximately 75 percent of Egyptian women were circumcised (Assad 1980; cited in Adler 1993: 49).

Cultures also vary concerning expectations related to sex among young people. For example, 84 percent of people in Ireland believed that sex before age 16 was always wrong; only one-third of the people in Sweden agreed (Widmer et al. 1998; cited in Galliano 2003: 173). Laws concerning the age at which young people can consent to sexual activity change over time, differentially affect men and women, and differ in regards to the type of sexual activity. For example, in Canada the *Criminal Code* outlawed intercourse with girls (boys were not mentioned) under 12. This age of consent for girls was raised to 14 shortly before 1900. It was not until 1988 that the law adopted gender-neutral language. The age of consent for anal sex, in contrast to other forms of sexual activity, is 18 years old, unless the partners are in a legal marriage. The higher age of consent for anal sex has affected gay men more strongly than others.

Expectations regarding sex between people of the same gender differ among cultures as well. Sixty-five percent of people in the Netherlands were accepting of sex between those of the same gender, while only 2 percent of those in Japan were accepting (Widmer et al. 1998; cited in Galliano 2003: 173). Same-sex behavior is illegal in at least 70 countries; in at least four of these countries, the punishment for homosexuality is death. Beliefs about sex among those of the same gender are often linked to how gender roles are constructed within a culture. For example, among the Sambia in Melanesia, young men are expected to perform fellatio on older men. This is based on the belief that young men must take in a certain amount of semen in order to conform to cultural expectations for **masculinity**. In Mexico and Brazil, a man's behavioral role in anal sex determines whether a man is considered homosexual. The penetrating partner is considered heterosexual, but the receiving partner is *maricone* (passive, like a woman).

What constitutes "sex" also varies. Almost all Caucasian heterosexual undergraduate students in the United States consider penile-vaginal insertion "having sex." Only about 80 percent consider penile–anal contact "having sex" and a mere 40 percent consider oral–genital contact "having sex" (Sanders & Reinisch 1999; cited in Galliano 2003: 174). There are also variations as to what constitutes homosexual behavior. In the United States, many (but not all) people believe that genital contact between women is "having sex." However, in Lesotho, Africa, "having sex" must involve a penis. While young women sometimes have relationships that include genital contact, this is not considered sex. During the 1950s, **marriage** to a man was compulsory for women but women also could choose another woman to be her *motsoalle*, or "special friend." These special relationships were celebrated with two ritual feasts held a year apart which involved dancing, eating, drinking, exchanging gifts, and validation of the commitment to each other from friends and family. The *motsoalle* relationship involved love, kissing, body rubbing, possessiveness, and sometimes genital contact, but were not considered sexual.

In some cultures, romantic love and marriage are separate concepts, while in others, these concepts are connected. Again, these concepts are often related to how a culture has constructed gender roles. For example, by 1900 in the United States, it was believed among white middle-class and wealthy people that romantic love should be the basis for marriage whereas earlier, major considerations were economic and social alliances between families. In Euro-American middle-class marriages, men have generally been older, better educated, and wealthier than their partners. African Americans have long based marriages on romantic love. Historical oppression of African Americans has led to lack of access to resources for both men and women, leading to greater economic parity among partners.

In Egypt, marriages are considered agreements between two families rather than individual choices and are not based on romantic love. Some Egyptian families select mates for their children and others are involved in approving their children's decisions. The bases for marriage choices are class, education, attractiveness, and moral factors. In some cultures, marriage and romantic love occur at the same time, but with different people. For example, in Brazil during the 1950s, most men lived with their wives and with another woman with whom they had romantic and sexual relationships. However, romantic and sexual relationships for married women outside of marriage were not accepted. In fact, men who suspected that their wives were having sex with someone else often murdered their wives in the name of "defense of honor."

In many cultures, each person is expected to marry one other person (monogamy). In many cultures, monogamous marriage is a heterosexual institution and most countries prohibit the marriage of two people of the same gender. In some cultures, a person can marry or partner with more than one person (**polygamy**), which often is related to gender roles. Polygyny, the most common form of polygamy, is when a man marries more than one woman. Polyandry is when a woman marries more than one man. In the United States, Mormons (members of the Church of Jesus Christ of Latter Day Saints) have a history of polygyny. Although polygamy was prohibited just before the beginning of the twentieth century, in 2003, an estimated 40,000 people lived in polygamous **families** (Galliano 2003: 137). In polygamous Mormon families, the man is expected to be authoritarian and to teach his family members religious values as well as resolve conflicts within the family. Wives are expected to manage the home and care for the children. Wives often develop strong relationships with one another and sometimes help find a new wife for the family. The man usually has a schedule for sleeping with the wives.

Another culture that includes polygamy is Tibetan society. While monogamy is the most common form of marriage, in some Western Tibetan groups such as Ladakh and the Nyinba, a woman sometimes marries several brothers. This prevents family lands from being divided. The woman is held accountable by society for the success or failure of the marriage. Toward the beginning of the marriage, the younger husband may be a child or adolescent. The woman initially treats him as a stepson and later initiates a sexual relationship with him. The younger husband often leaves the family to find a new wife.

Class status influences gender roles related to sex and love in various cultures. For instance, among wealthy Haitians, young men and women are able to socialize freely with one another at private country clubs, expensive restaurants, nightclubs, and through travel. In contrast, socialization among young middle-class men and women is not encouraged as parents worry that sexual interest among young men and women interferes with educational progress and career development. Among poor rural

Haitians, young women are not expected to socialize outside the home except for occasional social events during the day. Therefore, young men and women only have the opportunity to meet during village feasts or on the way to the market or other places. *See also* Childhood; Colonialism/Postcolonialism and Sex; Cross Dressing/Drag; Dating; Indigenous Peoples; Men's Movement; Pederasty; Romance; Sexism; Women's Movement.

Further Reading: Adler, Leonore Loeb, ed. *International Handbook on Gender Roles.* Westport, CT: Greenwood Press, 1993; Assad, Marie. "Female Circumcision in Egypt: Social Implications, Current Research, and Prospects for Change." *Studies in Family Planning* 11, no. 1 (1980): 3–16; Baird, Vanessa. *The No-Nonsense Guide to Sexual Diversity.* London: New Internationalist Publications, 2001; Beyrer, Chris. *War in the Blood: Sex, Politics, and AIDS in South East Asia.* London: Zed, 1998; Galliano, Grace. *Gender: Crossing Boundaries.* Belmont, CA: Wadsworth/Thomson Learning, 2003; Kendall, Kathryn. "Women in Lesotho and the (Western) Construction of Homophobia." In *Female Desires: Same-Sex Relations and Transgender Practices Across Cultures,* edited by Evelyn Blackwell and Saskia E. Wieringa, 157–78. New York: Columbia University Press, 1999; Lang, Sabine. "Various Kinds of Two-Spirit People: Gender Variance and Homosexuality in Native American Communities." In *Two-Spirit People: Native American Gender Identity, Sexuality, and Spirituality,* edited by Sue-Ellen Jacobs, Wesley Thomas, and Sabine Lang, 100–118. Urbana: University of Illinois Press, 1997; Lindsey, Linda L. *Gender Roles: A Sociological Perspective.* 4th ed. Upper Saddle River, NJ: Pearson Prentice Hall, 2005; Pilon, Marilyn. *Canada's Legal Age of Consent to Sexual Activity.* Parliamentary Information and Research Service, 2001. http://www.parl.gc.ca/information/library/PRBpubs/prb993-e.htm; Saunders, Stephanie A., and June M. Reinisch. "Would You Say You Had Sex If...?" *Journal of the American Medical Association* 281, no. 3 (1999): 276; Transgender Resources (& Much More). http://www.gendertalk.com/info/resource.shtml. Resources related to many different gender and transgender topics; Widmer, E. D., J. Treas, and R. Newcomb. "Attitudes toward Nonmarital Sex in 24 Countries." *Journal of Sex Research* 34, no. 4 (1998): 349–358.

Kathleen Rands

H

HETEROSEXUAL MARRIAGE.   *See* Marriage, Heterosexual

HETEROSEXUALITY.   Heterosexuality is the emotional and sexual attraction for those of a different gender—a sexual **desire** between a man and woman that satisfies an instinctual need. Heterosexual activities do not always lead to procreation, but provide opportunities for sexual release and interpersonal intimacy. Although emotions are usually associated with sexual arousal, among different cultures, backgrounds, beliefs, and understanding differ from one another and influence heterosexual practices within a community.

Heterosexuality is often assumed to be the sexual norm, but sexual orientation falls on a continuum from exclusively homosexual to exclusively heterosexual experiences. While some conclude the sexual preference is shaped by the culture and beliefs, the hormonal and genetic contributions to a person's sexual orientation cannot be overlooked. From the biological perspective, the increased secretion of the sex hormones from the adrenal glands is believed to help determined an individual's sexual orientation, although it is apparent much later in development. In fact, biologists suggest that heterosexuality, like **homosexuality** and **bisexuality**, is determined by our genes and hormonal influences even during prenatal stage. Although some argue that family and environmental influences have very little impact on sexual orientation, others believe that the social process of learning and modeling, social expectations, cultural values, traditions and peer pressure are important factors. The American Psychological Association states that heterosexuality is a combination of social, cognitive, and psychological factors that there is no one single cause for heterosexuality (or homosexuality) and that these factors shape our sexual identity at a very early age.

Partnering with a different gender for sexual activities and procreation, wherein human beings are categorized as either male or female, conforms to the idea of hetero-normativity. Here social institutions, ranging from the family to the **workplace**, assume such heterosexual pairing and any relationship outside this dichotomy is seen as abnormal. Because most religions and cultures believe the primary purpose of coitus is for procreation, it appeared only "natural" to have two genders that complemented each other, with each assuming particular **gender roles**. Although specific roles vary widely across cultures, the hetero-normative assumption appears within most cultures, including in traditional myths, rituals, and even language.

While most would agree that sex within heterosexual marriage is virtuous, different levels of acceptance for various sexual activities are found in different **religions**. Sex is not considered a shameful or a sinful activity if it is conducted in a **marriage** according to the Jewish law. Christianity complemented the Jewish understanding that marriage is monogamous. However, some extremist Christian sects such as the Esseenes, the Shakers, or the Nazareans regard sex as an inherently sinful activity and that heterosexual relations should be avoided altogether if one is to advance spiritually. In contrast, Hinduism considers sex as art as seen in Indian literature like the *Kamasutra* (Aphorism of Love) and sculptures carved on Indian temples that suggest a liberated society where people deal with sex openly. (Although some believe these sculptures serve as a reminder to the people to leave the feeling of sexual lust before entering the temple.)

Beliefs and understanding about heterosexuality vary widely across cultures. Within the tribal community of the Yap Island of the United States, there was a strong negative attitude toward sexuality. Intercourse was believed to cause weaknesses in men while, using similarly reasoning that health and sex were linked, women were strongly enjoined to avoid intercourse during **pregnancy** and afterward for several years. So, too, for the Manus of Papua New Guinea. Sexual activity of husband and wife is considered shameful and treated with the strictest secrecy. Women were so guarded about their menstruations that men denied their wives ever have their monthly cycles. Heterosexual relations are also treated with fear and anger among the Dobu of Papua New Guinea, where husbands are believed to be most vulnerable to female sorcery during intercourse.

Other cultures are sex positive. In the Polynesian society of the Central Pacific self-**masturbation** is encouraged at an early age and **premarital sex** is generally accepted. Often, song and dance expresses eroticism. The Mangaians of the Cook Islands also encourage premarital intercourse and it is important that the male satisfies his female partners, proving virility through the number of **orgasms** achieved.

Rules of sexual modesty, however, are observed everywhere and most cultures require that genitalia be covered or at least partially covered. Yet, again, what part of the body may be considered erotic, varies among cultures. For example, female breasts are considered sexually arousing in American and European cultures but for the Mangaians breasts are solely for feeding the babies and are not eroticized. However, women of the East Bay wear skirts that cover the thighs because these are considered erotic. Some females enhanced the eroticism by tattooing the inner part of the thigh. As for men, oiling their toned and tanned bodies and tucking scented leaves and branches in their clothing communicates sensual messages to the woman. In Middle Eastern societies and in many Islamic communities, women must cover themselves from head to toe. Wearing the Hijab, only the eyes are revealed, which are sometimes even shielded by a piece of thin cloth. And, in the Melanesian society of the southwest Pacific, women wear a shawl over their shoulders and breasts at night because it is believed that this is the apex of male sexual thoughts.

Beginning in the late 1940s and 1950s, there was a revolution in social awareness about human sexuality in the West. Surveys of modern sexual behavior by Alfred C. **Kinsey** and his associates followed a decade later by William Masters and Virginia Johnson's ground-breaking study, *Human Sexual Response,* revealed the nature and scope of heterosexual practices of Americans. At the same time, the development of antibiotics removed the threat of **sexually transmitted infections**, like gonorrhea and syphilis, while the availability of the contraceptive pill removed the threat of unwanted pregnancy.

Relaxation of sexual **censorship** resulted in more explicit heterosexuality in cultures, such as in **popular music** and **cinema**, as well as frank depictions of heterosexual activities through **pornography** in magazines, books, and films. Books with erotic content increased during the 1960s, leading to bans and protests. *Lady Chatterley's Lover* by D. H. Lawrence, for example, was confiscated and challenged in court. Non-fiction sex manuals, like *Sex and the Single Girl*, also appeared, as did explicit over-the-counter magazines such as *Playboy*, *Fanny Hill*, and *Hustler*. By the 1970s, people were freer to discuss their sexuality, engage in premarital sex, practice "wife-swapping," enjoy masturbation, and indulge in **pornography**. The traditional belief that sex between men and women is solely for procreation eroded.

Nevertheless, such scientific, technological, and social changes were not celebrated by all. Further, the increase in sexual transmitted infections along with the advent of **AIDS/HIV** created a more restrained sexual climate during the last three decades of the twentieth century. Heterosexual danger eclipsed heterosexual pleasure. The increase of sexual diseases alarmed countries and its citizens, thus inviting debates on abstinence-only **sex education** along with calls for a return to traditional sexual values such as **virginity** and **celibacy** and the return of the concept of romantic love. International conferences and meetings also were held to curb the alarming increases in diseases and **advertising** for and use of condoms were encouraged. In Japan, for instance, oral contraceptives are widely used and condoms account for 80 percent of **birth control** use. Japan also has comparably lower rates of AIDS than other countries.

With the increasing use of the **Internet**, beginning in the late 1990s, there has been an increase of cyber sex where one indulges in heterosexual activities. Although forms of "safe sex" behavior such as visiting different chat rooms or viewing **pornography on the Internet** is widely practiced, it also can lead to physical contact with various health and safety risks. *See also* Families; Indigenous Peoples; Romance; Sexual Science/ Sexology; Sociobiology.

Further Reading: Bhattacharyya, Gargi. *Sexuality and Society: An Introduction*. London and New York: Routledge, 2002; Ember, Carol R., and Melvin Ember. *Encyclopedia of Sex and Gender, Man and Women in the World's Cultures*. New York: Springer, 2004; Hascombe, Gillian E., and Morton Humphries. *Heterosexuality*. London: Gay Men's Press, 1987; Holmberg, Carl B. *Sexualities and Popular Culture*. Thousand Oaks, CA: Sage, 1998; Jackson, Stevi, ed. *Heterosexuality in Question*. Thousand Oaks, CA: Sage, 1999; Katz, Jonathan N. *The Invention of Heterosexuality*. New York: Penguin, 1996; Weeks, Vernon J. *Sexuality*. London and New York: Routledge, 1986.

Wah-Yun Low

HIRSCHFELD, MAGNUS (1868–1935). Magnus Hirschfeld, a German physician and author, was a pioneer of sexual research as well as a champion for the rights of persons of all sexualities and for related issues such as access to **abortion** and prevention of **sexually transmitted infections**. His many publications and public lectures, as well as an appearance in the first motion picture centering on the topic of **homosexuality**, made him a worldwide public figure. Hirschfeld's most original scientific contribution may be his *Zwischenstufenlehre* (theory of intermediate steps), which argued that every human being was composed of a unique combination of male and female aspects. Hirschfeld founded the *Wissenschaftlich-Humanitäre Komitee* (Scientific and Humanitarian Committee or SHC) in 1897 to fight for repeal of Paragraph 175 of the German Penal Code, criminalizing sexual relations between men. He published the first scientific journal dealing with intermediate sexuality, the *Jahrbuch für sexuelle*

Zwischenstufen (Journal of Sexual Intermediate Types), 1899–1923, and, in 1919, founded the *Institut für Sexuelwissenschaft* (Institute for Sexual Science) in Berlin, which was a major center for **sexual science** until destroyed by the Nazis in 1933.

Hirschfeld was part of the second generation of pioneers in the study of sexuality that included Karl Heinrich Ulrichs and Richard von Krafft-Ebing. By his time a gay subculture was developing in many European and North American cities. The fact that Hirschfeld established his medical practice in the Charlottenberg district of Berlin, center of that city's gay underworld, plus his status as a homosexual and, possibly, a transvestite, afforded him unique access and insight into people of differing sexualities.

The movement to win civil rights for homosexuals, in which Hirschfeld played a major role, was contemporaneous with a number of other reform efforts in Germany, ranging from the women's suffrage movement to macrobiotic diets and nudism, known collectively as the *Lebensreformbewegung* (Life Reform Movement). Hirschfeld was active in many of these causes, including the rights of unmarried mothers and their children, detection and treatment of venereal disease, legalization of **abortion**, and medical care for the poor.

The primary goal of SHC was the repeal of Paragraph 175 and its first activity in this regard was to prepare a petition with signatures of over 900 prominent Germans arguing for its repeal. This petition failed. In fact, Paragraph 175 remained until 1969. In keeping with Hirschfeld's belief that education and understanding would overcome prejudice against homosexuals (his personal motto was *"per scientiam ad justitiam,"* i.e., "through science to justice"), the committee also prepared and distributed educational materials. The first was the 1901 brochure *Was soll das Volk vom dritten Geschlecht wissen?* (What should people know about the third sex?); it is estimated that over 50,000 copies were eventually distributed. The SHC was unusual among homosexual rights organizations in including both male and female members. Notably, Hirschfeld joined Dr. Helene Stoecker, later a director of the SHC, in speaking out against the proposed extension, in 1909, of Paragraph 175 to outlaw same-sex relations between women.

Hirschfeld had considered a career as a journalist before entering medicine and research. A tireless writer and lecturer, he was often referred to in the popular **media** as "The Einstein of Sex." Among the first of over 500 published works was the 1897 pamphlet *Sappho und Socrates, Wie erklärt sich die Liebe der Männer und Frauen zu Personen des eigenen Geschlechts?* (Sappho and Socrates: How can one explain the love of men and women for people of their own sex?). Written with Max Spohr under the pseudonym "Dr med. Th. Ramien," this pamphlet argued for the acceptance of homosexuality and claimed, in the preface, to have been written at the request of a homosexual military officer who committed suicide on the eve of his marriage. In 1904, Hirschfeld published *Berlin's Drittes Geschlecht* (Berlin's Third Sex), a popular book about the primarily male homosexual subculture of Berlin. The term "third sex" refers to a popular conception of the time that homosexuals constituted a sex distinct from male and female. Hirschfeld, however, did not consistently endorse this point of view and, in *Zwischenstufenlehre*, argued against discrete categorizations of sexuality, although he continued to employ the concept because of its current popularity.

Hirschfeld introduced and popularized the term "transvestite" in *Die Transvestiten* (The Transvestites, 1910), asserting that transvestitism was a sexual variation independent of sexual preference. His greatest work may be *Die Homosexualität des Mannes und des Weibes* (The Homosexuality of Men and Women, 1914). Based on case histories and questionnaires collected from over 10,000 people, this pioneering, well-received work addressed the biological and sociological aspects of homosexuality along with its history in different parts of the world, including Europe, America, North Africa, and Asia.

The fate of Hirschfeld's ground-breaking Institute for Sexual Science (ISS) demonstrates how social and political climate can impact scientific research and social reform. Homosexual culture was largely suppressed in Germany during World War I, but the period that followed (often referred to as Weimar Germany) was marked by greater sexual freedom, including the development of openly gay subcultures in many cities. The ISS, which he gave to the German government in 1924, reflected Hirschfeld's broader interests in sexual matters. It offered marriage counseling, venereal disease treatment, **sex education**, vast collections of research materials, and a museum of sexuality. At its peak, over 20,000 people from all over the world visited annually and over 1800 consultations per year were performed. When the Nazis came to power, the ISS was one of their first targets, both because of the subject matter and because of Hirschfeld's status as a Jew, homosexual, and leftist (some Nazis also had Institute files). The ISS was broken into on May 6, 1933, and much of the collections removed; these were burnt in a public ceremony four days later, a process filmed by the Nazis and which appeared in contemporary newsreels (viewed by Hirschfeld himself in a Paris cinema). The building was then given to the Nazi Association of Jurists and Lawyers.

The critical and popular 1919 film *Anders als die Andern* (Different from the Others) also engendered great opposition and was banned from public exhibition in some cities. Directed by Richard Oswald and co-written with Hirschfeld, this was the first film whose primary subject was homosexuality. The story concerns a violinist (played by Conrad Veidt) who falls in love with his male pupil, is blackmailed by a former lover, and commits suicide after serving a jail sentence. Hirschfeld appears as a lecturer on behalf of homosexual rights.

Although his primary work was conducted in Germany, Hirschfeld traveled extensively. His first world travels predated his medical career: he attended the Columbian World Exposition in Chicago in 1892 as a newspaper reporter, and visited Italy and North Africa before returning home to Germany. He made a study tour of the USSR in 1926 and a world lecture tour in 1930, which included the United States, Japan, China, India, Egypt, and Palestine. The latter is chronicled in his *Die Weltreise eines sexualforschers* (The World Journey of a Sexologist, 1933). When Hirschfeld returned to Europe in 1932 he did not return to Germany due to the political climate. Instead, he traveled through Greece, Austria, and Switzerland before finally setting in Nice, France, where he died in 1935.

Hirschfeld participated in many activities that facilitated worldwide communication among physicians and scholars. In 1913, he addressed the International Congress of Physicians in London, which led to the formation of the British Society for Sexual Psychology in 1914, and to a SHC-like group in Vienna a year earlier. He also founded the International Conferences for Sexual Reform, the first of which was held in 1921 in Berlin, and the World League for Sexual Reform in 1928. The latter had worldwide membership of over 130,000 at its peak. *See also* Gay and Lesbian Movement; Politics; Sodomy; Transgender/Transsexual.

Further Reading: Gordon, Mel. *Voluptuous Panic: The Erotic World of Weimar Berlin.* Los Angeles: Feral House, 2003; Hirschfeld, Magnus. *The Transvestites: The Erotic Drive to Cross-Dress.* Translated by Michael A. Lombardi-Nash. Amherst, NY: Prometheus Books, 1991; Hirschfeld, Magnus. *The Homosexuality of Men and Women.* Translated by Michael A. Lombardi-Nash. Amherst, NY: Prometheus Books, 2002; The Institute of Sexual Science, 1919–1933. Magnus Hirschfeld Society, Berlin. http://www.hirschfeld.in-berlin.de/institut/en/index1024_ie.html

(accessed July 7, 2006). Online exhibition of photographs and text regarding the history of Hirschfeld's Institute for Sexual Science, 2002; Wolff, Charlotte, M. D. *Magnus Hirschfeld: A Portrait of a Pioneer in Sexology*. London: Quartet Books, 1986.

Sarah Boslaugh

HIV. *See* AIDS/HIV

HOMOSEXUAL MARRIAGE. *See* Marriage, Homosexual

HOMOSEXUALITY. Homosexuality, expressing sex and love between same-genders, has conceptually framed same-sex **desire** in some industrialized countries during the twentieth century. Between 1.5 percent and 2 percent of female population and between 3 percent and 4 percent of male population in the world are exclusively homosexual (Mackay 2000). Although the same-sex sexual (and ritual) contacts have occurred throughout history, it was not until the mid to late nineteenth century that those who were sexually attracted to the same gender were defined as "homosexual." As the construction of homosexuality changed from same-sex behavior to sexual identity, medicalization, particularly in the form of **psychoanalysis**, joined criminalization as typical societal responses. The twentieth century, not coincidentally, also witnessed the emergence of the homosexual rights movement, as gay men and lesbians began organizing to rescind laws and change medical opinions. Nevertheless, in some Middle Eastern countries same-gender sexual contact still can result in death penalty and homosexuality was only recently depathologized in Japan, South Korea, and China. Relatively few countries prohibit discrimination on the basis of sexual orientation or sanction same-sex **marriage**.

The modern homosexual emancipation movement began in 1897, when Magnus **Hirschfeld**, a Berlin doctor, founded the Scientific and Humanitarian Committee. The group presented a petition to the German Parliament for repealing Paragraph 175 of the Penal Code, enacted in 1871, prohibiting sexual conducts between men. This political movement spread throughout Europe and North America. In the Netherlands, J. A. Schorer, a liberal jurist established the Dutch Scientific Humanitarian Committee, to repeal Article 248. Edward Carpenter, a homosexual activist, was active in the British Society for the Study of Sex Psychology, founded in 1914 under Hirschfeld's influence. After World War I, the number of homosexual associations such as Freundschaft (friendship) and Klub der Freunde und Freundinnen (male and female) friends clubs increased, while the first state-chartered (albeit short-lived) Chicago Society for Human Rights was established in 1924 by Henry Gerber, who had visited Berlin following the war. There, too, was an increase in gay and lesbian novels, most notably *The Well of Loneliness* written in 1928 by Radclyffe Hall, an English novelist. Banned in many cities and countries, her novel was based on the theories of Richard von Krafft-Ebing, a German psychiatrist, and Havelock Ellis, an English sexologist.

In contrast to many Western societies, there had been no prohibition of homosexuality in most Eastern societies. In countries such as Thailand, those engaged in same-sex behavior were not considered deviant or persecuted. In Japan, same-sex sexual intercourse was not considered abnormal until at least the late nineteenth century (under the influence of European **colonialism**).

The worldwide Great Depression and the rise of fascism in Germany and other countries severely impacted the fledgling gay and lesbian movement, which largely ceased to exist by the mid-1930s. Oppressed liberality, together with the economic crisis, also restricted women's freedom to live and love as they liked. In 1933, Germany, though efforts to repeal Paragraph 175 a few years earlier nearly succeeded, banned homosexual-rights organizations, and Hirschfeld's Institute of Sexual Science was demolished with its valuable collection mostly destroyed. However, communities of homosexuals and social groups continued to flourish in Europe, Asia, and the Americas.

Studies into homosexuality continued throughout the twentieth century. Sigmund **Freud** suggested that sexual inversion including homosexuality was not innate, but a matter of object-choice in a psychic mechanism, which resulted in the treatment of homosexuals through extensive **psychotherapy**. However, unlike most medical authorities of the time, Hirschfeld argued that homosexuality originated from prenatal biological factors as did Havelock Ellis, in his book *Sexual Inversion*, which helped frame the arguments of the gay and lesbian movement. In 1948, *Sexual Behavior in the Human Male* had a worldwide impact. Alfred **Kinsey**, an American biologist, reported that 4 percent of white males were exclusively homosexual throughout their lives, 10 percent of the males were more or less exclusively homosexual, 30 percent had at least incidental homosexual experience or reactions over at least a three year period, and 37 percent of the total male population had at least some homosexual experience to the point of orgasm. Five years later, the companion volume, *Sexual Behavior in the Human Female*, disclosed that 2 percent of the females were exclusively homosexual, between 2 and 6 percent of the unmarried females and less than 1 percent of the married females had been somewhat exclusively homosexual, and 13 percent of the females had homosexual experience to **orgasm**.

Understanding of homosexuality was also influenced by the work of Evelyn Hooker, an American psychologist. Her research suggested that homosexuality, as a clinical entity, did not exist and its forms were as varied as are those of **heterosexuality**. Based on her investigation, with members of the Mattachine Society as subjects, she found that no significant psychological differences could be found between homosexuals and heterosexuals. Nevertheless, the prevailing thinking about homosexuality continued to be contoured by psychoanalysts who attributed homosexuality to pre-Oedipal conflicts.

In the same period, homosexual novels (for decades largely an underground phenomenon) gained greater prominence. In Japan, Yukio Mishima wrote *Kamen-no-kokuhaku* (The Confession of a Mask), a largely autobiographical work, and *Kinjiki* (Forbidden Colors), which featured a homosexual character. *Kamen-no-kokuhaku* was at first met with both applause and antipathy, and then acclaimed widely. Post-war America also found major publishers producing the works of Gore Vidal (*The City and the Pillar*), Truman Capote (*Other Voices, Other Rooms*), and Mary Renault (*The Charioteer*).

With the advent of the Cold War, the persecution of lesbians and gay men (as security risks) in the United States and England brought paradoxical effects. Although it had a chilling impact on the immediate post-war liberal environment, it also helped to foster awareness and identity among homosexuals, which resulted in the resurgence of the "homophile movement" in Europe and North America. As a result of this movement, England's Wolfenden Committee published its report, in 1957, recommending homosexual behavior between consenting adults in private should no longer be a criminal offence. This eventually resulted in the passage of the Sexual Offences

Act in 1967, decriminalizing male homosexual acts in private between two men. Two years later, Illinois became the first state in America to decriminalize homosexual behavior.

In China, whose society was traditionally tolerant of homosexuality, communism brought a relentless campaign to eradicate "decadent Western" homosexuality. During the Cultural Revolution (1966 to 1976) this oppression intensified as many lesbians and gay men were humiliated, tortured, and executed. In Vietnam, the concept of homosexuality came into wider use with the introduction of Western sexology in the 1950s and 1960s; lesbianism was found at all levels of the society and lesbian couples were tolerated by the society as "friends." In Japan, as early as 1952, the Adonisu-kai (Adonis Society) networked homosexual men through its publication, *Adonis*. Though its editors were aware of other publications such as *ONE*, a homophile U.S. magazine, unlike the homophile movement in America, it was not oriented to publicly organize gay men but to network them underground.

Although the **media** had been largely indifferent to polite protests of homophile bodies in United States during the 1950s and 1960s, once angry homosexuals stood up for themselves through violent protests, professional and public attitudes began to change. In 1969, police raided the Stonewall Inn and 200 working-class patrons (drag queens, gay men from developing countries, and a handful of lesbians) assembled in front of the bar and riots broke out in Greenwich Village. Along with other protest movements during the late 1960s, the "gay liberation movement" had a major impact on how professionals understood homosexuality.

The American Psychiatric Association (APA) was also not immune from such a trend. Though homosexuality appeared from the first issue of its nomenclature, *Diagnostic and Statistical Manual of Mental Disorders* (DSM), published in 1952, two decades later, in 1973, after three years of struggle within the association, the APA board of trustees deleted homosexuality, per se, from the *DSM-II*. The board, however, left room to treat patients uneasy about their sexuality under the classification of "sexual disturbance disorder" ("ego-dystonic homosexuality") from 1980 through 1986.

Homosexual organizations mushroomed worldwide during the late 1970s, impacting religious institutions as well as schools and the **workplace**. Many gay-centered Jewish organizations, for example, were established, including the World Congress of Gay and Lesbian Jewish Organizations. Although an increasing number of religious groups have changed their position regarding its sinfulness, in countries dominated by Islamic fundamentalism the situation remains difficult and dangerous for homosexuals and **transgender** persons. The 1979 Iran Revolution gave birth to the Islamic republic of Iran, where 4000 homosexuals have since been executed. In 1997, Qatar police deported gay foreign workers because they were gay. United Arab Emirates authorities, in 2005, arrested 26 men for attending a "gay wedding ceremony."

As the political, psychological, and religious changes occurred, biological study into homosexuality continued. In 1991, Simon LeVay, an American cerebral anatomist, published research showing that interstitial nuclei of the anterior hypothalamus is dimorphic with sexual orientation—at least in men—suggesting that sexual orientation has a biological substrate. Two years later, Dean Hamer, an American molecular geneticist, suggested that a gene at the edge of an X chromosome may contribute to sexual orientation. Sibling studies have supported these research findings. The brothers of homosexual men, for instance, have a 22 percent chance of being homosexual, while the brothers of heterosexual men have only 4 percent chance. The sisters of lesbians, similarly, have an enhanced chance of being lesbian. Further, concordance rate for identical twins is higher than the rate for fraternal twins. In one study (Bailey, Dunne, and Martin 2000) the rates were 24 percent for female monozygotic twins versus 10.5 percent for same-sex dizygotic twins and 18.2 percent for opposite-sex dizygotic twins; and 20 percent for male monozygotic twins versus 0 percent for same-sex dizygotic twins and 10.5 percent opposite-sex dizygotic twins. A substantial number of studies also have reported homosexual men tend to have more elder brothers than do heterosexual men. Researchers hypothesize that some women develop antibodies to male-specific antibodies with male fetuses, and that these antibodies affect the development following male fetuses in such a way as to heighten the likelihood of homosexuality.

The advent of **AIDS** as well as the rise of conservative governments resulted in policing homosexuality, which paradoxically politicized more homosexuals and their allies. Local and global movements driven by the AIDS crisis have progressed. In Japan, the AIDS crisis promoted gay youth to organize. The first gay-rights lawsuit against the Tokyo Metropolitan Government, having rejected the Japan Association for the Lesbian & Gay Movement's (OCCUR) overnight study meeting at a city-run youth hostel, was brought by OCCUR in 1991. The Tokyo High Court ruled, in 1997, that the city government should have given due consideration to homosexuals as a minority group, and its indifference and ignorance would not be tolerated.

In 1992, the World Health Organization deleted homosexuality out of the tenth revision of the International Classification of Diseases. In China, later in the 1990s, HIV/AIDS issues accounted for scholars paying attention to homosexuality. A condom for gay men, named "tonzhi" (it originally meant "comrade," but has now been appropriated to mean "gay"), is on the market.

Meanwhile, the South African Constitution banning discrimination based on sexual orientation was enacted in 1994 and Ecuador's new constitution, established in 1998, prescribed freedom from discrimination based on sexual orientation. During the first year of this century, in Germany, the few remaining gay survivors of the Holocaust became eligible for compensation. In South Korea, although one lesbian took legal action against her ex-partner to distribute the previous partner's property to her based on their de fact marriage, the court rejected the plea in 2004, saying the Korean Constitution provides that marriage is for a man and woman. Following the Netherlands, Belgium, and Spain, Canada became the fourth country to legalize same-sex marriage in 2005. The UK's Civil Partnership Act enforced in 2005 gives same-sex partners a legal guarantee and social admittance. *See also* Bisexuality; Gender Roles; Indigenous Peoples; Morality and Ethics; Politics; Religions, Eastern; Religions, Western; Sexual Science/Sexology; Sociobiology; Women's Movement.

Further Reading: Bailey, J. Michael, P. Michael Dunne, and G. Nicholas Martin. "Genetic and Environmental Influences on Sexual Orientation and Its Correlates in an Australian Twin Sample." *Journal of Personality and Social Psychology* 78, no. 3 (2000): 524–36; The International Gay and Lesbian Human Rights Commission. http://www.iglhrc.org/site/ iglhrc. An NGO aiming to secure the full enjoyment of the human rights of all people and communities subject to discrimination or abuse on the basis of sexual orientation or expression, gender identity or expression, and/or HIV status, July 2006; The International Lesbian and Gay Association. http://www.ilga.org. Much information on homosexuality in the world including the world legal map on LGBT legislations, July 2006; LeVay, Simon. *Queer Science: The Use and Abuse of Research into Homosexuality*. Cambridge, MA: MIT Press, 1996; Mackay, Judith. *The Penguin Atlas of Human Sexual Behavior*. New York: Penguin Putnam, 2000; Murray, Stephen O., and Will Roscoe. *Boy-Wives and Female Husbands: Studies of African Homosexualities*. New York: St. Martin's Press, 1998; Sullivan, Gerald, and Peter Jackson. *Gay and Lesbian Asia: Culture,*

Identity, Community. Binghamton, NY: Harrington Park Press, 2001; Swidler, Arlene. *Homosexuality and World Religions.* Valley Forge, PA: Trinity Press International, 1993; Tamagne, Florence. 2004. *A History of Homosexuality in Europe.* New York: Agora, 2004; Whitaker, Brian. *Unspeakable Love: Gay and Lesbian Life in the Middle East.* Berkeley: University of California Press, 2006.

Akihiko Komiya

HUMOR. Humor has generally been understood in the twentieth and twenty-first centuries as a practice that elicits amusement, entertainment, or laughter. Despite a common misconception that it is simply about "good times" or "fun," humor is a very important aspect of meaning-making in every society, especially when it is used to articulate and experiment with notions of love and sexuality. Depending on local customs and global influences, themes of love and sexuality in humor serve as a context for shaping, transmitting, and reinforcing categories of gender, class, race, and ethnicity. Conversely, these categories play a great role in influencing the appreciation, interpretation, and function of all forms of humor. Although humor itself is universal, there is not a universal joke. Because humor concerned with love and sexuality fulfills different functions for various people in diverse locations, what is amusing or funny in one context may not be so in another. This distinction is particularly evident when sexuality or love is the subject of humor. Humor is always contingent upon the changing values, beliefs, norms, attitudes, and stereotypes of any given culture and society.

Because it requires an ability to think critically about relationships within the environment, sexual humor has subversive and libratory potential. It can help raise social consciousness, reveal new perspectives, suggest better political alternatives, and bring about a more enlightened understanding among people. On the other hand, sexual humor is also a method of upholding cruel and hostile sentiments, oppressive social conditions, and stereotypical cultural assumptions. Among its many forms, humor is communicated through exaggeration, invective, understatement, cynicism, twists of logic, irony, disguise, deception, and appeal to superiority. These techniques are used in jokes, puns, tricks, drawings, anecdotes, skits, symbols, gestures, and countless other acts that are usually intended for an audience. Regardless of its purpose, reception, form(s), or techniques, humor is a powerful practice that impacts human relationships and carries social and political consequences.

Humor speaks volumes about the particular historical context in which it has been produced and circulated. Uses of sexual humor in vaudeville and burlesque theater, for example, provide a strong commentary about the racial, ethnic, gender, and class tensions within twentieth century America. During these times, the stage became a forum for humorous representations of gendered ethnic caricatures. For instance, humor was a method of representing Irish characters as belligerent drunks who would be too intoxicated to have sex with their wives; the Italians were portrayed as irresponsibly promiscuous who procreated too much; the Dutch were laughed at as sexually conservative and dumb; the Blacks were framed as lazy and having an overtly activated sexual drive; and the Jews were made fun of as being too clever, manipulative, dishonest, and sexually unskilled. While this humor emphasized the superiority of Whites and non-immigrant Americans, it was also a highly gendered commentary on heterosexual relationships. By suggesting that ethnic men constantly had problems with women, vaudeville and burlesque shows effectively staged women as nagging and demanding wives, as jealous and irrational girlfriends, as controlling and seductive vamps, and ultimately as regular victims of men's infidelities and broken promises. The most obvious interpretation of some of the American vaudeville and burlesque humor during that era was the stage as an outlet for resentment and aggression against the waves of new immigrants. As the humor of the day suggests, these people were seen as ethnic and racial "others." The fact that much of the humor reflected a misogynistic expression of heterosexual norms was also telling of an urban environment that was growing increasingly hostile to women and the new divisions of labor.

The relationship between humor and hostility can be traced back to Sigmund **Freud**. Extending his work on **psychoanalysis** to the arena of humor, Freud suggested that jokes provide people a socially appropriate opportunity to release our hostile and aggressive impulses toward others. He believed that the jokes of his day not only underscored an anti-Semitic climate, but more importantly were a disguised expression of otherwise repressed sexual feelings that were policed by late-nineteenth and early-twentieth-century European social prohibitions. Freud suggested that jokes, like dreams, are a direct route to the unconscious of repressed wishes for all of our sexual urges and desires for sexual pleasure. According to this theory, the pleasure principle makes us want objects that feel good, while the reality principle tells us to channel the energy elsewhere. Thus, since humans can't act on all of their sexual urges and aggressions, most desires for sexual pleasure become sublimated or repressed into a particular place in the mind. Jokes, including seemingly innocent slips of the tongue, represented to Freud a direct pathway to this place in the mind. Despite the limitations he placed on the very broad genre of humor, Freud's analysis of repressed sexuality has had a far-reaching effect into the social analysis of humor in much subsequent scholarship.

Freud remains relevant to contemporary understandings of social relationships. Male-to-male "jokelore" in Russian cities and villages of the Cold War era was largely aimed at relieving the tensions caused by either unfulfilled sexual **desire** or failed heterosexual relationships. Analysis of Soviet and post Soviet jokes suggests that humor, in this part of the world, was (and in many ways still is) a means of both asserting male control and distancing oneself from painful, sensitive realities. These everyday problems include: impotence (social and physical); lack of resources and opportunities (space, money, food); responsibilities (parenting and domestic life); and, female **infidelity** (changing gender dynamics and moral codes allowed for this). Although the themes and motifs of misogynic humor are an international phenomenon, evidence suggests that Soviet/Russian versions are angrier than in many other parts of the world. The most prevalent examples involve humor that relies upon sexist vocabulary and portrays women as promiscuous or frigid, unfaithful, treacherous, stupid, unprincipled, vain, lazy, and immature. A typical anecdote circulating in the Soviet Union in the 1950s and 1960s describes a husband making his way to the wrong home after drinking all night with his comrades (the problem of alcoholism appears throughout Russian humor). He winds up in the wrong neighborhood, in the wrong apartment, and in bed with the wrong wife, but gets the same bad sex and the same unpleasant lecture from this female stranger.

In the last quarter of the twentieth century, feminist scholars examined the patriarchal authority expressed within the creation and transmission of misogynist humor. Research shows that many societies police the exchange of humor by placing significant boundaries between the genders through regulatory religious and political institutions. Strict Muslim codes of gender conduct in many parts of the Middle East, for instance, have "officially" prohibited men and women from sharing sexualized comic exchanges in local spaces. Seen as a degradation of female pureness and male moral decency, the forces controlling Iran since the 1979 Islamic Revolution launched massive campaigns aimed at eliminating any traces of humor deemed inappropriate or sexually explicit. Although history suggests that even in the face of the most brutal regimes there is a subsequent rise of "underground" humor in private spaces, the overwhelming public disappearance of humor was felt across the Islamic Republic of Iran after the overthrow of Reza Shaw Pahlavi. Humor (particularly the sort that challenged the norms or **masculinity** of the leadership in any way) was a deeply and deadly contested site of struggle within the territories controlled by the Taliban. Scholars, however, are still searching for evidence that might suggest ways in which laughter became a method of resistance during this period of Afghanistan history. For example, as new information continues to make its way into public discourse, there is growing support that the Taliban regime was regularly the butt of jokes, even in the darkest of times. Behind closed doors frustrated citizens used humor to target everything from their spot checks for shaved armpits (a rule in Islam) to the hyper masculine protocols of Taliban "patrol units." Like others around the world, Afghans have used humor to channel dissent, voice aggression, and to distinguish themselves from their oppressors.

The notion of humor shared "behind closed doors" has been a familiar theme for lesbians, gays, bisexuals, and transgendered (LGBT) people in the last century. For example, by covertly inserting double entendre into **cinema**, art, and literature, "closeted" "queer" humor became a sort of sexually subversive joke to be shared only by those "in the know." As the political struggle for civil rights gained currency in the United States, Australia and New Zealand, Canada, the United Kingdom and some countries in continental Europe, LGBT people increasingly responded to the marginalizing effects of compulsory **heterosexuality** by using humor in more sexually explicit ways. As part of a late twentieth century movement to "come out" and differentiate themselves from the dominant heterosexual majority, LGBT humor has grown more visible. With its increasingly visible platform for humor, however, recent critics point out that humor based on homosexual characters is now guilty of reinforcing stereotypes. One illustration of the ambivalent impact of LGBT identified humor, which reproduces old and creates new identity myths, is:

Question: What does a lesbian bring on her second date?
Answer: A U-haul truck to move-in together.
Question: What does a gay man bring on a second date?
Answer: What second date?

As such humor continues to blend into more mainstream **media** outlets through various comedic genres in film and television, including popular situation comedies like *Will and Grace*, it remains to be seen what effects humor will have on homophobia and heteronormativity within this new century. Researchers are still debating whether LGBT forms of humor will spawn positive social change or reverse the progress of civil rights by further marginalizing difference.

The most current debates concerning the consequences of humor and its many uses is perhaps most significant on the subject of **Internet** humor. Certainly most global and multicultural in its reach, the Internet has spawned a new spectrum of opportunities and possibilities for the mass circulation of humor related to cultural trends. With its constantly morphing and dynamic form and content, online humor allows people to circulate jokes, funny songs, anecdotes, images, videos, and virtually any other form of humor while remaining both locally and globally situated. This is quite a change from times when humor was reserved only for the most specialized of people: the clown, the jester, the fool, and later the stand-up comedian or the identified author of anecdotes. These designations have changed with the seemingly endless humorous texts being disseminated, often anonymously, on the Web. One of the more compelling issues is whether humor on the Internet will have a Westernizing effect on the rest of the world. The potential consequences of this process will have an impact on attitudes towards love and sexuality. *See also* Censorship; Feminism; Gay and Lesbian Movement; Popular Culture; Race and Racism; Sexism.

Further Reading: Barreca, Regina. *They Used to Call Me Snow White—But I Drifted: Women's Strategic Use of Humor*. New York: Viking, 1991; Berger, Arthur Asa. *An Anatomy of Humor*. New Brunswick, NJ: Transaction, 1993; Durant, John, and Jonathan Miller, eds. 1988. *Laughing Matters: A Serious Look at Humour*. London: Longman, 1988; Freud, Sigmund. *Jokes and Their Relation to the Unconscious*. New York: Penguin, 1976; International Society for Humor Studies. See http://www.hnu.edu/ishs. Valuable links to books, joke blogs, newsletters, conferences and seminars, and various other resources relevant to humor studies.

Diana Fisher

I

IMPOTENCE. *See* Erectile Dysfunction

INCEST. Incest is sexual behavior or **marriage** among family members such as fathers and daughters/sons; mothers and sons/daughters; uncles/aunts and nieces/nephews; grandparents and grandchildren; and cousins. Sex or marriage between in-laws and adoptive relatives is also considered incestuous in some societies. Incest has been thought to be universally forbidden throughout history and across all cultures. While almost every culture in the world has an "incest taboo," which relatives are forbidden from having sexual contact varies. There, too, is evidence of cultures with no incest prohibition.

The notion of an incest taboo has been considered important by social scientists who have attempted to explain its origin and function. Some believe that the incest prohibition developed to prevent "inbreeding" (reproduction between blood relatives), which could potentially pass hereditary diseases to offspring. Sigmund **Freud** believed it prevented the disruption of family relationships; if incest were allowed, it would potentially cause jealousy between family members. However, the explanation for the incest prohibition that is most accepted within the social science community comes from Claude Levi-Strauss, who argued that the incest taboo encourages exogamy as **families** extend their social networks. Exogamy refers to a moral rule to select sexual partners and spouses from social groups other than those of whom one is a member. Forging links between families ensured that people would not marry within the family and hoard property and wealth.

Emphasizing a "universal incest taboo" could lead one to think that there must be uniformity among different cultures and their ideas about which family members are forbidden from having sexual relations. Although most cultures have rules that prohibit incest, different relatives are tabooed in each society. Thus, family members who are prohibited from having sexual relations in one culture would meet with cultural approval for marrying and having sexual relations in another. Some cultures, for instance, forbid distant cousins from marrying, while others prohibit only immediate blood relatives from having sexual relations or marrying. The incest prohibition also varies in terms of punishments handed out to offenders, ranging from mere social disapproval to shunning or even death.

In contemporary Europe, North America, and the United Kingdom, the incest prohibition is limited to immediate blood relatives, adoptive children, and step-relatives and is formally written into law, punishable by prison or fines. In the African Sudan, family is defined more broadly. For example, the Nuer forbid marriages between persons who have a blood relationship traced back to eight generations. If one has a common blood relative by one's great-grandparent's great-grandparent, then marriage is forbidden. The Nuer also consider sex between a man and his cousin on his father's side (father's sister's daughter) as worse than sex between a man and his own daughter or sister. Punishment of incestuous couples among the Nuer is thought to be handed out by God in the form of an unhealthy baby or a child that has an early death.

At the other end of the continuum are the Hoti from the Guiana region of Venezuela. The Hoti do not use blood relations as a criterion for defining family. Those who get along well enough to live together are members of a family, which may change throughout a lifetime. Hoti marriage has no special ceremony and simply involves people moving in with one another. Researcher Robert Storrie found that the Hoti might have three such marriages during their lifetimes and brother-sister marriages constitute 18 percent of Hoti couples. Moreover, no family members are forbidden from sexual relations or marriage. Thus, the existence of the Hoti challenges the idea that there is a universal incest prohibition and that such a taboo is an inherent or necessary part of human society.

What is defined as incestuous changes over time. For example, during the first three centuries (CE) of Roman rule of Egypt, the Egyptians tended toward endogamy (marriage within a tribe) including marriages between first cousins, uncles and nieces, and brothers and sisters. In fact, census documents from that time period reveal that 15 to 21 percent of recorded marriages were between full-blood brothers and sisters. Today Egyptians forbid endogamous sexual relations. In Europe and North America during the sixteenth and seventeenth centuries, England had such complex rules for who was related by blood or marriage that the ecclesiastical (religious) courts had to draw up tables to determine which relationships were forbidden. Today British incest laws are simpler, including only immediate family members and step-relatives.

The meaning of incest changes in the West in other ways as well. For example, the concern shifted away from worrying about behavior between adults to concern over adult sexual exploitation of children within the family. In the late nineteenth century, American social workers viewed incest as a problem of adult sexual exploitation of children, but assumed the practice only occurred in lower-class homes, due to overcrowding in apartment buildings. Throughout the twentieth century in the United Kingdom and North America, what was immoral about incest altered in that it became framed as **child abuse** and understood as not limited to the lower-class, but as crossing social class boundaries.

Social scientific studies of incest also turned away from theorizing the incest prohibition. Instead, researchers studied the prevalence and incidence of adult-child incest and its psychological effects, which are now understood as abusive. From this research, most sexual abuse is committed by men (90 percent) with family members constituting one-third to one-half of perpetrators against girls and 10 to 15 percent of perpetrators against boys.

Same-sex incest occurs between uncles and nephews, fathers and sons or between brothers. Some studies of people who have sought therapy from **mental health** providers, which are not considered reliable for measuring the prevalence of same-sex incest in the general population, have shown that gay men and lesbian women have disproportionately experienced incest during childhood. In one study on 942 adults, 46 percent of gay men reported having experienced same-sex sexual abuse during childhood (compared to 7 percent of heterosexual men), and 22 percent of lesbian women reported same-sex sexual abuse during **childhood** (compared to 1 percent of heterosexual women).

In multi-racial societies like the United States, there are no significant racial differences in the occurrence of incest within families. However, incest is more likely to come to the attention of authorities such as police or social workers when the family comes from a lower-status background such as being from a racial minority or when a family's socio-economic status is low. Further, the psychological dynamics of incest make it difficult for victims to disclose to others that they have been sexually abused— particularly when victims are ethnic minorities who fear being disloyal to their cultural group, as well as to their families. Since the 1970s, in North America and the United Kingdom, there have been incest "survivor" support groups ("survivor" is now the preferred term to "victim") to help those who suffered incest during childhood cope with negative psychological effects. *See also* Morality and Ethics; Psychotherapy; Religions, Western; Sociobiology.

Further Reading: Finkelhor, David. "The International Epidemiology of Child Sexual Abuse." *Child Abuse and Neglect* 18, no. 5 (1994): 409–17; Hutchinson, Sharon. "Changing Concepts of Incest Among the Nuer." *American Ethnologist* 12, no. 4 (1985): 625–41; Ingram, Martin. *Church Courts, Sex and Marriage in England, 1570–1640.* Oxford: Cambridge University Press, 1990; Parker, Seymour. "Full Brother-Sister Marriage in Roman Egypt: Another Look." *Cultural Anthropology* 11, no. 3 (1996): 362–67; The Rape, Abuse and Incest National Network (RAINN). http://www.rainn.org/. Includes statistics, news, events and programs, December 2006; Simari, Georgia C., and David Baskin. "Incestuous Experiences within Homosexual Populations: A Preliminary Study." *Archives of Sexual Behavior* 11, no. 4 (1982): 329–44; Storrie, Robert. "Equivalence, Personhood and Relationality: Process of Relatedness among the Hoti of Venezuelan Guiana." *Journal of the Royal Anthropological Institute* 9 (2003): 407–28; Voices in Action. http://www.voices-action.org/. An international organization providing assistance to adult and adolescent victims of sexual abuse, December 2006.

Nancy L. Fischer

INDIGENOUS PEOPLES. The term "indigenous peoples," in the most general sense, refers to any people native to a particular place or region. It can, therefore, include even persons from the First World. Because attitudes, perspectives, and practices related to love and sex are not static human universals but vary from place to place and change over time, understanding love and sexuality is always in context, or "indigenous."

The use of the term indigenous peoples in the twentieth and twenty-first centuries is more commonly and narrowly applied to the non-Western peoples from small societies. Sometimes referred to as "primitive" by anthropologists at the beginning of the twentieth century, those from small, Third World societies were believed to be at an earlier stage of social evolution than the West, and other technologically more developed societies. This evolutionary model was applied to matters of love and sex, as well as to **morality**. Supposed indigenous primitive promiscuity was juxtaposed with the ideal of a morally advanced heterosexual, formal marital monogamy.

This perception, however, rapidly changed as anthropological fieldwork suggested not only a lack of uniformity in love, sex, and relationship practices among so-called primitives but also a wide diversity in social, marital, and kinship systems and values associated with love and sex behaviors. With the repudiation of the notion that small

Dr. Margaret Mead visits with friends on a trip to Bali, Indonesia, 1957.
© AP Photo.

societies represented an earlier, more animal-like version of humanity than more developed, literate, state-based societies, any hope for a comprehensive, evolutionary theory of love and sex dissolved. None has replaced it.

Franz Boas and Bronislaw Malinowski were pioneering figures in early-twentieth-century anthropology. They encouraged the serious study of love and sex among their students. But this did not yield a thorough, systematic, and comprehensive cross-cultural program of study. Moral and religious value attachments limited the research. Researchers typically played up their informants' stated rules rather than their actual behaviors, which went unobserved. The result was most often a reporting of ideal rather than real sex and relationship life. Malinowski's *The Sexual Lives of Savages* is about the Trobriand Islanders with whom he spent two years. Though groundbreaking, it is less than satisfactory, in part, due to how his information was gathered and his inner struggles. Despite the suggestive title, the monograph is concerned with social institutions such as clan alliances as an outcome of **marriage** as with intimate relationships and sexual encounters.

Writing at about the same time, Margaret Mead, a student of Boas and the best-known anthropologist of the mid-twentieth century, devoted a major portion of her career to investigating and writing about love, sex, relationships, and family among indigenous peoples in the Pacific and elsewhere. She did so from a female perspective—and as someone who was actively, if not publicly, bisexual. Mead saw herself as a researcher and communicator with an activist intent. She was determined to broaden conventional views of sex and relationships in America and Europe by her non-Western examples. Her first book was *The Coming of Age in Samoa* (1927). Though fascinating, Mead's example of Manuan adolescent female sexuality does not tell us what indigenous adolescent female sexuality is like anywhere but in Samoa. Interestingly, Mead lamented that she found romantic love all but absent among the young girls she studied. Subsequent researchers to the area have suggested that Mead was wrong on this account; she likely underestimated emotional attachments between men and women because affection between spouses and lovers does not take place in public. Nevertheless, not just in Manua but among indigenous peoples, research accounts of passionate, romantic love are few if not non-existent.

In *Sex and Temperament in Three Primitive Societies* (1935), Mead compared **gender roles** among three New Guinea groups (Arapesh, Mundugumor, Tchambuli). She demonstrated that these roles and attitudes are neither inborn nor determined by the surrounding ecological environment but rather are a product of learning. They are cultural.

There is much that will never be known about indigenous peoples' pre-colonial sexual and relationship lives. In cases where history is not simply silent, the reliability of accounts recorded by Western researchers will always be questioned. Nevertheless, some generalizations about sexual practices can be made reliably.

In most cultures, **masturbation** by both male and female adolescents was considered acceptable, normal behavior. Following partner selection, judgments about masturbation varied widely but not on moral grounds. Among the Trobrianders, masturbation was not explicitly prohibited but considered a poor substitute for heterosexual intercourse and, therefore, unacceptable behavior for both males and females. Nevertheless, masturbation has not been seriously studied in most non-Western societies.

The range of choices for sexual partners, both sanctioned by forms of marriage and outside marriage, also varies widely. Some indigenous societies strictly regulate who shall have sexual relations with whom, while others are less concerned, but there is no hard and fast rule. Generally, marriage in small societies is more concerned with clan, kinship group and tribal alliances, and with group rules of inclusion and exclusion, than an individual's choice of marriage partner or, in the cases of **polygamy** and polyandry, partners. A prohibition of **incest** is nearly universal but the parameters of incest are not. Who, specifically, a person may or may not have sex with depends on who is considered a close relative—defined by local convention. Among the Trobrianders, a matrilineal society, children belong to their mother's clan. Therefore, sex between a man and his mother's sister (and her daughter) are prohibited while sex with his father's sister (and her daughter) is not. In some traditional Asian societies (China, India) the incest prohibition is considered to extend to anyone who bears the same surname.

No single posture for sexual intercourse is universally preferred. The most common sexual position for heterosexual intercourse cross-culturally is the man-on-top. Christians promoted this so-called "missionary position" as the only acceptable way to have sex. Among the Trobriand Islanders studied by Malinowski, the missionary position was considered uncomfortable and unnatural. Along with the Tallensi of Africa, the Karaja of South America and the Lepcha of India, among others, Trobrianders preferred a man-on-top position with the man squatting or kneeling between the legs of the woman who may be lying back prone or resting elevated on the man's hips. Because such a position is common in Pacific cultures, it is often called the "Oceanic position." Other peoples prefer side-by-side and face-to-face, or side-by-side while reclining, positions. In a few societies, such as the Bushmen of southern Africa and the Nambikwara and Apinaye of South America, rear-entry, the most common position among other mammals, is preferred.

Some indigenous peoples employ a wide repertoire of postures for copulation while others do not. In societies such as the Meru in Africa, where right and left hands are considered sacred and profane respectively, the male's left hand is usually designated for sexual uses. Erotic kissing, considered natural in the West, is completely unknown among such geographically diverse people as East African Somalis, the Siriono of South America, and the Lepcha of Asia. Similarly, oral-genital sexual practices—and their acceptability—vary as does supposed ideals from actual practices. Among the Ilahita Arapesh of Papua New Guinea, for example, men practice cunnilingus while supposedly terrified of menstrual contamination.

Beliefs about **homosexuality** and same-sex practices run the gamut cross-culturally. The vast majority of what is known about homosexuality concerns males. Some indigenous peoples violently disapprove while others expect and even demand homosexual behavior. The Zande of the Sudan institutionalized homosexual acts among men in the form of pederastic marriages while lesbian homosexual acts were punishable by death. Among the Lango in Uganda most homosexual acts, if found out, were punishable by death while marriages between two males, so long as one was a transvestite, were accepted. Although homosexual marriage was sanctioned, it was not always equal for both genders. Anthropologists in New Guinea and Melanesia have studied sexual relationships between boys and men. Beginning around the time of **puberty**, young males are prohibited from having sexual contact with anyone within their age cohort. Instead, they receive semen from older males, which is transferred through oral sex or anal intercourse. A specific relative such as an uncle may be the designated semen donor or many men from the group may function in this role. This practice of **pederasty** may last several years until such time as a young man is believed, by virtue of the passing of a specified period of time or by those in authority such as clan elders, to have received enough semen to enable him to marry, inseminate, and successfully father children. In some societies active **bisexuality** is expected to continue into mature adulthood; in others a transition to **heterosexuality** is expected as normative.

It is ironic that relatively little is known about lesbian sexual behavior cross-culturally because studies of the Aranda of Australia, Zulu and Nuer of Africa, Araucanians and Tupinamba of South America, Nahane and Achomawi of North America, Samoans and Easter Islanders of the Pacific, and the Chukchi of Siberia show a wide geographic range of societies that were at least tolerant of female same-sex relationships. Formal woman-woman marriage exists in more than 30 geographically diverse African populations. Typically, one woman pays the customary bride price for the other, as in heterosexual marriage, thereby securing her position as sociological "husband." With the aid of a male kinsman or friend of the female husband or a man of the wife's choosing, the couple may have children.

There are no reliable figures for the frequency of heterosexual activity although anecdotal accounts suggest a wide variation. The Yapese of Micronesia report having sexual intercourse on average once or twice a month while the Marquesans of Polynesia are supposed to be prodigiously sexual, with young men commonly reporting ten copulations in a day and one man having boasted of 31 in a single night.

Such stories play into Western myths and stereotypes about "primitive" peoples and sexuality. The notion, for instance, that there is an inverse relationship between brain size (and with it intelligence) and genital size (and with it virility and sexual appetite) has no basis in fact. While there is much we simply do not know and erroneous ideas persist, "primitive promiscuity," once posited as universal among indigenous peoples, is and ever was, a mere ethnocentric fiction.

Without documentary accounts of a society's sexual and relationship behaviors, reliable accounts of truly indigenous forms have been forever lost. Meanwhile, pre-colonial, indigenous peoples have forever been changed by Western **colonialism** with its institutions and sexual mores. But at the beginning of the twenty-first century anthropologists have rediscovered sexuality. Their new self-awareness and reflexivity along with an appreciation for the value of native self-representation have re-cast anthropological research. Attention is being given to structures of power relationships, "queer theory" and feminist critiques in the human sciences, the role of **AIDS/HIV**, and the politics of genital modification (mutilation). These areas suggest previously unexplored avenues for research and offer new perspectives on old data. Post-colonial, indigenous theory related to love and sexuality has not developed, however. *See also* Adolescence; Feminism; Race and Racism; Romance.

Further Reading: Francoeur, Robert T., and Raymond J. Noonan, eds. *Continuum Complete International Encyclopedia of Sexuality*. New York: Continuum International Publishing Group, 2004. Also available, updated, at: http://www.kinseyinstitute.org/ccies/; Janssen, Diederik F. *Growing Up Sexually, Vol. 1: World Reference Atlas*. Berlin, Magnus Hirschfeld Archive for Sexology. http://www2.hu-berlin.de/sexology/GESUND/ARCHIV/GUS/INDEXATLAS.HTM. The atlas contains thousands of footnoted references to practices and attitudes concerned with childhood and early adolescent sexualities from approximately 150 countries and over 560 ethnographic communities, February 2006; Lyons, Andrew P., and Harriot D. Lyons. *Irregular Connections: A History of Anthropology and Sexuality*. Lincoln, NE: University of Nebraska Press, 2004; Malinowski, Bronislaw. *The Sexual Life of Savages*. London: Routledge and Kegan Paul, 1929; Mead, Margaret. *The Coming of Age in Samoa*. New York: William Morrow, 1928; Mead, Margaret. *Sex and Temperament in Three Primitive Societies*. New York: William Morrow, 1935; Roscoe, Will and Stephen O. Murray. *Boy-Wives and Female Husbands: Studies of African Homosexualities*. New York: Palgrave Macmillan, 2001.

David Roth

INFIDELITY/EXTRAMARITAL SEX. Infidelity is a violation of the commitment to sexual loyalty by one or both members of a committed romantic relationship. Infidelity can take various forms, including sexual infidelity and emotional infidelity. Technological advances in the twentieth century have facilitated other forms of infidelity, such as phone/cybersex and viewing **pornography**. Although attitudes about infidelity differ between men and women and across cultures, infidelity constitutes a serious betrayal. Consequences can include mental/emotional suffering as well as termination of the relationship. However, the effects of infidelity can be overcome and healing is possible.

Regardless of culture, age, gender, marital status, or sexual orientation, a committed relationship usually includes a stated or implied promise of sexual (and perhaps emotional) loyalty to one's partner. Such commitment helps define and preserve the relationship. However, despite the explicit or implicit promise of intimate exclusivity, partners may be unfaithful and "cheat" on the other.

Infidelity can take various forms. In cases of sexual infidelity, sexual intimacy is diverted away from the committed relationship through sexual relations with another person. Other forms of infidelity include nonsexual physical relationships, emotional affairs, and liaisons via telephone or the **Internet**. With any kind of infidelity, intimacy that is typically reserved for the primary relationship is shared with another person without the partner's knowledge or consent. Extramarital sex or adultery is a specific kind of infidelity in which there is a betrayal of marital sexual exclusivity. Although most committed relationships include sexual fidelity, there are "open" relationships (also called "swinging"), in which partners agree that they can be sexually intimate with others, as long as the commitment to the primary relationship remains intact. In cases of **polygamy** and polygyny, sexual relations occur with more than one partner within the framework of committed relationships and with the knowledge of all parties involved.

Infidelity can occur with someone that is known personally or with someone that is not known, as with prostitution. Participation in phone/cyber sex, reading sexually explicit literature, and viewing pornography are other ways in which individuals can violate commitments to sexual exclusivity. Recent technological developments such as the Internet and mobile phones have increased access to pornography and potential affair partners. Some spouses regard Internet infidelity just as real and damaging as face-to-face affairs.

Infidelity can undermine the betrayed partner's sense of security and stability in a relationship; the emotional impact may be severe, including depression, anxiety, rage, symptoms of post-traumatic stress disorder (PTSD), and decreased self-esteem. For many couples, infidelity brings an end to the relationship. In marriage, adultery typically constitutes one of the most devastating acts of betrayal and may cause serious damage to the foundation of trust, loyalty, and security typically associated with marriage.

Almost all societies have implicit or explicit standards regarding extramarital sex. Historically, religious beliefs have had a strong influence on societal norms. Major **religions** of the world, including Catholicism, Islam, Protestantism, and Eastern philosophy have specific expectations of fidelity in **marriage**. There are also various legal implications with public and private consequences. In many countries such as the United States, Russia, Canada, Israel, and Poland, adultery represents grounds for **divorce**. Islamic law indicates that infidelity should be severely punished. However, four male Muslim eyewitnesses are required for conviction. Muslim women who have been unfaithful (identified by **pregnancy**) are punished (perhaps by public flogging or stoning), but men are often left unpunished because of a lack of evidence. Iran, Pakistan, Saudi Arabia, and Yemen punish adultery by death. However, there have been no recent executions unless other crimes were involved.

For many, sexual attitudes and practices shifted during the "sexual revolutions" of the 1920s and 1960s. Although attitudes in many countries during these periods became more liberal regarding certain sexual behaviors, societal views regarding extramarital sex have remained relatively stable throughout the twentieth century, with the vast majority of persons disapproving of it. A study of 24 nations found that only 4 percent of individuals surveyed report that marital infidelity is "not wrong at all." A 1994 cross-national comparison showed that 82 to 94 percent of respondents from Britain, the United States, Ireland, West Germany, East Germany, Sweden, and Poland condemn adultery, with West Germany being the most liberal (82 percent disapproving) and the United States being the most conservative (94 percent disapproving). Although there is a consensus across countries that extramarital sex is not acceptable, several nations, notably Russia, Bulgaria, and the Czech Republic, show considerably more tolerance. For example, only one of three Russians describe it as "always wrong," as compared to an average of two out of three persons from all 24 countries.

In spite of cultural standards forbidding extramarital sexual affairs, actual behaviors may vary. For example, marital fidelity is expected in the Hispanic culture. However, it is generally understood that the husband may have extramarital relationships. Likewise, men of financial stature in the Igbo society in Southeastern Nigeria see themselves as entitled when it comes to extramarital relationships and they display their girlfriends openly to their peers as a sign of status. However, their wives are forbidden to engage in extramarital affairs. In Thailand, long-standing traditions of commercial sex and a growing acceptance of **premarital sex** have contributed to infidelity. However, the **AIDS** epidemic in this country has led many to re-examine common views and behaviors regarding these practices.

Researchers have struggled to accurately assess the occurrence of infidelity among married and non-married couples. Research results on lifetime incidence rates of extramarital sex have shown great inconsistency, with findings and estimates ranging from rates as low as 1.5 to as high as 50 percent. Data collected in the 1940s in the United States by Alfred **Kinsey** estimated that nearly one out of two married men and one-fourth of married women commit adultery. There have been additional studies, with some supporting Kinsey's findings. Some researchers suggest that the incidence of infidelity increased during and following the two world wars; others note that there is not enough evidence to draw this conclusion. Conservative estimates from recent national surveys indicate between 20 and 25 percent of all married Americans will have sex with someone other than their partner.

Despite these discrepancies in research results, most scholars agree that infidelity is a common phenomenon in marriage. There is a clear discrepancy between attitudes and behaviors: a very high percentage of people disapprove of extramarital sex, but greater than 20 percent of married individuals admit to being unfaithful. Although infidelity has occurred throughout recorded history, the incidence of infidelity in the twentieth and early twenty-first centuries may be a manifestation of social changes that have elevated individual gratification above relational commitments.

Research across cultures shows that married men are more likely than women to report ever engaging in extramarital sex. In the United States, about one-quarter of married men and 10 to 15 percent of married women report engaging in extramarital sex. African American men and women have higher rates than Caucasian men and women. Additionally, men (Caucasian Americans, African American, and Hispanic) have higher rates of extramarital sexual affairs than women. About four percent of American men and two percent of women report engaging in extramarital sex during the past year. In contrast, a study in urban areas of China indicated that about 20 percent of men and 4 percent of women reported having extramarital sex during the past year.

Research in the United States conducted prior to the 1990s consistently revealed that men were more likely to engage in infidelity than women. However, a study by Wiedermen (1997) reported that there was no gender difference in lifetime incidence among men and women respondents younger than 40 years of age. Some hypothesize this may be due to the greater number of women in the **workplace**, providing greater opportunities to develop sexual relationships. Comparisons of data from two studies of female sexual behavior show some changes in prevalence rates among women in the United States during recent decades. The percentage of women reporting an extramarital affair increased twofold from the 1940s (15 percent) to the 1980s (37 percent).

Infidelity is not limited to married couples. The percentage of sexually active 16- to 45-year-olds (married and non-married) admitting to having been sexually unfaithful, are (in order of infidelity rates): United States (50 percent); Britain (42 percent); Germany and Mexico (40 percent); France (36 percent); and Spain (22 percent). Infidelity may begin prior to marriage when people are young. In a 2001 report of 14 countries, one-third of sexually active young people (40 percent of men, 28 percent of women) between 16 and 21 years of age experienced a sexual relationship with more than one person at a time. Teenagers surveyed from the following countries admitted to being unfaithful to a partner in a committed relationship: Thai males (52 percent), American males and females (43 percent), Greece (38 percent), the Czech Republic (38 percent), and British (31 percent).

Infidelity usually occurs in a relationship context that includes various factors that make the couple vulnerable, including: marital satisfaction, relationship roles and expectations, communication patterns, conflict-resolution style, and emotional and physical intimacy. For example, lower levels of marital satisfaction have been correlated with greater occurrence of infidelity. Cohabiting couples are also at greater risk for infidelity when compared with married couples, and couples in which one or both spouses have previously been divorced are at greater risk.

A couple's vulnerability may also involve individual and/or relational risk factors. Age, mental health/illness, physical well-being, self-esteem, attitudes about infidelity, religiosity, and gender are examples of individual risk factors. For instance, those with mental and/or emotional health conditions such as depression or anxiety are at a greater risk of having an affair. In addition, low self-esteem has been correlated with the occurrence of infidelity. Permissive attitudes toward infidelity increase a couple's risk and are more likely to occur in liberally minded individuals with low religiosity, premarital sexual experience, and premarital sexual permissiveness.

Men and women generally engage in infidelity for different reasons. A **desire** for emotional connection is often the most important aspect for women. Other factors include an unhappy marriage, the need for personal growth and self-fulfillment, and a desire for sexual fulfillment. In contrast, men report that sexual factors, rather than a need for greater emotional intimacy, are most important. In cases when infidelity includes both sexual and emotional intimacy, men typically begin with sexual involvement and move to include emotional, while the opposite is found with women. Furthermore, men tend to be more approving of affairs.

Couples who desire to stay together and mend the relationship may seek help through friends, clergy, self-help books, or professional counselors. In order for healing and reconciliation to occur, various steps must be taken by each partner. Unfaithful partners must take responsibility for their behavior and terminate the affair. Another crucial step in the healing process is a sincere apology by the offending partner. Healing is further facilitated as partners focus on factors that unify them as a couple and work to increase understanding and closeness. Eventually, forgiveness and a restoration of trust can occur. *See also* Aging; Free Love; Mental Health and Sex; Morality and Ethics; Sex Therapists; Sexism.

Further Reading: Glass, Shirley P., and Thomas L. Wright. "Sex Differences in Type of Extramarital Involvement and Marital Dissatisfaction." *Sex Roles* 12 (1985): 1101–20; Infidelity Facts. http://www.infidelityfacts.com/index.html. Information on infidelity and extramarital affairs, 2006; MacKay, Judith. "Global Sex: Sexuality and Sexual Practices around the World." *Sexual and Relationship Therapy* 16 (2001): 71–82; Penn, Christie D., Stacy L. Hernandez, and Maria Bermudez. "Using a Cross-Cultural Perspective to Understand Infidelity in Couples Therapy." *American Journal of Family Therapy* 25 (1997): 169–85; Scott, Jacqueline. "Changing Attitudes to Sexual Morality: A Cross-National Comparison." *Sociology* 32 (1998): 815–45; Wiederman, Michael W. "Extramarital Sex: Prevalence and Correlates in a National Survey." *Journal of Sex Research* 34 (1997): 167–74.

Stephen T. Fife and Gerald R. Weeks

INTERNET. From its beginnings in the late 1980s, the Internet has served as a means for people to establish sexual contacts, explore different forms of sexuality and sexual fantasy, and distribute and acquire information about sex and love. In technologically advanced societies, it has played a major role in educating young people about sex and love and in providing social support for sexual minorities and other marginalized groups. It has also changed the way people establish and maintain sexual and romantic relationships. In many places, however, concerns about pornographic materials have given rise to attempts to censor online content, which has affected access to important information on sexual health and the prevention of **sexually transmitted infections** and stifled open discussion of alternative sexualities and sexual identities. Recent studies indicate that more that 70 percent of 15- to 17-year-olds in the United States have used the Internet to access information about sexual health. Formal and institutional **sex education** sites make up only a small segment as serious discussions about sex and sexuality, love and **romance**, also take place on private websites, electronic bulletin boards, and web logs (blogs) as well as in virtual communities such as Cyberteens (www.cyberteens.com). Many argue that access to sexual content on the Internet has facilitated sexual health through providing people opportunities to explore sexual preferences and feelings as well as encouraging more candid discussions of sex.

This explosion of sexual content online has had a significant impact on the ways people communicate about and understand sexuality, especially within more traditional or conservative societies. In China, for example, web logs and bulletin boards contributed heavily to the sexual revolution of the 1990s, sparking spirited public discussions about both sexuality and gender roles. Similarly, chat rooms and online dating services in India have fundamentally changed the way many people approach finding a husband, wife, or life partner.

For many, sexual experiences on the Internet go far beyond accessing and distributing sexually explicit information, to the establishment of sexual and romantic relationships with others either close by or far away. Such relationships are formed in chat rooms, through email or instant messaging, through online **dating** services and matchmakers, and even in online gaming clans. One of the paradoxes of the Internet is that it is, on the one hand, a totally "disembodied" medium, and, on the other hand, one that seems to lend itself to representations and celebrations of the body and the establishment of an oddly embodied kind of intimacy.

One example of this can be seen in the rise of a new form of sexual interaction known as "cybersex." In its most basic form, cybersex consist of two or more individuals exchanging erotic messages via email, chat or instant messaging programs. More and more common, however, are multimodal forms such as televideo cybersex, in which individuals perform sexually for each other in front of webcams, and even the use of devices with which people can stimulate one another's sexual organs from a distance through appliances connected to their computers. The later form is known as "teledildonics," and, as with earlier online sexual pursuits, it is helping to spur technological innovation, particularly in the development of virtual reality (VR). Many people use the Internet not just for cybersex, but for seeking partners for face-to-face meetings, and even serious, long-term relationships. Online dating services and personal ad sites (Match.com and Friendster.com) are among the most popular sites on the Web. Nearly all large Web portals, like Yahoo.com, include space for users to look for sexual or romantic partners, and makers of instant messaging programs like ICQ heavily market their applications for finding potential mates. Initially a source of stigma or shame, finding partners through the Internet has become increasingly accepted, especially in the United States and Europe. In 2002, Match.com, the world's largest internet dating service, had an overall membership of over eight million, and it has been estimated that as many as a quarter of adults in the United States have used online dating services and personal ads.

Though many of the large North American online dating sites have gone international, there are also a large number of local sites all over the world geared towards the specific cultural environments in which they operate. In India, online services like Shaadi.com are replacing the small matchmakers who have traditionally helped families find suitable spouses for their children. In China, the online dating service of the nation's largest Web-portal, Sina.com, called "Club Love," is one of the country's more popular sites. Muslim specific sites like Arab2Love.com, Zawaj.com, and SingleMuslim.com tend to focus more on helping customers find potential husbands or wives rather than fun dates or quick sex. They often have a more religious tone, with information about customers' height and weight supplemented with statistics on how many times a day they pray or statements about their "relationship with Allah."

Such services are particularly useful to those whose physical circumstances make it difficult for them to meet potential partners. They also significantly broaden the selection of potential partners, magnifying users' chances of finding someone compatible. In some urban centers, online matchmaking has profoundly changed the way people socialize, giving rise to such phenomena as "hyperdating," arranging dates with many different partners in quick succession. It has also significantly facilitated the formation of international and intercultural romantic relationships.

The importance of computers and the Internet in sexual and romantic interaction is not limited to that which begins online. With the pervasiveness of electronic communication—emailing, chatting, instant messaging, and texting—in everyday life, online communication now plays an important part in helping people to manage and maintain their off-line relationships.

Online sexual materials and activities have been particularly influential in the lives of socially disenfranchised individuals such as sexual minorities and the disabled. For LGBT persons it has made available a wide range of information and emotional support, aided in the "coming-out" process, helped individuals to combat shame and discrimination, find friends and sexual partners, and discuss issues like HIV status. This is particularly important for sexual minorities living in rural areas or in societies in which alternative forms of sexual expression are severely stigmatized. The Internet has been an important factor in the growth of gay and lesbian communities and the promotion of LGBT human rights from China to the Middle East.

The Internet also provides new avenues for sexual and romantic expression for many disabled individuals, allowing them to overcome physical limitations in their search for partners. For people with disabilities that hamper mobility, for example, or for those with socially stigmatized disabilities, the Internet provides a way to meet people and establish relationships in a medium in which the physical body is not such a central factor in attraction and interaction. Moreover, there are websites for the disabled like Youreable.com that provide forums and personal ads.

Early cyber feminists like Donna Haraway have suggested that the Internet provides women with a significant tool for overcoming **sexism**, especially in societies in which their "real world" expressions of sexuality are limited or subject to a "double standard." Further, allowing individuals to transcend their gender through online "gender swapping" provides persons of any gender the opportunity to enter another virtual gender body.

Despite its potential benefits, there is a "darker side" to sexual interaction on the Internet. It has facilitated sexual exploitation, sexual harassment, and stalking. "Cyber-infidelity" has become an increasingly common threat to marriages and other committed relationships, and there are ample examples of adults using Internet tools like chat rooms and instant messaging programs to lure children and teenagers into sexual relationships. While the Internet has provided opportunities for LGBT people to access social support and fight for equal rights, it has also provided increased opportunities for the dissemination of hate speech directed at sexual minorities.

As the amount of sexually explicit content available on the Web has increased, so have attempts by governments and institutions to restrict its availability, especially to children, either through legislative means or though the technological methods such as filtering software. Different counties have approached such **censorship** attempts in different ways. In the United States, the government has taken a role in attempting to criminalize online "obscenity," passing the Communications Decency Act in 1996, which was struck down by the Supreme Court, and later, in 1998, the Child Online Protection Act, which, among other things, mandates that schools and libraries install software to block access to sexually explicit material. In places like China—which has the second-largest population of Web consumers after the United States—and Singapore, Saudi Arabia, Syria, and Libya, governments have adopted costly technological solutions in attempts to prevent Internet users from accessing sites with materials their governments find objectionable. Such censorship, however, is rarely effective. Technologically savvy persons have learned to confound these controls, accessing restricted materials, for example, through mirror sites or proxy servers; many children and teens, often more computer literate than their parents and teachers, have found ways to crack filtering software codes.

At the same time, attempts to restrict access to pornography can result in more limited access to legitimate educational materials. The use of filtering software at libraries and schools, for example, can prevent adults and teenagers from getting valuable information on issues like sex education, **HIV/AIDS** prevention, breast cancer, abuse recovery, and lesbian and gay issues. A 2002 study by the Kaiser Foundation found that most schools which employ Internet filtering software configure the it with settings that are so restrictive as to adversely impact students' access to health-related information. While such restrictions are often unintentional, in some cases they are part of efforts by certain political and religious groups to restrict young people's access to sexual knowledge. In other situations, government policies on restricting sexual content online have been used as an excuse to censor unpopular political speech.

The Internet has become an increasingly important tool for researching sexual behavior. Online tools provide researchers with ways of contacting a large, diverse population and research participants with ways of responding more anonymously. Research on "cybersex" and other virtual ways of interacting is providing valuable insights into sexual interaction in general, which can be applied to such areas as HIV/AIDS prevention. *See also* Infidelity/Extramarital Sex; Politics; Pornography; Pornography, on the Internet; Sociobiology.

Further Reading: Berry, Chris, and Fran Martin, eds. *Mobile Cultures: New Media in Queer Asia.* Durham, NC: Duke University Press, 2003; Cooper, Al, ed. *Cybersex: The Dark Side of the Force.* Philadelphia: Taylor and Francis, 2000; Dawson, Jeff. *Gay and Lesbian On-line.* Berkeley, CA: Peachpit Press, 1997; Electronic Frontier Foundation. http://www.eff.org.

An organization that advocates for online freedom of speech; Orr, Andrea. *Meeting, Mating and Cheating: Sex, Love and the New World of Online Dating.* Upper Saddle River, NJ: Reuters Prentice-Hall, 2004; Queer Resources Directory. http://www.qrd.org/qrd. One of the largest and most comprehensive Internet gateways for gay men and lesbians, providing links to pages on queer culture, activism, history, health, and other issues; Rideout, Victoria, Caroline Richardson, and Paul Resnick. *See No Evil: How Internet Filters Affect the Search for Online Health Information.* Menlo Park, CA: Kaiser Family Foundation, 2002; Teenwire.com. http:// www.teenwire.com. Sex education site for teens run by Planned Parenthood; Turkle, Sherry. *Life on the Screen: Identity in the Age of the Internet.* New York: Simon and Schuster, 1995; Waskul, Dennis. *Self-Games and Body Play: Personhood in Online Chat and Cybersex.* New York: Peter Lang, 2003; Waskul, Dennis, ed. *net.seXXX: Readings on Sex, Pornography and the Internet.* New York: Peter Lang, 2004.

Rodney Jones

INTERNET PORNOGRAPHY. *See* Pornography, on the Internet

INTERRACIAL/ETHNIC INTIMATE RELATIONSHIPS. Broadly speaking, interracial intimate relationships refer to sexual and/or love associations between two or more persons who are different because of shared histories, cultures, or physical features. The economic and socio-political power of each group helps establish a local racial hierarchy. The racial hierarchy, in part, determines which groups are socially acceptable for love relations and which for sexual liaisons. Racial preferences operate stronger in mate selection than in **dating** or for purely sexual liaisons as the first involves greater commitment. Deviating from intra-racial relationships may result in legal or social sanctions.

The eroticization of a racial minority group based on its shared histories, cultures, and physical features is exemplified by the interracial intimate relationships between Westerners and Asians. *Madame Butterfly* (written by John Luther Long in 1903, though more popularly associated with Giacomo Puccini's opera version), and its gay version *M. Butterfly* (Hwang 2000), focus on the theme of eroticizing orientalism. Westerners' eroticization of Asians focuses on their docility and submissive nature that are assumed to reflect Asian cultural characteristics—a common theme that was represented and continues to be portrayed in the **media**. Westerners generally assume all Asians shared a collective history that led to the development of these cultural traits. This assumption partly builds upon how "all Asians look alike": perceived physical features such as almond-shaped eyes, smooth skin, dark hair. Eroticizing orientalism leads Westerners to mistakenly view all Asians as possessing exotic physical features along with being passive, loyal, and submissive in relationships. Where interracial **marriage** is acceptable, Westerners often view Asian spouses as good providers or supportive homemakers. Where interracial relationships are acceptable, Westerners usually consider Asian sexual partners less demanding, compliant, and agreeable.

The degree to which interracial relationships are controversial or sanctioned depends on geographical and historical locations. The unequal relationships between white and black Americans are rooted in the history of slavery. The civil rights gained by blacks shortly after Reconstruction was short-lived as Jim Crow laws were enacted mostly in the South from 1877 to 1954. These prohibited interracial marriages; interracial cohabitation would result in imprisonment or a fine. A good portrayal of the

Essie Mae Washington Williams's book *Dear Senator: A Memoir by the Daughter of Strom Thurmond* is shown in this photo, 2004. Williams is the daughter of former U.S. Senator Strom Thurmond and a 16-year-old black maid who once worked for his family. Williams came forward in 2003 with the secret she had held for more than 70 years. © AP Photo/ Mary Ann Chastain.

reception of interracial relationships in the mid-1900s is found in *Strange Fruit*, a novel written by Lillian Smith (1944), a white anti-segregationist and lesbian. Weaved into the storyline is how a white man's sexual relationship with a black woman was tolerated as long as there was no mention of love or marriage. The life of the late ardent segregationist senator and presidential candidate Strom Thurmond is another example. Thurmond worked hard to preserve Jim Crow laws but, as a young adult, fathered a daughter with his black maid. The parentage was publicly acknowledged only after his death in 2003.

While this racial hierarchy and standards for interracial behavior continue in some communities within the United States, the Civil Rights movement has enabled racial minority members to achieve progress toward equality, resulting in black-white relationships being more accepted. Nevertheless, the legacy of slavery and a racialized sexual hierarchy also lends itself to the portrayal of black men and women—from **popular culture** to **pornography**—as possessing animalistic sexual energy, which may be dangerously exciting in bed but frightening and inappropriate in marriage.

These racial attitudes and behaviors are not confined to the United States. For example, non-Japanese Brazilians' preference for Japanese Brazilians as marriageable partners fluctuates with Japan's economic and political positions. In the early 1900s, Japanese were considered as acceptable but inferior substitutes for European workers. When Japan threatened global domination in World War II, anti-Japanese sentiment and ethnic discrimination intensified in Brazil. Opinions of Japanese Brazilians changed again when Japan arose as an economic power.

Other examples are evident in Asia where social stigma is attached to one group because of stereotypical perceptions as a result of the political and economic power of a country. Sri Lanka and the Philippines are major providers of domestic servants and construction workers to richer neighboring countries such as Singapore, whereas Thailand is known for its flourishing sex tourism. As a result, persons from a poorer country might carry a social stigma when interacting with those from a richer country. The perceived stigma enforces racial and ethnic stereotypes and negatively affects one ethnic or racial group's desirability as a marriageable partner but might falsely promote that group's attractiveness in sexual liaisons.

Scholars have theorized racial preference in mate selection using processes, such as acculturation, social mobility, or socialization. They assume that interracial relationships reflect one partner's desire to move up in the society or to be more accepted by the society through such associations. Implicit in these theories is a racial hierarchy that reflects racism and ethnocentrism. In addition, opportunities for upward mobility are not available to all groups as local racial dynamics affect different racial and ethnic groups' familiarity or propinquity of one another through differential social and sexual networking. Through immigration and globalization, different local racial hierarchies have begun to challenge one another as they come into contact.

Interracial relationships, whether love or sexual, are gaining more acceptance. Today few countries, if any, have laws against miscegenation. While legal sanctions rarely exist, social sanctions still prevail within some segments of a population. In cultures where family plays a role, the choice of a life partner is not necessarily an individual preference or decision. Also, within more homogeneous social groups or neighborhoods, dating or marrying an outsider may still be an issue. For instance, non-white men received more disapproval from their white female partners' friends and family than other groups and white females anticipated disapproval if dating members of low status groups rather than white men. Interracial relationships also have implications for the racialization of future generations. The one-drop-of-blood rule, for example, in early U.S. history and the whitening preference in Brazil demonstrate different philosophies of how to view interracial issues. The first views the miscegenation as losing its purity while the latter views it as an expansion of its group. *See also* Colonialism/Postcolonialism and Sex; Race and Racism.

Further Reading: Goldstein, Donna. "Interracial" Sex and Racial Democracy in Brazil: Twin Concepts? *American Anthropologist* 101 (1999): 563–78; Laumann, Edward O., John H. Gagnon, Robert T. Michael, and Stuart Michaels. *The Social Organization of Sexuality: Sexual Practices in the United States.* Chicago: The University of Chicago Press, 1994; Phua, Voon Chin, and Gayle Kaufman. "The Crossroads of Race and Sexuality: Date Selection Among Men." *Journal of Family Issues* 24 (2003): 981–94; Pinar, William. *The Gender of Racial Politics and Violence in America: Lynching, Prison Rape, and the Crisis of Masculinity.* New York: Peter Lang, 2001; Tsuda, Takeyuki (Gaku). "When Identities Become Modern: Japanese Emigration to Brazil and the Global Contextualization of Identity." *Ethnic and Racial Studies* 24 (2001): 412–32.

Voon Chin Phua

K

KINSEY, ALFRED CHARLES (1894–1956). Alfred Charles Kinsey was perhaps the finest and most widely recognized American sex researcher in the twentieth century. He was born to Alfred S. and Sarah Ann (Charles) Kinsey in Hoboken, New Jersey, on June 23, 1894. After battling rheumatic heart disease as a child, Kinsey left home at 18 to attend Bowdoin College where he earned an undergraduate degree in biology and psychology with honors in 1916. Shortly thereafter he entered Harvard University to pursue graduate study in zoology with an emphasis in entomology, earning his Doctor of Science degree in 1919. He quickly earned a solid reputation as a specialist in the phylogeny and taxonomy of gall wasps by publishing numerous scientific papers. In 1920, he accepted a position at Indiana University at Bloomington as assistant professor of zoology and was promoted to full professor nine years later. From nearly the inception of his career at Indiana University his wife and colleagues affectionately nicknamed Kinsey and regularly referred to him as "Prok," which was an abbreviation for *Professor Kinsey*. Ultimately, he became world-famous as a result of his books, *Sexual Behavior in the Human Male* (1948) and *Sexual Behavior in the Human Female* (1953). They discussed a variety of sexual practices and were best sellers with national and international acclaim. His research is still widely cited and he has been the subject of numerous biographies, biographical films, and documentaries. In 1921 he married Clara Bracken McMillan and had four children (Don, Anne, Joan, and Bruce). Although he remained married until his death, he had a complicated sexuality, and there is evidence that he was bisexual.

Kinsey had a reputation for being an extremely hardworking and meticulous biologist. He traveled extensively throughout the United States and Mexico in search of gall wasps, ultimately collecting approximately four million over many years to complete his taxonomical studies. He was a prolific researcher and writer, even authoring a few popular general biology textbooks.

Kinsey's career as a sex researcher began in 1938 as a result of the Indiana University Association of Women Students urging school officials to offer a course on **marriage**. Eventually, Kinsey was the faculty coordinator of this course in addition to teaching the biological foundations of sexuality with an emphasis on marriage. However, when Kinsey began doing library research to prepare for his presentations, he was unhappy and even "shocked by the dearth of scientific literature about sex and the misinformation spread by doctors and ministers" (gayhistory.com 1999). This led Kinsey to begin his research program in the area of human sexuality.

Faced with enormous pressure, primarily as a reaction to Kinsey taking sex histories of his students, the otherwise supportive university president, Herman Wells, gave Kinsey a choice of either continuing to take sex histories or to teach the marriage course. Kinsey announced his decision a month later to continue conducting sex histories, which led the hiring of his team of researchers in the 1940s: Clyde Martin, Wardell B. Pomeroy, and Paul Gebhard, all of whom were co-authors of Kinsey's landmark studies—commonly known as the "Kinsey Reports." Kinsey attracted money for his research from the National Research Council and the Rockefeller Foundation and his Institute for Sex Research was formally incorporated in 1947.

Dr. Alfred C. Kinsey, author of the well-known *Kinsey Report*, is shown with a copy of the book while on a visit to New York, 1948. © AP Photo.

Through the many years of collecting information about the sexual lives from thousands of interviews and questionaires of Americans, Kinsey and his associates published their findings about the incidences of **homosexuality**, **premarital sex**, bestiality, **masturbation**, infidelity/extramarital sex, oral sex, **bisexuality**, prostitution, **fetishes**, and so forth. For instance, Kinsey found that 37 percent of males and 13 percent of females had at least one homosexual experience leading to **orgasm**. Data about a variety of other sexual practices, detailed in vast statistical tables and commentary, revealed the vast diversity of human sexual experience.

While *Sexual Behavior in the Human Male* (1948) and *Sexual Behavior in the Human Female* (1953) were highly controversial at the time, they became best sellers and were translated into many languages. The significance of the male and female volumes was not only that they were the largest studies of sexual behavior to date, but they questioned the repressive and negative attitudes about sexuality preached by organized **religions** such as Judaism and Christianity and practiced by the medical establishment. Additionally, Kinsey's research findings and his insistence on depathologizing various sexual practices helped offer support for the early **gay and lesbian movement** in the United States.

Kinsey challenged a number of myths about sexuality. He debunked the belief that the majority of women were "frigid." Statistically, Kinsey found that a high percentage of women were sexually responsive and enjoyed orgasms (sometimes multiple ones) from a variety of sexual activities. Kinsey's research also shattered the public belief that nearly all married individuals were monogamous, revealing that many females (26 percent) and males (50 percent) engaged in extramarital sexual activities.

Kinsey's extensive research was met with much opposition, although Wells was skilled at quieting Kinsey's detractors at least by religious groups. Perhaps the biggest blow to Kinsey and his institute occurred when Senator Joseph McCarthy targeted foundations "on the grounds that they were providing funds to persons or organizations who had communist sympathies" (Weinberg 1976, p. 16). The end result was that the Rockefeller Foundation terminated its financial support, leaving the Institute for Sex Research with a meager grant from the National Research Council. Kinsey desperately tried to secure funding, but nearly all attempts were futile. "[G]rant-giving organizations gave him [Kinsey] either sympathy without money or treated him as though he were dangerously radio-active—which, indeed, he was from a political viewpoint" (Weinberg 1976, p. 16). Despite the financial crisis, however, research activities continued at the Institute.

Kinsey's work had global appeal and significance. He traveled extensively in Europe and delivered numerous lectures toward the end of his life. His work was translated into several languages, signaling his eminent and world-class reputation. In the spirit of his predecessors in sex research such as Magnus **Hirschfeld** and Havelock Ellis who fought against the tide of sexual conservatism and strove for sexual liberation, Kinsey left a lasting impact on scholars and non-scholars alike. In part, he paved the way for Masters and Johnson and other sexologists to do their sex research in the 1960s. Nevertheless, Kinsey's critics continue to attack him—fifty years after his death. Questions regarding his character assassinations as well as his research methodology and findings have almost without exception been debunked by serious biographers of Kinsey. *See also* Heterosexuality; Politics; Sexual Science/Sexology.

Further Reading: Bullough, Vern L. *Science in the Bedroom: A History of Sex Research.* New York: Basic, 1994; Gathorne-Hardy, Jonathan. *Sex: The Measure of All Things: A Life of Alfred Kinsey.* Bloomington: Indiana University Press, 1999; gayhistory.com. www.gayhistory. com/rev2/factfiles/ffkinsey.htm; Humboldt-Universitat zu Berlin. Kinsey, Alfred C., June Machover Reinisch and Margaret Harter. http://www2.hu-erlin.de/sexology/GESUND/AR-CHIV/SEN/CH15.HTM. Offers detailed biographical information about Kinsey and a comprehensive coverage of The Kinsey Reports and The Kinsey Institute; Jones, James. *Alfred C. Kinsey: A Public/Private Life:* New York: Norton, 1997; Pomeroy, Wardell B. *Dr Kinsey and the Institute for Sex Research.* New York: Harper & Row, 1972; Weinberg, Martin. S., ed. *Sex Research: Studies from the Kinsey Institute.* New York and London: Oxford University Press, 1976.

John P. Elia

M

MARRIAGE, HETEROSEXUAL. At its most basic level, marriage commonly unites a woman and a man as a socially recognized couple. This couple is then considered to form the basic building block of the family. Sexual relations resulting in **pregnancy** are often seen as the primary reason for couples to get married. While most societies share these characteristics, the particulars of marriage, such as the associated rituals, vary dynamically across time and culture. There are three main forms of marriage worldwide—monogamy, polygyny, and more rarely polyandry—and marriages are usually either civil or religious. The age at which individuals first marry and the percentages of people who marry have fluctuated over the last century and differ according to the society. However there has been a general global decrease in marriage rates and an increase in age of first marriage.

Almost all societies celebrate marriage in an elaborate way. A wedding acknowledges the couple's commitment to each other, symbolically demonstrates the uniting of the extended **families**, and allows the respective families the chance to display their wealth. In Ethiopia, the Karo people enhance a bride's beauty, and thus her status, by tattooing her abdomen with different symbols. In India, families often save their disposable income for the wedding celebration, while in Egypt a wedding costs an average of four times the annual per capita income, making marriage especially onerous for lower socio-economic groups.

Marriage often involves a multitude of exchanges. In many communities, women and men are valued for the complementary roles they assume in the household economy. If a woman's labor is highly prized, a man may be required to offer valuable goods, known as bridewealth, to the bride's family. Bridewealth is the most common form of all marital exchanges and it is found in more than half of the world's cultures. In Bugis society in Indonesia the groom's family must present the bride and her family with a selection of gifts, symbolically representing compensation to the wife's lineage for the loss of her labor and childbearing capacities, while simultaneously affirming the husband's family's social status. In some !Kung bands in Africa and among the Yanomamo in Brazil, a man may offer his labor to his bride's family, known as brideservice. Among Kalapur Rajputs in northern India and in many parts of Africa the bride's family may tender goods known as a dowry. Items such as jewelry, household utensils, clothing, and money, are usually transferred from parents to daughter at the time of marriage and form the bride's share of her inheritance.

There are three main forms of heterosexual marriage recognized throughout the world. Monogamy, the most common form of marriage in Western nations, permits a person to be married to only one spouse at a time. Polygyny allows a man to have more than one wife at a time; within many Middle Eastern societies men may marry up to four wives, as long as they can equally provide for them, ideally in emotional, affective, and financial terms. Polyandry is the rarest of the three main marriage forms, permitting a woman to have more than one husband at a time. Polyandry is found among Nyinba of Nepal where one woman can marry a group of brothers.

A less common type of marriage is an open marriage, popular in the United States during the 1960s, where each partner gives the other permission to experience physical intimacy with others as long as the primary relationship stays intact. Another variant on monogamous heterosexual marriage is polyamory, the practice of having more than one sexual loving relationship at the same time, with the full knowledge and consent of all partners involved.

Once married, the social status of the wedded couple is generally raised. With this increase in social status comes a set of obligations. In addition to supporting each other in times of economic hardship or ill health, spouses should consistently support and honor their partner, obligations which are especially important for couples with few financial resources.

Marriage means that the couple has obligations towards offspring and kin, both affinal (kinship connections through marriage or affinity) and consanguineal (kinship connections based on descent). In contemporary French society, both parents have equal obligations towards the raising of their children. This is a different situation from the early 1900s when French fathers were more often than not awarded custody of their children in the event of **divorce**. In parts of Pakistan, it is often the responsibility of a wife to look after the well-being of her elderly in-laws.

Marriage confers certain rights on both wife and husband. For instance, marriage sets out rights to property. In the early 1900s, New Zealand women necessarily forfeited the right to own property when they married. However, today they can choose between combining their property or keeping it separate. If property lawfully becomes equally owned, upon divorce it is equally divided. Alternatively, couples may choose to keep their property separate by signing a prenuptial agreement. Prenuptial agreements tend to be most popular among couples who have different levels of material wealth, such as a marriage between a rich celebrity and an ordinary person. Although prenuptial agreements are enforceable in some countries such as Canada, in Wales they generally remain unenforceable. In some societies, marriage is a prerequisite to the right to engage in legitimate sexual relations. In Yemen, only a lawfully wedded couple may engage in legitimate sexual relations and bear legitimate children. In some societies, though, the right to sexual legitimacy need not be sanctioned through marriage and it is acceptable, and even encouraged, for couples to have sexual relations and live together before getting married. For example, in Tikopia in the Solomon Islands in the 1930s, young people were expected to gain a great deal of sexual experience before marriage. In contemporary Norway it is generally assumed that a couple will live together before marriage and in Denmark sixty percent of first-born children are now born to unmarried parents. Marriage may also confer rights of unrestricted sexual access. Indonesian wives, for instance, cannot accuse husbands of rape. While in 1900 almost no country recognized marital rape, currently many counties, such as Portugal, do recognize domestic violence and rape within marriage and these offenses are legally punishable. However, punishment prescribed for spousal rape is often lighter than for other types of rape and the standard of evidence required for conviction is often higher.

Husbands and wives are expected to assume many roles within marriage. Simone de Beauvoir's *The Second Sex* was one of the first books to bring general awareness to the socially constructed roles of women and men and encourage women particularly to examine their role within marriage. Published in the period of post–World War II prosperity, Betty Friedan's 1964 *The Feminine Mystique* detailed how American women's activities centered on the home, ensuring the safety and welfare of their husbands, who brought income into the household from outside work. During the 1970s, many Western-based feminists, such as Germaine Greer and Gloria Steinem, rebelled against these strict ideals, making way for married men and women from the 1980s onwards to take advantage of more flexible choices between work inside and outside of the home—although **advertising** even in the first decade of the twenty-first century still placed an emphasis on wives as homemakers and husbands as providers.

Marriage tends to imply that a wife and husband will live together, but where the couple actually lives depends very much on the era and the cultural context. In the United Kingdom currently, newly married couples tend to establish their own homes (neolocal residence), although only around five percent of the world's societies are neolocal. Together with any children the couple may have, this unit is collectively known as the "nuclear family." In other societies, a couple may move in with the husband's family (patrilocal), such as in many parts of India and the Middle East, or they may move in with the bride's family (matrilocal), as practiced by matrilineal Minangkabau of Sumatra.

Some marriages are religious-based while others are civic-based. Sometimes a civil ceremony (where a couple is married by law) takes place during the religious one, such as in England and Spain. Sometimes the state requires a civil ceremony before the religious service, like Belgium and the Netherlands. Both civil and religious ceremonies ensure that both spouses affirm their will to marry and the procedures make the marriage legally valid and effective. Australia, as in some other countries, allows marriages to be held in private at any location, while others, such as Scotland, require that the civil ceremony be conducted in a place sanctioned by law (e.g., church, registry office) and to be public. Some cultures also recognize traditional custom weddings, as in some parts of Malaysia. In Ecuador, three forms of marriage are recognized: civil; religious; and free union where a man and a woman decide to form a family without undergoing any official ceremony.

There are many ways in which a woman and a man come to be married. In societies where marriage is about establishing lasting social relationships and bonds between extended families, such as in Bangladesh, the choice of marriage partner is often considered too great to be left to just two (usually young) people. Arranged marriages often have a class basis and are thus common among a society's elite, such as in the Tongan royal family. Arranged marriage has long been practiced in Saudi Arabia, but recently the nation's top religious authority banned the practice of forcing women to marry against their will. Arranged marriage can prove difficult if one partner is obliged to marry heterosexually and later identifies or transitions to the other gender, and/or realizes that they have same-sex sex desires.

In places where parents have less invested in who their children marry, arranged marriages are rare. In contemporary Germany, the choice of marriage partner is almost solely based on the notion of romantic love—a concept that developed over the last few centuries. The boundary between a free-choice and an arranged marriage is often blurred, though, as people tend to find partners within limited groups. In Singapore, individuals tend to be free to choose their marriage partner, but their choices are generally within a select group of appropriate potential spouses (e.g., someone of the same class and ethnicity).

During the boom years of the 1920s, the concept of **dating** emerged in many Western nations allowing women and men the opportunity to get to know potential spouses. Concomitantly, there was a freeing up of gender and sexual restrictions, which meant that couples in countries such as Austria were able to experiment with sex before marriage. To meet growing demand, numerous dating services subsequently opened up. The recent advent of the **Internet**, speed-dating (where individuals spend three minutes with a person before moving on to the next person), mail-order brides, and mobile-phone texting have combined to facilitate the meeting of potential spouses. Some of these commercial services exploit class and ethnic differences, for example by providing wealthy Western men with a means of meeting potential Russian brides.

In defining types of marriage many boundaries have been established. Societies tend to place restrictions on marriage to relatives, though the degree of prohibited relationship varies widely. In all contemporary societies marriage between brothers and sisters is officially forbidden. The consequence of the **incest**-taboo is exogamy, the requirement to marry someone from another group. Societies have, at times, also required marriage from within a certain group (endogamy). In the Middle East, patrilateral parallel cousin marriage is often preferred; a man should marry his father's brother's daughter. At times there have been proscriptions against interracial marriage. For example, the Jim Crow laws, established in the late 1800s in the United States, banned interracial marriage, and it was not until 1967 that interracial marriage was decriminalized throughout the United States.

Marriage is certainly not a static event and since 1900 there have been many changes. The devastating effects of both world wars and the Great Depression (1929–1939) resulted in people delaying marriage. One of the lowest rates of marriage ever recorded in Australia was in 1932. The prosperous years that followed saw Australia achieve its highest ever recorded rate of marriage in 1942, resulting in the "Baby Boom." Around the world the age of first marriage has been steadily increasing. In 1975, fifty seven percent of women in the United Arab Emirates were married by the age of nineteen; in 1995, only eight percent were. In 2005, the average age of first marriage in Australia was around 28. However, the positive correlation between poverty and early age of marriage is still acutely seen in countries like Mauritania where in 2000 sixty percent of women were married before the age of 24. Not only is there a general increase in the age of first marriage, but more people than ever before are choosing not to get married. Indeed, there is less reason to get married in a society that recognizes de facto relationships and permits civil unions, gives children born out of wedlock the same rights as children born within wedlock, and ensures that both parents provide spousal and child support, than in a society that does not recognize these factors. *See also* Domestic and Relationship Violence; Feminism; Free Love; Gender Roles; Interracial/Ethnic Intimate Relationships; Marriage, Homosexual; Polygamy/Polyamory; Religions, Eastern; Religions, Western; Romance; Women's Movement.

Further Reading: Bao, Jiemin. *Marital Acts: Gender, Sexuality, and Identity among the Chinese Thai Diaspora.* Honolulu: University of Hawaii Press, 2005; de Beauvoir, Simone. *The Second Sex* [*Le Deuxieme Sexe*]. Paris: Gallimard, 1949; Finlay, Henry. *To Have But Not to Hold: A History of Attitudes to Marriage and Divorce in Australia 1858–1975.* Annandale, New South Wales, Australia: Federation Press, 2005; Friedan, Betty. *The Feminine Mystique.* New York: Dell Publishers, 1964; Idrus, Nurul Ilmi. "Behind the Notion of Siala: Marriage, Adat and Islam among the Bugis in South Sulawesi." *Intersections: Gender, History and Culture in the Asian*

Context 10 (August, 2004); available at http://www.sshe.murdoch.edu.au/intersections/issue10/idrus.html; Ingoldsby, Bron, and Suzanna Smith, eds. *Families in Global and Multicultural Perspective*. Thousand Oaks, CA: Sage Publications, 2006; Kowaleski-Jones, Lori, and Nicholas Wolfinger, eds. *Fragile Families and the Marriage Agenda*. New York: Springer-Verlag, 2005; Marriage About. The New York Times Company: http://marriage.about.com. Has a number of links to articles and further information about marriage; The National Marriage Program. Rutgers University: http://marriage.rutgers.edu/publicat.htm. Posts information about marriage and has a good list of external links. Roy, Arun. *Marriage Customs and Ceremonies in World Religions*. Victoria, BC: Trafford, 2005.

Sharyn Graham Davies

MARRIAGE, HOMOSEXUAL. Love and intimacy have always existed between persons of the same sex and/or gender—sometimes validated by cultural recognition and, less frequently, by institutional and legal identity. While some societies have socially sanctioned and even culturally or religiously solemnized same-sex romantic partnerships most societies have limited the institution of legally licensed civil marriage to heterosexual pairs (though some have been accepting of **polygamy**). Homosexual marriage, or "same-sex marriage," became a subject of great controversy, with increasing international acceptance, in the late twentieth and early twenty-first centuries.

Into the early twentieth century, many societies had traditional arrangements in which intimate relationships of people of the same sex were recognized. For example, the Western phenomenon of "Boston marriages," involving intense intimate relationships between two women, allowed such couples to live, travel, and socialize together, and generally provide mutual support as domestic partners. Sometimes these relationships included a degree of legal recognition through contract, joint property ownership, and trusts or wills. Though their relationships were treated as acceptable under the pretense that they were non-sexual (though no doubt some were lesbian relationships), such "women-identified women" existed outside the scope of conventional heterosexuality in a bond that functionally paralleled marriage. Early-twentieth-century Paris, for example, provided a haven for an outstanding community of same-sex couples, both French and expatriate. Gertrude Stein and Alice B. Toklas established a renowned literary and artistic salon, while nearby American journalist Janet Flanner lived with her French girlfriend Georgette LeBlanc, and American heiress Natalie Barney and the poet Renée Vivien also held court. Sylvia Beach and her lover Adrienne Monnier were the proprietors of the Shakespeare & Company bookshop, legendary in the 1920s and 1930s as a home for the likes of James Joyce and Ezra Pound.

Formalized same-sex relationships also existed outside of the West. A Chinese practice of "sworn sisterhoods" continued into the twentieth century, in which two women could contract legal binding agreements of mutual intimacy and support, even including the joint adoption of children. There is some evidence of a similar practice of "bond younger brothers" among men in some parts of China. In several parts of Africa, a practice of "woman marriage" existed into the early twentieth century, whereby a successful older childless woman contracted with a younger woman to have children. The older woman might be married to a man or might not. Among the Nuer of Sudan, for example, the "woman-husband" married her wife in exactly the same way as a man marries a woman. A male kinsman or neighbor would be engaged to conceive children with the wife, and perhaps to offer ongoing assistance to the couple and child. He may

Lesbian couple Bathini Dambuza, left, and Lindiwe Radebe, right, show off their engagement rings as they pose on Constitution Hill in Johannesburg, 2006. Dambuza and Radebe want to take their relationship to the next level and get married after the South African parliament approves new legislation recognizing gay marriages. © AP Photo/Denis Farrell.

be rewarded for his service with a "cow of the begetting" at the time of the child's eventual marriage. A wealthy woman might have several wives and enjoy most privileges of a male head-of-household. Like any other husband, she could demand damages if a wife had relations with men without her consent. As the father of the children, she received "the cattle of the father," and her siblings would receive the other cattle, which go to the father's side in the distribution of bridewealth. The practice of "boy-wives" has also been noted among some African cultures, where an older male formally pairs with younger male via all the essential cultural protocols of marriage. Same-sex partnerships of these kinds became less acceptable by the mid-twentieth century, particularly under pressure from Western missionaries and colonial governments about **homosexuality** and **pederasty**.

Numerous cultures believe some people have the "spirit" of both male and female, thus taking on a **gender role** different from that conventionally assigned to their biological sex or adopting a "third gender" altogether. The intimate relationships of such people, often with partners considered to be heterosexual, might even be acknowledged through marriage. For instance, South Asian "hijra," formerly but somewhat erroneously equated with the European concept of "eunuch," is a person who does not fit the cultural norms of either gender. Hijra may live together in intimate family groups and may be involved with men who are considered heterosexual. Similarly, some Native American peoples have recognized, even venerated, "two-spirit" persons or "berdache" (which has somewhat offensive etymological roots). The relative tolerance of same-sex relationships among Native Hawaiians figured in the Hawaiian Supreme Court's 1989 decision in *Baehr v. Lewin*, where that court required equal protection guarantees extended to same-sex couples. The decision was effectively overruled, in 1997, by a referendum amending the state constitution.

Not surprisingly, however, many traditional and **indigenous peoples** are as conflicted as those living in modern societies in their attitudes toward personal relationships. For example, despite traditional recognition of "two-spirit" persons, a number of Native American tribes recently acted to limit legal marriage to one man and one woman. And, though the post-apartheid South African Supreme Court has mandated equal rights to same-sex couples based on the country's new constitution which prohibits discrimination on the basis of sexual orientation, a significant faction within the governing African National Congress has labeled homosexuality un-African and criticized the movement to legalize same-sex marriages.

The stigma against same-sex relationships is slowly eroding in the face of the modern **gay and lesbian movement**. The eventual changes in laws relating to **sodomy** statutes, discrimination in the **workplace**, and hate crimes have inevitably led to further demands for civil rights. Many same-sex couples feel the same emotional need that heterosexual couples do to have society recognize their commitment to each other. They also seek the security and financial benefits provided through the hundreds of legal advantages automatically available through heterosexual marriage. For example, in most of the United States, even through complex and expensive alternative legal arrangements, same-sex couples may not be fully able to share health and retirement benefits, take bereavement leave after a death in the family, file joint tax returns, benefit under property and inheritance laws, or visit loved ones in medical facilities. In addition, many same-sex **families** include children, whether the biological offspring of one of the partners or adopted, and require the protections and obligations of marriage under family law.

Same-sex marriage advocates parallel their cause with the earlier struggle to permit interracial marriage. Eventually, societies rejected the putative equality of anti-miscegenation laws that prohibited the marriage of a white to a person of color. Same-sex couples similarly seek the freedom to choose equally between male and female partners. The so-called "equal application" argument accepted in many cases permitting bans on same-sex marriage parallels an argument rejected in the U.S. Supreme Court decision in *Loving v. Virginia* (1967), for example, that a race-based ban that applies equally to Blacks and Whites is not a denial of equal protection because it applies to everyone. Thus, some have argued, a ban on same-sex marriage applies to all persons equally, both straight and gay.

An opposite approach, common among libertarians in particular, argues that the state should get out of the business linking legal benefits to any religious sacrament and should offer only civil recognition to all relationships, including those of heterosexual couples, leaving religious consecration a private affair. Some American states—New Jersey, New Hampshire, Connecticut, and Vermont—as well as foreign jurisdictions such as Denmark have established a legal status (often labeled "civil union") for same-sex couples (and sometimes heterosexual unmarried partners) that have essentially all the legal attributes of marriage without the word. However, no such jurisdiction has eliminated legal "marriage" for heterosexual couples so as to put same sex couples on an equal footing with opposite-sex couples.

Gay rights activist and scholar Michael Warner has cautioned that the fight for same-sex marriage may leave those who do not want to subject their intimate personal relationships to regulation by the state without a basis for claiming social respect or legal protection. Furthermore, even where there has been relative tolerance for or recognition of same-sex relationships, this did not mean an acceptance of all varieties of intimate relations. Often, tolerance extends only to those relationships that parallel stereotypical heterosexual monogamous pairs. Critics such as Warner argue the priority should be on making certain legal benefits now connected with marriage available to those in non-traditional relationships, whatever their orientation, or in no conventionally recognizable relationship form at all. He complains that a "sexual shaming" lurks behind the quest for same-sex marriage, making it consistent with efforts to close down bathhouses, stigmatize non-monogamous sexuality, and in some cases, impede safe-**sex education** by foreclosing discussion about healthy forms of non-monogamous relationships. The fundamentalist religious movement has spearheaded the traditionalist backlash against legal benefits for same-sex relationships. Some claim religious law only permits heterosexual marriage. Others claim that the government's interest in marriage is in promoting (and regulating) procreation, which they argue justifies refusing marriage to same-sex partners. This backlash has resulted in legislation and constitutional provisions prohibiting a jurisdiction from giving marriage benefits to same-sex couples. Several American states and the U.S. federal government have enacted prohibitions or severe limits on extending marriage beyond heterosexual pairs, and sometimes, as in the cases of Virginia and Wisconsin, even banned civil unions and domestic partnerships. This is not unique to the United States. Other countries, including Latvia, Poland, and Lithuania, also have recent enactments limiting benefits available to those other than heterosexual pairs and most countries allow for neither civil unions nor same-sex marriages.

Nevertheless, beginning with Denmark's recognition of civil unions in 1989, countries and jurisdictions throughout the world, especially in the advanced industrial democracies, have begun to establish legal recognition for relationships between same-sex couples. Full marriage rights were extended to same-sex couples in the Netherlands in 2001, and shortly thereafter in Belgium, Spain, Canada, and South Africa. The Supreme Court of the state of Massachusetts concluded that same-sex marriage could not be denied under that state's constitution, and the state legislature accommodated that ruling in 2004—after prolonged controversy and debate.

Other forms of civil recognition, some nearly identical to marriage without the name and some with substantially less benefits, have been established. By the first decade of the twenty-first century, civil recognition of same-sex relationships was available in Andorra, Argentina, Brazil, Croatia, Czech Republic, Denmark, Finland, France, Germany, Iceland, Israel, Luxembourg, New Zealand, Norway, Portugal, Slovenia, Sweden, Switzerland, and the United Kingdom; the Australian state of Tasmania, and the states of California, Connecticut, Hawaii, Maine, New Jersey, and Vermont; and the city of Washington, D.C. The European Parliament and European Courts of Human Rights have extended principles of nondiscrimination to same-sex couples and their families, which might lead to further extensions of rights and benefits with the European Union in future years. *See also* Interracial/Ethnic Intimate Relationships; Marriage, Heterosexual; Morality and Ethics; Politics; Religions, Eastern; Religions, Western.

Further Reading: Blackwood, Evelyn, and Saskia Wieringa, eds. *Female Desires: Same-Sex Relations and Transgender Practices across Cultures.* New York: Columbia University Press, 1999; Cox, Cece. "To Have and To Hold—Or Not: The Influence of the Christian Right on Gay Marriage Laws in the Netherlands, Canada, and the United States." *Law & Sexuality* 14 (2005): 1–50; Eskridge Jr., William N. *The Case for Same-Sex Marriage.* New York: The Free Press, 1996; Evans-Pritchard, E. E. *Kinship and Marriage among the Nuer.* Oxford: Clarendon Press, 1951; George, Robert P., and Jean Bethke Elshtain, eds. 2006. *The Meaning of Marriage: Family, State, Markets and Morals.* Dallas: Spence Publishing Company, 2006.

Ronald L. Steiner

MASCULINITY.   Masculinity is typically perceived as a natural and normative (the way things are and ought to be) mode of being for the group of humans defined as men. To achieve this naturalness and normativity the category of masculinity is linked to and grounded in two other socially constructed categories: maleness and manliness. Masculinity is an abstract category of being that is linked to femininity, while both are central to determining proper or improper expressions of sexuality and love. Understanding masculinity in the nineteenth and twentieth centuries requires an examination of the historical development of an idealized model of masculinity in Euro-Western knowledge systems, masculinity in other social locations, and its expression and links with femininity, **race** and **colonialism**. Theories of masculinity have burgeoned since the 1960s.

Thomas Laqueur investigated nineteenth and twentieth century Euro-Western science and philosophy. In *Making of Sex* (1990), he argued that a one-sex model dominated the understanding of human identity prior to 1800. In this model, the "sex" of the body, as determined by genitals, was understood to be singular: both the male and the female were perceived as having a penis and gonads. Although the male and female were considered to be one sex, however, the location of the penis and gonads was significant. In the male the penis and gonads were located on the exterior of the body, while in the female they were located in the interior of the body. Exterior location was considered better; genitals located on the interior were seen as a physiological malfunction. This view of male and female sex was largely established by the fourth century BCE philosopher and natural historian Aristotle, and the second century CE physician Galen. In this formulation of sex and sexuality, the male (and, therefore, men) represented the normative and proper outcome of human ontology (being), while masculinity was linked to this proper maleness (exterior penis and gonads). This pre-understanding of humanity shaped knowledge and experience, so that when confronted with the physiological reality that the vagina (Latin, meaning sheath) was not an inverted penis, it continued to be understood as such. Hence, what the anatomist or the midwife *saw* was an extroverted or introverted penis.

After 1800, this one-sex (male) and two-gender (men and women) model was replaced by the two-sex and two-gender model, wherein male and female are two distinct and opposite sexes and genders. Social changes occurring at the time, from the Enlightenment to the **women's movement**, contributed to this shift in understanding.

Although the two-sex and two-gender model still dominates Euro-Western knowledge systems and social organization, there have been and are different models of gender and sex. For example, in contemporary rural Malaysia, under the influence of Aristotelian theory embedded in the local Islamic anthropology, the one-sex and two-gender model continues to operate. Or, as with the Dine (Navajo) of the southwestern United States, a two-sex (male and female) and four-gender model (man, woman, man-woman and woman-man) was operative until colonization in the nineteenth century.

Yet, it is the two-sex model that dominates white, middle-class North America, in which it is of primary importance to differentiate between men and women as radically distinct and, therefore, opposites. Such perception allows for a distinct masculinity, one that is safely distanced from femininity. In this model, men who take on the feminine are a threat to proper masculinity as they blur the boundary between genders. In order that the borders between men and women remain secure, men who take on the feminine, either by emulating women or loving men, are not *proper* men. Such men often are disciplined by marginalization, laws against **homosexuality**, or violence, including bullying.

In the West, there is variation in the masculine category due to the interrelationship of gender, sex, and sexuality with other social categories, primarily class, race, and geo-political location. In a white racist society, for example, the masculinity of black men is represented as divergent from the masculinity of white men (of all classes). The presumed norm of white masculinity is evidenced by the under-representation in the popular **media** of those marked by race unless representation has to do with crime or social dysfunction, in which case such groups are overrepresented. Criminalization links hypersexuality to black maleness (the black male body), which then defines black masculinity as divergent and, therefore, deviant. Black maleness, defined as aggressive and overly/overtly sexual, is represented as hypersexual as depicted in films like *Shaft* (1971, 2000) or *Mandingo* (1975). However, when black masculinity is linked with black femininity, it connotes impotency, as it is seen to be delimited by black femininity. Such depictions of black femininity are visible in popular media stereotypes such as the asexual black mammy, the emasculating black Sapphire, and the sexually manipulative Jezebel.

Children learn forms of masculinity and the means by which boys—defined as male upon birth by reference to the penis—are seen to become (or not become) men. Equally, girls and women learn to reward boys and men for their performance of proper (again defined by race and class) masculinity. Such reinforcement was visible when women in England during the First World War presented non-enlisted men they encountered with a white feather of cowardice.

The indoctrination of masculinity is generally not enforced seriously until children reach **puberty**, but this depends on cultural location. For example, among the Nso' in the hills of Cameroon, boys and youth learn to avoid carrying a hoe, as this is a feminine object given to a young woman by her husband in the marriage rite. It is she who will till the fields, and he who will oversee the field, having been given rights to land through his male kinship relations.

Lee Tamahori's 1994 film *Once Were Warriors* presents the violent gender politics of the Maori people produced by their oppression and by the feminization of Maori masculinity under British colonial rule in New Zealand during the nineteenth century. The "white man's burden," defined as the necessity for him to uplift—via the lash and the cross in equal measure—the "primitives" who surrounded him in "remote" places such as India, New Zealand, Australia, or Africa, meant close contact with the contagion of the "native." Here, the white civilized British man, seen as the epitome of humanity, was exposed to the sexual vagaries found in the worlds he had "conquered" This kind of linkage between the white feminine and the racialized male other, who represents sexual excess, is visible in the film *She* (1965), based upon Ryder Haggard's late-nineteenth-century novel of the same name. In this film the protagonist, a young and innocent white man named Leo, enters mystical Africa and the realm of the white SHE (Ayisha) who has lived for centuries. SHE tyrannically rules the "savage" black men (and women) who serve her and who revel in their savagery. SHE is beautiful and Leo, bedazzled, loses sight of the civilized world of white English men. To save Leo SHE is destroyed while the "savage natives" are disbanded. Leo, saved from a return to the primitive, embarks for England, but the state of his soul is very much left in question.

The exposure to the sexually excessive "other" put British masculinity at risk, raising the fear of devolution (the reverse of evolution found in Robert Louis Stevenson's 1886 novel *The Strange Case of Dr. Jekyll and Mr. Hyde*). Deviating from the white British norm was translated into sexual excess and confusion as these others were perceived by him as yet-to-be-fully evolved. Contact, then, meant that British men risked reverting to a more primeval masculinity such as found in Rudyard Kipling's 1890 short story "The Mark of the Beast," set in India.

As one counter to colonial masculine anxiety, the British demonized Maori culture. The colonizers portrayed Maori men and women as both perpetrators and victims of a demonic way of life, rooted in perceived sexual promiscuity and flawed Maori masculinity and femininity. Tamahori's film depicts the consequences of Maori machismo (the necessity for the masculine to dominate the feminine), such as the impossibility of loving relations between husband and wife, father and daughter, brother and sister, and mother and son. Prior to colonialization in New Zealand, the Maori peoples held a two-sex and multiple-gender model that shaped their relations. Although Maori society was highly structured, based on kinship relations, age and gender, gender was not central to establishing status. Rather it intersected with and was subsumed by kinship relations and age as more important to establishing vertical and horizontal relations among the Maori.

Heart of Darkness, written by Joseph Conrad and first published in 1899 (and as a novella in 1902), is a representation and condemnation of the brutality of Belgian colonization in the African Congo. Although critical of colonialism, Conrad was, nonetheless, shaped by the imperialist masculine racism of his adopted country of England. Implicit in his tale of the journey into the unexplored center of Africa is the constant threat to proper white masculinity brought about by penetration into the heart of darkness. The heart of this darkness, like emotion itself, designated the feminine in the Euro-Western two-sex and two-gender model; the darkness of this heart referred to the primordial blindness of the unenlightened African male and female whose excess of emotion and sexuality threatened proper white British masculinity. Marlow, the novel's protagonist, expresses both **desire** for, and fear of, the "cavorting" to the sound of the drums of "prehistoric" black men and women. He risks his "modern" white masculinity in the face of the primeval masculinity (and femininity) and inhabits and travels further into the darkness of the jungle.

The fragility of the category of masculinity is a motif found in a number of different cultural locations. Among the Sambia of Papua New Guinea, young boys are removed to the men's clubhouse to undergo extensive rites of passage. These rites remove from the boy the feminine contagion acquired through living in close approximation to female kin. The rites of passage consist of a series of separate ritual actions that ensure the boy is properly masculinized. The rites are elaborate, and the associated myths complex, but at the center is the necessity that boys be transformed into men and evince the proper masculinity of the adult Sambian man, put at risk by the contamination of feminine blood. One such rite is that young boys imbibe the semen of their elders in order to become masculine. Through such rites, the boy will be protected from the feminine as he engages in various relationships with women from marriage and sexual engagement, to his wife's menarche, to the birth of his children.

Such ritual play is similar to the ritualized activity of the protagonists in the 1999 film *Fight Club* (U.S.). Central to the story is the feminization, through consumerism, of young adult men (all classes and races). In one of the opening scenes of *Fight Club* the protagonist, Jack, is seen sitting on the toilet in a well-decorated bathroom. Phone in hand, he is about to order a pair of slip-covers. In a voice-over he comments, "Like everyone else, I had become a slave to the IKEA nesting instinct." The viewer is cued to Jack's lack of masculinity by both his posture, sitting rather than standing at a toilet, and his activity, shopping by phone. In order to define and claim proper masculinity, the protagonist and his alter ego initiate a fight club. Here "the rules are simple" and the results are unmistakable: feminine men are transformed into masculine men through agonistic (competitive and combative) ritual. In a sense, the feminine is beaten out of them.

The link between normative masculinity and violence is one of the strongest mythological signifiers of "true" masculinity across many cultures. In the current Euro-West this link is achieved by reference to the hormone testosterone, in other locations, such as the Maori, to the figure of the warrior. Such links have led to expectations and acceptance of masculine violence perpetrated on women, children, other less dominant men, and colonized peoples, and to practices such as warfare, torture, rape, murder, serial killing, and bullying. However, the normalization of a violent masculinity has been scrutinized and rejected by those working in queer theory, men's studies, and women's studies. What they have argued for is an understanding of multiple masculinities with none of them signifying as true for all times and all places.

See also Cinema; Cross Dressing/Drag; Erectile Dysfunction; Feminism; Gender Roles; Indigenous Peoples; Men's Movements; Pederasty; Prisons, Sex in; Sports.

Further Reading: Butler, Judith. *Gender Trouble: Feminism and the Subversion of Identity.* New York and London: Routledge, 1999; Calimach, Andrew. "Androphile Gay History Project: The World History of Male Love." http://www.androphile.org/index.html. A grassroots project concerned with compiling and disseminating the vast cross-cultural history of male/masculine homosexuality, December 2005; Centre for Research on Gender and Sexuality. Liz Eno. http://crgs.sfsu.edu. The cumulative work of an interdisciplinary community from the University of San Francisco interested in producing and sharing germane knowledge on sexuality and gender, September 5, 2006; Connell, Robert. *Masculinities* 2nd ed. Berkeley: University of California Press, 2005; Conrad, Joseph. H*eart of Darkness.* London: Hesperus Press, [1902] 2002; Goheen, Miriam. *Men Own the Fields, Women Own the Crops: Gender and Power in the Cameroon Grassfields.* Madison: Wisconsin University Press, 1996; Herdt, Gilbert, ed. *Rituals of Manhood: Male Initiation in Papua New Guinea.* New Brunswick, NJ: Transaction Publishers, 1998; Hooks, Bell. *We Real Cool: Black Men and Masculinity.* New York and London: Routledge, 2003; Laqueur, Thomas. *Making Sex: Body and Gender from the Greeks to Freud.* Cambridge, MA: Harvard University Press, 1990.

Darlene M. Juschka

MASTURBATION. Masturbation is the intentional self-stimulation of one's genitals for sexual gratification. Slang terms for masturbation include: beating off, choking the chicken, jacking off, jerking off, jilling off, polishing the pearl, pushing the button, and wanking; technical terms include auto-eroticism and genital manipulation. Sexual partners who manually stimulate each other's genitals engage in mutual masturbation. Masturbation, in general, is widespread, and perhaps the most widely shared sexual expression. One study of college-age females and males in the United States concluded that 64 percent of women and 98 percent of men masturbated. In terms of frequency, females reported masturbating five times per month and their male counterparts averaged twelve times monthly (Kelly 2006). Prominent sex researchers such as Alfred C. **Kinsey**, and William Masters and Virginia Johnson reported that a high percentage of females and males engaged in this sexual activity.

Anti-masturbation sentiments have long been widespread, evidenced in Judeo-Christian religious tracts and thought throughout the Western world due to its non-procreative form of sexual expression. In keeping with the negativity of religious doctrine regarding masturbation, medical doctors deemed autoerotic activity to be a root cause of many medical disorders. There was such alarm about this sexual practice during the mid-nineteenth century that a number of devices were created to eliminate this seemingly depraved practice such as "erection alarms, penis cases, sleeping mitts, bed cradles to keep the sheets off the genitals, hobbles to keep girls from spreading their legs" (Laqueur 2003: 46). Laqueur also notes that capitalism and technology rose to the challenge to create a plethora of contraptions to join in the campaign against masturbation, which culminated in approximately twenty U.S. patents for such apparatuses. Taking the alleged harmful effects of masturbation seriously, dietary and lifestyle suggestions were offered in the service of prevention.

At the close nineteenth century, John Harvey Kellogg, a medical doctor and moral crusader, invented corn flakes—and a line of breakfast foods—to prevent masturbation and dampen misguided sexual **desire** and excitement, in general. He believed that bland foods helped in this effort. Along the lines of Sylvester Graham earlier in the nineteenth century, Kellogg did not reject sexual pleasure altogether; however, he postulated that excessive sexual excitement had harmful effects on the body. According to Graham and Kellogg, while sexual pleasure needed to be kept in check, it was acceptable in moderation so long as it was connected to procreation.

The twentieth century witnessed a shift in thinking about masturbation as fewer medical professionals believed that it could cause physical maladies. For instance, Sigmund **Freud** argued that masturbation was a normal part of psychosexual **childhood** development. However, he and other psychoanalysts believed that pursuing masturbation into adulthood interfered with developing healthy romantic and sexual relationships. Havelock Ellis, a British sexologist in the early twentieth century who coined the term autoeroticism, represented a radical departure from the previous conceptions about the linkage of masturbation to disease and moral decline. He believed that masturbation was not only harmless for adults, but could aid in relaxation. Attitudes about masturbation internationally have varied depending on locale and historical period. China and Japan, for example, espoused similar views about the vices of masturbation during the late nineteenth and early twentieth centuries. Based on Western medical professionals' discourse on masturbation, East Asians saw this sexual practice as potentially weakening the health of their nations.

Attitudes about this sexual practice have changed dramatically. Recent sexological studies in China and Japan reveal that masturbation is widespread, without negative medical or psychological consequences, and there is an increasingly relaxed attitude about it. In China, for example, masturbation is a topic studied in Chinese **sex education** and generally viewed as a normal form of sexual expression at any stage of the lifespan. Along similar lines, some Latin Americans have traditionally denigrated masturbation, but in recent years sexuality educators have espoused it as a form of safer sex, signaling a shift in attitudes about this sexual practice. In the South Pacific, the Lesu women will masturbate openly and without shame if they become sexually aroused and have no partners with whom to have sex. In this cultural context, it is common for children to engage in this practice free from disapproval—and it is a topic that is freely discussed. This reflects a casualness about masturbation that is uncommon in other parts of the world.

Masturbation is becoming a much more widely discussed topic as evidenced by not only websites, blogs, and other media but also due to the significant amount of scholarship that is being produced on masturbation. Recent research indicates that not only does masturbation occur throughout the lifespan, but also young people are masturbating earlier today than in the past (Hyde & DeLameter, 2006). Researchers and sex therapists have also used masturbation to assist individuals to overcome sexual difficulties. Masters and Johnson have long suggested that the squeeze technique be used to prevent premature ejaculation in males. Lopicolo and Lobitz advanced the concept of *directed masturbation*, a sex therapy technique to help women deal successfully with difficulties reaching **orgasm**. Research studies throughout the twentieth century have consistently revealed that masturbation has been widely engaged in by females and males, the young and the aged, and across all demographic categories. In the late twentieth century, various masturbatory techniques have been recommended by sex therapists to help those with sexual dysfunctions and promote sexual pleasure in their clients' lives. Besides the incidence of masturbation and the clinical aspects of it, a number of scholarly works have appeared ranging from historical treatments to literary analyses.

Even though sex researchers have documented how common masturbation is as a healthy form of sexual expression that crosses all sexualities, genders, social classes, and ethnicities/races, many individuals who masturbate continue to feel guilty and uneasy about it. This has political as well as personal impact. For instance, Joycelyn Elders, former United States Surgeon General, was fired in the 1990s for suggesting that children learn about masturbation in their sexuality education classes in public schools to help prevent **sexually transmitted infections**, including HIV, and to stem the tide of unintended teen pregnancies.

There are, however, many present-day international efforts to celebrate masturbation as a viable, healthy, and pleasurable sexual outlet. In Japan, there is a national masturbation day. Many websites boast about May being International Masturbation Month in which, among other activities, people are encouraged to get involved in masturbate-a-thons, various forms of self-loving, and mutual sexual play. Additionally, there are a plethora of internationally-based websites that discuss everything from female and male masturbatory techniques to the best kinds of sex toys to use during sexual self play. In the United States there are sex clubs that cater to masturbation such as the San Francisco Jacks, international icon and masturbation advocate, Betty Dodson, who wrote *Sex for One*, currently has an **Internet** site devoted to all aspects of self pleasuring, and a wide variety of sex toys specifically for masturbatory purposes. Access to many of these venues, however, are restricted to adults and are more likely found in metropolitan areas. *See also* Adolescence; AIDS/HIV; Celibacy; Sexual Science/Sexology.

Further Reading: D'Emilio, John, and Estelle B Freedman. *Intimate Matters: A History of Sexuality in America*. New York: Harper & Row, 1988; Hoshii, Iwao. *The World of Sex: Perspectives on Japan and the West—Sex in Ethics and Law*. Vol. 4. Woodchurch, England: Paul Norbury Publications Ltd, 1987; Hyde, J., and J DeLameter. *Understanding Human Sexuality*. 9th ed. Boston, MA: McGraw Hill, 2006; Kellogg's Cornflakes. http://www.rotten.com/library/sex/masturbation/kelloggs-conflakes/. Provides an overview of John Harvey Kellogg's views about masturbation and sexual excess, with special attention paid to how his cornflakes would serve as a corrective to such sexual "afflictions." It also briefly provides historical information of North American views about masturbation during the nineteenth century; Kelly, Gary F. *Sexuality Today: The Human Perspective*. 8th ed. Boston: McGraw Hill, 2006; Laqueur, Thomas W. *Solitary Sex: A Cultural History of Masturbation*. New York: Zone Books, 2003; Planned Parenthood Federation of America, Inc. "Masturbation—From Stigma to Sexual Health." http://www.plannedparenthood.org. A comprehensive history of masturbation in Europe and the United States, providing information about masturbation across the lifespan, health benefits of masturbation, and offers an extensively bibliography. Robinson, Paul. *The Modernization of Sex: Havelock Ellis, Alfred Kinsey, William Masters and Virginia Johnson*. Ithaca, NY: Cornell University Press, 1989; Smits, Gregory J. "Supplement #1: A Brief Account of Masturbation as a Medical/Moral Disease in Western Europe & the U.S., 18th–Early 20th Centuries as an Aid in Understanding a Similar Obsession with Masturbation in East Asia During the Late 19th and Early 20th Centuries." http://www.east-asian-history.net/textbooks/MJ/sup1main.htm, 2005; Wiesner-Hanks, Merry. *Christianity and Sexuality in the Early Modern World: Regulating Desire, Reforming Practice*. New York: Routledge, 2000.

John P. Elia

MEDIA AND SEX. Media flows through culture, reproducing it; and produces its own cultural forms. Love and sex have been perpetual themes in media of all kinds: music, film, popular press, and, since the 1950s, video and television. Since cultures are not static, examining media portrayals provides insights into cultural practices and ideals about matters such as love and sex, which are specific to particular moments in time and place. For example, in Anglo-American societies media portrayal of

homosexuality was the material of underground publications until the latter decade of the twentieth century whereas Japan has had a substantially longer history of representing homosexuality in its media. The liberalization of Western social values around gender and sexuality, influenced particularly by feminist and **gay and lesbian movements** in the 1970s, not only removed sex from the exclusive realm of **heterosexuality** but also from the confines of **marriage** and "true love." Accordingly, by the beginning of the twenty-first century substantially more diverse representations of sexuality and **romance** peppered the media in print and on the screen. Romance, traditionally deemed "feminine," was not so much dead as rewritten into a narrative that blended the "new sexualities" with the romantic endeavours of finding the one to live with "happily ever after," or at least for as long as possible.

These shifting patterns in the portrayal of love and sex can clearly be seen in historical and cultural analyses of women's and girls' magazines. Women's magazines in various forms pre-date the twentieth century and, although likely to have been produced in many countries, documentation in the literature is largely limited to Western countries and Japan. Japanese, North American, British, and European magazines of the early to mid 1900s (e.g., *Jogaku sekai; Woman's Journal; Harper's Bazaar* and *Cosmopolitan; My Weekly; Woman's Weekly; Home Chat; Elle*) focused on topics related to the home that accorded with women's limited social position as housewives and mothers. On the other hand, British and North American fiction allowed women to escape from the mundane into a world of romance and erotic fantasy where passion, sensuality, and torrid, adulterous affairs could be vicariously experienced. The passionate desires of fiction were not matched with topics about women's sexuality or sexual desires, although the British *Ladies Companion* aired the issue of **sex education** in 1922 and, in 1938, *Good Housekeeping* discussed meanings of Freud's work on women's sexual desire as "natural." More often though, even matters of sexual and reproductive health were not deemed appropriate and women who had the courage to write in asking for sexual information were dismissed. In contrast, African American women's magazines (e.g., *Ringwood's Afro-American Journal of Fashion, Half-Century Magazine for the Coloured Home and Homemaker*) tended toward a stereotypical construction of black women as hypersexual.

Magazines for younger women (e.g., *Seventeen* and *Mademoiselle* in North America, *Jackie* in the United Kingdom, *Bravo* in Germany, *Shojo* magazines in Japan) emerged from the 1930s through the 1950s. Less focused on domestic life than women's magazines, these concentrated on the interests of the "single girl" and teenage life, including fashion, beauty, work and "dating." Magazines for young women played an influential role in schooling them into heterosexuality and the "arts" of traditional femininity designed to please males. Despite the "sexual revolution" of the 1960s, embodied in a youth culture with messages of "**free love**," peace, and freedom, teen magazines remained faithfully romantic through this and much of the next decade. Whether in North America, the United Kingdom, or Germany, the common romantic narrative told of girls waiting anxiously to attract a boyfriend, then, having "caught" him, wondering anxiously if he would be lost to a more attractive girl,

The Patty Duke Show, which ran on ABC from 1963 to 1966. Courtesy of Photofest.

leaving them brokenhearted and "back on the shelf." On television, the *Patty Duke Show*, first appearing in the United States in 1963, incorporated much of the material seen in magazines like *Jackie*. Cathy Lane, played by Patty Duke, depicted a "perky," "cute" teenager whose romantic life is captured in episodes with titles such as "Too Young and Foolish to Go Steady," "Going Steady," "The Boy Next Door," "Patty and the Eternal Triangle," and "Every Girl Should Get Married." Like the heroines of *Jackie*, Cathy faced anxieties around fidelity, attractiveness, and whether other girls would lure her boyfriend away.

As girls waited patiently for boys to notice them in magazine and TV storylines, substantial changes were occurring for women in the "real" world that gained the attention of men in a markedly different fashion. During the 1970s, second wave **feminism** (1960s–1980s) began to unsettle traditional patterns of a compliant and passive femininity. "Girl Power" meant being active, ambitious, and in control. The antithesis to romantic passivity, Girl Power contributed to the decline of romance in girls' magazines (at least in its classical girl-meets-boy, love-overcomes-all, happily-ever-after form). For example, the British magazine *Just Seventeen*, unlike *Jackie* that preceded it, dispensed with love stories altogether, working on the premise that the increasingly independent, confident girl market no longer wanted to read "soppy" love stories. Similar patterns have been observed in studies of North American magazines. Love did not completely disappear, but a girl's identity was no longer exclusively tied up in being a boy's girlfriend. Pop stars rather than the boy next door emerged in magazines as girls' objects of **desire**. Nevertheless, in Germany, *Bravo* continued to include "Foto-Love-Stories" in which a beautiful girl (updated as both love-seeking and sex hungry) meets handsome (and now also "horny") boy. *Bravo*'s updated "romance" perhaps typifies teen girls' magazine content in the 1970s and 1980s regarding sexuality's inextricable tie to love and commitment.

For older women, on the other hand, *Cosmopolitan* was revolutionary in including explicit sexual material in its pages. Much of its revolution can be attributed to Helen Gurley Brown who turned the magazine's focus to sex and the single girl, normalizing **premarital sex**. By 1972, the magazine expanded to a British production and, in subsequent years, extended its publication to a further 27 countries. Each version "sold" the "Cosmo girl" brand of independence, power, and fun—in sex, work, love, and self-presentation, clearly incorporating some feminist values. In the same year as the launching of the British *Cosmopolitan* (1972), Australia's *Cleo* magazine pioneered, at least in that country, a male centerfold and in the same issue instructed women on "how to be a sexy housekeeper." Such frankness on sexual matters evolved more slowly in magazines targeting younger women, where through the 1970s and early 1980s sex was covered more educationally through topics such as **pregnancy**, or implicitly via relationship features about **dating**. Addressing older teenagers and young women, American magazines *Mademoiselle* and *Glamour* rivalled *Cosmopolitan* and *Cleo* with explicit topics such as ejaculation and talking too much when having sex.

The growth of sexual content in magazines begun in the 1980s continued through the 1990s and into the new millennium. Television, somewhat lagging behind magazine culture in terms of portraying sexual content, caught up in the 1990s when sitcoms, dramas, soaps, and reality shows began to incorporate sex scenes, some more graphic than others. Now women were being addressed more often as sexual subjects who wanted, pursued, and enjoyed sex and less so as sexual objects available for the sexual pleasure of men. Nor were discussions and portrayals of sex confined to romantic involvement, heterosexuality, and sexual intercourse. Magazines began to include articles on lesbian sex, oral sex, and sex with strangers, all of which also featured in the television sitcom *Sex and the City*. So, too, did magazines, television soaps, and teen dramas (e.g., UK's *Eastenders*, Australia's *Heartbreak High*, New Zealand's *Shortland Street*) more regularly incorporate storylines about teenage sex—especially safer sex, **abortion** and teen pregnancy—from the start of the decade.

Perhaps the clearest indication of the loosening of classical romantic narratives in the 1990s was the emergence of more diverse sexualities that deviated from conventional heterosexual romance. More marked on television than in women's and, especially, teen magazines, lesbian and gay sexualities made sometimes fleeting (e.g., soaps such as *Eastenders*, *Coronation Street*) and, at other times, more stable appearances (e.g., *Shortland Street*, *Bad Girls* [UK], *Buffy the Vampire Slayer* [U.S.], *The O.C.* [U.S.]). Just as we can only infer the influence of the **women's movement** on changing portrayals of women's sexuality in the media so, too, must we be tentative about the influence of the gay rights movement in bringing sexual diversity to our screens and coffee tables. At the same time, British social researchers have observed an increasing "fashionability" and certain "chic" about gay and lesbian identities amongst "straight" men and women, as seen for example in the popularity of gay bars for women's "hen" nights. Predating the "fashionable" status of homosexuality in the United Kingdom, girls in Japan have reportedly been avid consumers of the comic *Yaoi*, in which the protagonists are homosexual males, since the 1980s.

It would be a mistake, however, to assume that romance is "dead" in the media of the millennium. The popularity of "Mills and Boon" romances shows no signs of decline, the romantic comedy on the **cinema** and television screen continues to attract audiences and even the modern girl or woman represented in teen/women's magazines finds room in her independent, confident life to ponder love and **marriage**. But perhaps what has changed in popular media is that representations of romance are no longer a necessary prerequisite to sex (e.g., *Sex and the City*), no longer completely confined to heterosexuals (e.g., *The O.C.*; *Bad Girls*), and no longer, in their heterosexual form, necessarily male-initiated. These transformations of romance accompany radical changes in representations of gender, most particularly the ever-increasing portrayal of girls and women as "action chicks" in and out of the bedroom. Picture a rescripting of Tarzan and Jane where, swinging through the vines, Jane fancies Tarzan, she invites him to have sex with her, she falls in love with him, and he contemplates having children but returns to swinging through the jungle alone. It may not be a bestseller but transformations of romance and formations of the "new" sexual woman in the media make it a definite script possibility. *See also* Gender Roles; Internet; Popular Culture; Popular Music.

Further Reading: Carpenter, Laura. "From Girls into Women: Scripts for Sexuality and Romance" *Seventeen* Magazine, 1974–1994." *Journal of Sex Research* 35, no. 2 (1998): 158–68; Currie, Dawn. *Girl Talk. Adolescent Magazines and Their Readers*. Toronto: University of Toronto Press, 1999; Davis, Glynn, and Kay Dickinson, eds. *Teen TV: Genre, Consumption and Identity*. London: British Film Institute, 2004; Girls, Women and Media Project. Tamara Sobel. http://mediaandwomen.org. Resources on how media represent, serve and impact on girls and women, 2006; Inness, Sherrie, ed. *Millennium Girls: Today's Girls around the World*. Lanham, MD: Rowman & Littlefield, 1998; McRobbie, Angela. *Feminism and Youth Culture*. Basingstoke: MacMillan, 2000; Pearce, Lynne, and Jackie Stacey, eds. *Romance Revisited*. London: Lawrence & Wishart, 1995; Rooks, Noliwe. *Ladies' Pages: African American Women's Magazines and the Culture That Made Them*. New Brunswick: NJ: Rutgers University Press, 2004; Sato, Barbara. *The New Japanese Woman: Modernity, Media and Women in Interwar Japan*. Durham, NC: Duke University

Press, 2003; Walker, Nancy. *Women's Magazines 1940–1960*. New York: Bedford/St. Martin's, 1998; White, Cynthia. *Women's Magazines 1693–1968*. London: Michael Joseph, 1970.

Sue Jackson

MEN'S MOVEMENTS. Men's movements, focusing on men's rights and entitlements, duties, problems, and hegemony or powerlessness, are a relatively recent development, emerging mostly in the United States and principally in the last quarter of the twentieth century with various goals, methods, and ideologies. This development has been primarily due to the massive changes in gender relations escalating since the 1950s, and the shifts in the balance of power between the genders, with attendant shifts in male roles and gender/sexual identities and definitions of **masculinity**. The influence of the men's movement on concepts of sex and love can be traced through the twentieth century: from the definition of society as a patriarchy (male dominance, often conceptualized as oppressive, rather than protective, of women) to the **women's movement** emerging first in the early years of the century to demand political enfranchisement to the second wave developing in the late 1960s to the pro-feminist men's movement focusing on men as *being* a hegemonic, violent, and sexist problem (notably the National Organization of Men against Sexism) to the pro-male movements which define men as *having* problems, notably the National Coalition of Free Men, the gay rights movement, the mytho-poetic movement, the Promise Keepers, and the Million Man March (although they did not agree on the problems, nor the solutions). The global struggle for women's rights is now complemented, particularly in North America, by struggles for men's rights. But the issues persist globally to greater or lesser degree.

At the beginning of the twentieth century, several models of men and masculinity were embodied in **popular culture**. While distinct, they were not necessarily mutually exclusive and reflected Victorian concerns with health, work, and moral virtue. The slogan *mens sana in corpore sano*, a healthy mind in a healthy body, summarized a common theme in this range of beliefs and values. These included: the hero advanced by Thomas Carlyle; the self-made man, articulated by Benjamin Franklin referring to both wealth and virtue; the athletic Christian, the paradigm of muscular Christianity favored by Charles Kingsley in England and presented most famously in "Tom Brown's School Days"; the gentleman, the ideal described by John Henry Cardinal Newman; and the model of self-reliance of R.W. Emerson and Rudyard Kipling. By the end of the century, however, both the ideals and the values were very different.

Reflecting these different ideals, the same era witnessed the rise of many men's organizations oriented towards business, health, religion, and **sports**. These included the Kiwanis, the Shriners and the Rotary Club, the YMCA and other Christian groups, the Olympic Games (re-invented in 1896) and, soon afterwards, the Boy Scouts (established in 1908 in the United Kingdom and 1912 in the United States).

During the early part of the century most of these organizations, events, or sports were either integrated, like the business groups, or developed separate organizations, as with the YMCA/YWCA and the Girl Guides (established in 1912 in the United States and 1922 in the United Kingdom), or separate "leagues" as with sporting events like the Olympic Games (women participated from 1912), Wimbledon and sports teams from the municipality to the university.

Following the second wave of the women's movement in the late 1960s, the men's movements emerged a decade later, although with partly contradictory approaches to men. In the United States, the modern gay rights movement was galvanized by the

1969 Stonewall riots in New York City. Although there were fledgling anti-discrimination movements in North America from the 1930s to the 1950s, the Lambda Legal was not established until 1973 to combat sexual orientation discrimination. In the United Kingdom, the Wolfenden Commission recommended the legalization of **homosexuality** in 1957 and it was legalized in 1967 (Canada in 1974).

The gay rights movement was also furthered by the decision by the American Psychological Association, in 1974, to drop the definition of homosexuality as a "sexual deviation" from the *Diagnostic and Statistical Manual of Mental Disorders-III*. This decision effectively redefined homosexuality as within the normal range of sexual orientations. The outbreak of **AIDS/HIV,** in the early 1980s, saw attitudes harden in the United States, which was reflected in the 1986 U.S. Supreme Court ruling in *Bowers v. Hardwick* upholding the criminalization of men having sex with men. The gay community rallied against these twin threats, arguing for increased funding for medical research, and demanding equal rights in law.

By the early twenty-first century, there was a shift in public attitudes about homosexuality. In 2003, the Supreme Court overturned its 1986 ruling in *Lawrence v. Texas*. Opinion polls tracked a rapid decline in homophobia and a rise in gay-affirmative attitudes. High profile **media** celebrities were coming out, several popular television programs, like "Queer Eye for the Straight Guy," were airing, and some Hollywood movies received popular and critical success, notably *Brokeback Mountain* and *Capote*. Although the issue of same-sex **marriage** remains controversial in the United States, same sex marriages became legal in Belgium, the Netherlands, Spain, Canada, and South Africa, and civil unions are recognized in Argentina and the United Kingdom.

The men's movement also emerged from other concerns during the 1970s. The National Organization of Men against Sexism (NOMAS), formed in 1975, "advocates a perspective that is pro-feminist, gay affirmative, anti-racist, dedicated to enhancing men's lives and committed to justice." Incorporated in 1985, the organization is "deeply supportive of men who are struggling with the issues of traditional masculinity" and "strongly support[s] the continuing struggle of women for full equality" (www. nomas.org). In contrast to the John Wayne model of tough, stoic, laconic, traditional masculinity, the "New Age Man" is committed to women's equality and in touch with his emotions.

In contrast to NOMAS, the National Coalition of Free Men (NCFM), founded two years later, is committed exclusively to equal rights for men. Its mission is "to foster compassion, respect and understanding for all men," and to look "at the ways that sex discrimination affects men and boys" (www.ncfm.org). Among its concerns are parenting and **divorce**, Selective Service Registration and the Draft, physical and **mental health**, education, domestic violence, reproductive rights and paternity fraud, negative media portraits, misandry, and more. Although both organizations are concerned with issues of men's health, NCFM is principally concerned with men's rights, and the wrongs done *to* men, and the need to reform society. NOMAS is principally concerned with the rights of women, gays and minorities, the wrongs done *by* men as the hegemonic sex, and the need to reform men.

The turning point in raising men's awareness, however, was the publication of *Iron John* in 1990. Poet Robert Bly uses one of the Brothers Grimm's tales to illustrate his Jungian perspective on the status of men today as "soft." In his view this is primarily due to persistent father absence as a result of work, taking the father away from the family since the industrial revolution, to divorce and loss of custody, to imprisonment or early death, perhaps by homicide or suicide, or emotional absence due to **drugs or alcohol**. Bly went on to found the mytho-poetic movement and the ManKind Project. The Project runs 38 centers worldwide offering New Warrior Training Adventures to nearly 3,000 men every year offering to connect head and heart, to turn men from a material life to an interior life, and emphasizing such values as stewardship, responsibility, courage, integrity, and masculine energy.

This movement was paralleled in the same year by the formation of the Promise Keepers (PKs) by University of Colorado football coach Bill McCartney. The PKs were formed to create "godly men" and committed to keeping seven promises: "Honoring Jesus Christ"; "pursuing vital relationships with other men ... to help him keep his promises"; "practicing spiritual, moral, ethical and sexual purity"; "building strong marriages and families through love, protection and biblical values"; "supporting his church"; "reaching beyond any racial and denominational barriers"; and "influencing his world" (www.promisekeepers.org). The movement expanded rapidly with mass rallies at **sports** arenas across the country, culminating in about 700,000 men gathering in Washington in 1997. Since it declined equally rapidly due perhaps primarily to financial mismanagement, the PKs have not created a permanent political movement.

In 1995, Louis Farrakhan and the Nation of Islam, which is very influential in the United States and the Caribbean, organized the Million Man March. Echoing the 1963 March on Washington led by Martin Luther King, this march called for black unity, brotherhood, renewed commitment to family, community, and nation, and urged participants to register for the vote. Black celebrities from across the United States participated and there was widespread support for the goals of the march. There has been no equivalent march anywhere else in the world on such men's issues.

All six of these men's movements assume that men are in some sort of crisis. However, there is little agreement on the type of crisis (religious or secular, personal, cultural or political), or on how to resolve it. Most are individualistic in their approaches, so their impact for social change is personal rather than political and, therefore, severely limited. For the NCFM, the problems are primarily systemic discrimination and unequal rights on the basis of gender. For the gay rights movement the problems are social: homophobia and systemic discrimination on the basis of sexual orientation. Bly does not address discrimination or the disposability foregrounded by the NCFM or the spiritual crisis underscored by the Promise Keepers and the Million Man March. Men's problems are more of a familial problem and, therefore, psychological, in his view. For both the mytho-poetic movement and the Nation of Islam the issues are primarily men's duties and responsibilities, not men's rights nor men's psyche. Yet in all this, there is more blame than praise of men. Simultaneously, the *Journal of Men's Studies* was founded in the United Kingdom in 1992 and *Men and Masculinities* in the United States in 1998. As a result, an increasing number of authors have written specifically about men from a range of theoretical and ideological perspectives, concerned variously with men's health and the health system, the education and legal systems, issues around divorce, as well as custody and Parental Alienation Syndrome, the justice system (the high male incarceration rates and recidivism rates), high male suicide rates, accident rates and homicide rates, the homeless, misandry, and violence, along with a general critique of male values and culture. Some organizations, mirroring such concerns, have developed with specific political goals. The Fathers 4 Justice (F4J) movement, for instance, emerged in the United Kingdom demanding recognition of father's rights after divorce and has spread to much of the world. In Washington, the Men's Health Network highlights the high male death rate, the gender gap in longevity, and the lack of resources invested in men's health. *See also* Cinema; Gay and Lesbian Movement; Gender Roles; Politics; Religions, Western; Sexism.

Further Reading: Bartkowski, John P. *The Promise Keepers*. New Brunswick, NJ: Rutgers University Press, 2004; Bly, Robert. *Iron John*. New York: Addison-Wesley, 1990; Braver, Sanford. *Divorced Dads: Shattering the Myths*. New York: Tarcher Putnam, 1998; Farrell, Warren. *The Myth of Male Power: Why Men are the Disposable Sex*. New York: Simon and Schuster, 1993; Kimmel, Michael. *Manhood in America: A Cultural History*. New York: Free Press, 1996; Nathanson, Paul, and Katherine Young. *Legalizing Misandry: From Public Shame to Systemic Discrimination against Men*. Toronto: McGill-Queen's University Press, 2006; Sommers, Christina Hoff. *The War against Boys: How Misguided Feminism Is Harming Our Young Men*. New York: Simon and Schuster, 2000; Synnott, Anthony. "In Praise of Men." In *Exploring Gender in Canada*, edited by Beverly Matthews and Lori Beaman, 51–55. Toronto: Pearson/Prentice-Hall, 2007.

Anthony Synnott

MENTAL HEALTH AND SEX.   Mental health refers to a sense of psychological well-being as well as the absence of psychological disorders, including depression, anxiety, post traumatic stress disorder, and other diagnosable conditions. Feelings of love and attachment are strongly related to good mental health. Moreover, within intimate relationships, more frequent sexual interactions are associated with more positive feelings about the relationship. Yet, love is not always linked to sex and emotional well-being. Whether or not a person engages in sex, physical ability and comfort with sexual behavior is connected to mental health. For some, sexual experiences have a positive effect on mental health; for others, such as those who have been sexually assaulted, sex may have a negative effect. Depression and other mental health problems may contribute to diminished sexual drive or interest. Further, medications used to treat some mental health conditions may cause sexual problems. Finally, the link between sex and mental health varies over historical time and across cultures.

Historically, a society's definition of acceptable sexuality is often tied to the labeling of certain groups as sexually deviant and mentally ill. Mental health and sex, then, are inextricably connected. For example, in the early decades of the twentieth century, women's sexuality in the West was highly controlled, as it was in the previous century. Sexuality was incongruent with the presumed physical frailty and emotional vulnerability of white, middle and upper-class women. When these women expressed interest in sexuality, they were often viewed as mentally deranged. "Normal" women engaged in sex only as a necessary evil necessary for procreation. Many women labeled as "sexual" at this time were institutionalized or treated medically (with treatments ranging from blood lettings to clitoridectomies for their "mental illness"). However, during the same period, women of color and poor women were viewed as naturally sexual, which was attributed to their more primitive, animal-like nature. Further, doctors routinely performed gynecological experiments on women of color, choosing these women due to racist views of personhood. Other cultures, including some countries in Asia and the Middle East, shared similar views of controlling women's sexuality during this period and attributed sexuality in women to mental illness. However, these views of women and sexuality were not shared globally. In some countries, including Russia, the link between female sexuality and mental illness was largely absent in the early 1900s.

Sigmund **Freud**, perhaps the most prominent psychiatrist of the nineteenth and twentieth centuries, asserted that sexuality was central to the medical condition of hysteria, defined by uncontrollable outbursts of emotion, with the disease based on repressed infant sexual trauma. Over time, Freud modified his view and eventually argued that rather than actual and frequent sexual trauma occurring during infancy, children possessed their own sexuality and sexual **desire**, which was central to his theory of the Oedipal Complex. This included a belief in the existence of the libido, or "sexual mental energy" (Meissner 1993: 237). In 1905, Freud invented the stages of psychosocial development as his blueprint for sexual development.

From the early twentieth century to the 1970s, medical and psychological professionals labeled non-heterosexual sexual relations as deviant and indicative of mental illness. The American Psychological Association's *Diagnostic and Statistic Manual of Mental Disorders* included **homosexuality** as a psychiatric illness until 1973. Other countries, such as China, have more recently revised their diagnostic manuals. However, homosexuality continues to be viewed as a mental as well as moral abomination in many nations and some stigma and labels for non-heterosexual individuals, such as "Gender Identity Disorder" for **transgender** individuals, continue to exist throughout psychiatric literature. Although there have been gains in societal acceptance (or, at least tolerance) of gay, lesbian, bisexual and transgender individuals, queer youth often have a higher level of psychological distress than do their heterosexual counterparts. Most evidence points to the social stigma associated with their sexual status/identity as contributors to psychological distress.

In the latter part of the twentieth century, Western views about sex changed significantly. During the 1960s, the sexual revolution emphasized sexuality as natural and sexual **desire** as healthy. Contemporary views of sex were often linked to love, but not necessarily to one particular lover. "**Free love**" and the sex that went with it became a predominant theme of Western culture. Despite these changing views of women's sexuality, many Western and non-Western countries continue to restrict women's sexual and reproductive rights. Some nations connect mental illness to female sexuality. In New Guinea, for example, hyper-sexualization among women is still viewed as the main symptom of mental illness. In some countries like Pakistan, women face jail time or execution for sexual behavior, including adultery or **premarital sex**.

The pharmaceutical industry played an important role in the transition toward integrating views of sex with mental health by introducing oral contraceptives. Western women's greater control over reproduction contributed to the view of women's sexual desires as a healthy and normal part of life. Consequently, women (particularly married women) who did not desire sex were deemed sexually repressed, an emotional condition that warranted medical and psychiatric intervention. Clinicians and researchers included the absence of sexual desire as a symptom of mental health problems, particularly depression.

As pharmaceutical companies attempted to solve mental health concerns, problems around sexuality were sometimes created. Many medications given to patients suffering from depression, for instance, had sexual side effects, including reduced sexual desire and sexual functioning. In one study, among patients with major depression, 40 percent of the women and 50 percent of the men had decreased sexual interest after taking anti-depressant medication. Thus, medications used to treat mental health problems, such as Paxil, Prozac, and Wellbutrin, among others, may contribute to the problems of those already experiencing a loss of sexual desire or functioning from depression or other mental health conditions. Other **drugs**, notably Viagra, were marketed for **erectile dysfunction**, which may precipitate depression and anxiety.

Other mental disorders are also correlated with sexual dysfunction. One U.S. study found that people with panic disorders have a higher likelihood of sexual disorders, with three-fourths reporting some type of sexual problem, including sexual aversion disorder. In addition, one-third of those with social phobia in the study reported sexual disorders.

Within the general United States population, up to 40 percent of women may be classified as having some sort of sexual dysfunction, and up to 20 percent of men experience erectile dysfunction. These statistics vary cross-culturally, according to many studies like the Global Study of Sexual Attitudes and Behaviors (GSSAB). A study of 29 nations using the GSSAB—including countries such as New Zealand, Morocco, Spain, and Hong Kong—focused on sexual dysfunctions such as premature ejaculation, erectile dysfunction, or lack of sexual interest. These studies posited a relationship between quality of life and sexual functioning. In Brazil, for example, a study of men 18 years of age or older found an erectile dysfunction rate of 45 percent among the men. Further, researchers compiling data from the GSSAB analyzed chronic premature ejaculation in men by regions of the world. They found the highest rate of premature ejaculation occurring in men in Southeast Asia, with 30 percent of men reporting this problem. The lowest rate was 12 percent, in the Middle East. Europe, Latin America, and Non-European Western countries reported statistics nearing the higher end of the scale.

Another study, using GSSAB data and investigating nine Asian countries, found at least one sexual dysfunction in one out of five men and one-third of women, ages 40 to 80. Similar problems of sexual dysfunction are also noted in Brazil and other countries with varying frequency. The sexual problems reported in these studies may, as the researchers believe, be correlated with depressive symptoms leading to decreased sexual interest or other sexual "problems," as defined by the research. Sexual and mental problems may also occur in individuals due to sexual victimization in **childhood**, **adolescence**, or adulthood.

Sexual violence is a global phenomenon affecting the mental health of many people. Women and children are more likely to be victims of rape and other forms of **sexual abuse** and assault. In the United States, approximately 17 percent of women and 3 percent of men have experienced an attempted or completed rape. The Center for Disease Control found that, among U.S. high school students, 7 percent of white students, 10 percent of Hispanic students, and 12 percent of African American students had been raped. In the United States, 45 percent of all women sexual violence survivors meet the criteria for post-traumatic stress disorder.

Sexual violence is also common in war-torn countries such as Liberia and Sudan. For example, the World Health Organization reports that, in the Bosnia-Herzegovina ethnic conflict, occurring between 1992 and 1995, up to 50,000 Muslim women were raped as a strategy of war. In Liberia, one of every two women surveyed had experienced sexual violence at the hands of a solider or fighter.

Both short- and long-term mental health issues often arise from sexual assault, including anxiety, post-traumatic stress disorder, borderline personality disorder, depression, and attempted or completed suicide. Rape significantly increases the risk of suicide among rape survivors. Suicide is attempted 13 times more often among individuals who have been raped than among those who have not. Among male survivors of rape, the rate of completed suicide is nearly 15 times higher than for other males. Some survivors of sexual assault experience psychosomatic symptoms such as headaches and sleep disorders that occur as a result of stress from the assault. Other survivors may experience flashbacks of rape, including the emotions, smells, and sounds that occurred during the assault. Further, a mental health problem known as "dissociative identity disorder" sometimes occurs in survivors of childhood rape. These survivors have at least two separate identities, splitting their identities to cope with the abuse. Of course, **pregnancy**, physical trauma, and **sexually transmitted infections** resulting from assault further contribute to mental health problems in this population.

A number of studies point to the high prevalence of mental health problems among sex workers (including "voluntary" sex workers). In Kerala, India, for example, 40 percent of sex workers experienced mental health problems, including mood disorders, schizophrenia, depression, anxiety, post-traumatic stress disorder, and suicidal tendencies. In a California study, two-thirds of the sex workers interviewed exhibited signs of post-traumatic stress disorder, sometimes resulting from childhood and/or adult sexual victimization. Research suggests that individuals who were sexually victimized in the past or who had pre-existing mental health problems are overrepresented among sex workers.

Some types of sexual behavior may be viewed as "risky" in the sense that they are associated with an increased risk of mental health problems. These risky behaviors include early onset of consensual sex, unprotected sex, failure to use **birth control**, having multiple sexual partners, and acquiring sexually transmittable infections. These behaviors may have particularly adverse consequences for children and teenagers. Mental health problems are also associated with an increased risk for using alcohol and other illicit drugs that may further contribute to engaging in risky sexual behaviors.

Although mental health and sex may impact each other negatively, the connections between sex, love, and mental health are often very positive. Studies from around the world show that individuals with close social ties have better mental health and lower mortality rates than their peers. The social tie that seems to be most strongly associated with psychological well-being is a marital relationship. Falling in love and establishing close intimate ties provide some of life's most exhilarating experiences. *See also* Aging; Bisexuality; Child Abuse; Domestic and Relationship Violence; Fetishes; Heterosexuality; Humor; Incest; Infidelity/Extramarital Sex; Masturbation; Orgasm; Pederasty; Prostitution; Psychotherapy; Race and Racism; Sex Therapists; Women's Movement.

Further Reading: Aggleton, Peter, Jane Hurry, and Ian Warwick, eds. *Young People and Mental Health.* Chichester, England: John Wiley & Sons, 2000; Chu, James A., and Elizabeth Bowman, eds. *Trauma and Sexuality: The Effects of Childhood Sexual, Physical, and Emotional Abuse on Sexual Identity and Behavior.* Binghamton, NY: Haworth Press, 2002; Dean, Carolyn J. *Sexuality and Modern Western Culture.* New York: Twayne, 1996; Ehrenreich, Barbara, and Deirdre English. *For Her Own Good: Two Centuries of the Experts Advice to Women.* New York: Anchor, 2005; Meissner, William M. "Psychoanalysis and Sexual Disorders." In *Handbook of Human Sexuality,* edited by Benjamin B. Wolman and John Money, 286–311. Northvale, NJ: Jason Aronson, 1993; Phillips, Kim M., and Barry Real. *Sexualities in History: A Reader.* New York: Routledge, 2002; Wilton, Tamsin. *Sexualities in Health and Social Care.* Buckingham, England: Open University Press, 2000; World Health Organization. http://www.who.int/en. Current cross-cultural information on several topics including sexual health, sexual violence, and mental health, January 2007.

Jennifer Zaligson

MORALITY AND ETHICS. Sexual ethics and sexual morality are inherently difficult issues to discuss, as they are deeply rooted in an individual's beliefs about right and wrong. Ethics are based upon a person's values and are the standards by which they judge his or her actions as well as those of others. Where ethics is the systematic approach to right or wrong, morality is considered the means by which behavior is measured and controlled. In effect, morality is the law of ethics—or the code of conduct put forward by an individual, group, or society. Ethics guide the actions, which are judged to be moral or immoral depending on the observer's perspective. Sexual ethics would include what is "good" to do or be sexually, as well as what is "bad;" sexual morality is the code of conduct that is generated by a group or society that enforces the sexual ethics of that group. Two major issues involving sexual ethics and sexual morality are **birth control**, and same-sex **marriage**, which can be examined from four very different perspectives: Western Medical, Distributive Justice, Buddhist, and Islamic.

Although women across the globe have been practicing birth control for centuries, the twentieth century saw the advent of hormonal birth control methods. Indeed, the expansion of those methods in the twenty-first century has created options that have replaced daily pills with weekly patches and monthly injections and vaginal rings. Perhaps the greatest moral and ethical issue that arose from this medical advancement was the separation of procreation from sexual expression. This separation, along with a woman's ability to control her own reproductive life, led to unique issues in what is fundamentally "right" about sex, and who should get to decide what laws or guidelines govern behavior.

The world's relationship with birth control has been rocky and complicated, made even more so by **politics**, changing social mores, and beliefs about the sanctity of potential life. Despite the demands for birth control methods and information, moralizing legislation, like the Comstock Laws of the late-nineteenth and early-twentieth-century United States, made contraceptives difficult for many women to obtain. Even in recent years, some pharmacists refuse to fill prescriptions that contradict their religious beliefs. Internationally, Roman Catholic opposition to contraceptives is still highly influential in medicine, even though many Catholic women continue to use birth control.

Western Medical ethics (beneficence "do good" and non-malfeasance "do no harm") were established to promote the science of medicine and the betterment of public health. Historically, non-malfeasance has been woven into ethical patient care. Though not a legal mandate, the code serves as a guideline for the health care profession. From this perspective, the sexual morality of any issue might be based upon the potential harm that such actions might inflict upon the self or others.

Considering the ethics of non-malfeasance, it is logical for people to accept the use of contraception. With extremely few exceptions, **pregnancy** is significantly more injurious to a woman's health than approved pregnancy prevention measures. However, there are known risks and possible side effects to many methods, particularly those that are hormonally based. Thus, using this particular ethic offers a mixed result.

Distributive Justice, posited by ethicist John Rawls in the twentieth century, is another framework through to view ethical issues. Based on a principle of equity, it proposes: each person has claim to equal rights and to liberties that are extensive, fair, and compatible to the liberty and rights of others; social and economic inequalities must be of greatest benefit to the least advantaged and be attached to offices and positions open to all under conditions of fair equality of opportunity. Employing this principle, basic rights should not be infringed upon, even for the benefit of greater society. The morality of sexual behaviors, then, is judged upon the access of all people to equitable resources. In addition, an act's morality is based upon the consideration of whether it will impede another individual's basic rights.

As it relates to birth control, from Rawls's perspective each individual should be given equal opportunity to succeed. This correlates in a number of ways to the matter of contraception. Allowing women to manage their fertility enables the historically disadvantaged gender to compete academically and professionally. Also, through the use of contraception, births can be planned, limiting the number of children and creating greater access to limited resources.

Buddhism, a third framework, is built upon the concepts of individual enlightenment and personal responsibility. Though varied in practice and beliefs, Buddhist ethics are largely built upon the Five Precepts, which serve as voluntary guidelines for life. The third of these is most often cited when dealing with issues related to sexual ethics: a "willingness to be aware of the suffering caused by sexual misconduct and undertaking the training to refrain from using sexual behavior in ways that are harmful to myself and to others" as well as a commitment to "attempt to express my sexuality in ways that are beneficial and bring joy."

Early Buddhist texts did not mention birth control. Overpopulation was not yet a concern in Asia. Large families were highly valued and Buddha considered the number of children a person had to be a personal choice. Personal choice can be supported by the increased power given to women to choose their individual reproductive destiny. There are no express prohibitions against contraceptive use. Because Buddha aimed to end the problem of suffering in the world, his teachings would be supportive of the use of contraceptives if a pregnancy or resultant offspring would cause hardship. Finally, the attempt to express sexuality in ways that bring joy would also offer positive support from a Buddhist sexual ethic for the separation of reproduction from sexual pleasure.

With regard to sexuality, Islam's premise is to support the fulfillment of sexual urges in a way that is considered responsible and pleasing to God. This is determined through the reading and interpretation of the Qur'an, which is believed by Muslims to be the words of God delivered to the Prophet Mohammad. **Marriage** is a highly valued practice and **celibacy** is considered to be in opposition with God's commandments. Sex is highly recommended in the Qur'an and is considered, along with marriage, a sign of God's power and blessing. From an Islamic ethical perspective, sexual ethics are determined entirely by what is considered to be pleasing to God.

Although Islam has a general prohibition against **abortion**, contraception is allowed within the parameters of marriage. The methods must be chosen through mutual consent between husband and wife and must be reversible. Islamic sexual ethics would be at odds with providing contraceptive access to unmarried Muslim women.

Perhaps one of the greatest forces of the twentieth and twenty-first centuries on the morality and ethics of sex and love has been the globalization of society and the push toward cultural pluralism that has occurred. As influences of international travel, intercultural cooperation, and international publications increase, individuals are examining the world and its peoples from a more global perspective. As this occurs, ethics and morality, which are often derived from historical and religious belief systems, become relativistic and individualized. The challenge is determining whose ethics become the moral codes that guide our behavioral interactions.

Same-sex romances have existed throughout history, with varying degrees of social acceptance. Often the response of the general population to love relationships outside of **heterosexuality** is negative. Worldwide, the issue of marriage equity has arisen, with nations divided about the support of "marriage" or equivalent relationships for same-sex couples.

A Western Medical ethic would likely examine social science and medical research, looking for evidence that would suggest "harm" that would affect any individuals who might be associated with same-sex relationships. Historically, many researchers have looked to find evidence or lack of evidence of psychosis in homosexual and bisexual people or to find it in their offspring and in children raised in their homes. No overwhelming body of research literature has found any such evidence of "harm." Although this ethical framework is one that often supports same-sex relationships, many individuals from this perspective also support a "separate but equal" perspective of "civil unions" that frames same-sex relationships outside of the boundary of what is considered to be traditional "marriage."

According to Rawls's idea of political liberalism, equality in issues like same-sex marriage is not an issue of morality, but rather an issue of allowing a society to hold and freely discuss opposing political beliefs. Lesbians, gays, and bisexuals are likely to have an inequitable portion of resources in the form of income and social services, which is in direct contradiction to the aims of distributive justice. This is due to the general absence of financial support of children. Thus, a Rawlsian perspective would argue that same-sex marriage must be, in all ways, equal to that of other-gendered marriages.

Homosexuality and **bisexuality** are not explicitly discussed by Buddha, as the terms we now use to discuss these phenomena did not exist at that time. The issue is further complicated by Buddhism's great variations among believers. The romantic lives and personal opinions on same-sex marriage of followers are largely their personal concern, as is the overall search for enlightenment. From this perspective, many Buddhist sexual ethics would neither support nor oppose same-sex marriage. It would allow each individual practitioner to seek his or her path toward enlightenment. This sense of individual freedom further complicates a discussion of morality, as it does not clearly identify a code of sexual behavior.

Alongside Judaism and Christianity as one of the Abrahmic theologies, Islam condemns homosexuality on the basis of particular interpretations of religious texts. As with any religion, individual members may have differing beliefs and behaviors counter to the tenets of their creed. As a result, there is historical evidence of same-sex relationships in the Islamic world dating back centuries, although it is of limited use to view these events from a Western perspective. As a result, Islam would, almost universally, condemn homosexuality. Same-sex marriage would likewise be dismissed. *See also* Religions, Eastern; Religions, Western.

Further Reading: Al-Akili, Muhammad. *Natural Healing with the Medicine of the Prophet by Imam Ibn al-Qayyim al-Jawziyya*. Philadelphia: Pearl Publishing, 1996; Baumeister, Roy F., and Julie Exline. "Virtue, Personality, and Social Relations: Self-Control as the Moral Muscle." *Journal of Personality* 67, no. 6 (1999): 1165–94; Gert, Bernard. *Morality*. New York: Oxford University Press, 1998; Pardue, Peter A. "Buddhism." In *International Encyclopedia of the Social Sciences*, edited by David Sills, 176–84. New York: Macmillan, 1968; Rawls, John. *A Theory of Justice: Revised Edition*. Oxford: Oxford University Press, 1999; Rizvi, Sayyid Muhhammad. *Marriage and Morals in Islam*. Scarborough: Islamic Education and Information Center, 1994; Shryock, Richard. "Freedom and Interference in Medicine." *Annals of the American Academy of Political and Social Science* 200, no. 45 (1938): 32–59; Sorensen, A. *The Value of Value—in Ethics and Morality*. Copenhagen: Department of Management, Politics and Philosophy, Copenhagen Business School, 2005; Religioustolerance.org. Ontario consultants for religions tolerance. B. A. Robinson. http://www.religioustolerance.org. A relatively broad source for multiple faith perspectives on contemporary issues, April 2006 [last date updated]; Tyrer, Louise. "Introduction of the Pill and Its Impact." *Contraception* 59, no. 1S (1999): 11S–16S.

Donald A. Dyson, Timaree Schmit, and Tameca N. Jackson

O

ORGASM. The human orgasm can create the most intense erotic pleasure that a male or female experiences without recourse to drugs. It is a tantalizing short experience (some 5–50 seconds) and dissolves body boundaries thus uniting lovers in a unique way. Because of this it is often regarded as the ultimate expression of emotional and physical love between heterosexual or homosexual lovers, although it can also be used by an individual for his or her private sexual pleasure.

Orgasm can be self-induced (auto-**masturbation**), initiated by a sexual partner of either sex (masturbation), induced by coitus, or activated by vibrating devices applied to the genitals. Few have the rare ability to create an orgasm simply by exciting themselves mentally through fantasy. Orgasms occur without having to be awake, for they can be experienced during sleep in both males (so-called "wet dreams") and females. They are normally induced in willing (consensual) sexual partners and are often thought to be dependent on needing the subject's cooperation, but they can also be induced by sexual stimulation in both male and female non-willing (non-consensual) subjects by force, fear, or because of an impaired resistance to the stimulation (sleep, **drugs**, alcohol, or even hypnosis).

Marked differences exist between the high frequency of masturbation to orgasm in males compared to females and in the ease by which males can induce and have orgasms compared with the greater difficulty experienced by females. This is especially so during coitus where approximately 50 percent of females do not achieve orgasm from penile thrusting alone.

Males have no difficulty in identifying when they have an orgasm for it nearly always occurs with the ejaculation of semen. In the case of females, especially those who are having their first or early orgasms, the recognition of the activity is not so clear-cut. Even though it is a highly subjective experience, individuals can misjudge an extremely high level of sexual arousal for an orgasm or they can lie—without objective evidence of its occurrence there is no way of knowing the truth.

Clearly a definition would be useful as a template so that personal experience can be compared and matched. The difficulty starts here for who should define what an orgasm is? If an individual's self-report is unreliable, we must turn to those who study the activity, namely physiologists, endocrinologists, psychologists, and, more recently, brain imagers. Despite this impressive list it has been surprisingly difficult to establish a definition of orgasm that is universally acceptable. The best that we can do is to create a working definition as follows:

An orgasm is a variable, transient peak sensation of intense pleasure, creating an altered state of consciousness which is usually accompanied by involuntary, rhythmic contractions of the pelvic muscles often with anal contractions and myotonia (muscle contractions) that resolves, sometimes partially, the sexually induced tension and genital vasocongestion usually with a feeling of well-being and contentment.

In relation to males, with the orgasmic contractions of the pelvic muscles, semen normally is ejected, while in women, uterine contractions usually occur.

Although a few pioneering orgasm studies using questionnaires, interviews, and case histories occurred in the early part of the twentieth century (Ellis, Van de Velde, Dickinson, **Kinsey**), they now are mainly of historical interest. The scientific study of orgasm could be said to have begun with the laboratory investigations of William Masters and Virginia Johnson who studied 7,500 female and 2,500 male orgasms between 1954 and 1966. They created a model for the human sexual response cycle that included an excitement, plateau, orgasmic, and resolution phase (the EPOR model). Later modifications included addition of a desire phase and amalgamating the excitement and plateau phases, creating a DEOR model. In brief, during sexual arousal there is an increase in the heart rate, blood pressure, and breathing in both sexes. Blood is redirected to the genitals so that they become engorged, creating penile erection in males and clitoral and vaginal engorgement in females, the latter facilitating vaginal lubrication that allows painless penile penetration during coitus. All these changes reach a maximum just before the orgasmic phase takes place.

In the male orgasm the bladder is closed off by sphincter contraction to prevent entry of semen. The smooth (involuntary) muscle of the capsules surrounding the testis, prostate, and seminal vesicles contracts forcing the various secretions and the spermatozoa into the prostatic urethra. A feeling of impending ejaculation ("ejaculatory inevitability") occurs and the subsequent ejaculation cannot consciously be stopped. Within a second or two contractions of the urethra propel the semen along to the base of the penis. Finally, powerful repeated contractions of the pelvic striated (voluntary) musculature then squeeze the urethra and forcibly squirt the semen from the penis. Concomitant with these contractions are throbbing waves of extreme pleasure (the actual orgasm) whose intensity gradually dies away. Most males groan/vocalize at each contraction. Although orgasm and ejaculation nearly always occur together, their physiological mechanisms are known to be distinct. Without the striated muscle contractions (just the smooth muscle contractions) ejaculation is of a dribbling type and the pleasure experienced greatly reduced.

It is possible to have an orgasm without ejection of semen ("dry ejaculation"). This happens when multiple ejaculations deplete the semen pool, with various drugs and with low testosterone levels. Orgasm is thus not dependent on the accumulation or pressure of semen in the male genital tract. The first orgasm of a sexual scenario is usually the most intense and pleasurable and there is an immediate period after its occurrence when another cannot be experienced—technically called the post-ejaculatory refractory time (PERT). The duration of the PERT varies; it can be short in young males (minutes) but gradually gets appreciably longer in **aging** males (hours).

According to Masters and Johnson female orgasm is initiated with a transient sensation of "suspension" or "stoppage" followed by a thrust of intense sensual awareness at the clitoris then radiating out into the pelvis. It is followed by a sensation of suffusion of warmth first in the pelvis, which then spreads to the rest of the body. Finally, involuntary contractions in the vagina and lower pelvis, often described as "pelvic throbbing," occur related to contractions of the striated muscles around the vaginal entrance (introitus). Many women feel the waves of pleasure with the latter throbbings, but not all perceive such contractions yet still claim they have orgasms. PERT does not occur in females who can have multiple (serial) orgasms with ever-increasing pleasure. Some females expel a glandular, prostatic-like fluid from their urethra during orgasm (female ejaculation), which can be mistaken for urine.

Orgasmic uterine contractions sucking up the sperm have been claimed to hasten their transport along the female genital tract and, controversially, to allow better retention of those from a chosen high-ranking male. These proposals ignore the fact that pregnancies occur in non-orgasmic women and by artificial insemination. Moreover, the cervix and uterus are elevated during arousal from the vaginal floor, preventing such rapid sperm transport. In fact, the fastest sperm transit is actually in the unaroused female, and arousal delays it.

When people describe their orgasms in writing and any gender clues are removed others cannot identify whether a particular description is written by a male or female. This suggests a common mental activity. Brain imaging is just beginning to identify similarities and differences between the sexes. There are differences, however, between male and female orgasms: females can have multiple orgasms separated by a very short interval while males normally cannot; female orgasms can be much longer than the males; male and female pelvic muscle contractions show different patterns; the male orgasm once initiated always runs to completion but the female's can end if the sexual stimulation inducing it is stopped.

Much has been written about the types of female orgasms, especially those produced from clitoral compared to vaginal stimulation. Many females report that they experience different feelings when the two sites are stimulated separately. Orgasms from clitoral stimulation are described as "warm, ticklish, electrical and sharp" while those produced by vaginal stimulation are "throbbing, deep, soothing and comfortable." Early laboratory observations by Masters and Johnson did not reveal any physiological differences. However, later studies by Perry in a single subject recording muscular contractions showed those during orgasms induced by clitoral stimulation and those from stimulation of the anterior (upper) wall of the vagina, where the so-called G spot is found, were different. The mechanics of coitus suggest that penile thrusting would stimulate simultaneously both the anterior vaginal wall and the clitoris through traction on ligaments attached to its base producing orgasms from joint clitoral and vaginal stimulation. The whole subject of the types of female orgasm is fraught with very limited physiological studies but much speculation, some of it overly influenced by sexual **politics**.

The assumption, probably unwarranted, is that males do not have a typology of orgasm. There are reports, however, that orgasms from penile stimulation differ from those obtained by digitally stimulating the prostate gland per rectum. This technique is not usually employed in most heterosexual sexual scenarios but is often used in homosexual ones. No laboratory comparison of the two possible types exists but anecdotal reports describe the prostate-induced orgasms as being "deeper," more widespread, and lasting longer.

While coitus and orgasm are often thought of as "natural acts," society and culture can have a significant impact on them. This is especially so in relation to the acknowledgment of female sexual pleasure and her orgasmic potential. In cultures that are censorious about female sexual pleasure, women have difficulty in becoming orgasmic, but in those that expect women to have orgasms like men, the women experience orgasms more easily.

Most of our knowledge of the influence of society and culture on sexual behavior comes from anthropological studies of tribal societies. Those that foster female sexual potential, such as the Mundugumur (Papua, New Guinea) and Mangaian (Cook Islands, South Pacific), encourage their women to have orgasms and, in the latter, males are instructed how to stimulate them for maximum pleasure. Males who cannot give their partners an orgasm are not held in high esteem. Other societies, like the Arapesh (New Guinea), have no word for the female orgasm. Sambian men (New Guinea) deny that female orgasm exists and accord the clitoris no function or importance and never mention it publicly. In a number of sub-Saharan African countries men have no interest in giving females orgasms and prefer coitus with unlubricated vaginas that women have to prepare by instilling drying agents. This makes coitus painful and, thus, the attainment of female coital orgasm is impeded.

Orgasm can be easily self-induced by males for pleasure. Because it is concomitant with the expulsion of sperm, moralists and some religions condemn such activity as self-abuse, indicating moral weakness or lack of self-control. Undertaking the activity solely for the purpose of procreation becomes virtuous while its activation simply for pleasure is sinful. In many societies, males who profess masturbating are scorned and, because of fear of public ridicule, it becomes a secretive and often guilt-ridden activity. In the West, those who masturbate, especially young men, are given pejorative names (wanker, tosser, jerk-off, toss-pot) and regarded as inadequate, supposedly as the only way they can obtain sexual relief; such epithets are not applied to women who masturbate.

Modern attitudes to human sexuality regard adolescent **masturbation** as a necessary part of healthy sexual development benefiting later adult erotic activity. Its positive use is as a learning technique to experience the responses of the body and explore what pleases one most. *See also* Heterosexuality; Indigenous Peoples; Mental Health and Sex; Sex Therapists; Sexual Science/Sexology.

Further Reading: Ford, Cleland S., and Frank A. Beach. *Patterns of Sexual Behaviour*. London: Eyre & Spottiswoode Ltd, 1952; Francouer, Robert T., and Raymond J. Noonan. *The Continuum Complete International Encyclopedia of Sexuality*. New York: Continuum International, 2004; Levin, Roy J. "Sexual Arousal—Its Physiological Roles in Human Reproduction." *Annual Review Sex Research* 16 (2005): 1–31; Mah, Kenneth, and Yitzchak M. Binik. "The Nature of the Human Orgasm: A Critical Review of Major Trends." *Clinical Psychology Review* 21 (2001): 823–56; Masters, William H., and Victoria E. Johnson. *Human Sexual Response*. Boston: Brown & Company, 1966; Meston, Cindy M., Roy J. Levin, Marca L. Sipski, Elaine M. Hull, and Julia R. Heiman. "Women's Orgasm." *Annual Review of Sex Research* 15 (2004): 173–257.

R. J. Levin

P

PEDERASTY. Pederasty is often subsumed within the generic category of intergenerational sexual acts, practices, and identities. Unlike pedophilia, which defines adult male or female attraction to a prepubescent girl or boy under thirteen, and korephilia, which denotes adult female attraction to girls, pederasty specifically defines emotional, intimate, and physical adult male attraction to teenage boys. The contested issues generated by such relationships across a number of academic disciplines, **media**, and cultures give crucial insights into shifting contemporary attitudes related to gender, sexuality, class, race, and most significantly age relations, throughout the twentieth century. Contemporary Western understandings of, and meanings on, pederasty have invariably (yet problematically) drawn on a Classical Greek lexicon, where the term "paiderastia" denoted an asymmetric pedagogical and erotic relationship between an adolescent boy (pais) and an adult male lover (erastes). However, over-reliance on such archaic meanings obscures diverse cross-cultural manifestations of pederastic sexual practices and intimate loving relationships involving adult men and adolescent boys. These have been widespread in different cultures, where they were devoid of a Western homosexual label or social stigma. Historical and cross-cultural variations on pederastic relationships (including the older and younger partners involved) can be explained by differing conceptions of **childhood** and **adolescence**, sexual behavior, class, gender, and various unique, context-specific factors. Such relationships reflected structural power dynamics within the societies in which they were negotiated; many also provided and inspired a rich literature and iconography celebrating male youth aesthetic beauty, reciprocal desiring subjectivities, and close intimate friendships.

Explanations for pederasty vary, and the meanings associated with such relationships are hotly contested. Factors commonly cited include: transferring special charisma to the younger partner; an asymmetric sexual order in which older males inseminate younger; patriarchal and militaristic social systems; adopting particular sexual identity and gender roles; and a youth's coming of age. Strong associations can be seen in pre-twentieth-century pederasty and class. For example, Central America Mayans ritually prescribed pederasty according to political and social ascension, in which noble youth were constructed as objects of **desire** by the leaders of society. European ethnographers in nineteenth-century China described sexual and intimate relations between mandarins and their servant boys, alongside widespread male youth prostitution, and Japanese pederastic practices lasted up until the early twentieth century within religious communities and in Samurai warrior codes.

Late-nineteenth-century Europe witnessed a revival in interest in classical antiquity. In Victorian Britain and Imperial Germany, many educational and cultural elites adopted Platonic notions of "Pedagogical Eros," with paternalistic emphases on mentoring. In early ethnographic interpretations, such "high" European conceptions of intergenerational male love were contrasted with non-European "base" sexual practices, which were depicted as "immoral" and "primitive" (Bleys 1996: 185). Despite such claims, there has been an extensive and long-standing tradition of pederastic relationships between European men and boys in various non-European locations (notably North Africa, Sri Lanka, and the Far East). Recent labeling of such relationships as "child sex tourism" fails to adequately address the extent to which many non-European cultures tolerated and even embraced the educational, financial, and friendship benefits of such contacts.

There is also strong evidence of a thriving underground artistic and literary pederastic movement called the Uranians in the nineteenth and early twentieth century. UK Pederastic themes also emerged in the literature of key writers during this period (Alger and Melville in the United States, Houseman and Wilde in the United Kingdom, and Goethe and Mann in Germany). Whereas in many of these pederastic, cross-class relationships, older middle-class partners often eroticized working-class boys as "transgressive other," contemporary writers (Whitman and Carpenter) provided an alternative, idealistic framework of a democratic cross-class, cross-generational ideology based on male comradeship. In his 1908 anthology of poems, "Iolaus-anthology of friendship," Carpenter dedicates a whole section to Whitman's poetry and philosophy. The theme of male comradeship comes across in Whitman's "Leaves of Grass" (1891) poem, and throughout his life, Whitman established several intense intergenerational friendships, notably when helping wounded young soldiers in the U.S. Civil War.

Pederasty has also been linked with patriarchal **gender roles**. For example, Evans-Prichard conducted a study of sexual relationships between young warriors and boys amongst the Azande of Sub-Saharan Africa. These were organized in fighting units between "abakumba" (married men) and "aparanga" (bachelors) who lived together in barracks. In South Africa, Zulu boy-brides ("inkothsare") accompanied miners on their work. Pederastic attachments even extended to formal marriages between men and boys amongst the Egyptians, Western Australia Aborigines, Inuit, Algerians, and Greek Orthodox Albanians. A long-standing pederastic tradition also exists to the present day in many Arab countries, with a common lexicon in Arabic, Farsi, Turkish, and other languages for adult males who are attracted to boys. Although such ties were instituted and maintained through intimate and romantic associations, they were explainable by factors such as inheritance rights and the segregation of women. Finally, the Melanesian model construed sexual contacts between adult males and boys through the ritual transference of semen to facilitate the male lineage. The Sambia believed femaleness to be innate unless men intervene as "secondary socializers" (trainers, enforcers, teachers, elders and shamans) through ritual procedures in the form of initiation practices to protect them from female contamination, and promote strength.

It has been a widely held view by historians of sexuality that paradigmatic shifts took place in western Europe away from pederastic to androphile (adult male same-sex or gay) relationships as the dominant modes of homosexual desire. By the early twentieth century, in Europe and the United States, an emerging body of moral and scientific literature maintained that the seduction of boys could impair their "normal" physical and emotional development. In the UK, after a series of sexual **scandals** involving high-profile figures and male youth prostitutes, increasing attention was paid to the seduction of youths by men. Pre–World War I Canada also witnessed an upsurge in middle-class fears of working-class boys being "led astray" by "fallen men."

The social and political context of post-1945 North America was especially conducive for constituting young people within Cold War discourses. Here special attention was paid to "vulnerable youth," with fears that **homosexuality** was predatory, wreaking physical and psychic havoc on youth. Homosexuality was constituted as "un-American" and a danger to children, who were in turn, held up by conservatives as a metaphor for the very future of the West and the associated family and gender roles it represented.

Modern-day critics have imposed late modern victimological discursive formulas, whereby all male lovers of youth are stigmatized as sex offenders, and all initiatory or willing younger partners labeled victims. In contrast, pederastic historians like Brongersma have imported historical sexual practices into modern-day sexuality debates and overly eulogized the romantic and positive aspects, while failing to accept critical aspects of pederastic relationships, including potential power imbalances and harmful consequences. Nevertheless, quantitative research suggests positive accounts from younger males in pederastic relations, conventionally silenced in dominant victimological positions.

Claims for young peoples' sexual rights outside protectionist frameworks highlight discrepancies in the way young people are presented as active agents in some areas, yet constituted as unknowing dupes in sexuality. Here the general sex-negative, ageist Western cultural scripting for adult-child sexual relationships (including state intervention and professional pastoral monitoring) is heavily criticized by child liberationists. Liberationists argue that although children are subservient to adults in all areas of social life, their rights in certain contexts (including financial and political) are institutionally recognized, and youth should be allowed to experience loving and sexual relations with whosoever they choose. Many European counties have reduced their ages of consent, and there is increasing evidence of a lowering of the age at which children have their first sexual experience.

Nevertheless, "boylover" movements, for example, the North American Man Boy Love Association (NAMBLA), have largely failed to achieve their demands for abolishing age of consent legislation, or generate acceptance for man-boy relationships. Their attempts to inject a counter-discourse of man-boy love, in contrast to stressing man-boy sex, have also failed to allay public suspicions. The impetus for maintaining the current injunctions on such relationships can be explained by a long-running campaign by the **gay and lesbian movement** to remove the stigmatic association of homosexuality with the seduction of youth and pedophilia. The near universal adoption of child sexual abuse (CSA) positions by national and global organizations, together with mounting stories drawn from male survivors of abuse, has further entrenched popular attitudes against such relationships. *See also* Child Abuse; Colonialism/Postcolonialism and Sex; Indigenous Peoples; Mental Health and Sex; Politics; Sex Crimes; Sexual Abuse and Assault.

Further Reading: Bleys, Rudi. *The Geography of Perversion: Male-to-Male Sexual Behavior Outside the West and the Ethnographical Imagination 1750–1918.* London: Cassell, 1996; Brongersma, Edward. *Volume 1 Loving Boys. A Multidisciplinary Study of Sexual Relations Between Adult and Minor Males.* Amsterdam: Global Academic Publishers, 1986; Evans-Prichard, Edward. "Sexual Inversion among the Azande." *American Anthropologist* 72 (1970): 1428–34; Herdt, Gilbert. *The Sambia: Ritual and Gender in New Guinea.* Chicago: University of Chicago, 1987;

IPCE. See http://www.ipce.info/ipceweb/Library/overview.htm. Research articles, references, and annotated bibliographies; Murray, Stephen. "Southwest Asian and North African Terms for Homosexual Roles." *Archives of Sexual Behavior* 24, no. 6 (1995): 623–29; Rind, Bruce, Robert Bauserman, and Philip Tromovitch. "A Meta-Analytic Examination of Assumed Properties of Child Sexual Abuse Using College Samples." *Psychological Bulletin* 124 (1998): 22–53.

Richard Yuill

POLITICS.　　Politics is the process of group decision-making. Sexuality and politics have often been considered to be of opposite natures: sexuality being among the most private of individual activities and politics an essentially public concern. Yet, the two have had an intimate relationship throughout history and their connection has become even more prominent through the democratization and mass-mobilization of politics. The interaction between sexuality and politics has taken place in two main ways. First, politicians of the twentieth and twenty-first centuries have, like their counterparts in earlier eras, attempted to control and regulate sexual activity and **gender roles**. Political concerns and goals have led to the passing of laws promoting or banning various sexual practices and modes of love. But the relationship has also gone the other way as the political process itself has been influenced by issues of gender and sexuality. This can be seen most prominently in increasing participation of women in the political process in countries around the world. It can also be demonstrated by the injection of sexual themes, language, and metaphors into the political process, even when this process is itself not about sexuality.

Beginning in the eighteenth and nineteenth centuries, many states claimed ever-greater powers to regulate their citizens' personal and sexual behaviors. The state often supported religious leaders who claimed to promote or protect a mode of family life they considered under threat from social or technological change. By 1900, many states around the world had outlawed heterosexual **sodomy**, homosexual sex of any kind, contraception, and **abortion**. Non-Western states that did not traditionally revile **homosexuality** often adjusted their legal codes in this way in order to conform to European standards. This was often required in trading agreements and treaties. Thailand, for example, outlawed sodomy in the first decade of the twentieth century for this reason, although its Buddhist religion had long tolerated individuals of same-sex, transvestite, or transgendered identities, together called *katoey*. This standardization along Western lines was a prominent feature of the first half of the twentieth century, as states claimed increasing power over their citizens' sexual behaviors because of the idea that the citizen's body and behavior was of essential importance to the welfare of the state.

During the last half of the twentieth century, many countries re-evaluated their legal codes. This re-created local differences, traditions, and values. Thailand, which decriminalized homosexuality in 1956, is home to one of the world's most vibrant and public homosexual and **transgender** communities. Other countries, like India, have maintained their colonial legacy outlawing sodomy despite local efforts to rescind Section 377 of Indian Penal Code, which was enacted by the British 150 years ago.

Many countries that still restrict their citizens' sexual activities do so largely because of pressure from local religious authorities. In Iran, homosexuality is still illegal under the country's strict interpretation of Islamic law, and is punishable by death in some cases. But the state sponsors and even mandates gender reassignment surgery for male-to-female transgendered persons, based on the idea that they could then pass as women and enter into heterosexual marriages.

Some states also claim such power over reproduction and child-bearing. Eugenic policies (the selective breeding of human beings with the supposed purpose of improving the intelligence and health of society) became quite popular in many countries during the first half of the twentieth century, with almost all Western societies adopting programs that encouraged **marriage** among the wealthy or highly educated, in the hopes that this would produce more intelligent offspring. Many countries, including Denmark, Finland, France, Iceland, the United Kingdom, Norway, and Switzerland, passed laws to forcibly sterilize people deemed mentally or physically deficient. The United States had one of the most comprehensive programs in the world. The U.S. Supreme Court declared, in the 1927 case *Buck v. Bell*, that individual states could sterilize those they deemed mentally unfit. Between 1907 and 1963, the United States sterilized over 64,000 people. Sweden, which sterilized a similar number of people, later paid reparations to the victims; no such compensations have been provided by the U.S. government.

The most comprehensive and extreme eugenic program, however, was enacted in Germany from 1933 to 1945. The Nazis used some tactics already common in other countries, both "positive" (increase birth rates among favored segments of the population) and "negative" (sterilization) eugenics, but they expanded these policies to an unprecedented scale. In many ways, political control of sexuality and family life was at the heart of the Nazi program. A 1933 Law for the Prevention of Hereditary Diseased Offspring required doctors to report on their patients' mental conditions and family status, and it created over 400 Genetic Health Courts to rule on whether these people should be sterilized. During the first four years of this law, over 400,000 people were victimized. The Nazis also promoted sexual activity and child-bearing among "Aryan" segments of the population by providing incentives for childbearing, instituting medals and awards for mothers similar to military honors, and establishing "Fountain of Life" homes to support single mothers and mothers of children fathered by men of the SS, an elite corps of armed soldiers within the Nazi Party. Nazi eugenic policies eventually led to the Holocaust, in which over six million Jews across Europe were murdered.

After the German defeat in 1945, knowledge of the regime's crimes discredited eugenics across the world. Nevertheless, some programs continued for decades, including many targeting indigenous, rural, or poor communities. As late as 1996 to 2000, Peru sterilized over 230,000 rural poor as part of a compulsive family planning program.

The common element to all these cases is the state's claim that its political interests are more important than the personal interests of its citizens. Laws concerning sexuality and family life can therefore change over time according to what politicians believe a state requires. During the first years of Communist Rule in China, 1949–1962, **families** were encouraged to have as many children as possible based on Mao Zedong's idea that "the more people, the stronger we are." This dramatically increased the Chinese birth rate, but also led to wide-scale famine when food supplies could not be similarly increased. After Deng Xiaoping took charge of the party, in 1978, a new population policy encouraged a one-child family. While it was never illegal to have more than one child, families who chose to do so risked losing state benefits in education and health care and often paid fines. Also, especially in rural areas, the policy has led to increased rates of infanticide and forced **abortions**, especially of female babies, and forced sterilizations of women who have already had children.

Partially because previous policies were so successful, creating negative population growth in some areas, and partly due to unforeseen consequences (small families increased reliance on the elderly and state support), the one-child policy has been modified. Chinese families in some cities and of certain education levels are being again encouraged to bear children.

In earlier centuries, political decisions and laws about sexual behavior would have been made by a relatively limited group, which consisted of tribal elders, landed or hereditary nobles, economic elites, or religious leaders. Additionally, with few exceptions, these decision-makers were all men. Beginning in the early twentieth century, women for the first time gained the right to vote and to stand for public office. A century later this is nearly universal.

The women's suffrage movement originated in Great Britain, one of the oldest and most advanced democracies. It had traditionally barred women from voting partially because of stereotypes about women being more emotional, less logical, and more easily deceived than men. Additionally, many voting laws in Great Britain and elsewhere required property ownership, which also was denied to women. Paradoxically, the suffrage movement made its biggest advances only when it disavowed universal suffrage, which challenged class and racial prohibitions as well.

Women's suffrage was at first a purely European phenomenon. But the first governments to grant women access to the vote were actually located farthest from Europe's center. British colonies in the Pitcairn Islands and New Zealand had already granted suffrage in the nineteenth century. In 1907, Finland elected 17 women to be the world's first female members of parliament. France and Belgium, in contrast, did so shortly after the Second World War, leaving Switzerland (1971) and finally Lichtenstein (1984) as the last European countries to restrict voting to men only. Around the world, many new governments created in the wake of de-colonization granted women's suffrage from the moment of their establishment.

Today, most countries' election laws give men and women equal voting rights, but some exceptions remain. In Lebanon, women may vote if they have completed an elementary education, while men are required to vote whether they are educated or not. Officials in Saudi Arabia, where men and women remain strictly segregated in all realms of public life, shifted course on women's voting in 2005. At the beginning of the year they declared that the ban against women would remain in place, but in the November 2005 municipal elections they allowed women for the first time to vote and run for office. Some countries also take marital status into consideration in their voting requirements, which in effect deprives many women and men of their votes based on their unmarried status. In Bolivia, married people of 18 years and older are required to vote, while unmarried individuals cannot vote until they are 21. The small Himalayan kingdom of Bhutan grants one vote per family in its elections, which effectively bars many women from voting because of their subordination to male heads of the household.

Since winning equal political rights, women have entered government not only as voters, but as office-holders and officials themselves. Over the course of the last century, women became heads of state, prime ministers, and leaders of governments in such diverse locales as Argentina, Chile, Germany, Guyana, Haiti, Iceland, Ireland, Latvia, Liberia, Nicaragua, Panama, the Philippines, and Sri Lanka. Many people expected or feared that women would bring a new, softer tone to the political world. Ironically, many of the most famous female politicians have been of the "Iron Lady" variety, a phrase the Soviet media coined in reference to the British Prime Minister Margaret Thatcher (1979–1990). Thatcher, as well as other "Iron Ladies" such as Israel's third Prime Minister Golda Meir (1969–1974) and Indian Prime Minister Indira

Gandhi (1966–1977 and 1980–1984), demonstrated that women could serve equally in the government.

One way in which politics has been changed by the growing prominence of sexual and gender matters in public discourse are the ways in which politicians have used these subjects as political metaphors or arguments. Worldwide, political operatives have exposed or alleged sexual behaviors of their opponents in order to discredit them and remove them from office. Those behind the allegations may or may not be genuinely outraged over the behavior, but their primary motivation is usually one of politics and not **morality**.

A German case, in 1907, set the standard for this tactic. The Eulenberg affair, named after the diplomat and noble Count Phillip of Eulenberg, involved a clique of homosexual officials close to the German Kaiser Wilhelm II. Proponents of military and imperial expansion feared that these men were trying to moderate German foreign policy. They seized on evidence of homosexuality to drive the moderates from political control. From 1907 to 1909, over twenty officers were dismissed after being found guilty of homosexuality. Six committed suicide after being threatened with blackmail. Eulenberg himself fell sick and retired from public life. Germany then proceeded on its military expansion and confrontational diplomatic tone, which eventually led to the outbreak of the First World War, the fall of the German Empire, and the abdication of the Kaiser. Although the journalists and politicians behind the **scandal** did not have these goals in mind, many people at the time recognized their political motives. As Eulenberg's wife said, "They are striking at my husband, but their target is the Kaiser."

The Nazis built on this heritage in the 1930s to defame and discredit those who opposed them, including military officers, Catholic priests, and even some leaders of the Nazi party, including Ernst Roehm who commanded the Nazi Storm Troopers. Similar cases have been seen around the world, such as a 2001 incident in which the Taiwanese politician Chu Mei-feng was secretly videotaped having sex with a married man. The 47-minute tape was distributed by papparazzi magazines and over the **Internet**, effectively ending her political career.

In all these cases, the injection of sexual themes into the political process is used to argue about the character, competence, and morality of political figures. The Taiwanese case and others like it also show the powerful combination of media and political interests. Perhaps the best example is U.S. President Bill Clinton's affair with a White House intern. Once sex was brought into the equation, the nation was captivated. Republicans pointed to the affair as an example of Clinton's alleged immorality and claimed that he could not be trusted to use power responsibly due to his sexual appetites and his attempts to cover up the scandal. They used a sensational allegation about Clinton's private sexual behavior to argue against his public policies. *See also* Birth Control; Colonialism/Postcolonialism and Sex; Indigenous Peoples; Religions, Eastern; Religions, Western; Women's Movement.

Further Reading: Apostolidis, Paul, and Juliet A. Williams, eds. *Public Affairs: Politics in the Age of Sex Scandals.* Duke University Press, 2004; Genovese, Michael A., ed. *Women as National Leaders.* Newbury Park, CA: Sage, 1993; Hartmann, Heidi, ed. *Gendering Politics and Policy: Recent Developments in Europe, Latin America, and the United States.* Binghamton, NY: Haworth, 2005; Mbakpuo, C. Victor. *The Conscience of a Nation: Clinton, Sex, and Politics Around the World.* BookSurge, 2006; Mouton, Michelle. *From Nurturing the Nation to Purifying the Volk: Weimar and Nazi Family Policy, 1918–1945.* Cambridge: Cambridge University Press, 2007; Revles, Daniel J. *In the Name of Eugenics: Genetics and the Uses of Human Heredity.* Cambridge, MA: Harvard University Press, 1995; Women in Politics. Inter-Parliamentary Union.

http://www.ipu.org/iss-e/women.htm. Documents historical membership of women in politics and promotes their current participation, January 2007.

Andrew Thomas Wackerfuss

POLYAMORY.   *See* Polygamy/Polyamory

POLYGAMY/POLYAMORY.   Polygamy is the cultural and religious practice of having multiple **marriage** partners; polyamory is the recently coined term for a social movement of people who embrace responsible non-monogamy as a relationship model. Although both connote multiple sexual partners, polygamy and polyamory signify distinctly different forms of non-monogamous sexual and loving partnerships and have been used to describe a variety of social groupings. Polygamy, in which each spouse may marry more than one partner, has realized many forms in different historical periods and cultures. However, most cultures do proscribe specific rules on partnerships and the ways in which individuals relate to one another within the marriage. Polyamory, coming into use in the late twentieth century in the United States, is a relationship model allowing for multiple sexual partners, with all members communicating openly with one another and everyone is aware of each other's relationships. Both polygamy and polyamory reject monogamy. In a sample of ethnographic data, scholars found that 77 percent of the world's cultures had at some point practiced polygyny, 17 percent had been entirely monogamous, and 1 percent had practiced polyandry.

The term polygamy surfaced in the sixteenth century from Greek to mean "many marriages." In the twentieth-century, it meant the state of being married to or desiring multiple marriages. Additionally, polygamy chiefly is applied to the custom of a man with multiple wives (polygyny), which contrasts to a woman who customarily marries multiple men (polyandry).

Polyandry is rarer than polygyny. It is usually typified by physical environments where high populations put extreme pressure on a limited agricultural system. This social organization works to limit population growth and is commonly found in the Himalayan areas of South Asia, although polyandry has occurred in various African, Oceanic, and Native American cultures. Fraternal forms of polyandry often involve multiple brothers marrying the same woman and organizing kinship around the male family members (a patrilineal household).

Polygyny has been practiced by many different cultures throughout history. Polygynous societies are generally organized around the family, which ideally includes one husband and multiple wives. Households are usually organized with the wives and children living with or near one another and the husband having sexual relations with all of the women, although not always equally. Many African societies have practiced polygyny for centuries. Although Western influences have curbed the practice, many countries still tolerated or encouraged the practice throughout the twentieth century. Even where it is legal, only a small percentage of the population practiced polygyny, due to the relative balance of men to women at any given time. Thus, individuals who practice polygamy are marked with a higher social status in Africa. Yet even marriages that are monogamous in a polygynous society may transition to polygyny at any point.

The most famous example of polygyny in twentieth-century America occurred in Mormon areas of Utah. Via a series of bills and federal court cases, the United States government struggled to criminalize polygamy during the latter half of the nineteenth century. The government revamped immigration procedures in 1891, banning

A Latter-Day Saint poses on the porch with his six wives in Salt Lake City, ca. 1915. Courtesy Library of Congress.

polygamists from entering the United States, and its immigration policy was exercised heavily during the early part of the twentieth century. The head of the Church of Latter Day Saints (the Mormons) officially denounced the marital practice as recently as 1904 and the government prosecuted those who openly practiced polygamy. Those who favored polygamy had to be cautious. Throughout the 1930s and 1940s, fundamentalist groups formed new communities in remote parts of Utah and Arizona, all organized primarily around the issue of plural marriages.

Although polygamous groups have experienced varying legal responses from state authorities, enforcement of laws has at times been strong. In 2006, authorities arrested Warren Jeffs, a leader of a polygamous group who was rumored to have anywhere from 40 to 70 wives. The charges pressed against him addressed the arrangement of marriages between minor girls and older men, a practice that is amongst the most highly criticized aspects of fundamentalist Mormon polygamy customs. The arrangement of marriage for girls under the age of 18 has become the key legal focus against polygamy in the twenty-first-century United States.

Polygyny faced other complex social responses in the twentieth century. African society continued to see the practice challenged by the spread of Christianity during the era of colonialism that ended only in mid-century. As Islam tolerates and sometimes encourages polygamy, this marital practice becomes a debate around which religious and political lines are drawn. Many Western feminists, for instance, argue that a society constructed around households of one man and many wives exploits women and devalues them socially and sexually. Proponents counter that polygyny offers a stable social network and religious grounding, which does not repress women. Nevertheless, the economic difficulties in supporting multiple wives as well as changing social mores have led to a decline in practicing polygamous families throughout Africa.

Polyamory emerged as a term in the early 1990s, yet the origins of the term remain uncertain due to the nature of **Internet** communication. Public discourse around non-monogamy, however, dates back into at least the nineteenth century. Proponents of the **free love** movement spread their message of sexuality freed from traditional social expectations alongside socialist and anarchist lectures throughout the mid-1800s into the twentieth century. Outspoken women stood alongside their male counterparts in public forums arguing for the social and sometimes legal freedom to have sexual relations that were not necessarily monogamous. In fact, many believed that sexual freedom represented the ultimate liberation for women. Public criticisms of monogamy continued into the 1920s, with café culture and bohemian lecture circuits providing a forum for discussions of sexual freedom. From the 1930s through the 1950s, public discussion for non-monogamy ebbed during an era of social and political conservatism, but in the 1960s, discussions of free love resurfaced. Some within the growing **gay and lesbian movement** also criticized monogamy. Many gay men, in particular, made free sexuality a key part of their public political expression.

During the 1960s and 1970s, heterosexual and bisexual couples and individuals experimented with group marriages, often becoming public about their practices. Scholars studying American group marriages distinguished between their subjects' social groupings and polygynous forms. They argued that polygyny was patriarchal and oppressive to women, and that a commitment to gender equality marked the new forms of group marriage.

As the term polyamory emerged in the early 1990s, chat rooms, publications, and social organizing converged around the new polyamorous identity. Polyamorists differentiated themselves from polygamists by relying on the same points that group marriage proponents had articulated decades before. They characterize their relationships as built on honesty and communication. They often discuss dominant marital practices as "serial monogamy," pointing out that most people love several others during the span of their lifetimes. Although the polyamorous community first appeared to be centered on the United States, international communities, organizations, and conferences have begun to appear. Despite its rapid growth, polyamory remains a fringe practice in marital relationships.

Individuals with a wide range of sexual identities participate in polyamory, including gay men, lesbians, heterosexuals, bisexuals, and others. It is often aligned with **bisexuality**, partly due to the notion that bisexuals have equal **desire** for both genders and that polyamory offers the opportunity to fulfill bisexual desire. Despite the diversity of sexual identity found in the polyamorous community, traditional gay and lesbian activists invested in the legalization of same-sex marriage have distanced themselves from it. However, many queer activists readily embrace polyamory (even if they do not practice it), favoring a unified sexual freedom movement for consenting adults.

Although sexual freedom is a fundamental principle in polyamory, most practitioners argue that sexuality is but one component of their lifestyle model. Most put forth love and connection as key motivators, underscoring the possibilities for both personal growth and community-building. Polyamorists argue that by dealing openly with jealousy, personal growth and a deeper intimacy are rewards for their relationship model. They emphasize the benefits of sharing resources and flexible family models for childrearing. Most important for polyamorists is the idea of a relationship structure that is fluid. By accommodating a diverse set of emotional and physical needs, many polyamorists feel that their relationship model offers an authentic, individual, and adaptable relationship model that allows for a community of people deeply invested in one another. *See also* Child Abuse; Families; Heterosexuality; Politics; Religions, Eastern; Religions, Western; Women's Movement.

Further Reading: Altman, Irwin, and Joseph Gnatt. *Polygamous Families in Contemporary America*. Cambridge: Cambridge University Press, 1995; Anapol, Deborah. *Polyamory: The New Love Without Limits*. San Rafael, CA: Intinet Resource Center, 1997; Blum, William G. *Forms of Marriage: Monogamy Reconsidered*. Nairobi, Kenya: AMECEA Gaba Publications, 1989; Constantine, Larry L., and Joan M. Constantine. *Group Marriage: Marriages of Three or More People, How and When They Work*. New York: Collier Books, 1973; Cott, Nancy F. *Public Vows: A History of Marriage and the Nation*. Cambridge, MA: Harvard University Press, 2000; D'Emilio, John, and Estelle Freedman. *Intimate Matters: A History of Sexuality in America*. Chicago: University of Chicago Press, 1998; Easton, Dossie, and Catherine A. Liszt. *The Ethical Slut: A Guide to Infinite Sexual Possibilities*. San Francisco: Greenery Press, 1997; The Institute for Twenty-First Century Relationships. The Foundation of the National Coalition for Sexual Freedom. http://www.lovethatworks.org. Background on polyamory and other forms of non-monogamy activism; most information is from the United States.

Lara Kelland

POPULAR CULTURE. Popular culture can be defined differently, which shapes how representations of sex and love are perceived. One way to define popular culture stresses its commercial appeal, focusing on the industrially produced content of the **media** via radio and television programs, movies, **popular music**, and the **Internet**. This definition often carries with it traces of fifteenth and sixteenth century "popular" and the idea of inferior cultural practices by the "common people." Later it implied something deliberately manipulated to ensure its popularity. These rather negative ideas about popular culture are often apparent in the discussions about popular culture where critics lament what they see as the shallowness of the latest love song or when they fear the influence that popular culture has on the sexual morals of society or when those who build media content around the notion that "sex sells." These rather negative ideas about popular culture are often apparent in the discussions about it where critics lament what they see as the shallowness of the latest love song, or when they fear the influence that popular culture has on the sexual morals of society, or when critics condemn those who build media content around the notion that "sex sells." A second important definition of popular culture focuses on "the people" as a culturally distinct group with its values, beliefs, and traditions. It is often close to definitions of folk culture. Thus, people refer to black, gay, youth, Asian, and other popular cultures. Governments, agencies, and activists sometimes seek ways to use the mass media and the arts to disseminate culturally relevant social welfare and sexual health care messages just as commercial enterprises seek to produce and market music, film, and other forms to various cultures.

Popular cultural forms of love and sex change over time and within contexts. In the early twentieth century, for example, German cabaret performances often challenged the limits of sexual **desire** and gender. Cabaret artists played across the boundaries of gender and the cabaret was a relatively safe space for a diversity of sexual desires. However, in the United States, vaudeville was a place for "ribald" entertainment and "wholesome" family entertainment, attempting to appeal to middle-class morals and titillate. On the one hand vaudeville had developed in the nineteenth century as a contrast to the coarse saloon entertainments of the frontier, but on the other hand vaudeville shows were not above including saucy acts such as The Barrison Sisters who were billed as "The Wickedest Girls in the World." In multi-ethnic New York, vaudeville minorities were often the performers and the punch lines of risqué **humor**. For example, performing using "black face" or heavy Yiddish accents was a staple of the vaudeville stage. Irving Berlin's early work, however, did not follow this tradition as the "naughty" protagonists of songs, such as My Wife's Gone to the Country (1926), were often white, middle-class men and women. This caused some critics to scold him for making fun of the institution of **marriage**.

Although the vaudevillian stage could often be a place where sexual stereotypes about minorities were reinforced, it was also a site where African American women sang the Blues, challenging erasures and stereotypes about black sexuality and love. Ma Rainey, Bessie Smith, and Gladys Bentley sang frankly about sex and sexuality with songs such as "Prove It on Me Blues" and "'Taint Nobody's Bizness If I Do." In lyrical interpretations and styles of performance these women asserted black women's right to choose, define, and express desire and love.

If sex was the subject for stage performances and musical recordings, it also helped the bottom line for newspapers. Building on nineteenth-century "yellow journalism," which emphasized **scandal** and sensational reporting, newspaper publishers developed "jazz journalism," which focused on sex, Hollywood gossip, and crime for tabloid sales. One of the most successful newspapers of the time, The Daily News, promised its readers "New York's most beautiful girls every morning." These newspapers also gained popularity in Britain, and the tabloid, in newspaper, magazine, and television formats, continues today.

During the 1930s and 1940s relatively conservative ideas of love, sex, and **romance** within popular culture affirmed a sexual division of labor in which men were dominant. However, these were expressed differently through various media. For example, U.S. men's magazines turned away from Victorian ideas of romance and commitment. Magazines such as Esquire displayed a great deal of mistrust towards women who, as they viewed it, trapped men into marriage. Similar views emerged in post–World War II men's magazines in Australia and Britain. Within this thoroughly heterosexual universe of men's magazines, women decorated its pages as "cheesecake" for men's enjoyment.

In the Caribbean similar views were expressed through Trinidadian calypsos. Calypsonians boasted of their heterosexual prowess and ability to control many women, yet at the same time berated "modern women" for not being virtuous. Female audiences also were being coached on the value of sexual virtue in radio dramas in the United States. Romance soap operas often pitted women of virtue against a host of dramatic problems, especially women of easy virtue. Virtuous women had to work hard at attaining "true love," which comprised a steady heterosexual, monogamous relationship. In Our Gal Sunday (1937), the title character, Sunday, an orphan, must deal with the social challenges of marrying a British aristocrat, and in The Romance of Helen Trent (1933), Helen's romantic pursuit showed love was possible for a virtuous woman over thirty-five.

The decades of the 1950s and 1960s were ones of great change. It was the period of decolonization in Asia, Africa, and the Caribbean and the Civil Rights movement in the United States. As former colonies of Europe cast off imperial control, novels and plays, in particular, expressed their independent national identities. Writers such as Ngugi Wa Thiongo, Chinua Achebe, George Lamming, and Wilson Harris emerged with literary works challenging **colonialism** and racism. Post-colonial writers such as Michelle Cliff and H. Nigel Thomas would come later to challenge sexual hierarchies.

The 1950s and 1960s were also the period of "Rock and Roll." In the United States, the Blues began to find a mainstream audience when an injection from hillbilly music transformed it into Rock and Roll. African American singers such as Little Richard and Chuck Berry attracted white audiences, crossing the lines of segregation in U.S. society. Moralists condemned the barely concealed or sometimes unconcealed joy of sex in the lyrics, making this musical form even more attractive to youth. Conservative commentators in Britain and Australia bemoaned not only the sexually charged rebellion of the music but also its affront to "true British-ness" or "true Australian-ness." Music promoters and executives set about finding and promoting singers who could put a white face on this music. Some singers, like Elvis, maintained its sexual energy while others, such as Pat Boone, sang sanitized covers of the African American hits, or, like Paul Anka, sang about safe teen romance and love. Nevertheless, in most cases this music was produced and performed by males.

Throughout the twentieth century women have challenged male efforts to control the image and bodies of women. Madonna's explicit play with her sexuality and image has been taken by many as challenging this, just as other musicians in other music genres have articulated their sexual independence: Salt-N-Pepa and Queen Latifah in Hip Hop; Calypso Rose, Alison Hinds, and Denise Belfon in Calypso and Soca; and Lady Saw and Tanya Stevens in Dancehall Reggae. Even girls' magazines, which have traditionally been criticized for their focus on makeup, shopping, and boyfriends have, at times, emphasized female assertiveness and sexual independence.

One can never guarantee how audience members might use popular culture in their definition of sexual and gender identity. Female Jeli pop singers in Mali, for instance, perform songs that preach female patience and submission yet many of their female fans enjoy these songs because these emphasize tradition. Nevertheless, those same female fans enjoy lives that are much more independent than the lives depicted in the lyrics. Audiences can reinterpret popular cultural representations to meet their needs, thus women frequently make their own meanings of sexist and/or homophobic media portrayals. For example, lesbian and **drag** king performers and their fans can use the strict gender roles in country music to challenge heteronormativity.

In fact, popular culture has provided a variety of opportunities for lesbian, gay, bisexual, and **transgender** (LGBT) challenges to heteronormativity. In the United States and Europe, the dance music scenes provide a valuable space for queer public performance as does the women's music festival scene. However, popular cultural forms have also been used to assert and reassert heterosexual norms. For example Jamaican dancehall music has been severely criticized for homophobic lyrics. LGBT organizations in Britain and the United States have targeted musicians such as Beenie Man, Buju Banton, Elephant Man, and TOK for anti-gay lyrics. Although the criticisms are valid, the defense of the artists often ignore the diversity and complexity in Jamaica and gloss over the homophobia in Britain and the United States.

Developing countries have used popular culture and the media as part of their strategies of sexual health. For example, since the late 1970s Sistren, a women's theatre collective in Jamaica, has been engaging in street theatre to tackle issues such as gender inequality, domestic violence, rape, and teen pregnancy. Radio soap operas in Tanzania and Malawi, too, have been used to focus on family planning and to educate about **AIDS/HIV**. These popular broadcasts air on community radio stations that are relatively small and volunteer-run. *See also* Advertising; Cartoons and Comics; Cinema; Fashion; Pornography; Sports.

Further Reading: American Variety Stage Vaudeville and Popular Entertainment 1870–1920. The Library of Congress. http://memory.loc.gov/ammem/vshtml/vshome.html. Multimedia anthology including sound records, playbills, and motion pictures, October 1998; Chin, Timothy S. "Jamaican Popular Culture, Caribbean Literature, and the Representation of Gay and Lesbian Sexuality in the Discourses of Race and Nation." *Small Axe* 3, no. 5 (1999): 14–33; Davis, Angela Y. *Blues Legacies and Black Feminism: Gertrude "Ma" Rainey, Bessie Smith and Billie Holiday.* New York: Vintage Books, 1998; Hamm, Charles. *Irving Berlin: Songs for the Melting Pot: The Formative Years, 1907–1914.* New York: Oxford University Press, 1997; Laurie, Ross. "Fantasy Worlds: The Depiction of Women and the Mating Game in Men's Magazines in the 1950s." *Journal of Australian Studies* 56 (1998): 116; McRobbie, Angela. "More! New Sexualities in Girls' and Women's Magazines." In *Back to Reality? Social Experience and Cultural Studies,* edited by Angela McRobbie, 190–209. Manchester: Manchester University Press, 1997; Ram, Anjali. "Framing the Feminine: Diasporic Readings of Gender in Popular Indian Cinema." *Women's Studies in Communication* 25, no. 1 (2002): 25; Rohlehr, Gordon. "Images of Men and Women in the 1930s Calypsos: The Sociology of Food Acquisition in a Context of Survivalism." In *Gender in Caribbean Development,* edited by Patricia Mohammed and Catherine Shepherd, 223–89. Barbados: Canoe Press, 1999; Williams, Raymond. *Keywords: A Vocabulary of Culture and Society.* Rev. ed. Oxford: Oxford University Press, 1985.

Susan Harewood

POPULAR MUSIC. Privately, music is a self-expressive avenue for characterizing one's own (or one's culture's) feelings and understandings about life situations. Its amateur creators produce "authentic" and highly relevant forms of music. Publicly, popular music at the turn of the twentieth century was performed by professional musicians and singers in large civic venues for the entertainment of audiences loyal to a fading Victorian ethic that frowned upon self-pleasure and free expression. However, as the arts began to challenge this Western ethos, public music adapted to satisfy smaller, differently civic venues like cabarets, saloons, and burlesque halls. Here, lyrically, love could be erotic and sexual, sex passionate and liberating, and identity (represented by female impersonators, cross-dressers, and black-face performers), just a complicated aspect of civic life. Over time, these alternative venues enabled musical composers and performers alike to expand upon and reshape their musical roots.

As a true American art form and taproot of popular music, jazz became a genre identified early on as "Negro music" associated with primitivism, rebelliousness, sensuality, and moral decay. Competing with culturally sentimental mainstream music, early jazz and its amalgam of African American folk/blues tied to West Africa and Caribbean music spread as its creators and performers migrated north from New Orleans. Its audience grew thanks to the player piano, sound recordings and eventually, radio play. Jazz provided young people of the 1920s and 1930s with a new soundtrack for social discourse and self-expression in a direct line of communication between performer and listener. Swing jazz (epitomized by Louis Armstrong) was predominantly dance music suggesting and popularizing culturally subversive fads and feelings across race and social class. Love and sex were often conflated in both the lyrics and delivery style of popular female vocalists like Sophie Tucker and Victoria Spivey.

For the most part, jazz was a largely urban, middle class musical phenomenon among young adults poised to usher in the coming popularity of the "big band" era. However, representations and social constructions of jazz music coincided with new recording, film and radio technologies, bringing other music genres into public awareness. Largely indigenous and territorial, these "hillbilly" (white country & western) and "race" (black rhythm & blues) musics also represented more dissonant cultural understandings of sex and love than those of mainstream music. The particular configuration of African American jazz, blues, and folk music combined with the remarkable black American writers and visual artists to produce the "Harlem Renaissance" of the 1920s and 1930s in New York City. Musically, this epoch introduced audiences to many "sissy" (gay), "bulldagger" (lesbian), and transvestite entertainers accompanied by superb musical talents like Fats Waller, Count Basie, and the vocalist Ma Rainey.

Around the world, the 1930s and 1940s produced economic, political, and social unrest as nations and cultures clashed amidst a global industrial and technological juggernaut. Musically, the growing popularity of the radio, jukebox, and personal phonograph player combined with the emergence of microphonic amplification and increasing electronic recording facilities to introduce and spread popular music throughout the United States and, eventually, the world. Paradoxically, these technologies helped to uproot popular musics from their territorial bases and direct them toward their inevitable confrontation with mainstream culture. In addition to popular dance numbers, the pure drive and emotional groove of urban jazz along with the sensual cries and earthy lyrical images of rural blues would soon be available to listeners everywhere.

David Bowie as Ziggy Stardust. Courtesy of Photofest.

During these war years, popular music in the United States continued largely to reflect the sensibilities of a young, White, increasingly hedonistic middle class audience. Love was understood as a romantic ideal and premarital relationships as unacceptable—unless justified as love. The "big band" era in the United States and Europe made live music available well beyond urban centers, bringing together growing audiences eager to listen, dance, and socialize. Other audiences were drawn to the authentic genuineness of country and R&B songs that spoke of love as yearning and hurtful, women as long-suffering and forgiving, and life as a struggle and challenge. At the same time, love could be foolish, sex promiscuously delicious, and women could feel complete and satisfied without a man.

By the 1950s, popular music belonged to an emerging youth culture. For this generation, listening became as important as dancing, and AM radio connected them to a growing array of musical genres. Vocalists like Frank Sinatra, Nat "King" Cole, Rosemary Clooney, and Patti Page connected to listeners' lives through their lyrical voices. Yet racism continued to stifle widespread access to African American artists, and "covers" (white artists recording tunes written and sung by blacks) continued to flourish. Listening and record-buying audiences among both white and black youth fought this commercial control and played a major role in popularizing a racially charged new music: rock and roll. Despite the compelling sights and sounds of Chuck Berry, Bill Haley, and Little Richard, it was Elvis Presley (a southern white-who-sounded-black singer) who did the most to make and eventually break the dangerous originality in this new American musical form. Elvis produced a string of hit records in three different charts (R&B, pop, and C&W), popularizing "crossover" hits and an eventual "Creolization" of musical genres, themselves.

Early rock and roll produced a media synergy among television, recordings, radio, and film that forever changed popular music's social and cultural perspectives on love and sex as well as race and gender. Here, relationships were represented as experimental, sex as enjoyable, and love as a passing opportunity. Elvis Presley personified the role of popular music artist as performing artist, providing sufficient lyrical romanticism to assuage the cultural mainstream and simultaneously provoke cultural misfits with his sexually suggestive stage presence and vocal delivery. Ultimately, the lyrical realism and raw musical and performative energy of rock and roll invited its audience to rethink common standards of behavior about themselves and their sex/love intentions toward others.

The music industry quickly diminished this dangerous shift by exploiting this new youth market with softer, more commodified versions of rock and roll known as pop rock, teen pop, or simply, rock. Though pop rock music, banal in structure and lyric, offered three-minute tales of romanticized love, recording technologies enabled record producers to create unique signature sound styles. These included Phil Spector's "wall of sound," Barry Gordy's "Motown sound," and the "Memphis sound" of Stax Records. Peppered with the presence of singular geniuses like Ray Charles and James Brown, U.S. pop music was both enhanced and pulled back toward its R&B roots through "soul music."

In addition to soul, the 1960s produced an outgrowth of rock and roll stylistic tributaries as more artists created their own music. Popular music expressed the romantic ideal for telling it like it is (blues), speaking from the heart (country), testifying (gospel), and expressing social responsibility (folk). Nevertheless, today's "rock myth" is rooted most deeply in the "British Invasion" of the United States during the early 1960s led by the Beatles. Their music (along with numerous others, including the Rolling Stones, the Kinks, and The Who) emerged from a post–World War II desire among British teens and young adults to produce new, personal forms of music addressing everything from romantic love to social alienation and critique. The overwhelming popularity of these groups and their music reshaped Western teen cultural attitudes toward appearance, attitude and behavior, not to mention musical expectations.

Within the United States, multiple streams of musical influence continued to proliferate, with Bob Dylan questioning mainstream social, cultural, and political values, the Beach Boys harmoniously encouraging teen fun and freedoms, Ray Charles popularizing a hybrid of C&W and R&B music of relationship concerns, and foreign language novelty tunes from Europe and Asia entering the aural landscape. During the late 1960s, youth eagerly consumed rock music's expanding catalog of increasingly edgy R&B, social protest and drug-embracing psychedelic rock anthems, and sweet soul music in large indoor and outdoor venues, becoming convinced during this decade of their own cultural uniqueness when "all you need is love," and all you needed to "light my fire" was a willingness to "feed your head" with pills that would remove your sexual inhibitions, resulting in "hot fun in the summertime."

By the end of the 1960s, rock had reached a high water mark for this new generation's alternative cultures of protest, good times, and difference. Musical performance had trumped the significance and quality of musical relevance as audiences sought to "connect" not only with performers but also with their counter-culture peers. Appealing melodies and inviting beats enhanced singers whose evocative lyrical rendering sought out listeners' private feelings while exposing cultural anachronisms regarding sex, drugs, race and social class. Whether through the soul tunes of The Shirelles's "Will You Still Love Me Tomorrow?" or The Supremes's "Love Child," the British music of the Animals's "House of the Rising Sun," or the Broadway musical *Hair*'s tunes "White Boys" and "Black Boys," many recording artists of the 1960s seemed to be questioning "cultural business as usual."

Rock music fragmented during the 1970s into soft, hard, country, jazz, and progressive sub-genres, each with its own nuanced styles, elements, and audiences. That decade also produced new genres like funk, punk, and new wave. Flamboyance and gender disobedience played a significant role for many of these artists. David Bowie, like Little Richard and Mick Jagger before him, proved difficult to genderize, metamorphosing over the years into various performing personae (each with a different musical style). The early 1970s was marked by what some have called "bisexual chic," with David Bowie leading the way. Although later he would say it was a mistake identifying as bisexual, he

> had no problem with people knowing I was bisexual. But I had no inclination to hold any banners or be a representative of any group of people. I knew what I wanted to be, which was a songwriter and a performer, and I felt that [bisexuality] became my headline over here for so long. America is a very puritanical place, and I think it stood in the way of so much I wanted to do. (http://www.blender.com/guide/articles.aspx?id=366, paragraph 15)

Michael Jackson, too, would become a mysteriously gendered artist in subsequent years. Patti Smith, the Runaways, and Chrissie Hynde followed the 1960s groundbreaking Susie Quatro into the male-dominated world of hard rock and punk, while body piercings and very long hair became commonplace among mainstream male rockers. Glamour and flash appeared in virtually all pop music of the decade—from the unusual makeup and leather outfits of stadium rockers Alice Cooper and Kiss to the outrageous costumes and on stage behaviors of funk-oriented Sly and the Family Stone and Parliament; and from the pop rock campy costumes of Elton John to the curiously gendered and clearly erotic soul rock of Prince. Many pop performers abandoned convention when it came to gender, sexuality and love, including the visually curious gendering of Tiny Tim, the (homo)sexual mimicry of Freddie Mercury and Queen, and the commentaries on race, sex and drugs contained in the Rolling Stones's hit, "Brown Sugar."

These "glam" elements of pop music became most conspicuous over time in their association with disco. The discothèque's thudding beat, complex lighting effects, and open invitation for physical enjoyment created a uniquely welcoming atmosphere for public identity experimentation of all sorts, eventually shifting the liberties and sensibilities of fans and performers alike. From the homosexual camp of the Village People and eroticism of Donna Summer to gender-bending Boy George (who denied he was gay), representations of sex and sexuality would further heighten the performative and transgressive impact of disco music and spawn numerous derivatives, including house, Euro, Italo and Hi-NRG techno-music of the 1980s and 1990s.

Technology and media sped changes in the sound and face of 1980s popular music throughout the West. The introduction of the Sony Walkman and the digital CD musical format in 1979 would revolutionize the artist-audience relationship in short order. The 1980s emergence of MTV in the United States resulted in a growing market for European white pop music, thanks to the global popularity of Michael Jackson's songs and accompanying choreography. Indeed, Jackson's representations of pop music as curiously gendered and sexually explicit performance art would prove central to many of the decade's biggest stars, including Madonna. Along with her titillating sexual lyrics, Madonna's on- and off-stage pleasure-seeking interactions with males and females alike would serve to shape and promote her popularity as a musical performer among her millions of fans.

Nonetheless, the U.S. pop music scene also grew conservative. Members of the U.S. Congress and their spouses produced a high-profile effort to place warning labels on recordings with "offensive" lyrics. Christian artists introduced faith-based contemporary spiritual/folk, pop, and rock tunes to a growing audience that would, by the century's end, be purchasing Christian heavy metal and rap—two genres popularized during the 1980s with sounds, performance styles and lyrical images representing violent and intolerant attitudes toward most cultural and social conventions. **AIDS/HIV** emerged early in the decade to be read by some as a punishment for sexual hedonism, and several major events featuring live, all-star performances in simultaneously satellite-linked venues around the globe raised millions of dollars for Ethiopian famine victims and, in the United States, for family farmers. Similar large-scale efforts in Canada would raise funds in the 1990s for people living with AIDS/HIV.

Multiple forms of pop music flourished during the 1980s as the international influence of MTV grew, making images as important as sound, "packaging" as necessary as musical content. The visual demeanor and message of black rap and white heavy metal were no less important than the wardrobe and choreography of new wave pop, for form had finally triumphed over substance and popular music had become "show business." Rap music, in particular, received considerable "degrees of popular cultural freedom" from the music industry, achieving commercial success despite what many mainstream critics and audiences saw as rap's disgusting lyrics and misogynistic messages about women as sex objects and subservient beings, not to mention its unmistakable disdain for mainstream law and order, homosexuality, or love that had anything to do with romance, commitment or family.

During the 1990s, rock lost serious popular ground to rap, dance, and pop music. Established artists like Melissa Etheridge and k.d. lang would, among others, publicly share their lesbian identities without fear of losing popular appeal. Country and Western songs and artists grew in popularity, as did "grunge" and alternative rock. Teen music returned to popularity with acts like the Backstreet Boys and Britney Spears, and international or "world musics" (e.g., *reggae*, *ska*, and *salsa*) entered popular western markets during that decade, invited by hugely successful recordings and global tours of Paul Simon accompanied by musicians and singers from South Africa and Latin America. World musics favored folk-based, dance-oriented contributions from the Caribbean region, Central and South Americas, and numerous African countries, later including "pure pop" efforts from Asia, India, and eastern Europe.

Beyond their sounds, world music lyrical themes challenged the dominant message within Western pop that hedonistic love and sexual gratification defined being young and popular. Globalization resulted in disappearing cultural and social traditions— situations that world music stylistically and lyrically represented in complex combinations of exuberance and angst. Whether from Latin America, China, Turkey or Thailand, these musics were also political and social in nature, with clear messages about nationalism, civil rights and personal freedoms. Thematically, songs were often more culturally complex than western pop, offering listeners contested spaces for cultural and social representations and understandings—for example, between women's liberatory emotional and sexual freedoms from oppressive patriarchal societies and their personal desire to control their own destinies. *See also* Homosexuality; Popular Culture.

Further Reading: Brett, Philip, Elizabeth Wood, and Gary C. Thomas, eds. *Queering the Pitch: The New Gay and Lesbian Musicology.* 2nd ed. New York: Routledge, 2006; Clarke, Donald.

The Rise and Fall of Popular Music. New York: St. Martin's Press, 1995; Cook, Nicholas, and Anthony Pople, eds. *The Cambridge History of Twentieth-Century Music.* Cambridge: Cambridge University Press, 2004; Frith, Simon. "Why Do Songs Have Words?" *Contemporary Music Review* 5 (1989): 77–96; Grove Music Online. Oxford University Press. 2006. http://www.grovemusic. com. Authoritative information about music. Ruhlmann, William. *Breaking Records: 100 Years of Hits.* New York: Routledge, 2004; Swiss, Thomas, John Sloop, and Andrew Herman, eds. *Mapping the Beat: Popular Music and Contemporary Theory.* Malden, MA: Blackwell, 1998.

J. Dan Marshall

PORNOGRAPHY. Pornography originated from the ancient Greek words "porni" and "grafi," meaning "writings about prostitutes." In the twentieth and twenty-first centuries "pornography" denotes the depiction of sexual activities via assorted **media** intended to cause sexual arousal. It often has pejorative connotations, referencing materials subject to state regulation. "Erotica," in contrast, is often used to demarcate materials that are merely sexually graphic. Pornographic media includes books, magazines, films, cartoons, and the **Internet**, comprising one of the world's largest industries. Advances in the technologies of photography and film in the twentieth century made the mass production of sexually explicit images inexpensive; the development of the Internet in the late twentieth century facilitated international access and distribution of these materials. Taboos against pornography are declining in Europe and North America as a result of social revolutions that eroded religious association of sex with love and **marriage**, while prohibitions remain strict in most areas of Latin America, Asia, India, the Middle East, and Africa. The legal status of pornography also varies across nations, according to cultural standards of obscenity, the age of consent, state and religious jurisdictions, and sexual liberalism. There are few international prohibitions against pornography, apart from those related to human trafficking and child pornography, reflecting wide cultural disagreement about the social impact of pornographic materials, and the precedent of respecting national sovereignty to adjudicate this dissent.

Pornography laws differ greatly from one nation to another, exhibiting various understandings of sexual morality and state jurisdiction. Nearly all nations have laws prohibiting child pornography and typically require that participants in pornography be over the age of 18. However, the contextual content of the laws against child pornography depend upon local norms and it is widely available. Some nations are stringent, such as Canada, where it is illegal to even depict someone as under 18 in a pornographic film, and legislation has been proposed that would make it a crime to not only distribute and possess child pornography, but to do Internet searches for it. Other countries, such as England and Germany, raised the otherwise lower age of legal consent (which is 16 and 14, respectively) to 18 for participating in and consuming pornography. However, some nations allow younger persons access to pornography such as Sri Lanka (age 13 and older), the Netherlands and Switzerland (16 and older), and Finland (15 and older).

Denmark was the first country to legalize "hardcore" pornography in 1969, defined as patently offensive because of its graphic or violent nature. In countries such as China, Singapore, Vietnam, and most Middle Eastern countries all sexually explicit materials are banned, including the American magazine *Playboy*, and there is no distinction drawn between erotica and pornography. In contrast, most European countries and the United States have loose legal restriction of adults creating and consuming sexually explicit materials of all sorts, although some nations ban gay and lesbian pornography, bestiality/zoophilia, or those depicting violent sadomasochism, rape, or demeaning acts such as "scat," which involves defecation or urination. Hungary and Norway prohibit showing genitalia on magazine covers, domestic television, and cable television. Until the early 1990s, Japan exercised a ban on showing adult genitalia, requiring that pubic hair be scratched out of all pictures, but this restriction is no longer enforced and pornographic magazines are readily available in public vending machines. And, in Japan, as in most of Europe, photographs of nudes are not uncommon in the mainstream media. Many other countries such as France and the United States employ a rating system to distinguish "X-rated" or "blue films." A few countries such as Brazil require the use of condoms in pornographic films, most others, including the United States, do not.

Pornography in the twentieth and twenty-first centuries has rapidly evolved through the advent of photography, film, and the Internet, the latter of which has created new and complex international markets for pornography. Currently there is little international regulation of this market. The notable exceptions are India and China, both of which actively censor international pornography and prosecute consumers. Most phone sex numbers called from India are to businesses run in the United States, Hong Kong, and Australia. India has blocked access to international numbers used for phone sex and is using technology to stop people accessing Internet pornography from other countries. The penalty for purchasing, sending, publishing or creating pornography is a minimum two-year prison sentence and fine of 2,000 rupees. Likewise, China gives strict jail sentences for downloading movies with pornographic content.

The Internet and the increased availability of personal computers allow many individuals an audience to freely distribute and promote their works of pornography. One market that has increased as a result is animated or cartoon pornography, which is the portrayal of illustrated fictional characters in erotic or sexual situations. These animation sites on the Internet fall into three broad categories. "Hentai," translated meaning "strange" or "perverted" and sometimes referred to as "ecchi," uses the hard-core Japanese school of the art style known as "anime" that may appear in "magna" (comic books) or film. The Americanized version of hentai, are parody renditions of famous cartoons and comics such as Disney characters. In the United States animated pornography also includes adult computer games, which have existed since the early 1980s, such as "Custer's Revenge" and "Playboy: The Mansion."

Animated and virtually simulated pornography often depicts acts that are legally prohibited, including rape, **incest**, and sex with children, frequently perpetrated by aliens or mythological creatures. Because there is no harm to actual persons, these forms are rarely prosecuted.

Cultural preferences and ethnic norms are evident in other types of pornographic materials. In pornographic film, the United States is known for parodies of Hollywood films and classic stories, with actresses increasingly featuring surgical enhancements such as breast implants. European and Japanese women are said to have a more "natural" appearance and pornographic films have stronger realism. The pornography industry in the United States has genres of heterosexual **fetishes** that include bondage/ Dominatrix, pregnant and lactating women, elderly or obese women, and adults portraying themselves as children. "Ethnic" women, distinguished as being non-white, are often portrayed as exotic and animalistic, mirroring ethnic stereotypes that emerged from historical events such slavery, imperialism, and wars. In the United States, Europe, and Malaysia voyeurism is increasingly popular, in the form of reality

Protesters on 7th Avenue not far from Times Square in New York picket the theater where the pornographic film *Deep Throat* is being shown, 1980. © AP Photo/Dave Pickoff.

television, ostensibly leaked celebrity sex films, as well as sex films of everyday people either willingly performing or reportedly caught under stealth. Japan is noted for *bukkake*, a practice wherein a series of men take turns ejaculating on the face of a woman sitting, kneeling, or lying down. The semen is left on the face until all the men have completed the routine. In rare cases the target is a man, and a new variant depicts lesbian women ejaculating or in some cases urinating on one another. Another Japanese subgenre is *tamakeri* in which a female kicks a man in the testicles and is slapped vigorously by the man in response.

Fetishism in pornography, or the use of an inanimate object for sexual stimulation, reveals cultural standards of beauty and sex appeal. Shoes and feet are common fetish items employed in pornography, most notably in the West are stockings, garter belts, and high heels, although homosexual men also report a preference for sports socks and sneakers. Knee-high socks are often combined with different types of uniforms. Spandex leggings and leotards are similarly fetishized, as are tight, shiny garments made of leather, rubber, or PVC piping. The Japanese term *zentai* refers to a spandex suit covering the entire body, eroticized both for its form fitting nature and the sensation created for the wearer. In addition to clothing, fetish pornography can be addressed to physical traits, accessories, disabilities, and bodily fluids. Sometimes, whole cultures can develop the fetish to such an extent that it is no longer perceived as a fetish but merely as an inherently sexual quality, as in the United States for lingerie or women lacking body hair.

In the early twentieth century pornography featuring non-heterosexual relations was often unavailable, due to a combination of stringent prohibitions and a lack of a market. The categories of lesbian, transsexual, bisexual, and inter-sexual were either emerging as new cultural concepts, and/or treated as medical pathologies. Some of the first gay porn films appeared near the beginning of the twentieth century in the United States, but comprised only 1 percent of the genre, while lesbianism appeared in about 20 percent of erotic films. Homosexual relations were illegal in many countries throughout

Europe prior to this time, and the rise of the Nazi Party in Germany had tightened restrictions against "sexual deviance" that had flourished within the Weimar Republic, including restrictions on **homosexuality** and pornography. In the United States pornography was driven underground due to the legal influence of officials such as Anthony Comstock, a U.S. postmaster who successfully persuaded Congress to ban the transport of materials deemed "obcene, lewd, or lascivious" through the mail via the Comstock Law. Novels such as *The Well of Loneliness*, *Lady Chatterley's Lover*, *Histoire D'O*, and *Lolita*, now acclaimed for their literary merit, were banned in many countries and their authors brought up on obscenity charges. By 1956, the U.S. Congress had passed 20 obscenity laws that were variations of the Comstock Law.

The twentieth century saw a gradual ebb of this trend in the United States, via a series of legal rulings that refined and reversed earlier laws against heterosexual and homosexual pornography. In 1933 federal judge John Woosley overturned a former ban on James Joyce's novel *Ulysses*. In the 1957 case *Roth v. United States*, the Supreme Court developed a new test of obscenity that extended First Amendment protection to materials dealing with sex in a manner not appealing to "prurient interest." During the 1960s, the Supreme Court developed more liberal tests for obscenity, determining that pornography rights and protections are conferred by age, and that sexually explicit material with even minor social value is speech protected under the First Amendment. Current governing standards, established by the 1973 case *Miller v. California*, restricts obscene materials that lack serious literary, artistic, political, or scientific value, as determined by both local and national community standards.

The reliance on community standards to determine what is obscene in the United States and elsewhere is reflected in the disparate treatment of homosexual and heterosexual pornography throughout the world. Although homosexual pornography has attracted less attention from anti-pornography activists than heterosexual materials, some countries consider it more "obscene" and subject it to greater legal restrictions or consider it a fetish. Included in the first materials seized under the 1992 *R. v. Butler* obscenity Canadian law were lesbian erotica. Despite the tendency to be perceived as more deviant and obscene, gay and lesbian pornography companies have taken strong initiatives to combat the spread of **AIDS** by requiring condom usage.

In the twenty-first century it is possible to find a wide range of pornographic materials featuring non-heterosexual relations. Similar to heterosexual materials, variations in gay and lesbian pornography fall along lines of age preferences, ethnicities, body characteristics, sex acts, and set types such as westerns and **prisons** as well as sex between races. Pornography often blurs the traditional boundaries of sexual orientation. Some mainstream pornography aimed at heterosexual men contains lesbian scenes. In Japan lesbian pornography is commonly characterized as "straight." In many other nations, pornography depicts bisexual women and men as lesbian and gay, whereas heterosexual and lesbian women may be portrayed as bisexual, contributing to a lack of clear standards for distinguishing sexual orientation and identity.

Bestiality, or sexual acts between humans and animals, is banned in Finland and was recently banned in the Netherlands due to new animal-welfare laws. It is unrestricted in many other countries, including the United States, where laws against sex with animals vary by state, and tend to fall under animal cruelty statutes.

Women's rights groups around the world argue that pornography not only encourages violence against women and children, but itself constitutes violence against the women and children used in its production. In the mid-1980s, feminists Andrea Dworkin and Catharine MacKinnon pushed for legislation that would have permitted women to sue pornographers in civil court when they could demonstrate harm from the production or use of pornography. This legislation was defeated in Minnesota, but was successful in Canada as *R. v. Butler*.

Anti-pornography supporters cite many studies showing that pornography leads to desensitization to violent and misogynist practices, but dissenters cite many studies suggesting that pornography usage is benign. U.S. commissions appointed by President Lyndon Johnson in 1970, and by Ronald Reagan in 1984, yielded conflicting conclusions. Milton Diamond and Ayako Uchiyama report that increased permissibility of pornography in Japan has correlated with decreased incidence of **sex crimes** from 1970 to 1994. Berl Kutchinsky reports similar results for the United States, Denmark, Sweden, and the Federal Republic of Germany from 1964 to 1984. Pornography proponents such as Salman Rushdie, novelist, and Larry Flynt, publisher of the American magazine *Hustler*, contend that permissiveness of pornography is an important measure of liberal democracy. *See also* Cartoons and Comics; Censorship; Cinema; Feminism; Pornography, on the Internet; Race and Racism.

Further Reading: Bhaumik, Subir. "India Rebels 'Making Porn Films.'" *BBC News* (August 27, 2005) at http://news.bbc.co.uk; Diamond, Milton, and Ayako Uchiyama. "Pornography, Rape and Sex Crimes in Japan." *International Journal of Law and Psychiatry* 22, no. 1 (1999): 1–22; Encyclopædia Britannica, Inc. "Pornography." *Britannica Concise Encyclopedia*. Answers.com. http://www.answers.com/topic/pornography, January 15, 2007; Gongoli, Geetanjali. "The Regulation of Women's Sexuality through Law: Civil and Criminal Laws." *Global Reproductive Health Forum: Re/productions #2*; Kher, Anuradha. "Is It OK If India Says Yes to Pornography?" *Asia Media News Daily* (August 14, 2004); Kutchinsky, Berl. "Pornography, Sex Crime, and Public Policy." *Sex Industry and Public Policy*, Conference Proceedings. 1991; McDougal, Dan. "Executive Deaf to Call for Inter-net Porn Study." *The Scotsman*, February 2, 2004; Wikimedia Foundation, Inc. "Pornography." *Wikipedia, The Free Encyclopedia*. http://en.wikipedia.org/w/index.php?title=Internet_pornography&oldid=100416 221, January 13, 2007.

Maureen Sander-Staudt

PORNOGRAPHY, ON THE INTERNET. Internet pornography offers sexually explicit images, video, text, and chat to visitors of electronic Web sites. Today, many people experience sexuality and relationships as mediated communication, which may include the exchange of sexually explicit words or images. Since the development of the World Wide Web and the graphic browser in 1995, the production and distribution of commercial **pornography** as digital image exchange has become a popular form of adult entertainment provided by e-commerce entrepreneurs. Internet pornography is now the most visible and controversial expression of pornography. It differs from older forms of image-based pornography because users access this digitized product through globalized Web-based distribution channels. Web sites also encourage customers to directly interact with images or give feedback to porn actresses/actors through chat rooms, mailing lists, or Web cams. Internet porn encourages Web users across cultures to become active by writing feedback on message boards, or watching Web-based "live" striptease while chatting with the model involved.

Estimates on the actual size and revenue of the Internet pornography industry are difficult to obtain. The Web currently hosts hundreds of thousands of "feeder" sites, or

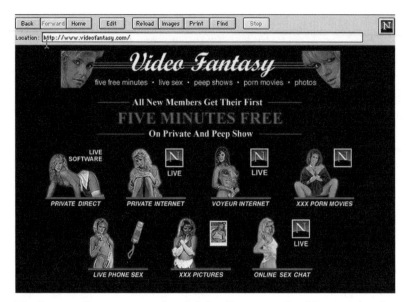

The Supreme Court unanimously ruled that Congress violated free-speech rights when it tried to curb smut on the Internet, as seen in this screen shot taken from an adult web page, 1997. The justices unanimously agreed that Congress's effort to protect children from sexually explicit material goes too far because it would also keep such material from adults who have the right to see it. © AP Photo/VideoFantasy.com.

websites that offer free pictures to customers, whereas the number of actual "membership" sites is considerably lower. Being one of the major entertainment industries on the Internet, one could estimate that the Internet porn industry's annual income ranged somewhere between five and ten billion dollars during the year 2001, but it would be hard to determine what that figure would be today (Zook 2003).

The content of Internet pornography reflects the wide variety of sexual interests of users. Although, for the most part, these cater to adult males, there has been growth of smaller "niche" porn sites, such as a Web site featuring pornography made by lesbian women for lesbian women. Here, pornography distribution is often combined with other activities such as information-sharing and community activism. Pornographic products are also distributed and shared through non-commercial channels: newsgroups, web logs, pod casts, or peer-to-peer platforms of exchange. These non-commercial Web platforms have been targeted recently by governments for their dissemination of illegal products, and pirated or taboo images, such as child pornography.

Internet pornography's transnational reach has caused havoc amongst conservative governments and consumer groups, specifically in cultures where sex workers and pornographic products are socially stigmatized and/or stringently monitored by law. For instance, in May 2006, the Indonesian government proposed to pass a hard-line conservative anti-pornography law, spurred by politicians and Muslim groups angered by the influx of "degenerate" Internet products. In contrast to the muffled response from Indonesians, in 2003 student groups marched in Tehran to protest the government's ban of a hundred thousand pornographic websites. In mainland China, after four years of censorship measures, the Chinese government is reported to "win the war on

Internet pornography" by further detaining Web users and by closing down domestic websites. However, initiatives to either ban or protect Internet pornography are also taking place in Western countries, such as the European Union's proposal to create a "Safer Internet Forum," where users can learn about and report harmful Web content.

Internet pornography also has stirred debate among intellectuals around the world. Feminist Catharine MacKinnon has argued that pornography in cyberspace is more pervasive and interactive than conventional means of distributing pornography. All forms of pornography production, according to her, exploit women's labor and damage female and male psychology, particularly when accessed by minors and children. In contrast, Mireille Miller-Young, who looks at representations of gender and **race** in Internet pornography, argues that women of color can use the Internet pornography industry to gain greater control over their labor and representation. Even though they have to compete with slick operations sponsored by production companies, they can more easily design their sites and stay away from misogynist Web sites, which present black women as an "underclass" ready to be dominated by male pimps and customers. Independent pornographers include assertive women and feminists who present their more dynamic and personalized versions of sexiness and cultural identity.

Despite the promise of democratization within the Internet, pornography is causing an enormous backlash in Internet platforms for autonomous expression, sharing, and freedom of speech. For instance, the U.S. government collaborates with American Internet service providers and search engines to closely monitor web traffic. Following a congressional report showing peer-to-peer networks being used for the trading of child pornography, there has been a widespread crackdown on such networks with surveillance tests on the networked computers of individuals and student communities.

In other countries such as the Philippines and China, the government has made decisions to ban video games and shut down all traffic taking place in cyber cafes. Since the new wave of Internet porn industries makes use of such Web-based communication tools to develop its more diversified culture of free expression, body imaging, and autonomous representation of race and gender, it is unclear if the new players of the porn industry will survive within the current climate of corporate expansionism and moral backlash. *See also* Feminism.

Further Reading: The Art and Politics of Netporn: http:/www.networkcultures.org/ netporn; First International Conference on Internet Pornography. Organized by Institute of Network Cultures, Hogeschool van Amsterdam. Contains an archive of relevant scholarly articles, Web sites, and an up-to-date mailing list, October 2005; Jacobs, Katrien. "Pornography in Small Places and Other Spaces." *Cultural Studies* 18, no. 1 (2004): 67–84; Lane, Frederick, III. *The Entrepreneurs of Pornography in the Cyber Age.* New York: Routledge, 2000; MacKinnon, C. A. "Vindication and Resistance. A Response to the Carnegie Mellon Study of Pornography in Cyberspace." *The Georgetown Law Journal* 83, no. 5 (1995): 1959–67; Miller-Young, Mireille. "'Because I'm Sexy and Smart!': Black Web Mistresses Hack Cyperporn." *Cut-Up Media Magazine.* September 26, 2005; available at http://www.cut-up.com/news/detail.php?sid=416; Suicidegirls. http://www.suicidegirls.com. A pornographic Web site that encourages women with "punk" appeal to be porn models, while creating their profiles through bios and daily Web journals; Ven-Hwei, Lo, and Ran Wei. "Third-Person Effect, Gender, and Pornography on the Internet." *Journal of Broadcasting and Communication* 46 (2002, March): 13–46; Williams, Linda. *Porn Studies.* Chapel Hill, NC: Duke University Press, 2004; Zook, Matthew. "Underground Globalization: Mapping the Space of Flows of the Internet Adult Industry." *Environment and Planning* 35 (2003): 1261–86.

Katrien Jacobs

PREGNANCY. Pregnancy is the carrying of developing offspring, one or more embryos or fetuses, within the female body. Specifically, human pregnancy occurs by fertilization of the female egg by the male sperm, which travels to the woman's uterus and implants in the uterine wall where it grows for the next approximately nine months or forty weeks and ends with childbirth. Signs of pregnancy are a missed menstrual period after penile-vaginal intercourse, nausea or morning sickness, increase in the size and tenderness of the breasts, darkening of the areolas around the nipples, increased frequency of urination, increased size of the abdomen, softening of the cervix, a positive pregnancy test, detection of a fetal heartbeat, feeling the fetus moving, and visualization of the fetus through ultrasound. To date, men cannot get pregnant.

Historically, pregnancy occurred through penile-vaginal intercourse during the woman's fertile time where the man's erect penis was inserted into the woman's vagina and he ejaculated his sperm. Then, the sperm traveled up through the woman's vagina, cervix, uterus, and fallopian tubes to fertilize the woman's egg released from one of her ovaries. However, new advances have been made throughout the last century to aid partners of all kinds in getting pregnant in ways other than penile-vaginal intercourse when infertility problems arise.

Any number of fertility problems can occur in either the female or male making pregnancy difficult, if not impossible to attain. Over the past 30 years, fertility specialists have developed a multitude of ways to aid partners in becoming pregnant. However, assessments and treatments are costly, unlikely to be covered by insurance, and not available in all countries. Fertility treatments often raise emotional, religious, moral, legal, and ethical concerns. Fertility medications and surgery are two of the mild options used to treat both females and males who have potentially viable eggs and sperm. If it is determined that either the eggs or sperm are not viable or that the woman's body is unsuitable for pregnancy, then other treatment options may be explored.

Intrauterine insemination (IUI), or artificial insemination, is a procedure where the sperm is injected into either the cervix or uterus to get them closer to the egg. This procedure may be used when a man's sperm count is low or when a woman's cervical mucus is not permitting the sperm to swim through to meet the egg. Another highly complex and expensive treatment option is in vitro fertilization or IVF. The first successful joining of the egg and sperm outside the body in a test tube and then transferring the embryo into the woman's uterus to grow for the remaining nine months was done in 1978. Since then, IVF has become a lucrative business and the last option for partners to have a biological baby.

If fertility medications, surgery, IUI, and IVF have been either unsuccessful or not an option, partners may explore the option of obtaining donor eggs, donor sperm, or even donor embryos. The emotionally and legally taxing decision to use such options is often made by women and men who have fertility issues that cannot be resolved, same-sex couples, and/or single parents. Once the donor eggs, sperm, or embryos have been obtained, the woman goes through the IVF process and the final embryo(s) are transferred into her uterus so that she may still experience the pregnancy, though the child may not be completely biologically hers.

One final option partners may consider beside adoption is surrogacy. A surrogate is a woman who conceives and carries a child for someone else, or goes through IVF with another woman's embryo, carries the child, and then gives the child to the partners for whom she carried. Surrogacy is often used with gay couples, as well as straight couples who cannot physically carry a pregnancy.

As pregnancy options have changed dramatically since 1900, so has the intimacy component in the pregnancy process. Enjoying the intimacy of trying to get pregnant often gets lost with rigorous fertility treatments. It is important to communicate about intimacy when going through fertility treatments since the pregnancy process can become very mechanical and stressful.

Penile-vaginal intercourse to attempt a pregnancy is available and acceptable across countries, cultures, and religions (if done at an acceptable time point in life). However, fertility treatments are very costly (anywhere between approximately $10,000 and $35,000 U.S. dollars) and not available and/or acceptable everywhere. Most fertility rates have progressively dropped throughout the century and there has been an increase in the age of women waiting until later in life to get pregnant.

Multitudes of factors have had an impact on fertility rates throughout the last century. The World Health Organization has tracked global fertility rates. Table 1 represents many of the larger countries for which data are reported. The World Health Organization also reported fertility statistics by geographical region in 2004 as well as the adolescent fertility percentages, as seen in Table 2.

Yet, the Population Reference Bureau reported in Table 3 a fertility rate comparison amongst major geographical regions in the world. Fertility rates are higher in the developing countries, particularly in Africa, than in the developed countries. However, the majority of countries have experienced a decline in the fertility rates although several European countries have experienced a slight increase in their fertility rates. A variety of factors have contributed to the flux in fertility rates, including: elevated governmental services, political policies, increased age at **marriage**, **gender role** changes, more contraceptive options, greater use of contraceptives, and decreased mortality, as well as gains in women's health, education, and rights.

In the 1950s, India's government instituted family planning policies to slow population growth. China implemented the "one-child policy" in 1979 to slow its

TABLE 1 Total Fertility Rates: 1993 and 2003 (per woman)

Country	1993	2003
Canada	1.7	1.5
China	1.9	1.8
Ethiopia	6.8	6.1
France	1.7	1.9
Germany	1.3	1.4
India	3.8	3.0
Mexico	3.1	2.5
Nigeria	6.3	5.4
Russian Federation	1.5	1.1
South Africa	3.4	2.6
Thailand	2.1	1.9
Turkey	3.1	2.4
United Kingdom	1.8	1.6
United States of America	2.1	2.1
Vietnam	3.2	2.3

TABLE 2 Fertility Rates by Geographical Region and Proportion of Adolescent Fertility

Geographical Region	Total Fertility Rate (per woman)	Adolescent Fertility Proportion (%)
African region	5.3	11.7
Region of the Americas	2.3	12.8
Southeast Asia region	2.8	10.0
European region	1.6	8.4
Eastern Mediterranean region	3.7	10.0
Western Pacific region	1.8	1.9

TABLE 3 Fertility Levels in Major World Regions: 1950 and 2003 (children per woman)

Region	1950	2003
Africa	6.7	5.2
Asia	5.9	2.6
Latin America and Caribbean	5.9	2.7
North America	3.5	2.0
Europe	2.7	1.4

population growth. However, 88 countries worldwide have offered financial assistance including tax breaks, free or subsidized childcare, low cost housing loans, and cash payments to **families** to help defray the cost of children.

Adolescent or teen pregnancy is defined as pregnancy if a girl is less than 20 years old. Views on adolescent pregnancy differ based on culture. For young women in South Asia, the Middle East, and North Africa, adolescent pregnancy has been the norm due to marriage immediately after menarche. In these cultures, adolescent pregnancy is not considered problematic. However, in Western societies, adolescent sexual activity and pregnancy rates have sharply increased, particularly since World War II. In these cultures, adolescent pregnancy is viewed as a growing problem. One explanation for the increase in adolescent pregnancy rates is earlier onset of menarche. Reasons for earlier onset of menarche include obesity, depression, stress, increased use of insecticides, generally improved environmental circumstances, exposure to endocrine-disrupting chemicals, smaller families, gradual change in world temperature, drop in incidence of disease, and sedentary lifestyle. Obesity and insecticides influence estrogenic activity in girls triggering the onset of puberty. The age of decline is mostly universal, though the rates of decline are slower in the less developed countries.

Cultural, socioeconomic status, rural or urban location, and time period all influence attitudes about pregnancy. In Hispanic cultures, some believe in the "evil eye" phenomenon. Here, a female relative may stay with the pregnant woman during prenatal visits as well as for up to 40 days after childbirth to prevent harm to the mother and child from someone staring at them. Women in the Haitian culture hold the belief that "werewolves" can consume babies before they are born or harm small children, and, therefore, may not seek health care until the time of delivery. In Indian culture it is tragic if the woman does not produce a son since the male is the one who cares for the parents in their old age and participates in death rituals to ensure the parents pass into the afterlife. Both the Hmong tribe in Laos and Cambodian culture believe in reproduction starting in adolescence and continuing late into the reproductive years. Women in both of these cultures often will not seek medical care until the end of pregnancy, if they seek medical care at all.

A woman's body goes through tremendous change, physically and hormonally, during and after pregnancy. These changes not only affect her, but can also affect her partner as well. Each woman and each pregnancy are different. Some women report increased attraction to and from their partner, whereas others note that their partners pull away during pregnancy. Libido may increase or decrease depending on the emotional and physical state of the woman. As the body grows and changes, particularly after the fourth month of pregnancy, new sexual positions may need to be explored to not only keep the woman off her back, but also to make room for the expanding abdomen. After the fourth month, lying on the back can impede the blood supply to the fetus.

Some women feel beautiful with their expanding abdomens and others feel fat and unattractive. How they feel about themselves may determine the role intimacy plays in their relationships. For some, all sorts of sexual activities will be appealing; for others, cuddling or being held will be the extent of intimate activity. Regardless of the level of **desire**, sexual activity should be discussed with a health care practitioner throughout the stages of pregnancy to ensure the safety of the woman and fetus(es).

Sexuality is just as important before and during pregnancy as it is in the postpartum period. Once the child(ren) is born, the woman's body does not immediately return to pre-pregnancy state. Physically, a woman may still look approximately five months pregnant after giving birth. This appearance will change as the uterus shrinks back to its original size. Penile-vaginal intercourse is not recommended for six to eight weeks after childbirth in order to allow the female reproductive organs to heal. For those women who choose to breastfeed, they and their partners may experience a variety of feelings over the functionality of the breasts versus the sexual nature of the breasts. Communication is essential in this time of transition.

Depression and bleeding after childbirth caused by tiny pieces of the placenta remaining in the uterus are potential complications after childbirth. Depression, often manifested in the woman pulling away from the child or withdrawing internally, is easily treated by a health care practitioner. Retained placenta requires the woman to undergo a dilation and curettage (D & C) to stop the bleeding. *See also* Abortion; Adolescence; Birth Control; Mental Health and Sex; Puberty and Puberty Rituals.

Further Reading: Luttrell, Wendy. *Pregnant Bodies, Fertile Minds: Gender, Race, and the Schooling of Pregnant Teens.* New York: Routledge, 2003; Meyers-Thompson, Jackie, and Sharon Perkins. *Fertility for Dummies.* New York: Wiley, 2003; Nichols, Francine, and Elaine Zwelling. *Maternal-Newborn Nursing.* Philadelphia: Saunders, 1997; Paget, Lou. *Hot Mamas: The Ultimate Guide to Staying Sexy throughout Your Pregnancy and the Months Beyond.* New York: Gotham, 2005; Population Reference Bureau. "Population Bulletin." www.prb.org. A reference for population statistics and cultural changes, 2004.

Carey Roth Bayer

PREMARITAL SEX. Premarital sex refers to voluntary sexual activity before **marriage** that typically follows a script, progressing from kissing to petting, including manual or oral stimulation of the genitals to **orgasm**, to intercourse. However, associating premarital sex mainly with those who engage in sexual intercourse prior to marriage ignores the varying influences of culture, love, and expectations regarding marriage. All societies restrict or control sexual expression to some extent. The focus on premarital sex likely results from cultural emphases valuing **virginity** among females and the wish to limit out of wedlock births. Thus, the focus of premarital sex implies a focus on women's sexuality as well as a presumption of **heterosexuality**.

Studies of premarital sex focus on the time frame following physical maturation at **puberty** (for women, first menstruation or menarche) to the time when individuals enter marriage. Depending on the culture, this time frame can be very brief, such as when teenagers marry during **adolescence**—a custom in some Asian or African countries that is now declining. Within most industrialized countries, where menarche typically occurs by age thirteen and where the average age at first marriage is increasing, the time frame is ten years or more.

The last century has witnessed dramatic shifts in how marriages are formed in Western culture as well as among the vast populations of India and China, as the influence of parents and communities has waned in favor of individual choices based on love and attraction. Reiss (1980) described four basic cultural standards:

- *Abstinence* in which premarital sex is seen as wrong under all circumstances.
- *Double Standard* under which premarital sex for women is more discouraged than for men.
- *Permissiveness with Affection* allows for premarital sexual activity for men and women in the context of a committed loving relationship.
- *Permissiveness without Affection* in which premarital sexual activity is acceptable for men and women regardless of whether a relationship exists.

With a shift towards love and attraction from 1900 to the new century as the determinants of a marital relationship, there also has been a shift away from abstinence and a double standard to acceptance of premarital sexual activity where there is a loving relationship.

Premarital sexual activity in the United States increased significantly during this time frame, as assessed by a range of studies, which, while differing in sampling and measurement dimensions, provide related information. The most careful measurement of premarital sexual activity is the percentage of individuals who were virgins on their wedding night. However, a number of other measurements are clearly related including: the average age at loss of virginity; surveys of current sexual behavior of never married members of a group; the number of children conceived before marriage; and, the **abortion** rate among single women.

The best-known and most widely cited studies include the pioneering work by Alfred **Kinsey** as well as the much more scientifically constructed and landmark study by Laumann and his colleagues towards the end of the century. In an early study, Kinsey asked married women born before 1900, from 1900 to 1909, from 1910 to 1919, and from 1920 to 1929 whether they were virgins on their wedding night. Nearly three out of four women born before 1900 reported being virgins on their wedding night. For women born in the next three decades the figure declined to roughly 45 percent (Kinsey, Pomeroy, Martin, and Gebhard 1953). A more recent study contrasted women born from 1933 to 1942, from 1943 to 1952, from 1953 to 1962, and from 1963 to 1974 and found a continuing decline in the percentage of virgins on their wedding night, from 55, to 33.8, 27.4, and 30 percent, respectively (Laumann, Gagnon, Michael, and Michaels 1994).

This shift away from virginity at marriage raised the concern that it might also reflect a greater movement away from monogamy. According to Kinsey, however, even those opposed to premarital sex were more accepting if the couple intends to marry. The implication is that intercourse is more acceptable with someone you love or for whom you care deeply. The Laumann study validated this for the later born groups. The study showed that women born between 1933 and 1942 had engaged in coitus with only their spouse and one other man almost 92 percent of the time; and with the 1963 to 1974 group about three-fourths of the women had sex only with their spouse and one other male at the time of marriage. The same women sampled by Laumann reported that their first sex partner was a spouse or someone with whom they were in love 83 percent of the time; and an additional 13 percent was with someone they knew well but with whom they were not in love. "Love" (or a deep emotional attachment) was the most important criterion for engaging in first sex.

Sexual behaviors liberalized over the course of the twentieth century. For example, the percentage of individuals who report having engaged in intercourse by age 19 steadily increased. For women born before 1911, 6 percent reported engaging in intercourse by 19, by the 1950s the figure rose to 55 percent, and by the 1980s it was 83 percent. Similarly, there were increases in the incidence of sexual activity other than intercourse as seen in the heterosexual script of Americans. The well-known baseball analogy of kissing as first base, breast manipulation as second base, manual stimulation of the genitals as third base, and intercourse as home plate remains current. Kissing (90 percent) and manual stimulation of the genitals (77 percent) was reported as part of the first experience of women who engaged in sex voluntarily. Perhaps the greatest change in sexual foreplay is the increase in couples who report engaging in oral sex. In the middle of the century, about one in every ten married couples reported engaging in oral sex; by the 1970s, roughly half of teenagers and young adults were doing so. Two decades later, 70 percent of teens and young adults experienced oral sex. For teens and young adults, oral sex may be their "new third base." More recent studies about the rate of oral sex among teens show somewhat lower numbers.

Two recent phenomena among teens and young adults may reflect liberalization towards sexual permissiveness without affection: "friends with benefits" and "hooking-up." In the former, young adults may pair up for occasional sex without the requirement of monogamy or a loving relationship. Hooking-up refers to a pattern of engaging in some type of sexual activity, which may or may not include intercourse, with just a casual acquaintance or relative stranger, and there is no expectation of a continued relationship beyond the sexual encounter.

There has been an equal amount of research measuring attitudes towards premarital sexual activity. In 1992, the Laumann survey assessed beliefs about premarital sex; when asked whether premarital sex is always or almost always wrong, women born in earlier cohorts were more likely to answer in the affirmative (1933 to 1942, 53 percent; 1943 to 1952, 31 percent; 1953 to 1962, 31 percent; 1963 to 1972, 22 percent). Men in the same age cohorts were less likely to see premarital sex as wrong (36, 26, 21, 16 percent, respectively). This change in attitudes mirrors changes in sexual behavior before marriage. In a study of sexual attitudes in industrialized nations (Widmer, Treas, and Newcomb 1998), attitudes towards premarital sex in the United States were comparable to Ireland, Northern Ireland, and Poland. Attitudes in these countries were more liberal than attitudes in the Philippines (76 percent disapproved of premarital sex), but were more conservative than in Scandinavia and eastern European countries where less than one-in-ten disapproved of premarital sexual activity.

Between 1900 and 1950 anthropologists and other social scientists studied the varieties of sexual expression in different cultures. For a vast number of the world's inhabitants living in Asian cultures such as China, India, and Japan, the first experience with sex occurred following an arranged marriage where the couple had little or no opportunity to know one another, and even less opportunity for love or sex play to occur. In some Islamic cultures, virginity at marriage is prized and there are severe restrictions on female sexuality. Experience with premarital sex for females can have dire consequences including being killed by one's family.

In other cultures, such as the Pacific Islands, **childhood** sex play has been an expected part of adolescence with little or no disapproval of premarital sexual activity. Children in these more permissive cultures may have the opportunity to witness the sexual interactions of adults and may mimic the behavior prior to puberty. There is little emphasis placed on virginity and, in at least one culture (Trobriand), premarital intercourse is encouraged to assess sexual compatibility.

Since mid-century, there have been dramatic cultural changes in Asia, resulting both from political and social upheavals and exposure to Western culture and values. In China, for instance, The Marriage Act of 1950 outlawed arranged marriages and instituted a government policy of monogamy based on free choice. In the decade following the number of arranged marriages dropped from 70 to 27 percent, and by the mid-1960s there were almost no marriages arranged, although families did continue to play some role in about half of the marriages. Other behaviors also changed. In the early 1990s somewhere between 12 and 40 percent of Chinese women experienced premarital intercourse. In Hindu India, there has been a similar decline in arranged marriages with a significant minority of men (43 percent) and women (37 percent) believing in choice of marriage partner (Hatfield and Rapson 1996). In Japan, there is a significant amount of choice of whom to marry although families still play a significant role. Further, one-fourth of Japanese females reported engaging in intercourse by age 18 (Alan Guttmacher Institute 1998).

While arranged marriages may be on the decline in some parts of the Muslim world, strongly fundamentalist subcultures maintain severe restrictions on female sexuality. In sub-Saharan Africa, female circumcision is still practiced. In some cases, the clitoris is excised in the belief that women will not be tempted by sexual **desire** and will remain chaste until marriage. In some of these more restrictive societies, the stress on female virginity and the segregation of the sexes until adulthood may limit the sexual exploration of adolescents to members of the same sex, despite religious and civil prohibitions.

Studies of sexual behavior in Central and South America find patterns of sexual behavior that are similar to North America for males where the majority report engaging in intercourse by their early to mid-twenties. However, unlike North America, females in Central and South America do not engage in premarital sex at the same levels as males. For instance, in Mexico 86 percent of males, age 20–24, report engaging in sex compared to 39 percent of females. This may reflect the existence of the double standard where males have greater sexual freedom than females and men may frequent prostitutes for their first sexual experience.

Although premarital sex generally implies heterosexuality, sex before marriage may include homosexual experimentation. A recent study (Ellis, Robb, and Burke 2005) of U.S. and Canadian college students found that 12.5 percent of males and 8 percent of females reported intimate sexual experiences with members of the same gender. Further, an even greater number reported same-sex fantasies (21 and 26 percent, respectively). Studies of premarital sex that ignore the variety of sexual experimentation will miss a significant proportion of sexual behavior since almost every study of cross-cultural sexuality has found evidence of homosexual activity. Cultural changes in the West resulting in recognition of civil unions and marriages of same-gendered couples also will widen the definitions of premarital sex. *See also* Celibacy; Dating; Infidelity/Extramarital Sex; Religions, Eastern; Religions, Western.

Further Reading: Ellis, Lee, Brian Robb, and Donald Burke. "Sexual Orientation in United States and Canadian College Students." *Archives of Sexual Behavior* 34 (2005): 569–81; Evans, Harriet. *Women & Sexuality in China: Female Sexuality and Gender since 1949.* New York: Continuum, 1997; Ford, Clellan S., and Frank A. Beach. *Patterns of Sexual Behavior.* New York: Harper and Row, 1951; Guttmacher Institute. "Into a New World: Young Women's Sexual and Reproductive Lives." http://www.guttmacher.org/pubs/new_world_engl.html. International research, policy analysis, and education regarding sexual and reproductive health; Hatfield, Elaine, and Richard L. Rapson. *Love and Sex: Cross-Cultural Perspective.* Boston: Allyn and Bacon, 1996; Kinsey, Alfred C., Wardell B. Pomeroy, Clyde E. Martin, and Paul N. Gebhard. *Sexual Behavior in the Human Female.* Philadelphia, PA: Saunders, 1953; Laumann, Edward O., John H. Gagnon, Robert T. Michael, and Stuart Michaels. *The Social Organization of Sexuality: Sexual Practices in the United States.* Chicago: University of Chicago Press, 1994; Paul, Elizabeth L., Brian McManus, and Allison Hayes. "'Hookups': Characteristics and Correlates of College Students' Spontaneous and Anonymous Sexual Experiences." *The Journal of Sex Research* 37 (2000): 76–88; Reiss, Ira. *Family Systems in America.* 3rd ed. New York: Holt, Rinehart and Winston, 1980; Widmer, Eric D., Judith Treas, and Robert Newcomb. "Attitudes toward Nonmarital Sex in 24 Countries." *The Journal of Sex Research* 35 (1998): 349–58.

Christopher Flynn

PRISONS, SEX IN. "Prison sex" has been the stuff of popular culture, academic research, public health and correctional policy throughout the twentieth and early part of the twenty-first centuries, yet its relationship to love has been overshadowed by the concentration on sensational sex. Much of the attention to prison sexuality in the early parts of the twentieth century focused on prison rape and adaptations to deprivation. In the latter part of that century and into the twenty-first century in the United States and other countries (especially Australia), attention broadened to include concerns with **masculinity**, disease transmission and control, as well as the relationship between prison sex and **homosexuality**. Popular culture reflected these themes, with particular attention to the forced dimension of same-sex behavior in jails and prisons. The concern with sexual assault in corrections culminated in the creation of the Prison Rape Elimination Act of 2003 in the United States.

Sex and prisons conjure up a range of images. From the frequent setting for an X-rated video to a Congressionally created commission, there is a stock of cultural, personal, administrative, and academic knowledge about the subject. Yet, it remains one of the most elusive topics in the professional literature. There are several dominant narratives about sex in correctional settings (detention, jails, and prisons), including "prison sex" as a form of coercion, a form of risky sexual behavior, a form of currency, and a form of exploration. However, "prison love" is not in that list, as it is a rare theme of most discourses on prison sex and only a rare theme in the arts world.

In the late seventeenth through the mid-nineteenth centuries, prior to the development of the modern penitentiary form of prison, sex was likely more common among those imprisoned in European and early North American prisons. Because of debtors' prisons and the low threshold for criminal activity punishable by incarceration, whole **families** and women were imprisoned. The Crown/State did not provide regular food, clothing, or medical care to those imprisoned. Some were able to sustain themselves without resorting to less than desirable means. For women, particularly, sex was a commodity that could be traded for sustenance, food, and perhaps freedom. For what may be considered a lucky few, a promise to trade sex bought passage to a hard, but promising new life in the American colonies and later Australia.

With the advent of the Quaker-inspired penitentiary, isolation, hard work, and penitence were rewarded with rations and shelter. The development of separate jail and prison facilities for men, women, and children would ideally lead to less bartering of sex for the necessities of daily life inside. Food and water are not, however, the only commodities for which one can barter. A common theme in the accounts of prison sex involves the trading of sexual activities for cigarettes, **drugs and alcohol**, "junk food," toiletries, clothing, and, of course, security.

Sex as coercion has emerged as one of the primary themes around prison sex. For example, the "old timer" loans the new inmate money or goods for a period of time, and when the newcomer is unable to pay up, the debt is settled through sexual favors. This may or may not involve the outright threat or use of force. Such sex may be provided directly to the person from whom the "loan" was received, or that person may "sell" the debt to another for collection.

A variation on the coerced "sale" of sex is also seen in the price paid for protection of some inmates by others. After a real or perceived threat by another inmate or inmate group, an individual may form an alliance with another inmate who can promise protection from a beating or rape. The only price is to provide sexual services to the protector. While it appears one is "buying" protection, this is still considered coercion.

Sometimes prison sex is the use of rape as a form of power or revenge, as popularized in media such as *Born Innocent, American History X*, or *Oz*. These events may range from an individual exerting power over a victim, to a gang or group using sexual violence to control an individual or a setting. There are, of course, allegations and instances in which correctional officers have been known to "look the other way," to punish individual inmates, or to reward inmate gangs for keeping order in an institution.

There are some who take a "MacDworkin" approach to sex, arguing that all sexual contact inside correctional facilities is coercive. The move to make all sex between correctional officers and prisoners illegal is one example of this, and some would extend this to any inmate with inmate sexual contact. In this way, the arguments for banning all sexual activity inside prisons takes on a different tact than the more "penological interest" approach, but achieves the same outcome—all sex is forbidden; love is no excuse.

Concern with sexual coercion, generally termed "prison rape," led to passage of the Prison Rape Elimination Act of 2003 in the United States. This congressionally mandated ten-year program seeks to provide the first nationally comprehensive study of rape in correctional settings (juvenile detention, local jails, and state and federal prisons). Additionally, the National Prison Rape Elimination Commission will develop standards for responding to and eliminating sexual violence in correctional institutions.

Although there have been periodic "outbreaks" of various **sexually transmitted infections** (STIs) among those in jails and prisons over the decades, the arrival of **AIDS/HIV** in the population in the early 1980s generated a great deal of fear and debate that continues to the present. Rates of HIV among prison populations are generally several times higher than observed in the community in most countries/states that report this information (e.g., Australia, Canada, Mozambique, Malawi, the United Kingdom, and the United States). This is due to the concentration of individuals whose risk behaviors in the community place them at high probability of contracting HIV and hepatitis C (HCV).

There is also documented STI transmission within correctional facilities, though there is considerable debate over just how significant this level of transmission is. In the United States, intra-prison transmission of HIV among African American men has become almost an article of faith in explaining the growth of HIV among African American women in the community, even in the face of underwhelming empirical support for this idea. A few studies have also documented the transmission of syphilis and hepatitis B among prisoners.

The STI transmission issue has been met in a variety of ways. For example, the Australian state of New South Wales has introduced condoms through vending machines located in residential areas and do not penalize consensual sexual relations among inmates. Queensland and West Australia, however, do not condone sexual relations among inmates and/or distribute condoms. Throughout the United States, sexual relations among inmates are almost universally forbidden, and the handful of state prison systems and local jails that provide condoms still penalize those who are observed having sex, at least in theory.

The least well-developed theme in the academic prison sex literature centers on sex as an expression of love between individuals. There is a remnant of the taboos about same-sex relations, especially male-to-male. Some authors suggest that stories of same-sex prison love were integral to the development of gay and lesbian identity in the later part of the 1900s. For instance, some literary critics contend that stereotypes of aggressive prison lesbians helped to shape certain acceptable lesbian roles in the free world and other depictions made lesbian behaviors more acceptable in mainstream culture.

Transgender prisoners are almost always mentioned as rape victims, health care, or security problems—never in relation to loving relationships. Perhaps *Kiss of the Spiderwoman* is the exception to this prevailing norm regarding transgender prisoners.

Lesbian and female same-sex relationships are about the only area of prison sexuality in which the concept of love is applied on a more than occasional basis, even rising to the status of a "homonormative" environment. Some would say that the relationships among females in prison were the first to rise to scientific interest. The more caring and familial relationships among female prisoners observed by some comes closest to a free world concept of loving relationships discussed in the prison sex literature. Others have argued that while expressions of care, concern, and love may be present in these relationships, these are only temporary manifestations of inmates being "gay for the stay."

Conjugal visits for heterosexual prisoners are a rarity in the United States. They are more common in Latin American and European countries where they are believed to preserve family cohesion and reduce the incidence of same-sex behavior inside. The extent to which conjugal visitation achieves any of its desired outcomes remains a matter of debate, but little research. The restrictive nature of some programs renders them almost unused, and they remain as rare as legal condoms in many prison systems.

Since so much of the narrative about sex inside revolves around coercion, it is also possible that some researchers doubt that a genuine affection could develop among incarcerated individuals, or between the incarcerated and their captors. In essence, such behaviors are more likely to be an adaptation to an "unnatural" situation, or a

"Stockholm syndrome" response to a captor. Popular imagery of male inmates seducing female staff in hopes of either gaining prestige among their fellow inmates or as a means to escape, dominate the "love" theme, keeping it related to the coercion theme.

Alfred **Kinsey**'s and his colleagues' interviews with imprisoned men suggest that the development of loving relationships among male inmates takes a relatively long period of time, that is, several years, to find a partner inside with whom one can build a strong, loving bond—if ever. Those interviews were conducted at a time when same-sex relationships were themselves the subject of criminal prosecution and rushing into a sexual relationship with another inmate can have dire consequences. *See also* Heterosexuality.

Further Reading: Eigenberg, Helen, and Agnes Baro. "If You Drop the Soap in the Shower You Are on Your Own: Images of Male Rape in Selected Prison Movies." *Sexuality & Culture* 7, no. 4 (2003): 56–89; Hensley, Christopher, ed. *Prison Sex: Practice & Policy.* Boulder, CO: Lynne Reinner Publishers, 2002; Herman, Didi. "'*Bad Girls*' Changed My Life: Homonormativity in a Women's Prison Drama." *Critical Studies in Media Communication* 20, no. 2 (2003): 141–59; Human Rights Watch. *No Escape: Male Rape in U.S. Prisons.* http:// www.hrw.org/reports/2001/prison. Provides gripping personal narratives by individuals sexually assaulted in prisons, 2001; Kunzel, Regina G. "Situating Sex: Prison Sexual Culture in the Mid-Twentieth Century United States." *GLQ: A Journal of Lesbian and Gay Studies* 8, no. 3 (2002): 253–70; Maeve, M. Katherine. "The Social Construction of Love and Sexuality in a Women's Prison." *Advances in Nursing Science* 21, no. 3 (1999): 46–65; National Prison Rape Elimination Act. http://www.nicic.org/Library/020686. The text of the Prison Rape Elimination Act of 2003—United States; New South Wales Justice Health Inmate Health Survey. http://www.justicehealth.nsw.gov.au/pubs/Inmate_Health_Survey_2001.pdf. Contains data on prisoner sex and sexual assault experience, pre- and during incarceration, with links to articles on sex in prisons; Potter, Roberto Hugh, and Richard Tewksbury. "Sex and Prisoners: Criminal Justice Contributions to a Public Health Issue." *Journal of Correctional Health Care* 11, no. 2 (2005): 171–90; Seal, David Wyatt. "HIV-Related Issues and Concerns for Imprisoned Persons throughout the World." *Current Opinions in Psychiatry* 18, no. 5 (2005): 530–35; Stop Prison Rape. http://www.spr.org. A non-profit organization dedicated to providing support for victims of sexual assault while incarcerated, research and advocacy with several studies and links to research; Struckman-Johnson, Cindy, and D. L. Struckman-Johnson. "Sexual Coercion Rates in Seven Midwestern Prison Facilities for Men." *The Prison Journal* 80, no. 4 (2000): 379–90.

Roberto Hugh Potter and Richard Tewksbury

PROSTITUTION. Prostitution is the monetary exchange (or its equivalent) to a person or persons in return for their engagement in one or more sexual acts, for the sexual gratification of those who have paid or are expected to provide some type of payment. Some writers and commentators find the very term "prostitute" just as pejorative as terms such as "whore" or "hooker" (or if male, terms such as, hustler, rent boys, trade, or gigolos), preferring "sex worker." Some sex worker activists, however, have tried to reclaim "whore" in the same way as some gay male activists have reclaimed "queer." Males who are "managers" or live off the earnings of female sex workers are known as "pimps" or "ponces" and a female manager (usually only typical in a brothel context) is a madam, or in some Asian contexts, mama-san. Pimps do not typically feature in the context of adult male prostitutes and are not a universal phenomenon among all female sex workers around the world. Increasingly, as a result of liberal print **media** and **Internet** outlets many female sex workers can more easily bypass working with pimps.

While money-based exchange is by far the most common basis for such sexual transactions throughout the world, there remain some locations where non-monetary based exchange still persists to some degree. In Senegal there exist *diola* women, who typically have had one or two children before **marriage**, or *bassari* women, for whom there is some measure of duty to spend the night with a guest to their village. Some countries also have religion or state-sanctioned cultural institutions and norms that effectively facilitate prostitution, but not explicitly by that name. For example, Iran has a penal code (effective since 1925) in which prostitution itself is not a crime, though advocating it, aiding and abetting a woman to enter prostitution, or operating a brothel is strictly illegal on pain of execution. However, a temporary marriage, *mutïa*, where men may get married to a woman for a few hours or less, is legal. Hence, in practice, men visiting prostitutes can be rendered completely permissible so long as it operates under the conditions of *mutïa*. In many other countries, regulations and statutes intended to eliminate, reduce, or contain male and female prostitution are bypassed by using other terms for such services such as **advertising** as escort agencies and massage parlors.

Undated photo of Lily Langtry. Courtesy of the Library of Congress.

Men and women have been selling sexual services to each other for many centuries in wholly independent, state-owned or church-owned enterprises, or under various gradations and types of federal, state, or municipal regulation. The legal status and degree of social stigma associated with prostitution since 1900 has exhibited enormous variety from country to country and in some cases from city to city. Over the course of the twentieth century there have been social changes (e.g., female emancipation and legalization of homosexual activity) and public health concerns (primarily syphilis, gonorrhea, and subsequently **AIDS/HIV**) which have, in some locations (e.g., the Netherlands), led to increasing liberalization, and in others (e.g., the United States), greater restrictions on the practice of prostitution. Fear of **sexually transmitted infections** has also been linked to the growth in demand since the Victorian and Edwardian era for child prostitutes who were assumed (often wrongly owing to widespread deception) to be clear of such infections.

During the first decade of the twentieth century, within Paris's wealthy society it was still not uncommon to find females finding "protectors" among the banking, financial, military, government, and aristocratic male elite who would pay their bills in return for companionship and sexual services. London, too, had a smaller pool of discreet courtesans who fulfilled the same function, with Lily Langtry being the best known. Washington, D.C., had its elite prostitutes, operating under the guise of lobbyists who stayed in town during the Congressional session. Prostitution in the service of the elite was also found in Southern India. The practice of *devadasi* involved the "**marriage**" of some adolescents to a religious deity or temple where they provided prostitution services to upper-caste members. The practice was only made illegal in the late 1980s.

In most countries the more mainstream market in the early twentieth century, as indeed now, comprised both street-based and off-street (including brothel-based) prostitution. In 1902, New Orleans instituted Storyville (named after Alderman Sidney Story), which provides an early example of a sex work toleration zone. It was devised to help the city enjoy the economic benefits of this industry, but also to restrict "nuisance" or "disturbance" to the wider residential community. Further, while many countries and cities around the world now have printed or Web-based "erotic guides" to various brothels or individual prostitutes, New Orleans had its publications at the turn of the century.

Between 1910 and 1915, the Women's Christian Temperance Union helped to influence a wave of bans and restrictions on prostitution in most of the United States. Storyville's services were discontinued by the Federal Government in 1917 following a decree that closed all brothels within five miles of a naval base. Probably due to a persistent gender imbalance as well as its status as not then a full state of the union, prostitution remained legal in Alaska till 1953. It remains legal in some counties of Nevada, which famously host a number of celebrated ranch-style brothels. The entire course of the history of prostitution indicates that complete bans typically do not work. At the dawn of the First World War similar concerns to those of the U.S. military were also evident in Germany. Yet closure of brothels was considered to be likely to adversely affect troop morale. Accordingly, mobile military brothels were a common feature behind fighting lines. Red-light brothels were for non-commissioned officers and the lower ranks of soldiers and blue-light brothels were for officers. Such brothels featured Medical Corp personnel dispensing condoms, collecting payments for the madam, and providing a brief medical inspection of the troops. Formal or informal military brothel operations or franchises, either on or off-base, were a feature of the Japanese military in the 1930s, as well as the U.S. military in connection with the Philippine occupation, the Korean and Vietnam wars, and with United Nations troops in Bosnia.

The continued existence of paid sex markets remains subject to fierce debate and engenders hotly contested views surrounding the nature of what constitutes an appropriate public policy towards prostitution. Partly, this is a result of the analytically unhelpful and deliberately misleading conflation of the enormous range of prostitution markets by some commentators, lobbyists, politicians, and activists into one single, seemingly homogeneous market. Sex markets involving minors, which support hard drug dependency, and where coercion and enslavement of sex workers by means of violence or economic and psychological threats by pimps and traffickers occur, are often "placed" in the same market as adult voluntary transactions.

Nevertheless, consensual adult sex markets attract bitter dispute across the religious-moral-political spectrum. The "abolitionist" camp contends that since most sex work is supplied by women, it has been harnessed as a means of reinforcing the power role of men over women and, in so doing, subordinates females even further. The "sex work" camp argues that selling sexual services can be a legitimate work choice, warranting protective legislation to improve working conditions and a reduction in the social stigma associated with such markets.

For many individuals, however, prostitution is simply an economic survival strategy or a means of income diversification. It potentially offers relatively higher returns compared with many other income sources that are deemed to be realistically available. Relatively higher monetary returns, however, may merely reflect the higher risks associated with working as a prostitute (in terms of sexual health and physical violence from some customers).

Surveys of prostitutes and their customers typically reveal that a significant proportion, or in some cases the majority, are likely to be in relationships or married. The use of prostitutes by individuals in existing relationships is motivated by a range of factors, including a need to satisfy a higher frequency of sexual contact than one's relationship partner is willing to make, a need for variety, or a **desire** to engage in specific sexual activities, which the existing relationship partner is not prepared to countenance. It may also provide a sexual outlet during bouts of marital conflict (a "sexual refuge" motive) or an outlet for other forms of stress and tension. Using a prostitute may satisfy all these needs without the need for any emotional complications, since the existing relationship may, in general, provide adequate companionship and emotional support. Indeed, unlike the heroine in the 1990 movie *Pretty Woman*, prostitutes typically maintain emotional detachment from clients. Since many consumers of prostitution services are in existing relationships, they are more likely to endure considerable social disapproval if discovered. In the United States, street-based prostitution accounts for approximately one-in-five working prostitutes and 85 to 90 percent of those arrested for prostitution related offenses have worked on the street (Prostitutes' Education Network 1999). Community action against such prostitution may feature vigilante patrols to harass prostitutes and potential clients, or the use of cameras, hand-held video equipment, and manual recording of vehicle number plates. These actions allow for "naming and shaming" tactics in local newspapers and other **media** or direct contact with the family and spouses of discovered "curb crawlers." There is typically a greater risk of discovery since the street market is the most likely to be affected by episodic, though typically pre-announced clampdowns and offensives by police against street crime, or even more durable area-based "zero tolerance" initiatives such as those encouraged by Mayor Rudolph Giuliani in New York during his term of office.

Many countries, states, or city authorities continue to experiment with a variety of strategies to regulate or control prostitution. These include toleration zones or licensing of sex workers and prostitution enterprises or brothels. Yet even with a legalized market, regulatory enforcement is still necessary. City authorities typically require the management and containment of prostitution activity to "shield" nearby residents or other elements of the community from its real or perceived negative effects. This generally means delimiting the hours of business and/or spatial margins of prostitution activity. Within such zones, illegal sex workers and enterprises typically continue to operate in the same way that illegal traders operate alongside legal traders in other markets. They may gain from tax evasion, offering banned (e.g., under-aged sex) or higher-risk premium services (unsafe sex) not permitted in the legal market. In such an illicit context, sex workers who have failed health checks may be under pressure to work illegally and organized crime enterprises may try to use their talents in coercion to "manage" sex workers for generating third-party gains. Nonetheless, proponents of legalization hope that illegal market demand can be reduced to a residual hardcore base that can be more easily targeted by the police with their existing resources. *See also* Child Abuse; Scandals; Sex Crimes.

Further Reading: Brock, Rita, and Thistlethwaite, Susan. *Casting Stones: Prostitution and Liberation in Asia and the United States.* Minneapolis, MN: Fortress Press, 1996; Collins, Alan, ed. *Cities of Pleasure: Sex and the Urban Socialscape.* London: Routledge, 2006; Gebhard, Paul, and Alan Johnson. *The Kinsey Data: Marginal Tabulation of the 1938–1963: Interviews Conducted by the*

Institute of Sex Research. Philadelphia: Saunders, 1979; Prostitutes' Education Network. Prostitution in the United States—The Statistics. http://www.bayswan.org/index.html. A measured introduction to some key issues and facts relating to prostitution, 1999; Tannahill, Ray. *Sex in History*. London: Book Club Associates, 1990.

Alan Collins

PSYCHOANALYSIS. Psychoanalysis refers to both the theory and practice of interpreting psychological symptoms to effect healing. It is most commonly and accurately associated with the Austrian neurologist Sigmund **Freud**, whose published works on mental disorders such as hysteria established the field as a "scientific" discipline, introducing terms such as the "subconscious," "Oedipus Complex," and "Freudian slip" into everyday vocabulary. Freud's frank discussion of the importance of sexuality to the development of the individual personality attracted notoriety to the field in the scientific and wider community of late-nineteenth-century Europe. Specifically, his theory concerning the Oedipus complex in the development of the male child—and indeed the underlying assumption that children were capable of sexual feelings at all—has been the focus of intense interest. There is a significant historical coincidence between the development of psychoanalysis and clinical terms to describe a host of often female mental conditions, as well as increasingly "scientific" definitions of the newly invented terms "**homosexuality**" and "**race**." This has ensured an ongoing relationship between psychoanalysis and **feminism**, queer theory, and postcolonialism.

Early theorists viewed hypnotism—a practice that enjoyed some popularity during the nineteenth century—as the undisputed therapeutic approach to treating subconscious maladies like hysteria. They also maintained an intense focus on certain mental illnesses, such as lethargy, catalepsy (a seizure or trance), and hysteria (predominantly a female condition). Lastly, late-nineteenth-century explanations for mental illness moved away from the medieval belief that these conditions were caused by the build up of "an unknown bodily fluid," substituting a similarly unknown "mental energy." It was these speculations that Freud organized into a scientific discipline of psychoanalysis.

Freud proposed that "normal" adulthood for the human individual is the result of the successful completion of a number of stages or phases of "libidinal development," taking place during **childhood**, between the ages of 18 months and three years. He suggested that the abnormally long development period in human young (compared to those of other species) requires mastering basic bodily processes such as satisfying and mastering the immediate desires for eating and excreting (the famous "oral" and "anal" phases). In each of these phases, the infant becomes "fixated" upon the stimuli associated with the impulse: the mouth (the oral stage); the anus (the anal phase). Successful completion of one stage is necessary for the progression of the infant to the next stage, and consequently his or her development. Thus, the phrase describing an orderly, obsessive or obstinate person as "anally retentive" as a result of being fixated in this stage, has entered the popular vocabulary.

In subsequent years, Freud added the central dimension of sexuality to his conception of the developing human personality. "Triebe" (drives) were converted, he hypothesized, through the individual's psyche, into "wishes" via a multi-stage process. There were two principle drives motivating the human organism: the drive to copulate and thus reproduce (*eros*), and the drive toward extinction or death (*thanatos*). It was

Freud's preoccupation with the first of these drives upon which the bulk of much subsequent psychoanalytic work and criticism was to be based.

The second important proposition of psychoanalytic theory is the notion that successful progression to adulthood requires that the child move through a sexual conflict. The Oedipus Complex—named after the Greek tragedian Sophocles's play about a king who unknowingly kills his father in order to marry his mother—dramatizes this conflict. The infant develops an erotic attachment to mother, the primary giver of material and emotional nourishment. Later in life, the child recognizes a competitor for mother's affections (father), which creates a feeling of childhood hostility toward the father. The successful resolution of this conflict, according to the psychoanalysts, marks the transition into a psychologically "healthy" adulthood.

Importantly, this model of a child's psychosexual development admits neither the possibility for female sexual **desire** nor homosexual desire of any form. It implies a heterosexual relationship between a male child and his female parent, which is disrupted by sexual competition from another male. Although Freud later proposed a second phase, the "Electra Complex" (after Oedipus's sister) to describe a similar conflict in the female child, he was never entirely comfortable with the idea of feminine sexuality in its own right. As feminist critics have argued, Freud assumes the male child as the developmental "norm." Most notable among feminist examinations of psychoanalytic theory is the work of Bulgarian-French feminist and psychoanalyst Julia Kristeva. While preserving the basic features of the psychoanalytic developmental model, she conceptualized the "abject," that which the psyche must exclude to remain whole. This process was essentially directed toward defining the boundaries between the individual's body and the outside world. The mastery of bodily orifices and fluids has an important role to play, but she extended her notion of the "abject" to include femininity. Kristeva argued that the feminine was defined as "Other" by Western societies in general, and especially psychoanalysis, in order to construct a sense of individual identity. Despite Freud's claim that this identity is universal, Kristeva proposed that it is a heterosexual male of which he speaks—an identity formed in large part by not being feminine.

Other theorists have drawn similar comparisons to the representation of ethnic Others in the Western imagination. The most long-lasting of these theorists is the French-Algerian Frantz Fanon. Having studied in France during the 1940s and qualified in 1951 as a psychiatrist, Fanon was not strictly a psychoanalyst. However, his work drew on the psychoanalytic principles in its suggestion that historical and cultural situations such as **colonialism** impacted on the psychic state of the individual. *Black Skin, White Masks* and *The Wretched of the Earth* emphasized the previous role of cultural background in the treatment of mental illness, providing the foundation for later psychoanalytic work on the psychology of race.

The developmental aspects of psychoanalytic theory are highly influential in psychological practice and research to this day, largely due to the work of the Austrian born psychoanalyst Melanie Klein who published *The Psychoanalysis of Children* in 1932. Her main contribution to psychoanalytic thought (besides how children might profit from psychoanalysis) is object-relations theory. This branch of psychoanalysis focuses on Freud's theory that the individual always satisfies desire through a particular medium or object. In the case of the pre-oedipal child, this is usually the child's mother. Later in life however, the object can be any thing or person that satisfies these desires. Perhaps the most academically influential proponent of psychoanalytic principles was the French analyst Jacques Lacan. He was persuaded by Freud's developmental stages as a means of explaining how the individual self or "subject" is formed. However, as a Freudian revisionist, he railed against the prevailing psychological wisdom of the 1920s, which focused on "ego psychology." Lacan stressed a return to the core Freudian conceptions of the unconscious not as a single, unified entity, but the product of a web of identifications. Central to these identifications was the function of language, which he theorized as originating from the separation of a child from mother. His most famous theoretical contribution to psychoanalysis, however, is the "Mirror Stage." Generally around 12 months of age, the child acquires the ability to sense its individual "self." Lacan describes a hypothetical situation in which a child looks into a mirror and realizes that this image is not a baby, but a representation or projection of its own self. Thus, as the child becomes aware that it has an existence separate from that of its parent, it instinctively develops language as a way of "reaching out" into the world and filling this gap. This structure forms the basis for Lacan's subsequent discussions on language and identity.

The reputation of psychoanalysis in psychological circles declined during the 1980s and 1990s. Nevertheless, techniques based largely upon its central tenets are still widely practiced in the United States, Europe, and other Western democracies. The clichéd popular image of the "talking cure," whereby a patient seeks healing from an analyst "on the couch," bears very little resemblance to the experiences of the majority of psychological practitioners and their patients. The history of psychology is associated with the rise of modern industrial societies and the massive social upheavals they create. The end of the nineteenth century also saw an increased interest in the biological sciences, which sought to explain human behavior. Psychology is often associated with these developments. It is perhaps for these reasons that psychoanalytic thought arose in the industrialized Western world, and its continued dominance in those countries today is a reflection of this economic inequality. *See also* Heterosexuality; Mental Health and Sex; Psychotherapy.

Further Reading: Bieber, Irving. *Homosexuality: A Psychoanalytic Study.* New York: Basic Books, 1962; Bristow, Joseph. *Sexuality.* New York: Routledge, 1997; Ellenberger, Henri F. *The Discovery of the Unconscious.* New York: Basic Books, 1970; Fine, Reuben. *A History of Psychoanalysis.* New York: Columbia University Press, 1979; Foucault, Michel. *History of Sexuality.* London: Penguin, 1990; Gedo, John E., ed. *Freud, the Fusion of Science and Humanism: The Intellectual History of Psychoanalysis.* New York: International Universities Press, 1976; International Psychoanalytic Society. http://www.psychoanalysis.co.uk. Information on the current status of psychoanalytic thought and practice, November 2006; Mitchell, Juliet. *Psychoanalysis and Feminism.* London: Penguin, 2000; Nye, Robert. *Sexuality.* Oxford: Oxford University Press, 1999.

David Nel

PSYCHOTHERAPY. Psychotherapy is a theory and method of healing that uses psychological or mind-focused treatments as opposed to somatic or body-focused treatments to relieve nervous and mental symptoms. As a discipline, medicine has resisted psychotherapy because it took medicine outside of somatic treatments. In general, communication between therapist and patient is a key part of the treatment process. Psychotherapy is important because it has played a key role in mediating self-development, and in regulating sexuality and love within particular social and cultural norms. Historically, under the influences of law, legislation, and social mores, the forms of discourse on sexuality have been controlled in psychotherapy and psychiatry—just as they have been regulated in mainstream culture and society. Psychotherapists and psychiatrists, like physicians and educators, have been expected to speak about sexuality, especially the sexuality of children, in terms that relegate any discussion of sexuality and love to the parameters of heterosexual development and other-sex attraction. Indeed, psychotherapy and psychiatry have promoted **heterosexuality** and procreation as sociocultural norms. Moreover, they have placed alternative sexual identities and love practices in the realm of pathology and within a discourse on the dangers of sexual perversions. This is perhaps most evident in the historical discourse on **homosexuality** as a mental affliction requiring diagnosis and therapy.

During the late nineteenth century, homosexuality was constituted as a psychiatric category and a dangerous species. Carl Westphal's 1870 article, *Archiv für Neurologie*, addresses what he called contrary sexual sensations. During the subsequent century, psychiatry and psychotherapy reflected law and tradition, considering homosexuality to be an affliction of the normal sexual instinct. Homosexuality was deemed pathological; it was taboo and something to be constrained and corrected through treatment. This categorization of homosexuality as pathology remained the medical standard in North America until 1973. In that year, the American Psychiatric Association (APA), as a branch of medical science, removed homosexuality from its *DSM-III* (*Diagnostic and Statistical Manual of Mental Disorders*, 3rd edition). The APA acknowledged there was an inadequate scientific database to support the assertion that homosexuality is pathological. Nevertheless, the World Health Organization did not remove homosexuality from the list of mental disorders in the *International Classification of Diseases* (ICD) until 1992. This impacted nations like the United Kingdom that follow the ICD. For example, until recently, psychoanalytic training institutes in the United Kingdom refused to accept homosexuals for training. Heterosexist bias and homophobic attitudes remain prevalent in psychotherapy.

Despite these moves to reclassify homosexuality, to this day orthodox psychotherapy maintains that homosexuality is pathological, and it affirms a complementary, male-female model of gender and sexuality that locates love and "normal" sexual development in heterosexual terms. Orthodox psychotherapy finds some support for its theory and method in current versions of the DSM and the ICD, at least in terms of pathologizing gender identities not aligned with biological sex. While diagnoses like Gender Identity Disorder remain in classifications of pathologies, the medicalization of gender identity will significantly impact the lives of trans-identified persons for whom sexuality and love mediate the complexities of gender and sexuality. Diagnosing and treating homosexual orientation and gender identity as pathological are substantially grounded in culturally based heterosexism, homophobia, and transphobia.

This exposes the need for extensive clinical investigation to improve the scientific foundations of psychotherapy. The reliance on case studies or anecdotal evidence instead of scientific evidence that can be empirically replicated has always been considered to be a key weakness of psychotherapy. Psychotherapy has also lost medical value because its discourse has primarily been about males and their development and clinical issues; generally, its present theory and method are not valid for females. Moreover, psychotherapy, emerging as a theory and practice available to the middle and upper classes that could access it, has been considered to be exclusionary and class-biased. Today, psychotherapy works best when it considers the influences of history, culture, morality, class, and gender, and when it accommodates the complexities of sexuality and love in treating individuals.

The history of pathologizing homosexuality in psychoanalytic psychotherapy indicates problems permeating contemporary **psychoanalysis**. At the core of these problems is the fact that much of psychoanalysis rests on Sigmund **Freud**'s hypotheses, some of which have been invalidated or made questionable by other areas of the medical sciences including the neural sciences and clinical and developmental psychology. Nevertheless, Freud's work remains central to the theory and method of psychoanalytic psychotherapy. The effectiveness of psychotherapy, Freud believed, depended on a patient freely choosing therapy (not at the request of significant others like parents), and the patient's openness to change, with no preconceptions of the direction that psychoanalysis would take.

By the mid-1920s, Freud had developed four hypotheses constituting the cornerstones of psychoanalytic theory and method: there are unconscious mental processes; sexuality and the Oedipus complex (a phase of psychosexual development marked by a strong **childhood** attachment for the parent of the other gender) are important; infantile experiences are significant; the mind is a site of resistance and repression. Resistance and repression, according to Freud, are cornerstones of psychoanalysis since evidence of repression always followed signs of resistance in therapy.

Despite psychotherapy's historical efforts to diagnose and treat homosexuality as an affliction, there is no evidence that Freud considered homosexuality to be pathological. Indeed his earlier theorizing, particularly evident in the first essay of his 1905 book *Three Essays on the Theory of Sexuality* (revised in 1920), positioned homosexuality as part of normal development, just another expression of sexuality. Even though Freud ambiguously cast heterosexuality as the desired outcome of psychosexual development in his later theorizing, he never decided whether homosexuality was a valid sexual orientation or evidence of pathology. Nevertheless, psychoanalysis after Freud was more orthodox, locating homosexuality as an aberration of **heterosexuality**. This exclusionary perspective has made psychotherapy for homosexuals problematic, even dangerous, as theorists may maneuver clients toward the adoption of accepted gender norms and socially acceptable sexual behaviors.

In recent decades in the United States, psychiatry has been distancing itself from psychotherapy. One move has been toward a biomedical model of psychopathology or mental illness. In part, this has been an oppositional response to U.S. psychiatry's marked involvement with Freudian psychoanalysis from 1920 to 1960. It has also been an expression of the discipline's desire to gain credibility as a medical specialty. However, the contemporary biomedical perspective in psychiatry dismisses a social-science conception of mental illness and rejects the influence of cultural variations, blaming the client when therapy doesn't work. It, too, has engendered opposition. Other positions, like those emanating from cultural psychiatry, have been gaining ground. In fact, since the 1960s individual and cultural differences pertaining to race, ethnicity, gender, religion, ability, and sexual orientation have become a focus of multicultural therapeutics. Some therapists would like multiculturalism to become a fourth force in psychotherapy alongside the traditional schools of psychoanalysis, behaviorism, and person-centered humanism.

Exploring the link between culture and psychotherapy has ramifications for clinical practice. In treating a client, culturally grounded psychotherapy acknowledges variables associated with ethnic and cultural diversity as well as problems arising from a therapist's cultural ignorance and fear. For example, culturally sensitive therapists recognize that culture involves integrated and patterned systems of values, beliefs, and behaviors. They are more cognizant of the impact of matters like spirituality and religion and more likely to consider cultural aspects of afflictions like grief, trauma, and loss. These therapists do not consider any form of psychotherapy to be immune from the influence of culture. Even psychoanalytic psychotherapy, they note, never thrived in the conservative culture of old Vienna where it originated. Thus, culturally sensitive therapists gauge the influence of culture on all therapies, even those like cognitive-behavioral therapy, which is considered to have universal applicability of theory and method. They acknowledge culturally-specific therapies, which have arisen from certain sociocultural environments and eras. One example is Rapid Integrated Therapy that emerged in China during the Great Leap Forward movement in the 1960s. It focused on building self-confidence and social integration as part of the therapy's political demand for rapid healing and recovery.

While mainstream psychotherapy plays catch up with culture, orthodox psychotherapy, especially as it has developed in Canada and the United States, continues to pathologize homosexuality and legitimize reparative therapies purported to cure homosexuals. Although all major Canadian and U.S. health and mental-health associations have declared that homosexuality is not a mental illness, issued resolutions, policy statements, revised ethical codes to this effect, and published position statements noting the lack of evidence to support the efficacy of reparative therapies (and warning of their possible harm), orthodox psychotherapy promotes their use. Further, conservative politicians and religious groups, seeking to limit gay civil rights, have used so-called reparative therapeutic evidence in media campaigns and court cases to claim that homosexuality is freely chosen and changeable. *See also* Sex Therapists; Transgender/Transsexual.

Further Reading: Caplan, Eric. *Mind Games: American Culture and the Birth of Psychotherapy.* Berkeley: University of California Press, 1998; Friedman, Richard C. *Male Homo Sexuality: A Contemporary Psychoanalytic Perspective.* New Haven, CT: Yale University Press, 1988; Jacobs, Michael. *Sigmund Freud.* 2nd ed. London: Sage Publications, 2003; Lee, Richard M., and Manual Ramirez III. "The History, Current Status, and Future of Multicultural Psychotherapy." In *Handbook of Multicultural Mental Health: Assessment and Treatment of Diverse Populations,* edited by Israel Cuéllar and Freddy A. Paniagua, 279–309. San Diego: Academic Press, 2000; Maguire, Marie. *Men, Women, Passion and Power: Gender Issues in Psychotherapy.* 2nd ed. New York: Brunner-Routledge, 2004; Marsella, Anthony. J., and Ann Marie Yamada. "Culture and Mental Health: An Introduction and Overview of Foundations, Concepts, and Issues." In *Handbook of Multicultural Mental Health: Assessment and Treatment of Diverse Populations,* edited by Israel Cuéllar and Freddy A. Paniagua, 3–24. San Diego: Academic Press, 2000; Marshall, Sue. *Difference and Discrimination in Psychotherapy and Counselling.* London: Sage Publications, 2004; Psychotherapy Networker. http://www.psychotherapynetworker.org/index. html. This online U.S. magazine contains articles of contemporary interest, and information about courses, conferences, and resources for continuing professional development in psychotherapy; Sigmund Freud—Life and Work. http://www.freudfile.org. Provides essays and papers on Freud's biography, self-analysis, and work; on the psychoanalytic movement; and also on individuals with whom Freud interacted in his development of psychoanalysis; Wen-Shing, T., and Jon Streltzer. *Culture and Psychotherapy: A Guide to Clinical Practice.* Arlington, VA: American Psychiatric Publishing, 2001.

André P. Grace

PUBERTY AND PUBERTY RITUALS. Puberty is a life stage in which humans move from sexual immaturity to maturity. Prepubescent boys and girls may experience sexual **desire**, but they are unable to become parents. The popular imagination associates puberty with a hormone-driven "discovery" of the other gender, followed by several years of "boy-craziness" or "girl-craziness." However, any such sudden, dramatic surge in heterosexual interest seems to be the product of social expectation rather than hormones; most people report that they first experienced heterosexual or same-sex desire at a much younger age. Socially, puberty is the beginning of the transition to adult roles and responsibilities. Some of the transitions occur overnight, and others gradually, over a period of years, but at the end the child has adopted adult interests, activities, costumes, and forms of address—and is often expected to fall in love and enter heterosexual **marriage**. Puberty rites are ritualized activities that mark some aspect of the transition: a certain age (e.g., turning 16), a certification (the first driver's license), or an experience deemed evidence of maturity (a first date).

The age at which puberty begins varies, depending on the individual's genetic makeup, environmental factors, and social expectations. However, there is evidence that it has been generally decreasing. In 1840, the mean age for entering puberty in England was 16.5 for girls and 17.5 for boys. Today, 97 percent of girls in the West have their first menstruation by age fourteen; for boys the same percentage show their first increase in testicle size by age thirteen. However, the duration of puberty has remained fairly constant, about five years for girls and six years for boys.

The significance of puberty in the social life of the community has also changed considerably. Prior to the twentieth century, barely pubescent boys and girls were treated as adults, able to marry, have children, own property, and make valid legal and political decisions. During the last century, an increasingly specialized division of labor has made high school and even college attendance mandatory in many countries, adding between five to ten years between biological pubescence and social maturity. Instead of entering adulthood, pubescent children now enter **adolescence**, a sort of buffer zone with its own norms, occupations, and activities.

Traditional societies, such as found in contemporary Melanesia and Amazonia usually mark the onset of puberty as a specific, dramatic, and often painful event. Pubescent children might be subject to tattooing, scarring, piercing, or circumcision. They might be starved, deprived of sleep, isolated from other members of the tribe, entombed in a sort of symbolic death and resurrection, or sent into the wilderness for an arduous spirit journey. Afterwards the transition is complete: yesterday's child is universally acknowledged as an adult.

During the first half of the twentieth century, pubescence was marked by ritualized changes in costumes and activities even in industrialized countries. At the end of childhood, boys would switch from short pants to long pants, and girls would switch from skirts to dresses. However, as the increased productivity of late capitalism led to a wider variety of consumption choices for everyone, it became increasingly difficult to mark a specific style of hat, pants, or skirt "for children" or "for adults," and the practice largely faded away.

Today, few of these instantaneous puberty rites survive. The Japanese *genpuku* and *mogi* and the Korean *gwalye*, coming-of-age ceremonies for pubescent boys and girls, gradually faded away during the nineteenth century. Some arduous puberty rites survive in rural and underdeveloped areas, where they are almost universally condemned. Often these are outlawed. One rarely sees a woman of the Ainu people of northern Japan with a tattooed chin, and Navajo parents who sent their son on a wilderness quest would draw the wrath of child welfare agencies. In many East African communities, pubescent girls mark their entrance into adulthood by receiving a clitoridectomy (ritual removal of the clitoris). Human rights agencies denounce the practice as "genital mutilation."

Children living in contemporary societies do not enter adulthood instantly, at carefully defined moments, as in traditional societies; instead, they enjoy a gradual increase in responsibilities and privileges. For instance, in Connecticut children under the age of fourteen may not work outside the home. Fourteen and fifteen-year-olds may work part-time. Sixteen and seventeen-year-olds may work full-time, but their jobs must end by 10:00 P.M. Finally, at age 18, they can work until late at night.

No contemporary puberty rite represents a definitive, unambiguous moment of transition between **childhood** and adulthood: whether it is a driver's license or a first date, college graduation or the ability to vote, all parties realize that there is still a long way to go before the boy becomes a man and the girl becomes a woman. In fact, in contemporary societies, milestones tend to be repeated across the lifespan. Contemporary jobs usually do not last for our entire life, but change every few years, requiring a return to school for additional certification and degrees. Few people select a single lifelong romantic partner at age 18; they continue dating through their twenties and thirties; and some change partners nearly as often as they change jobs.

However, some societies have retained or re-invented the puberty rite as a marker of significant milestones on the road to adulthood. Japan designates the second Monday in January as *Seijin No Hi*, "Coming Out Day," to commemorate those who have reached the age of twenty. In Australia and New Zealand, "Twenty-Firsts" are sometimes celebrated. A Jewish boy becomes *bar mitzvah*, a "son of the law," on his thirteenth birthday; a non-Orthodox Jewish girl becomes *bat mitzvah* on her twelfth. They are then allowed adult privileges in the synagogue, including reading the Torah and helping to constitute a minyan, the minimum number of adults necessary for services.

Many other puberty rites mark milestones in the transition from childhood to adult social categories. Some mark educational achievement: high school graduation, college graduation, or joining a fraternity or sorority. Others mark the onset of an adult privilege or responsibility: the first job, the first car, registering for military service, becoming old enough to purchase tobacco or alcohol, or moving into one's first house or apartment. However, most involve heterosexual **desire** or practice. Parents anxiously await evidence that their child is "growing up" by expressing an interest in girls/boys. Other adults often inquire, "Do you like girls/boys yet?" First dates are causes of celebration, and any delay past the age of 15 or so is cause for alarm. The child's first dance, first kiss, first experience of falling in love, first rejection—all are subject to intense scrutiny, parental advice, and wholehearted acclaim from family, friends, and every social institution, as long as the object of interest is a member of the "opposite sex." The first experience of heterosexual intercourse is not necessarily acclaimed by parents (though in some countries fathers are rumored to take their sons to brothels on their sixteenth birthdays), but it is acclaimed by peers and by the society at large as the moment of "becoming a man" or "becoming a woman."

Becoming old enough to be heterosexually married is cause for more formal celebration in many countries, with significant differences in social class. Among the upper classes in England, France, and their former colonial empires, girls who reached the age of 18 became debutantes. Their "coming out" into adult society was celebrated at elaborate parties called debutante balls (deb balls in Australia, debuts in the Philippines). Many debutante balls are still held every year, usually in the fall, such as the "Bachelor's Cotillion" in Cincinnati or the "Debutante Club Ball" in New Orleans.

Less affluent parents gave their daughters "Sweet Sixteen" parties, commemorating their eligibility for marriage, or at least for heterosexual romantic relationships (the expression "sweet sixteen and never been kissed" derives from the practice). In Cuba, aristocratic families held elaborate parties, or *quinceañeras*, for girls on their fifteenth birthdays, to mark their entrance into adulthood. The custom has been adopted in other parts of Latin America, including Brazil (where it is called *Festa de Quinze Anos*), and in Hispanic communities in the United States. A similar ceremony in Spain, *Los Quintos*, commemorated boys' eligibility for military service at the age of 18, but it rarely occurs today.

Since these milestones and celebrations assume explicitly that every adolescent is heterosexual, gay and lesbian adolescents usually participate along with their heterosexual peers, bowing to the pressure to like girls/boys and ask or accept dates with them. Some do not even recognize that they are gay or lesbian until after they have acquiesced to the pressure to select a heterosexual marriage partner. If they manage to find same-sex relationships at all, they are usually clandestine, conducted without the knowledge or support of parents or friends. As a result, they are excluded from the rituals of adolescence, and often must re-invent them in adulthood, going through a "delayed adolescence," with a network of friends substituting for parents and high school peers. Sometimes they believe that they are perpetually adolescent, just "playing around" instead of embarking upon the "serious business" of heterosexual **romance**. *See also* Dating; Heterosexuality.

Further Reading: Bancroft, John, and June Machover Reinisch. *Adolescence and Puberty.* Oxford: Oxford University Press, 1990; Growing Up Sexually. See http://www2.hu-berlin.de/sexology/GESUND/ARCHIV/GUS/GUS_MAIN_INDEX.HTM. A vast compendium of bibliographic information on sexuality among children and teenagers, February 2006; Martin, Karen A. *Puberty, Sexuality, and the Self: Boys and Girls at Adolescence.* New York: Routledge, 1996; Raphael, Ray. *Men from the Boys: Rites of Passage in Male America.* Lincoln: University of Nebraska Press, 1988; Van Gennep, Arnold. *The Rites of Passage.* Chicago: University of Chicago Press, 1961.

Jeffery P. Dennis

R

RACE AND RACISM.   Race, as an idea, and racism, in the form of discrimination and physical control based on ideas of racial superiority or unfounded fear of different human groups, very often involve sex, and sometimes "love." As part of the colonial expansion of European nations beginning in the fifteenth century, the categorization of newly encountered human populations and cultures relied on defining presumably natural differences. In the encounters between the colonizers and the colonized, visible differences of "race"—including skin tone, hair type, and body features—became synonymous with biological and cultural difference. In deeming these differences markers of race, non-European and non-white cultures were deemed "other," an "exotic" difference typically eroticized and thus also colonized on the level of sexuality. European colonizers used notions of cultural and racial inferiority to their advantage, to justify violent enslavement and exploitation of natural resources, including the appropriation of women's bodies by force. What resulted then from these violent sexual encounters were multiracial populations around the world, a blending of European blood with that of populations from Africa, Asia, and the Americas. Indeed, some of the first instances of cross-racial "love" in the world involved a violent sexuality.

As more racial and cultural groups began to intermarry and offspring demonstrated multiracial characteristics, the idea that race is unchanging and based on biology began to lose validity. But there were violent reactions against these changes, in the form of counter-attacks and racial violence from groups like the Ku Klux Klan in the United States, founded at the end of the Civil War. In the classic 1915 U.S. film *Birth of a Nation*, a white woman is depicted as the presumed natural target of a formerly-enslaved African man. The film reinforced the racist notion that men of African descent are "natural" sexual predators and white women's bodies the natural victims of such sexual assaults. Under these exaggerated racialized fears of sex between men of African descent and white women, government and institutions of power held on to racist notions and designed de jure and de facto policies that gave more privileges to Whites.

Race has been invoked powerfully throughout the world by enacting anti-miscegenation laws. Miscegenation, the process of mixing different races or ethnicities, especially through **marriage**, has been illegal in many countries for centuries. Since the eighteenth century, U.S. states passed anti-miscegenation laws, sometimes using passages from the Bible to justify them. The U.S. Supreme Court first upheld the constitutionality of anti-miscegenation laws through the 1883 case of *Pace v. Alabama*. It was not until the *Loving v. Virginia* case that the Court ruled anti-miscegenation laws unconstitutional in 1967. Nine years earlier, the Lovings, identified as a "colored" woman and a white man, had been arrested in the middle of the night in their Virginia home for violating that state's miscegenation law. By the time the Supreme Court offered its ruling, 16 states still had laws prohibiting racial intermarriage, demonstrating the anxieties of many in the United States about racial mixing, again, between African Americans and Whites. Yet, it was not until November 2000, 33 years after the Supreme Court had ruled these laws unconstitutional, that Alabamans voted to overturn its anti-miscegenation laws. Still, a full 40 percent of those voters wanted to keep these nineteenth-century laws in place.

Other countries have also relied on anti-miscegenation laws to protect the idea that "whiteness" is superior to all other racial classifications and to defend the notion of white racial purity. During its Nazi regime, Germany passed its Anti-Semitic Nuremberg Laws, targeting the German Jewish population, which it considered sexually immoral. These statutes forbade marriages between the "racially pure" "Aryan" Germans, considered to be superior, and Jews, deemed a lower or sub-human population. In addition, the laws required the forced sterilization of those members of society the German state thought unfit to reproduce, including those of mixed-race. German fascist policies also held deeply homophobic values, with lesbian women and gay men being targeted and placed in concentration camps—in part for their unwillingness to sire children. Racial differences, sex, gender, and **homosexuality** in particular, thus, have been very closely linked to Fascist culture in Germany.

More recently, South Africa used race as a form of social control of different bodies, also in conjunction with sexuality, through the enactment of apartheid laws in 1948. These laws specifically prohibited marriage between non-whites and whites, while they also set aside the best jobs for "white-only." To determine classification into "black" (African), white, or colored (of mixed descent), government workers used physical appearance, social acceptance, and descent inconsistently. World protest and boycotts brought this system of institutionalized racial discrimination to an end formally between 1990 and 1994. The historical legacies continue in the drastic class differences between whites and blacks today. At the same time, anxieties about the racial mixing or sexual procreation between Africans and those of European descent remain high. And yet, South Africa is one of the few countries in the world to legalize same-sex marriages, regardless of race, with its Constitutional Court requiring that this mandate go into effect by the end of 2006. With this ruling, South Africa joined the Netherlands, Canada, Belgium, Spain, and the one single U.S. state of Massachusetts.

In the Americas, racial mixing through heterosexual crossings remains a reality today. In Brazil, based on the fact that there have never existed legalized barriers against racial mixing, there remains the myth of a racial democracy. With a greater racial fluidity and flexibility than in the United States, Brazilian intermarriage is very common. Nevertheless, the overwhelming majority of those crossings are between white and brown—"pardos"—and between brown and black; white and black intermarry at a much smaller rate, suggesting the still significant polarization between these two groups.

Popular images of Brazilian life depict a tropical paradise of equal access for all—whites, blacks, and multiracial individuals of multiple shades—yet the higher incomes, educational opportunities, and housing standards remain concentrated among overwhelmingly white populations. Throughout Latin America the pattern is unmistakably the same: while ideas of racial mixing such as *mestizaje* have been popular for decades, the lighter shades remain closer to resources and privilege while the darker ones, including the indigenous, remain largely poor and disempowered.

As the German Nazi example and the more contemporary South African show, race and sexuality have also interacted in same-sex, gay and lesbian cross-cultural relations. As the historian Estelle B. Freedman has found, in the first half of the twentieth century, state officials and criminologists were concerned about the cross-race romances between white and black women inmates in the United States. Their reports singled out African American women as the presumed masculine or aggressive partner and their white lovers as the feminine, "normal" ones. Across national borders, same-sex relations have been taking place between mostly White, United States and Europe based tourists and peoples of color through the growth of the tourism industry. For several decades, European and U.S. tourism to a wide array of destinations including Brazil, Thailand, Mexico, and the Caribbean has constructed local men's bodies as an exotic sexual commodity for white gay and bisexual men. In these transnational same-sex relations, the local body is simultaneously eroticized and exoticized, as just another natural resource that can be purchased in the global market.

Racist beliefs about "lower" and "higher" races influenced the eugenics movement in the first half of the twentieth century. The resulting social policies included forced sterilization, cross-racial marriage restrictions, and immigration restrictions for certain populations. Eugenics and other racially motivated political movements sought to "improve" the race, typically those from white European descent, by controlling those non-white bodies deemed inferior. By 2006, no countries had laws against interracial marriage, yet race and racism remain central ideas in questions of love, sex, and marriage, especially as more and more national groups crisscross the globe in search of work and political stability. As people from different regions and cultures increasingly come into contact, they share the intimate space of their bodies and desires.

Young people across the world are in contact more than ever before with different cultural, racial, and national groups, often from former colonized regions of the world. The encounters often turn violent, as were the December 2005 attacks on people of presumed Arab and Mediterranean descent by young white men in Sydney, following the presumed assault on two lifeguards by Lebanese youth. In France, one month earlier, second- and third-generation French youth of Arab and Muslim descent rioted against discrimination and police brutality. At the same time, more youth in multiracial urban centers socialize and organize across their ethnic differences and different languages, and often make social justice part of their joint work. In a recent study on young Iranians in Los Angeles, researchers found differences between **religions** and genders in young women's and men's attitudes about mate selection. Muslim Iranians, the researchers found, were more liberal about dating outside their group than were Jewish Iranians. Male Iranians, on the other hand, regardless of religion, were more liberal or "Americanized" than young Iranian women. In a more globalized society, racial anxieties pertaining to sex, love, and possible intermarriage remain. But there are also some signs that young women and men, compared to their parents, are more tolerant and understanding about cultural groups different from their own. *See also* Bisexuality; Colonialism/Postcolonialism and Sex; Interracial/Ethnic Intimate Relationships.

Further Reading: Alexander, M. Jacqui. "Imperial Desire/Sexual Utopias: White Gay Capital and Transnational Tourism." In *Pedagogies of Crossing: Meditations on Feminism, Sexual Politics, Memory, and the Sacred*, 66–68. Durham, NC: Duke University Press, 2005; Appelbaum, Nancy P., Anne S. Macphersen, and Karin Alejandra Rosemblatt, eds. *Race and Nation in Modern Latin America*. Chapel Hill: University of North Carolina Press, 2003; Applied Research Center. http://www.arc.org. A New York, Oakland, and Chicago-based research and policy center advancing interracial understanding and racial justice, including those pertaining to multiracial populations and cross-racial relations; Daniel, G. Reginald. *Race and Multiraciality in Brazil and the United States*. State College: Pennsylvania State University Press, 2006; Freedman, Estelle B. "The Prison Lesbian: Race, Class, and the Construction of the Aggressive Female Homosexual, 1915–1965." In *Sex, Love, Race: Crossing Boundaries in North American History*, edited by Martha Hodes, 423–43. New York: New York University Press, 1999; Hannassab, Shedeh, and Romeria, Tidwell. "Intramarriage and Intermarriage: Young Iranians in Los Angeles." *International Journal of Intercultural Relations* 22, no. 4 (November 1, 1998): 395–408; Herzog, Dagmar. *Sex after Fascism: Memory and Morality in Twentieth-Century Germany*. Princeton, NJ: Princeton University Press, 2005; Mohamed, Adhikari. *Not White Enough, Not Black Enough: Racial Identity in the South African Coloured Community*. Athens: Ohio University Press, and Cape Town: Double Storey Books, 2005; Pascoe, Peggy. "Miscegenation Law, Court Cases, and Ideologies of 'Race' in Twentieth-Century America." In *Sex, Love, Race: Crossing Boundaries in North American History*, edited by Martha Hodes, 464–90. New York: New York University Press, 1999; Riggs, Marlon T. (Producer and Director) [Videotape.] *Ethnic Notions: Black Images in the White Mind*. Berkeley, CA: California Newsreel, 1987; Telles, Edward E. "Racial Distance and Region and Brazil: The Case of Marriage among Color Groups." *Latin American Research Review* 28, no. 2 (1993): 141–62.

Horacio N. Roque Ramírez

RACISM. *See* Interracial/Ethnic Intimate Relationships; Race and Racism

RAPE. *See* Domestic and Relationship Violence; Sex Crimes

REICH, WILHELM (1897–1957). An Austrian born psychiatrist and political psychologist known for his study of human sexuality and emotions, Wilhelm Reich was born on March 24, 1897, as the first son to his cattle farming parents who lived on a large tract of land in the Ukraine, in what was then the Austro-Hungarian Empire. The relationship between Wilhelm and his extremely jealous father was coldly distant and brutal, which contrasted with his near incestuous relationship with his mother, who had a secret love affair with Wilhelm's private tutor. Reich experienced deep guilt over his **desire** to protect his mother, who committed suicide when the relationship was discovered, from the ravages of his father and the need to disclose and end his mother's affair. Sent to study in an all-male school, Reich's father, gravely despondent over the events, attempted suicide by drowning only to die soon after with pneumonia. At the age of 17, Reich, parentless and penniless, returned to the farm. A year later, in 1915, Germany invaded his region and he lost forever his last ties to his family and **childhood**. After serving in the Austrian army, Reich entered medical school at the University of Vienna. He studied neuropsychiatry under the Nobel Prize winner, Professor Wagner-Jauregg. He also met Sigmund **Freud,** who allowed him to begin seeing his patients in 1919. Reich became a member of the Vienna Psychoanalytic Association a year later and received his medical degree in 1922. Reich's first major book, *The Function of the Orgasm* (1927), greatly influenced his contemporaries as well as future practitioners and writers ranging from Fritz Perls and A. S. Neil to Saul Bellow and William S. Burroughs. However, he is best known for his concept of "orgone," understood to be a distinct type of primordial bio or life energy released at the time of **orgasm**. Hoping to reconcile Freudian and Marxist theories with his conviction that the body and sexual health are fundamentally related to both the psychological health of the individual and the political well-being of society, he alienated both psychoanalysts and Marxists. He died in a Pennsylvania prison on November 3, 1957.

As Freud's chosen student, the charismatic Reich challenged the psychoanalytic concept of "libido," the psychological source of desire, to study its physical expression. Reich posited that sexual problems were core in a diagnosis not symptomatic of an underlying psychology. He argued in *The Function of the Orgasm* that failure to achieve orgasm could itself produce neurosis. Hence, the libido was more that a mere concept; it was energy—energy often repressed resulting in individual and societal neuroses. In contrast, when total discharge of bio-energy happened ("orgastic potency"), there was less rigidity in psychological persona ("muscular armoring") and social mores ("sexual repression"). Unlike Freud in *Civilization and Its Discontents*, Reich argued that "you don't think from the standpoint of the state and the culture, but from the standpoint of what people need and what they suffer from" (http://www.wilhelmreichmuseum.org/biography.html). Thus, rather than adapting sexual instincts to the culture, Reich favored altering culture to fit human sensual needs.

Mary Boyd-Higgins, Director of the Wilhelm Reich Museum in Maine, displays an exhibit of the workings of the Orgonomic Energy collection, 2000. A conference on Orgonomic Functionalism was held at the museum shortly thereafter. © AP Photo/Michael C. York.

The physiological process of phallic erection provided the beginning formula for Reich's great scientific discoveries that predate efforts to understand **erectile dysfunction** and male orgasm. He identified four essential stages for male orgasm: tension, build-up, discharge, and relaxation. However, Reich argued that recovery from sexual impotency, now known as erectile dysfunction, should not be restricted to the inability to hold erections and have ejaculations. Rather, the goal should be orgiastic potency: "the complete surrender to the flow of biological energy without any inhibition, the capacity for complete discharge of all dammed-up sexual excitation" (Reich 1948: 79).

Reich left Germany in 1933 with the Nazi takeover and the next year he started the *Zeotscjroft fur politische Psychologie and Sexualokonomie* (*Review of Political Psychology and Sexual Economy*), which he edited for four years before emigrating to New York in 1939. He later settled on a 160-acre farm in Maine where he conducted research and taught. It was in the United States that Reich developed several devices for the control of orgone energy. The best known of these is the orgone energy accumulator. This six-sided 5 foot × 2.5 × 2.5 box was framed by alternate layers of metallic (e.g., iron, aluminium) and non-metallic materials (e.g., cotton, wool or plastic) which allegedly could collect and distribute orgone energy. This device, he determined through measurement, resulted in treatment for burns without scarring, cancer cases did not develop anemia, and the patient's blood and body mass improved.

Following a critical 1947 article, "The Strange Case of Wilhelm Reich" that appeared in the leftist magazine the *New Republic*, the U.S. Food and Drug

Administration began an investigation of the orgone energy accumulator and a ten-year effort to prohibit practice of his medical treatment and censor of his scientific ideas. The United States District Court at Portland, Maine issued a complaint against Reich on February 20, 1954, charging that the accumulator ("sex box") was a fraud and questioning the existence of orgone energy. When Reich refused to discontinue his work and the work at Orgonon (the research site at his Maine farm), he was sentenced to two years in prison for criminal contempt. A year earlier, as a result of a court decision, nearly all of Reich's books—nearly six tons—had been burned at the Gansevoort Street incinerator in Manhattan on August 23, 1956. No U.S. newspaper protested this unprecedented state **censorship** of academic material, so reminiscent of 1933 Nazi destruction of the library and research of Magnus **Hirschfeld**. Reich died on November 3, 1957, in the Federal Penitentiary at Lewisburg, Pennsylvania.

Reich's concept of the orgone and the failure of humans to express themselves in sexually and emotionally honest ways extended beyond individual psychoanalysis to political psychology. His books, such as *Listen Little Man*, *The Sexual Revolution*, and *People in Trouble*, described the mass pathology resulting from an overly masculinized culture that prevented the movement of this energy through the blocking of emotion. This collective neurotic disorder is best exemplified in Reich's writings through his criticism of fascism and cultural institutions, such as religion, that proscribe sexual freedom. In *The Mass Psychology of Fascism*, for example, he wrote: "My medical experience has taught me that adolescents who are sexually sick have an unhealthy appreciation of the legend of Jesus."

An advocate of **sex education** and pioneer for mental hygiene centers, especially for working class youth, in 1929, he formed the Socialist Society of Sexual Advice and Sexual Research and two years later founded the German Association for a Proletarian Sexual Policy. In a 1931 brochure, *The Sexual Struggle of the Young*, he linked the sexual interests of young people with the need for a socialist revolution promoting a radical liberation of individual behavior. He also was a strong supporter of **birth control**, **divorce** rights, and serial monogamy (he had three wives during his lifetime). In 1932, he published *The Invasion of Compulsory Sexual Morality*, a sociological study based on the work of the anthropologist Bronislaw Malinowski. Reich was a strong advocate of sex education, arguing that forbidding sex—including among children and adolescents—is a result of society's anti-sexual attitude, which prevents young people from growing up as nature intended while allowing for repression of sexual energy into a culture of oppression.

Not surprisingly, Reich's work has found greater reception among young people, although Reichian (Orgone) therapy still is practiced by some psychiatrists and psychologists and The American College of Orgonomy publishes the *Journal of Orgonomy*. His ideas were embraced by beat novelists like William S. Burroughs ("The Job"), radical educators such as A. S. Neil (his Summerhill School is based, in part, on this), as well as various artists. His ideas, for instance, are found in popular culture such as music by Patti Smith ("Birdland"), Miles Davis ("Orgone"), Kate Bush ("Cloudbusting"), or Hawkwind ("Orgone Accumulator"), and the play *Wilhelm Reich in Hell* (http://www.wilhelmreichinhell.com). *See also* Mental Health and Sex; Psychoanalysis; Sex Therapists; Sexual Science/Sexology.

Further Reading: Boadella, David. *Wilhelm Reich: The Evolution of His Work*. Chicago: Regnery, 1973; Mann, Edward. *Orgone, Reich and Eros: Wilhelm Reich's Theory of the Life Energy*. New York: Simon & Schuster, 1973; Mann, Edward, and Ed Hoffman. *The Man Who Dreamed of Tomorrow: A Conceptual Biography of Wilhelm Reich*. Los Angeles: J.P. Tarcher, 1980;

Ollendorff, Ilse. *Wilhelm Reich: A Personal Biography*. New York: St. Martin's Press, 1969; Orgone Biophysical Research Lab. James DeMeo. http://www.orgonelab.org. Current research on the "orgone," with an extensive bibliography of Reich's work and writings about Reich, 2006; Orgone Energy. The Skeptic's Dictionary. Robert Todd Carroll. http://skepdic.com/ orgone.html. A counter website "debunking" the "pseudoscience" of Reich, 2006; Raknes, Ola. *Wilhelm Reich and Orgonomy*. New York: St. Martin's Press, 1970; Reich, Wilhelm. *The Function of the Orgasm*. Translated by T. P. Wolfe. New York, 1927/1961; Reich, Wilhelm. *Character-Analysis; Principles and Technique for Psychoanalysts in Practice and in Training*. Translated by Theodore P. Wolfe. New York: Orgone Institute Press, 1933; Reich, Wilhelm. *The Mass Psychology of Fascism*. New York: Orgone Institute Press, 1940; Reich, Wilhelm. *The Sexual Revolution*. New York: Noonday Press, 1962; Reich, Wilhelm. *Wilhelm Reich: Selected Writings*. New York: Farrar, Straus & Cudahy, 1960; Sharaf, Myron. *Fury on Earth: A Biography of Wilhelm Reich*. New York: Da Capo Press, 1994; Wyckoff, James. *Wilhelm Reich: Life Force Explorer*. Greenwich, CT: Fawcett, 1973.

James T. Sears

RELIGIONS, EASTERN. The Eastern religions—here identified as Hinduism, Buddhism, Taoism, Confucianism, and Shintoism—are rich in their iconographic, ritual, doctrinal, and cultural expressions of the mutuality of sex and love. Although often as culturally patriarchal as the West, they tend to be more eros-affirming than their Western counterparts (located in their mystical traditions), with their iconographies and theologies of the *hieros gamos*, the sacred union of male and female. In contrast to the Western dualism of a radical essential distinction between God and creation, the Eastern religions' view of sexuality is based in understanding that the deepest part of the human being, indeed, the entire creation, shares an identity with the divine transcendent. In other words, each creature has within it the seed of the Eternal, so that the goal of spiritual practice in the East is the realization of this original identity, as opposed to, as in the West, the healing of a broken relationship.

Hinduism formally came to North America in 1893 with the arrival of Swami Vivekananda, a student of Sri Ramakrishna who, after speaking to the Parliament of World Religions, planted the seeds of the Vedanta Society. During the last half of the twentieth century, two other forms of Hinduism were introduced to the United States. Maharishi Mahesh Yogi (with help from the Beatles) introduced Transcendental Meditation (TM), which spawned the Students International Meditation Society (SIMS), and the International Society for Krishna Consciousness (ISKCON, or Hare Krishnas).

The cluster of Indian religions associated with Hinduism is the most eros-affirming of Eastern religions. The *bhakti* (devotional) and *tantric* traditions stand out. Sensual pleasure (*kama*) is one of the four goals of Hindu devotion; the others are virtue (*dharma*), financial well-being (*artha*), and spiritual liberation (*moksha*). *Bhakti*, "devotion" to the gods, is elucidated clearly in the Narada Bhakti Sutras where "ultimate love" (*parapremarupa*) is described in its manifestations and stages. This incarnate love leads to "perfection, immortality, fulfillment" and is known in the following five relationships: servant-master, friend-friend, parent-child, husband-wife (as between Rama and Sita in the *Ramayana*), and lover-beloved. Within these five manifestations are eleven forms, from attachment to divine attributes to the most sublime (and paradoxical), the longing of separation.

This sensual, erotic longing for the Beloved frees the Self to discover its true unity with the All; it is the truest and freest of loves. In the "Yoga of Devotion," *Bhagavad Gita* 12, the paradox is resolved as Divine Love—both subject and object of all human

Dark blue Buddha Samanthabadra with his consort yab-yum appears in this mural painting located in the Namchi monastery, Sikkim, India. © Art Directors.co.uk/Ark Religion.com.

love, a love that demands complete devotion and is the source of such devotion. The sexual longing for the Divine Beloved is described as a union, or, as the *Chandogya Upanishads* famously puts it, "*Tat tvam asi*" ("Thou art That!"); Atman (the immanent Eternal seed within the Self) *is* Brahman (the transcendent Cosmic Eternal).

Krishna's tryst with Radha (in the *Gita Govinda*) demonstrates this most erotic and passionate of loves beyond social convention, family honor, conscience, commandment, ritual, and morality, and beyond religion itself. Mahatma Gandhi's lifelong devotion to the *Bhagavad Gita*, his complex marital choice of **celibacy,** and his strategic use of fasting uses sexual themes and symbols from the *bhakti* tradition.

Tantric groups have continually grown in the West in the last 30 years. The *tantric* traditions understand the Eternal Divine as manifested in the animation of the masculine (Shiva, potential energy, transcendence) by the feminine (Shakti, kinetic energy, immanence). This union of supposed opposites is accomplished through a variety of erotic rituals and techniques, including various *mantras* (chants), *mandalas* (geometric meditation designs), *mudras* (hand positions), and, in the so-called "left hand path," the "sacramental" breaking of ritual and social taboos, particularly with regard to **food** and sexual intercourse (*maithuna*). In the last half of the twentieth century, the use of psychotropic **drugs** in the West was added. Sexual union is both the means and the manifestation of spiritual union, the holistic—mind, body, spirit—realization of union with the divine.

During the 1970s, Sannella's *The Kundalini Experience*, following Wilhelm **Reich** (who called the *kundalini* "orgone energy" in the 1930s), Carl Jung, and others, studied the physiological, psychological, and sexual manifestations of this energy. In contrast to Western religious understanding, Eastern religions view the human body and all its senses not as obstacles but rather as means by which the potential energy (the *kundalini*) works its way up the *sushumna* (ethereal spine) through various chakras (energy centers). At the crown of the head is the ultimate union of Shiva and Shakti, bliss, and the consciousness of *tat tvam asi*.

Tantric practice is differentiated from *bhakti* in that in *bhakti* the longing for the Beloved is experienced as relationship, whereas in *tantra*, there is consumption, union, and the erotic bliss of lover and Beloved—a difference between relationship and identity. *Tantric* texts, like the well-known *Kama Sutra*, describe the forms, rituals, and aesthetics of this erotic union. The Divine Feminine, Shakti, encompasses the entirety of the cosmos, and thus is beyond duality. Therefore, the goddess tradition is strong in *tantric* devotion, particularly the dark and wild Kali. Warrior and mother, the breaker of all taboos, yet upholder of the good, she signifies a powerful sentiment within Hindu **feminism.**

Rita Dasgupta Sherma describes Shiva's and Shakti's fierce intercourse as follows: "Shiva, the I-awareness of God, 'enters' Shakti, God's dynamic, creative matrix, and the universe of infinite possibilities comes to be" (in Manning et al. 2005: 32). The erect *linga* standing within the circular *yoni* symbolizes this erotic dance of destruction and creation. The great saint Sri Ramakrishna was a devotee of the goddess.

Arranged **marriages** and **abortion,** especially of female fetuses, are concerns of contemporary practitioners of Hinduism. Although the caste system is officially outlawed, given the patriarchal nature of Indian society, arranged marriages within one's socio-economic class (*jati*) are still common. Abortion, too, especially of female fetuses, particularly in northern India, is still a major social problem.

Fault lines about the West's influence on sex and culture in contemporary Indian society are exacerbated by Indian film and theater culture. It's sexually explicit **advertising**, as well as the controversially erotic themes and content (e.g., Deepa Mehta's 1996 film, *Fire*, which showed a lesbian relationship between two sisters-in-law, Sita and Radha, names of two goddesses), have caused many public protests.

In the last quarter of the twentieth century, Buddhism has experienced a renaissance throughout the contemporary world. Factors in this revival include:

1. Buddhism's psychological, adaptive nature among the traditionally religious as well as for those spiritual "seekers" outside of religious institutions
2. The growing influence of H.H., the Dalai Lama as a universal spiritual leader among the Western cultural elite
3. A new "Western Buddhism"
4. The growing "conversion" movement among the Indian *shudra* caste
5. The renewal of Buddhist life and practice in response to modernization throughout Asia

Buddhism views human sexuality holistically as part of a human being's desires, fears, needs, and intentions. Buddhists seek self-transformation through liberation (*moksha*) from rebirth into this life of sensual pleasure, including the clinging (*tanha*) to the impermanent. Liberation manifests in ever-increasing compassion (*karuna*) for all sentient life, so both action and intention are central to Buddhist moral principles. Buddhists believe that liberation from ego (the Buddha-verse as infinite compassion) can be experienced in this life (*nirvana*), and this includes one's sexual existence.

The two Buddhist ethical precepts pertaining to human sexuality are the mandates against harming another and sexual misconduct. Human sexuality, in itself, is not at issue because it belongs to a general proscription against **desire** for anything transient or harmful, thereby leading to suffering and dissatisfaction (*dukkha*). Thus, behaviors such as adultery and rape are specifically forbidden. The goal, both communal and individual, is enlightenment, "waking up" (*bodhi*).

In more traditional southern Theravadan monastic communities, sexual pleasure and gratification is a part of the larger problem of desire, so **celibacy** remains the norm to purge oneself of such impulses. These monastics also condemn **homosexuality,** especially since the rise of the **AIDS/HIV** epidemic. But in other parts of the Buddhist *lay* world, while recognizing the inherent temptations of sexual longing and pleasure, sex is understood as a natural extension of an authentic human life, physically and emotionally, thereby encouraging loving-kindness (*metta*) and mindfulness in all things, including one's sexual life.

In *Vajrayana* ("Diamond Vehicle"), the Buddhist Tantrism found in Tibet, Nepal, and central Asia, *samsara* (the transitory and illusory) is *nirvana,* the Eternal. Like its Indian counterpart, the goal of sexual expression, pleasure, and **orgasm** is the complete emptying of one's natural illusory consciousness until all that remains is the "really Real," an Emptiness (*sunyata*) that is full within the heart-mind (*citta*), similar to the French denotation of orgasm as *le petite morte*. The erotic poetry of the controversial twentieth-century Tibetan master, Gedun Chopel, *The Tibetan Arts of Love*, reflects this view. Paradoxically, sex in Buddhism is repressing and celebrating. So-called "Red Thread Zen," for instance, focuses on the transgressing of sexual taboos, thereby cultivating spiritual energy in sexual pleasure. The famous Zen master Ikkyu wrote: "A woman is enlightenment when you are with her; when the red thread of both your passions flares inside you, you see." Bernard Faure (1998: 98–99) characterizes this as "desire as enlightenment." According to Faure, "The logic of transcendence that characterizes Mahayana Buddhism implies ... a transgression of all fixed rules.... Instead of rejecting desire and sexuality, it is better to transmute them through meditation."

Generally, Buddhists understand issues like marriage, **masturbation,** oral sex, and contraception as religious only insofar as they harm another living being or participate in sexual misconduct, on the one hand, or lead to an attitude of genuineness, contentment, and a more compassionate life.

Twentieth-century Confucian and Taoist history is complex. The People's Republic of China (1949) and the Cultural Revolution (1966–1976) saw the rise of policies of industrialization, population control, public education, the role of Western **media**, the relation between the individual and the state, and the increasing encroachment of Western ideals of human rights. Yet, most advances for Chinese women in education and social status have been the fruits of the state, not religion.

Because Confucianism has been a force for traditional **gender roles,** most of women's advancements in the second half of the twentieth century were state-mandated. The Marriage Law (1950) and the Great Leap Forward (1958) brought new status within marriage and the social order, as well as educational, economic, and work opportunities; but the Five Goods Program (1956) was a short-lived return to traditional sex roles.

Confucianism, the core of Chinese culture, is family-ism; of its five primary relationships, three are family-based and patriarchally defined—father-son, brother-brother, husband-wife. The woman's role is defined by "three obediences and four virtues" (*san cong si de*), binding a woman to her father, then husband, and eldest son after her husband's death, and whose virtues were morality, proper speech, modest manner, and diligent household work.

Since the end of the Cultural Revolution, there has been an awkward marriage between the communist state (as it modernizes and emerges as a global trading partner) and a revival of its patriarchal Confucian tradition. On the one hand, women's rights have improved under a secular government policy; on the other hand, while female chastity is still the ideal, prostitution and **divorce** are on the rise. Women, not men, are the ones punished for violating the one-child policy, and are the expected subjects of contraception, including sterilization.

Critics of Confucian patriarchy, once held in contempt, are now grudgingly earning respect. (Activist Lu Hsiu-lien, imprisoned for feminist reforms, is now Vice-President of Taiwan, for example.) Feminists are making inroads in the arts, professions, and the academy, particularly in sexual science and cultural studies. The so-called "New Confucians," like Harvard's Tu Weiming, are redefining Confucian ideals for a modern, post-Enlightenment Chinese world.

Taoism subtly emphasizes the individual, especially the *yin*, female principle, reinforcing Chinese patriarchal stereotypes of women as soft and yielding. In contrast to *Tao-chia*, the philosophical branch of the *Laozi* (*Tao te Ching*) and *Chuangzi*, *Tao-chiao* combines Chinese alchemical traditions of immortality, yogic exercises, and sexual-spiritual intercourse rituals.

Douglas Wile (in Manning et al. 2005: 77) describes the new hermeneutics of the *I Ching*, the *Classic of Changes* as "the fundamental identification of *yin* and *yang* with male and female gives the work a cosmo-sexual cast," whose yang and yin lines and trigrams represent the penis, vagina, and various sexual positions. These sexual rituals (*fang-chung shu*) develop the semen's essence (*jing*) and potency as the elixir of immortality (*nei-tan*), animate the entire cosmos, and complete the harmonious union of earth (female) and heaven (male) in the eternal *tao*.

Shinto, the "Way of the *Kami*," parallels traditional Japanese culture. Shinto's appreciation for sex comes from its creation mythology wherein fertility is considered participation in the spiritual energy and power of the *kami*. The fertility celebration *Kanamara Matsuri* (the Festival of the Steel Penis), originally dedicated to pray for fertility and sexual safety, now raises money for **AIDS/HIV** research.

Post-war reconstruction, economic development, and industrialization in Japan have increasingly Westernized its culture, including sexual values. For example, the presence of traditional *geisha* in Japanese society is rapidly declining, except in larger cities, along with so-called "love hotels" and bathhouses. **Prostitution**, although illegal, prospers; **divorce** is on the rise; and the Japanese sex industry is a $20 billion annual business. Further, an agreement between Japan and Korea was finally settled in the 1990s following a lawsuit filed by the Korean Council for Women Drafted for Military Sexual Slavery, compensating Korean women for being used as "comfort women" (sex slaves) during World War II in officially-sanctioned Japanese military brothels.

The Eastern religions reflect diverse views concerning **homosexuality**. Although still taboo in Hinduism, the Gay and Lesbian Vaishnava Association deals with *tritiya-prakriti* (LGBT) issues. *Hijras*, male transvestites, although marginalized, still have ritual functions. Alan Sponberg (in Manning et al. 2005: 54) relates the famous account of the Dalai Lama's 1997 ambiguous conversation with American Buddhists on the subject. Originally, he stated that "gay and lesbian sexual activity was 'wrong,' but then added that homosexual sexual orientation 'is not improper' in itself." Later he added that "if two males or two females voluntarily agree to have mutual satisfaction without further implication of harming [the] other, then it is OK." *See also* Families; Morality and Ethics; Women's Movement.

Further Reading: Bornoff, Nicholas. *Pink Samurai: An Erotic Exploration of Japanese Society*. Vermont: Trafalgar Square Publishing, 2001; Cabezon, Jose Ignacio. *Buddhism, Sexuality, and Gender*. New York: State University of New York Press, 1991; Faure, Bernard. *The Red Thread: Buddhist Approaches to Sexuality*. Princeton, NJ: Princeton University Press, 1998; The Gay and Lesbian Vaishnava Association. http://www.galva108.org/index.html. Articles, resources, and on-line groups to support GLBT hindus and vaishnavas; Lynch, Owen M., ed. *Divine Passions: The Social Construction of Emotion in India*. Berkeley: University of California Press, 1990; Manning, Christel, and Phil Zuckerman, eds. *Sex and Religion*. Belmont: Thomson Wadsworth Publishing, 2005; Ruan, Fang Fu. *Sex in China: Studies in Sexology in Chinese Culture*. New York: Springer Publishing Company, 2003; Runzio, Joseph, and Nancy M. Martin, eds. *Love, Sex, and Gender in the World Religions*. Oxford: Oneworld Publishing, 2000; White, David Gordon. *Kiss of the Yogini: "Tantric Sex" in Its South Asian Contexts*. Chicago: University of Chicago Press, 2003.

L. Michael Spath

RELIGIONS, WESTERN. The Western religions—here identified with the monotheistic traditions of Judaism, Christianity, and Islam—have historically sent mixed signals to their adherents with regard to the origin, expression, regulation, and spiritualization of human sexuality. On the one hand, in each of the traditions, one can find rich iconographic, poetic, hymnic, and cultural expressions of the beauty of human sexuality: a participation in God's ongoing work of creation; a manifestation of divine love; a symbol of union with God. On the other hand, influenced by a neo-Platonic dualism, often these very sexual longings and manifestations have been, at best, distrusted and, at worst, understood as arising from a fallen, sinful creation. Both views reinforce the power that human sexuality has had and continues to have in Western religious symbols, myths, and identities.

Generally speaking, Christianity has emphasized "right belief" throughout its history. It focuses on orthodoxy, the tension between law and freedom, the concomitant role of the Spirit, with its origins in Paul's letters to the Romans and Galatians, traced through the Church fathers, the Reformation, and Enlightenment, up to the present discussion among the various Christian denominations. Judaism and Islam, on the other hand, have emphasized the ethical imperative. They focus on orthopraxy, the centrality of, respectively, *halakhah* and *Shariah*. Nevertheless, all three traditions were founded and sustained in patriarchal contexts. However, just in the last century, many who identify with these traditions have begun to question, re-evaluate, and critique these traditions. This is especially the case regarding the relationship between and identification with sexual "**morality**" and the cultures in which they were first formulated.

Presently, about six million Jews live in Israel, another six million in the United States, and one million throughout the world. Contemporary Judaism, however, varies in its understanding of sexual ethics. Reform and Reconstructionist Judaism were nineteenth- and twentieth-century "reform" movements combining an emphasis on "ethical monotheism" with its Jewish cultural manifestations in the West. Reconstructionism emphasizes that Judaism is an "evolving religious civilization" that observes *halakah* as an important cultural sign.

Conservative Judaism combines a respect for the authority of *halakhah* with an understanding of the need for its development and situational application. Modern Orthodoxy, despite its very small minority status, has become a significant theological and political force within Judaism. Although not formally structured to be so, it is the "establishment religion" of the Israel state today, wielding great legislative and social influence.

The *halakhah* arises out of a covenantal relationship between G-d and G-d's chosen people, Israel. According to Jewish tradition, *halakhah* reveals itself anew in succeeding generations with questions that changing contexts bring. Thus, rabbinical, biblical commentaries (Midrash) and social and legal rabbinical commentaries (the Talmuds) result in community ritual, moral, and spiritual legislation. These have developed to such a degree in the rabbinical movements that many religious Jews believe that a dual Torah, written (biblical) and oral (Talmudic and midrashic), serves as revelation. Hence, these serve as the basis for a variety of interpretations on sexual as well as social, cultural, and spiritual teaching.

Within the last 20 years a resurgence of the popularity of Jewish mystical spirituality has gained notoriety. In conjunction with a rise in a generic, mystical, and evolutionary consciousness-raising in the West, it has attained a certain celebrity status by the likes of

Bishop Gene Robinson, the Episcopalians' first openly gay bishop, smiles after giving his first service, 2003. © AP Photo/Jim Cole.

Madonna, Barbra Streisand, Demi Moore, Mick Jagger, and Britney Spears. Serious study of kabbalistic texts such as the *Iggeret ha-Kodesh*, *Zohar*, and, of course, the biblical *Song of Songs* are offered as vehicles for expanded consciousness, and even immortality. These sensual texts also promise Tantra-like sexual satisfaction and, thereby, union with G-d.

Sexuality and spirituality is not the sole province of Kabbalism, as the Central Conference of American Rabbis (Ad Hoc Committee on Human Sexuality) affirmed in 1998.

> A relationship may attain a measure of *kedusha* (holiness) when both partners voluntarily set themselves apart exclusively for each other, thereby finding unique emotional, sexual and spiritual intimacy .... *Kiddushah* may be present in committed, same gender relationships between two Jews; ... these relationships can serve as the foundation of stable Jewish families, thus adding strength to the Jewish community. ("On Homosexuality," http://www .faqs.org/faqs/judaism/FAQ/10-Reform/preamble.html Question 18.3.8)

The rabbis originally meant this as an affirmation of heterosexual intimacy within **marriage**. But this statement, like the Talmuds, has been read differently by Jewish believers. Feminist theologian Rachel Adler "envision[s] new rituals of marriage ... as an egalitarian partnership, a 'covenant of lovers'" (in Manning et al. 2005: 102–3).

Within Reform and Reconstructionist circles it has been interpreted as allowing for (and affirming) such loving, monogamous, and long-lasting non-marital and same-sex relationships as well. Through their exclusive commitment, partners find "holiness" (*kodesh*). In contrast, Orthodox Judaism views heterosexual intimacy exclusively for procreation, downplaying its pleasure-providing capacity.

Given these plural understandings of sexuality and spirituality, these traditions vary on their views about contemporary sexual issues like **homosexuality**, **birth control**, and **abortion**. Orthodox Judaism condemns homosexuality, although it reserves its harshest language for male homosexuals. It forbids birth control by mean (as well as **masturbation**'s "spilt seed"); although Orthodox halakhic interpretation allows it for women if **pregnancy** is life-threatening. Conservative Judaism supports full civil rights for lesbian, gay, bisexual, and transgendered individuals, but rejects their ordination. Reform and Reconstructionist Jews not only support full civil rights, but also same-sex unions and the ordination of openly gay and lesbian rabbis. Reform Judaism also promotes responsible family planning through any means of birth control. Abortion, however, is allowed under various circumstances within Jewish *halakhah*. Thus, from Orthodox to Reform and Reconstructionist Judaism one finds the continuum between permitting abortion to protect the life of the mother to an absolute support for a "woman's right to choose."

Christians number approximately 2.4 billion adherents but with many religious denominations. Like Judaism, Christianity is monotheistic in belief but pluralistic on sexual attitudes. To discuss human sexuality within a Christian context, one must understand that recently fault lines have shifted from divisions between Occidental and Oriental Christianities (East and West) to those between North and South. The rise of the Religious Right, the growth of non-denominational congregations, especially so-called mega-churches, the increasing secularization of Europe, and the evangelistic explosion of conversions in Africa and Latin America have brought a more conservative Christian ethical understanding worldwide, particularly with regard to human sexuality.

Although all Christians give the Bible a primacy of place, the view that the Bible is the literal and inerrant word of God ("literalists" or "traditionalists") stands in contrast to those Christian believers who assert the importance of interpretation of this sacred text ("progressives"). In the last two centuries, with the rise of historical criticism particularly, there has been a variety of hermeneutical models in understanding the context of the biblical witness as well as its function in contemporary ethical application.

Traditionally, Christianity taught that the full expressions of intimate, sexual love in intercourse take place in the context of a monogamous, heterosexual, lifelong marital union, which is open to the potential of procreation. In contemporary Christianity worldwide, Christian sexual ethics has taken center stage in denominational studies, dialogues, church resolutions, controversies, and even splits.

Lines have been drawn between those who interpret the Bible more literally, in accordance with traditional cultural understandings and following church tradition or canon law, and those who understand the Bible as a living document whose spiritual truths must be reinterpreted in a new setting. These lines have also appeared between a more traditional, conservative South (Latin America, Africa, and in evangelical missions in the Far East) and North (particularly Europe and Canada, although also in the United States). And these lines are intra-denominational as well, with more traditionalist and progressive factions present in every church. Issues of human sexuality are at the forefront of Christian ethical self-reflection and cultural engagement in virtually every denomination.

With Roman Catholicism being the most notable exception, most Christian denominations support the use of artificial contraception. Roman Catholics oppose it arguing that every sexual act be open to the possibility of the creation of life; the only birth control they support is "natural family planning," the so-called "rhythm method." For those denominations supportive of artificial means, their position is dependent on their understanding of abortion. They ask, "At what point of the sexual and biological process does the artificial means of birth control prevent the pregnancy?" Those conservative denominations that believe life begins at conception and, therefore, have adopted a very strict anti-abortion stance, oppose all means of contraception after the fertilization of the egg. Progressives take a more nuanced approach, understanding that family planning is a moral imperative.

These same fault lines can be seen in the issue of abortion, between the two poles of the so-called pro-life and pro-choice positions. All Christians recognize that human beings are created in God's image with the presumption to protect and preserve life. However, they differ with regard to the "rights" and "value" of the fetus and the mother, the rights and value of the woman's other relationships, the advancement of the **pregnancy**, the means of conception, as well as the woman's medical, social, emotional, relational/familial, and financial well-being. Protestants, who interpret the Bible more literally for ethical guidance, as well as Roman Catholics and Orthodox Christians, reject abortion for all but the most limited circumstances (the life of the mother, perhaps rape or **incest**). In contrast, those who interpret the tradition in light of Jesus's gospel ethic of love and compassion, allow for greater latitude in the conscience of the mother and her family to make her decision, again all the while realizing the tragic nature of the choice given the fall of creation. All Christians realize the necessity of reforming the social conditions that lead to such tragic choices, and a more supportive social and ecclesial infrastructure that would embrace the mother, the family, and the to-be-born child.

Finally, in the last two decades, particularly in the United States and Europe, **homosexuality** has taken center stage as a defining cultural, ethical, and theological issue in Christianity. The more conservative, traditionalist denominations and their mission churches in Latin America, Asia, and Africa oppose all homosexual practice. For example, the Roman Catholic Church teaches that although homosexual orientation is considered an "inclination '*propensio*'" and homosexual persons "must be accepted with respect, compassion, and sensitivity," nevertheless "tradition has always declared that homosexual acts are intrinsically disordered" and that "same-sex loving acts are an intrinsic moral evil" (*The Catechism of the Catholic Church*, Paragraphs 2357–2359). Therefore, same-sex "marriage" is rejected as an ontological impossibility and the ordination of openly gay priests is forbidden. However, it has been the Southern Baptist Convention, which condemns homosexual behavior as "a manifestation of a depraved nature and a perversion of divine standards ... outside the will of God," that has been at the forefront by encouraging boycotts of companies that appear to be too "gay-friendly," such as Disney in 1996.

The Anglican Communion splits along North-South lines, too. When the Episcopal Church of the United States of America (ECUSA) ordained the first openly gay bishop, New Hampshire's Gene Robinson, they affirmed the blessing of committed relationships of LGBT persons, and it was roundly condemned by traditionalists within its own ranks, as well as the majority of sister Anglican churches worldwide, particularly in the growing African Anglican church. This set off a worldwide Anglican conversation about homosexual orientation among unions, clergy, and bishops. Meanwhile, the United Church of Christ has taken a further step as an "open and affirming" denomination that "supports local, state and national legislation to grant equal marriage rights to couples regardless of gender ... welcoming [LGBT persons] and encouraging their participation in every aspect of the mission and ministry of the church" (*In Support of Equal Marriage Rights for All*, UCC General Synod, Atlanta, Summer 2005).

With 1.4 billion adherents, Islam is the world's second largest religion. From the revelation of the Qur'an and the *Sunna* (practice, tradition) of the Prophet in the seventh century, to Shariah law, codified in the ninth and tenth centuries, all govern the Muslim view of human sexuality. The Prophet taught the revolutionary view that marriage was the only proper context for sexual intercourse in a contractual (in contrast to the previous proprietary) relationship with the husband, thus liberating women.

Human sexuality is celebrated in Islam within heterosexual marriage. Monogamy is the ideal, although the Qur'an allows for *polygyny*, up to four wives, as long as they are treated equally. In many culturally Islamic societies, patriarchal conditions remain for Muslim women, that forbids women from religious leadership, separates them from men in prayer, and that restricts their access to education, employment, and other social, political, and sexual expressions outside of the home. Yet increasingly, in progressive Muslim circles, Islamic feminists bypass the later interpretations of the Shariah to return to the original Qur'anic revelation and Sunna of the Prophet, that women are "twinhalves" of men (*Hadith*, Al-Tirmidhi, 113; Ahmad, 25663) and that all people "are equal, like teeth in a comb" (*Hadith*, Ibn Hajar, Fath al Bari, 1:658–659; 3:204–205). Given this Islamic feminist hermeneutic based in the Qur'an and Sunna, scholars are reinterpreting family law, reproductive rights, female genital mutilation (*khitan*), homosexuality, and HIV in the Muslim world.

Birth control is permissible in Islam. Traditionally, *coitus interruptus* (*'azl*) is permitted as long as the wife is satisfied sexually. Also, any method that prevents the fertilization of the egg is acceptable, including the "Pill," condom, diaphragm, as well as the rhythm method. Irreversible methods of contraception, however, are forbidden. Further, all four Islamic law schools agree that abortion is forbidden once the *ruh* inhabits the fetus. Nevertheless, interpretations differ as to when that occurs. Some say four months, others 42 days—"When 42 nights have passed on *nutfah* (when sperm and egg mix), Allah sends an angel to form it; he creates its ears, eyes, skin, flesh, and bones" (*Hadith*, Imam Muslim, 33: 6392). Still others say that the *ruh* enters the fetus immediately as the fertilized egg is implanted in the uterus and, therefore, abortion is completely forbidden.

Homosexual behavior (*liwat*) is strictly condemned by the Qur'an and *hadith*, and every Islamic law school, subject to a variety of punishments depending on the law school. Traditionally, the Egyptian Hanafite School recommendations range from no physical punishment to flogging while the Saudi Hanbali School urges stoning. Homosexual behavior among men is viewed as extramarital sex (*zina*), similar to adultery; lesbian sex (*sihaq*) is forbidden, too, but Islamic law is virtually silent about it (calling it lewd or indecent), focusing virtually exclusively on male-male intercourse.

Finally, a minority of Muslim progressive scholars declare "the gates of *ijtihad*" (independent legal reasoning) to be open again, as opposed to traditionalist Muslim jurist majority that codified the Shariah in the tenth century, and thus employ an historical-critical-contextual hermeneutic. Bypassing the Shariah, they base the Islamic sexual ethic on Qur'anic attitudes. Thus, they affirm gender equality and healthy same-sex relationships. In virtually every Muslim country, LGBT communities—*Imaan* in Britain, *Al-Fatiha* in the United States, and the informal but very influential *Queer Jihad*—are slowly and quietly becoming more visible. In many Muslim capitals, the gathering places for LGBT individuals are well known, such as Hashemiya Square in Amman, Tahrir Square Gardens in Cairo, and Taksim Square in Istanbul. LGBT Muslims, caught between their faith and their sexuality, find these views of the Qur'an very liberating. *See also* Colonialism/Postcolonialism and Sex; Families; Feminism; Gender Roles; Infidelity/Extramarital Sex; Polygamy; Sexism; Sodomy; Women's Movement.

Further Reading: Beattie Jung, Patricia, Mary E. Hunt, and Radhika Balakrishnan, eds. *Good Sex: Feminist Perspectives from the World's Religions*. Piscataway, NJ: Rutgers University Press, 2000; Gauch, Suzanne. *Liberating Shahrazad: Feminism, Postcolonialism, and Islam*. Minneapolis: University of Minnesota Press, 2006; Magonet, Jonathan, ed. *Jewish Explorations of Sexuality*. Providence, RI: Berghahn, 1995; Manning, Christel, and Phil Zuckerman, eds. *Sex and Religion*. Belmont, CA: Thomson Wadsworth, 2005; Nelson, James B., and Sandra Longfellow. *Sexuality and the Sacred*. Philadelphia: Westminster John Knox Press, 2006; Roald, Anne Sofie. *Women in Islam: The Western Experience*. Oxford: Routledge Press, 2001; Stuart, Elizabeth. *People of Passion: What the Churches Teach about Sex*. London: Cassell, 1997; Urban, Hugh. *Magia Sexualis: Sex, Magic, and Liberation in Modern Western Esotericism*. Berkeley: University of California Press, 2006; Vanderbilt University. "The Carpenter Program in Religion, Gender, and Sexuality." http://www.vanderbilt.edu/divinity/carpenter/index.html. Provides links to over 35 interfaith sites, and statements from the religious traditions about their views of human sexuality.

L. Michael Spath

RITUALS.   *See* Puberty and Puberty Rituals

ROMANCE. Romance is a strong and ardent involvement between two people, characterized by a mix of emotional and sexual **desire**, hopefully leading to **marriage**. The vision of romance as the ideal form of love has been dominant in Western society from the nineteenth century. However, socio-historical developments, such as the two world wars, the gay/black/women's liberation movements of the 1960s, and the gradual increase of sexual freedom have brought about meaningful changes in the concept of ideal romantic relationships. Although the original view of true romance as destined to last a lifetime is still dominant, sexual intercourse prior to marriage, unthinkable in the nineteenth century, has become socially accepted. As the concept of romance has its origin in Western society, it is not easily applicable to non-Western cultures, especially those that reinforce the notion of heterosexual marriage as a contract between **families**. However, in the process of globalization, adoption of romance ideals in some non-Western countries is taking place.

Romance stems from romantic love, born often at "first sight," in which a fusion of souls and bodies is reached, hence the expressions "soul mate" or "twin soul." Romantic love is different both from erotic love, driven by sexual desire only, and from forms of love void of sexual drives, such as familial love, platonic love, or friendship. "Romance" is often used as synonymous of "romantic love," but it slightly differs from it in that it is always returned, while romantic love can be one-sided.

Romance became a recognized passion in Europe in the Middle Ages (fifth through sixteenth centuries). However, for generations it was discouraged as a legitimate route to marriage, which had as its main purpose economic and political alliances between families. Young people were constantly warned against the danger of following emotions instead of acting according to practical considerations. Romance as a legitimate route to marriage was accepted in some measure among the power classes, where economical and political interests in combining marriages were less substantial. However, not much is known about it.

Social acceptance of romance began in the second half of the nineteenth century, when romance novels became popular. Their plots typically spread over a number of years as lovers meet and overcome different obstacles, finally marrying and living happily ever after. England became the cradle of romance novels during the reign of Queen Victoria (1837–1901). Industry and technology flourished within the British Empire, giving rise to a large urban social class—the bourgeoisie—who could read and write. Heterosexual love, however, was associated with a strict **morality**, blessed by the church, and leading to marriage approved by the lovers' families. Since romance symbolized the union of two people aspiring to create a family to celebrate God's will, lovers were supposed to maintain a chaste relationship until marriage. The political and religious establishment had a conspicuous interest invested in encouraging this vision of romance as it discouraged carnal relationships, disapproved by the church and by the Victorian regime, and encouraged unions between people belonging to the same social class, thus acting as a control mechanism on young people.

In the United States, romance emerged in the eighteenth century when people began basing their marital choices more on emotional considerations than social calculations. At the beginning of the twentieth century, as women began attending college in greater numbers, **dating** and petting (but not sexual intercourse) became accepted prior to marriage.

Romantic vision depicts different images of the two "ideal" genders. Women were considered to be devoid of sexual drives and motivated by elevated thought and feelings. Men were supposed to be less moral and chaste than women and subject to carnal drives, which would calm down when they found a pure love and became worthy of it, under the positive influence of the beloved. Under the pretense of exalting women's morality, this viewpoint provided legitimacy to men expressing sexual drives, mostly with prostitutes and lower-class women, while women of the higher socio-economic classes were kept under strict control.

Throughout the first half of the twentieth century, during the first wave of the **women's movement**, females in the United States and in the United Kingdom challenged this romantic vision, claiming that it damaged women, as it overshadowed their inferior position. British writer Mary Wollstonecraft, considered the grandmother of **feminism**, advocated the social and moral equality of the sexes and even dared to acknowledge the existence of women's sexual desires, thus undermining the idealistic vision of the pure, non-sexual woman, which was basic to romance ideals. This was an era when women were robbed of independence and self-respect and made totally dependent on men. Women had no civil rights, could not vote or own property, and husbands exercised legal power over their wives to the extent that they could imprison or beat them with impunity. **Divorce** and child custody laws also favored men and women were not allowed to enter professions such as medicine or law.

World War I enhanced feminist movements, as women ably filled the work tasks of men who were in the army. Indeed, after the war, women obtained the right to vote in most Western countries together with some other civil rights. Women began to adopt a more realistic view of romantic relationships, demanding more equality between genders.

In the course of the twentieth century, the concept of romance became secular and void of its religious implications. Carnal passion was acknowledged as an integrant part of romance as practices like petting prior to marriage began to be accepted as legitimate, not only in North America, but also in most European countries. Western societies began to accept love as the only legitimate route to marriage. Romance, in its more modern version, began to hold a central position in **popular culture**, nurtured through the **cinema**, love songs in **popular music**, television, and modern romance novels. Life without romance was not considered worth living.

Other social forces brought further changes to the romantic vision, especially the "second wave" of the women's movement, beginning in the early 1960s through the late 1980s. Provocative feminist authors published evocative books with titles like *The Female Eunuch*, *Sexual Politics* and *Our Bodies, Ourselves*. Like the first wave of activists, these women challenged the glorification of heterosexual **marriage**, the wifely submission to the husband's will, and the double moral standard, which allowed sexual freedom for men, even married ones, while women were condemned as immoral for the same behavior. Given the gains in suffrage and property ownership from the first wave, the new slogan was "the personal is political." Movement leaders now encouraged women to understand all aspects of their personal lives as reflecting a basic inequality between genders, which laws alone could not eliminate.

Feminist ideas have influenced both the women's and **men's movements**, introducing more realistic views of love relationships. Nevertheless, romance as ultimate ideal is still dominant. Romantic love is considered especially valuable if it lasts a lifetime, perpetuating the nineteenth-century ideal through twenty-first-century technology. Popular culture, especially Hollywood movies, exerts a strong influence on people from all social classes in grasping even improbable romantic plots with happy-endings as real and achievable. Movies and television series, like Jane Austen's *Pride and Prejudice* taken from romantic nineteenth-century love stories, still appeal to the larger public.

Romance novels by writers such as Charles Dickens and Emily Brontë are still very popular, especially in North America, where it is the best-selling genre.

Romance culture has been criticized also for perpetuating sexual and racial prejudices. Until recently, same-sex romance was condemned although, with a growing legal, medical, and political legitimacy, these relationships have become more accepted in society and in popular culture. A further critique of romantic popular culture relates to its racism. In countries with a history of domination over other cultures, such as Britain, the United States and South Africa, it is rare to see a movie dealing positively with **interracial/ethnic intimate relationships** such as *West Side Story* and *Jungle Fever*. However, as interethnic marriages become more accepted, change is to be expected in the future.

Within non-Western countries, acceptance of romantic ideas remains limited. In Japan, romantic ideas have spread and romance has gained legitimacy, especially among the more educated classes and in big cities. However, traditional cultures and groups, especially those in which religion is dominant, such as fundamentalist Muslim or Orthodox Jews, still choose to enforce parental matchmaking and see women's **virginity** as a precondition to marriage. Thus, romance is discouraged—and in some countries even punished with death. In other non-Western countries, like India, romance is considered legitimate between people belonging to the same social class, if there is parental approval. *See also* Premarital Sex; Religions, Western; Sexism; Workplace.

Further Reading: Fass, Paul, F. *The Damned and the Beautiful: American Youth in the 1920s.* New York: Oxford University Press, 1977; Galician, Mary-Lou. *Sex, Love, and Romance in the Mass Media: Analysis and Criticism of Unrealistic Portrayals and Their Influence.* Mahwah, NJ: Erlbaum, 2004; Illouz, Eva. *Consuming the Romantic Utopia.* Berkeley: University of California Press, 1997; Lystra, Keren. *Searching the Heart: Women, Men, and Romantic Love in Nineteenth-Century America.* New York: Oxford University Press, 1989; Mondimore, Francis M. *A Natural History of Homosexuality.* Baltimore: The Johns Hopkins University Press, 1996; Psychology Today. Bruce Kanner. http://www.psychologytoday.com/articles. Academic articles regarding actual social issues, such as developments in interpersonal and romantic relationships, March–April 1995; Seidman, Steven. *Romantic Longings.* New York: Routledge, 1991; Shumway, David. R. *Modern Love: Romance, Intimacy, and the Marriage Crisis.* New York: New York University Press, 2003; Zeldin, Theodore. *France, 1848–1945. Vol. I, Ambitions, Love, and Politics.* Oxford: Clarendon, 1973.

Diana Luzzatto

S

SANGER, MARGARET (1879–1966). Margaret Sanger founded the **birth control** movement in the United States and was an influential advocate worldwide for women's access to reproductive and gynecological health care. Sanger's experiences as a public health nurse in New York City convinced her that women's inability to control the number and timing of their children was a major contributor to poverty and high infant and maternal death rates. Among her many accomplishments, Sanger opened the first birth control clinic in the United States, founded the American Birth Control League, and organized the first World Population Conference. Sanger was a tireless advocate for women's reproductive rights internationally, from her travels to Japan in the 1920s to promote birth control alongside the Japanese feminist Kato Shidzue, to her travels in Europe, Africa, and Asia four decades later to advocate use of the newly available birth control pill.

Margaret Sanger's activities empowering women to control their fertility have also improved the lives of men and children. In the most practical sense, giving women the ability to control their fertility has ameliorated many social problems caused by or contributed to by overpopulation. In a more philosophical sense, by redefining women's sexuality and removing its inevitable link with reproduction, Sanger freed both women and men to express themselves sexually.

Margaret Sanger, 1922. Courtesy of Library of Congress.

Margaret Sanger was born in Corning, New York, in 1879. Her father, Michael Higgins, was a stonecutter and labor organizer for the Knights of Labor. His radical political views alienated potential employers, including the Catholic Church, and hindered his ability to support his family. Sanger's mother gave birth to 11 live children and had 7 miscarriages before dying from tuberculosis at age 50. Due to the family's poverty, Sanger was unable to pursue a career as a physician, and despite her obvious academic talent, she trained as a nurse and began her career at White Plains Hospital. She married the architect William Sanger, with whom she had 3 children, and in 1911 the Sangers moved to New York City.

Active in radical politics in New York, William and Margaret were friends with labor leaders such as Elizabeth Gurley Flynn and Big Bill Haywood. Margaret began working for the Visiting Nurses Association among the poor on the Lower East Side of Manhattan, which provided her with a first-hand view of grinding poverty and its effect on people's lives. She became convinced from this experience that women's inability to control the size of their family produced a multitude of evils: it destroyed any chance for women to develop as free individuals, it produced vast numbers of children whose parents could not take care of them, and the resulting overpopulation led to other social evils such as malnutrition, child labor, **child abuse**, and **incest**.

Sanger wrote "What Every Girl Should Know" for the Socialist newspaper *The Call* in 1912–1913. In this column, she frankly discussed topics such as menstruation, **pregnancy**, **sexually transmitted infections**, and **masturbation**. It was declared to be obscene under the Comstock Laws, which made it illegal to disseminate information about birth control through the mail. In 1914, Sanger began publishing *The Woman Rebel*, a monthly periodical which published six issues in the spring and summer of 1914, and whose declared aim was to fight everything which enslaved women, including **prostitution**, **marriage**, uncontrolled fertility, and wage slavery. Given Sanger's focus on working class women, she was less concerned with issues such as suffrage, which she considered primarily relevant to the middle class.

The March issue of *The Woman Rebel* included an article titled "The Prevention of Contraception" which the post office declared to be obscene, and Sanger and her husband were indicted for publishing obscene material. She fled to Europe while he remained in New York and served 35 days in jail. While overseas, Sanger took the opportunity to observe birth control practices in Europe, particularly those available in the Dutch clinics run by Dr. Johannes Rutgers.

Margaret Sanger returned to the United States in 1915 and the charges against her were eventually dropped. She opened the first birth control clinic in the United States in Brownsville, New York City, on October 1916, modeled after clinics she had observed in the Netherlands. She was arrested and eventually served 30 days in jail. This case turned into a victory for the birth control movement when, in 1918, the Court of Appeals ruled that physicians could give contraceptive advice "to cure or prevent disease." Birth control clinics became legal if staffed by a physician. Sanger continued to establish clinics in New York City, including one in Harlem in 1930, which was endorsed by leading members of New York's African American community.

Sanger founded the monthly periodical *Birth Control Review* in 1917, which continued irregularly until 1940. It carried articles by noted authors such as H.G. Wells, Olive Schreiner, and Havelock Ellis, and frequently carried articles which connected birth control with other progressive topics. For instance, articles in a special issue devoted to child labor argued that without access to birth control poor **families** had no choice but to have large numbers of children, who due to poverty would have to begin work at an early age, thus creating a pool of surplus labor which suppressed wages and perpetuated their poverty.

Sanger founded the American Birth Control League and served as its first president. She also organized the first American Birth Control Conference in 1921. The last day of this conference was planned as a public forum at Town Hall in Manhattan. When the conference organizers arrived, they found the doors to the hall locked. Sanger and Mary Winsor were arrested, although charges against them were later dropped when the order to close the hall was traced to officials in the Catholic Church. The incident was heavily covered in the newspapers and the publicity may have benefited the birth control movement.

Sanger was ahead of her time in insisting that women had the right to sexual desires and their expression: in fact her contemporary Mabel Dodge said that Sanger was "the first person I ever knew who was openly an ardent propagandist for the joys of the flesh" (Chesler 1992: 96). Sanger divorced William Sanger in 1920 and married the self-made millionaire Noah Slee in 1922. Besides these two marriages, she had a number of well-publicized affairs with prominent men, including Havelock Ellis and H.G. Wells.

In *Happiness in Marriage* (1926), Sanger argued for a new model of marriage in which a couple would get married only after having experienced other relationships and would practice birth control and share household chores and childrearing. The second half of the book describes the reproductive organs and mechanics of sexual activity and gratification, information not generally available at the time outside medical textbooks. Sanger discussed only heterosexual relationships in her work and is not known to have had any lesbian relationships, although surviving letters indicate that she inspired feelings of what we would now term "romantic friendship" with one or more female friends, including Dr. Marie Equi and Stella Browne.

Sanger believed the **desire** of women to control their fertility was not limited by ethnicity, nationality, or social class, and throughout her life traveled extensively to advocate for birth control. Her ideas were particularly well-known in Japan, which she visited several times beginning in 1922, and the Japanese birth control advocate Kato Shidzue, later the Baroness Shidzue Ishimoto, became known as "the Japanese Margaret Sanger." Sanger's visit to India in 1935–1936, where she addressed the All-India Women's Conference and met with Mahatma Gandhi, was also well-publicized. Into her 80s, Sanger continued to travel as an advocate for birth control. She toured Europe, Africa, and Asia in the 1960s to publicize the birth control pill. Sanger also founded several international conferences and organizations that furthered the cause of birth control, including the first World Population Conference in 1927 and the International Planned Parenthood Foundation in 1952. *See also* Feminism; Sex Education; Women's Movement.

Further Reading: Chesler, Ellen. *Woman of Valor: Margaret Sanger and the Birth Control Movement in America.* New York: Simon & Schuster, 1992; Reed, Miriam. *Margaret Sanger: Her Life in Her Words.* Fort Lee, NJ: Barricade Books, Inc., 2003; Sanger, Margaret. *What Every Girl Should Know.* Springfield, IL: United Sales Co., 1920. Reprinted with an introduction by Joy Johannesen. New York: Belvedere, 1980; Sanger, Margaret. *Happiness in Marriage.* New York: Brentanos, 1926. Reprinted Old Saybrook, CT: Applewood Books, 1993; Sanger, Margaret. *The Autobiography of Margaret Sanger.* New York: W.W. Norton, 1938. Reprinted: New York: Dover Publications, 2004; The Truth About Margaret Sanger. Jon Knowles. See http://www.plannedparenthood.org/pp2/portal/files/portal/medicalinfo/birthcontrol/bio-margaret-sanger.xml. Discussion of Sanger's relationship with the African American community, her position on eugenics, and refutation of allegations that she promoted birth control out of racist motives, October 2004.

Sarah Boslaugh

SCANDALS.   Scandals are incidents that are judged to be morally offensive and evoke intense public attention and indignation. A scandalous event need not be real; mere allegations of wrong-doing can produce reactions just as intense as those actions based in reality. Rumors and misunderstandings usually surround "real" scandals, inflaming stronger reactions and keeping scandals alive in people's consciousness. Scandals can surround many aspects of social life. However, violations of sexual or

President Clinton in a 1995 photo with then White House intern Monica Lewinsky that later appeared in a report by Independent Counsel Kenneth Starr. © AP Photo/ OIC.

relationship norms, such as engaging in homosexual behaviors or having an extramarital sexual relationship, are common basis for scandals.

One of the most highly publicized scandals in the late twentieth century was the "Clinton-Lewinsky scandal." President Bill Clinton had a sexual relationship with a White House intern, Monica Lewinsky. To make matters worse, President Clinton denied the allegations, which later proved to be true. These events eventually led to the impeachment of the president in 1998. Thousands of pages of testimony from Ms. Lewinsky and President Clinton, including highly explicit details of their sexual encounters, were published on the **Internet**.

While the Clinton-Lewinsky scandal elicited intense reactions within the United States and forever tainted the reputations of those intimately involved, persons in other countries, such as France, could not understand why Americans were so upset about the president's indiscretions. They were more fascinated with Americans' reactions to the scandal than the actual relationship between Clinton and Lewinsky. Further, the reaction to this affair was far more intense than had been witnessed for earlier presidents, such as President John Kennedy, who was widely reputed to have had extramarital affairs. Thus, the Clinton-Lewinsky event illustrates scandals are dependent upon both cultural and historical contexts, and they are public rather than private matters often fueled by **media**.

Scandals are also rooted in social customs and expectations, telling us much more about a society and its expectations than about the individuals or groups that are involved in improper behavior. This suggests that no behavior is inherently immoral, whether it is deemed scandalous depends upon the cultural context in which it occurs.

Consider the act of adultery or having sexual relations with someone other than one's spouse. Reactions to such behavior can range significantly. In countries such as the England and Scotland, adultery is grounds for **divorce** but is not considered a crime. Similarly in the United States, unless the case involves someone famous or someone for whom such actions are forbidden—such as a Catholic priest—an adulterer may be subject to disapproval by others but is rarely ostracized or publicly punished. In some Islamic countries, however, such behavior may be punishable by death. This practice recently drew intense reaction from countries around the world when Safiya Hussaini, a divorced Nigerian woman, was accused of committing adultery and sentenced to death by stoning in 2002. The stoning was postponed until she could wean her 13-month-old daughter (it was this **pregnancy** that served as "proof" of her **infidelity**). In her case, she was acquitted in large part due to protests from human rights groups along with a bizarre legal defense that claimed Hussaini had actually been impregnated by her former husband before the divorce, even though the child had been born more than year after the divorce (her attorneys argued that the period between conception and birth can take up to seven years). Other women and men have not been so lucky, even in cases in which a woman's "adultery" was the result of rape.

Even within a given society, the same sexual behavior can have very different meanings, depending upon how the act is defined. Although in some Islamic countries having multiple sexual partners may be severely punished if it is defined as "adultery," polygyny—the marriage of one man to two or more women—is legal (though rare). Polygyny is also practiced by a sect of Mormons in the United States (these marriages are not legally recognized by the government) but adultery is impermissible. Further, it is permissible for Mormon men to have multiple wives but it would be scandalous for any married Mormon woman to engage in sex with a man who was not her husband. Thus, social factors such as gender or religion significantly shape a culture's reaction to various behaviors.

Scandals are also dependent upon historical contexts. In many countries during the first half of the twentieth century, **marriage** or sex with someone outside one's racial or religious group was considered unnatural and immoral, and such unions would certainly be scandalous. In some cases, such relations were considered not just scandalous but illegal. In Nazi Germany, for instance, a 1935 law outlawed marriages among Jews and non-Jews. As part of South Africa's apartheid movement, laws were passed in 1949 and 1957 that made it illegal for Whites to marry or have extramarital relations with Blacks. In the United States, interracial marriages were illegal and punishable by fines or prison terms as late as 1967. Over time, however, interracial relationships have gained greater acceptance and are more common. According to the U.S. Census, in 1960, fewer than 1 percent of marriages in the United States were interracial; by 1980 it rose to 2 percent; and by 2000, 6 percent of marriages were interracial. In addition, 3 percent of marriages included one Hispanic and one non-Hispanic individual. While some may still disapprove, these interracial relationships no longer evoke public outrage.

The fact that scandals are culturally and historically determined can also been seen in attitudes towards gay and lesbian relationships. Same-sex marriages are legal in several countries, including Belgium, the Netherlands, Canada, and parts of the United States. Nevertheless, homosexuality has been and remains a controversial issue and revelations of homosexuality among public figures are almost certain to lead to scandal. In the past, these revelations often led to legal investigations and arrests (as was the case of political leader Heinrich Rutha, who was arrested in Czechoslovakia during the 1930s for engaging in homosexual acts, along with 12 other men implicated in the scandal). In the United States, such a scandal is more likely to spell the end of a public figure's career but seldom results in arrests as in the cases of Congressman Mark Foley and the Reverend Ted Haggart in 2006.

When more than one sexual or relationship norm is violated there is even greater potential for scandal. Nowhere is this clearer than in the scandals involving Roman Catholic priests who have been accused of pedophilia and **pederasty**. **Sexual abuse** scandals involving Catholic priests have been documented around the world, including Canada, South Africa, Hong Kong, Ireland, Poland, Central America, Germany, the United States, and Austria. The scandal has grown even wider with the discovery that many of these incidents were deliberately "covered up" by church officials.

One might assume that over time a wider range of behaviors becomes more permissible and, therefore, are less likely to result in scandal. This is not always true. Certain taken-for-granted and invisible behaviors can become scandalous as social norms, laws, and awareness shift. Sexual harassment, for example, only entered into the language of Western cultures during the latter part of the twentieth century. Since then, awareness of sexual harassment has spread beyond the West, such as in Japan and Africa. Of course, behaviors that many would consider sexually harassing existed long before there was a name for them. But until they were named and made visible, they did not have the power to erupt into major scandals.

If scandals are cultural in nature, it follows, too, that they are public rather than private matters. There is no scandal unless the behavior becomes subject to public scrutiny and reaction. It may be the case that individuals involved feel extreme guilt, shame, or anger, but these are private reactions. A scandal occurs when private behavior—that is intended to remain private—becomes public. Scandals need not be widely publicized and may involve just a small group of individuals, such as a family, but if the behavior in question is not made known to persons other than those directly involved, it will not evoke a scandal.

The ability to broadcast news of a person's or group's indiscretions worldwide and in a matter of seconds is critical to igniting and continuing a scandal. In countries such as the United States, the news **media** and **Internet** have taken precedence over other mechanisms (e.g., rumor-mills or legal proceedings) in constructing and perpetuating popular scandals. Of course, news of improper behavior still can and does occur on the small-scale and may shock a group or community, but technology makes it possible to delve into the private lives and shortcomings of persons known to us only by reputation.

Major scandals are only possible in open societies that have a free press. Widespread scandals simply cannot exist when the media are under state control. For instance, in China, where the press is controlled by the government, there is little information about improper behavior (unless it involves an international scandal, such as spying, in which case the country with the open press is responsible for publicizing the event). Even in some open and democratic countries, the media is not likely to publicize information about the private lives of public figures. In Germany, for instance, it is illegal for media to publicize details about the sexual lives of public figures. In fact, the United States and Britain are unusual in the sense that virtually every aspect of a public figure's private life is available for public scrutiny.

Whether a scandal is broadcast to just a few or to the world, one of its main functions is social control. Scandals help clarify moral boundaries and control individuals' behaviors by showing what happens when rules are broken. The fear that one's illicit behavior may become known publicly is often enough to make an individual conform to social expectations. Although scandals serve to reinforce social norms, they can also serve to challenge and change them. Scandals may be more likely to occur during times or in societies where norms and social expectations are changing rapidly. People may be testing the boundaries of appropriate behavior and there is greater social anxiety and conflict surrounding people's behavior. Some groups will want to reassert traditional norms while others will contest these. Thus, scandals become an important arena in which battles over **morality** are fought.

Another function of scandals is power and control. Persons in high-level or highly visible positions are much more likely than those less-known to have their indiscretions publicized in the media, not only because they are better known but because they have more to lose and for others to gain from exposing their wrongdoing. The Clinton-Lewinsky affair would probably never have become widely publicized if there were not powerful individuals who had political interests in damaging the president's reputation or ousting him from political office.

A scandal evokes outrage and moral indignation but it also functions as a form of social entertainment and bonding. Not all individuals are outraged by an individual's behavior—and even if they are, they may still find the incident titillating. Scandals bring people together to discuss, debate, and dispute what did or did not happen. No matter how horrific the behavior, when the scandal involves a high-profile person or persons, it will almost certainly become fodder for talk shows and stand-up comedy.

Although scandals have the potential to destroy careers and reputations, they can have the opposite effect. Consider the case of a millionaire in the United States who was publicly embarrassed when a videotape of his daughter having sex with her partner was broadcast through the Internet. Undoubtedly, what made this so scandalous was not that his daughter was sexually active or even that there had been a tape made. The scandal was that someone in such an elite position was publicly embarrassed by the sexual exploits of a child. That short-lived scandal propelled a relatively unknown woman, Paris Hilton, into a twenty-first-century celebrity. *See also* Race and Racism; Religions, Western; Sex Crimes.

Further Reading: Adut, Ari. "A Theory of Scandal: Victorians, Homosexuality, and the Fall of Oscar Wilde." *American Journal of Sociology* 111 (2005): 213–48; Apostolidis, Paul, and Juliet A. Williams, eds. *Public Affairs: Politics in the Age of Sex Scandals*. Durham, NC: Duke University Press, 2004; Esser, Frank, and Uwe Hartung. "Nazis, Pollution, and No Sex: Political Scandals as a Reflection of Political Culture in Germany." *American Behavioral Scientist* 47, no. 8 (2004): 1040–71; Gamson, Joshua. "Normal Sins: Sex Scandal Narratives as Institutional Morality Tales." *Social Problems* 48, no. 2 (2001): 185–205; Halpern, Diane. "Sex, Lies, and Audiotape: A Cognitive Analysis of the Clinton-Lewinsky Scandal." Psi Chi, the National Honor Society in Psychology. http://www.psichi.org/pubs/articles/article_65.asp, Winter 2001; Lull, James, and Stephen Hinerman, eds. *Media Scandals: Morality and Desire in the Popular Culture Marketplace*. New York: Columbia University Press, 1998.

Liz Grauerholz

SEX CRIMES. Sex crimes are most commonly behaviors that "knowingly cause another person to engage in an unwanted sexual act by force or threat" (LaborLawTalk. org). In addition to being a violation of a legal statute, most sex crimes are also seen as a transgression of cultural morals and social norms. The definition and punishment of sex crimes have been largely dependent on culture and history. Although some sexual behaviors may or may not be considered a sex crime in various cultures (e.g., exhibitionism, **cross dressing**, use and distribution of **pornography**), there are a few sexual behaviors that have been almost universally considered illegal.

Sexual acts between an adult and a minor are almost universally condemned, although the definition of an "adult" and "minor" varies across cultures. In the majority of industrialized nations, an adult who can give legal consent for their sexual behaviors is a person at least sixteen years old, although it can range from as young as twelve years old in Mexico to twenty-one in Madagascar. Pedophilia is the intense sexual attraction toward prepubescent or pubescent children. According to the American Psychological Association, a pedophile is someone over the age of 16 who has persistent, recurring attractions to persons at least five years younger. Legally in the United States, one is considered a child sex offender for acting on these sexual urges (although some research indicates that sexual urges are not present in most convicted sex offenders). Most perpetrators of child sex crimes are family members or individuals known to the child, and almost always men. It is estimated that one in four girls and one in ten boys will be the victim of a sexual crime before they reach adulthood; the number of these crimes actually reported is significantly lower.

Although sexual behaviors with children are considered crimes in most countries, there are regions of the world in which they are accepted social norms. For example, in the Sambian tribe of Papua New Guinea, the act of fellatio is performed by an adolescent boy on an older male in the tribe as a rite of passage into manhood and a full member of the tribe. In Zambia, there are also initiation ceremonies that involve a young girl preparing for marriage by learning how to sexually pleasure a man and performing such acts. Because these are accepted cultural rituals, there is no legal recourse for sex acts between adults and children.

There are also cultural variations in the way sex crimes with children are prosecuted. In the United States, Canada, western Europe, and Australia, legal punishments for pedophilia involve a mandatory jail sentence. Early treatment for sex offenders included surgical castration or aversion therapy, which delivered shocks upon viewing arousing pictures or thoughts to quell their desires. More recently, treatment of sex offenders has included cognitive behavioral therapy and the option of chemical castration, using anti-androgen pills to suppress the sex drive in men. Also, because of Megan's Law, which was passed nationwide in the United States in 1996, databases of information on registered sex offenders are made available to the public. Similar registries exist in some countries, such as Canada, yet in other countries, such as Spain, there is no public release of sex offender profiles.

Sex acts with children in many less-developed areas of the world are less likely to be prosecuted. Over the course of the twentieth and twenty-first centuries, sex tourism has largely profited on the selling of sexual acts with minors. The global sex trade industry has trafficked (moved and sold) an estimated two million girls and boys worldwide, some as young as five years old. Once sold to a brothel, a child prostitute may service as many as 30 customers per week, and are at highly increased risks of **sexually transmitted infections**. Sex tourism is most often found in regions with high rates of poverty and little resources for economic development, such as eastern Europe, Mexico, parts of Central America, the Philippines, Nepal, Cambodia, and Thailand. Sex tourists are usually males from North America and western Europe. Although most countries have laws against sex tourism, they are widely under-enforced, due to law enforcement agents' use of child prostitutes or because of the economic revenue it brings to the country.

Rape and sexual assault are also widely defined and prosecuted as sex crimes. Rape is a forcible sexual act with penetration, whereas sexual assault is a forcible sexual act without penetration. In both cases, the sexual act is generally committed under the duress, force, or threat of the victim. In general, approximately 90 percent of convicted rapists are male and 10 percent are female. Although data on the actual prevalence and rates of rape and sexual assaults are extremely hard to verify, due to the under-reporting of such crimes, it is estimated that roughly one in four women and one in seven men will experience rape or sexual assault sometime in their lives. Largely due to fear or stigma, male, gay and lesbian, non-white, and poor victims are especially thought to under-report the frequency of **sexual abuse and assault**.

Legal definitions and punishments of rape vary widely around the world. For example, in Costa Rica, Guatemala, and Ecuador, the defendant's punishment in dependent on the worthiness of the victim's testimony and whether she is considered to be chaste. In Peru, sentences decrease in severity as the age of the victim advances, with very little punishment for the rape of older women. In Pakistan, a woman can also be convicted of adultery for rape. Rape is often interpreted and judged differently based on the way in which the act was committed. For example, rape and sexual assault are perceived as more harmful and damaging when the perpetrator is male (than female) and the victim is female (than male).

A majority of rapes and sexual assaults are committed by an acquaintance rather than by a stranger. An estimated 84 percent of perpetrators are someone the victim knows or has dated. However, a common myth is that the majority of perpetrators are strangers. Biases exist in perceptions of what constitutes a typical rape or assault scenario. A stereotypically common perception is that rape victims are white, female, heterosexual, and young, and are raped by a stranger who is non-white, male, and sex-crazed in a dark alley. These stereotypical perceptions have an impact on whether one believes or sympathizes with a victim. Further, individuals tend to see stranger rape as more serious and damaging than an acquaintance rape, and support a greater degree of severity and punishment for the perpetrator.

Racial biases also play a large role in the judgment of these crimes. Researchers find that people sympathize more with white victims than black victims, and interracial rape involving a black male perpetrator and a white female victim is perceived to be the most serious. An examination of alleged rapes committed in the American South during the first half of the twentieth century shows that black men suffered extremely severe punishments (maximum prison sentence, lynching, death) compared to the punishments given to white defendants such as a fine or twelve-month sentence.

Another public perception is that only unmarried women can be raped or assaulted. In many parts of the world, it is seen as a husband's unrestricted right to have sex with his wife. That is, a husband cannot legally rape his wife. There are high incidence rates of spousal rape in developing countries such as India, Colombia, Haiti, and Nicaragua. Often, when women have no other means of financial and social support, they feel powerless in fighting against the assault and are much less likely to report it. In the United States, this idea was long supported as well until 1975 when South Dakota deemed it illegal for a husband to have non-consensual sex with his wife.

In the several decades since the 1970s, as more awareness and research has been committed to understanding rape and sexual assault, it has been commonly accepted that rape and sexual assault is not about sex or lust, but about power and control. The perpetrator rapes and sexually assaults to send a more overt message of power and intimidation to the victim. Rape and sexual assault is often used to victimize lesbian and bisexual women because of their sexual orientation.

Historically, rape and sexual assault have been weapons of war. Soldiers from one group, culture, or country may systematically rape and assault women of an enemy group. Documented mass rapes have occurred in Japan and Germany, during World War II, and in more recent conflicts in Sierra Leone, Bosnia, and Rwanda. Such rape sends a message to the opposing side's men that they failed to protect their women and children while dehumanizing victims. It is often more violent than non-war rape.

Another commonly cited sex crime is **sodomy**: as oral or anal sex between members of the same sex, although the term has historically been used to describe any sexual act that is unnatural or abnormal. The Catholic Church in England first deemed sodomy a crime and a sin in the 1500s. It was considered an "offense against God" in the United States's colonies and continued as a crime in some states until the early twenty-first century. Punishments ranged from fines to life sentences. Some states did not consider oral sex between women (cunnilingus) a crime, ruling that "without a penis, there could be no sodomy."

Following World War II, amidst the anti-communism and anti-homosexuality ideologies of McCarthyism, there was a rise in the number of sex crimes prosecuted as well as a strengthening of laws against sodomy. However, Alfred **Kinsey** documented the frequency of so-called immoral sexual behaviors. In 1961, Illinois became the first state to overturn its law prohibiting sodomy, followed by Connecticut and twenty-one other states. There were continual fights in many other states, primarily between gay activists and state legislatures, to overturn sodomy laws as recent as 1995. Finally, the U.S. Supreme Court decision in 2003 voted to overturn sodomy laws that were still present in Texas as well as twelve other U.S. states, which protect the private sexual behaviors between two consenting adults.

Globally, sodomy is illegal in many countries. Criminal sentences range from paying a fine (e.g., Algeria, Mali), to 3–5-year jail terms (e.g., Ethiopia, Morocco), to life imprisonment or death (e.g., India, Nepal, Nigeria, Sudan, Afghanistan, Saudi Arabia, United Arab Emirates). Homosexual acts are legal in most countries in Europe. Gay and lesbian and human rights activist groups have been extremely committed to challenging international laws prohibiting homosexual acts and relationships, and have pushed, albeit unsuccessfully, for a unified resolution by the United Nations to punish governments for human rights violations based on sexual orientation. *See also* Child Abuse; Domestic and Relationship Violence; Incest; Infidelity/Extramarital Sex; Internet; Pederasty; Polygamy/Polyamory; Prisons, Sex in; Puberty and Puberty Rituals; Race and Racism.

Further Reading: Brownmiller, Susan. *Against Our Will: Men, Women, and Rape.* New York: Simon and Schuster, 1975; Donovan, Roxanne, and Williams, Michelle. "Living at the Intersection: The Effects of Racism and Sexism on Black Rape Survivors." *Women and Therapy* 25, nos. 3/4 (2002): 95–105; Door, Lisa Lindquist. *White Women, Rape, and the Power of Race in Virginia, 1900–1960.* Chapel Hill: University of North Carolina Press, 2004; Koss, Mary P., Lori Hiese, and Nancy Felipe Russo. "The Global Health Burden of Rape." *Psychology of Women Quarterly* 18 (1994): 509–37; LaborLawTalk.com. "Sex Crime." http://dictionary.laborlawtalk.com/sex_crime, 2006; Milillo, Diana Marie. "Rape as a Tactic of War: Social and Psychological Perspectives." *Affilia: Special Issue on Women, War, and Peace Building* 21, no. 2 (2006): 196–205; Painter, George. "The Sensibility of Our Forefathers: The History of Sodomy Laws in the United States." http://www.sodomylaws.org/sensibilities/introduction.htm, 2005; Pharr, Suzanne. *Homophobia: A Weapon of Sexism.* Berkeley, CA: Chardon Press, 1997; SexCriminals.com. http://www.sexcriminals.com. This site provides a sex offender registry list for the United States and Canada, a comprehensive list of articles, discussion polls, and links to related sites, 2006.

Diana Milillo

SEX EDUCATION. Although information on the biology and social norms of sex may come from family, peers, and religious leaders, sex education is curriculum sponsored by organizations, institutions, and governments primarily for the prevention of disease and unwanted **pregnancy**. Sex education emerged at the turn of the twentieth century in several nations with various forms instituted in many other countries during the mid to late twentieth century.

In the United States, books on sexual health for adults were prevalent by the 1880s and materials for male and female adolescents came onto the market a decade later, although no books were intended for both genders. Efforts to educate youth about the dangers of **premarital sex** grew as purity crusaders and medical professionals alike imparted information on the duties of **marriage**, the dangers of **prostitution**, **homosexuality**, and **masturbation**, and the basics of hygiene.

In 1912, the National Education Association recommended that teachers' colleges include sexuality education. By 1917, the American Social Hygiene Association (founded 4 years earlier) sought to reduce venereal disease by promoting abstinence from extramarital sex, which began to be included in public school curricula. By the 1920s, 540 normal schools were teaching some form of sexuality education, instructing teachers on how to teach human reproduction and the dangers of **sexually transmitted infections** (Mooney 1974).

Purity crusaders, hygienists, and educators continued to agree on the necessity of sex education as gender and sexual mores were changing in urban settings of the 1920s and 1930s throughout the world. Norway's government mandated instruction on human reproduction in 1939. (The curriculum expanded in 1971 to address sexual **desire**, masturbation, homosexuality, contraception, family planning, **abortion**, and venereal disease.) In 1942, Sweden recommended public schools include sex education on the biology of human reproduction and sexual hygiene. By 1956, this curriculum was compulsory. Today Sweden's curriculum covers issues of intercourse, masturbation, contraception, and pregnancy at its earliest level—children ages 7 to 10 years.

By the 1940s, in the United States, the curriculum expanded from lessons on biology, hygiene, and disease prevention to discussions on appropriate **gender roles** for domestic relations. What began as an experimental curriculum on family relations in a small New Jersey community, in 1941, was later adopted as basic principles for sex education by the American Health Association in 1947. A decade later, sex education was less focused on disease prevention and was oriented toward promoting values and behaviors for married life. In 1965, the family life version of sex education became compulsory in all schools accepting federal funds. Although more schools had access to funding for family life education, the emergence of any sex education curriculum into American schools was slow. Five years later, only 6 states required sex education and implementation was limited. Sex education did not become widespread until 2001, when it was estimated that 60 percent of youth experienced a more comprehensive version of sex education in schools (Francoeur 2001).

Opposition to compulsory sex education in U.S. schools became a hallmark issue for the growing New Right and Christian organizations during the 1960s. In 1964, the Sexuality Education and Information Council of the United States (SEICUS) was founded to counteract this opposition and to promote comprehensive K–12 sex education, emphasizing issues of pleasure, safety, and choice. As the years passed, the debate polarized over appropriate messages regarding premarital sex, abortion, homosexuality, and masturbation.

By the late 1980s, as **AIDS/HIV** became recognized as a threat to all people and not limited to certain "risk groups," public schools began to implement opt-in/opt-out policies, giving parents the right to take their children out of sex education classes—a major concession to the growing conservative movement in the country. In some school districts, however, students' continued to receive a broad sex education approach addressing **sexism** and homosexuality as well as disease and pregnancy. Despite concessions, American conservatives effectively lobbied for federal funding to abstinence-only-until-marriage education, which began with the Adolescent and Family Life Act (1981) and later expanded, in 1996, with the Abstinence Education Act.

Debates over appropriate messages spread worldwide as abstinence-only curricula became a stipulation in the Global AIDS funding policy of 2003. The impact of HIV/AIDS, however, had already moved many governments to integrate sex education in its schools. In June 1981, for instance, soon after the first HIV/AIDS cases were discovered in Uganda, sex education commenced. Five years later, Uganda became the first African nation to address the disease by investing in sex education, training, counseling networks, treatment centers, and testing.

Sex education programs in schools and on the radio were expanded in 1990 by the Ugandan National Task Force on AIDS and additional funds through the United Nations Joint Program on AIDS (UNAIDS). Condom sales were subsidized as education and public service messages were increased. HIV/AIDS prevention was boosted in 1997 by same-day testing and counseling services. Uganda is one of few nations to report 100 percent of teachers trained in life skills-based HIV/AIDS education.

U.S. policy interventions also impacted Uganda. In 2001, with financial support from the United States, this African government launched the Presidential Initiative on AIDS Strategy for Communication to Youth, which provided abstinence-until-marriage messages through assemblies, classroom activities, and rallies. Uganda's ABC program asks people to abstain, be faithful, and use condoms.

In contrast to Uganda, although the AIDS pandemic came late to South Africa, slow government response allowed the disease to spread. HIV/AIDS, identified in South Africa in 1980, was regarded as a black problem by the Apartheid government. Beginning in 1990, South African schools have been able to include HIV/AIDS prevention messages. However, these programs have been met by resistance from parents who believe it will corrupt their children. The post-Apartheid government did not formally address the epidemic until 1992 with a free National Helpline, founded after President Nelson Mandela addressed the National AIDS Convention of South Africa (NACSA). Mandela's successor, President Mbeki, initially admitted to the seriousness of HIV/AIDS in 1995. However, five years later, he addressed the AIDS epidemic as a problem of poverty instead of infection of HIV. Some blame Mbeki's skepticism as hindering successful promotion of prevention messages. The increase of AIDS orphans and the reality of 60 percent of new infections among people aged 15 to 25 has brought increased government involvement through the Department of Welfare. Education strategies now target youth to influence high-risk attitudes and behaviors.

As rapid increases in HIV/AIDS cases in the 1980s prompted many countries to adopt sex education to curb the pandemic, some nations began to address issues of population control and the rights of women through sex education initiatives. In 1974, Mexico developed sex education to address its growing population. The content has remained a contested issue between messages promoting sex for procreation within marriage and economic pressures from rapid population growth. Private and public school students are required to include sex education, but this policy is not implemented consistently. Since the 1980s, sex education has been supplemented by non-governmental organizations, which stress the need for culturally relevant information and try to reach those women who did not complete school. By 1987 access to sex education and family planning was still limited for low-income women, but coverage was further supplemented by coalitions between local programs and non-profits. Most family planning services are available through the Planned Parenthood affiliate Fundación Mexicana para la Planifiación Familiar or government health agencies run by the Ministry of Health and the Mexican Institute for Social Security. Programs now target areas impacted by mass migration—mainly along the U.S.–Mexican border.

Poverty greatly increases the risk for unintended and/or premarital pregnancy and also reduces the chances of survival for people with AIDS. Lack of development and disruption of access exacerbates both the hardships of poverty and the seriousness of unintended pregnancy and maternal and prenatal health.

Issues of population growth and public health promoted a renewal of sexual discourse in China. As early as the second century BCE, Chinese philosophy promoted sexuality as a means to spiritual harmony. With the cultural revolution of communism in 1949, sexual liberality of Eastern religions was suppressed and the spread of sexually transmitted infections remained low until the first case of HIV/AIDS in 1985. From the Chinese revolution through the 1970s, few books were published on the topic of sex; those that were focused on love, marriage, medical conditions, and dysfunctions. During the 1980s the China Sexology Association was established and more sex manuals were published. These have since become popular in China and are the main source of sexual information for couples. Manuals stress that it is natural to marry, to be sexually active, and that good sex occurs with simultaneous **orgasm**.

Sex education was first instituted in Shanghai schools in 1981. The initial curriculum focused on contraception and family planning and later expanded to address hygiene and sexual **morality**. Sex education was instituted nationwide in 1988. The curriculum evolved as the government became aware of changing sexual ethics among Chinese youth, including increases in teen pregnancy, sex crimes, and sexually transmitted diseases. After decades of exclusion from public life, sex education is now implemented from fourth grade to middle school. Students may have a less limited view of sexuality as textbooks are reported to be more scientific in their approach to topics of masturbation, contraception, harassment, HIV/AIDS, and homosexuality.

Unlike China, Thailand has remained a sexually liberal society although public discussion about sex is taboo. Sex education in Thai schools did not begin until 1978 and has remained limited to reproductive biology and sexually transmitted disease. In 1989, under external pressure by non-governmental organizations, the Thai government adopted condom promotion programs for sex workers and introduced sex education in public schools to reduce teen pregnancy and decrease HIV infection rates. Thailand's Basic Education Curriculum of 2001 integrates sex education within the existing health and physical education courses. Its focus is more on anatomy and diseases than masturbation, contraception, and homosexuality. Non-profits as well as academic institutions are currently developing programs to train educators and develop curriculum that will make sex education programs relevant to students' lives. *See also* Birth Control; Politics; Race and Racism; Religions, Eastern; Religions, Western.

Further Reading: Francoeur, Robert. *International Encyclopedia of Sexuality*. New York: The Continuum Publishing Company, 2001; McMillan, Joanna. "Doing It by the Book: Natural Tales of Marriage and Sex in Contemporary Chinese Marriage Manuals." *Sex Education* 4, no. 3 (October 2004): 203–15; Melody, Michael Edward, and Linda Mary Peterson. *Teaching America About Sex: Marriage Guides and Sex Manuals from the Late Victorians to Dr. Ruth*. New York: New York University Press, 1999; Mooney, Elizabeth. *The School's Responsibility for Sex Education*. Bloomington, IN: Phi Delta Kappa, 1974; Moran, Jeffery P. *Teaching Sex: The Shaping of Adolescence in the 20th Century*. Cambridge, MA: Harvard University Press, 2000; Nimkannon, Oratip. "New Models for Sexuality." *Bangkok Post*. http://www.bangkokpost.net/education/site2006/cvjl1806.htm. Describes the state of sex education in Thailand; Planned Parenthood Federation of America, Inc. *Reproductive Health and Rights in Mexico*. http://www.plannedparenthood.org/about-us/international-work/reproductive-health-and-rights-in-mexico.htm. Explains the state of sex education in Mexico, 2006; "Sex Education in Norway." International Planned Parenthood Federation. European Regional Information 7, no. 4 (1978): 3–4; Stephenson, Joan. "AIDS in South Africa takes Center Stage." *Journal of the American Medical Association* 284, no. 2 (2000): 165–68.

April Niver

SEX THERAPISTS. Sex therapists provide **psychotherapy** for sexual dysfunction—the term used for problems in any of the phases of the sexual response cycle. Sex therapists do not focus upon sexual deviations such as **child abuse**, but work on sexual functioning in adult, consensual relationships. This focus includes working with homosexual couples, but the large majority of couples seeking sex therapy are married, heterosexual couples. Although sex therapy is largely a Western phenomenon, sex therapists practice throughout the world, but with varying degrees of acceptance.

There are several phases of the sexual response cycle, each of which may be associated with problems, which sexual therapists can treat. The problems in the **desire** phase are low sexual drive and aversion to sex. People with true low sexual drive (low level of interest or even a total lack of interest) typically only engage in sexual activity to please their partner and avoid disrupting their love relationship. Aversion to sex means not only lacking interest in sexual activity but finding it to be upsetting and unpleasant.

The problem in the arousal phase for men is **erectile dysfunction**, which refers to inability to reach or to sustain erection of the penis. For women, arousal dysfunction is shown by a lack of vaginal lubrication and the other physical aspects of arousal. For men and women, the lack of physical arousal may or may not be accompanied by a lack of psychological and emotional feelings of excitement and pleasure.

In the orgasmic phase of sexual function, women may be unable to reach **orgasm**. Men may also have problems in reaching orgasm, but much more common is "premature ejaculation," which refers to the man having orgasm so rapidly that sexual activity is not satisfying for him or for his partner. In extreme cases, the man may reach orgasm before entry of the penis into the vagina.

There is one other problem that is treated by sex therapists. Vaginismus is pain a woman experiences due to involuntary spasms (painful contractions) of the muscles that surround the vagina. This is not caused by physical problems but results from a fear reaction to the entry of the penis.

The rates of occurrence of sexual dysfunctions vary cross culturally. However, the rates of male dysfunctions do not seem to vary as much across cultures as those of the female. Cultures vary less in their attitude toward male sexuality than in the attitude

Human sexuality researchers William H. Masters and Virginia E. Johnson Masters are pictured before a broadcast of NBC's "Meet the Press" in Washington, DC, 1979. © AP Photo/ Cook.

regarding female sexuality. Thus, social anthropologists have classified cultures according to how the culture views female sexuality.

The United States is considered to be moderately positive regarding female sexuality. In several research studies done over the last fifty years, it has been consistently been found that ten to fifteen percent of adult, sexually active women have never had an orgasm in any way. Cultures that are moderately negative about female sexuality include some strongly Catholic European nations like Ireland and Poland. In these cultures, up to 40 percent of women have never had an orgasm.

There are some North African and Middle Eastern cultures that are classified as extremely negative about female sexuality. In these cultures, the rate of total lack of orgasm in women appears to be as high as 80 percent. In some of these cultures young women routinely are given what used to be called "clitoral circumcision" (now referred to as "female genital mutilation"). In its most severe form, there is complete removal of the clitoris and stitching together of the vaginal lips—the labia. This procedure is done to insure **virginity** and chastity in women. Not surprisingly, the rate of lifelong lack of orgasm appears to be 100 percent in women who have had this procedure.

At the other end of the classification are some South Pacific island cultures. Female sexuality is valued in much the same way our culture values a woman having a good education, being a good mother, or having a good job. In these cultures, the rate of women never having had an orgasm is below 5 percent.

Sex therapy was developed in the Western world in the final years of the nineteenth century. The pre-eminent sex therapist was Richard von Krafft-Ebing, a Viennese psychiatrist. In the theoretical approach to sexual problems taken then and into the early years of the twentieth century, the cause of sexual dysfunction was "moral degeneracy." Childhood **masturbation**, it was thought, essentially exhausted the sexual response mechanism. Texts of the time contained supposedly scientific facts like "the loss of one drop of semen is equivalent to the loss of seven drops of blood." Treatment consisted of procedures like having children wear metal mittens or restraining garments that made it impossible for them to reach their genitals when they were put to bed at night. For adults, plenty of healthy, outdoor exercise was recommended. Additionally, the adults should not eat spicy, protein loaded foods. Kellogg and Graham each wrote that their cornflakes and their crackers could help prevent and cure sexual problems.

Sigmund **Freud** was the next major figure in the field of sex therapy. According to his psychoanalytic theory, children go through stages of sexual development, from oral, to anal, to the phallic or "Oedipal" phase. The Oedipal phase involves the child (around age 2 to 3) having sexual feelings towards their parent of the other gender. If these feelings are not resolved by identifying with the same sex parent, the result is sexual dysfunction in adulthood. For example, the adult man with an unresolved Oedipal complex will have erectile dysfunction since all women are symbolically equivalent to mother. Sexual feelings toward the mother equivalent causes "castration anxiety." Treatment consists of hundreds of hours of psychotherapy to resolve the feelings towards the parents. But, this therapy was never very successful. In fact, men are more likely to develop erectile dysfunction late in life after many years of not having a problem. Focusing on early **childhood** then is illogical and ineffective.

The next development in sex therapy was the work of the behaviorists, such as Joseph Wolpe. They viewed dysfunctions as caused by anxiety about sexual performance. Treatment, therefore, focused upon anxiety reduction, by teaching deep muscle relaxation techniques, which the patient would then do while visualizing pleasurable sexual activity. These techniques were moderately effective. The anxiety reduction approach worked best with erectile failure, in which anxiety about performance is a major element. However, success with female dysfunctions was limited.

Greater success with female sexual dysfunctions came with the work of cognitive psychotherapists, including Albert Ellis. If a person has deeply held beliefs that sexual activity is somehow wrong or immoral, he argued, just attempting to reduce anxiety will not succeed. In cognitive therapy, the person's belief system, self esteem, view of the world, and overall thought system are addressed through procedures such as discussion with the therapist, reading educational materials, and viewing appropriate videos. The therapist does not impose another value system upon clients, but rather helps them examine how much of their belief system has been imposed upon them, rather than reflecting their own informed, free choice.

The field of sex therapy advanced with the groundbreaking work of William Masters and Virginia Johnson who argued that a complete sexual history is crucial. This includes both what the patient learned as a child about sexuality and more recent life history events that may interfere with sexual functioning. Treatment then can focus on negative attitudes and beliefs about sex. In the Masters and Johnson's program, couples came to St. Louis for two weeks of intensive, daily treatment. This allowed for changes to be made in their marital and sexual interactions that were be hard for couples to make in more standard, once-a-week therapy.

Masters and Johnson emphasized that once a sexual dysfunction begins the person experiences "performance anxiety" and takes a self-evaluative "spectator role" when they make love. Failure leads to greater failure that ensures a self maintaining cycle. This cycle ends when the couple stops trying to have a complete sexual experience and begins "therapy homework" by doing "sensate focus body massage." Here they can just enjoy physical pleasure with each other without the pressure of performing sexual intercourse. Masters and Johnson also developed specific sexual techniques for the partners to use which directly dealt with their dysfunction. For instance, premature ejaculation is treated by having the couple manually stimulate the penis until the man is moderately to highly aroused. The penis is then briefly squeezed, where the head joins the shaft. Stimulation is paused for another 30 seconds or so and then resumed. This "squeeze and pause" procedure is repeated several times before being carried through to the point of the man reaching orgasm. Over successive practice sessions, the number of squeeze and pause sequences needed for the man to have a long duration of stimulation before reaching orgasm is reduced, until none are needed. Then, this procedure is repeated with entry of the penis into the vagina. The procedure is successful in virtually 100 percent of cases of premature ejaculation. Their therapy was extremely successful and revolutionized professional thinking about sexual problems.

One major issue about the effectiveness of the Masters and Johnson treatment program involves the somewhat restricted range of persons they treated. First, patients who had any medical problems as factors in their dysfunction were screened out.

Perhaps more importantly, it was required that the couple have a happy, stable marital relationship. However, many couples with sexual dysfunctions do show marital distress, so there were questions raised as to how applicable their model was to the majority of cases seen in actual clinical practice where, in some cases, marital distress may actually be the major source of the dysfunction. Therefore, it may well be necessary for marital therapy to precede or be included in treatment of sexual dysfunction using the techniques developed by Masters and Johnson.

Joseph LoPiccolo adapted an integrative model to serve a broader range of couples. Couples are not excluded from therapy because of marital distress or medical issues. In addition to the elements of the Masters and Johnson approach, marital distress is confronted around issues such as power and control, conflict resolution, emotional closeness, intimacy, trust, and basic level of romantic love. Medical issues, such as heart disease, neurological disorders, and side effects of medications also are addressed. Additionally, what might be called "real life" issues are examined. These include the time and emotional stresses of both partners being full-time employed while also having children, and financial problems. In the work of most therapists, patients are seen once per week as they continue with their real life responsibilities during the course of therapy.

While sex therapists focus primarily upon heterosexuality, there has been some sexual therapy done with homosexual couples and individuals. Although many of the issues confronting homosexual couples are similar to those of heterosexual ones, issues of societal and familial rejection of homosexuality complicate treatment of sexual problems in gay men and lesbians. A person in a heterosexual **marriage** may be able to seek support from a family member when the relationship is troubled and, perhaps, receive helpful support, advice, or a suggestion to seek marital therapy. A person in a homosexual relationship in this situation, however, is likely to be told the relationship is "unnatural," cannot be expected to work, and should be ended. *See also* Sex Education; Sexual Science/Sexology.

Further Reading: American Association of Sex Educators, Counselors, and Therapists. http://www.aasect.org. This interdisciplinary organization's site includes resources, links, and FAQs on human sexuality,   December 2006; Ellis, Havelock. *Reason and Emotion in Psychotherapy.* New York: Lyle Stuart, 1962; Greene, Beverly, and Gregory Herek. *Lesbian and Gay Psychology: Theory, Research, and Clinical Applications.* Thousand Oaks, CA: Sage, 1994; Krafft-Ebing, Richard. Reprint editor. *Psychopathia Sexualis.* New York: Arcade, 1998; LoPiccolo, Joseph. "Postmodern Sex Therapy." In *Comprehensive Handbook of Psychotherapy,* edited by Florence W. Kaslow and Jay Lebow, 411–36. Vol. 4. New York: Wiley & Sons, 2002; Masters, William. H., and Virginia. E. Johnson. *Human Sexual Inadequacy.* Boston: Little Brown, 1970; Wolpe, Joseph. *Psychotherapy by Reciprocal Inhibition.* Stanford, CA. Stanford University Press, 1958.

Joseph LoPiccolo

SEXISM.   Sexism is any act, attitude, or institutional configuration that systematically subordinates or devalues women. Built upon the belief that men and women are constitutionally different, sexism takes these differences as indications that men are inherently superior to women, which then is used to justify the nearly universal dominance of men in social and familial relationships, as well as politics, religion, language, law, and economics. Furthermore, this perceived right to dominance results in a thinly veiled right to exert force when necessary to maintain men's superior status. Sexism embeds in love and sex across cultures, from traditional **heterosexual** marriage vows and courtship rituals to levels of tolerance regarding **infidelity** and **domestic/ relationship violence**.

At the philosophical level, sexism is based on dualistic thinking that conceives of **masculinity** and femininity as opposites, along with many other dualisms such as: White/Black; heterosexual/homosexual; civilized/savage; logical/emotional. Even though these terms are portrayed as opposites, they are not deemed equal. In each dualism the first term is dominant. Members of the dominant categories (male, White, heterosexual, husband) typically can harness greater socio-cultural-linguistic resources to regulate sexual policies, laws, doctrines, and traditions that keep the members of the second terms (female, Black, homosexual, wife) in a subordinate position. Dominance, then, in the form of sexism, is written into marital property laws, woven into courting traditions, and built into the language of **romance**.

Feminists argue that sexism is neither natural nor benign, but an ideological state imposed, managed, organized, propagandized, and maintained by force. It is arguable that any socializing process creates structures that both limit and enable individuals, but not all such structures are oppressive. In oppressive systems one group is asymmetrically and unjustly disadvantaged to the benefit of another. Sexist ideology posits men as strong and aggressive, women as weak and passive. Thus, the male is to *act* as initiator in courtship, marriage proposals, and sex. The female's role is to *respond* to that which the male initiates.

One of the key theoretical advances aimed at mitigating sexist oppression came about in the 1970s through conceptualizing the distinction between sex (biological/ physiological differences of men and women) and gender (the differential socialization and cultural expectations that govern the acceptable behavior of men and women). Gendered expectations are essentialized notions of socially acceptable "feminine" and "masculine" behavior. Because gender is constituted within cultural norms, sex-marking and sex-announcing behaviors vary considerably not only between men and women, but among women in different countries, races, classes, religions, subcultures, and time periods. For instance, clothing is a primary sex-marking and sex-announcing convention in most societies, but the ways in which it has been used to do so have differed over time and geographical locations. In Asia both husbands and wives have worn pants for centuries, but men who wore pants in Greece and Rome were considered effeminate. By the fourth century women in the Western world were wearing pants, which they adapted from Persian clothing, but by the Middle Ages ladies exchanged their pants for dresses and their suitors wore the breeches. In the United States during the nineteenth century, proper ladies wore dresses except when horseback riding, when they wore trousers that were completely hidden by full skirts. During the same period, however, working class wives, laboring alongside their husbands in farming, mining, or ranching, wore trousers.

Gendered roles govern "appropriate" behavior in everything from **dating** and marriage to the freedom with which one may converse with in mixed groups. Because essentialized feminine behaviors elicit expectations of weakness, submission, and emotionality, rigid gender roles have restricted women's psychosocial, educational, and professional development throughout the twentieth century. Most professions, for instance, barred women (except for teaching and nursing) during the first half of the twentieth century. Not only were women denied intellectual development, but they had little recourse for supporting themselves financially, making heterosexual marriage a necessity for the vast majority of women. Furthermore, until the early 1970s, it was illegal in most U.S. states to prescribe contraceptives to single women or to married women without the husband's approval. Tied into a cycle of **pregnancy**, birth, lactation, and child rearing, married women had little time or energy for developing themselves intellectually or professionally.

Educational access often serves as a barometer for sexist attitudes. That is, in areas where male dominance is most pronounced women are denied equal opportunities in education. Alarming gender gaps persist to this day. In sub-Saharan Africa, South Asia, East Asia and the Pacific, 83 percent of girls do not attend school. In 2002, this translated into 24 million girls in sub-Saharan Africa and 23.5 million South Asian girls (http://www.scoop.co.nz/stories/WO0404/S00211.htm). Without an education, girls and women in these areas are particularly vulnerable to exploitation in sex trafficking. Those who escape **prostitution** have few options available to them outside of conventional heterosexual marriage.

Rigid **gender roles**, however, hinder more than heterosexual women's development. Proscriptions against same-sex attraction and gender expression that deviates from socially constructed norms marginalize lesbians, gay men, bisexuals, and transgender (LGBT) persons. In many societies they are endangered physically as well as emotionally. For example, **sodomy** is a crime in many countries in Africa, the Asian Pacific, and the Middle East with punishments varying from fines to imprisonment to death. Far more common than judicial punishment, however, are threats of violence from strangers, peers, or even family members and the difficulties of entering into long term loving relationships. Even in countries where same-gender civil unions or marriages are legal, sexist attitudes or assumptions remain, such as the expectation that one partner will be dominant or prohibitions against adoption by same-sex couples.

Gendered role expectations also inflict harm on heterosexual men. By limiting the expectations of the husband/father role to a sexually dominant breadwinner and "benevolent dictator," men often have difficulty forming emotionally stable and supportive relationships with women and developing into nurturing caregivers of their children. Because masculine expectations include strength, lack of emotion, control, and aggressiveness, men are expected to initiate sexual relationships. The social expectations for women are to be sexually passive, but responsible for emotional support and nurturing. This gendered division of emotional labor means that men frequently are unable to reciprocate with demonstrations of caring, leaving their partners emotionally bereft. Further, these men may allow themselves to be touched and cared for only during sexual intercourse.

Even though there is a great deal of variation in gendered roles among cultures, there are commonalities in sexist structures. Religious teachings generally fuel many sexist practices relating to sex and love. In Christianity, Judaism, and Islam, the husband is viewed as both the spiritual and actual head of the family, while the wife is expected to be modest, obedient, and subservient. Traditional Christian wedding vows solemnized this difference: the man promised to "love and protect" and the wife promised to "serve and obey."

However, religious tenets often become enshrined in cultural traditions and laws, taking on a life of their own quite apart from their religious foundations. Such has been the case with the man's role as head of household, which has been codified in ways that deviated substantially from "loving and protecting." In English Common Law, for instance, husbands could chastise wives "within bounds." Men were also exempt from accusations of spousal rape because the law provided that wives could not refuse sex with their husbands. This Common Law definition of rape remained in effect in the

United States until the 1970s, when many, but not all, states modified their rape statutes.

Similarly, teachings in the major religions of Christianity, Judaism, and Islam counsel women to be chaste. In many cultures, however, the virtue of chastity mutated into rites in which brides must prove their **virginity**. In some cultures it is still customary for relatives to inspect the bed clothes for blood following consummation of marriage as proof that the bride was a virgin, even when grooms are presumed to be sexually experienced.

In spite of the fact that social expectations regarding virginity have relaxed enormously in many Western countries, little has changed in countries where Islam is the predominant religion. Many Muslim women do not feel safe in public without wearing the burqa for fear of "inflaming men's lust." It is especially important for Muslim women to be circumspect because women who bring charges of rape risk counter-charges of adultery, punishable by stoning. Further, despite the Qur'an's teachings that husbands treat their wives with respect, there are thousands of reported cases of "bride burnings"—a form of domestic abuse often disguised as an accident or suicide. These women are burned to death over wealth because their husbands or in-laws are unhappy with the size of the dowry that accompanied them into the marriage. So, too, are instances increasing of so-called "honor killings," exacted by family members when women or girls are raped or commit **sex crimes**.

It would be a mistake to assume that all Islamic countries have responded to honor killings in the same way. Although most have no official state positions on this practice, Jordan, Morocco, and Syria legally sanction honor killings. On the other hand, Dubai integrates religious teachings into a thoroughly modern society, legally granting women equal justice under the law.

The effects of sexism remain especially pernicious in war-torn regions. Gender-based violence historically has been, and continues to be, integral to military conquests. During the 1990s women in the heavily militarized state of Chiapas, Mexico endured sexual harassment, rape, forced prostitution, and compulsory servitude in military camps. Systematic rape has been part of the war strategy in places like Bosnia and Darfur.

There is also a connection between natural disasters and sexual violence against women. A rise in gender-based violence ripples through communities around the world, as sexist dispositions consider violence toward women to be an acceptable way for men to relieve sexual tension. Consequently, while catastrophes like the Asian tsunami create vulnerability and stress for everyone, women are further threatened by the increased likelihood of male violence during crises.

Comprehending the limits that sexism imposes upon healthy development is the first step toward change. Because gender is both changing and changeable, social transformation of oppressive sexist institutions and practices is possible. Thus, altering the sexual socialization and educational experiences for both women and men can mitigate sexism and promote a healthier and more just world where romance and love are mutually expressed between two equal partners. *See also* Advertising; Fashion; Feminism; Humor; Men's Movement; Religions, Eastern; Religions, Western; Women's Movement.

Further Reading: Connell, Robert. *Masculinities*. Berkeley: University of California Press, 2005; Frye, Marilyn. "Oppression." In *The Politics of Reality: Essays in Feminist Theory*, 1–16. Freedom, CA: Crossing Press, 1983; Heldke, Lisa, and Peg O'Connor, eds. *Oppression, Privilege, and Resistance: Theoretical Readings on Racism, Sexism, and Heterosexism*. New York: McGraw-Hill, 2004; Lorde, Audre. "Sexism: An American Disease in Black Face." In *Sister Outsider*, 60–65.

Freedom, CA: Crossing Press, 1988; MADRE online. MADRE: Human Rights for Women Worldwide. See http://www.madre.org/articles/index.html. Descriptions of global activism for human rights for women and families, 2004.

Susan Birden

SEXOLOGY.   *See* Sexual Science/Sexology

SEXUAL ABUSE AND ASSAULT.   Sexual abuse and assault encompass a range of behaviors, considered both criminal and non-criminal, perpetrated against women, children, and men. Sexual abuse in which a child is raped or assaulted by an adult is a crime; however, similar behavior between siblings or between pre-adolescent peers is not. While sexual assault is defined by a single act of perpetrator against victim, typically sexual abuse presumes a relationship of domination/subordination involving more than one act, over time, in which real or perceived differentials of power and vulnerability exist. Children, the elderly, and the disabled/incapacitated are at greatest risk of sexual abuse because of their degree of vulnerability and dependence on others. Sexual abuse may involve physical force—but often victims are threatened, coerced, or manipulated by the perpetrator to engage in behavior against their will.

Sexual assault includes verbal, visual, or any behavior that compels (physically or psychologically) an individual to participate in unwanted sexual contact or attention, including inappropriate touching, vaginal, anal, and oral penetration, sexual intercourse, rape, attempted rape, child molestation, forced **prostitution**, voyeurism, exhibitionism, **incest**, stalking, and sexual harassment. Sexual assault may occur in many different situations involving a family member, a friend, an acquaintance, a date, or a stranger and does not discriminate on the basis of age, gender, class, marital status, or sexual orientation. Sexual assault is an act of violence imposed upon another; the victim is not responsible for the act nor is she or he to blame.

Data on **child abuse** is a difficult to ascertain given that children are often not able to describe an assault or to realize that what occurred may represent a sexual assault. In a representative sample of over 3,000 U.S. adults, roughly 12 percent of men and 17 percent of women, reported being touched before they reached puberty either by older adolescents (between fourteen and seventeen) or adults over the age of eighteen. For the women who reported being touched, the perpetrator was a male over eighteen in 63 percent of the cases. The most common sexual offense against the women respondents was genital touching (90 percent of the time), with kissing, oral sex, and vaginal intercourse occurring less frequently (31 percent, 10 percent, and 14 percent, respectively). In the same survey, more than one in five women and one in twenty men reported being forced to do something sexual as adults. The majority of sexual assault cases go unreported and, of those reported to police, an even smaller percentage are successfully prosecuted. Of the adults sexually touched as children, only one of four girls and one of six boys told someone. Among the minority of rapes reported to police, one out of two results in an arrest; 80 percent of those arrested are prosecuted; and approximately 60 percent of the prosecutions result in a conviction. Perpetrators of sexual assaults are overwhelmingly male. Of the women touched sexually as children, in only 4 percent of the cases was the perpetrator female. The only exception to the data that males are the perpetrators was in the reporting of cases of males touched as children; 45 percent of the time, the perpetrator was an adolescent female between fourteen and seventeen and 9 percent of the time a woman eighteen and over. Of the 4 percent of adult males who reported being forced to be sexual, the perpetrator was more likely to be male than female. Among the more than 20 percent of females who report being forced, the perpetrator was male nineteen out of twenty times. While males may be coerced sexually by females, the majority of cases of men who report sexual assaults are reporting an assault by another male.

Perpetrators of the sexual assaults of both men and women are generally known to the victim. Of those who sexually touch children, the perpetrator is a stranger to the child for fewer than 8 percent of girls and 5 percent of boys. The most likely perpetrator of a sexual assault of both boys and girls is an older relative or family friend. In the sexual assault of adults, the perpetrator is most likely someone with whom the victim is in love or knows very well.

Sexual assaults and rape are widespread across the globe. A cross-cultural analysis of ninety-five societies concluded that **gender-role** socialization and a hierarchical power structure of male dominance normalizes and perpetuates a social climate in which girls and women are conditioned to accept responsibility and assume blame for events in which they are sexually victimized. Many girls and women live in fear of being raped and, if victimized, minimize or deny the existence or degree of their trauma.

Due to the prevalence of female abuse and assault, the issue of sexual violence has frequently been portrayed as a women's issue. However, a shift in our understanding of sexual assault as primarily an act of aggression and violence rather than an act motivated by sexual need, in addition to recent changes in the legal definition of rape as anal or vaginal penetration by a penis, has expanded our awareness that boys, adolescent males, and men may also be victims of sexual abuse and assault. Data from Western and cross-cultural studies revealed that adolescent males reported having been coerced or forced into sexual relationships with older adult males, often by figures of authority in the community such as teachers, employers, religious leaders, or neighbors.

In nations that are experiencing social conflict or war, there is a greater likelihood of sexual abuse or assault. In World War I, the German army invaded Belgium and France and the rape of girls and women was widespread. During the World War II, the Jewish women in German-occupied territories were subject to rape and murder. The Japanese army sexually assaulted and raped women in China and Korea; often Chinese and Korean women were forced into **prostitution**, servicing Japanese soldiers. Members of the U.S. armed forces sexually assaulted and raped Vietnamese women during wartime. At the end of the twentieth century, rape was a part of armed conflicts in many parts of the world, including the genocidal war in Rwanda in which rape and murder of Hutu and Tutsi was widespread. From areas as varied as Kosovo, Congo, Darfur, and Iraq, there have been ongoing and continued reports of rape as occupiers sexually assault the citizenry of the occupied land.

Rates of coercive sex may increase as a result of economic and cultural factors. Forced marriages result in unwanted sex for young brides. In areas with high levels of poverty, women are coerced into sex in exchange for money or goods by older, wealthier males. Women from impoverished areas are offered remunerative jobs and, instead of receiving appropriate work, are forced into laboring as sex workers.

The consequences of sexual assault and rape may vary considerably depending on the age of the victim, the relationship to the perpetrator, the extent of physical violence and threat to life, and the context in which it occurs. Victims of childhood sexual abuse may report continuing and ongoing distress into adulthood that affects relationships and social functioning. Victims of sexual abuse and assault report more sexual partners and sexual variety coupled to less satisfaction in their sex lives. Acute stress reactions may include numbing, disorientation, withdrawal, and increased anxiety. Given their stage of development and because most perpetrators are male, some adolescent male survivors may experience confusion regarding sexual identity or engage in inappropriate attempts to reassert **masculinity** through increased aggressiveness and destructive or antisocial behavior. Some survivors of childhood sexual abuse and assault may exhibit traumatic sexualization in which they develop more liberal sexual attitudes and engage in more consensual sex at a young age which may increase their risk for re-victimization as adults. Adolescent males and females also are at greater risk of developing self-harming behaviors, eating disorders, and substance use disorders. Long after the initial event, some survivors may experience symptoms of post-traumatic stress disorder including flashbacks to the initial event while awake or nightmares while sleeping, increased anxiety and arousal, avoidance of stimuli that are reminiscent of the event, and disruptions in mood, behavior and relationships.

Cultural, socioeconomic, and political issues are essential realities in any discussion of preventing sexual abuse and assault. However, early education regarding non-consensual touch, an examination of gender prescriptions, and awareness of and attention to power imbalance between females and males in any society are important steps in affecting the occurrence of sexual violence. While resolution and healing from sexual abuse and assault is an individual and multidimensional process, some important aspects of recovery may include working through intense feelings associated with the abuse or assault; integrating the assault experience as an aspect, rather than a definer, of the survivor's life; accepting the reality of the assault and acknowledging the traumatic nature of the event; perceiving support from others; and finding positive meaning through the traumatic experience. *See also* Domestic and Relationship Violence; Infidelity/Extramarital Sex; Internet; Mental Health and Sex; Pederasty; Prisons, Sex in.

Further Reading: Brownmiller, Susan. *Against Our Will: Men, Women and Rape.* New York: Simon and Schuster, 1975; Finkelhor, David, and Patricia Y. Hashima. "The Victimization of Children and Youth: A Comprehensive Overview." In *The Handbook of Youth and Justice,* edited by Susan White, 49–78. New York: Kluwer Academic/Plenum, 2001; Jejeebhoy, Shireen J., and Sarah Bott. *Non-consensual Sexual Experiences of Young People: A Review of the Evidence from Developing Countries.* New Dehli: Population Council, 2003; Koss, Mary. "Acquaintance Rape: A Critical Update on Recent Findings with Application to Advocacy." http:vip.msu.edu/theCAT/CAT_Author/MPK/Colorado.html, 2000; Laumann, Edward O., John H. Gagnon, Robert T. Michael, and Stuart Michaels. *The Social Organization of Sexuality: Sexual Practices in the United States.* Chicago: The University of Chicago Press, 1994; Rape, Abuse, & Incest National Network (RAINN). http://www.rainn.org/statistics. The nation's largest anti-sexual assault organization and has been ranked as one of "America's 100 Best Charities" by *Worth* magazine; Sanday, Peggy R. *Female Power and Male Dominance: On the Origins of Sexual Inequality.* New York: Cambridge University Press, 1981; Whaley, Rachel B. "The Paradoxical Relationship between Gender Inequality and Rape: Toward a Refined Theory." *Gender and Society* 15 (2001): 531–55; Worell, Judith, and Pamela Remer. *Feminist Perspectives in Therapy: Empowering Diverse Women.* 2nd ed. Hoboken, NJ: Wiley, 2003.

Christopher Flynn and Karla Soukup

SEXUAL SCIENCE/SEXOLOGY.   Sexual science is the study of human sexuality. Also known as sexology, it refers to knowledge, attitudes, beliefs, feelings and/or behaviors in relation to biological sex/gender (male, female, intersexed), erotic/sexual orientation (what, who, when, how, people get "turned-on"), **gender roles** (masculine, feminine, both), and relationships with self and others. Although the terms are often used interchangeably, sexual scientists and sexologists usually approach the study of sexuality from different mindsets. Today, sexual scientists are generally trained and work in the natural sciences (biological and physical sciences) and use quantitative methods for their research. In contrast, researchers who identify as sexologists most often are educated in the humanities and work in the social sciences such as psychology, women's studies, and history, using qualitative methods. Since its inception, sexual science has been based upon and remains organized by the ideas and beliefs of Western scientific thought. However, in the United States, sexual science does not have full academic status, and no major degrees can be earned in this field of study.

Sexual science was established at the end of the nineteenth century. In Berlin, Iwan Bloch called for the creation of a multidisciplinary approach to the study of human sexuality. In establishing the field of sexual science/sexology, he included the term "love." Despite its inclusion, with the exception of Havelock Ellis, most researchers of the time such as Magnus **Hirschfeld**, Sigmund **Freud**, and Cleilia Mosher, emphasized studying sexual behaviors as problems and looked for a scientific understanding of them.

Today, most research about love is separate from research about sexuality. Biochemistry and neurosciences look at the ways in which the brain and the nervous system communicate with one another. Researchers such as Thomas Lewis and Helen Fisher, seeking to explain the process of love, employ biochemistry, neuroscience, and neuro-imagining (the study of the brain via high tech pictures). Some exceptions to the separation of love and sex research do exist, but one must look at a variety of resources outside the studies of sexuality such as *The Handbook of Sexuality in Close Relationships*.

Prior to World War II, sexological research was often undertaken to normalize a wide variety of sexual behaviors such as **homosexuality** and **masturbation**. This trend became more public with the establishment of the Kinsey Institute after the war and the publication of the infamous Kinsey reports. Alfred **Kinsey**, whose expertise was the scientific study of the gall wasp, began studying human sexuality based on questions raised (and the lack of research knowledge to answer them) through an undergraduate course he taught at Indiana University for married students or those contemplating **marriage**. This course began five years after Emily Mudd, in 1933, helped establish the Marriage Council of Philadelphia as a place to inform women about birth control and to develop a training program for those working in human relationships.

Although Kinsey was a progressive thinker, his work and that of **sex therapists** Masters and Johnson highlights a male bias that still exists in sexual science as well as a prejudice toward sexual behaviors which are quantifiable over the more complex understanding of human sexuality, including sexuality in relationships. The careers of these pioneering sexologists also illustrate the power of culture and **politics** as funding issues, media controversies, and religious backlash impacted their work.

Accompanying the growth of the field of sexual science, professional organizations were established in the United States. Although much overlap exists among groups, their differences illustrate particular purviews of sexology. Nevertheless, much of the widely disseminated research about sexuality remains concentrated on medical and biological explanations.

In 1957, the Society for the Scientific Study of Sex (SSSS) was founded to encourage the rigorous scientific study of sexuality. While this organization focused on research, seven years later, the Sexuality Information and Education Council of the United States (SIECUS) and its counterpart in Canada were established to provide the public access to sexual knowledge, lobbied for comprehensive sex education in schools and promoted access to information for professionals. Established in 1967, the American

Association of Sex Educators, Counselors, and Therapists (AASECT) promotes understanding about sexuality and certifies professionals working in education, research and psychotherapy. In contrast, the Society for Sex Therapy and Research (founded in 1975), is limited in scope to professionals who have clinical or research interests in human sexual concerns.

Other nationally based groups can be found in other regions of the world, including the Council for Education and Study on Human Sexuality which published *Sei-to-sei-no-kyouiku* (Human Sexuality and Education) in Japan, the Finnish Association of Sexology, and African Regional Sexuality Resource. There, too, is the World Association of Sexual Health, which was founded in Paris in 1978 as the World Association of Sexology, building upon the legacy of sexological congresses hosted by Hirschfeld and Moll before World War II. This organization's name change is an example not only of the prominence of focusing on physiological processes over psychosocial concerns but the influence of culture and politics on sexual science.

The emergence of organizations to fill gaps in content or to affect changes in the direction in sexual science was also evident in the formation of the National Sex Forum (NSF) in 1968. NSF, which reflects a humanistic approach to sexuality, expanded in the 1970s with the establishment of the Institute for Advanced Study of Human Sexuality. This private non-sectarian graduate school prepares sexologists through interdisciplinary study.

Scholarly journals were also established as a way to report, discuss, and distribute information about sexuality. The first journal, aptly named *Sexology*, was founded by Hirschfeld. It corresponded with the creation of the Institute for Sexual Science in Berlin and it remained in publication, in the United States, throughout the 1970's. Other organizations also publish journals like the *Archives of Sexual Behavior* (SSSS), the *Journal of Sex Education and Therapy* (AASECT), and *Contemporary Sexuality* (AASECT). In addition, due to the multi-disciplinary nature of sexology, other journals are dedicated exclusively to sexuality issues, including the *Journal of the History of Sexuality*, *Journal of Lesbian Studies*, and the *Journal of Sex Education*.

Also during the 1970s, the works of Michel Foucault and Luce Irigaray infused the burgeoning fields of women's studies, gender studies, and queer studies with the idea that sexuality and gender are concepts that are constructed differently across time and cultures. As a result of social construction theory as well as the research being generated by scholars from an array of academic disciplines, challenges to biological bias and heterosexism (a belief that all people are or should be heterosexual) in traditional sexological research flourished.

The impact of social construction upon the understanding of human sexuality continues to provide new areas of research. Thus, sexuality research is understood to occur in a variety of disciplines. In geography, for example, which is not often associated with sexuality, the emphasis on space and how all relationships (including those with people) are spatial, has brought insights into how spaces are sexualized through concepts like the "geography of **desire**," or studies of the geographic distribution of lesbian, gay, bisexual and transgender (LGBT) people.

However, due to a cultural bias that prefers natural science research (as compared to the humanities), sexuality researchers whose work favors biological and physical sciences are often touted as experts while other studies are often objected to as unscientific or ignored or simply dismissed. Especially within the multidisciplinary field of sexual science, it is important to approach it critically. Several critical questions should be considered when evaluating sex research: Was the research design adequate or appropriate for the research question? Who were the participants? What were the questions or measures used in the research? What do the results mean? Who funds the research? What are the motivations for the researchers in undertaking the project?

An example of the importance of using critical thinking to evaluate sexuality research comes from an analysis of the introduction of the drug Viagra at the end of the twentieth century for the treatment of **erectile dysfunction**. Evaluation of Viagra and the pharmaceutical industry also illustrates the complexities of sexuality as well as the conflicts that can occur in sexual science.

The original purpose of the research on Slidenafil Citrate (generic Viagra) was to look at its effects on chest pain. Scientists found the drug had little impact on heart pain but had a curious side effect—improving blood flow to the genitals. Improved blood flow to certain areas of the penis can result in erections. Having made this discovery about Slidenafil, researchers at Pfizer (the pharmaceutical company undertaking the original heart pain research) had to figure out what to do with the results. Researchers created a new study (to which they already had the answer) focused on sexual functioning to determine how often participants could achieve an erection adequate for intercourse and how often that erection was maintained after penetration.

Slidenafil Citrate (generic Viagra) does not produce erections. When accompanied by sexual stimulation, the drug can help facilitate erections. Despite this knowledge by the manufacturer, the drug has been presented to the general public as a pill that solves the problem of impotence (i.e., the inability to get an erection). In addition, a mass media campaign which launched the drug was aimed at changing the language of "sexual dissatisfaction to sexual dysfunction" (Loe 2004: 51). Thus, Viagra has been promoted as a drug that produces erections when the research indicates that what it actually does is help facilitate blood flow that, when combined with sexual stimulation, may result in erections. In spite of the inaccuracy of the message, a once flailing industry has become a multibillion dollar business.

This boost to the pharmaceutical industry occurred despite the knowledge that sexual functioning difficulties for men and women are often the result of physiological and/or psychological issues. A thorough critique of the Viagra research as well as the broader impact of the release of Viagra was undertaken by Leonore Tiefer and colleagues. In response to the limited and androcentric (male-centered) model being used by researchers and the pharmaceutical industry, Leonore Tiefer and other feminist researchers and practitioners established the campaign for "A New View of Women's Sexual Problems." Briefly noted, the New View promotes a broad, multidimensional understanding of issues pertaining to women's sexual functioning. Furthermore, this model offers a wide range of options to incorporate and/or modify changes in sexual functioning beyond the popping of a pill. Recently, this New View model has also been applied to males to promote a broader conceptualization of male sexual functioning.

Further Reading: Brown, Michael. "Geography." *GLBTQ Encyclopedia.* http://www .glbtq. com/social-sciences/geography.html, 2004; Bullough, Vern L. *Science in the Bedroom.* New York. Basic Books, 1994; Coleman, Eli. *Sexology and Sex Research: Towards an Interdisciplinary Study of Human Sexuality.* http://www.gfmer.ch/Medical_education_En/PGC_RH_2006/pdf/Sexology_research_Coleman_2006.pdf, 2006; FDA Talk Paper (March 27, 1998): http://www.fda.gov/cder/consumerinfo/viagra/; Frayser, Suzanne G., and Thomas J. Whitby. *Studies in Human Sexuality: A Selected Guide.* Littleton, CO. Libraries Unlimited, 1987; Harvey, John H., Amy Wenzel, and Susan Sprecher, eds. *The Handbook of Sexuality in Close Relationships.* Mahwah, NJ: Lawrence Earlbaum, 2004; Irvine, Janice. M. *Disorders of Desire.* Philadelphia: Temple University Press, 1990; Loe, Mieka. *The Rise of Viagra.* New York: New York University Press, 2004;

Magnus Hirschfeld Archive of Sexology. http://www2.hu-berlin.de/sexology. Includes information about the archives and its history, on-line course, critical dictionary on sexology, and surveys; Neil, James. *Qualitative versus Quantitative Debate.* http://www.wilderdom.com/research/QualitativeVersusQuantitativeResearch.html, July 5, 2006; Working Group on a New View of Women's Sexual Problems. "New View of Women's Sexual Problems." Vol. 3. http://www.ejhs.org/volume3/newview.htm, 2000; Ogden, Gina. *The Heart and Soul of Sex.* Boston: Shambhala, 2006; Reiss, I. "Evaluating Sexual Science: Problems and Prospects." *Annual Review of Sex Research X* (1999): 246–71; Wiederman, Michael, W. *Understanding Sexuality Research.* Belmont, CA: Wadsworth/Thompson Learning, 2001.

Lisa B. Schwartz

SEXUALLY TRANSMITTED DISEASES (STDs). *See* Sexually Transmitted Infections (STIs)

SEXUALLY TRANSMITTED INFECTIONS (STIs). Sexually transmitted infections (STIs), often interchangeably referred to as sexually transmitted diseases (STDs), were generally known in the early twentieth century as venereal diseases (VD) or social diseases, a metaphor for the moral decay of society. Change in the terminology to STDs in the latter half of the century concurred with medical advancements in diagnosis and treatment. More recently, the term STIs is used as it is inclusive of infections with or without symptoms, as many STIs in women are asymptomatic. The human immunodeficiency virus (HIV) and its resultant disease, **AIDS**, are included in this definition. STIs, described as a formidable enemy of the human race in the previous century, remain a major public health problem despite medical advances. STIs are about contagion and sex, fear and passion, hate and love —the fundamentals of being human. Notions of disease and sex are rooted in dimensions of culture and gender. The fear of contagion for a disease linked to sex often evokes social prejudices that act as a powerful force of exclusion, justified by social understandings of disease and acceptable sexual behaviors.

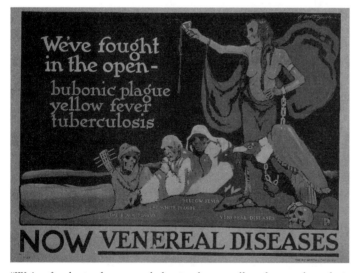

"We've fought in the open—bubonic plague, yellow fever, tuberculosis —now venereal diseases." Emaciated human figures, representing various diseases, cower beneath a partially nude female figure chained to a vulture, representing venereal disease, ca. 1918. Courtesy of Library of Congress.

STIs consist of 20 infections caused by bacteria (e.g., gonorrhea, syphilis, and chlamydia infections), viruses (e.g., HIV, herpes simplex, human papilloma, hepatitis B), fungi (e.g., candida albicans), or parasites (e.g., trichomoniasis). When left untreated, these may result in serious complications such as infertility, cancers, and death. These STIs cause a range of symptoms such as genital ulcers, genital warts, urethral and vaginal discharge, lower abdominal pain, and neonatal conjunctivitis. For pregnant women, STIs may cause stillbirths or blindness, lung damage, and death in the newborn. Importantly, the risk for HIV infection is increased by three to five times when other STIs are present.

Transmissions generally occur through the mucous membranes of the penis, vulva, and to a lesser extent the mouth, during vaginal, anal, and oral sex, or through any other activities between people where semen, vaginal fluids, saliva and/or blood are exchanged. Mother-to-child transmission accounts for most non-sexual transmission of STIs. Unprotected sex, multiple sex partners, and intravenous (IV) drug use are the main transmission modes. Substance use increases the likelihood of unprotected sex and indiscriminate sexual partner involvement.

STIs can be effectively managed through early diagnosis, treatment, and prevention and through maternal, child, and family planning services that includes antenatal syphilis screening. Clients with STIs are motivated to refer their sexual partners for treatment, and lately through patient-delivered partner therapy. STIs are diagnosed with blood tests that assist treatment. In contexts with limited laboratory facilities, STI treatment is based upon a diagnosis made from a group of symptoms and signs. Bacterial STIs are easily treated but virus infections remain incurable though symptoms are managed. The vaccines against hepatitis B and HPV are not available in resource-poor settings.

In many parts of the world today both socio-cultural and medical understandings of sex and disease shape the different responses to STIs. Disease is not only understood in terms of bio-medical "germ" theories, but may be viewed as a punishment for wrongdoing or caused by some mystically polluting force that has entered the body, and from which the body has to be cleansed. An STI may be interpreted as the result of the transgression of sexual taboos, the violation of cultural norms and values regarding sexual behavior, or bewitchment through sexual intercourse. These still common understandings inform various responses to symptoms and care like the use of laxatives, the washing of genitals with disinfectants or herbal concoctions, or having sex with a virgin. In South Africa, traditional healers are often consulted to address the causes of the STI while the health care system is sought to cure the symptoms. Some self-treatment and traditional practices may complicate diagnosis and delay medical treatment thereby increasing the likelihood of STI transmission to others and re-infection by an infectious partner.

Culture and religion define appropriate and acceptable expressions of sexuality and society sanctions those who transgress these moral codes and values. Social and cultural gender norms differentiate women from men and define the ways in which women and men should interact in society and with each other. In Western countries, Christianity's standard of heterosexual monogamous sexual partnership means that other expressions of sexuality are viewed as sinful or immoral. **Colonialism** imposed these standards on traditional societies in Africa and parts of Asia which practiced **polygamy** and other sexual practices. Today, in many societies cultural images of femininity and **masculinity** are dominated by fertility, male dominance, sexual prowess, and female submissiveness. This determines expressions of sexuality and meanings of STIs. For example, in early twentieth century Europe a STI was considered a rite of passage into manhood; it is still common worldwide. For women a STI might imply a failure to satisfy her sexual partner or denote promiscuous behavior on her part.

Twentieth century technological and medical advances brought increasing control over STIs. This commenced with the discovery of the bacteria causing syphilis in 1905, followed by the introduction of the Wasserman blood test for the diagnosis of syphilis. Salvarsan was first used for the treatment of syphilis in 1909 and the introduction of penicillin during World War II paved the way for effective antibiotic treatment for bacterial STIs.

Along with control of disease came greater control over human beings. The public health movements of the early twentieth century in Britain, United States, and Russia, advocating stronger STI control, were motivated by ideas of national and military efficiency as well as by gender and class issues. Medical treatment and moral instruction were central to VD control. Prostitutes (later called sex workers) were blamed for STI transmission and for the moral decay of society, while men were portrayed as the innocent victims. In China, for instance, **prostitution** was banned in 1949 when the Communist Party gained power, and through punitive control China was declared VD-free in 1964 until the post-Maoist era. Such attempts to regulate prostitution failed and consideration of the social causes of STIs ignored. However, women, young women, and sex workers continue to be blamed for STIs, particularly in contexts where great gender disparities pertain. STIs continue to be tainted with ideas about wrongdoing and risk emerging from socio-cultural and medical understandings, ignoring that STIs are often acquired through mutually pleasurable and loving sex.

The latter half of the twentieth century has been described as a permissive sexual era characterized by the early onset of sexual intercourse, widespread youth sexual activity, and an acceptance of **premarital sex**. As advances in medical technology that managed the negative consequences of sexual behavior occurred, sexual activity was not exclusively for the purpose of reproduction. The introduction of chemical contra-ceptives in the 1960s was a turning point for women and contributed to the emancipation of female sexuality. Men's greater sexual freedom over women also declined with the growing women's movement as tolerance increased for alternative sexual expressions with the advent of the **gay and lesbian movement**. The revolution in sexual attitudes and behaviors witnessed in Europe and the United States soon extended to other parts of the world.

STI incidences worldwide mirrored these changes. However, these were not equally distributed across societies. The World Health Organization (WHO 2001) estimated that of the 340 million new cases of curable STIs that occurred worldwide in 1999, the largest number were in South and Southeast Asia, sub-Saharan Africa, Latin America and the Caribbean. The poor, women, MSWM, IV drug users, and young people are most vulnerable.

Women in sub-Sahara Africa, India, and parts of Asia, in particular, are disproportionately infected and affected by STIs, stemming mostly from gender inequalities and poverty. Their subordinate status limits their ability to negotiate condom use, or to claim monogamy, or safer sex from their partners. Inequalities often bring economic exclusion because of limited access to education and employment opportunities and force destitute women into sex work or the engagement in transactional sex for food and shelter for themselves and their children. Gender-based violence, unsuccessful partner referrals, limited access to condoms, and associations of disease with a lack of trust or love further increased vulnerability to STIs.

When people are unable to access relevant information or health care services due to social prejudice, age, or poverty, early diagnosis and treatment of STIs are delayed and there is a greater risk for the development of complications. Prevailing social prejudices against **homosexuality** and IV drug use, for instance, can prevent people from seeking health care because of a fear of stigma and discrimination. Because youth sexual activity is often frowned upon, young people might not have adequate access to health information or be able to access condoms and youth-friendly health care services. Poverty, too, largely limits health services, such as ineffective antenatal syphilis screening, and restricts availability of drugs that contribute to STI complications.

The practice of safer and protected sex is vital in preventing STIs. Current global control is driven by a strong public health agenda prescribed by the WHO. Better epidemiological data and more surveillance of STIs and sexual behaviors will identify those who engage in risky behaviors and better enable effective public health strategies. These, however, are often challenged by the social and interpersonal dynamics of sexual relationships and the socio-cultural contexts that shape individual responses to STIs. In southern Africa, for instance, attempts to link condom use with love and care of partner have not yet yielded the desired effects. Nonetheless, some success has been achieved by control strategies in the developing world, as curable bacterial STIs started to decline from 1993.

The twenty-first century has witnessed shifts from bacterial to viral etiology of STIs while ulcers of herpetic origin dominate in the developing world. Further, the control over STIs offered by medical science is diminishing as drug-resistant bacterial strains are introduced in more and new communities through globalization and virus infections remain incurable. While new antimicrobial agents, microbicides, and effective vaccines are urgently needed, STIs continue to be influenced by driving social forces that support the cycle of STI vulnerability: prejudice, gender inequality, and poverty. *See also* Drugs and Alcohol; Religions, Western; Sex Education; Sexism.

Further Reading: Centre of Disease Control. http://www.cdc.gov/std/default/htm. Range of information about STIs; DeMaria, Alfred. "Challenges of Sexually Transmitted Disease Prevention and Control." *Clinical Infectious Diseases* 41 (2005): 804–7; Evans, David. "Tackling the 'Hideous Scourge': The Creation of the Venereal Disease Treatment Centers in Early Twentieth-Century Britain." *Social History of Medicine* 5, no. 3 (1992): 413–33; Hart, Graham, and Kaye Wellings. "Sexual Behaviour and Its Medicalisation in Sickness and in Health." *British Medical Journal* 324 (2002): 896–900; Meyer-Weitz, Anna, Priscilla Reddy, Wies Weijts, Bart van den Borne, and Gerjo Kok. "The Socio-Cultural Contexts of Sexually Transmitted Diseases in South Africa: Implications for Health Education Programmes." *AIDS CARE* 10, no. 1 (1998): S39–55; Meyer-Weitz, Anna, Priscilla Reddy, Bart van den Borne, Gerjo Kok, and Jacques Pietersen. "Determinants of Multi-Partner Behaviour of Male Patients with Sexually Transmitted Diseases in South Africa: Implications for Interventions." *International Journal of Men's Health* 2, no. 2 (2003): 149–62; Schmid, George, Richard Steen, and Francis N'Dowa. "Control of Bacterial Sexually Transmitted Diseases in the Developing World Is Possible." *Clinical Infectious Diseases* 41 (2005): 1313–15; Wasserheit, Judith N. "Epidemiological Synergy—Interrelationships between Human Immunodeficiency Virus Infection and Other Sexually Transmitted Diseases." *Sexually Transmitted Diseases* 19, no. 2 (1992): 61–77; World Health Organisation. *Global Prevalence and Incidence of Selected Curable Sexually Transmitted Infections.* 2001. http://www.who.int/hiv/pub/sti/who_hiv_aids_2001.02.pdf, 2001.

Anna Meyer-Weitz

SOCIOBIOLOGY. Sociobiology and evolutionary psychology are a broad area of interest concerned primarily with the study of mind and behavior as they evolve through time for the survival and success of the individual in his/her social, cultural, and physical environments. Sociobiology can be conceptualized in terms of evolutionary theory, inclusive fitness theory, and natural selection theories. Natural selection is a powerful driving force that ensures the survival and success of living organisms. However, the principles of evolution cannot only be applied to biological processes but social psychological ones as well, such as love and mate selection. During the past several decades, the sociobiological perspective on love has gained increased attention and states that cross-culturally, human beings are governed by principles of attraction and mate selection that focus on the conception, birth, and survival/success of their children. Sociobiology, thus, uses principles of biological evolution and natural selection to understand human social behaviors.

According to traditional sociobiological conceptions in mate selection, marital bonding, and family formation, males tend to prefer female marital partners based primarily on the latter's degree of physical attractiveness and their biological readiness for successful pregnancy and birth. Females, on the other hand, tend to prefer male marital partners who are good financial/material providers. This, according to sociobiologists, is a stable marital/familial pattern that has evolved through thousands of years to ensure female impregnation, successful birth, and the survival/success of children.

Even though **homosexuality**, at first glance, does not fit into the sociobiological conceptions of mate selection, marital bonding, and family formation outlined above—since gay and lesbian couples are only able to have children through adoption or artificial insemination—it, too, conforms to general sociobiological premises. For example, in their daily interactions and routines, most gay and lesbian couples are identical to heterosexual couples although more equitable and less traditional. Gay and lesbian partners' cohabiting, marital, and family bonds are dependent on their level of interpersonal commitment for prolonged monetary, material, emotional, and sexual investment in their relationship. This, in turn, ensures their survival and success as a marital unit and even as a familial one in case of children.

Most sociobiological conceptions use natural selection processes to explain change over time. Evolutionary or Darwinian-based theories are determined by three interacting principles of change: variation, selection, and retention. In the social psychological process of love, mate selection, and **dating**, variation is exposing oneself to a pool of available mates, either directly through face-to-face interaction settings, such as those of work, school, and leisure or virtually through an artificial/symbolic medium, such as a personal computer as in the case of cyberdating. Selection refers to the process of successfully choosing an appropriate partner from the large number available in natural or virtual environments. Various courting mechanisms, learned through socialization, aim at maximizing rewards, such as physical attractiveness, sexual satisfaction, and money/material goods. Using effective strategies to successfully carry out and complete the dating process is an example of retention. This may occur first virtually, by taking advantage of the many benefits offered by virtual nearness in the **Internet** environment, and then in actual face-to-face interactions.

Prior to the cyberdating revolution, from colonial times up until the beginning of the twentieth century, most courtship and dating were done under the close scrutiny and control of the family. Although prospective spouses met and engaged in some fun activities, they were under the watchful eyes of their elders, who prohibited any form of sexual activity. The advent of new technology, particularly the telephone and the automobile, revolutionized the courtship and dating process. Youth were now free to talk to and get to know each other for long periods of time as well as drive away from the scrutiny of parents and relatives. This resulted in the dramatic increase in the frequency of sexual intimacies, such as petting and intercourse. This freedom to court, date, and even engage in some forms of light-core sexual intimacies was amplified by the rise of individualism and material culture, the decrease of religiosity, and the rise of the entertainment culture. For example, young people started frequenting dance halls, bars, and clubs for late night sensual dancing while listening to the tunes of revolutionized beats of **popular music**, such as those of rock and roll. They also began to smoke and drink, attend the **cinema**, and wear fashionable clothing and **cosmetics**. All of these contributed to a more liberal dating ethic.

The evolution of the dating process extends back to prehistoric times whereby daily living was largely nomadic in nature and survival-oriented. As such, the process of interpersonal mating developed on an episodic basis whereby individuals paired just to satisfy their instinctual drives for sexual gratification and procreation. With the passage of time, however, and as stable agrarian-oriented societies evolved, episodic instinctual/gratification oriented mating turned mimetic whereby the focus of attention evolved from the environment to the physical body and personhood. As individuals found themselves in stable dwellings in small settlements, they had more time to interact with each other, thereby developing stable patterns of social interaction. These patterns, in turn, were replicated and passed on from one person, and one generation, to another through mimicking. Agrarian living was more stable in terms of its physical locale, increased probabilities for individual survival and success, and allowed more time for bodily concerns. For example, individual mating was not randomly determined based on the environmental availability of mates but was organized around rituals involving elaborate props, dance, body paints, costumes, and artifacts. These mating ceremonial practices were, in turn, encoded in memory and biologically transmitted from one generation to the next. This began the evolution of the dating culture.

As these agrarian cultures evolved into kingdoms and empires, highly sophisticated communicative systems of shared meanings, known as language, emerged. Oral and written communication, in turn, facilitated the evolution of detailed cultural systems of mores, norms, and folkways. These provided a set of dos and don'ts related to interpersonal relationships, including mating and dating. For example, various spoken and unspoken rules and regulations evolved about who, when, and how to date/marry, the details of the marital ceremony and contract, the nature of the couple's sexual life, the birth and raising of children, inheritance rules, relationships with in-laws, relatives, and friends. The mating, dating, and marital processes were no longer left to the environmental whims of physical presence/availability and satisfaction/satiation of instinctual drives (as in prehistoric episodic clans). Neither were they left to reproduction and the acting out of simple rituals of the body (as in primitive mimetic tribes).

Mythic cultures and societies thus have evolved to present-day postmodern, postindustrial service-oriented symbolic cultures characterized by an almost exponential increase in both hard and electronic copy informational knowledge. The widespread and relatively inexpensive availability of reliable mechanical and electronic machinery and devices, coupled with the presence of effective and efficient transportation systems, reduced work hours and increased disposable income, material comforts, and luxuries. These, in turn, significantly contributed to the evolution of highly individualistic pleasure-oriented cultures of painless problem resolution and short-term gratification. In such cultures, impersonal communication through such means as telephones, cell phones, text messages, emails, chatrooms, message boards, and Web cams (initially starting out as viable tools to meet the demands of fast-paced modern living) have gradually evolved to become dating tools.

Through sociobiology, we can conceptualize the use of the personal computer as a sophisticated written and pictorial communicative means to our evolutionary end of emotional, psychological, and reproductive survival. Through the widespread availability of such **media**, individuals can satisfy their emotional and psychological needs for interpersonal relatedness and sexual gratification virtually and sometimes even anonymously. Here begins the evolution of the culture of cyberdating with virtual nearness as its major characteristic.

Virtual nearness tends to increase the frequency of contact between prospective cyberdaters and, by extension, the degree of their exposure to one another. In turn, the more their online exposure, the more likely it becomes for them to exchange positive cyberdating interactions and evaluations. Here, interactivity is the direct digital interface between a cyberdater and a cyberdating system in order to bring about some on-screen change. Such change takes place by bringing up the personal profiles of cyberdaters who subscribe to that particular site, screening these profiles according to the initial cyberdater's tastes and preferences, and viewing different texts, pictures, and video clips for closer inspection and final mate selection.

Within a virtual dating environment users feel as if they are transported into a real-life dating scene, a phenomenon known as telepresence, where they experience time distortion and enjoyment. This creates flow experience: losing oneself in cyberspace whereby the cyberdaters become so taken by the flow of their romantic inclinations and online actions that they forget who they are and how long they have been logged in. To facilitate a sense of flow, online cyberdating site creators go to great lengths to make their web sites appealing, stimulating, and responsive to cyberdaters.

Cyberdating may be particularly appealing to special populations, such as shy individuals, physically, emotionally, or psychologically challenged persons (due to short-term or chronic health conditions or old age), or people living in rural areas. For such populations, cyberdating becomes an effective means to their dating ends by allowing them to have access to a relatively large population of potential dates with the added advantage that they can get to know each other in relative anonymity.

Since cyberdating encounters are anonymous and the physical presence of the individuals is not required, physical personhood is substituted for a constructed virtual self. This self-fluidity of selfhood, in turn, allows the person behind the computer screen to be anything or anyone he/she wants. This results in the construction of exaggerated or even grossly false projections of the cyberdaters' true selves bringing about all sorts of misunderstandings. Since cyberdaters ultimately meet person-to-person, they may be disappointed to find that their virtual partner fails to fulfill physical, psychological, or emotional expectations. In some cases, the cyberdaters' exaggerations and lies may even serve more sinister purposes of financial or sexual exploitation or even abuse. Nevertheless, the projection of different virtual selves may prove beneficial by providing cyberdaters with the short-term psychological satisfaction of being the center of attention and perhaps even admiration from others, who, in real life, they may not have been able to attract as potential dating partners.

Overall, cyberdating allows individuals to search for and secure emotionally, psychologically, and sexually satisfying relationships with potential dating partners and increase their chances for reproductive survival. As individuals become increasingly affected by technology, they will continue to pursue cyberdating at even greater rates, employing the quickly evolving technological means to their dating and marital ends. This will result in their being exposed to a wider population of potential dating and marital partners not only more broadly within their societies and cultures but across others as well. Therefore, rates of **interracial/ethnic relationships**, marriages, and births are likely to increase with significant sociobiological changes in the make up of the genetic pool. Evolutionarily speaking, this will result in the creation of future non-homogenous, non-indigenous generations of individuals who will be biologically better fit in terms of physical attractiveness, intelligence, physical health, and resistance to illness.

Further Reading: Buss, David. 1999. *Evolutionary Psychology*. Boston, MA: Allyn & Bacon, 1999; Caporael, Linda. "Evolutionary Psychology: Toward a Unifying Theory and a Hybrid Science." *Annual Review of Psychology*, 52 (2001): 607–28; Center for Evolutionary Psychology. http://www.psych.ucsb.edu/research/cep/index.html. A web site dedicated to linking the largest and most active communities of researchers in evolutionary psychology; Csikszentmihalyi, Mihaly. *Beyond Boredom and Anxiety: Experiencing Flow in Work and Play*. San Francisco: Jossey-Bass, 2000; Darwin, Charles. *The Expression of the Emotions in Man and Animals*. Chicago: Chicago University Press, 1965.

Andreas G. Philaretou

SODOMY. Sodomy may be defined as sexual intercourse between two people involving anal or oral copulation, though it frequently refers to anal sex between two men and is often used synonymously with homosexual sex. The term "sodomy" has a long history as an indicator of sexual activity; its genesis extends even further back. While North Americans generally are familiar with the Hebrew Bible's injunctions said to be directed against **homosexuality**, the ancient Greek understanding of sexual behavior was quite different in its openness to same-sex behavior, despite its gendered nature. Biblical passages have been the main reference for condemnation of sodomy as well as homosexuality in the Western tradition, including in the United States today, given its religious traditions. Nonetheless, Western civilization has had an alternative approach to human sexuality that emphasized intimate friendship rather than carnal relations, though it was displaced by Western Christianity and was not to be recaptured until the nineteenth century by literary figures and early sex researchers.

According to the French philosopher and historian of ideas Michel Foucault, "homosexuality" did not exist prior to the nineteenth century, because it was not until then that this term or discourse about sexuality in general was invented. This neologism entailed that one who engages in sodomy was a specific type of person, a sodomite, whose character and/or moral worthiness are determined by his engaging in this sexual activity, making him ripe for clinical intervention. The implication of this is that, prior to late modernity, persons were not understood to have a sexuality, and their personalities were not sexualized.

Indeed, in Western civilization, generally only male-female intercourse was considered sexual behavior, while all other forms of behavior involving the genitals were regarded as non-sexual though they were often given a moral valence, usually subsumed under the category of sin in the Western, Christian tradition. The predominant sin at issue was sodomy, coined by Peter Damian, an eleventh century monk and theologian, specifically to refer to any illicit sexual activity among the clergy, a term that down through the centuries has come more narrowly to refer to a specific sexual act—anal intercourse—between two males. Damian chose the appellation sodomy because, he thought, only the specter of a terrible fate such as befell biblical Sodom would deter men of religious orders who, despite having taken a vow of celibacy, continued to engage in sexual activity with women. Hence, a geographical place reference became transformed into a term to indicate illicit carnal activity, and this found its way into church law, which itself found its way into common law.

In early modern European society sodomy was deemed a crime; it was punishable by death in Britain, for example. The *locus classicus* in Anglo-American law regarding sodomitical behavior is William Blackstone's 1769 *Commentaries on the Laws of England*, Volume 2, Book IV, Chapter 15, which refers to "the infamous crime against nature … an offense of so dark a nature … the very mention of which is a disgrace to human nature … a crime not fit to be named." Blackstone's *Commentaries* were a part of the common law tradition the American colonies inherited from England, and maintained in great measure until well into the 1800s.

As law in the United States became increasingly codified into statutes, and many common law notions discarded, the crime of sodomy was widely maintained, though to indicate illicit, not specifically homosexual sexual activity that occurred secondarily alongside other crimes, such as rape and public sex. Perpetrators of sodomy did not come to be regarded as particular types of people until religious discourse gave way to the medical discourse of psychology, emerging in the late nineteenth century. That a private sexual act of anal intercourse between two consenting males caused physical, palpable injury was never the motive for these laws; rather, it was to indicate a moral preference in the law for certain sexual activities and, now by implication, certain persons—heterosexual persons—who, presumably, did not perform acts of sodomy, or any sexual acts outside of **marriage**.

The scientific understanding of homosexuality was at its most advanced in Weimar Germany, where Magnus **Hirschfeld**'s Scientific-Humanitarian Committee compiled innumerable studies in the new field of sexuality. Most of these were destroyed in 1933 in a Nazi backlash against the social activism associated with this research intended to provide a rational basis for the elimination of the infamous Paragraph 175, a statute against same-sex activity. Homosexual sexual activity was decriminalized first in Denmark in 1930 and in Sweden in 1944. Criminal sanctions very gradually came to be seen as irrational and inhumane in much of Europe, mostly through court rulings as legislators were disinclined to go against popular opinion despite well-known reports such as the 1955 British Wolfenden Report's recommendations against continuing to discriminate against consensual homosexual acts.

During the period of the 1950s and 1960s scientific research resumed, casting long-entrenched social understandings of sexuality into considerable doubt, especially the notion of sexual deviancy. This gradually brought homosexuality into respectability in terms of a research topic, and gay and lesbian persons into some measure of self-respect from which they could further advance their legal and political claims, and live their lives more openly. During the 1970s viable and enduring homosexual communities were established in North America and Europe, in which gay men and lesbians could assert membership and pride as valued citizens. The spirit of the **gay and lesbian movement** was one of liberation from social strictures. In the academy, sexuality studies emerged and theoretical focus was turned away from explaining homosexuality and toward the nature of social prejudice directed against gays and lesbians. Nevertheless, laws against sodomy remained on the books throughout the United States and in many countries, where they were used at will to discriminate against suspected gay individuals, whose private lives often were ruined by public exposure or by the threat of **scandal**.

Public opinion gradually changed to view homosexuality as a normal manifestation of human sexuality, and gays and lesbians as just as worthy of civil liberties and civil rights protections as any other group of American citizens. The constitutional protection of privacy in the United States was viewed as especially important; many gay rights activists advocated that securing protection for private consensual sexual activity between adults would fit in nicely with emerging privacy law. Nonetheless, though sodomy laws were struck from the books in several states, starting with Illinois in 1960, they remained in many other states and frequently specified sodomy as between two members of the same gender, activity that is non-procreative.

Gay liberation alongside lesbian **feminism** took root in European countries such as in Scandinavia, The Netherlands, Germany, Italy, and France, during the 1970s and 1980s, promoting civil rights for gay persons. The last two decades of the twentieth century witnessed the decriminalization of homosexual activity between consenting adults, which Canada had already done in 1969 and which 15 European Union states accomplished by the year 2000, with the United Kingdom and several former Soviet states in eastern Europe following suit shortly thereafter. The 1996 constitution of South Africa, that shares the United States's inheritance of British common law, was the first in the world to recognize gay rights. The emergence of the European Union and with it the Treaty of Amsterdam, implemented in May 1999, included Clause 13, which banned discrimination on the basis of sexual orientation.

The onset of **AIDS/HIV** in the early 1980s was catastrophic for the gay and lesbian community, though in time the community was strengthened by it and its effects reversed—with the exception, of course, of the hundreds of thousands of lives lost to this disease. One curious matter about the early understanding of AIDS is that it was seen through the lens of gay male sexual promiscuity. Thus, the disease was not merely medicalized, but moralized as well, with some viewing it a natural consequence of unnatural sexual activity, or even a punishment from God. Although there are still persons who identify or justify AIDS as God's wrath, many members of religious communities have responded with grace and charity to the suffering of their fellow human beings, with the side-effect of triggering many denomination-wide conversations regarding the status of gay persons in this or that religious community, and in the eyes of the god they worship.

In the United States the gay and lesbian movement suffered some of its greatest defeats and victories. The U.S. Supreme Court's 1986 ruling on the Georgia sodomy statute in *Bowers v. Hardwick* had effects on the continuing failure to get the federal *Employment Non-Discrimination Act* passed through the United States Congress and on passage of the *Defense of Marriage Act* in 1996. These weighed against social acceptance of gay and lesbian people and their families because of this close identification of gay persons with an illegal activity.

In 1986, the Supreme Court was faced with the question of whether Georgia's sodomy statute was constitutional. The statute was gender neutral and made no distinction between heterosexual and homosexual sodomy or between single and married couples. In its 5–4 decision, the Court found that there was no constitutional right to homosexual sodomy, yet asserted that the statute could not be enforced as written against heterosexual couples owing to the violation of constitutionally protected privacy rights. The Court held that popular morality alone can provide the basis for a law and the nation's Christian inheritance proscribed sodomy. This ruling—for which the non-legal rationale was provided in a concurring opinion by Chief Justice Burger, who cited the Christian Bible as well as Blackstone—made possible the identification in the law of homosexual behavior and homosexual persons, the presence of one signaling the presence of the other, completely reducing the person to a sexual act, which this decision stated could be criminalized. Therefore, the hard-won gains in understanding and legal protection of prior decades were jeopardized, since to protect a gay person or confer a benefit upon him or her could be construed as protecting a criminal or condoning criminal behavior in any state that had a law against sodomy.

It was not until the 2003 Supreme Court's recent decision in *Lawrence v. Texas* that *Bowers v. Hardwick* was finally overturned, depriving states of the power to criminalize consensual sodomy among couples of any sexual orientation due to the invasion of privacy and the liberty interests entailed. In *Lawrence v. Texas* the Supreme Court further eroded the idea still ensconced in the laws of thirteen states that popular morality alone can provide a legitimate basis for law, here, against sodomy. The Court in *Lawrence* overturned the earlier *Bowers* decision by ruling that Texas's anti-sodomy statute, which penalized only same-sex sodomy, was an unconstitutional invasion of privacy and a violation of the guarantees of equal protection.

The decision in *Lawrence* to strike down sodomy statutes reflects profound changes in U.S. society, at least in its legislation and jurisprudence, where anti-gay bias once had official sanction that could be relied upon in the absence of sound public policy analysis or legal argument. It is no longer sufficient to claim an anti-gay bias, regardless of how widely it may still be shared among the citizenry, as a cover for legislation that burdens gay persons. This has rendered gay persons more equal subjects of the law, and no longer simply and without question the object of punitive measures or other derogations based on their sexual activities, including sodomy.

Numerous nations in the developing world continue to proscribe sodomy or homosexuality, often providing brutal punishments including death for gay persons in some Muslim countries such as Pakistan, Iran, and Saudi Arabia. Approximately 19 states in Africa continue to proscribe homosexual sexual activity in their law, many doing so only for sodomy between men. *See also* Morality and Ethics; Pederasty; Politics; Puberty and Puberty Rituals; Religions, Eastern; Religions, Western; Sex Crimes; Sexual Science/Sexology.

Further Reading: Foucault, Michel. *The History of Sexuality. Volume I: An Introduction.* Translated by Robert Hurley. New York: Vintage/Random House, 1990; Hartman, Keith. *Congregations in Conflict: The Battle Over Homosexuality.* New Brunswick, NJ: Rutgers University Press, 1996; Jordan, Mark D. *The Invention of Sodomy in Christian Theology.* Chicago: University of Chicago Press, 1997; Pronk, Pim. *Against Nature? Types of Argumentation Regarding Homosexuality.* Translated by John Vriend. Grand Rapids, MI: Eerdmans, 1993; Sodomy Laws. http://www.sodomylaws.org.

Gordon A. Babst

SPORTS. Sports have become a worldwide phenomenon attracting people worldwide as spectators and participants. The relationship between sport, love, and sexuality has been present throughout the twentieth century—reinforced by the shifting social and cultural milieu of the time. Over the past century, as cultural norms for sex and love have evolved, so have sports and athletics. Athletic participation, sports, and sexuality have influenced one another. This influence is evident by the emerging role of the athlete as a sex symbol, the increasing number of women in sports, and an increase in public interest in and perceptions of the role of **masculinity** and femininity in sports. The common factor among athletics, transcending **race** or class, is the sexual images associated with sport participation. Although much has changed in the culture of sports, sex and love have mutually evolved, becoming more present in the social norms and patterns of societies. The omnipresence of sex in society, particularly in the United States, has allowed for more dialogue and openness about sexuality, creating an environment in sports that forces athletes to confront their sexuality, sexual behaviors, and sexual images.

Sports, sexuality, and love are intricately connected and this interaction can be complex due to increased feelings of love and **romance** that often emerge between players and with players and their coaches, which can have a lasting and transformative impact. The relationship between sports, love, and sex is seen and felt in many countries, among men and women, and within different cultures and ethnicities. Because the United States is home to many prominent professional sports leagues for men, such as the National Football League, and due to its racial and ethnic diversity, the cross-cultural influence is particularly evident in U.S. amateur and professional sports.

Track and field Olympic gold medalist Mildred Babe Didrikson pitches for New Orleans of the Southern Association against the Cleveland Indians, 1934. © AP Photo.

The most striking transformation of both sports and sex has been the increasing participation of women and girls and the clear shift in perceptions of the female role in society. In the early 1900s, women's development in sports was characterized by specific events that exhibited strength and activity, two otherwise non-feminine characteristics. In 1900, the first 19 women competed in three sports (tennis, golf, and croquet) at the Olympic Games in Paris, France. Margaret I. Abbot was the first American woman to win an Olympic gold medal in golf. Three years later, Eleanor Roosevelt enrolled in the Junior League of New York where she taught calisthenics and dancing to girls.

Despite the distinct accomplishments of certain women and emerging groups of women teams, physical educators of that era strongly opposed competition and intense activity for women, fearing that it would make them less feminine, less desirable to men, and damage their female reproductive organs. Following this philosophy, in 1914, the American Olympic Committee formally forbade women's athletic competition in the Olympics, making the floor exercise the only exception (but women had to wear long skirts).

This was not enough to prevent the rise of women in sports. In that same year the first national swimming championships for women were held by the Amateur Athletic Union. Slowly, women became integrated in the world of activity and sports, participating in golf, tennis, swimming, and bowling. The Women's International Bowling Congress, founded in 1916, became the oldest and largest women's sports organization in the world. Other accomplishments made way for women's involvement in a variety of activities, such as Bessie Coleman becoming the first African American licensed pilot in 1921.

Gradually and across the globe the movement of women into sports was characterized by a larger social movement propelled by the women themselves. Banned from the Olympic Games, a group of French women staged their version of international games for women, the *Jeux Olympiques Feminine du Mond*. In 1921, 300 women from five countries competed in track and field as well as basketball. The resistance to the integration of women in sports continued, however, and, in 1931, the

American Baseball Commissioner banned women from professional baseball after 17-year-old pitcher Virne Beatrice "Jackie" Mitchell struck out Babe Ruth and Lou Gehrig in an exhibition game. Baseball, the Commissioner decreed, was "too strenuous" for women; the ban lasted until 1992.

Still, female athletes emerged, the most famous being Babe Didrikson who was accomplished in just about every sport. Many sports writers condemned her for being too "manly." In fact, Didrikson's success in athletics and sport earned her number ten ranking among North American athletes of the twentieth century by Sports Century. However, as early as 1930, and to some extent continuing through the late 1950s, women's roles were still defined by feminine qualities and their various responsibilities as caregivers for their husbands and families. The emergence of female athletes called into question those qualities and provoked much social criticism. Didrikson competed at a time when women's roles were just beginning to evolve from "homemakers" defined by their roles as wives and mothers, to a period when some women preferred to be known for their independence and individuality. Still, in many parts of the world, women still serve domestic needs. Therefore, participating in sports is not an option, as this would be considered the "father's" role in the family, and inconsistent with what is acceptable behavior for a wife and mother.

What Babe Didrikson accomplished as an individual woman in sports, the passage of Title IX accomplished for women collectively. Passed in 1972, Title IX governs the overall equity of treatment and opportunity in education and prohibits the exclusion of participation in a federally funded activity based on sex. The most significant impact of this law has been in athletics and Title IX has provided girls and women at all levels of education the opportunity to participate in sports which, in turn, has helped the public accept and prepare for the developing professional leagues for women.

As the boundaries for women in sports became more permeable, the restrictions toward women's sexuality were also challenged. This occurred in two distinct ways. Some females violated the qualities of femininity with more masculine behaviors. These athletes, such as tennis star Billie Jean King, did not adhere to the strict stereotypes of femininity and did not cater to their external image in traditional feminine ways. At the same time, women challenged the notion that sports were damaging to women's femininity. A talented and skilled female athlete could be successful in athletics while maintaining her femininity. In the 1968 Winter Games, for instance, Peggy Fleming won the gold medal in the free-skating program, instantly becoming an icon for the beautiful female athlete. This idea of traditional femininity existing with athleticism opened the door for the possibility of the sexual athlete, the female whose athletic accomplishment contributed to her sex appeal.

Male athletes also have enjoyed increasingly high status levels as role models, sex symbols, and public heroes. For example, in Mexico and Latin America men's soccer is extremely popular among men and women spectators, and athletes are often idolized for their athletic prowess and aggressive style of play.

As the century progressed, the status of the professional athlete became linked with sex and sexuality. In addition to the money they earned as a professional, top athletes received millions of dollars for **advertising** endorsements, often using swimwear or formal clothing to enhance sex appeal and promote products. The athlete as a sex symbol also occurred in other countries among men and women. In England, soccer player David Beckham is admired as much for his sex appeal as for his athletic capabilities, and Russian tennis player Anna Kournikova has never won a tournament title yet maintains her popularity and model-like status for her looks and sexy body.

Many of these international athletes are popular among men and women in their own countries, and they are admired in the United States more for their image and sexuality than for their talent.

On college and high school campuses athletes are the most popular and most visible students and exist in a sphere separate from other non-athletic students. A student athlete can achieve popularity and a high status among peers, despite social class, ethnicity, physical appearance, or academic achievement.

The high status experienced by many athletes results in amorous relationships, which are both significant and superficial. The idolization of professional athletes by children and teenagers creates a false sense of love by the fans toward the athlete. Fans spend a large amount of money and time fostering their "love" for a particular athlete. Pictures adorn bedrooms, and jerseys and other athletic apparel have become popular items. It is more likely for younger fans to feel greater infatuation with athletes. However, at any age, the bond with a fan's favorite athlete, although superficial, can be strong.

On high school and college campuses, male and female athletes find a connectedness in their athleticism that often provides a starting point for a loving relationship. Among female athletes and sport teams, this connectedness can be the beginning of many lesbian experiences. Although a common athletic background does little to guarantee the love will last, the shared experiences and values that accompany sports allow for bonding and social connection among athletes.

Because of the positive image of athletic participation, the pressure to participate in sports and athletics is often felt, particularly by young males. However, not all sports are equally valued. In the United States more physical and aggressive sports such as football and men's basketball enjoy a higher status than swimming or tennis. Internationally, soccer is the most popular sport; skill and success as a soccer player brings the highest status. This stratification is felt among high school and college athletes, where the most popular and well-known students play the high-status sports, as well as among professional athletes in high profile sports who garner the most endorsements and media time.

The culture of sports for boys and men establishes masculinity and reinforces **heterosexuality**. For young boys, this is learned with the first introduction into little league baseball or youth football. The nature of competition and winning, which implies conquering and dominance, have come to reflect the social standard for masculinity. As such, sports may be one popular way to establish and define masculinity and demonstrate male sex status; competing on traditional athletic teams (such as baseball, football, hockey, and basketball) has become an important cultural component in society. Thus, the more young men adhere to the values of sport and succeed within the institution of sport, the more they establish an acceptable sexual identity with their peers.

There are many negative values associated with participating in sports, such as the acceptance of violence that exists within many team sports. Often violence is not only a part of the game; it seems to be a necessary component. The aggression exhibited in sports is not only legitimate and validated by the rules of the game, but is desirable by opponents and spectators. Strength and power, validated by the culture of sports, becomes a part of the culture of masculinity.

This extreme masculinity has implications for patriarchy and **homosexuality**. The tendency for male sports to be more aggressive, more violent and, generally, more physical, reinforces the notion that men are the dominant gender and are entitled to a more powerful role than women. Where sports allow a certain tolerable level of violent behavior, that same behavior becomes problematic when it is carried into other aspects of life. Public incidents involving team members engaging in sexually explicit, violent, and other inappropriate behaviors with men and women demonstrates the negative outcomes.

The reinforcement of male heterosexuality is present in the defined values of aggression and dominance. The perception of a gay male as effeminate and weak contradicts the perception of a successful athlete—and what is considered manly in sport. Around the world, in the sports dominated by men (football, soccer, baseball, and basketball), the notion of a gay man achieving success in those sports goes against what is perceived as acceptable. There are a few athletes in those sports who have openly talked about their sexuality. For example, former NFL players David Kopay (1975), Roy Simmons (1992), and Esera Tuaolo (2002) are the *only* three former NFL players who have been open about being gay. In contrast, sports such as swimming, along with those requiring athletic skills like dance, are more susceptible to a "gay" image. Nevertheless, there are elements and opportunities in sport that provide male-bonding. Sports allow for closeness among men that is not acceptable in other facets of life. As teammates, men are able to share an intimacy through locker room jokes and even physical connections, such as hugs after victories, which are denied to them through the rigid standards of masculine heterosexuality.

If heterosexuality dominates the culture of male sports, homosexuality dominates the culture of female sport. Athletics go against what most societies consider feminine. The very nature of athletics, in which girls and women wear short hair, or pull back long hair, and wear little or no make-up during practice or competition, continues to call into question their femininity. In societies with such strict adherence to gender roles women can, very easily, develop masculine qualities. Female participation in sports may be seen to blur the lines between femininity and masculinity. As a response to these blurred lines, the lesbian has become the focus of attention and often the scapegoat, or exception to the feminine rule.

Throughout the middle of the twentieth century, institutions offering women's sports implemented a heterosexual component to avoid the lesbian stigma. Physical education programs developed an integration of school dances in efforts to help women cultivate their femininity. Softball and basketball tournaments continued to feature beauty pageants and many leagues had dress codes that prevented female athletes from wearing men's clothing. Despite these efforts, the stereotypical image of a lesbian athlete persisted and was often reinforced when opponents of women's sports ridiculed skilled athletes as unnatural. This effect seeped into the larger culture as competitiveness, aggression, independence, and strength were seen as uncharacteristic of womanhood.

The emphasis on heterosexuality, however, did little to change the image of female athletes. The lesbian label is very pervasive, especially in sports such as softball and basketball. The stigma of lesbianism in female athletics makes it difficult for heterosexual women who fear being labeled a lesbian to overcome what they perceive are negative stereotypes. These women often wear clothes and makeup to emphasize their femininity, and they may engage in sexually promiscuous behaviors with men to "prove" their heterosexuality. Paradoxically, the stigma makes it more acceptable, and sometimes easier, for athletes to be more open about their lesbianism. Many young athletes experience both ends of this spectrum as they struggle to come to grips with their own sexuality. Professional basketball player Sheryl Swoopes is an example of someone who experienced this transition. However, it is still much more likely for a female athlete to be open about her homosexuality than a male athlete.

Although the linkage of mannishness with lesbians and athletics created a negative image that prevented some heterosexuals from participating in sport, it also created a safe place for lesbians to develop their culture. Sport participation provided a women's-only space to develop a sense of individual and collective identity. The All-American Girls Professional Baseball League (1943–1954) is an example of how sport provided a new opportunity for women to develop relations with each other in ways independent from their homes or the males in their lives. For some females, this became a welcome introduction to their lesbian culture, while others tried hard to evade the lesbian-in-sport stereotype.

Whether due to the stark presence of masculine values for male sports or the existence of a lesbian culture in female sports, North American society is more accepting of lesbian athletes than gay male athletes. Over the last half of the twentieth century, more female athletes have acknowledged they are lesbian or bisexual than male athletes. The males who have publicly admitted they are gay or bisexual are participants of sports more accepting of non-violent behavior, where aggression is not as much of a component. Bill Tilden, the tennis player in the 1920s and 1930s, Greg Louganis, the diver of the 1980s, and professional baseball players Glenn Burke (1982) and Billy Bean (1999) are some of the better-known gay male athletes. Lesbian athletes, such as Babe Didrikson, Billie Jean King, Martina Navratilova, and Amelie Mauresmo are socially more accepted, regardless of the sport they play. *See also* Bisexuality; Gender Roles; Sexism; Women's Movement.

Further Reading: American Association of University Women: St. Lawrence County Branch. History of Women in Sports Timeline—2006. http://www.northnet.org/stlawrenceaauw/time17.htm. Chronology of women in sports starting from 776 BCE, outlining social, cultural, individual, and political events, October 2006; Anderson, Eric. *In the Game: Gay Athletes and the Cult of Masculinity*. Albany: State University of New York Press, 2005; Birrell, Susan, and Cheryl L. Cole, eds. *Women, Sport and Culture*. Champaign, IL: Human Kinetics, 1994; Brandy, Susan J., and Anne S. Darden. *Crossing Boundaries: An International Anthology of Women's Experience in Sports*. Champaign, IL: Human Kinetics, 1999; Gay Sports. http://www.gaysports.com. News, articles and information on issues of sport for gays and lesbians from topics of fitness, recreation, outdoors, Olympics, and professional sports, November 2006; Griffin, Pat. *Strong Women, Deep Closets: Lesbians and Homophobia in Sport*. Champaign, IL: Human Kinetics, 1998; Lenskyj, Helen. *Out of Bounds: Women, Sport and Sexuality*. Toronto: Canadian Scholars Press, 1987; Messner, Michael A. *Power at Play: Sports and the Problem of Masculinity*. Boston: Beacon Press, 1992; Nelson, Mariah B. *The Stronger Women Get, the More Men Love Football: Sexism and the American Culture of Sports*. New York: Harcourt Brace, 1994; Suggs, Welch. *A Place on the Team: Triumph and Tragedy of Title IX*. Princeton, NJ: Princeton University Press, 2005.

Cheryl Getz and Lorri Sulpizio

STDs. *See* Sexually Transmitted Infections

STIs. *See* Sexually Transmitted Infections

T

TRANSGENDER/TRANSSEXUAL. Individuals who cross-dressed and/or lived as a gender different from their birth gender have been documented in many cultures and time periods. But how these experiences have been interpreted by both outside observers and the individuals themselves has varied greatly, even within a specific society. The meanings attached to gender identities continue to expand and diversify today, as more and more youth seek ways to describe their feelings and beliefs beyond binary sex and gender categories and openly identify as transgender or trans.

Although source material is often limited, historical evidence suggests that a number of early societies recognized cross-**gender roles** and/or multiple genders. For example, Hindu and Muslim cultures on the Indian subcontinent have traditionally had a special social space for Hijras, anatomic males who dress and live as women, but who do not seek to pass and are known for sexually suggestive behavior considered culturally inappropriate for biological women. As part of their religious beliefs, Hijras have their genitals removed. This experience leads to comparisons with transsexual women, who often seek to change their "male" genitalia in order to be seen as women and/or fully express their female identities. But Hijras, historically and today, identify as neither men nor women.

Many indigenous cultures in North and South America also embraced gender diversity. From the outset of their arrival in the Americas in the sixteenth and seventeenth centuries, Europeans reported on the visibility of individuals who adopted cross-gender roles, including having sexual relations with and marrying people of the same biological gender. These outside observers were particularly horrified by women-men (males who partially or completely assumed culturally defined women's roles), whom they subsequently referred to as "berdaches" (an adaptation of the Arabic and Persian words for a male prostitute or "kept boy"), assuming that these individuals were the effeminate male sexual partners of other men. However, within their respective societies, women-men and men-women (females in men's roles) were viewed as neither men nor women, but as additional genders that either combined male and female elements or existed completely apart from binary gender categories. Thus, relationships between cross-gendered and non-cross-gendered individuals of the same biological gender were considered to be what anthropologist Sabine Lang (1998: 210) calls "hetero-gender" relationships and not same-sex sexual relationships, as many Europeans, and later European Americans, believed.

Medical professionals and researchers in Europe and the United States began to focus on cross-gendered identities in the late nineteenth century in response to the growing

Athena, 20, who was born a man, is seen with her mother in Tehran, 2004. In 1976, the supreme leader of Iran, Ayatollah Ruhollah Khomeini, imposed a fatwa to allow people with hormonal disorders to change sex if they wished, as well as change their birth certificates. © AP Photo/Alexandra Boulat/VII.

visibility of urban communities of people who lived at least part-time as a gender different from their assigned gender. The sexologists considered such individuals to be "gender inverts"—that is, to have a gender the opposite of or inverted from what was expected. Included in this group were individuals whose primary expression of inversion was considered to be their attraction to others of the same gender. Not until the turn of the twentieth century did sexologists begin to separate sexual identity from gender identity and recognize that individuals who transgressed gender norms were not necessarily what they described as "homosexuals."

The central figure in developing the concept of gender identity was German physician Magnus **Hirschfeld**, who coined and popularized the term "transvestism" (Latin for cross dressing) with his 1910 book *The Transvestites*. A transvestite himself, Hirschfeld argued that transvestites were not fetishists, but were overcome with a "feeling of peace, security and exaltation, happiness and well-being ... when in the clothing of the other sex" (1991: 25). Challenging the claim by other sexologists that transvestites were homosexuals and almost always men, Hirschfeld demonstrated that transvestites could be male or female and of any sexual orientation. However, he did not distinguish between people who crossdressed but identified as their birth gender ("transvestites," now referred to as "cross dressers") and people who identified as a gender different from their birth gender and who lived cross-gendered lives, which included cross dressing.

The latter group began to be categorized as "transsexuals" in medical literature in the late 1940s and early 1950s through the work of American psychologist David O. Cauldwell and endocrinologist Harry Benjamin. Cauldwell believed that transsexuality was a mental illness and opposed "sex change" surgeries, but Benjamin recognized that **psychotherapy** was largely unsuccessful in changing someone's inner sense of gender and advocated hormone replacement therapy and gender confirmation surgeries to bring the bodies of transsexuals into harmony with their minds.

The medical debates about transsexuality entered Western popular discourse in 1952, when Christine Jorgensen became an international celebrity for being the first person from the United States publicly known to have a "sex change." Jorgensen transitioned in Europe, where transformative surgeries had been performed as early as 1882. Through the efforts of Hirschfeld's Institute for Sexual Science in Berlin, "sex change" operations reached a peak in the early 1930s. In the United States, only a handful of doctors privately performed transformative surgeries prior to 1950, and through the 1960s few of the country's transsexuals could gain access to surgery, even though hundreds of transsexual women sought assistance in the wake of the publicity given to Jorgensen's transition.

The reluctance of the American medical profession to perform surgeries stemmed not only from unfamiliarity and inexperience with female-to-male (FTM) and male-to-female (MTF) genital reconstruction procedures, but also from castration anxieties and the pathologizing of transsexuality. Most surgeons, who were male, could not fathom removing a healthy penis and testes, even for a transsexual woman. Benjamin's research notwithstanding, other physicians, especially psychoanalysts, continued to consider transsexualism a mental illness best treated through therapy rather than surgical intervention. The prevalence of this point of view among clinicians led to transsexuality, under the category of "Gender Dysphoria," being added to the third edition of the American Psychiatric Association's *Diagnostic and Statistical Manual of Mental Disorders* (*DSM*) in 1980. This diagnosis remains in the latest version (2000) of the *DSM* as "Gender Identity Disorder."

The inclusion of transsexuality in the *DSM* means that hormones and surgeries are paid for under the state medical plans in Canada and some European countries. But in the United States, transsexual-related procedures are rarely covered by insurance companies, which severely limits the access of individuals who want to transition, especially poor and young people, to necessary health care. As a result, some MTFs and FTMs turn to illicit sources, such as risky, non-prescription hormones and unlicensed providers of breast implants or mastectomies. The prevalence of job discrimination against transsexual women, because of misogyny and because they may be less effective in "passing" than transsexual men, makes it even more difficult for them to gain access to appropriate medical services.

In addition, poor transsexual women, especially those of color, are more likely to experience harassment and physical and sexual assault, and because some turn to sex work to support themselves and pay for transitioning, they also have higher rates of HIV infection and alcohol and drug abuse. For example, the 2000 Washington D.C. Transgender Needs Assessment Survey (Xavier, Bobbin, Singer, and Budd 2005) involved more than 250 self-identified transgender people, three-fourths of whom had been born anatomically male and almost all of whom were people of color. The study found that only 58 percent of the participants were regularly employed, and 15 percent reported losing a job because of anti-transgender discrimination in the **workplace**. About a third of those surveyed indicated that they had been the victim of a transphobic or homophobic hate crime. Nearly half the sample used illegal drugs, and one-fourth acknowledged that they were HIV-positive, including almost a third of the MTF respondents.

While transsexual men are less subject to misogyny, they still encounter transphobia, especially when they are "out" or recognized by others as transsexual. For instance, like transsexual women, they frequently face discrimination from health care providers, such as hostile questioning from insensitive medical professionals when they seek a gynecological exam. Doctors have also been slow to develop effective surgical techniques to create a functioning phallus, perhaps because male physicians want to limit who can possess what they see as the "true" sign of manhood.

But many transsexual men, who are typically recognized by those around them as male after taking testosterone and having mastectomies or "top" surgeries, do not feel that they need to have genital or "bottom" surgeries to be "real men." Likewise, a significant number of transsexual women undergo hormone replacement therapies and may have breast implants, but do not have or desire further medical intervention. Thus the traditional expectation that transsexual individuals pursue complete surgical transformation is inaccurate. A more inclusive understanding is that transsexual men are men who have lived in female bodies and transsexual women are women who have lived in male bodies.

At the same time, many younger transgender people who describe themselves as genderqueer are challenging the entire transsexual paradigm—that individuals recognize themselves as the "opposite" gender and begin to identify and present as that gender. Refusing to accept a gender binary, genderqueers do not feel that they have to reject all of the traits associated with their birth gender and move to the other gender extreme. Instead, they may blend or bend gender in appearance, dress, and/or expression, or present as androgynous. Genderqueer individuals use a wide variety of terms to characterize their gender and sexual identities, including third gendered, bi gendered, non gendered, gender blender, femme queen, transdyke, transfag, boygirl, trannyboi, and androgyne.

More and more people are coming out publicly as transgender at the outset of the twenty-first century and often doing so at younger ages, due to information and support being readily available through web sites, **Internet** chat rooms, and, in many places, local trans and trans-supportive youth groups. It is becoming increasingly common today for high school, junior high, and even elementary school students in many Western countries to be open with their friends and family about their transgender identities and to express these identities in a myriad of ways. As a result, transgender communities are not only growing in size, but also becoming more diverse and more visible. *See also* Drugs and Alcohol; Fetishism; Heterosexuality; Homosexuality; Mental Health and Sex; Prostitution; Psychoanalysis; Religions, Eastern; Sex Therapists; Sexual Science/Sexology.

Further Reading: American Psychological Association. *Diagnostic and Statistical Manual of Mental Disorders.* 4th ed., Text Revision. Washington, DC: Author, 2000; Benjamin, Harry. *The Transsexual Phenomenon.* New York: Julian Press, 1966; glbtq: An Encyclopedia of Gay, Lesbian, Bisexual, Transgender, and Queer Culture: http://www.glbtq.com. A free, online encyclopedia that includes a number of articles on transgender topics; Hirschfeld, Magnus. *Transvestites: The Erotic Drive to Cross Dress.* Translated by Michael A. Lombardi-Nash. Buffalo: Prometheus Books, [1910] 1991; Lang, Sabine. *Men as Women, Women as Men: Changing Gender in Native American Cultures.* Austin: University of Texas Press, 1998; Meyerowitz, Joanne. *How Sex Changed: A History of Transsexuality in the United States.* Cambridge, MA: Harvard University Press, 2002; Nanda, Serena. *Neither Man Nor Woman: The Hijras of India.* Belmont, CA: Wadsworth, 1990; TransBiblio. http://www.library.uiuc.edu/circ/transgender_bibliography/transbiblio.htm.

An extensive bibliography of print, audio-visual, and online resources related to transgender issues and people; Xavier, Jessica M., Marilyn Bobbin, Ben Singer, and Earline Budd. "A Needs Assessment of Transgendered People of Color Living in Washington, DC." In *Transgender Health and HIV Prevention: Needs Assessment Studies from Transgender Communities Across the United States*, edited by Walter Bockting and Eric Avery, 31–47. New York: Haworth Press, 2005.

Brett Beemyn

TRANSSEXUAL. *See* Transgender/Transsexual

VIOLENCE. *See* Domestic and Relationship Violence

VIRGINITY.   Although the common definition of virginity—not having had sexual intercourse—in principle applies equally to both genders, the Latin root word "virgo" meaning "maiden," or unmarried woman, underscores the concept's historical reference to female sexuality. Today, in many cultural contexts virginity is particularly associated with female sexual innocence. The status of virginity, too, is markedly different for men and women and varies from culture to culture. Female virginity has historically been most highly valued in patriarchal societies where **marriage** involves the giving of dowries. In these societies the bride's family provides material wealth or goods for the newlyweds, linking control of a girl's sexuality to the protection of familial lineage and wealth. During the twentieth and twenty-first centuries, the value on female virginity in industrialized European countries has steadily declined as an emphasis on and investment in a girl's education replaced the association between marriage, property exchange, and the regulation of a girl's sexuality. In these contexts, "love" presents personal characteristics and qualities of mind as more important than virginity. Ideas about virginity, nevertheless, remain central to family planning and reproductive health policies, illustrating formative moral, legal, and religious doctrines in any given culture.

In many contexts around the world medical examiners seek to determine virginity by physical inspection of the female genitals despite its unreliability. Such examinations suppose that a loss of virginity is evidenced by a perforation of the hymen—a usually crescent-shaped, very thin membrane that partially closes the vagina in women or girls who have never experienced sexual intercourse—and that this perforation would be physically noticeable. However, the texture and elasticity of this membrane differs so markedly among women as to be a poor indicator of virginity. Hymens have on occasion been found to survive the birth of a child and not all virgins have intact hymens. These examinations, violating a woman's human rights when conducted against her will, can be painful, humiliating, and traumatic and, moreover, possibly destroy the condition they seek to confirm.

Virginity examinations are still tacitly condoned in Turkey within a variety of public institutional settings such as state run orphanages, vocational high schools, and **prisons**. In 1995 the Turkish Ministry of Education issued a statute stating that proof of "un-chastity" was a valid reason to expel women from the education system. The statute was

Steve Carell (as Andy Stitzer) stars in Judd Apatow's 2005 film, *The 40-Year-Old Virgin*. Courtesy of Photofest.

rescinded in 2002 after five students attempted suicide rather than be subjected to such tests. Turkish women, however, remained without full protection from virginity testing, a protection recognized by most member countries of the European Union.

Even though an intact hymen is not a reliable indicator of virginity, some women who live in societies that place a high value on virginity feel compelled to have hymen reconstructive surgery in order to be considered a virgin at the time of their marriage. It is estimated that as many as two percent of Guatemalan women have undergone this procedure, very often in medical clinics that evade government regulation. Not only are these operations very expensive by Guatemalan standards, they are often performed in unsanitary conditions by doctors who do not inform their patients of the significant health risks involved. Although there is substantial bilateral support in Guatemalan Congress for a new law on family planning and reproductive health that would do much to ameliorate the current situation, it has been contested by a socially conservative president.

Family, state, and religious beliefs in most societies during the first half of the twentieth century dictated that a woman should remain a virgin until married and then practice heterosexual activities strictly within the chaste confines of marriage. Around mid-century, a number of social trends emerged that significantly impacted practices and conceptions of virginity in the latter part of the century. The general availability of condoms by the 1950s and the introduction of the **birth control** pill in the 1960s helped inaugurate the "**free love**" ideologies. These developments, in turn, bolstered the **women's movement**, which championed a woman's freedom to make choices regarding her own body and freedom from sexual and domestic violence.

Nevertheless, the subjective experience of first intercourse in a late twentieth century Western cultural context often differs significantly for women and men. While men tend to view their first intercourse with the positive connotations of a gain in **masculinity** or ascendance to manhood, women are more likely to perceive the experience negatively as a definitive loss of virginity. Under these normative heterosexual conditions, women tend to passively facilitate access to adult male sexuality rather than constituting active agents in the expression of their sexuality. Men are more likely to report having felt a sense of accomplishment following the occasion of first heterosexual intercourse, though they may also perceive women as having the power to disrupt or withhold the facilitation of their masculine sexual identity.

Western attitudes concerning love and sex during the late twentieth and early twenty-first centuries have been characterized by an unprecedented permissiveness that persists in marked contrast to the generally prohibitive attitudes toward sexuality that existed at the beginning of the twentieth century. Rather than harboring strict injunctions against expressions of sexuality, an implicit yet equally stringent command to enjoy is now pervasive in Western culture. Exemplary of this predominant cultural trend is the recent Hollywood blockbuster *The 40-Year-Old Virgin*. The movie portrays a man who has remained celibate not out of fidelity to any religious doctrine or cultural attitude condemning **premarital sex** but as the result of a supposedly private pathology. His co-workers consider it no less than a moral obligation to initiate him into the world of heterosexual relations and, by implication, to adulthood. The central message of the movie concerning the loss of one's virginity is concisely encapsulated by its advertising taglines "Better late than never" and "The longer you wait, the harder it gets."

Pronounced conservative reactions against such freedoms emerged with increasing intensity towards the end of the century. Particularly in the United States, religious groups have sought to reinstate prohibitions limiting **heterosexuality** to the conjugal bed. Since the 1990s the increasing momentum of abstinence-only **sex education** initiatives spearheaded predominantly by Evangelical Christian organizations such as the Southern Baptist Convention has lead to a marked increase in the cultural valuation of virginity. In 1997, the Abstinence Clearinghouse was founded as a nationwide resource for abstinence-only sex education. It has collaborated with the Centers for Disease Control to regulate the implementation of abstinence-only sex education in public schools. In 2005, it was awarded 167 million dollars in public funds by the U.S. federal government.

Prominent Evangelical abstinence programs like True Love Waits and Silver Ring Thing, established in 1993 and 1995, respectively, have popularized the practice of virginity pledges to deter young people from engaging in premarital sexual intercourse. For those who have already had sex, these groups offer the opportunity to symbolically reclaim their virginity by pledging to remain chaste until marriage. It is estimated that over 2.5 million adolescents have made a virginity pledge since 1993. There is some evidence indicating that such programs have greater success in populations where the pledge identity constitutes a minority position within a non-pledging majority. In contexts where the pledge identity constitutes a majority, the pledge promise is seen to be less efficacious at preventing or delaying premarital sex.

Embedded within the Evangelical religious discourse is the view of virginity as a sacred gift only to be given to one's spouse at the time of marriage. One significant consequence of this discourse is how it has affected the possibilities for the elaboration of gay and lesbian sexual identities. Traditionally, gay and lesbian sexualities have fallen outside the purview of discourses on virginity since this term is defined in an exclusively heterosexual manner. As a result, gay and lesbian sexualities have often been associated with promiscuity by conservative heterosexual mores since they do not occur within the institution of marriage. The renewed valuation of virginity spurred by Evangelical abstinence-only sex education movements has encouraged some gay and lesbian youth associated with these movements to appropriate the category of virginity in order to counteract their degrading default status of being considered sexually promiscuous. Some gay and lesbian people see this as a deeply problematic solution insofar as it does nothing to disrupt the determination of their sexualities by normative heterosexual standards. *See also* Adolescence; Celibacy; Childhood; Cinema; Domestic and Relationship Violence; Religions, Eastern; Religions, Western; Romance; Sexism.

Further Reading: Amico, Michael. "Gay Youths as 'Whorified Virgins'." *Gay & Lesbian Review Worldwide* 12, no. 4 (July/August 2005): 34–36; Ayse, Parla. "The 'Honor' of the State: Virginity Examinations in Turkey." *Feminist Studies* 27, no. 1 (2001): 65–88; Holland, Janet, Caroline Ramazanoglu, Sue Sharpe, and Rachel Thomson. "Deconstructing Virginity—Young People's Accounts of First Sex." *Sexual and Relationship Therapy* 15, no. 3 (2000): 221–32; Holtzman, Deanna, and Nancy Kulish. *Nevermore: The Hymen and the Loss of Virginity.* Northvale, NJ: Jason Aronson, 1997; Pearson, Marcia L. "A Blemish on the Modern Face of Turkey." *North Carolina Journal of International Law & Commercial Regulation* 28, no. 3 (2003): 663; Roberts, Hannah. "Reconstructing Virginity in Guatemala." *The Lancet* 367, no. 9518 (April 2006): 1227–28; Schlegel, Alice. "State, Property, and the Value on Virginity." *American Ethnologist* 18, no. 4 (1991): 719–34.

Christopher R. Bell and Kate Briggs

WOMEN'S MOVEMENT. The term "women's movement" denotes a diverse and fluid range of individuals, groups, and organizations that share a belief in women's equality. In addition to economic and political equality, a key link among feminist initiatives across different locales throughout the twentieth and the start of the twenty-first centuries has been advocacy for changes in laws and cultural practices that regulate love, sex, and sexuality. During this period, women's movements emerged in response to profound social shifts that have accompanied modernization. Beginning with the promotion of equal rights as related to nationalism and the rapid pace of Western industrialization at the onset of the twentieth century and culminating in the intensification of globalization by the century's end, these disruptions have provided opportunities for locally based women's movements to coalesce. These movements have emerged from the disparate and distinct needs of women in particular cultures, in specific **race**, class, and ethnic groups, and in national contexts. They also have offered openings for a dispersion of ideas on sex, sexualities, and love through a wide variety of means—from informal networks, pamphlets, and books to international institutions, transnational organizations, and the **Internet**. Working together across cultural divides has been a challenge for women's movements. There have been debates and conflicts related to sex and sexualities, and divergent views about cultural practices and their relationship to equality. Some of these have prompted individuals and groups to rethink their ideas, and others have blocked cooperation.

At the start of the twentieth century, a broad array of groups and individuals in the women's movement debated sex, sexuality, and love. The movement's diversity—marked by social class, the presence of men in some groups and organizations, and religious differences—sparked initiatives on **prostitution**, **birth control**, **abortion**, **homosexuality**, love, **marriage**, and **divorce**. Although lesbians were present in women's movements at the time, their involvement and specific concerns were not openly discussed or addressed.

Lesbian sexuality did not emerge from the silence that surrounded it until the 1970s. However, in the first decade Johanna Elberskirchen and Anna Rüling of Germany were among the first lesbian feminists to speak publicly about their sexuality and relate it to women's emancipation. Other activist lesbian feminists, such Sara Josephine Baker in the United States, created informal networks through clubs and other women's organizations.

At the onset of the twentieth century participation in divergent sex reform initiatives was not uncommon among feminists. Some imagined a more moral world

Women representing the different cultures of the world hold the "peace torch" during the opening ceremony for the Non-Governmental Organizations Forum on Women at the Olympic Stadium in Beijing, 1995. © AP Photo/Anat Givon.

that restrained **heterosexuality**, while others championed hetero- and homosexual freedom. Helene Stöcker founded the pioneering sex reform organization League for the Protection of Motherhood (1905) in Germany. She joined radicals who were at the helm of the socialist women's movement to organize against the German government's regulation of prostitution.

In Germany, female prostitutes registered with the police and submitted to regular medical examinations. Similar laws existed in the United Kingdom and in France as governments aimed to address the spread of venereal diseases through the control of women's bodies. That prostitutes were regulated by the police, while men purchased their services without consequence, was seen as a form of discrimination—a manifestation of an institutionalized sexual double standard—that the movement sought to abolish. Feminist organizing against government control of prostitution spread through the work of an international organization—the International Federation for the Abolition of State Regulation of Prostitution, and the public speaking campaigns of organizers such as Josephine Butler in the United Kingdom. The Federation developed branches in Italy, France, Switzerland, Germany, Belgium, India and the United States and its ideas were circulated through books, newspapers, and *The Shield*, the International Federation's journal.

The sexual double standard, which manifested itself in culturally specific ways, was a critical issue that feminists around the world confronted during the opening decades of this past century. Feminists in Egypt and Syria, for example, critiqued cultural practices that were discriminatory to women—such as **polygamy** and the veil—arguing that they stood in opposition to the meaning of Islam. These ideas circulated through the Arab world with the aid of newspapers, books, and the travels of individual feminists. In the United States, Great Britain, and Germany, where the idea of romantic love flourished across social classes and racial and ethnic groups, **sex education** was advocated in the early twentieth century as a means for women to learn about their bodies so that they too could enjoy sexual pleasure on par with men. A **free love** movement, which included feminists such as Olive Schreiner in South Africa, the poet Lesbia Harford in Australia, anarcho-feminists Emma Goldman in the United States and Ito Noe in Japan, argued that women should be free sexual agents and that the institution of marriage itself bound women in unequal relationships to men. He Zhen, a Chinese feminist, who was also influenced by anarchism, critiqued Confucian ideals of love and marriage, arguing that women should be free to have multiple lovers, at the same time that she denounced excessive sexual freedom.

Linking heterosexual sex to **pregnancy** meant that fertility control emerged as an early issue. Contraceptives were available in Denmark and England, but access especially for poor women was very limited. Socialist feminist physicians, including Hope Adams in Germany, performed illegal abortions for working-class and poor women. And, in the Netherlands, feminists worked on distributing contraceptives to women who could not afford them. Only in the Soviet Union was abortion legal for a short period after the revolution, beginning in 1920; Stalin banned it in 1936. In Great Britain, the English Women's Co-operative Guild supported legalizing abortion in 1934.

In countries where Catholicism was a major force—such as Argentina, Italy, and Spain—feminist sex reform and fertility control initiatives found little support until the last third of the twentieth century. In the face of the Comstock Law in the United States, which made contraception and the distribution of birth control literature illegal, women such as Margaret **Sanger** pushed for legalization and helped establish the American Birth Control League (1921). Sanger also opened an illegal birth control clinic and published her ideas widely in the socialist press. Marie Stopes, a Scottish feminist, who supported full equality in marriage and whose 1911 book *Married Love* was banned in the United States, was influenced by Sanger and opened a birth control clinic in London in 1921. Not all work on birth control was aimed to advance a purely feminist agenda; Sanger and Stopes also used eugenic arguments that influenced support for the issue. During the 1920s birth control and abortion became increasingly available to women who could afford to pay for them, even when they were explicitly outlawed.

In China, too, women were concerned with issues related to the sexual double standard. Here as in many other counties, nation-building was an impulse that led to feminist activities. How could the nation progress if women's feet were bound? At the turn of the century there were initiatives against foot binding, which was legally banned in 1911. Jin Yi published *Women's Bell* in Shanghai in 1903, arguing for women's rights including freedom from arranged marriage. The Women's Rights Recovery Association, which was against male control of women, polygamy, and concubinage, also appeared. After the May Fourth Movement (1919–1921), a rapidly developing women's movement argued for marital reforms and the end of arranged marriage. Laws were slowly reformed throughout the 1930s in China, enforcing the idea of heterosexual monogamy, and providing women with rights in divorce and the ability to select marital partners. After the revolution, in 1949, and particularly during the Cultural Revolution, sex and love were not major topics of feminist discussion although contraception was available to women.

During the 1960s and 1970s advocacy for women's equality coincided with the growth of other progressive social movements interested in changing how sex, sexuality, and love were experienced. In 1963, Betty Friedan's *The Feminine Mystique* galvanized middle-class suburban women to begin to look at the "problem with no name," a dissatisfaction that these women felt about their daily lives and a "yearning" for deeper fulfillment and meaning. By the mid-to-late 1960s young women who had been active in the Civil Rights movement and the Anti-War Movement objected to men treating them as domestic workers and sex-objects. Feminists such as Robin Morgan and Shulamith Firestone distinguished their feminist activism from the male-dominated New Left when they advocated for the development of autonomous women's groups. Both radical and moderate groups proliferated, including the broad-based National Organization for Women (NOW), founded in 1966. For the generation of women, who came of age after the pill was approved in the United States in 1960, heterosexuality was increasingly tied to pleasure as the association between sex and pregnancy continued to weaken.

In England, France, Italy, and Germany women agitated on multiple fronts for sexual equality through mass demonstrations, lobbying, and extra-legal tactics. As a result of these efforts, women gained the right to abortions in France (1975), Italy (1978), and, under particularly strict limitations, in Spain (1985). In Argentina, after nearly a century of feminist struggle, the right to divorce was won in 1987 and access to contraception was finally legislated in 2003.

These movements were influenced and informed by works calling into question the institution of heterosexuality and linking it to gender inequality. The S.C.U.M. Manifesto, in 1967, argued that nothing short of the elimination of men would free women from oppression. Kate Millet's book, Sexual Politics, proposed a sexual revolution that would free women from patriarchy. In 1970, Shulamith Firestone's The Dialectic of Sex, asserted that sex and class were at the root of women's subordination, that men's power over women in the family along with women's roles needed to be addressed, and that reproductive technologies would liberate women from dependency on men for childbearing. The Australian feminist Germaine Greer (The Female Eunuch) argued that women were desexualized by the misogyny that was practiced by men and internalized by women. The family, she thought, was the primary site of women's oppression in that it robbed them of agency. Added to these ideas was the publication of Ingrid Bengis's Combat in the Erogenous Zone, which explored the dynamics of sexuality, from heterosexuality to violence against women.

Demythologizing the female **orgasm**—from an emphasis on penile penetration of the vagina to clitoral stimulation—was an important part of the dialogue as was the separation of love and sex. The women's health movement, which grew rapidly in the United States and internationally, has supported this effort over the last 35 years by providing resources like Our Bodies, Ourselves—a book adapted by women to local cultures in dozens of countries that provides the knowledge women need for sexual and reproductive control.

Lesbian feminists, in particular, critiqued the institution of heterosexuality. Although lesbianism was not against the law in many of the countries where lesbian initiatives emerged, it was a sexuality that had not been acknowledged. Heterosexism in the movement caused serious conflicts. Groups such as the Furies organized and published on lesbianism in the early 1970s in the United States, advancing lesbian visibility both inside the women's movement and in the larger society. In Ireland lesbian feminists emerged from Irishwomen United as a distinct group and worked on public recognition, lesbian community-building, and the social acceptance of lesbian sexuality.

The specific concerns of black women were also hidden in the predominantly white women's movement. In response to racism, especially in the United States in the

1970s, black women began to establish their cross-class feminist groups working on issues of specific concern to them. For some women, the critique of heterosexuality belied their racial identities and also paradoxically obscured the racialized problems of sexual objectification and sexual stereotyping that black women specifically faced. At the same time, groups such as the Combahee River Collective advocated for the concerns of black lesbians as they also reached out to a diversity of women of color in the Third World.

Highly organized local and global efforts throughout the 1970s and 1980s focused on ending all forms of sexual violence against women, including **incest**, rape, and sexual harassment. Groups inside the movement also engaged in debates and direct actions against pornography, which touched off controversies inside the movement about what constitutes liberating and/or non-sexist sexual practices for women. In 1976, the International Tribunal on Crimes Against Women was held in Brussels. Some 2000 women from 40 countries participated and discussed a battery of **sex crimes** against women from rape to female genital mutilation (FGM).

1975—International Women's Year—was the year of the UN's first conference on women. Significant in the mid-seventies were the tensions between the agendas of women in the Third World and those in the United States and western Europe. Third World feminists launched incisive critiques on the Western developmental model, pointing to the North-South divide, U.S. hegemony, and the need for localized feminisms that could address specific cultural and national mechanisms of subordination. Based on recommendations from the conference, the UN instituted the Decade for Women (1975–1985), which provided resources and mechanisms for raising feminist issues internationally. The conferences have had parallel non-governmental organization (NGO) forums, which have become as important as the official state-led conferences for the international women's movement. At the mid-decade conference, women began to raise issues of sexuality. Sexual violence against women, FGM, and trafficking in women and girls were among the issues that were discussed. By the UN Conference on Women at the decade's end, **pornography** and "deeply rooted" cultural practices that discriminate against women were on the agenda. Other UN conferences, such as those on Human Rights (1992) and Population (1994), have also been pivotal for the growth and accomplishments of a global women's movement.

It was not until the UN held the Fourth World Conference on Women in Beijing, in 1995, however, that issues of sexuality emerged in force. The health section of the conference's Platform of Action stated that "human rights of women include their right to have control over and decide freely and responsibly on matters related to their sexuality, including sexual and reproductive health, free of coercion, discrimination and violence" (Platform for Action, 2006, paragraph number 96).

In addition to UN sponsored activities, many feminist networks emerged globally. They included academic organizations, governmental agencies, and activists from grass-roots groups, national and international organizations. Women working on violence against women organized international "Take Back the Night" marches, which increased awareness about sexual violence and what could be done to eliminate it.

Throughout the 1980s and 1990s as local women's movements in the West began to wane, feminist initiatives in the Third World and international feminist organizations grew. The Internet helped facilitate communication among women's groups. Islamic feminists, for example, in predominately Muslim countries and across the globe began organizing against male power over women both in the family and in marital relationships. As a result of Moroccan women working to reform traditional family law, the Moroccan Parliament mandated equality between men and women in the family and provided for the possibility of a woman being granted custody of her children in a divorce. In Zimbabwe today, women organizing around the Musasa Project, have begun to resist the customary laws that allow polygamy.

In the late 1990s and into the next century individual feminists and women's groups in North America and Europe began to address some new issues related to sexualities. Transsexuality challenged some feminists' ideas about gender identity, while others welcomed queer sexualities and engaged in support of transsexuality. Trafficking in women from Asia, Russia, and eastern Europe emerged as an international feminist issue. This was especially true after the end of communism in the East. In the Czech Republic a loose network of feminists began to work on issues such as prostitution, and they have raised awareness about the problems of lesbians and single mothers.

Feminists have also rallied against the continual chipping away of the right to abortion in eastern European countries, most of which had legalized abortion under communism in the 1950s. The 1990s witnessed funding cuts and increasing limitations on access to abortion. In parts of western Europe, abortion rights remain very limited, especially in countries where Catholicism dominates. Since abortion rights were granted in the United States, in 1973, women have been struggling to maintain those rights, despite continued attempts to limit them. The year 2005 also saw lesbians in the United States organize in support of same-sex marriage, while feminists in Egypt have continued to protest the sexual double standard that denies women sexual pleasure, and a nascent women's movement in Russia continues to work through both the residue and myths of Soviet sexophobia. *See also* Censorship; Domestic and Relationship Violence; Families; Feminism; Gender Roles; Men's Movement; Politics; Religions, Eastern; Religions, Western; Sexism; Sports; Transgender/Transsexual; Workplace.

Further Reading: Antrobus, Peggy. *The Global Women's Movement: Origins, Issues and Strategies.* London: Zed Books, 2004; Basu, Amrita. *The Challenge of Local Feminisms: Women's Movements in Global Perspective.* Boulder, CO: Westview Press, 1995; Freedman, Estelle. *No Turning Back: The History of Feminism and the Future of Women.* New York: Ballantine/Random House, 2001; Isis International. http://www.isiswomen.org. Isis was formed in 1974 to advance the work of women's movements across the globe; McBride Stetson, Dorothy, ed. *Abortion Politics, Women's Movements and the Democratic State. A Comparative Study of State Feminism.* Oxford: Oxford University Press, 2001; Platform for Action. The United Nations Fourth World Conference on Women. http://www .un.org/womenwatch/daw/beijing/platform/health.htm#diagnosis.

Anne Lopes

WORKPLACE. Even though sexual flirting and **dating** are often commonplace at work, love and sex are not usually directly associated to the workplace in most cultures. This is due to the naturalized division of the private and public spaces along with the assumption that organizations and work are rational, not emotional sites. Accordingly to this division, within industrialized countries of North America and Europe from the early 1900s to the middle of the twentieth century (mainly before World War II), male workers predominated in the workplace. Although women were present in auxiliary tasks such as maids, secretaries, and nurses, it was in the private domain of the household where love and sex were thought to be confined. Even in rich countries, women and children of the poor classes (as well as non-white males) were enrolled in dangerous and very low-income work activities in the recently born industries, particularly during the first decades of the twentieth century. Around the world the timing as well as the social and cultural contexts varied. Non-industrialized and traditional societies preserved a rural division of labor in Latin America, Asia, and Africa. In these regions love and sex arrangements conformed to a highly structured class or caste hierarchy.

The early 1900s marked the beginning of the spread of technological transformations around the world, which created new job opportunities for men and women. Although predominantly rural societies continued traditional forms of gender relationships, within industrialized countries, especially in urban environments, these began to change. The introduction of new technologies in the factories and other workplaces turned obsolete the need for physical strength, allowing women to enter the production line and perform a greater variety of tasks. Similarly, the invention of domestic appliances (e.g., dishwasher, refrigerator, vacuum cleaner, washing machine) facilitated household duties and freed women from the time consuming housekeeping. Also, the spread of the communications, beginning with the telegraph, followed by the telephone, radio, television and the **Internet**, disseminated ideas of gender equality in the workplace along with Western values associated with romantic love.

These technological innovations were accompanied by cultural, economic, and political changes, which also influenced workplace gender positions. In the 1920s, for instance, great economic growth and the **women's movement** influenced more liberal relationships between men and women, albeit mainly in upper classes and in the arts. The emergence of fascist political regimes (Italy and Germany) and the economic crises of the 1930s (the 1929 economic crash in the United States), however, brought a workplace conservatism that changed only during and immediately following World War II—and then later with the emergence of the social movements of the 1960s. In some countries, like the United States, women took on traditionally male roles in the workplace during the war. Most returned to their domestic roles following the conflict, creating a "baby boom" of historical proportions. During the 1950s and 1960s, however, there was also an undercurrent of rebellion as the women's and Civil Rights movements re-emerged along with other social movements to challenge traditional workplace relationships. These included the Beat-turned-Hippie movement that questioned, among other elements, capitalistic society's way of life and traditional family morals, and the **gay and lesbian movement**, fighting against discrimination and expanding the traditional concept of **families**.

Some historians consider the women's movement as the most important social event of the twentieth century because it denounced the sexual inequality of opportunities in society—both in public and private spaces. Feminists questioned the moral link between sex and **marriage**, in part, due to the advances in medicine such as antibiotics and **birth control**, which, in turn, allowed women to enter into the workplace full time. Economic and cultural globalization spread the impact of this movement in the latter twentieth and early twenty-first centuries.

These movements generated conservative resistance in societies with strict division of gender and sexual roles. Within fundamentalist Muslim societies and conservative Christian and Jewish sub-cultures, traditional dress, gender roles, and divisions between the public and private spheres still exist. In fundamentalist religious countries, most of the Arab world, and some African countries, women have very few rights and there is an extreme inequality of opportunities.

In Western societies, as the model contemporary worker is no longer linked to one company with escalated positions, increased responsibilities, and higher wages, love and sex arrangements in family life have changed. Single men/women and couples without children are more common (given their mobility) than the traditional family of the early and mid-twentieth century, which usually had three or more children. Dual career households are also more common, although the couple's emotional needs and careers expectations may go in different directions causing shift from marriage to cohabitation.

Most people will spend more than one third of their adult lives in the workplace; about 30 percent of co-workers in the West will date at some point of their careers. Marriages and romantic relationships begin (and end) in the workplace, although some companies have policies that restrain such relationships as do laws in some countries related to sexual harassment or discrimination based on gender. Even here, however, the enforcement of these policies and laws is, at best, uneven. Further, workplace harassment and discrimination against homosexual and transgender workers are common. Jokes, insults, and insinuations along with traditional assumptions regarding masculinity and femininity affect the quality of workplace life and the possibilities for advancement. Additionally, those gay men who are effeminate or those who cross-dress are more visible in feminine professions such as hairdressing and fashion design while those who choose to enter professions such as medicine, law, the clergy, education, or engineering often remain in the closet. Relatively few countries and localities have adopted anti-discrimination policies to protect sexual minority workers, although protection against discrimination of workers on the basis of HIV status is more common, and the United Nations and the European Union have been influential. Other affirmative policies have been implemented by many companies, notably in the technology and entertainment sectors.

There also is still a marked division between men and women in high-quality and well-paid jobs. This is linked to the sexual division of production/reproduction tasks in which raising children and domestic activities (cleaning, laundry, and meals preparation), in most societies, are still considered as mainly women's responsibilities. They are aggravated by differences in the education between men and women. Latin cultures and poor countries are generally characterized by an increased inequality of opportunities. Also, countries that have experienced long slavery periods, such as Brazil, or discriminatory dictatorships, such as South Africa's apartheid regimen, associate color discrimination to sexual inequality in social divisions of labor. In Brazil, a white man earns more money than a white woman who earns more than a black man who earns more than a black woman.

Most democratic countries had implemented anti-discriminatory laws and programs by the end of the twentieth century. In Japan and South Korea, for example, the introduction of capitalism and democratic regimes occurred after the World War II. The rapid shift from a highly hierarchic, almost feudal society, to a democratic political regimen and a capitalist market culture has not significantly altered the dominant male position in society or the association of masculinity with the workplace environment. In China and North Korea, the communist regimen has imposed more equal opportunities for men and women, but there is a lack of liberty and a persistence of traditional values and little likelihood of workplace advancement (although this is changing in some parts of China, notably economic free zones). Neveretheless, there is an absence of women in the political elite and the practice of abandonment of baby girls in China due to the population control policies remains. *See also* Religions, Eastern; Religions, Western; Romance; Sexism.

Further Reading: Bauman, Zigmunt. *Liquid Modernity*. Cambridge: Polity Press, 2000; Hobsbawn, Eric. *Age of Extremes: The Short Twentieth Century 1914–1991*. London: Michel

Joseph & Pelham Books, 1994; Goetzman, Gary; Utt, Kenneth; Bozman, Ron (Producers), and Demme, Jonathan (Director). *Philadelphia*. U.S.: TriStar Pictures, 1993; Greenwald, Nana; Skoll, Jeff; Wechsler, Nick (Producers), and Caro, Niki (Director). *North Country*. U.S.: Warner Bros, 2005; International Labor Organization. http://www.ilo.org/public/english/gender.htm. Presents gender equality promotion policies and programs, giving access to documents, articles, news and statistics related to gender and sexuality issues at work, August, 2006; Kumar, Krishan. *From Post-Industrial to Post-Modern Societies: New Theories of the Contemporary World*. Oxford: Blackwell Publishers, 1996; Powell, Gary N., and Sharon Foley. "Something to Talk About: Romantic Relationships in Organizational Settings." *Journal of Management* 24, no. 3 (1998): 421–48; Riordan, Daniel, C. "Interaction Strategies of Lesbian, Gay, and Bisexual Healthcare Practitioners in Clinical Examination of Patients: Qualitative Study." *British Medical Journal* 328 (2004): 1227–29; Sennett, Richard. *The Corrosion of Character: The Personal Consequences of Work in the New Capitalism*. New York and London: Norton, 1998.

Henrique Caetano Nardi

Selected Bibliography

Abbott, Elizabeth. *The History of Celibacy*. New York: Da Capo Press, 2001.

Adam, Barry D., Jan Willem Duyvendak, and André Krouwel, eds. *The Global Emergence of Gay and Lesbian Politics: National Imprints of a Worldwide Movement*. Philadelphia: Temple University Press, 1999.

Apostolidis, Paul, and Juliet A. Williams, eds. *Public Affairs: Politics in the Age of Sex Scandals*. Durham, NC: Duke University Press, 2004.

Bailey, Beth. *From Front Porch to Back Seat: Courtship in Twentieth-Century America*. Baltimore: Johns Hopkins Press, 1988.

Baird, Vanessa. *The No-Nonsense Guide to Sexual Diversity*. London: Verso, 2001.

Bancroft, John, and June Machover Reinisch. *Adolescence and Puberty*. Oxford: Oxford University Press, 1990.

Basu, Alaka Malwade, ed. *The Sociocultural and Political Aspects of Abortion: Global Perspectives*. Westport, CT: Praeger, 2003.

de Beauvoir, Simone. *The Second Sex* [Le Deuxieme Sexe]. Paris: Gallimard, 1949.

Benjamin, Harry. *The Transsexual Phenomenon*. New York: Julian Press, 1966.

Bhattacharyya, Gargi. *Sexuality and Society: An Introduction*. London: Routledge, 2002.

Blackwood, Evelyn, and Saskia Wieringa, eds. *Female Desires: Same-Sex Relations and Transgender Practices across Cultures*. New York: Columbia University Press, 1999.

Brett, Philip, Elizabeth Wood, and Gary C. Thomas, eds. *Queering the Pitch: The New Gay and Lesbian Musicology*. 2nd ed. New York: Routledge, 2006.

Brownmiller, Susan. *Against Our Will: Men, Women, and Rape*. New York: Simon & Schuster, 1975.

Bullough, Vern L. *Science in the Bedroom*. New York: Basic Books, 1994.

Bullough, Vern L., and Bonnie Bullough. *Cross Dressing, Sex, and Gender*. Philadelphia: University of Pennsylvania Press, 1993.

Butler, Judith. *Gender Trouble: Feminism and the Subversion of Identity*. New York: Routledge, 1999.

Chesler, Ellen. *Woman of Valor: Margaret Sanger and the Birth Control Movement in America*. New York: Simon & Schuster, 1992.

Connell, Robert. *Masculinities*. 2nd ed. Berkeley: University of California Press, 2005.

Cott, Nancy F. *Public Vows: A History of Marriage and the Nation*. Cambridge, MA: Harvard University Press, 2000.

D'Emilio, John, and Estelle B. Freedman. *Intimate Matters: A History of Sexuality in America*. New York: Harper & Row, 1988.

Ehrenreich, Barbara, and Deirdre English. *For Her Own Good: Two Centuries of the Experts Advice to Women*. New York: Anchor, 2005.

Evans, Harriet. *Women & Sexuality in China: Female Sexuality and Gender since 1949*. New York: Continuum, 1997.

Ford, Clellan S., and Frank A. Beach. *Patterns of Sexual Behavior*. New York: Harper and Row, 1951.

Foucault, Michel. *The History of Sexuality. Volume I: An Introduction*. Translated by Robert Hurley. New York: Vintage/Random House, 1990. Originally published in 1987.

Freedman, Estelle. *No Turning Back: The History of Feminism and the Future of Women*. New York: Ballantine/Random House, 2001.

Freud, Sigmund. *Three Contributions to the Theory of Sex*. New York: Dutton, 1962.

Friedan, Betty. *The Feminine Mystique*. New York: Dell Publishers, 1964.

Galician, Mary-Lou. *Sex, Love, and Romance in the Mass Media: Analysis and Criticism of Unrealistic Portrayals and Their Influence*. Mahwah, NJ: Lawrence Erlbaum, 2004.

Garber, Marjorie. *Vice-Versa: Bisexuality and the Eroticism of Everyday Life*. New York: Simon & Schuster, 1995.

Gathorne-Hardy, Jonathan. *Sex: The Measure of All Things: A Life of Alfred Kinsey*. Bloomington: Indiana University Press, 1999.

Gedo, John E., ed. *Freud, the Fusion of Science and Humanism: The Intellectual History of Psychoanalysis*. New York: International Universities Press, 1976.

Greenberg, Jerrold S., Clint E. Bruess, and Debra W. Haffner. *Exploring the Dimensions of Human Sexuality*. 2nd ed. Sudbury, MA: Jones & Bartlett, 2004.

Harvey, John. H., Amy Wenzel, and Susan Sprecher, eds. *The Handbook of Sexuality in Close Relationships*. Mahwah, NJ: Earlbaum, 2004.

Hatfield, Elaine, and Richard L. Rapson. *Love and Sex: Cross-Cultural Perspective*. Boston: Allyn and Bacon, 1996.

Hirschfeld, Magnus. *The Transvestites: The Erotic Drive to Cross-Dress*. Translated by Michael A. Lombardi-Nash. Amherst, NY: Prometheus Books, 1991.

Hirschfeld, Magnus. *The Homosexuality of Men and Women*. Translated by Michael A. Lombardi-Nash. Amherst, NY: Prometheus Books, 2002.

Holmberg, Carl B. *Sexualities and Popular Culture*. Thousand Oaks, CA: Sage, 1998.

Hunter, Ian, Stephen Heath, Colin MacCabe, and Denise Riley, eds. *On Pornography: Literature, Sexuality, and Obscenity Law*. London: Macmillan, 1993.

Irvine, Janice. M. *Disorders of Desire*. Philadelphia: Temple University Press, 1990.

Krafft-Ebing, Richard. *Psychopathia Sexualis*. Reprinted. New York: Arcade, 1998.

Laqueur, Thomas. *Making Sex: Body and Gender from the Greeks to Freud*. Cambridge, MA: Harvard University Press, 1990.

Laqueur, Thomas W. *Solitary Sex: A Cultural History of Masturbation*. New York: Zone Books, 2003.

Laumann, Edward O., John H. Gagnon, Robert T. Michael, and Stuart Michaels. *The Social Organization of Sexuality: Sexual Practices in the United States*. Chicago: University of Chicago Press, 1994.

Lenskyj, Helen. *Out of Bounds: Women, Sport and Sexuality*. Toronto: Canadian Scholars Press, 1987.

Lull, James, and Stephen Hinerman, eds. *Media Scandals: Morality and Desire in the Popular Culture Marketplace*. New York: Columbia University Press, 1998.

Lyons, Andrew P., and Harriot D. Lyons. *Irregular Connections: A History of Anthropology and Sexuality*. Lincoln: University of Nebraska Press, 2004.

Mackay, Judith. *The Penguin Atlas of Human Sexual Behavior*. New York: Penguin Putnam, 2000.

Manning, Christel, and Phil Zuckerman, eds. *Sex and Religion*. Belmont, CA: Thomson Wadsworth Publishing, 2005.

Masters, William. H., and Virginia. E. Johnson. *Human Sexual Inadequacy*. Boston: Little, Brown and Company, 1970.

McCarthy, Barry, and Michael Metz. *Men's Sexual Health*. New York: Routledge, 2007.

Melody, Michael Edward, and Linda Mary Peterson. *Teaching America About Sex: Marriage Guides and Sex Manuals from the Late Victorians to Dr. Ruth*. New York: New York University Press, 1999.

Meyerowitz, Joanne. *How Sex Changed: A History of Transsexuality in the United States.* Cambridge, MA: Harvard University Press, 2002.

Mitchell, Juliet. *Feminism and Psychoanalysis.* New York: Basic Books, 2000.

Moore, Susan, and Doreen Rosenthal. *Sexuality in Adolescence.* London: Routledge, 1993.

Moran, Jeffery P. *Teaching Sex: The Shaping of Adolescence in the 20th Century.* Cambridge, MA: Harvard University Press, 2000.

Nye, Robert. *Sexuality.* Oxford: Oxford University Press, 1999.

Orr, Andrea. *Meeting, Mating and Cheating: Sex, Love and the New World of Online Dating.* Upper Saddle River, NJ: Reuters Prentice Hall, 2004.

Patton, Cindy. *Globalizing AIDS.* Minneapolis: University of Minnesota Press, 2002.

Petersen, J. *The Century of Sex: Playboy's History of the Sexual Revolution, 1900–1999.* New York: Grove Press, 1999.

Phillips, Kim M., and Barry Real. *Sexualities in History: A Reader.* New York: Routledge, 2002.

Pinar, William. *The Gender of Racial Politics and Violence in America: Lynching, Prison Rape, and the Crisis of Masculinity.* New York: Peter Lang, 2001.

Ramakers, Micha. *Dirty Pictures: Tom of Finland, Masculinity, and Homosexuality.* New York: St. Martin's Press, 2000.

Robinson, Paul. *The Modernization of Sex: Havelock Ellis, Alfred Kinsey, William Masters and Virginia Johnson.* Ithaca, NY: Cornell University Press, 1989.

Roy, Arun. *Marriage Customs and Ceremonies in World Religions.* Victoria, BC: Trafford, 2005.

Runzio, Joseph, and Nancy M. Martin, eds. *Love, Sex, and Gender in the World Religions.* Oxford: Oneworld Publishing, 2000.

Sanger, Margaret. *My Fight for Birth Control.* London: Faber, 1932.

Sears, James. *Behind the Mask of the Mattachine.* Binghamton, NY: Haworth, 2006.

Sears, James, ed. *Youth, Sexualities and Education.* Westport, CT: Greenwood, 2005.

Strong, Bryan, Christine Devault, Barbara W. Sayad, and William L. Yarber, eds. *Human Sexuality: Diversity in Contemporary America.* New York: McGraw-Hill, 2004.

Tannahill, Ray. *Sex in History.* London: Book Club Associates, 1990.

Wiederman, Michael W. *Understanding Sexuality Research.* Belmont, CA: Wadsworth/Thompson Learning, 2001.

Wolff, Charlotte. *Magnus Hirschfeld: A Portrait of a Pioneer in Sexology.* London: Quartet Books, 1986.

Index

Boldfaced page numbers indicate main entries.

About the Editor and Contributors

Pamela Autrey earned her PhD in curriculum theory at Louisiana State University, where she studied gender issues and their effects on learning in elementary schools. She teaches in the public Montessori magnet program in Baton Rouge, Louisiana.

Gordon A. Babst is Associate Professor of political science at Chapman University in Orange, California. He received his PhD in political science in 1996 from Claremont Graduate University and has focused his scholarship on issues of justice, religion, and sexual minorities. His first book, *Liberal Constitutionalism, Marriage, and Sexual Orientation* (2002), argued that bias against same-sex couples was ultimately religious in nature, not based on sound social scientific findings, and so to make policy on that basis was to indulge in the shadow establishment of religion.

Carey Roth Bayer, Ed.D, RN, Assistant Professor of research in the Center of Excellence for Sexual Health at the Morehouse School of Medicine, earned a Bachelor's of Science in nursing from Xavier University, a Master's in adult education, and a Doctorate in human sexuality education, both from Widener University.

Brett Beemyn, PhD, is Director of the Stonewall Center at the University of Massachusetts, Amherst. Brett-Genny has published and spoken extensively on transgender college students and trans-inclusive campus policies. Recent publications include "Trans on Campus: Measuring and Improving the Climate for Transgender Students" in *On Campus with Women*" and a special issue of the *Journal of Gay and Lesbian Issues in Education* on "Trans Youth." Brett-Genny is currently working on what will be the largest study of transgender identity development in the United States.

Christopher R. Bell is a graduate student at the University of West Georgia in Carrollton. His research focus is on recent developments in continental philosophy and the history of psychoanalysis. He earned his undergraduate degree from Brown University in English literatures and cultures.

Susan Birden is an Associate Professor of educational foundations at SUNY-Buffalo State College. Her current research interests include the role of confession in classroom settings, especially regarding issues of sexuality. She is author of *Rethinking Sexual Identity in Education*.

Anthony F. Bogaert is Professor of community health sciences and psychology at Brock University in St. Catharines, Canada. He has published extensively on various aspects of human sexuality. He is on the editorial board of *Archives of Sexual Behavior* and is a recipient of Brock University's Chancellor's Chair for Research Excellence.

Sarah Boslaugh, PhD, MPH, is a senior statistical data analyst in the Department of Pediatrics at Washington University in Saint Louis. She has published a number of technical and professional articles and books and is currently editing *The Encyclopedia of Epidemiology*.

Kate Briggs, PhD, is a psychoanalyst and writer teaching in psychology at the University of West Georgia in Carrollton. Her Doctorate was a study of sublimation and sexual difference in Freud, Klein, and Lacan and her publications include writings on feminism and art.

Bryan N. Cochran received his PhD in clinical psychology from the University of Washington in Seattle. He is an Assistant Professor of psychology at the University of Montana in Missoula. Current areas of research are LGBT mental health, substance abuse treatment, and psychotherapy process. Some of his representative publications appear in the *American Journal of Public Health* and the *Journal of Homosexuality*.

Alan Collins is Professor of economics at the University of Portsmouth in the United Kingdom. He specializes in the analysis of social and environmental policy in urban settings.

Jennifer Craik is Professor of communication and cultural studies at the University of Canberra, and Adjunct Professor of fashion and textiles at the RMIT University, Melbourne, Australia. Current research projects include fashion and national identity, the culture of fashion accessories, and contemporary arts and cultural policy. Her most recent book is *Uniforms Exposed: From Conformity to Transgression*.

Joshua Paul Dale received his PhD from the University of Buffalo. Currently, he is a lecturer in the English Department of Tokyo Liberal Arts University. His research interests include transnational cultural studies and narrative nonfiction in addition to Lacanian psychoanalysis, gender studies, and theories of sexuality.

Sharyn Graham Davies is Senior Lecturer in the School of Social Sciences at Auckland University of Technology in New Zealand. Her current research interests revolve around issues of gender and sexuality, particularly in Indonesia. Sharyn has published articles in the *International Social Science Journal* and *Journal of Gender Studies* as well as her book, *Challenging Gender Norms: Five Genders among Bugis in Indonesia*.

Jason Del Gandio, Ph.D., is a lecturer in the Department of Strategic and Organizational Communication at Temple University in Philadelphia. He specializes in rhetoric, critical studies, and the philosophy of communication, with a current focus on the global justice movement, the rhetoric of dissent, and Italian socio-political thought.

Jeffery P. Dennis is Visiting Assistant Professor of sociology at Lakeland College. He is the author of *The Culture of Silence* (2007), *Queering Teen Culture* (2006), and a number of articles on masculinity and sexual identity.

Donald A. Dyson, MSS, PhD, is an Assistant Professor in the Widener University Program in Human Sexuality and an adjunct faculty member at Widener's Center for Social Work Education. He specializes in the areas of ethics, multiculturalism, reproductive health, and professional training of practicing sexologists. His research includes work on motivation and unsafe sexual behaviors as well as condom beliefs.

John P. Elia (Ph.D. in education, UC Davis, 1997) is Associate Professor and associate chair of health education at San Francisco State University. He serves on the editorial boards of several journals, and is associate editor and the book review editor of the *Journal of Homosexuality*. His current research interests include school-based sexuality education and queer popular culture. He is currently co-editing a book entitled *Sexuality, Power and Education: Intervening in Schools and Communities*.

Stephen T. Fife is an Assistant Professor of marriage and family therapy at the University of Nevada, Las Vegas. His research focuses on processes of change in psychotherapy, conceptualization and treatment of interpersonal conflict, treatment of infidelity, and forgiveness. He also has a private practice in Las Vegas.

Nancy L. Fischer is an Assistant Professor of sociology and metro-urban studies at Augsburg College in Minneapolis, Minnesota. She has conducted research on the meaning of incest in contemporary Western culture. She is a co-editor of *Introduction to the New Sexuality Studies* along with Steven Seidman and Chet Meeks.

Diana Fisher is a Lecturer in the Departments of Communication and Liberal Studies at California State University, Los Angeles. She earned her PhD in cultural studies at Claremont Graduate University in 2004 and is currently researching how Soviet and Russian immigrants have used collective memory, humor, and everyday micropractices to create an ethnic enclave in the city of West Hollywood, California.

Christopher Flynn, PhD, is a licensed clinical psychologist and currently Director of the Cook Counseling Center at Virginia Tech. His clinical and research interests include relationships and sexuality among college students.

Cheryl Getz is Director and Assistant Professor in the Leadership Studies Program in the School of Leadership and Education Sciences at the University of San Diego. Her primary teaching responsibilities are in the area of higher education administration. Her research focuses on college student development, social identity, and group dynamics.

Debra Gimlin is a Lecturer in the Sociology Department at the University of Aberdeen. Her research interests include gender, identity, and the body and body management. She is the author of *Body Work: Beauty and Self-Image in American Culture* (2002).

Sarah Goodfellow received her PhD in 2004 from Penn State University, funded in part by the NSF, and studies scientific and medical models of senescent sexuality. After holding a post-doctoral position at Michigan State University, she now lives in Atlanta and is an Adjunct Professor of the history, philosophy, and the sociology of science at Michigan State.

André P. Grace is a Professor of educational policy studies at the University of Alberta, Edmonton, Canada. His current research interests include legal, legislative and educational policy contexts of inclusive education for sexual minorities. An in-press publication in the *Journal of Homosexuality* is an article titled "The Charisma and Deception of Reparative Therapies: When Medical Science Beds Religion."

Liz Grauerholz is a Professor of sociology at the University of Central Florida in Orlando. Her areas of interest include gender, families, social psychology, and teaching/learning. She is co-author of *Sociology of Families* and numerous articles on sexual harassment, popular media, and the social influences on student learning.

Susan Harewood lectures in communication at the Barbados Community College and in cultural studies at the University of the West Indies. Her research focuses on communication, popular culture, and gender. Her work has appeared in a number of journals including *Cultural Studies*, *Critical Methodologies*, *Social Economic Studies*, and the *Harvard Educational Review*.

Sharon Horne is an Associate Professor of counseling psychology at the University of Memphis. Her research and teaching interests include domestic violence; gay, lesbian, bisexual, and transgender issues; and international cross-cultural research and practice. She has published and presented widely on violence against women.

Sue Jackson is a Senior Lecturer in the School of Psychology at Victoria University of Wellington, New Zealand. Her major area of research and publication is the representation of young women's sexuality in the media and its influences on how young women negotiate sexuality in everyday life.

Tameca N. Jackson, LICSW, is a doctoral student in human sexuality at Widener University studying religion and sexuality. She founded Epiphany Enterprise, a social and therapeutic service company, and has extensive experience working to improve the health of the nation's underserved. Jackson is an active community member and advocate supporting women's personal and sexual health care, LBGTQ rights, education and awareness.

Katrien Jacobs is Assistant Professor at City University of Hong Kong. She is a scholar, writer, and activist in the field of digital art and culture who has published widely on Internet pornography, sexuality, art, and censorship. She has a PhD in comparative literature and media, with a thesis on dismemberment myths and rituals in 1960s/1970s body art and performance media. She recently finished her book *Libidoc: Journeys in the Performance of Sex Art*, featuring the work of 27 artists, with tales and commentaries by the double-narrator "Libidot" and "dr jacobs."

Rodney Jones is an Associate Professor in language and communication at City University of Hong Kong. He has written extensively on computer-mediated communication, cyber-sex, and the discursive construction of sexual identities.

Darlene M. Juschka is Associate Professor and Coordinator in women's studies and adjunct professor in religious studies at the University of Regina. In her interdisciplinary work, she brings together feminist theorizing, ritual and myth studies, and the new phenomenology of religion. Currently, she is working on a monograph titled *The Semiotics of Gender: Political Bodies/Body Politic*, while more recently published works include "Spectacles of Gender: Enacting the Masculine in Ancient Rome and Modern Cinema" in the *Journal of Religion and Theology* (2005) and her edited and annotated text, *Feminism in the Study of Religion*.

Lara Kelland is a third-year doctoral student at the University of Illinois at Chicago. Her research looks at American social movements in the nineteenth and twentieth centuries and the ways in which activists used collective memory to build political identities.

Shannon Kelly, MA, COTC, is a practicing clinician in the field of addiction treatment and is the clinical director of an outpatient addiction treatment center in Georgia. She has published articles on psychoanalysis, ethics, and clinical practice.

Didi Khayatt is Professor at York University's Faculty of Education. She is the author of a number of articles and one book. She is interested in various issues of equity, including gender, race relations, and sexuality.

Akihiko Komiya is research fellow of the Japan Society for the Promotion of Science. He is doing comparative study of (homo)sexuality and education between UK and Japan.

Wendy Korwin is a Ph.D. student in American Studies at the College of William and Mary. Her dissertation research focuses on child readers and public libraries, 1876–1920.

Sharon Lamb, Ed.D., is Professor of psychology at Saint Michael's College in Colchester, Vermont, and a clinical psychologist in private practice in Shelburne, Vermont. She is the author of *The Trouble with Blame: Victims, Perpetrators, and Responsibility*, *The Secret Lives of Girls*; *Packaging Girlhood*; and *Sex, Therapy, and Kids: Addressing Their Concerns through Talk and Play*. She has also edited three books on victimization, moral development, and forgiveness. Currently, she is a member of the American Psychological Association's Task Force on the Sexualization of Girls and is Co-director of the steering committee for the Anti-Violence Partnership at the University of Vermont.

R. J. Levin is Honorary Research Associate at the Sexual Physiology Laboratory, Porterbrook Clinic, Sheffield, Yorkshire. He was previously Reader in physiology in the Department of Biomedical Science, University of Sheffield, Sheffield, Yorkshire, from 1977 until his retirement in 2000.

Anne Lopes is Professor of political theory at Metropolitan College of New York. She was active in the women's movement in the 1970s and 1980s and has written on women's movements in Germany. She is co-author of *Men's Feminism: August Bebel and the German Socialist Movement* (2000).

Joseph LoPiccolo is a clinical psychologist who is a Professor in the Department of Psychological Sciences at the University of Missouri, Columbia. He does research and has written in the area of sexual dysfunction. He has received the Alfred Kinsey Research Award from the Society for the Scientific Study of Sexuality and the Masters and Johnson Memorial Award from the Society for Sex Therapy and Research.

Karen Lovaas is Assistant Professor of speech and communication studies at San Francisco State University. She is on the editorial board of the *Journal of Homosexuality* and was coeditor of *Queer Theory and Communication: From Disciplining Queers to Queering the Disciplines* (2003). She is lead editor for an upcoming issue of the *Journal of Homosexuality* on The Contested Terrain of LGBT Studies and Queer Theory. She is currently co-editing *Sexual Identities and Communication in Everyday Life* with Lee Jenkins.

Wah-Yun Low is Professor of psychology at the Health Research Development Unit, Faculty of Medicine, University of Malaya, Kuala Lumpur, Malaysia. She graduated with a Bachelor of Arts (Hons.) from the National University of Malaysia and earned her Master of Science (M.Sc) and Doctorate in medical psychology from the University of Surrey, England. Her research and writing revolves around human sexuality and sexual and reproductive health and aging.

Diana Luzzatto is a social anthropologist and senior lecturer at the Academic College of Tel-Aviv-Yafo. Her major research interests are gender, sexuality, the body, and youth culture, on which issues she has published in professional journals.

J. Dan Marshall is a Professor of education in Penn State University's Educational Leadership Program. His scholarly interests range from general curriculum studies and initial teacher preparation to popular music.

Barry McCarthy, PhD, is a Professor of psychology at American University, a diplomat in clinical psychology, and a certified marriage and sex therapist. He has published over 70 professional articles, 19 book chapters, coauthored 11 books, and presented over 250 professional workshops both nationally and internationally.

Melina McConatha-Rosle is currently studying for her PhD at the University of Delaware in the Department of Human Development and Family Studies. Her research primarily focuses on gender issues within the family, family violence, and disabilities studies. She is passionate about integrating the intersectionality of race, class, and culture into her research and continues to be an advocate for the equal treatment of women in the field of family and disabilities studies.

Anna Meyer-Weitz is a Professor in the school of psychology at the University of KwaZulu-Natal, Durban, South Africa. She earned graduate degrees in psychology at the University of South Africa and her Doctorate in health promotion and health education from the University of Maastricht, The Netherlands. More biographical information is available at *Marquis Who's Who in the World*.

Diana Milillo is a social psychologist who researches and teaches about the psychology of gender, sexism, violence against women, and sexual orientation. She is currently an Instructor of psychology at Nassau Community College.

Adena Miller is a graduate student at the University of British Columbia in the School of Social Work and Family Studies. Her research interests include the divorce process and post-separation parent-adult child relationships.

Henrique Caetano Nardi is Professor at the Social Psychology Graduate and Undergraduate Program of the Federal University of Rio Grande do Sul (www.ufrgs.br) in Porto Alegre, Brazil. He has a PhD in sociology. His interdisciplinary program of research explores public politics on health, gender, education, sexuality, and work issues. His most recently published book is *Ética, Trabalho e Subjetividade* (*Ethics, Work and Subjectivity*).

Llewellyn Negrin teaches at the University of Tasmania, Australia, where she is head of and Senior Lecturer in art and design theory. As well as teaching courses on Fashioning and Imaging the Body, she has published articles concerned with feminism and fashion and postmodern theories of the body and the role of beauty in contemporary culture in journals such as *Theory, Culture & Society*; *Body & Society*; *The Journal of European Cultural Studies*; *Philosophy & Social Criticism*; *Feminist Theory*; *Hecate*; and *Arena*.

David Nel is a graduate of the University of Western Australia in English. He is currently researching a dissertation provisionally entitled "The Measure of Love: Science, Sex and Subjectivity in the Fiction of Jeanette Winterson." His research interests include feminist theory, philosophy, and literature, with a particular slant on the role of subjectivity in literary production, literature and science, queer studies, and literary history.

Caryn E. Neumann is a Visiting Assistant Professor of history at Denison University in Granville, Ohio. A former managing editor of *The Journal of Women's History*, she earned a Doctorate in women's history from Ohio State University.

Sylvia Niehuis is Assistant Professor at Utah State University. She earned her undergraduate and graduate degrees in psychology from the J.W. Goethe University, Germany, and her Doctorate in human ecology from the University of Texas at Austin. She publishes in a variety of peer-reviewed journals, such as *Personality and Social Psychology Bulletin* and the *Journal of Family Communication*.

April Niver is a PhD candidate in educational leadership and policy studies at Arizona State University. She has taught on schooling and culture, action research, human sexuality, and writing. Her research explores sex educators' experiences of conflict. Niver has also written on horror films and the European health education network.

Gilad Padva teaches at the Film and TV Department at Tel Aviv University, Israel, and Hadassah College, Jerusalem. He publishes extensively about representations of gender and sexualities in contemporary cinema, television, visual communication, and popular culture.

Émilie Paquin grew up in Quebec City, Canada. She obtained a bachelor of arts in history and women's studies from the University of Ottawa in 2004. She is currently completing her history P.D. at the University of Sydney, Australia. Her thesis is a comparative study of social hygiene organizations in Canada and Australia.

Andreas G. Philaretou, PhD, PMCMFT, CFLE, is an author and lecturer and currently an Associate Professor of psychology in the School of Humanities and Social Sciences at Cyprus College. He received his B.S. and M.S. in sociology, and his PhD in human development from Virginia Polytechnic Institute and State University (Virginia Tech). In addition, he earned a Post-Master's Certificate in Marriage and Family Therapy (PMCMFT) and has been certified as a Family Life Educator (CFLE).

Voon Chin Phua is Assistant Professor of sociology at Gettysburg College. His research interest is on race, sex, and sexualities. His work has been published in the *Journal of Family Issues*, *Men and Masculinities*, and *Culture, Health and Sexuality*.

Lyndy A. Potter is an Australian and U.S.-trained clinical psychologist whose research specializes in the long-term impact of childhood trauma. She now devotes her time to providing support to the international community of individuals with progressive multiple sclerosis and their caregivers through her Web-based forum.

Roberto Hugh Potter is a sociologist/criminologist currently working at the intersection of corrections and public health. His work focuses on understanding the social worlds of custody and medical staff and the impact this has on inmate health status and health disparities in communities disproportionately affected by the criminal justice and public health systems. He has worked as a state and federal researcher and manager, as a manager in the community-based organizational sector, and as an academic at U.S. and Australian universities. He earned his Doctorate in sociology from the University of Florida in 1982.

Horacio N. Roque Ramírez teaches LGBT histories, Chicano/Latino Studies, and oral history at the University of California. His work has appeared in *The Journal of the History of Sexuality* (2003), *CENTRO: Journal of the Center for Puerto Rican Studies* (2007), and *Queer Migrations: Sexuality, U.S. Citizenship, and Border Crossings* (2005).

Kathleen Rands is a doctoral student at the University of North Carolina at Chapel Hill. She is interested in sexuality and gender in schools, linguistic diversity, critical multicultural education, and teacher preparation.

David Roth is Co-Director and Therapist at The Center for Relationships and Sexuality, Allentown, Pennsylvania, and Adjunct Professor of theology at Caldwell College. He is a fellow of the Royal Anthropological Institute.

Lorena L. Russell is an Assistant Professor in the Department of Literature and Language at the University of North Carolina at Asheville, where she specializes in queer theory and postcolonial studies. She has most recently published essays in *Considering David Chase* (2007) and *Considering Alan Ball* (2006) and is completing a manuscript on Angela Carter, Fay Weldon, and Jeanette Winterson.

Maureen Sander-Staudt is an Assistant Professor of philosophy at Arizona State University in the Department of Integrative Studies. She publishes in the areas of applied ethics, gender studies, and bioethics, and is the author of several articles. Her most recent publications are on the topic of the politics of caregiving.

Annesa Flentje Santa, M.A. is a doctoral student in the clinical psychology program at the University of Montana, Missoula. Her research interests include underserved populations, particularly LGBT individuals, and substance abuse treatment.

James T. Sears is Professor of education at Penn State University and specializes in sexuality issues in curriculum studies and U.S. history. He earned an undergraduate degree in history from Southern Illinois University, a graduate degree in political science from the University of Wisconsin, and his Doctorate in education and sociology from Indiana University, which awarded him its Outstanding Alumni Award. Sears's scholarship has appeared in a variety of peer-reviewed journals; he is the author or editor of 18 books and the editor of the two-volume international encyclopedia, *Youth, Education, and Sexualities* (Greenwood, 2005). Sears has taught in the departments of education, sociology, women's studies, and the honors college at several universities, including Harvard University, Trinity University (Texas), Indiana University, the College of Charleston, and the University of South Carolina. He has also been a Research Fellow at the Center for Feminist Studies at the University of Southern California, a Fulbright Senior Research Southeast Asia Scholar, a Research Fellow at the University of Queensland, and a consultant for the J. Paul Getty Center for Education and the Arts. His biography is included in the *Dictionary of International Biography*, *Who's Who in American Education*, *Contemporary Authors*, and *Who's Who in America*.

Timaree Schmit is an Ed.D. student in human sexuality at Widener University and has worked in the field as an HIV prevention counselor and tester, peer sex educator, sex advice columnist, and volunteer for various sexuality and social justice organizations.

Lisa B. Schwartz, PhD, is an AASECT-certified sex therapist and a licensed marriage and family therapist. She maintains a private psychotherapy practice in Bucks County, Pennsylvania. For more information, please see her Web site at www.sexualconcerns.com.

Karla Soukup, M.S., is a licensed marriage and family therapist. Most recently, she has served as the Assistant Director of Trinity Counseling and Training Center, New Orleans, Louisiana.

L. Michael Spath is Assistant Professor of religious studies at Indiana University-Purdue University, Fort Wayne, Indiana. He teaches in the areas of comparative spirituality and religion and culture. He is the Director of the Middle East Peace Education Project and a co-founder of the Institute for the Study of Christian Zionism. His recent research has been in the dialogue between Sufism and Zen Buddhism.

Ronald Steiner, PhD, J.D., serves as an Associate Professor of political science at Chapman University, where he teaches courses on law and politics. In addition, he has served as a judicial clerk on the U.S. Court of Appeals for the Ninth Circuit, worked as a litigator in the Los Angeles offices of a major international law firm, and served in 1999–2000 as Deputy Counsel for California Governor Gray Davis's Blue Ribbon Advisory Commission on Hate Groups.

Lorri Sulpizio is a faculty member and the head women's basketball coach at San Diego Mesa College in California. She is currently working toward a PhD in leadership at the University of San Diego. Her research interests include leadership in sports and athletics, as well as issues in gender and sexuality.

Anthony Synnott is Professor of sociology at Concordia University in Montreal and author of *The Body Social* (1993), *Shadows* (1996) on social problems, and co-author of *Aroma: The Cultural History of Smell* (1994).

Richard Tewksbury is Professor of justice administration at the University of Louisville. He holds a Ph.D. in sociology from Ohio State University. He is author/editor of 11 books and more than 150 scholarly articles and chapters. His research focuses on men's sexuality, institutional corrections, and the intersection of sex, gender, and sexuality. Dr. Tewksbury is the 2006 recipient of Peter Lejin's Correctional Research Award from the American Correctional Association and the 2005 Educator of the Year for the Southern Criminal Justice Association.

Maria Thestrup is currently pursuing her PhD in clinical psychology at American University. Her primary clinical and research interests relate to the topic of stress and coping. She has received her MA in psychology and has worked for several years within the field of social work.

Bahira Sherif Trask, PhD, is a faculty member in the Department of Individual and Family Studies, University of Delaware, and a policy scientist in the Center for Community Research and Service. She has a PhD in cultural anthropology from the University of Pennsylvania and a B.A. in political science from Yale University. Dr. Trask is interested in the interrelationship of work, gender, and belief systems in culturally diverse families, the conceptualization and redefinition of non-Western families when compared to Western families, and the pivotal role of economics in families.

Andrew Thomas Wackerfuss is a PhD candidate at Georgetown University. He currently teaches World Civilization while finishing the final chapters of his dissertation, "The Stormtrooper Family: How Sexuality, Spirituality, and Community Shaped the Hamburg SA."

Matthew Waites is Lecturer in sociology in the Department of Sociology, Anthropology and Applied Social Sciences at the University of Glasgow, Glasgow, Scotland. He researches on lesbian, gay, and bisexual politics in the United Kingdom and globally, works on the editorial board of two journals: *Sociology* and *Sexualities*, and is author of *The Age of Consent: Young People, Sexuality and Citizenship*, and co-editor, with Jeffrey Weeks and Janet Holland, of *Sexualities and Society: A Reader*.

Gerald R. Weeks is Professor and Chair of the Department of Counseling at University of Nevada, Las Vegas and in private practice. He is a Clinical Member of the American Association of Marriage and Family Therapy, and is board-certified by the American Board of Professional Psychology and the American Board of Sexology. He has published 17 professional textbooks in the fields of sex, marital, and family therapy.

Elizabeth Whitney is currently writing about DIY aesthetics in feminist and queer performance communities. Her recent publications have appeared in the journals *Text and Performance Quarterly* and *Liminalities: A Journal of Performance Studies*, and the anthology *Casting Gender: Women and Performance in Intercultural Contexts*. Her solo performance work on gender and popular culture has been seen at colleges and universities, festivals, and gallery spaces throughout the United States and Canada. She is a Scholar in Residence in the Institute for Liberal Arts & Interdisciplinary Studies at Emerson College in Boston.

Reiko Yeap, a junior lecturer at International Medical University, Malaysia, holding a BA degree in psychology from the University of New Brunswick, Canada, and an M.Sc. in psychological research from the University of Wales, United Kingdom, is currently working towards a PhD at University of Malaya, Malaysia. His research areas include public attitude and perception toward psychology and mental health, the role of media in shaping beliefs and behaviors, and interpersonal communication. He has co-authored and presented studies concerning communication skills training in Malaysia.

Gust A. Yep is Professor of speech and communication studies and human sexuality studies at San Francisco State University. He recently co-edited *Queer Theory and Communication* and co-authored *Privacy and Disclosure of HIV in Interpersonal Relationships*.

Carrie Yodanis is an Assistant Professor in the School of Social Work and Family Studies at the University of British Columbia. She studies gender dynamics and intimate violence in marriage from a cross-national perspective.

Richard Yuill recently completed his doctoral research at the University of Glasgow, Scotland, on "Male Age-Discrepant Intergenerational Sexualities and Relationships." He has taught at the University of Glasgow and Cumbernauld College and is currently involved in independent research on age, sexuality, and masculinity, with an essay on pedophilia in *Encyclopedia of Sociology* (2006).

Jennifer Zaligson is a PhD student in the Department of Sociology at the University of Texas at Austin. Her research focuses on gender and sexuality, domestic violence, relationships, and health. For her master's thesis she examined domestic violence shelter responses to LGBTQ survivors. She is currently working on an article about the impact of health changes on relationship quality in long-term gay, lesbian, and heterosexual couples.